MARYLAND

A Guide to the Old Line State

MARYLAND

A GUIDE TO THE OLD LINE STATE

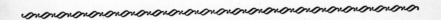

Compiled by workers of the Writers' Program
of the Work Projects Administration
in the State of Maryland

AMERICAN GUIDE SERIES

ILLUSTRATED

Sponsored by Herbert R. O'Conor, Governor of Maryland

OXFORD UNIVERSITY PRESS · NEW YORK

THE UNIVERSITY OF MARYLAND
State-wide Sponsor of the
Maryland Writers' Project

FEDERAL WORKS AGENCY
JOHN M. CARMODY, *Administrator*

WORK PROJECTS ADMINISTRATION
F.C.HARRINGTON, *Commissioner*
FLORENCE KERR, *Assistant Commissioner*
FRANCIS H. DRYDEN, *State Administrator*

HERBERT R. O'CONOR
GOVERNOR

EXECUTIVE DEPARTMENT
ANNAPOLIS, MARYLAND

It gives me pleasure on behalf of the State to present the Maryland Guide, which has been prepared by the Maryland Writers' Project, Work Projects Administration.

Compiled, as it was, by a large group of writers who were able to devote much time to exploring not only the usual sources of information for such a work as this, but also the lesser used and therefore possibly even more valuable channels of personal contact and community tradition, this Guide presents a comprehensive record of the State, its people and their historical background. Furthermore, there is included a complete inventory of the resources of Maryland, which should prove valuable for many purposes. Not a few of the facts included herein are being presented for the first time in a work of this nature.

From the date of the first settlement at St. Mary's City back in 1634, Maryland and Marylanders have made history and established traditions, the record of which as presented herewith should serve as a continuing reminder and incentive to the people of our State today.

From the humble beginnings of 1634, and particularly in the last fifty years, Maryland has made great progress along many lines, industrially, agriculturally and in a broad cultural sense. Much, of course, remains to be done. Our people need but to carry on, however, in the traditional Maryland spirit to solve the problems confronting the State today and to add additional prestige to the name of our great commonwealth.

Marylanders who would have better knowledge and understanding of our State will find the Maryland Guide a ready and authentic encyclopedia. Those residing outside our State or travelling within its borders, will find the Maryland Guide replete with every possible type of desirable information.

I most heartily commend this volume and take pleasure in extending my sincere congratulations to all who have had a part in its preparation.

Sincerely,

Herbert R. O'Conor

Governor

Preface

MANY individuals have generously co-operated with the staff of the Maryland Writers' Project in the preparation of the *Maryland Guide*. To these, and to the civic, historical, educational, and commercial organizations throughout the State who have aided the staff, grateful acknowledgment is due.

The staff of the Writers' Project in Maryland owes an expression of gratitude to Dr.Joseph L. Wheeler, Librarian of the Enoch Pratt Free Library. While work on the guide was in progress, the project was quartered in the central branch of the library, and the library employees at all times extended every possible courtesy. In addition, Federal, State, and city agencies have consistently made their resources available to the project.

Among the many individuals who generously gave specialized help and advice to the staff, and to whom the entire project is indebted, are: I.Duke Avnet, Dr.Florence E. Bamberger, Morris Barroll, Frank L. Bentz, the late George F. Bragg, Joshua Clayton, Mrs.Charles E. Cockey, C.L.Dail, Henry T. Dielman, George Doyas, Dr.N.Bryllion Fagin, James W. Foster, H.Findlay French, Francis D. Friedlein, the Right Reverend Edward T. Helfenstein, Bishop of Maryland, Miss Elizabeth Henry, Robert Goldsborough Henry, Dr.Zadok P. Henry, Rear Admiral Guy Hicks, U.S.N.(ret.), Macgill James, Dr.Paul Jones, Fiske Kimball, Dr.Edward B. Mathews, the late J.E.Metzger, Mrs.Robert Moffett, Dr.Earl R. Moses, Carl Murphy, Sidney L. Nyburg, Earle W. Orem, Otto Ortmann, Dr.J.Hall Pleasants, Judge Mason Shehan, J.Alexis Shriver, Dr.Guy Steele, S.Broughton Tall, Tench Tilghman, Charles J. Truitt, Dr.William Urie, Fred G. Usilton, Mark S. Watson, Wallace Williams, and Lieutenant Commander Chester C. Wood, U.S.N.

Research and careful study have revealed to the staff of the project, as every student of Maryland history has recognized, that much of the source material on the State is conflicting and in many instances misleading and ambiguous. Every effort has been made to avoid errors of omission and commission, but it is natural to assume that the material included in the *Maryland Guide* is not perfect. Factual and statistical material for the book has been gathered over an extended period and it is possible, therefore, that occasional outdated items may be encountered.

This one book obviously can not be definitive or complete. The story of Maryland and its people is too rich, too eventful, too filled with the stuff of which books are made, to be encompassed in one volume. It is to be hoped that the *Maryland Guide* will serve as a springboard for others, an inspiration to Marylanders to search more deeply into and to write more fully of their native State.

H. BOWEN SMITH
State Supervisor, Maryland Arts Project

April 30, 1940

FRANK J. REALL
State Supervisor, Maryland Writers' Project

Contents

Part IV. Appendices

Maps

General Information

Railroads: Baltimore & Ohio R.R. and the Western Maryland Ry. serve western Maryland. Pennsylvania R.R. with various divisions serves the Eastern Shore. Both have trunk lines between Washington and New York by way of Baltimore.

Bus Lines: Intrastate lines connect principal towns and cities; interstate lines include Blue Ridge Transportation Co. (between seaboard and Great Lakes), Capital Transit Co. (between Laurel and D.C. over US 1), L.& A.Bus Lines (between Cumberland and New Creek, W.Va., Cumberland and Hyndman, Pa.), Maryland Coach Co. (between Baltimore and Hanover, Pa.), Nevin Midland Lines (between Baltimore and D.C. and over US 1, 140, and 15), Peninsula Transit Corp. (between Baltimore and Norfolk, Va., Baltimore and Reedville, Va.), Pennsylvania Greyhound Lines (eastern seaboard), Red Star Lines, Inc. (between Salisbury and Philadelphia, Ocean City and Baltimore through Salisbury), Safeway Trails, Inc. (eastern seaboard over US 1 and 40), Somerset Bus Co. (between Pittsburgh, Pa. and Washington, D.C. through Cumberland, Johnstown, Pa., and Clarksburg, W.Va., Winchester, Va., and Washington, D.C.).

Airlines: American Airlines, Eastern Air Lines, Imperial Airways, Ltd. (between Baltimore and Bermuda), Pan American Airways (between Baltimore and Bermuda, also transatlantic in winter), Pennsylvania-Central Airlines. Emergency landing fields near most cities and towns.

Water Transportation: Ferry service from Baltimore and Annapolis to the Eastern Shore; steamboat service daily between points on Chesapeake Bay; weekday sailings to Wilmington, Del., and Chester and Philadelphia, Pa., through Chesapeake and Delaware Canal; regular coastwise steamship service to Atlantic, Gulf, West Indian, and Caribbean ports. Several intercoastal and transoceanic freight lines carry passengers.

Traffic Regulations: Speed limit on open road, 55 m.p.h. on dual highways, 50 m.p.h. on remainder; 20 m.p.h. in larger towns and 25 m.p.h. in thinly populated towns. Nonresident licensed driver (from states having reciprocity) may operate auto. No person under 14 years of age permitted license. Trailers and towed vehicles must display one red light visible to rear for distance of 200 feet. Commissioner of Motor Vehicles, Baltimore, telephone University 3900. Maryland State Police enforce motor vehicle laws.

Accommodations: Hotels in all larger towns; tourist houses numerous in and near cities and most larger towns; overnight camps in all parts of State; camp sites in State forest reserves and parks.

Climate: Somewhat diversified owing to topography; mean temperature 53.8°. Summers are quite warm throughout the State, though the temperature seldom goes above 90° in the hilly regions. Sudden local thunder showers frequent. Winters in the Chesapeake Bay section are mild, with abundant sunshine and relatively light average snowfall; zero temperatures very rare; mountain winters, however, are rigorous with heavy snowfall and frequent zero temperatures.

Poisonous Plants, Reptiles, and Parasites: Poison ivy grows profusely in most sections of the State, generally along fences and about trees in open land. Poison sumac, though not so plentiful, is sometimes found in swampy places. Timber rattlesnakes are fairly common in the mountains, and copperheads are occasionally seen in the vicinity of streams throughout the State. Woodticks sometimes carry rabbit fever (tularaemia) and spotted fever; these diseases can be acquired by contact with dead animals. Puttees are recommended for hikes through wooded or brushy country and rubber gloves should be worn in cleaning wild rabbits. Careful search should be made for the ticks immediately after return to camp or home; remove ticks with tweezers and destroy.

Information Bureaus: Tourist Development Bureau of the Baltimore Association of Commerce and local commerce associations, hotels, railroads, service stations, and automobile associations give information on travel, resorts, recreational opportunities, and road conditions.

Recreational Areas: The Catoctin Recreational Area and the fourteen State forests and parks (*see map*) provide opportunities for hiking, picnicking, and camping. The former and several of the latter have tent sites, trailer sites, and cabins; tents and cots rented in the Swallow Falls State Forest. The Appalachian Trail, extending from Maine to Georgia, passes along the crest of South Mountain. Larger municipalities maintain parks with facilities for picnicking, swimming, golfing, playing tennis, and riding. Chesapeake Bay and its tributaries have some 3,000 miles of water front and 2,430 square miles of inland waters affording splendid opportunities for swimming and boating. Large numbers of yachts and boats annually engage in races and regattas. Summer colonies and public bathing beaches are numerous, and countless small shore houses are rented. The State's only ocean beach is near Ocean City.

Fires: By law entire responsibility for costs and damages are placed upon those lighting fires; loss of control over fire is considered proof of carelessness or neglect.

Fishing and Hunting: The numerous tributaries of Chesapeake Bay and the rugged mountainous country together afford abundant opportunities for hunting and fishing. License required for hunting and for fishing in non-tidal waters.

Fishing license issued to persons over 14 years of age: nonresident $5, plus 50¢ fee for Conservation Fund, resident $1.25; three-day (consecutive) license for Deep Creek Lake $2.25 (apply Garrett Co. Court House, Oakland, or game warden, Rainbow Inn, on lake). Fishing button must be worn. No license required for sport fishing or crabbing in tidal waters; boats and equipment available at numerous points for bay fishing and at Ocean City for deep sea fishing.

Commercial fishing permitted only to residents.

Hunting licenses: nonresident $15.50 (state-wide), nonresident property owner $5.50 (state-wide), or $1.50 in county where property is held; resident $5.25 (state-wide), $1.25 (county of residence). Hunting permitted on all lands except game preserves, U.S. Military and Naval Reservations, and posted private lands. (For detailed information on fishing and hunting, and for booklets of laws and regulations, consult Conservation Department of Maryland, Munsey Building, Baltimore, or local game warden.)

Races: Pari-mutuel betting at 4 major (one-mile) tracks (Bowie, Havre de Grace, Laurel, and Pimlico) and 6 half-mile tracks (Bel Air, Cumberland, Hagerstown, Marlboro, Taneytown, and Timonium). Whippet races at Brooklandville.

Calendar of Annual Events

JANUARY

| No fixed date | at Hagerstown | Exhibition of Cumberland Valley Artists, Washington County Museum of Fine Arts |

MARCH

Twenty-fifth	at St.Marys City	Maryland Day Celebration Commemorates Landing in 1634 of First Settlers
No fixed date	at Baltimore	Spring Concert, United German Singers, Alcazar
No fixed date	at Hagerstown	Photographic Exhibition, Washington County Museum of Fine Arts

APRIL

First two weeks	at Bowie	Spring Race Meet
First-Thirtieth	at Baltimore	Maryland Artists' Exhibition, Baltimore Museum of Art
First Saturday	at Glyndon	Junior Cross-Country Race, over J.W.Y.Martin Estate
First Saturday	at Monkton	Point-to-Point Race at My Lady's Manor
Last two weeks	at Havre de Grace	Spring Race Meet
Second Friday	State-wide	Arbor Day
Third Saturday	at Hereford	Grand National Steeplechase, Whittingham Estate
Fourth Saturday	at Glyndon	Maryland Hunt Cup Race, Martin Estate
No fixed date	at Upper Marlboro	Marlborough Hunt Club Horse Show

| No fixed date | at Towson | Azalea Show, Towson Nurseries |
| No fixed date | at Historic Estates | Tours of Maryland Gardens and Homes, Federated Garden Clubs of Maryland |

MAY

First two weeks	at Baltimore	Pimlico Spring Race Meeting, Preakness Ball (see Baltimore *Annual Events*)
First Saturday	at Pikesville	McDonogh School Horse Show
Eighth	at Bethesda	National Capital Horse Show, Congressional Country Club
Twenty-third	at Ellicott City	Howard County Horse Show
Thirtieth	at Hagerstown	Antietam Battlefield Memorial Day Exercises
No fixed date	at St. Margaret's (near Annapolis)	St. Margaret's Hunt Club Spring Horse Show
No fixed date	at Bel Air	Bel Air Flower Show
No fixed date	at Centerville	Flower Show, Queen Annes Garden Club
No fixed date	at Chestertown	High School and College Teachers' All-Maryland School Men's Golf Tournament, Chester River Yacht and Country Club
No fixed date	at College Park	University of Maryland Field Day
No fixed date	at College Park	University of Maryland Pony Show
No fixed date	at Elkton	Cecil County Fox Hunters' Association Dog Show
No fixed date	at Frederick	Frederick Garden Club Flower Show
No fixed date	at Frederick	Semiannual Maryland-Virginia Aberdeen-Angus Cattle Show, Fairgrounds (also held in November)
No fixed date	at Frederick	Frederick County Rural Schools Music Festival

No fixed date	at Garrison	Garrison Forest School Horse Show
No fixed date	at Granite	Woodstock Hunt Club Spring Horse Show
No fixed date	at Hagerstown	Hagerstown Livestock Auction (also held in November)
No fixed date	at Le Gore	Flower Show, Woodsboro Woman's Club
No fixed date	at Pikesville	Baltimore County Kennel Club Dog Show
No fixed date	at Pocomoke City	Flower Show, Woman's Club of Pocomoke City
No fixed date	at Salisbury	Flower Show, Wicomico Women's Club

JUNE

Thirteenth	State-wide	St. Anthony's Festival (see Baltimore calendar)
Fourteenth	at Baltimore	Flag Day Celebration, Flag House
Third week	at Annapolis	June Week Exercises at Naval Academy
No fixed date	at Bel Air	Harford County Pony Show, Benefit of Harford Memorial Hospital, Fairgrounds
No fixed date	at Hagerstown	Flower Show, Armory
No fixed date	at Hyde Station	Long Green Valley Horse Show, Palmer Estate
No fixed date	at Taneytown	Carroll County Agricultural and Fair Association Exhibition

JULY

| Third week | at Hagerstown | Hagerstown Fair and Race Meet |
| Thirtieth | State-wide | Maryland Yacht Club Annual Cruise (see Baltimore calendar) |

No fixed date	at Chestertown	Chester River Yacht and Country Club Regatta
No fixed date	at Gibson Island	Summer Carnival, Benefit of the Little Protestant Episcopal Chapel, St.Christopher's by the Sea (only time open to public)
No fixed date	at Gibson Island	Miller Memorial Race, Gibson Island Club; Star Boat Races
No fixed date	at Havre de Grace	Regatta of the Havre de Grace Yacht Club
No fixed date	at St.Michaels	Miles River Yacht Club Regatta
No fixed date	at Mountain Lake Park	Mountain Choir Festival, Mountain Lake Park Amphitheater
Last week	at Bel Air	Bel Air Race Meet

AUGUST

First week	at Bel Air	Bel Air Race Meet
No fixed date	at My Lady's Manor	Ladies' Tilting Tournament; Dog and Pony Show
Second and third week	at Cumberland	Cumberland Race Meet
Fifteenth	at Hyde	State-wide Tilting Championship Tournament, St.John's Church
Last week	at Marlboro	Marlboro Race Meet
Second Wednesday	at Cordova	St.Joseph's Catholic Church Tilting Tournament (only one on Eastern Shore)
Second Saturday	at Ellicott City	Horse Show, Doughoregan Manor (5 miles beyond Ellicott City on Route 40)
Third Saturday	at Tilghmanton	Washington County Tilting Tournament
Third Saturday and Sunday	at Rock Hall	Annual Regatta Rock Hall Yacht Club

No fixed date	at Easton	Regatta of the Chesapeake Bay Yacht Club
No fixed date	at Middletown	Ayreshire Field Day, Frederick County Ayreshire Breeders' Club
No fixed date	at Oxford	Tred Avon Yacht Club Regatta
No fixed date	at Salisbury	Eastern Shore Net Tourney
No fixed date	at Taneytown	Carroll County Fair and Races

SEPTEMBER

Fifth	at Sparks	Sparks Horse Show
Labor Day	at Centerville	Horse Show, Queen Annes County Horse Breeders' Association
Labor Day	at St. Margarets	Annual Tilting Tournament (near Annapolis)
Second week	at Timonium	Timonium Fair and Race Meet
Twelfth	State-wide	Old Defenders Day (see Baltimore calendar)
No fixed date	at various locations	Chesapeake Bay Fishing Fair
Twelfth	at Union Bridge	Union Bridge Horse Show
Nineteenth	at Timonium	Baltimore County Humane Society Horse Show
No fixed date	at Chestertown	Flower Show, Kent County Homemakers Clubs
No fixed date	at Ellicott City	Fall Flower Show, Howard County Garden Club
No fixed date	at Fair Hill	Fox Catcher Hunt Club Race Meeting
No fixed date	at Fair Hill	Cattle Show of the Cecil County Jersey Cattle Club
No fixed date	at Gibson Island	Cedar Point Race, Gibson Island Yacht Club
No fixed date	at La Plata	Charles County Fair
No fixed date	at La Plata	Tobacco (Queen) Festival
No fixed date	at Salisbury	Two-Day Fall Flower Show, Wicomico Garden Club
No fixed date	at White Hall	County Fair of the White Hall Fair Association

OCTOBER

First-Thirty-first	at Laurel	Laurel Fair and Race Meet
Second-Third	at Worthington Valley	Horse Show, Worthington Valley Hunt Club
Second week	at Frederick	Frederick County Fair and Races
Thirty-first	at Hagerstown	Halloween Celebration; Mummers' Parade
No fixed date	at Bel Air	Harford County Fair
No fixed date	at Hagerstown	Hagerstown Symphony Orchestra Concert
No fixed date	at Baltimore	Baltimore Live Stock Show, Union Stock Yards
No fixed date	at Centerville	Queen Annes County Poultry and Game Show, Armory
No fixed date	at Chestertown	Chestertown Day
No fixed date	at Easton	Mummers' Parade

NOVEMBER

First two weeks	at Baltimore	Pimlico Fall Race Meet
Last two weeks	at Bowie	Fall Race Meet
No fixed date	at Frederick	Semiannual Maryland-Virginia Aberdeen-Angus Cattle Show, Fairgrounds (also held in May)
No fixed date	at Hagerstown	Hagerstown Livestock Auction (also held in May)
No fixed date	at Taylor	Harford Hunt Races and Livestock Fair, Elkridge-Harford Hounds

PART I
Maryland's Background

Maryland, My Maryland

PROBABLY no other State in the Union has produced or will produce a man who in his will set aside several hundred thousand dollars for a university auditorium decorated with murals of one-time reigning beauties he had known. Each figure of a more glamorous day was to be painted at the height of her beauty, the bequest specified. Although there may be difficulty in finding an artist—or a group of artists—intrepid enough to attempt the task, some day Maryland will have, immortalized for the benefit of Johns Hopkins University students, representatives of an era Baltimoreans still think of tenderly and with regret for its passing. Although many non-Marylanders like to call the State English and for that matter, many visiting Englishmen say it is reminiscent of home, this sort of thing is almost Viennese in its grace and urbanity. This is an echo of the South that carried over into Maryland after the War between the States; a flavor still an integral part of the State's charm.

To pick out one adjective or even a group of adjectives, and say, 'This is Maryland,' is, of course, impossible. Natives rarely try to define the State's individuality; 'outsiders' try too hard, and, to existing knowledge, have not yet succeeded. English? Yes; for its conservatism, stolidity. Southern? Yes; in its frequent lassitude, its willingness to sacrifice prospects of progress to known, safe comforts. Northern? Yes; in its occasional outbursts of efficiency and industry. Maryland is all of these, and more.

Maryland is the Eastern Shore to New Yorkers who have found haven in handsome Tidewater homes. Maryland is Harford, Baltimore, or Howard County to others who come for hunting and racing. Maryland is the Chesapeake Bay to fishermen and lovers of crabs and oysters. Maryland is terrapin and good whiskey to gourmets, and a beautiful woman to connoisseurs of feminine beauty.

Maryland is only Baltimore to thousands of Americans who pass through the State's metropolis and wonder at its rows of white steps, its remaining gas-lighted street lamps or its areas of crumbling residences. Or Maryland may be Annapolis to the tourist who comes to see the midshipmen during June week.

To the student and historian, Maryland recalls Poe, or Lanier, or clipper ships, or John Hanson, or Taney, or John Wilkes Booth, or Charles Carroll of Carrollton, or the burning of the *Peggy Stewart*, or the attack on Massachusetts troops in the streets of Baltimore, or bloody Antietam. To the romanticist, what State can surpass Betsy Patterson Bonaparte and Wallis Warfield, Margaret Brent and Anna Ella Carroll? Statesmen, soldiers, poets, beauties, teachers, doctors, parade through the State's history. Perhaps many more as great may yet be born and bred in Maryland.

How did all this begin? What are Maryland's roots and why are Marylanders what they are today?

Life that was close to the earth, work and sport on the Chesapeake Bay and others of Maryland's waterways—these provided the beginnings of the substantial body of folklore, folk-customs and folk-language, which through three centuries has become a subconscious, rarely recognized part of life in Maryland. Slave-life in southern Maryland and on the Eastern Shore also played a major role in enriching the State's folkways, for white children, cared for by Negro servants and spending their youth in the company of Negro children, naturally absorbed the influence of their associates.

When the early settlers pushed on into their unknown country, many found homes and a new way of life in western Maryland. From this hardier, more practical type of pioneer, who faced constant conflict with Indians and the daily hardship of earning a living in his rugged countryside, came another sort of folklore. Tall tales of great hunters—hunters of animals and men—crop lore and superstitions absorbed from the Indians, imported customs brought by immigrating Mennonites, Dunkards, and Amish from Pennsylvania—these, too, have been passed down to present-day Marylanders.

During the major part of the nineteenth century, Baltimore was second only to New York as port of entry for immigrants from Europe. Thousands of men, women, and children of nearly every nationality brought with them habits and customs of their native lands, and some of these folkways, too, became part of the native Maryland scene, until today it is difficult in most instances to trace *Marylandia* to its sources.

Probably the richest body of lore and language that is peculiarly Maryland's has sprung from the Eastern Shore, and is still current there. Since the livelihood of the natives might very often be dependent upon the results of a day's work on the water, it is only natural that portents should play a large part in the activities of crabbers, oystermen, and fishermen.

'It's bad luck to swear while fishing.' 'Don't go fishing in the sign of the Crab, fish won't bite then.' 'Spit on your bait for good luck.' 'Fish begin to bite when the dogwood is in blossom.' These and many similar expressions have come to be accepted and are faithfully observed.

Fishermen express their weather lore in an old bit of doggerel:

When the wind is from the north,
  Sailors don't go forth;
When the wind is from the east,
  'Tis neither fair for man nor beast;
When the wind is from the south,
  It blows the bait in the fishes mouth;
When the wind is from the west
  Then it's at its very best.

'If you would catch oysters, sing; if fish, be still.' This is an article of faith to which the Chesapeake oysterman strictly adheres, for he always sings at his work.

The influence of the moon is no more disregarded by watermen than by landsmen whose planting schedule may be based upon the position of the moon. For instance, crabbers say: 'Hard crabs have more meat in them during the increase than during the decrease of the moon.'

To Eastern Shoremen, a 'fly-up-the-creek' is a flighty, scatterbrained individual. To be 'as poor as gar broth' is to be poor, indeed, for the gar is a thin almost meatless fish, offering little nutritional value.

Familiar to both the Eastern Shore and southern Marylanders is the custom originating with Negro slaves of 'kotchin' Marse's Christmas gif.' Until recent years it was still part of the holiday season in old Maryland families. Faithful slaves—and later old retainers—competed with each other for the honor and advantage of being the first to shout 'Chrismus gif', Chrismus gif'' to members of the master's family. The winner, according to ancient custom, would be rewarded with an especially generous supply of presents.

After all the presents had been distributed, the Negroes would sing, including in their varied repertoire old favorites and new versions improvised for the occasion, with flattering personal comments directed toward the master, his wife, and his children. Clapping of hands, shuffling of feet, and rhythmic body movements generally accompanied such a song as 'Pattin' the Juber.'

Juber do, an' Juber don't,
Juber will an' Juber won't;
Juber up an' Juber down,
Juber all aroun' de town.

Sif' de meal an' gimme de husk,
Bake de cake an' gimme de crus',
Fry de pork an' gimme de skin,
Ax me when I'se comin' agin.
Juber, Juber, Juber-ee!

The synchronization of body rhythm to song has long been recognized as of economic value by those in charge of groups of Negro laborers. Beginning in the earliest days of the colony with slaves working in tobacco fields or busy at similar chores, the custom continues in Maryland and can still be observed among gangs of Negro workers along Baltimore's water front or any other group engaged in hard physical labor. A corn-husking song is an example of the older type of Maryland work-song:

> De Jack Snipe said unto de Crane,
> I wish to de Lawd dere would come rain;
> De wile Goose said unto de Swan,
> De comin' winter'll be sharp an' long.
>
> Dey say ole Marse is sick agen,
> He suffer many a' ache an' pain;
> When my old Marse's dead an' gone,
> Dis ole nigger'll stop huskin' corn.
>
> O, my ole Marse is good to me,
> An' when he dies, he'll set me free,
> We've possum fat an' 'taters too,
> Good enuf fo' me an' you.

An Eastern Shore and southern Maryland custom, which has spread throughout the rural sections of the State, is the tournament, a curious survival of a vanished age. Since earliest Colonial days, tilting tournaments have been held at Prince Frederick, Calvert County, and today it is possible to witness these colorful events at many county fairs, church carnivals, and horse shows. For years the only tournament in the East for women riders was held at My Lady's Manor, in Baltimore County.

At Prince Frederick, plumed knights, bearing the names of their ancestral acres, are clad in riding breeches and silk shirts, and each proudly flaunts a favor from his lady as with lance a-tilt he gallops down the field. Mortal combat is not the order of the day, however. The knight must merely transfix with his lance small metal rings suspended from overhead arches. Many of the lances are family heirlooms, handed down from generation to generation.

At the conclusion, the victor of the joust crowns his Queen of Love and Beauty, while runners-up select maids of honor to wait upon the Queen. The entire event ends with a picturesque square dance staged by the royal court, followed by a general dance for guests and spectators.

Headless blacksmiths, phantom black dogs, haunted houses—Maryland has its share of legends of this sort. Old houses, old families, old graveyards breed such lore, and the State's supply of antiquities is not alarmingly diminished. Probably one of Maryland's few claims to a unique ghost is that which deals with a mournful wraith who haunts the western border of the

State, striving to expiate a sin undiscovered until after his death. He moved a boundary marker, the legend goes, in all likelihood a story born at the time of the disputes between Maryland and Pennsylvania over territorial lines.

In the Middletown Valley section of western Maryland the fabulous 'snallygaster' flies into a little settlement of log cabins that served as slave quarters prior to the Civil War. The great bird preys upon Negro children out after dark, and on occasion has even been known to carry off a full-grown man to its lair in the near-by mountains. The name, those who have investigated the legend believe, may well have been a corruption of the German *schnellegeister*, meaning 'quick spirit,' since that section of the State has been heavily infiltrated with German families who migrated from Pennsylvania.

In the farther reaches of western Maryland, neighborhood woodchoppings are still popular, relics of pioneer days when small settlements lived on a communal basis, sharing their meager goods, their work, and their pleasures. On these occasions, the women prepare an elaborate meal, and a barrel of cider is conveniently placed near the workers, who neither expect nor receive any pay for their labors. The day usually ends with an old-fashioned square dance.

Customs and habits inherited from their Swiss and German forebears are still markedly evident among members of the Dunkards, the Mennonites, and the Amish sects in the northern central and western parts of Maryland. Utter simplicity—of life and of apparel—is the creed of these industrious people, most of whom are successful farmers.

Communities of Dunkards gather once a year for a Love Feast and Footwashing. Members of the congregation sit around a large table in the center of the church, and after singing a hymn, dip pellets of bread into a common dish of lamb stew, and eat sandwiches of roast lamb. Finally, each man removes his coat, takes up a towel, bathes and dries the feet of the man beside him, and gives his neighbor the 'kiss of charity' on each cheek. The women then perform the same ceremony. Basins used at the footwashing are kept in the church for this one purpose.

The Maryland idiom, with the exception of that native to the Eastern Shore, has been catalogued by Dr.Hans Kurath as Western American, the type of speech in general use among the overwhelming majority of Americans. 'When you get as far south as Maryland,' James Fenimore Cooper said in 1828, 'the softest and perhaps as pure an English is spoken as is anywhere heard.' This is owing, primarily, to the fact that the colony was first settled by immigrants from the British Isles. To the true Northerner, however, the accents of a Marylander have a pronounced suggestion of a Southern drawl, while to a Virginian or a Carolinian, the Marylander's pronounciation may frequently be tainted with the harshness of the Yankee tongue. Amiable raillery is aimed from every direction at residents of both shores of the State for their pronounciation of *Baltimore*, which from a native sounds something like *Bawlamur*.

Contributions made by Negroes to Maryland vernacular are highly vivid and colorful. For instance, the cuckoo is often called the 'rain-crow'; the domestic guinea-fowl is a 'guinea keat,' or merely a 'keat'; and the 'mammy-baby' is, in the language of the psychiatrist, one who has an Œdipus complex. The constellation Orion among old-fashioned Negroes is known as 'hellinyear,' probably a corruption of the 'elle and yard' colloquialism used generally in both Europe and America to designate Orion.

Many curious words and expressions heard frequently in Maryland have been imported by German settlers. To 'feel for' means to 'like,' as in 'they all felt for peaches'; while to 'try for' is the expression applied to running down a witch or hex.

In Baltimore's Lexington Market, the obsolete term 'levy,' meaning approximately $12\frac{1}{2}$¢, is occasionally heard. For instance, the huckster may offer his *Anaranel* (Anne Arundel County) strawberries at 'a levy a quart.' And the huckster himself is probably called an *a-rab*.

A 'spite lane' is a path between two 'spite fences,' built on either side of a boundary lane by neighbors not on friendly terms, and a 'growing hand' is the gift of a person who succeeds in making sickly plants thrive. 'As independent as a hog on ice' and 'lay low and chew pokeroot' are both homely bits of *Marylandia* which indicate their rural origin.

Marylanders who can trace their ancestry to the early period of colonization are *all* cousins, the outsider quickly concludes. Most of them actually are 'connections,' and when they aren't, they are 'kissing cousins,' which generally means that parents and grandparents were lifelong, intimate friends. The Southern custom of referring to a married woman by her maiden name still persists, and Negro servants who have for long periods been employed by the same families most frequently address their mistresses as 'Miss Mary,' rather than 'Mrs. Browne.'

Among its more distinguished ghosts, Maryland can point with pride to Lincoln, who has appeared rather often, in company with John Wilkes Booth, at sections of Baltimore County once frequented by the actor-assassin. Lamb's School, at Philopolis, numbered among its pupils Booth and his brother Edwin, and the name of the former may still be seen cut in the bark of trees near the one-time school building. The Civil War President, it seems, follows the ghost of Booth along the road leading to the schoolhouse, Lincoln pointing his finger accusingly at his murderer, who bows his head in shame.

These, then, are a few of the facets that gleam brightly, or now, perhaps, flicker only faintly out of the past. These make the color of Maryland, its taste and sight, its sound and fragrance. All these are intangible things, however, and still the exact, measured quality of this small stretch of land remains unnamed, uncatalogued.

Albert Cabell Ritchie, four times governor of Maryland, was born in Virginia. But one of the reasons he *was* governor four times in succession was because he represented—to most Marylanders—all the things they knew and couldn't explain about their State. He defined and expressed, by an inflection of his voice, the essence of the place he had made his home, when he ended many of his public addresses with the words, 'Maryland, My Maryland.'

Natural Setting

THAT they need not look for any other Terrestrial Paradice, to suspend or tyre their curiosity upon' was George Alsop's assurance in
1666 to prospective settlers of Maryland. Three centuries of settlement have dispelled the primitive charm of the early days, but the State's
actual endowment of natural wealth and beauty is only a little diminished.

The three major regions differ widely in topographic character. The
Coastal Plain is the tidewater country, low and level, 'full of Rivers and
Creekes'; almost any point affords view of some arm of the Chesapeake
Bay. The bay divides the plain lengthwise into the low-lying Eastern
Shore and the higher Western Shore. Westward is the Piedmont Plateau,
a broad, gently rolling upland; the larger rivers traversing it have cut
gorges, but most of the streams flow placidly at high level as far as the
Fall Line where the plateau drops to the Coastal Plain. From Catoctin
Mountain to the western border of the State is the Appalachian Mountain
Region, a succession of ridges and valleys. Most of these valleys are narrow; three of greater extent are grouped symmetrically to the Blue Ridge:
the Frederick Valley to the east (actually part of the Piedmont Plateau),
the Hagerstown Valley to the west, and the Middletown Valley between
its two main ridges.

The Coastal Plain has a surface composed of easily eroded sands and
clays. The Piedmont Plateau exhibits resistant rocks whose gently
rounded contours indicate a very protracted period of exposure to the elements. In fact, Maryland is part of one of the longest exposed areas of the
earth's surface.

Some of the oldest rocks known are exposed in the Piedmont Plateau.
During Archean time that region was part of a sea bed on which great
thicknesses of sediment accumulated. From sands and muds these have
been transformed by the stresses of millions of years into white marble and
quartzite, green serpentine, and brown and gray gneisses and schists. The
sedimentary layers were compressed and consolidated, folded up into
mountains, and injected with molten rock from the depths, which solidi-
fied to black gabbro, gray granite, and salmon-colored pegmatite.

During the Paleozoic era the Appalachian Mountain area was a long narrow trough covered for long periods by the sea. Changing conditions are reflected in alternations of sandstone, shale, and limestone at varying distances from the shore line. The warm climate of the Paleozoic era is attested by the fossil remains of a warm-water fauna, which includes the oldest species of coral (*Tetradium simplex* from the Devonian). As the trough became nearly filled with sediment, the region became a great swamp, covered with tree ferns and giant allies of the club mosses and scouring rushes, whose remains have given the State its principal mineral resource in the coal beds of Allegany and Garrett counties.

The Paleozoic era ended with stresses that buckled the Appalachian strata into a series of mountainous swells and troughs, and reversed the drainage as far as the line of the Blue Ridge. The Piedmont rocks were thrust bodily westward over the easternmost Paleozoic sediments, and were for the last time intruded by a large igneous mass, the Woodstock granite.

The first Appalachian Mountains probably attained Alpine proportions, but during the Mesozoic era they were eroded to their roots. Meanwhile the reversal of drainage progressed westward by stream capture. Early in the Triassic period there was an outburst of seismic energy. Along a great fault plane east of Catoctin Mountain, a broad area was dropped more than a mile, to form the floor of the Frederick Valley. The resulting hollow was completely filled with detritus. Toward the end of the period these detrital beds, as also the strong rocks of the Piedmont region, were riven by a series of faults, some of which were invaded by dikes of diabase. Erosion continued throughout the Triassic and Jurassic periods, until the whole of what became Maryland was worn down to become part of an almost flat plain that covered all eastern North America. The remnant of this plain in Maryland is the now deep-buried rock floor of the Coastal Plain.

The Cretaceous period began with a warping of the land that flooded the coast as far as the present Fall Line, but raised the inland region and gave new velocity—hence, cutting power—to the rivers. Thick deposits of sand, clay, and gravel were formed in the lagoons behind the barrier beaches lining the coast.

Maryland contains fossil records of the replacement of the earlier Mesozoic cycads, ginkgoes, and conifers by flowering plants. Early in the Cretaceous period the archaic types were dominant, though poplar, sassafras, sedges, and water lilies were present fairly early; by the end of the period a large number of modern genera had appeared.

All the main types of dinosaurs were represented in Maryland. The vicinity of Muirkirk, Prince Georges County, is one of the few places in

North America that have yielded remains of early Cretaceous forms. The flesh-eaters were *Allosaurus*, 34 feet long, and *Coelurus*, only about five feet long but built for speed and action; these were bipeds with long sharp teeth. Another biped, but of the plant-eating type, was the turtle-beaked *Dryosaurus*. Of the helpless wallowing type, which fed on succulent swamp plants, were two species of *Pleurocoelus*, one 30 feet in length, the other 12.

The cataclysmic disturbance ending the Mesozoic era had no effect in the area. The gently arched surface was gradually worn down once more to a low and monotonous plain (the Schooley Peneplain), with sluggish rivers winding across it in ever-changing courses. After the formation of this plain the land began to rise so gradually that the rivers were able to incise their meandering courses into the rock. A number of intrenched meanders remain along the Upper Potomac and its branches. In time the underlying rock structure of the Appalachian region had its effect on the river courses. Where the sandstones and other hard rocks came to the surface along the flanks of the truncated folds, ridges were formed whose crests were at the former plain level; they deflected the streams, which then carved valleys in the softer shales and limestones. The middle parts of the ancient swells, as well as the troughs between, are now valleys; the crests of the mountains lie near the level of the dissected plain, forming a remarkably even horizon. The harder, more low-lying Piedmont rocks have preserved a similar surface of more recent date.

The Eocene, Miocene, and Pleistocene epochs of the Cenozoic era have left sedimentary records in Maryland; during the Oligocene and the Pliocene epochs alternating with these, the land stood especially high, and deposits were formed far out on the continental shelf.

The Eocene is represented for the most part by greensands and greensand clays, deposited in quiet and fairly deep water. The climate of the time was warm, as shown by fossils of crocodiles, turtles, sharks, eaglerays, shellfish, and corals.

The Miocene formations of Maryland and Virginia furnish data for the whole Atlantic coast. The Calvert Cliffs, 30 miles long and up to 100 feet high, expose a continuous section of clays rich in marine fossils. A drawing of a shell from this place that appeared in 1685 in Martin Lister's *Historia sive Synopsis Methodica Conchyliarum* was the first illustration of an American fossil. Besides a multitude of shellfish, the fauna of the epoch included angelfish, sharks, turtles, crocodiles, whales, dolphins, gannets, and shearwaters.

Maryland was only indirectly affected by the Pleistocene glaciations.

Oscillations of the sea level, resulting from the growth and shrinkage of the ice caps, are recorded in wave-cut cliffs and wave-built terraces at varying heights. An early submergence caused barrier beaches to form near the Fall Line; upon withdrawal of the sea these barriers diverted the rivers, causing the Susquehanna to excavate the valley now occupied by Chesapeake Bay. During the emergent periods the shore line was as far out as the present 100 fathom line; the last of these was so recent that the ocean bottom is still covered with mixed deposits characteristic of dry land. The present distribution of land and water is not more than two or three thousand years old, and the shore line is still in the process of adjustment.

The Pleistocene fauna varied with the alternations of warm and cold climate. As a whole it was that of the present enriched by a number of large forms that are now either foreign or nonexistent. In the former category are the bison, cougar, peccary, and tapir; in the latter, three kinds of elephant (the northern and southern mammoths and a mastodon) and several of the ancient American horse.

CLIMATE

'The temper of the Ayre is very good,' says the anonymous *Relation* of 1635. Seasonal changes in Maryland are well marked but not severe. The mean monthly temperature ranges from 34° for January to 75° for July; the annual temperature varies from 48° in the extreme west to 57° in the extreme south, with a mean of 54° for the State as a whole. Zero weather occurs about once in three years at Baltimore, a little more rarely to the south, and much more frequently to the west. Rainfall is well distributed throughout the year, with a slight maximum in summer and a minimum in autumn; the annual average is 41 inches. The regions of heaviest rainfall are along the Chesapeake Bay shores and in Garrett County; the eastern part of the Appalachian region is relatively dry. Annual snowfall ranges from 16 inches at Easton to 66 inches at Oakland.

FLORA

The plant life of Maryland is a mixture of northern and southern species. Most of the State lies in the eastern belt of hardwood forests, but its extreme corners extend into the northern and southern evergreen zones. A little more than a third of its land area remains in forest, though cultivated lands, when abandoned, are only temporarily overrun by weeds, then give way to new forest growth.

Most of the species dominating the hardwood zone are diffused to some degree throughout the State. Black and white oak and beech are some-times found in pure stands, but mixed forest is more common. In many places black gum is predominant but chestnut and black walnut, formerly of equal or greater importance, have almost entirely disappeared, the former through the chestnut blight, the latter through lumbering. Other trees growing in fairly large numbers are the tulip poplar, yellow locust, pignut, hickory, and white ash. The more open woods are often festooned with virgin's bower (clematis) and honeysuckle, Virginia creeper, or the deceptively similar poison ivy. Three kinds of wild grapes are found and blackberry and raspberry bushes form dense thickets in some areas. In early spring wooded hillsides are carpeted with spring beauty, Carolina cranesbill, trailing arbutus, May apple, and early blue violet. Later appear wild roses, mountain laurel, spotted touch-me-not, and several native and foreign clovers. Conspicuous immigrants such as evening primrose and wild carrot bloom profusely in waste places. Toward fall the composites begin to dominate the landscape with black-eyed Susan, Maryland golden aster, and several varieties of goldenrod covering fields and roadsides.

The chain of serpentine barrens above the Fall Line is covered with patches of post oak, blackjack oak, and red cedar, interspersed with clumps of mountain laurel, sage willow, deerberry, and highbush huckle-berry. Fame-flower and a heatherlike variety of field chickweed are found only in these barrens.

The Coastal Plain shares with the middle zone not only the species hav-ing State-wide distribution, but it also has the chinquapin, American and slippery elm, hackberry, buttonwood, strawberry bush, dogwood, persim-mon, and fringe tree. The dominant evergreens in the southern half are the loblolly and scrub pine, locally called foxtail and spruce pine; the former is more common on the Eastern and the latter on the Western Shore. Other trees found only in the southern section of the Coastal Plain are the Span-ish and willow oak, laurel magnolia, and sweet gum. There holly grows to tree size; roadsides and forest edges are given a touch of vivid color by the trumpet creeper; and partridge pea, succory, and field balm are more com-mon than in the uplands.

The flora of the lower Eastern Shore shows Maryland's kinship with the South. Loblolly pine is thick in large pure stands and also in mixed stands with water oak, southern tupelo, and wax myrtle. Hercules' club, found at the edge of woods throughout the Coastal Plain, is most abundant in this section. The Pocomoke Swamp, a true dismal swamp that extends into Delaware, is the northernmost area where bald cypress is seen.

In the northern evergreen zone, confined to Garrett County, conifers are still completely dominant in a few places—white pine, spruce, and hemlock in the moist forests of the Glades, and hemlock along slopes with a northern exposure. The forest was originally somewhat mixed, and second growth seems to favor the hardwoods. Hardwood stands differ little from those of the east; since the disappearance of the once common chestnut the dominant species are red and white oak and sugar maple. Striped maple and yellow birch are localized here, but sweet birch spreads into the middle zone. Flowering plants in this and the middle zone are wake-robin, tall anemone, water-leaf, tall bellflower, and woodland sunflower; among those limited in Maryland to this region are bush honeysuckle, hobblebush, black snakeroot, papoose root, and narrow-leaved gentian.

FAUNA

The fauna of the State includes northern, southern, and oceanic species: the brown-headed nuthatch breeds in the extreme south; the mockingbird, fish hawk, and fish crow throughout the Coastal Plain; and the cardinal, Carolina wren, tufted tit, and many others on the Piedmont Plateau. The Appalachian region is a nesting ground for such northern birds as the chestnut-sided warbler, rose-breasted grosbeak, Wilson's thrush, and possibly the snowbird.

Shore and water birds, both resident and migratory, are abundant. Of the 41 varieties of ducks observed, about a dozen are common migrants; among the dozen or more that remain the year round are the canvasback, red-breasted merganser, blackhead, mallard, black duck, and wood duck. Geese and swans accompany the ducks in their annual migrations. The great blue heron is a regular summer visitant; the green heron is fairly common, and the black-crowned night heron sometimes becomes so in a few favorable places. Plovers, sandpipers, and rails are common on the marshes and beaches.

The bald eagle is seen in the vicinity of water, especially in the tidewater country but the golden eagle is much rarer and does not breed within the State. The soaring turkey buzzard is common the year round, and the black vulture is an irregular visitant to southern Maryland. Various hawks and owls, especially the latter, are seen even in city suburbs and large parks.

The State is well within the range of the ruby-throated hummingbird, which ventures at times into city gardens. The extinct Carolina paroquet formerly ranged as far north as the Potomac, but the last recorded specimen in this region was shot in 1865.

'There are likewise sundry sorts of Birds which sing, whereof some are red, some blew, others blacke and yellow,' Father White wrote. The early colonists could not fail to notice the songbird that bore their overlord's heraldic colors; Lord Baltimore himself is said to have observed it with great pleasure during his visit to Virginia in 1628. Although widely distributed, the Baltimore oriole has always been viewed with proprietary interest by Marylanders. In 1882 killing orioles or possessing them, live or dead, was forbidden by law; the same protection, later extended to all song and insectivorous birds, has resulted in a multitude of thrushes, finches, warblers, and sparrows through most of the State. The whippoorwill, chuck-will's widow, and nighthawk are fairly common, especially in the southern part of the State.

Large mammals have become rare. Timber wolves have utterly vanished and black bears are only occasionally reported in the mountains, but bobcats are still fairly common in the wilder parts of Garrett County. A handful of topographic names is the only reminder of the elk and woodland bison that once ranged down to the Fall Line. Nine Beaverdam Creeks memorialize the animal whose fur was once a staple article of commerce between Indians and whites.

The Virginia deer, eastern cottontail rabbit, raccoon, opossum, red and gray fox, and mink are found throughout the State. The Coastal Plain marshes offer a favorable environment to the rice rat and Virginia musk-rat; the latter is bred on several commercial fur farms. The fox squirrel lives chiefly below the Fall Line, the red and gray squirrels, woodchuck, wood rat, chipmunk, and otter above it. In the uplands, especially in the mountain zone, are the New England cottontail rabbit, snowshoe hare, and cloudland deer-mouse.

Six snakes have their northern limit in Maryland: the corn snake (red rat snake), yellow rat snake, brown king snake, striped water snake, water pilot (brown water snake), and scarlet snake. Though the last resembles and is often mistaken for the poisonous southern *elaps* (not found in Maryland), there are actually only two poisonous species in the State, the timber rattlesnake and the copperhead. The former is most common in the mountains north of Montgomery County; the latter is unevenly distributed in wet places throughout the State. The mountain or pilot blacksnake, which attains a length of more than seven feet, is more numerous than the black racer but is less widely distributed. The garter snake and ribbon snake are abundant throughout, the queen snake and water snake are common in the vicinity of streams, and the pine snake is seen only in the woods and sandy places of the Eastern Shore.

The diamond-back terrapin abounds in the marshes of the lower Eastern Shore. Another edible variety, less highly valued, is the wood terrapin found in moist upland woods. Among amphibians are several widely distributed species of frogs and toads, a peculiar tree frog (*Hyla evittata*) found only in the vicinity of Washington, the mud eel of the Coastal Plain, and the mud puppy of the mountain streams.

The fields and roadsides in summer are bright with butterflies. Large swallowtails are especially common in the eastern half of the State, with the zebra swallowtail in greatest numbers in the lower tidewater counties. The sulphurs, monarch, and painted lady are also more frequent in the east, leaving the mountain region to smaller and less brilliant types. In early summer one of the most conspicuous insects is the handsome but destructive Japanese beetle, which has spread over the State in great numbers during the past decade. The damage done by the seventeen-year locust—which is a cicada, not a locust—is now much less severe than formerly. There are three broods in Maryland: one swarm that appeared last in 1936 has wide distribution; a smaller swarm, due in 1940, is in the upper Potomac basin; and another, due in 1945, is in southern Maryland. None appears in the Eastern Shore, where the water table is too close to the surface for their burrowing larvae.

The streams and tidal waters are inhabited by 200 species of fish, a large number of them now classified as commercial or game fish. Every spring shad, alewives, croakers, and others ascend the bay on their way to the larger rivers to spawn. Off the Eastern Shore in the ocean are skate, sting ray, marlin, swordfish, and dogfish and other sharks; these at times wander into Chesapeake Bay.

The most conspicuous members of the invertebrate fauna are the edible blue crab and the oyster. Spider crabs and several varieties of shrimp and prawn are found in the lower parts of the Bay. Jellyfish—sea nettles and ctenophores—spread up the Bay in summer, a few remaining as late as November; they are sometimes troublesome at bathing beaches.

Perhaps the most fascinating inhabitants of tidal Maryland are the *Noctilucae*, tiny protozoa that give weird light with every movement of the waters.

The Indians

MUCH of Maryland's Indian history naturally concerns the tidewater region, the area of early settlement. There, peacefully for the most part but always uneasily, the colonists lived with four tribes or 'nations' as neighbors. Three of these, the Piscataways of southern Maryland and the Nanticokes and Pocomoke-Assateagues of the Eastern Shore, were of Algonquin stock and had similar dialects and customs. The fourth was the Susquehannock, or Sasquesahannock nation, an Iroquoian enemy of the Piscataway known in their own language as Andaste, Gandaste, Gandastoguez, or Conestoga. It was pressure from this tribe that forced the Piscataway into a defensive alliance with the white newcomers and enabled the early colonists to avoid serious clashes with other aborigines. Nevertheless Maryland's colonial history is sprinkled with stories of scalpings and of minor frontier forays. The Indian allies always blamed strays from other tribes for the thefts and occasional raids on isolated cabins; the colonists in turn occasionally had to make rather elaborate apologies to cover up the part played by some of the more reckless Europeans in disturbing the Indian peace. But there was never any serious breach of the compact on either side.

Little is known of the very earliest Marylanders; their skeletons have nearly all disintegrated and the white colonists did not collect even legends about them. There is evidence, however, that the area was inhabited for centuries before the historic Algonquin arrived and that the inhabitants had cruder artifacts than those used in the two or three centuries just before European contact. Relics of this early people include soapstone bowls, grooved axes, arrow points, and simple pottery, but no pipes.

According to their own tradition, the historic Algonquin arrived only some three centuries before the whites. Whether they destroyed, drove away, or absorbed the earlier groups is unknown. Somewhat later the upland regions were overrun by Iroquoian tribes. The Susquehannock, of this group, were still extending their conquests from the Susquehanna valley into the Chesapeake Bay country in the seventeenth century. In that century's early years the Susquehannock made themselves overlords of the Delaware, whose territory extended from Pennsylvania into the Eastern Shore peninsula, and forced the Western Shore Indians to retire from their lands east of the Patuxent River.

Anthropologists studying the skeletons of Maryland aborigines find little physical difference among the tribes; the average for their cranial index places them just within the longheaded group, and other characteristics are similar to those of most other Indians of the Atlantic region. The account of the Susquehannock written by George Alsop is therefore somewhat exaggerated: 'a people cast into the mold of a most large and warlike deportment, the men being for the most part seven foot high in latitude, and in magnitude and bulk suitable to so high a pitch; their voice large and hollow, as ascending out of a Cave, their gate strait and majestick.'

Also within the Coastal Plain and on its borders were several smaller tribes of uncertain affinity, which were absorbed by the others or driven away in early colonial times. Within the tribes were local groups and subdivisions, such as the Choptico, Mattawoman, and Choptank River or Locust Neck Indians; thus the provincial records mention what some later writers attempted to dignify as tribes. Some of these were important enough to be accorded separate treaties with the province, but upon such occasions as the election of tribal 'emperors' they manifested their true position as members of the several nations.

The mode of life of the Maryland Indians was basically the same as that of all northeastern tribes, with modifications that owed their development to local conditions and resources. They built true wigwams, round or apsidal huts of bark or mats over a framework of saplings; made grooved stone axes, used shell money, and made net-marked or incised pottery (the Susquehannock made collared jugs of the distinctive Iroquoian type, with a few peculiarities of their own). The fish and fowl teeming in the Chesapeake area stimulated the development of gear for their taking. Indian nets were in demand among the English, who were accustomed to make trips to the native villages to buy them. The making of baskets and mats was also highly developed. Cecil Lord Baltimore asked his brother Governor Leonard Calvert to order enough matting from the Indians, some 350 yards, to carpet his house. Log canoes were seaworthy enough to be bought, traded, bequeathed, and stolen by Englishmen. Their type was later developed by the whites into the modern Chesapeake Bay canoe, formed of several logs pinned together and hewn to shape. The fondness of the Indians for oysters and clams is evident today in the numerous shells found in their garbage pits and the large shell heaps along the shores. (The most notable of these shell heaps is the huge deposit on Popes Creek, the beginning of which dates back to prehistoric times.)

Blood relationship and the inheritance of chattels, honors, and rights were reckoned in the female line, from a mother's sons to her daughters' sons, her daughters' daughters' sons, and so on. The Susquehannock had full-fledged matrilineal clans of the Iroquoian type, with animal eponyms; but the Algonquin tribes had borrowed only the rule of descent. Among the latter chieftainship was elective among the brothers or nephews of the deceased chief. Each village had two chiefs and two councils, dividing between them the affairs of war and peace. The earliest records preserve the native titles: *Werowance* for the war chief, *Cockarouses* for members of his council, *Wisoes* for members of the council of peace—the name of the chief peace officer does not appear. In a short time the colonists had replaced these with a set of English titles considerably more august than the case demanded, but more familiar from their own political experiences: King and Councilors, Speaker and Great Men. Each of the three nations was under the primacy rather than the government of a high chief (*Tayac* or *Tallak*) who, as the superior of kings, was necessarily called in English an emperor. The Susquehannock government appears, on what slender evidence there is, to have been more nearly republican and to have been based on the clan system: treaties were signed on some occasions by all the clan chiefs, but on others by an official called the 'Chief Generall Counsellor of the Sasquesahanough Nation.'

Burial customs varied from period to period. According to Alsop, the Susquehannock put away their dead in seated position in pits roofed with bark. Some of the later Algonquin tribes kept the bones of chiefs and their families, wrapped in deerskin, in special wigwams called *quiacosan* houses. Also in the later period secondary burial was widely practiced; ossuaries containing bones of 250 to 600 persons have been uncovered. In single burials there were also wide differences of position; while the flexed position was most usual, extended or dismembered burials have also been found.

Before the colonization of Maryland, Virginian adventurers had laid the foundations of the fur trade. For a while the Potomac River Piscataway and Anacostin fared best in this traffic, since the Anacostin held a trade monopoly with the Iroquois, but late in the 1620's William Claiborne began to trade on the Chesapeake and later established a permanent post on Kent Island, to the advantage of other tribes. The coming of the colonists turned the tables again; Governor Leonard Calvert, having established friendly relations with the Emperor of Piscataway, bought the site and lands of Yaocomaco, a village whose people were on the point of retreating westward to escape the Susquehannock. This village became St. Marys, the first capital of Maryland.

The province was always careful to maintain good relations with the several divisions of the Piscataway, their bulwark against the warlike Susquehannock, and the Piscataway reluctantly accepted the alliance as a defensive measure of value to themselves. In time the colonists came to depend on them for scouts, hunters, and the like. The Jesuit missionaries who came with the first colonists made a fair number of converts among the natives, a few of whose descendants, somewhat mixed in blood, still survive in Charles and Prince Georges counties under the name of We-Sorts. Most notable of the early converts was the Emperor Kittamaquund, baptized in 1640. Having gained the 'throne and scepter of Pascattaway' by poisoning his predecessor Uwannis, he ruled for only a few years before his own death. Emperors as a rule were short-lived, for the Indians were expert poisoners. Once in confirming the election of a new native ruler, the governor stipulated with some acerbity that he must live longer than his predecessors.

The founding of the colony and the alliance between the English and the emperor did not lessen the pressure of the Susquehannock upon the Piscataway, but rather increased it by putting the former at a disadvantage in trade. The Marylanders' seizure in 1638 of Claiborne's trading post, the principal market for Susquehannock furs, aggravated the intertribal ill feeling and brought the colonists within its range. It was necessary to send military expeditions to the head of the bay in 1642 and 1643. On the second trip the militia managed to lose a quantity of arms, including two field pieces. This fact came to light when John Lewger, secretary of the province, issued over the absent governor's signature a commission to treat for their recovery. Upon the governor's return Lewger was summarily removed from office. About this time, however, events northward began to change the attitude of the Susquehannock toward the province and its Piscataway allies.

In 1647 the Susquehannock, called by Alsop 'the most Noble and Heroick Nation of Indians that dwell upon the confines of America,' offered their aid to the Huron against the Five Nations. The Huron were defeated and made captive or scattered. In 1651 the same offer was made to the Neutrals, who were likewise overthrown. The next year, to insure themselves against the same fate, the chiefs of seven Susquehannock clans made a treaty of peace with the province of Maryland. It was not until 1661 that they were hard pressed enough to apply for actual aid. In response to their appeal the government made a treaty of mutual assistance and sent a supply of munitions and a levy of untrained 'soldiers' who got into trouble with the Susquehannock chiefs and came home in a great hurry. The war dragged on from year to year, with what help in men and arms the provincial council could bludgeon out of an unwilling assembly.

By 1674 the issue had become so plain that the assembly decided that peace ought to be made with the Iroquois, even at the price of a war with the Susquehannock. The next winter the Five Nations destroyed the Susquehannock fort and carried most of the tribe into captivity. (The fort is reputed to have been exactly on the fortieth parallel, the original boundary of Maryland; its site figured in the dispute with the Penns.) A remnant took refuge near the Potomac in an abandoned Piscataway stockade. During the summer there were several murders, which were ascribed to Susquehannocks. A combined force of Virginians under Colonel John Washington—grandfather of George Washington—and Marylanders under Major Thomas Truman marched on the fort to demand an explanation. Five chiefs, coming out to parley under a flag of truce, were massacred. Truman was impeached for his participation in this crime but his punishment was light. The survivors withstood a long siege, then escaped to southern Virginia, killing on the way more than enough whites to repay the murder of their leading men. This incursion was one of the series of events which gave rise to Bacon's Rebellion. Later the Susquehannock returned to join those who had already submitted to the Five Nations.

Not all the colonists shared the government's good will toward the Indians; to some, especially to the Puritans who gradually came into control, they were Canaanites to be driven out. For protection against this element all Indian lands near the settlements were from time to time surveyed and resurveyed, and the English forbidden to settle on them. But the Indians were gradually weakened and as the number of settlers increased, safeguards of this sort availed little against the self-righteous arrogance of the newcomers. In the spring of 1697 the Piscataway Emperor Ochotomaquah and a large number of his people, giving up all hope of keeping their lands, went off to the mountains of Virginia, whence all the blandishments of the English failed to lure them back. They remained on the upper Potomac for 14 years or more, then drifted northward to take refuge in the Long House of the Five Nations. During these migrations the Piscataway came to be known by the Iroquois name of Conoy or Ganawese. Finally in 1735 the lord proprietary ordered that all existing reserves be erected into manors.

The Eastern Shore Indians, the Nanticoke and the Pocomoke-Assateague, were throughout their history exceedingly active as lobbyists. There was scarcely a session of the assembly at which their representatives did not appear with some complaint or other, asserting that the colonists were squatting on their land, lumbering in their woods, breaking their traps, or letting cows into their corn. For nearly twenty years Unnacokassimon, Emperor of Nanticoke (d.1686), escaping the usual fate of the Piscataway emperors, kept his people in order and insured protection of their rights at the capital. His successors were less able men; one, for reasons unknown, ran away to the Iroquois and was deposed by the tribe. The Pocomoke-Assateague, once powerful, were decimated by the atrocities of Colonel Edmund Scarborough of Virginia. The remnant gathered into a single large town at Askiminokonson opposite the present Snow Hill. For a while the title of Emperor of Assateague continued to be used in treaties, but in time the tribe combined with the Nanticoke.

In 1742, on the pretense of making an emperor, every Indian on the Eastern Shore disappeared into the marshes. Investigation revealed that a number of chiefs had become involved in a fantastic plot for a general uprising, fomented by an errant Shawnee chief, Messowan. The provincial government dissolved the empire, making the title of Emperor merely honorary, and placed each town directly under its own authority. Thereafter there was much agitation for permission to emigrate, and by the end of the decade a large part of the tribe had moved to the Susquehanna and become tributary to the Iroquois. This group moved slowly northward, and their descendants are now in Ontario, Canada. Of those who stayed in Maryland, one section lived on the Choptank reserve until 1798, when the State, having purchased all but 100 acres, parceled out this remainder among the four or five families left. The last survivor of the group is said to have died some time in the 1840's. Another remnant of the tribe, retaining next to nothing of native culture, has survived near Indian River in Delaware.

The central and western parts of the State were not thoroughly explored nor settled until well into the eighteenth century. The mountain region was never very heavily populated by Indians, but served chiefly as a hunting ground; settlements were confined to the Frederick and Hagerstown Valleys and the bottom lands of smaller valleys. The widespread migrations that had begun just before the end of the seventeenth century had affected this region, and the settlers found only a few bands of Shawnee along the upper Potomac. The principal villages were Caiuctucuc and King Opessa's Town; abandoned by the Indians before the middle of the eighteenth century, their sites were later occupied by Cumberland and Oldtown. As several branches of the Great Warriors' Path crossed the western part of the State, the settlers were often visited by parties of northern and southern Indians on the way to raid each other's towns. At times these parties met and there were engagements which local tradition has magnified into tremendous battles. During the French and Indian War, the uprising of Pontiac, and the Revolution, western Maryland was open to the attacks of 'foreign' Indians, who as a rule caused more fright than damage. Sporadic visitations from the Northwest Territory, similar to those experienced in other states, continued into the early part of the nineteenth century.

History

MARYLAND has been a political entity for 308 years. In the course of the first 144 it changed from wilderness thinly inhabited by people with a Stone Age culture to an English feudal domain, then to an independent state. During the next century and a half it gradually took its place in a union of states and further developed its natural and human resources. Any account of its history is bound to pay more attention to the events of that first period in which a pattern of life was set and problems developed that were to influence events of the second period. The key to Maryland history is compromise, involving enlightened toleration of opposing interests and views for the sake of domestic peace and prosperity. The province had every ingredient for the bitter struggles that disturbed other colonies for long periods, and on several occasions came close to open war, but common sense was always invoked to avert disaster. Dispassionate historians from other parts of the country have paid tribute to the wisdom with which the rulers and the leaders handled not only the Indians but also the conflicting religious, social, and economic interests. As far as human frailty permitted, Marylanders have lived up to the injunction in the royal charter that their laws should be 'Consonant to Reason.'

THE PROVINCE

At the time the *Ark* and the *Dove* bore the first Maryland settlers into the Great Bay of Chesapeake in the early spring of 1634, the bay with its rich bordering territory had long been known. Europeans had been nosing along the shores in pinnace, yacht, or bark—traders from Virginia since 1608, occasional Dutchmen after 1624, and long before either, the Spaniards; they had explored the whole Atlantic coast by 1526 and by 1556 had described the bay and named it Santa Maria. Sir Walter Raleigh knew of it at the time of his unsuccessful colonizing experiment from 1585 to 1587 at Roanoke, Virginia, and had instructed Governor Jones to explore it, possibly for a northwest passage to the Indies and definitely for a specially advantageous site for settlement.

When Calvert's company arrived, William Claiborne, an agent for some London merchants, had trading rendezvous on several islands in Chesapeake Bay and the Susquehanna River, and a large, well-supplied settlement about his headquarters on Kent Island. Henry Fleete, a rival, was also trading in Maryland, mostly along the Potomac; in five years of Indian captivity he had acquired a knowledge of native languages that was to be of great service to the first colonists.

George Calvert, projector of the Maryland colony, was born in Yorkshire about 1580. He was knighted in 1617 and became principal secretary of state to James I in 1619. The Calverts were a mercantile family of Flemish origin whose shrewd practicality and conservatism have in some measure left their mark on Maryland to the present day. Sir George's interest in colonial ventures was shown by his membership in the Virginia Company and his position on the board of the New England Company. Wishing to found a colony of his own he turned to Newfoundland, the fisheries of which had attracted transient fishermen for more than a century and projectors of colonies for nearly as long. In 1620 Calvert bought a large tract in the southeastern part of the island from another proprietor and this was patented to him by James I as the Province of Avalon on April 7, 1623.

As 'true and absolute Lords and Proprietaryes' Sir George and his heirs were to have great powers in Avalon. The province was to be held 'in Capite by Knights service'; a white horse was to be yielded whenever the king should visit it, also one fifth of all gold and silver mined. The lords proprietaries were empowered by special clauses of the charter to make laws, grant lands, raise armies, and establish ports, towns, and churches. There were no taxes payable to the crown, save for customs in English and Irish ports after ten years. The lawmaking power was made subject to the assent of the freeholders, who were to be assembled for the making of laws.

In 1624 Calvert professed adherence to the outlawed Church of Rome, thus becoming disqualified for public office. To keep him on the privy council, James made him Baron of Baltimore in the Irish peerage. Shortly afterward James died, but his successor, Charles I, was not unfriendly to the courtier.

Before long Lord Baltimore had made his attempt at colonization; he himself spent the winter of 1627 in Newfoundland and the next year took his wife and children out with him. But by the end of the second spring he was disgusted with 'his intolerable plantation at Newfoundland where he hath found between eight and nine months winter,' and sailed for Virginia. The Virginians were only moderately friendly, for it was apparent that

Calvert was looking for real estate with a better climate; his attention was first turned to lands south of the James but he later shifted his attention to the peninsula between the ocean and the bay. He sought a charter for this land and it was granted but before it had passed the seals he died (1632). This charter granting the peninsula and the land between the south bank of the Potomac and the fortieth parallel was issued by Charles I to 'Cecilius' Calvert, second Lord Baltimore, on June 20, 1632. It is told that though Calvert favored Crescentia (Land of Increase) as the name for his province he had tactfully left a blank for a name to be filled in by his sovereign. The king suggested the name of his queen.

The new charter was largely a duplicate of the old. The changes were in the direction of greater liberality; tenure was in simple fealty, with the return of two Indian arrows a year. Laws were to be subject to the assent of the freemen—not the freeholders. There were to be no crown taxes, but the customs moratorium was not renewed.

Baltimore opened an office in London and freely advertised the attractions of his province with the inducement of easily acquired land; and he cited instances of the eagerness of the Indians for the teachings of Christianity, mentioning Anglican and Puritan clergy to show that he welcomed other faiths than his own. For in addition to combating formal assaults upon his charter by Virginia partisans and others, he had to overcome various rumors, including those that he was transporting nuns and soldiers to the king of Spain, and that he intended to establish a Roman Catholic state in America.

Father Andrew White organized the Catholic part of the expedition—which probably composed less than half—and Calvert himself selected from all applicants those best fitted to promote the colony and keep religious and civil peace. After many delays caused by his opponents, some 200 colonists, consisting of gentlemen adventurers with their families, yeomen, artisans, and laborers, some with families, also indentured and other servants, finally sailed on November 22, 1633, with Cecil's twenty-five-year-old brother Leonard as governor.

The *Ark* and the *Dove*, parted by a severe storm shortly after leaving England, followed separately the circuitous route chosen, by way of the Canaries and Antilles, and were reunited at Barbados. After a brief stop in Virginia, reached on March 5, 1634, where they were kindly treated by Governor John Harvey despite some antagonism owing to Virginia interest in Maryland lands, the pilgrims went on up the bay.

Coming to anchor off an island in the Potomac—the colonists named it St. Clements but it was later renamed Blakistone—Leonard Calvert followed Lord Baltimore's instructions to make friends with the natives. The governor treated with the Indians, first at Piscataway, chief village of an Indian confederacy, and later at Yaocomico with the aid of Henry Fleete, the trader. The Indians of Yaocomico, greatly decimated and already planning to move out of reach of the fierce Susquehannock, sold their townsite to the English, turned over part of the wigwams and fields at once, and agreed to vacate entirely after the harvest. This ready-made settlement was renamed Saint Marys and made the capital of the province.

After the colonists landed in St.Clements the Catholic group celebrated the feast of the Annunciation on March 25. Setting up 'a great cross hewn from a tree,' the governor and other Catholics, wrote Father White in his *Relatio Itineris*, 'humbly recited on bended knees, the Litanies of the Sacred Cross with great emotion.' No chronicle of the first worship of the Protestants has been preserved, but they too, in the manner of the day, and according to their several faiths, must have held some service of thankfulness. The beauty of the primeval region, its fertility and resources, observed at the beginning of spring, could hardly have left any colonists unmoved.

Under the conditions of settlement offered by the proprietor, each person who came at his or her own expense (there were several women adventurers) received 100 acres of land. If the 'adventurer' transported fewer than five others, he received an additional 100 acres for each person over 16 years and 50 for each under that age. For transporting five settlers between 16 and 60 years, he received 2,000 acres. By this 'headright' system a wealthy man who brought ten, twenty, or more settlers was entitled to great tracts of land, even though after the first year the allowance for transporting five persons was cut to 1,000 acres. The large grants were often seated as manors, those who received them corresponding to the lords of manors in England, with the right to hold local court leet and court baron, and to numerous fees and fines, as well as to rents of tenants. Sixty-one such manors were granted during the seventeenth century. Artisans, besides their initial grants, were given extra land for practicing their arts as masons, brickmakers, carpenters, leather dressers. In addition to these classes of holdings, the proprietor made grants on different terms, especially to relatives and friends. All who held land in the province of Maryland—whether a manor, large freehold estate, or one of the fifty-acre tracts given indentured servants when their term of service expired—paid an annual quitrent to the proprietor, at first in pounds of good wheat, later in tobacco, for each 50 acres.

Claiborne had already protested against the Maryland grant, though he had only a trading license and no land patent. Efforts were made at first to conciliate him, but he would not admit Lord Baltimore's jurisdiction over Kent Island—the conflict became a minor war with a battle between Claiborne's *Cockatrice* and Maryland's little *St.Helen* and *St.Margaret* at the mouth of the Pocomoke River on April 23, 1635. The Marylanders were victorious in this engagment but were less successful in another encounter on May 10. Warfare was ended by acting-Governor Francis West of Virginia, who put both parties under bond to keep the peace. George Evelin appeared late in 1636 as agent for Cloberry and Company, Claiborne's principals, and soon supplanted him in control of the island. Thereafter Evelin urged the islanders to submit to Maryland and have the benefit of its liberal trading privileges, and finally induced Governor Calvert to send an armed expedition, which 'reduced' the island settlement.

The First General Assembly, which convened at St.Marys on February 26, 1635, passed a number of laws, which Lord Baltimore promptly vetoed on the principle that the assembly had no right to propose them. The next assembly, in January 1638, rejected the laws Lord Baltimore sent from England and passed others that were also rejected; however, on August 21 Lord Baltimore diplomatically conceded the right of initiative and delegated the power of assent to his governor.

These first assemblies were general, with all freemen bound to attend either in person or by proxy. As the growth of the colony made these folkmeets impracticable, as well as inconvenient, election of delegates gradually prevailed. In the same period the members of the Council, a permanent executive body, began to sit separately as the Upper House of Assembly.

The conflict in England between king and parliament, cavalier and roundhead, had more serious repercussions in Maryland than in other colonies. In February 1645, Captain Richard Ingle, an ardent parliamentarian, landed an armed force that seized St.Marys. Shortly thereafter, either in collaboration or independently, Claiborne seized Kent Island. Governor Calvert sought aid in Virginia, which royal colony eventually sent Captain Edward Hill with an order to bring back certain of the invaders. Hill stayed in Maryland with a rather mysterious commission as governor, received on July 30, 1646. The Ingle regime, severe at first, was by then on the wane. On July 31 the Catholic celebration of the feast of St.Ignatius with an artillery salute in the night resulted only in the confiscation of the 'papists'' arms and powder. The assembly called by Hill was in session when in December Leonard Calvert appeared with an armed force and captured the whole body. Hill was allowed to return to Virginia, and the assembly was continued. Claiborne tried to raise an expedition to retake Saint Marys, but the Kent Islanders would not follow him and he withdrew a second time.

Governor Calvert died June 9, 1647, leaving Thomas Greene in nomination as his successor and Mistress Margaret Brent as the sole executrix of his will. Mistress Brent (*see Tour* 11) was an energetic and capable woman who became his lordship's attorney and as such demanded (but was not granted) a seat in the Upper House of the Maryland assembly.

In an effort to placate the parliamentarians who were victorious in England, Lord Baltimore replaced Greene by the Protestant William Stone and gave a majority of Council positions to Protestants. As a safeguard to toleration he proposed the Act Concerning Religion which was passed with some Puritan amendments in April 1649. About the same time at Governor Stone's invitation, a group of Puritans left Virginia, where they were extremely unpopular, to settle by the Severn River. Their settlement, which they called Providence, included the site of Annapolis.

Charles I was beheaded in 1649. When the news reached Maryland, Greene, as acting governor in Stone's absence, followed Virginia's example in proclaiming Charles II king. Both Stone and the proprietary repudiated this action, but the harm was done. Commissioners, of whom Claiborne was one, were sent out to 'reduce' the Chesapeake Bay colonies. After 'reducing' Virginia they arrived in Maryland in March 1652. Governor Stone, parliamentarian though he was, refused to submit because the articles of submission violated the charter. He was unseated and replaced by a council, but reinstated in June. At first, despite Claiborne's lifelong enmity to Lord Baltimore, the commissioners acted with fair moderation. Stone, however, continued to insist strongly on the proprietary authority; wherefore in July 1654, the commissioners once more removed him and disfranchised all who had opposed them, which included the Roman Catholics. A new Act Concerning Religion passed in that year, withdrew protection from adherents of both 'papacy' and 'prelacy' (Anglicanism).

Cromwell had become Lord Protector in 1653 and had been proclaimed as such by Stone before his second removal. Early in 1655 the surprising news came that Cromwell wished Lord Baltimore to keep his province. Stone gathered an armed force to reduce the Providence settlement but was defeated and captured in the battle of the Severn, March 25, 1655.

The Puritans were now in complete control, but Cromwell's attitude did not change. Matters were settled on November 30, 1657, by an agreement between Lord Baltimore and representatives of the Maryland Puritans.

Josias Fendall was commissioned governor with instructions to renew the 1649 Act Concerning Religion and to compensate those who had suffered in the struggle.

Fendall took office without trouble in February 1658, the people being weary of a conflict that had brought business chaos. After two years of apparent quiet an assembly was convened in February 1660, the lower house of which declared at Fendall's instigation that it alone constituted the assembly, dependent on no other power in the province. Fendall promptly gave up his commission and received another from the assembly. This revolt was ended by the arrival in December of Philip Calvert with a commission as governor and an order from King Charles II, then on the throne, for all subjects to aid in re-establishing the proprietary authority.

This marked the beginning of thirty years of relative peace and prosperity. Settlement expanded rapidly along the bay and the principal rivers. There were no towns. The great estates near the bay and many of the larger number of small plantations along the tributaries shipped their produce from their own wharves. All land was held feudally for a quitrent of four shillings on each 100 acres. Until 1683 free transportation of settlers into Maryland entitled the transporter to acreage; thereafter a small 'caution money,' a sort of purchase price, was required. The purchaser obtained a warrant, had the land surveyed, and then received his patent. Both warrant and patent were transferable and divisible; land speculation, such as there was, was in warrants rather than in actual holdings.

Tobacco growing was the chief business in Maryland as in Virginia. Early attempts to make the province more self-sufficient by diversified planting had been abandoned. Tobacco largely replaced coined money as the medium of exchange. By 1667 expansion of the cultivated area had resulted in a glutted market and reduced prices, causing Maryland to join Virginia and North Carolina in ruling that 'no tobacco shall be sown, set, planted or anyway tended' in that year. The proprietary emphatically rejected this measure because of the harm it would do to 'the poorer sort of Planters (who are the most in number, and of whom the Lord Baltimore must have as tender a care as of the rich).' 'Cessation' was brought up more than once in the years that followed but was never adopted in Maryland.

The period was one of increased absolutism on the part of both the king and the lord proprietary. The important positions in the province were given to Calvert relatives and friends, mostly Roman Catholic. The Puritans were dividing into sects and no longer formed a powerful unit, but the large majority (composed of Protestants and those uninterested in religious affiliation) was forced into a certain unity by the Roman Catholic dominance in high places. Restriction of the franchise by a property qualification, adopted in or before 1681, was another source of grievance. Dissatisfaction was largely expressed in petty bickerings between the two houses of assembly, but from time to time the lower house uttered forceful and eloquent statements of its rights and immunities as the voice of the people.

Philip Calvert served as governor from 1660 to 1662, and Charles, son of Cecil, from 1662 to 1675, when his father died. Charles was the first of the lords proprietary to govern the province in person (1679–84).

With the rapid increase of trade which came in the period after the Navigation Act of 1660 was put into effect, the crown and the proprietary determined to regularize colonial trade, curbing the system by which a man could avoid the unpleasant customs duties by shipping from his own wharf on his own ship or that of any nation he chose. In 1683 an Act for the Advancement of Trade was passed, establishing towns—really customs houses —through which all imports and exports were supposed to pass. Some of the towns thus established never went beyond the paper stage, others had brief lives, yet others flourished for a century or so, and a few became centers of importance.

The planters did not submit easily to this curb and in time Maryland waters came to be policed by two sets of revenue officers, proprietary and royal. Minor friction was unavoidable and unending. James II, though a Roman Catholic, found little cause to exempt Maryland from his plans for bringing all colonies directly under the crown. Proceedings had been instituted against all proprietary charters when the Protestant Revolution gave the throne to Mary and her consort, William of Orange.

A group headed by the former clergyman John Coode staged its own revolution in Maryland, with the result that a government under royal control was set up in 1689. The charter was not revoked, Lord Baltimore's rights as chief landlord were untouched, but his political powers were suppressed. The excuse was that he might make Maryland a center of reaction and Jacobitism. One of the first acts of Francis Nicholson, the first royal governor, was to change the capital from remote St.Marys to the banks of the Severn, where he had Annapolis laid out. Royal governors administered the province from 1692 to 1715, when Benedict Leonard Calvert publicly renounced 'the Romish errors.'

The actual form of government was not modified by the revolution of 1689, but the spirit and manner of its operation were radically changed. The royal governors were devout advocates of the divine right of kings, who 'always Studied Loyalty to God Almighty's Vice Gerent on Earth.' There was much less concern for the good of the colonists as a whole and they were often reported as 'sour ill natured Incendiaries' moved by 'the restless antimonarchial Spirit of an ungovernable Faction.' Sale of public offices became the rule.

The first act of the royal government was a bill of establishment, imposing a tax of forty pounds of tobacco per poll to support the Church of England. Resentment by the growing number of nonconformists was partly responsible for the clause in the later Declaration of Rights, 'that the levying of taxes by the poll is grievous and oppressive, and ought to be prohibited.' There was no intention of abandoning general toleration, but the activities of Catholic supporters of the Stuarts brought suspicion and oppression upon Catholics in general.

The most progressive action of the royal government was its last assembly's thorough revision of laws, a much needed step as the province had outgrown the conditions responsible for many of them. A comprehensive body of laws was adopted, some of which remain in force to the present.

Throughout these changes in government the perpetual insurgence of the lower house continued to operate and gained measurably in dignity and effectiveness. There was an increasing consciousness of inherent rights as Englishmen and increasing objection to legislation that discriminated between residents of the British Isles and those of the province. Though the colony had turned its back on the neutral religious policy of the first Calverts, the act establishing the state church contained the clause 'that the Great Charter of England be observed in all points.' Other statements of no less vigor were elicited by almost every session of the assembly.

Boundary disputes with the Penns had begun upon the granting of Pennsylvania in 1681. Previous relations with the Swedes and Dutch on the Delaware had been for the most part friendly, with occasional protests that the land was Lord Baltimore's. In 1732 the two parties agreed on practically the present line, but with a starting point at Cape Henlopen. The survey was not begun until 1763, while border fights continued and occasionally resulted in bloodshed. Thomas Cresap, captured and taken to Philadelphia, remarked that it was 'the finest city in Maryland.' (Maryland has had boundary disputes on every side, and lost territory in all. The southern boundary agreement of 1874 gave a strip of the Eastern Shore to Virginia but preserved the whole Potomac to Maryland. The choice of the North Fork of the Potomac instead of the longer South Fork sacrificed a large area in the west and the fixing of the western boundary by the

Supreme Court in 1912 occasioned a final small loss, this time to West Virginia.)

Settlement of the region above tidewater had begun about 1700, and some hardy souls were moving into the western part of the province by about 1730. Sporadic raids by the Indians were no deterrent to the rapid filling up of the country. By the outbreak of the French and Indian War there was a fairly passable road through Maryland and Virginia to the neighborhood of Wills Creek—later Cumberland.

In the meantime, in 1749, a group of British merchants and Virginia planters—among them George Washington's half-brother Lawrence—obtained a royal grant of half a million acres south of the Ohio River and immediately prepared to start settlement and fur trading there. The French had already claimed the Mississippi Valley and regarded the country beyond the Alleghenies as their own, though they had made little effort to advance southward into it. Soon after the British subjects who had formed the Ohio Company established their first post, the French took action and began to build posts south of the Great Lakes and to interfere with British traders. Governor Dinwiddie of Virginia, who was a stockholder in the new company, sent an expedition in 1753–54 to oust the French from the post they were building at the head of the Ohio River; the expedition was driven off and Dinwiddie tried to get help from the other colonies and also from England to protect the Ohio Company lands. Governor Sharpe did his best to persuade the Maryland Assembly to raise funds and troops but the Marylanders were unconcerned about the fate of Virginia real estate. Under pressure various measures were eventually passed but Sharpe had to veto them because the assembly stubbornly insisted on levying against the private income of the proprietary for part of the expenses.

When England became aware that the war in progress with France for many decades had again reached a dangerous point in America, troops were sent out under General Edward Braddock, with orders to drive the French back north of the Great Lakes. Under pressure from abroad most of the colonies reluctantly made arrangements to raise militia to reinforce the regulars. Braddock hurried to Frederick Town, prepared to clear up the trouble beyond the mountains in short order. His stubborn refusal to take advice on frontier conditions resulted in his death shortly after he crossed the mountains in 1755 and in the rout of his troops. The French and their Indian allies then began raids in western Maryland that gave the province its first taste of real frontier warfare. Still the assembly refused co-operation in the new war, even removing the provincial militia from control of the British commander. The raids from the west were minor and sporadic so there was never any great danger to the province though considerable uneasiness persisted until after the French had at last been driven from America in 1763.

There had been attempts in the past to make the colonies contribute to empire defense, but the chief contributions had been for warfare in America and had come largely from the colonies on the Canadian frontier. During this last of the wars with the French in America the British had begun vigorous enforcement of trade laws to prevent the northern colonies from contraband trading with the enemy. This had drawn attention to the volume of colonial trade. The war had also made clear the need for providing a more profitable system of administration of the colonies and for forcing them to bear their share of empire costs. On the whole the new laws did not inconvenience Marylanders—even though they did put a high duty on the wines imported from Spain and Portugal—but other factors were stirring them to great dissatisfaction in their relations with the mother country. The net of debts to English merchants was becoming unbearable and the absence of colonial currency was adding to business difficulties. Increase in the number of dissenters forced to support an established church whose representatives were often merely interested in their comfortable berths provided further unrest.

Thus Marylanders were ripe for action when the Merchants' Committee of Philadelphia asked them in 1769 to join in the movement (begun in New England) to ban importations from the mother country until the Townshend Acts, imposing further taxes, should be revised. The people of town and county responded promptly. A convention meeting in June drew up a contraband list of goods under levy and of luxury articles; it was the most drastic adopted in any colony. Basic commodities of many kinds were included, as well as gauze, ribbons, millinery, and manufactured silk. Among the necessities exempted from the agreement were blankets of not more than five shillings cost—for the Indian trade, in part—shoes of not more than four shillings, cheap cutlery, nails, and tools. The long list is not only indicative of how little was manufactured in Maryland at the time but also of what goods were considered essential to life; among the limited number of articles that could be imported were sewing silk, 'Wig-Cauls,' boneware combs, and stoneware 'Bottles, Jugs, Pitchers, and Chamber-Pots.'

The agreement was broken in Maryland only after violations in other colonies had made it useless. Though violated, the compact resulted in repeal of the Townshend Acts in 1770, which lessened colonial tension. Maryland was fairly quiet until 1774 when news of the Boston Port Act, the misguided measure intended to clean up that hotbed of smuggling and defiance, reached this province. First Annapolis, then other centers and the counties, entered into an agreement to unite with other colonies in support of Boston. The Marylanders went beyond all other colonies that had renewed the nonimportation pledge, suspending exportation, boycotting any other colony not joining the agreement, and forbidding all lawyers to bring suit for any debt due to a British merchant from a Marylander. Delegates to the First Continental Congress were also appointed. When the Continental Association was formed in the same year—1774—Maryland was the first of the plantation colonies to take action on joining it. How vigorously the nonimportation agreement was complied with—and enforced—is evident from the records; English imports to Virginia and Maryland dropped from £528,738 in 1774 to £1,921 in 1775. One of the few articles that a captain attempted to smuggle into Maryland was a tombstone; the committee sitting on the case firmly crushed sentiment and ordered it destroyed. Balls were discontinued and various other social events, including the Jockey Club races, unbecoming at such a serious time, were called off. As Governor Eden reported dolefully, he firmly believed the Marylanders would persist in the agreement not to buy or sell until Boston was relieved 'in spite of every inconvenience . . . and the total ruin of their trade.' The need of 'something more sensible than supplications' was becoming plain, and in November 1774 the Provincial Convention declared 'that a well-regulated militia, composed of the gentlemen, freeholders, and other freemen, is the natural strength and only stable security of a free government'—a statement which survives almost word for word in the present Declaration of Rights.

The Provincial Convention became by degrees a provisional government. Its members, five from each county, were elected annually. Between sessions executive power was vested in a small committee of safety. Members of this committee and delegates to the Continental Congress were elected by the convention. For a time the old and the new governments existed side by side.

Troops were raised in 1775 for the defense of the northern colonies, and nearly 250 privateers operated out of Chesapeake Bay ports—including such craft as the *Black Jack*, the *Irish Gimblet*, the *Bacchus*, and the *Sturdy Beggers*. Money contributions were fairly generous.

The Provincial Convention was reluctant to make the break with England, but public sentiment was vehemently insistent. On July 3, 1776, a resolution was adopted (but not entered in the journal till the 6th) 'that the King of Great Britain has violated his compact with this people, and they owe no allegiance to him.' Samuel Chase, William Paca, Charles Carroll of Carrollton, and Thomas Stone—Maryland's delegates to the Continental Congress—had already been empowered on June 28 to vote for independence—'provided the sole and exclusive right of regulating the internal government and police of this colony be reserved to the people thereof.' On the same day a special convention was ordered 'for the express purpose of forming a new government by the authority of the people only.'

The constitutional convention met on August 14, 1776; the Declaration of Rights was adopted on November 3, and the first State constitution on November 8. The government thereby instituted was closely patterned on that which it superseded. The general assembly consisted of two houses, a house of delegates and a senate. All elections were annual; the governor could have only three consecutive terms and thereafter must step down for four years; senators were elected by the indirect method. The franchise was limited by a property qualification, but free Negroes had at first the right to vote. Thomas Johnson, the first governor under the new regime, took office March 21, 1777.

Maryland troops saw service at first in the North, especially in the Battle of Long Island (August 27, 1776), and later in the Southern campaigns that ended the war. Save for sporadic appearances of raiding parties on the Chesapeake, Maryland was only once invaded. In the late summer of 1777 Admiral Howe's fleet sailed up the bay and landed an army at the head of Elk River. The Continental Army hastened south, and additional Maryland troops were raised. The armies met on Brandywine Creek in the battle that opened the way for the British capture of Philadelphia.

It was during the Revolutionary War that Maryland received the nickname by which it is best known to scholars and historians—the 'Old Line State.' The soubriquet was earned, according to some historians, because of Maryland's regular 'troops of the line.' In this connection, military writers have stated that the troops of the old Maryland Line ranked among the finest in the Continental Army and were 'held in admirable discipline,' as distinguished from the militia, which fought mainly in guerilla fashion.

In 1777 foreign officers began to appear to aid the American cause. Count Casimir Pulaski organized 'Pulaski's Legion' at Baltimore in 1778; Baron Johann de Kalb, who accompanied Lafayette, met his death while leading Maryland troops in the battle of Camden, South Carolina, in 1780. Lafayette himself spent much time in Maryland in the months preceding the final campaign of 1781, assembling troops and supplies and awaiting the arrival of the Count de Grasse with the French fleet. On October 19, 1781, de Grasse wrote to Governor Thomas Sim Lee: 'I have just desired General Washington to send me back my troops, of which probably he will no longer stand in need, as Lord Cornwallis has surrendered.' Six months after this decisive victory Great Britain began to negotiate for peace. The treaty, signed at Paris on January 20, 1783, was ratified by the Congress of the Federation sitting in Annapolis on January 14, 1784.

INDEPENDENCE TO CIVIL WAR

Though the Revolution had freed Maryland from the exactions of a medieval landlord, freed the traders and producers to sell and buy wherever they could find an advantageous market, and removed the burden of supporting a state church, it had not solved the basic problems that had helped turn the province to revolt. The fertile Tidewater lands, which had given colonial prosperity and built the magnificent houses in Annapolis and on the plantations, had been overworked by careless cultivation and the exhausted soil itself was disappearing, carried away by every rain to silt up the rivers that had formed the intra-province trade routes. Moreover, in spite of increased wheatgrowing on the Piedmont, the State was not producing enough foodstuffs for its own use; nor was it producing enough wheat and tobacco to pay for quantities of food and manufactured goods from other States and abroad. Slavery was becoming a serious burden as the fertility of the tobacco lands was reduced, and was already having disturbing social results (*see The Negroes*). Banking and currency were in chaos and the need for long-delayed public improvements was creating great irritation.

Although in 1777 it had 'long and impatiently expected that a Confederacy would have been founded,' the assembly, fearful of increasing the power of large States, refused to assent to the Articles of Confederation unless the western lands, 'wrested from the common enemy by the blood and treasure of the thirteen States, should be considered as a common property, subject to be parcelled out by Congress into free, convenient and independent governments.' Though the question was still undecided early in 1781, the State characteristically empowered its delegates in Congress to sign the articles rather 'than by an over perseverance, incur the censure of obstinacy.' It was made clear, however, that there was no drawing back from the position taken; and in the end the Maryland idea prevailed.

In 1785 Maryland, recognizing the need for co-operation, issued a call to Virginia, Delaware, and Pennsylvania for a conference on revenues. Virginia responded with a call to all the States. Commissioners from New York, New Jersey, Pennsylvania, Delaware, and Virginia met at Annapolis on September 11, 1786, to consider the condition of the nation. They agreed to request all of the States to send delegates to a convention at Philadelphia in May of the following year to revise the Articles of Confederation. Maryland had authorized no commissioners to the convention to which it was host, believing that the meeting 'may be misunderstood or misrepresented in Europe, give umbrage to Congress, and disquiet the citizens of the United States.'

The State's delegates to what came to be called the Constitutional Convention of 1787 were James McHenry, Daniel Carroll, Daniel of St. Thomas Jenifer, John Francis Mercer, and Luther Martin. Only the first three were signers of the Constitution, but Martin was the most active in debate, particularly as the representative of a small state, on the question of securing to all states equal representation in the Senate. Despite his continued objections (during the debates for ratification of the Constitution) to clauses he believed dangerous to State rights, a State convention at Annapolis gave Maryland's ratification on April 26, 1788.

Already in 1783 Maryland had sought to have Congress lodge permanently in Annapolis, offering it 'the Stadt House and Public Circle,' a mansion for its president, and thirteen dwellings for its members. Congress responded to the extent of holding at Annapolis the sessions at which Washington resigned his commission and the peace treaty was ratified. During the discussion of a site for the capital in 1789, Maryland and Virginia passed acts ceding lands on the Potomac and advancing large sums for public buildings in case of acceptance. Maryland's share, $72,000, was raised partly by the sale of the vacated Choptank Indian lands and the reserved lands west of Fort Cumberland. The act of Congress accepting the site was passed July 16, 1790, and the first boundary marker of the District of Columbia was set up April 15, 1791.

The census in 1790 found 319,728 people in the State, 13,503 of them in Baltimore—six times as many as in old Annapolis. Baltimore had become powerful enough to dominate the congressional election in September of that year, in which each representative was elected by state-wide vote. The result so frightened the counties that on December 19 they forced through a law dividing the State into districts and confining the voter's choice to residents of his district.

In the rush of commercial activity which followed independence a number of banks were established, chief of which were the Bank of Maryland (1790), the Baltimore branch of the Bank of the United States (1793), and the Bank of Baltimore (1795). When a lull in the European wars (1802–03) brought exports down to $5,100,000, a local belief developed that insufficient banking facilities were part of the cause and the Union Bank of Maryland was founded in 1804. Resumption of the war caused exports for Maryland ports to rise in a few years to $14,500,000.

The conflict in Europe was profitable to Marylanders in other fields; many engaged in privateering, a source of local wealth but an irritant to the powers at war. Great Britain began to deal heavily with American privateers, and also to violate American shipping rights. The passage of the Embargo Acts in 1807—an attempt to keep America out of war—aroused stormy agitation for secession in the Northern States, whose trade was temporarily hurt thereby though their manufactures gained great advantage. Maryland, already a shipping state but still primarily agricultural in its interests, stood with the government and South in favor of vigorous action.

The division, economic at base, expressed itself also in the alignment of political parties. In 1800 the newly organized Republican (Democratic) party had triumphed over the Federalists in Maryland as elsewhere in the South. In the following year the State constitution had been amended to give the suffrage to 'every free white male citizen' of voting age. Property restrictions had been partly removed (wholly in 1810) and the suffrage had been enormously extended, though free Negroes were disfranchised. The Federalists, among them Samuel Chase, were much disturbed by this extension of popular power. Chase, then associate justice of the Supreme Court of the United States, was accused of including political comments in his charges to juries; articles of impeachment were drawn in March 1804. At his trial, early in 1805, the prosecution was not well managed and he was acquitted by a Senate containing a large Republican (Democratic) majority.

War was declared on June 18, 1812, two days after England had revoked the offending Orders in Council. The *Federal Republican* of Baltimore printed a denunciation of the war that provoked a chain of bloody riots (*see Baltimore*), the leaders of which were never brought to justice. By the shock of these outbursts Maryland was driven back into the Federalist ranks. Nevertheless vigorous measures were taken for the defense of state and nation. Maryland troops first saw service in the fruitless Canadian campaign of 1812. The Chesapeake was invaded in February 1813 by Admiral Sir George Cockburn. Little damage was done for more than a year; a few plantations and villages were raided, but privateers seem to have been little impeded. In August 1814 a large force under Cockburn and

Major General Robert Ross was sent up the Patuxent and thence over-land toward Washington. This army met the Americans at Bladensburg on August 24, inflicted on them the rout known as the 'Bladensburg Races,' and passed on to burn the public buildings of Washington.

From the national capital the British turned their attention to Balti-more, 'the great repository of the hostile spirit of the United States against England.' On September 12, after landing the army on North Point at the mouth of the Patapsco, the fleet sailed up the river to bombard Fort Mc-Henry. Both movements failed. (The sight of the flag still waving over Fort McHenry at dawn of September 14 was the inspiration for Francis Scott Key's 'Star Spangled Banner.') Thereafter there was only desultory raiding in the Chesapeake until news of the Treaty of Ghent arrived in February 1815.

The war had interrupted the growth of industry, commerce, and in-ternal improvements, and caused banks everywhere, but especially in Maryland, to suspend specie payments from 1814 to 1817. Thereafter de-velopment was resumed with great vigor. The next twelve years witnessed the completion of the National Pike to the Ohio (1818), beginning of work on the Baltimore and Ohio Railroad and the Chesapeake and Ohio Canal (both July 4, 1828), and opening of the Chesapeake and Delaware Canal (*see Transportation*).

The increase of population in Baltimore, especially population of for-eign non-British birth, raised the fear of domination in the counties, whereas in fact the city was grossly under-represented at Annapolis. More-over, the smallest county had the same representation as the most popu-lous. A movement for apportionment of delegates by population, as in Congress, and for direct popular election of the governor had begun shortly after the war. When the Federalists were overthrown in 1819, the matter was brought up in the assembly, but the counties refused to 'place the great agricultural State of Maryland at the feet of the merchants, the bank speculators, the brokers, the lottery office keepers, the foreigners, and the mob of Baltimore.'

For many years this attitude helped to retard the enfranchisement of Jews—though they were less than two hundred in number but concen-trated mostly in Baltimore. Solomon Etting had begun the struggle in their behalf in 1797; Thomas Kennedy of Washington County in 1818 in-troduced a bill for enfranchisement that was defeated. But agitation con-tinued and the so-called 'Jew Bill' was passed in 1826.

The waning Federalist minority in the counties finally disappeared, and the State constitution was amended in 1837 to provide for direct popular election of governor and senators and for apportionment according to population. Baltimore city was to have six delegates, as many as any county could have. In the succeeding century the Baltimore delegates have increased to thirty-six, but the city is still much under-represented. The governor's term was increased to three years without immediate re-election. The State was divided into three districts from which governors were to be elected in rotation; this arrangement lasted until 1864.

The rather erratic operations of the Bank of the United States, and especially the irregularities of its Baltimore branch, caused national concern. An investigation of the branch in 1818 compelled it to restrict its activities, and a law passed in that year required any bank with its head office outside the State to print its notes on stamped and taxed paper. Maryland's suit against this branch for nonpayment of the tax reached the United States Supreme Court; Chief Justice Marshall regarded the bank as part of the Government and ruled that the law was void because the power to tax implies the power to destroy. The Federal Government and the Constitution, he said, were created not by the States but by the whole people—notwithstanding that 'No political dreamer was ever wild enough to think of breaking down the lines which separate the States, and of compounding the American people into one common mass.'

The era of expansion and wild speculation in canals, railroads, and public lands culminated in the 1830's. The first sign of the impending crash was the failure of the Bank of Maryland and two rural banks in 1834. Receivers of the Bank of Maryland made no report for seventeen months; agitation over the matter resulted in five days of rioting. During the depression of 1837–42 Maryland found that it must either repudiate its debts or increase taxes. The property tax, heavy during the Revolution, had been levied only five times thereafter, and for small amounts; most of the State's revenues came from licenses, fees, and fines. In 1841 the property tax was levied in earnest; ever since it has been the principal source of revenue.

The acute industrial depression brought with it labor difficulties although the State was not then so heavily industrialized as to have serious trouble from this source (*see Labor*).

The presence in Baltimore of union groups, however, and of considerable numbers of recent immigrants from non-English speaking countries caused considerable distrust of the city in the counties and made them unwilling to liberalize the State constitution for many years. This fear of the city had other sources, however, because as Baltimore developed into a commercial and industrial city its interests differed from those of the agricultural counties. The counties were particularly critical after a series of disgracefully riotous elections had brought the city to the unfavorable notice of the nation. Wide publicity had been given to the common practice of 'cooping' a supply of well-alcoholized voters for use as 'repeaters.' The Native American or Know-Nothing party, established about 1844 to combat such evils in this as well as other cities, soon became their most glaring exponent; the reforms for which it was founded were lost sight of and it became anti-Catholic and anti-foreign. The tumultuous elections of 1856 aroused the more conscientious citizens in Baltimore, as well as in the counties, to try to do something about conditions. The reform movement was not successful until 1860, when the assembly ejected its Baltimore members as illegally elected and put the city police under direct State control.

In the midst of this turmoil the State succeeded in 1851 in replacing its much-amended but still inadequate constitution with one embodying the results of seventy-five years of experience. This second constitution was in force until 1864.

In the increasingly bitter economic struggle between North and South, Maryland occupied a middle position, Baltimore sharing the industrial and commercial interests of the North, the agrarian interests of the South. The general policy of Marylanders was, as always, one of compromise. Slavery had by this time no great hold upon the State and there was active opposition to it among the farmers of the Piedmont; in 1860 there were very nearly as many free Negroes as slaves.

John Brown's raid on Harpers Ferry, conducted from a base in Maryland in 1859, did much to weaken the State's conciliatory attitude. Nevertheless, upon the secession of the Southern States, the citizens and press, if not the vacillating State government of the time, expressed themselves clearly for the peaceful restoration of the Union. When the South Carolinian palmetto flag was flown by some agitators in Baltimore, a newspaper remarked that 'If ever—which God forbid—a time shall come when our people shall be unwilling to let the flag of the Union float over them, Maryland has a banner of her own, red with the glories of the Revolution . . . which she can unfurl, and be proud of its memories, though she sorrow for the need of its return.'

Yet coercion of the seceding States was not favored. On April 19, 1861, the eighty-sixth anniversary of the Battle of Lexington, Massachusetts troops were attacked by a large crowd while marching from one Baltimore railroad station to another. The frightened recruits opened fire, killing twelve. The result of this demonstration was a close military supervision of the State for the duration of the war.

The next night the railroad bridges north of the city were burned by police, militia, and citizens, to prevent more such clashes. John Merryman, a militia lieutenant, was arrested for complicity in this 'treasonable' act. Writs of habeas corpus had been disregarded in two other cases, therefore his counsel made his petition directly to Chief Justice Roger B. Taney. The chief justice journeyed to Baltimore to issue the writ. General George Cadwallader asserted that he had authority to suspend it and ignored a summons for contempt. The chief justice then rendered in writing his decision that the President was not empowered by the Constitution to suspend the writ of habeas corpus, nor to authorize others to do so.

Although Maryland remained in the Union and contributed a fair share to its defense, there were whole regiments of Marylanders and a notably large number of Maryland officers in the army of the Confederacy. On May 23, 1862, the First Maryland Regiment, C.S.A. met the First Maryland Regiment, U.S.A. in the Battle of Front Royal, Virginia. The Union regiment, retiring slowly in the face of superior numbers, was thrown into hopeless confusion by a stampede of New York cavalry and obliged to surrender.

Early in September 1862 Lee's army occupied Frederick and a proclamation was issued that 'Marylanders shall once more enjoy their ancient freedom of thought and speech.' McClellan hastened up from Washington and met the Confederates in the battles of South Mountain, September 14, and Antietam (or Sharpsburg), September 16–17, forcing them to retire across the Potomac.

The Confederate armies were on Maryland soil again late in June 1863, on the advance which was checked in the Battle of Gettysburg, July 1–3, 1863.

The third invasion of Maryland in July 1864 was less friendly than the others, owing to the destruction of property in the South by the Federal armies. An indemnity of $20,000 was levied upon Hagerstown and one of $200,000 upon Frederick. After the Battle of the Monacacy, July 9, in which Union forces were defeated, the Confederate forces passed close to Baltimore and Washington, and raiding parties destroyed communications to the North and burned Governor Augustus W. Bradford's house near Baltimore.

In the midst of the conflict and while public opinion was largely suppressed the State adopted the constitution of 1864, permeated by the bitter animus of the extreme Unionists who were in power, but embodying a number of sound reforms. Slavery was abolished in terms adopted nationally a few months later for the Thirteenth Amendment. The governor's term was increased to four years without a no-re-election clause, gubernatorial districts were abolished, and provision was made for registration of voters.

THE STATE MATURES

Domination of the radical Unionists had been broken when military control was withdrawn at the end of the war. The wartime constitution had been superseded in 1867 by the constitution that is still in force, which embodies the progressive features of the previous constitution but omits its harsh measures of repression. The downfall of the Republicans left the Democratic party in control for many years. Though Negroes to the number of about 36,000 voted in 1870, casting their votes for the party that had restored the privilege taken from them in 1802, the Democrats remained in power.

The decade following the war, with its commercial and industrial boom and its dizzy heights of speculation, was a period of overt engagement in politics by the great corporations, resulting in many grants of special privilege and much political corruption. Rivalry between the Pennsylvania and the Baltimore and Ohio railroads was intense. Oden Bowie, president of the projected Baltimore and Potomac Railroad Company, which had come under Pennsylvania control, became governor in 1868; during his term of office the road was nearly completed, with a main stem between Baltimore and Popes Creek according to its charter, and a branch from Bowie to Washington which has become a main artery between North and South.

Maryland representatives in Congress consistently protected the interests of the railroad chartered in the State. When the subject of a government-built railroad between New York and Washington, discussed since 1861, was broached in Congress in 1871, Senator George Vickers and Representative Francis Thomas denounced the plan as exceeding the Federal power to regulate commerce and to establish post offices and post roads and 'interfering with the reserved rights of the States.' Transportation interests continued to dominate the State for many decades. Arthur P. Gorman, president of the Chesapeake and Ohio Canal Company, with I.Freeman Rasin of Baltimore, controlled State politics from 1869 to 1895. Gorman became United States senator in 1881 and narrowly missed nomination for the presidency in 1892. It was Rasin who disorganized the Workingman's Party by finding a job in his office for its leader, 'Honest Joe' Thompson—who thereupon became known as ex-Honest Joe.'

The panic of 1873 was the beginning of a long-continued depression which forced the railroads as well as other industries to take drastic measures of economy. The Baltimore and Ohio Railroad Company's announcement of a wage cut in 1877 resulted in a series of riots at Martinsburg, West Virginia, Cumberland and Baltimore (*see Labor*).

Growing resentment of the domination of the 'Third House,' as the Gorman-Rasin machine was called, resulted in a Republican victory in the State election of 1895. This overturn was due in large part to the 'Fourth House,' the newspapers. Citation of a reporter for contempt upon refusing to tell a grand jury the source of his information aroused the Journalists' Club to seek protective legislation. In 1896 the assembly passed an act to protect reporters and other newspaper men from being compelled to disclose the source of any news or information procured for publication in any legal or legislative proceeding in the State of Maryland. Under this immunity the newspapers became such a power that in 1905 a press historian could boast: 'The fear of the press is greater than the fear of the law. Through the press there is law.'

In the Spanish-American War, Maryland troops were denied the opportunity to distinguish themselves in action, their only casualties being victims of typhoid fever in the southern cantonments where they were held in reserve. The most noteworthy local repercussion of the war was the anger aroused by what seemed the deliberate and malicious slighting of a victorious naval officer from Maryland. Commodore Winfield Scott Schley had commanded during the Battle of Santiago de Cuba, while Captain W.T. Sampson was absent on an attempted visit to the army chief. The transfer of credit to Sampson and subsequent aspersions upon Schley's courage and leadership drew numerous and vehement complaints in newspapers and elsewhere.

The opening decade of the twentieth century witnessed a series of attempts to regulate and offset the solidly Republican Negro vote. It was revealed that enumerators for the 1900 census in Republican-controlled counties of southern Maryland had falsified the figures. An extra session of the assembly called in 1901 ordered a State-conducted census. A 'white supremacy' platform met with popular approval in the gubernatorial election of 1903. A constitutional amendment was proposed the following year, whereby a registering voter must prove literacy by reading part of the Constitution, and explain it satisfactorily to the registration officials. The latter provision aroused suspicion of its possible use for other purposes—since even the Supreme Court of the United States differs on its interpretation of the document—and caused defeat of the amendment. Suspicion once aroused did not subside; subsequent amendments were defeated in 1909 and 1911, and the 'white supremacy' movement was dropped for fear of opening the way to arbitrary registration methods.

A marked change at the turn of the century was the successful defiance of the political machine by individual candidates. Isaac Lobe Straus gained control of the House of Delegates and secured passage of a corrupt practices law, a primary election law, and other progressive legislation. Edwin Warfield, who became governor in 1904, supported the proposal that the will of the people expressed in primary elections should govern the assembly in its election of United States senators. The plan was adopted, though later Maryland did not ratify the Seventeenth Amendment.

Austin L. Crothers, a machine candidate, showed independence after he became governor in 1908. Progressive moves under his administration were the creation of a public service commission and the passage of a child labor law. The public service commission law was widely assailed as 'socialistic,' but the governor said emphatically that he wanted the law 'administered by conservative men.' Similar objections were made to the efforts to pass workmen's compensation laws. A co-operative insurance law introduced by State Senator (later Congressman) David J. Lewis, the first of its kind in the country, was passed in 1902 but found unconstitutional after less than two years of operation. Lewis continued his efforts for more than a decade, building up a body of public opinion that overcame the determined and overt opposition of certain mercantile and industrial groups; the workmen's compensation act became law in 1914.

When the United States entered the World War a Maryland Council of Defense was formed to co-ordinate civilian war work. Its task was made especially difficult by the influx of thousands of soldiers, construction workers, shipbuilders, and other war workers. The Maryland war measures were drafted by Attorney General Albert C. Ritchie, who was soon thereafter made general counsel to the United States Industries Board.

State administration has made notable progress in efficiency and economy since 1919 when Albert C. Ritchie was elected to the first of his four terms as governor. He attacked the problem almost immediately, appointing a commission and calling in outside experts to plan a reform of the executive department. When the experts submitted their plan he refused to follow it in full because it 'did not take sufficient account of the experience, conditions and usages of this State,' and added, 'In a word, we want for Maryland a Maryland form of government.' The plan as eventually adopted in 1922 reduced the number of separate agencies from about eighty to fourteen.

For many years the principle of local option had been gaining ground in the towns and counties, though Baltimore remained pugnaciously 'wet.' The temperance sentiment was strong enough to secure the State's ratification of the Eighteenth Amendment in January 1918. Very soon, however, resentment of the Volstead law as 'an unnecessary and drastic Federal infringement on their State and personal rights' turned Marylanders against the amendment, and Ritchie became its outstanding opponent.

It was at this time that the term 'Free State' was coined to express the ancient Maryland tradition of autonomy, individual liberty, and laws 'Consonant to Reason.'

In recent years a number of agencies have been breaking down the old antagonism between the agricultural counties and the commercial and industrial center, Baltimore. The radio and motor cars, the increase in the size of commuting areas, and recently rural electrification aided by the Federal Government, have brought the opposing groups to a better understanding of each other and each other's problems and interests.

Sanction in law for the flag and anthem of the State, accorded in the present century, has been no more than a recognition of their still stronger sanction in long-continued popular acclaim. The brilliant Calvert colors, 'brought ashore with great solemnitie' in 1634, have been the Maryland flag for three centuries, officially until the Revolution, and thereafter in the esteem of the people until the General Assembly restored them to official use in 1904. In like manner the General Assembly of 1939 gave official recognition to the song which the Nation had regarded for nearly eighty years as the State's battle hymn, 'Maryland, My Maryland.'

Racial Elements

MARYLAND is predominantly English in ancestry and cultural heritage. In 1790, when the first census of the United States found 319,728 people living in the State, all but 7 per cent of the white population—which comprised 62 per cent of the whole—was of British birth or ancestry.

The 61 per cent of the 1790 population listed as British was not wholly English in origin; on the basis of family names, 2.4 per cent of the total population was listed as Irish and 6.5 per cent as Scottish. Of the 7 per cent of the 1790 white population not British by birth or ancestry, 6 per cent was German, largely sectarians who had fled from persecution in the homeland. The French, the Dutch, and the Jews each contributed fractional percentages.

The population of Maryland has increased steadily but without spectacular spurts and much less rapidly than in many other States. Though Baltimore was for many years one of the leading ports of entry, the State retained proportionately fewer immigrants than did other receiving centers of the Atlantic seaboard. In 1930 when foreign-born comprised 11.6 per cent of the total population of the United States, somewhat less than 6 per cent of Maryland's 1,630,543 inhabitants were of foreign birth, with two-thirds of them living in Baltimore. At the same time, in spite of the influx of Negroes from the Deep South during and after the World War, the percentage of Negroes was only about half of what it was at the time of the first census.

The preponderance of British settlers at the time of the 1790 census—when the population was already between a fifth and a sixth of what it was to be in 1930—was a result of the conditions of settlement. The province, established in part as a haven for Roman Catholic refugees from Britain, later offered haven to other dissenters from the Established Church, and also accepted political opponents of the Commonwealth.

Throughout nearly two centuries political and religious refugees have continued to form a large part of Maryland's immigrants; many of the Germans who arrived after the 1848 upheaval in their homeland left Europe for political reasons, and the Russian and Polish Jews who came in such numbers around the turn of the twentieth century were fleeing both religious and political persecution.

The 52 per cent of the total population of the new State classified as English composed three quarters of the dominant race of the State and gave it its cultural pattern. It was a fairly representative group, ranging from gentry to criminals. In early days, younger sons of good family drew large tracts of fertile land through the influence of friends and relatives, and most had come over to develop them.

Among the very large number of indentured servants were many teachers, scholars, skilled craftsmen, half-trained apprentices, sons of clergymen and businessmen—adventurous souls who were willing to do whatever was required of them for a few years in return for passage to America and the small stake, at first guaranteed by law, that would be theirs when their contract period was over. Many of these were soon able to take their place beside the people who had arrived under more favorable conditions. Of the considerable number of settlers who came over as 'criminals' to work out their sentences on the plantations, probably a majority were paupers, debtors, and political and religious offenders caught in the net of harsh laws. They, too, in time had their chance to enter the free life of the province, and some were able to reach positions that would have been closed to them in their native land. Those criminals who preferred to make livings by continuing to prey on others, and those unfortunates who could not manage to prosper even on the rich lands of the province, became the criminals and paupers of the colony or drifted westward to live on the fringe of settlement.

But regardless of social status in the homeland, the majority of the immigrants of all classes before long helped to form a society that was English in culture. Within a few decades the province had been sprinkled with estates reminiscent of those in England. As soon as possible—which usually meant as soon as enough land had been cleared to produce large crops of tobacco—landed Marylanders had built substantial houses and furnished them with rugs, silver, hardware, china, and draperies brought back on the ships that had taken the tobacco to London. Most of those who could afford it had sent their sons, and some of them their daughters, to England for education, insuring the province a continuing culture of the kind they considered most desirable. Englishmen visiting the province felt at home; here were the house parties, the horse races, the hunts, the talk of politics, agriculture, and the theater—as well as the conservatism —they had always known. And in spite of natural modifications, much of the Maryland of provincial days remains. Even Baltimore, with its considerable population non-English by birth or ancestry, is frequently considered more reminiscent of London than any other large city in the United States; it has received its immigrants slowly enough to digest them and convert them to its viewpoints and customs while accepting the stimulation the newcomers offered.

The German migration to Maryland began in 1684 with the arrival of a small body of Labadists, mystics from Friesland. By 1710 the Germans had been recognized as so desirable that the assembly declared that they should be free from paying any 'publick, county or parish levy' for a period of one year. In 1732 the fifth Lord Baltimore, Charles Calvert, outdoing the offers being made to Germans by neighboring colonies, made the munificent proffer of two hundred acres in fee, subject to a nominal rent, to any head of a family who should settle between the Patapsco and the Susquehanna within three years; and to each single person between the ages of fifteen and thirty, one hundred acres on the same terms. This offer induced many Germans from Pennsylvania to move to the fertile lands of Frederick and Washington counties and others to come directly from Europe.

During the nineteenth century Germans continued to come in such numbers that today there are about 90,000 people in the State who retain enough of their cultural identity to be classified as Germans or German-Americans. There were two periods when immigration from Germany was particularly large; the first was after the Napoleonic wars, when artisans, peasants, and business men were driven out by famine and taxes, the second after suppression of the revolution of 1848, when scholars and other members of the intelligentsia left the country as political refugees. The arrivals of this second period had considerable influence on Baltimore life, supplying the brains for various businesses and stimulating thought and music.

From Revolutionary times, however, Germans have been active in Maryland industrial enterprises. In 1785 John Frederick Amelung established his glass factory at Frederick, and Knabe and Stieff are Maryland names long associated with the manufacture of pianos. The first sugar refinery in Baltimore was founded by Garts Leypoldt in 1796, and the first brewery in the town was operated by W. Barnitz. The printing firm of A. Hoen, in existence for more than a century, is well known for its map printing; and Ottmar Mergenthaler, a Baltimorean, invented the linotype.

Most of the earliest Irish settlers in Maryland were Roman Catholic, but Irish Protestants arrived later. As early as 1684 the name of County of New Ireland was given to a tract now in Cecil and Harford counties.

This territory was composed of New Connaught, New Leinster, and New Munster, with farms recorded under such south Ireland names as Cork, Clare, Limerick, Dublin, and Wexford.

Though Irishmen were relatively few they were leaders in the building of Baltimore, and before the Revolution many merchants, educators, and professional men of the little town were Irish by birth. Outstanding Marylanders of Irish origin were Charles Carroll, the signer; Charles Carroll, the barrister; John Carroll, first archbishop of Baltimore; John Allison, pastor of the First Presbyterian Church and a chaplain of the Continental Congress; Dr.Henry Stevenson, who introduced inoculation for 'winter feaver' (smallpox) into Baltimore; Commodore Joshua Barney, first to raise the Stars and Stripes, which he flew at the masthead of the sloop *Hornet*; and David Poe, grandfather of Edgar Allan Poe. Three Irishmen —George Brown, William Patterson, and Robert Garrett—were responsible for the inception of the Baltimore & Ohio Railroad.

Protestant Irish immigration continued into the early part of the nineteenth century though the Irish influx that began after the War of 1812 was largely Roman Catholic. During the years 1846–50, following the Great Famine, when one-third of Ireland's 6,000,000 inhabitants migrated, the greater number came to America through the ports of Boston, New York, and Baltimore. Many of these immigrants found work in Maryland on the canals and railroads before making their way to Allegany and adjacent counties to become miners and farmers.

The Irish of Maryland formed the nonsectarian Hibernian Society (not to be confused with the Ancient Order of Hibernians) in 1817 '. . . to do all acts, matters and things as are or shall be necessary for the purpose of affording charitable assistance and advice to such emigrants from or natives of Ireland arriving at or residing in any part of Maryland.' In about a decade the municipality of Baltimore appropriated $260,000 to bring Irish immigrants to this port, entrusting the choice of families to the Hibernians.

The first French settlers in Maryland came from Nova Scotia in 1755 when the unfortunate Acadians were scattered. James Ryder Randall, the author of *Maryland, My Maryland*, and Dr.Basil L. Gildersleeve, the eminent philologist, were descended from these settlers through Rene le Blanc, the notary whose Baltimore descendants today use 'White' as their family name. A second French group arrived in 1793, when about 1,500 people left Santo Domingo because of the race war in that island and settled in Baltimore with what remained of their slaves.

Although the founder of Maryland displayed more liberality in civil and religious matters than did the Puritans in New England, early religious freedom in Maryland was limited to Christians. For this reason Jews did not settle in the province to any extent before the Revolution. Those who came generally established themselves in the cities, though Dr. Jacob Lumbroso, a Portuguese physician and the first Jew to arrive (1656) settled in St. Marys County. Today Baltimore's Jewish population numbers approximately 75,000 and is prominently identified with the city's commerce and industry. Jews have also contributed substantially to the cultural life of the city. They have given many objects of art to the various museums of Baltimore and notable support to musical organizations.

Poles began to settle in Maryland during the Civil War and today there are about 34,000 people of Polish birth or descent in Maryland, largely in Baltimore. The Poles work chiefly as laborers and metal workers. In the spring and summer some families go into the counties to pick berries, peas, and beans, successively.

The post Civil War Polish immigration originated in what was Prussian Poland (Posen Province) and was caused primarily by the collapse of the Central European grain market, arising out of the importation of cheap American wheat. The descendants of this group to this day call themselves *Prusski* or *Pozmaniocy*. A second period of Polish immigration in 1890 can be traced to Galicia; and a third, between 1905 and 1914, was the aftermath of the Russian Revolution of 1905.

The first Czech resident of Maryland was Augustine Hermann, who settled in Cecil County in 1640 on a large tract of land granted in return for his services as a mapmaker. It was about 1860 that Czechs arrived in such numbers as to form a small colony. The 1930 census reported 7,652 of Czechoslovak birth or parentage in Baltimore. A large number are tailors and shoemakers, though among the skilled craftsmen are wood carvers, wrought iron workers, and cabinet makers.

The *Baltimore Town and Fell's Point Directory* of 1796-7 contains such names as Bringaiole, Cafenave, De Luce, La Cafagne, evidence that Italians were here during the eighteenth century. In the 1840's and 1850's some Ligurians from the smaller seaports around Genoa and a few political refugees and adventurers settled in the city. But it was not until 1890 that a steady influx of Italian immigrants took place. Today the great majority of Maryland Italians live in Baltimore, but a few have scattered to other centers, where they are active in the small trades, operating fruit-stands, restaurants, and grocery stores. The bulk of the Italians, aside from the normal second generation percentage in law and medicine, work in factories and on construction.

Lithuanians first began to settle in Baltimore in 1876 and they and their children now number about 9,000. A majority of the first generation does tailoring, but the young people are entering office work.

The 1930 census listed some 17,000 Russians in Baltimore, of which the great majority are Jews. Other national groups in Maryland are relatively small. Five hundred Finns live in Baltimore and the Ukrainian colony established about 40 years ago at Highlandtown, now numbers about 1,200. The first Baltimore Greeks were nine boys who arrived in an American brig as refugees from the Turkish massacre of 1822. One of these boys became the father of George Partridge Colvocoresses, who was graduated from the Naval Academy and who, from 1905 to 1907, was commandant of midshipmen there. The 1,200 Greeks now in Baltimore are chiefly in the food trades.

Except in the industrial centers there are few people of foreign birth or parentage outside Baltimore County. Italians work in the quarries near Port Deposit, and Slavs—chiefly Poles and Ukrainians—in the mines of western Maryland. In 1914 a Slavic farming colony was established near Augustine Hermann's old manor on the outskirts of Chesapeake City.

Only one group of early Maryland settlers has descendants who have never given up their distinguishing customs: these are the Amish living near Grantsville in Garrett County. The German-Swiss Amishmen, Mennonite fundamentalists, came to Maryland from Pennsylvania during the eighteenth century. The present-day Amishmen, like their forefathers, are farmers whose products find ready market in neighboring towns. Like their forefathers, they consider education as a useless frippery and scorn participation in government. They are easily identified by their clothes, which have a homemade plainness. The women wear shawls, small bonnets, and dark-colored, full-skirted dresses, the men long coats and broad hats. Amish clothing is always fastened with ties and hooks, rather than buttons, and the men always wear a beard but no mustache. (These idiosyncracies are relics of passive resistance to civil government in Switzerland, where buttons and mustaches were taxed.) There is another small Swiss group in Frederick County on farms cleared in 1761.

The 1930 census report listed 977 foreign-born inhabitants of Maryland under the heading 'All others.' Among them are a few Latin Americans, some Rumanians and Hungarians. Also in this group are a few members of other races—a handful of Japanese and a larger number of Chinese.

The Negro

THE Negroes form the largest group in Maryland not British in origin. Though their history is interwoven with that of the whites from the first days of settlement, it remains separate. Among the hardy voyagers who disembarked at St.Clement's Island in 1634 were John Price, a Negro, and Mathias Tousa, a mulatto, who had been taken aboard in the Barbados when the English vessels stopped for supplies. By the beginning of the eighteenth century Negro slaves were numerous in the colony and by the time of the Revolution nearly a third of the population of the State was Negro, for the most part laborers on the plantations. Though the high wages of the World War period brought numerous Negroes to Baltimore from the Deep South and also from the Maryland counties, Negroes now form only 16 per cent of the total population of Maryland.

Maryland early took official cognizance of the evils of slavery and of the danger of swelling its population with members of another race. In 1783 the slave trade was prohibited by State law and in 1787 Luther Martin of Maryland endeavored to have a clause limiting or banning the trade placed in the National Constitution. It was a matter of economics, however, that had reduced the slaves to 12 per cent of the population by 1860; Maryland tobacco plantations had become increasingly unproductive (*see Agriculture*) and the care of slave families from infancy to old age was becoming a serious burden. Long before the Civil War many families had begun to free their slaves, and by 1860 freed slaves formed 13 per cent of the population.

'Free' Negroes, however, were not entirely free. At times they were restrained by law from working at certain occupations, or from selling tobacco and other commodities without a certificate from a justice of the peace. Again they were prohibited from keeping dogs, carrying firearms, attending religious services (unless conducted by a licensed or ordained white minister), belonging to secret orders, or selling spirituous liquors. If convicted of any of these offenses, Negroes could be banished from the county or State.

Perhaps the leading abolitionist working in Maryland was William

Lloyd Garrison, who, during the winter of 1829–30 published in Baltimore *The Genius of Universal Emancipation*. In a series of vitriolic articles he lashed out at slave-owners, owners of ships carrying slaves, slave dealers, and Northern sympathizers with slavery. In the reaction that followed the brief appearance of the paper, Maryland, fearing the growing abolition sentiment, passed increasingly severe laws governing slavery, restricting manumission, and rigidly limiting the movements of slaves.

Among the leading figures in American Negro history were several Marylanders, including Benjamin Banneker (1731–1806), the astronomer; Frederick Douglass (1817–95); Harriet Tubman (1815–1913); and Frances E.W. Harper (1825–1911).

Banneker, a free Negro and first of his race to receive a presidential appointment, was named to assist Major Andrew Ellicott in a survey of the boundaries of the 'Federal Territory.' In 1761 Banneker whittled from wood the first clock made in Maryland and in 1792 published an almanac for which he constructed his own tables. The early years of Frederick Douglass (*see Literature*) were marked by insecurity, harsh treatment, and constant change of ownership. In 1838 he made his escape to New England, where he became one of the Anti-Slavery Society's most eloquent propagandists. The fact that he was himself an escaped slave made his position perilous, and he was sent abroad to lecture, chiefly in Great Britain where he received much attention and where he remained until 1847 when he was 'ransomed' by two Englishwomen. Returning to America with funds subscribed by British admirers, he for many years published the abolitionist paper, *The North Star*. In 1871 he was appointed a member of the territorial government of the District of Columbia; later he was made a United States marshal and still later recorder of deeds in the District. He also served as minister to Haiti.

Harriet Tubman, variously called the 'heroine of the Underground Railroad' and 'the Moses of her people,' escaped from her Eastern Shore master into Pennsylvania when she was about twenty-five. She first returned to assist members of her own family to freedom, and later so extended her activities that between three and four hundred liberations are credited to her. She so infuriated the slave-owners that a price of $40,000 was set on her head.

Frances Ellen Watkins was born of free parents in Baltimore. By about 1853 in Little York, Pennsylvania, she had become interested in the Underground Railroad and she later lectured against slavery in Philadelphia, New Bedford, and Boston. On September 28, 1854, she was engaged as a permanent lecturer by the Anti-Slavery Society of Maine. In 1860 in Cincinnati she married Fenton Harper. After the Civil War she continued to lecture on various subjects and spent much time in the South as a representative of the Women's Christian Temperance Union.

Josiah Henson, whose life story provided material for Harriet Beecher Stowe's *Uncle Tom's Cabin* and whose descendant, Matthew Henson, accompanied Peary to the North Pole, was also born in Maryland.

The problem that had confronted Negroes freed during the first half of the century faced all Negroes in Maryland after the Civil War—that of earning a living. Personal services, common labor, and farming were the three fields with which the Negro was most familiar, and those easiest for him to penetrate. A few, particularly in the country, were blacksmiths and carpenters. Brickmaking and oyster shucking constituted seasonal occupations. There were also Negro stevedores, and at one period following the war, Negroes practically monopolized the ship caulking trade and hod carrying.

Today the occupational distribution of Maryland Negroes has not changed radically. It is true that a number of business and professional men have overcome their economic and social handicaps, but in 1930 Maryland had only one Negro lawyer to every 8,375 Negroes and one Negro doctor to every 2,800 Negroes. In the field of public service are relatively few Negroes and the majority of these are teachers. In the municipal government of Baltimore, where Negroes comprise more than a fifth of the population, they have little share of jury service and the possibility of election to the City Council is remote, although there have been infrequent instances of such occurrences. No Negro has ever been elected to the Maryland State Legislature and until 1938, when one woman and three men were appointed to the Baltimore force, there were no Negro police.

As elsewhere, discrimination against Negroes in official position exists both on a numerical basis and, at least among teachers, in regard to salaries. A 'jim-crow' law segregating whites and Negroes on public carriers applies on steamships carrying passengers within the State and on electric cars running 20 miles beyond the limits of a city, but the law specifies that accommodations be of equal quality. Segregation is practiced in both public and private educational institutions, and in most cases the facilities for Negroes are not as good as those for whites. Though attempts to enforce housing segregation by law have been unsuccessful, practical segregation has forced the Negro to pay high rentals in deteriorated districts. Custom decrees that the color line be observed in theaters, restaurants, and, to some extent, in stores.

The Maryland Negro finds many industrial and commercial fields barred to him, in part because of the widespread theory that it is unwise or impossible to mix Negroes and whites at work. In refuting this, Negro leaders point out that the State's first union of brick-masons was formed by whites and Negroes; that one-third of the members of the first brick yard workers' organization were Negroes; and that both whites and Negroes are included today in such organizations as the Longshoremen's Association.

In 1869 the first Negro state labor convention in the United States met in Baltimore and recommended a nation-wide organization of Negro labor. Five months later a national assembly met 'to consolidate colored workingmen of the several States, to act in co-operation with our white workingmen in every State and in every territory of the Union who are opposed to distinction in the apprenticeship laws on account of color, and to act co-operatively until the necessity for separate organization shall be deemed unnecessary, and to petition Congress for the exclusion of coolie labor.' There is, however, no further record of this early movement after the national convention.

When prospects of jobs with high wages brought an influx of Negroes during and after the World War period, they increased the Negro population of Baltimore by more than a third and had definite economic and social effects on the life of the city. Overloading that part of the labor market open to Negroes, the immigration lowered the wage level of all unskilled labor and in later years swelled the ranks of the unemployed. With their farm backgrounds and with standards of living set in small, rural communities, many of the newcomers had difficulty in adjusting themselves to city life.

In Maryland as elsewhere social and economic handicaps have helped to make dependency, delinquency, and disease important factors in the Negro 'problem.' In 1934 Negroes, who constituted approximately one-sixteenth of the total population, formed more than 40 per cent of the persons on relief. More than 75 per cent of the illegitimate births reported to the city health department are Negro and 40 per cent of the children taken to juvenile court are of this race.

The percentage of Negroes in Baltimore who reach the age of sixty-five years and thus become eligible for old-age assistance is only one-half that of the whites reaching the same age—some indication of the poor health conditions among members of the race. Recent reports showed that the city's death rate from tuberculosis was the highest in large American cities. Baltimore's health commissioner, laying the blame for this situation largely on bad housing conditions for Negroes, pointed out that the Negro leath rate from tuberculosis in Baltimore was 245.2 per 100,000 in 1937 as against a white death rate of 63.6.

Although the social and economic bases of these conditions have not peen touched, several groups are at work attempting to better the conditions of Maryland Negroes. Among such organizations is the Urban League, the Baltimore branch of which was founded in 1924; its objective is to improve relations between the races. The Baltimore body has made an effort to interpret this rather broad program in relation to local problems.

Maryland is the only State with a permanent interracial commission, consisting of ten white and nine Negro members, to consider questions concerning the welfare of Maryland Negroes, and to recommend legislation and sponsor movements toward the improvement of relations between the races. The members of the commission, which was inaugurated in 1927, serve for six years without pay and are appointed by the governor with the consent of the State senate.

The Federation of Maryland Organizations is still another group attempting to secure social justice for the Negro, and the *Afro-American*, published twice weekly, carries on a militant campaign for Negro rights.

Religion is always a vital factor in Negro life. In the Colonial period Negroes and whites of Maryland worshiped in the same buildings, but gradually Negroes organized themselves into separate congregations, chiefly Baptist and Methodist, which at first were served by white pastors. In addition to the Protestant congregations, there are now four Negro Roman Catholic parishes with a membership of about 12,000.

Among Negro religious schools is one maintained by the Oblate Sisters of Providence (*see Religion*). Its Baltimore school, founded in 1828, is now attended by the daughters of well to do Negroes of Baltimore and other cities.

Religious cults have had increasing influence among Negroes in the postdepression period. More than three score 'churches' with congregations of about a dozen each are housed in small dwellings or in abandoned stores. This movement has been stimulated by the success of a former Baltimorean, Father Divine, who was born in Georgia. A generation ago George Baker was mowing lawns in Baltimore's suburbs. About 1907 he experienced a 'recombustion' and announced himself as the 'Messenger.' He moved his sphere of activity to New York City, where he became the guiding spirit of a communal experiment that offered his followers the advantages of church, boarding house, and employment agency—all under one roof. Father Divine's organization today claims a membership of 2,000,-000, both Negro and white, with more than 150 'kingdoms' scattered over twenty-three States, the District of Columbia, and four foreign countries

Another local cult leader is a mulatto, C.M.Grace, known as 'Bishop,' 'Father,' or more often simply 'Daddy.' He heads forty or more missions in various parts of the country. Contrary to usage in the Divine cult, finances are stressed in the Daddy Grace movement. Collections are 'lifted at all services, and should the offering be meager, commodities under the proprietary name of Daddy Grace are offered for sale.

Northwest Baltimore, where approximately 125,000 Negroes live, is Baltimore's 'Harlem.' Within a comparatively small area are two hospitals, numerous churches, schools, theaters, markets, stores, confectionaries, hotels, restaurants, and night clubs, all, with few exceptions, conducted for and by Negroes. Cultural entertainment available to the Negroes of Baltimore includes concerts by a Negro municipal band, a Negro symphony orchestra, a Negro chorus of some 300 voices, and drama by a little theater.

In the counties of Maryland, particularly on the Eastern Shore and in southern Maryland, the Negro lives under much the same conditions his ancestors knew. Oyster shucking, crab-picking, truck farming, work in canneries—these are his chief means of earning a meager livelihood. Dependent largely upon the generosity of a white employer or landowner, he is generally described in the phrase, 'Sure, I love niggers, the old-fashioned kind, that know their place.' Of the sixteen recorded lynchings in Maryland since 1885, eleven have occurred in southern Maryland or on the Eastern Shore.

Inextricably involved in the general social and economic affairs of the State, Maryland Negroes believe that solution for their troubles is expressed in the statement of editorial policy by the *Afro-American*: '. . . when colored citizens get their share of jobs in industry, in municipal, State and Federal departments, they will have, ipso facto, solved most of their other problems.'

Agriculture

'THIS I can say,' wrote Father White in his narrative of the first voyage to Maryland, 'that the soil appears particularly fertile, and strawberries, vines, sassafras, hickory nuts and walnuts we tread upon everywhere in the thickest woods.' That was in 1634. Today Maryland, one of the smallest States in the Nation, produces large crops of foodstuffs and other agricultural products on its limited but fertile acres.

Any comparative study indicates how relatively well off Maryland farmers are. Ninety-nine acres in size, the average farm is valued at $5,500. The average cash return to the State's 44,412 farms in 1935, which was a median year, was more than $1,600, or a total farm income for that year of $73,557,000. The average throughout the South was less than half this figure. This prosperous condition is largely due to the great diversity of crops; the prevalence of ready-cash crops and specialties with large markets closely accessible; the short-haul transportation, much of it by water; and the fertility of much of the farm land.

The State can be divided into four principal regions, according to types of soil, climatic conditions, nearness to markets, and means of transportation. The first two sections developed, southern Maryland and the Eastern Shore, lie on the Coastal Plain that forms about three-fifths of the State's area. This comparatively level peninsula with its alluvial deposits has lands with good surface and water drainage. The north-central region, which contains some of the State's best farming lands, is on the Piedmont plateau, where undulating hills dip into fertile valleys. Western Maryland is mountainous, ranging from 500 to 3,400 feet in height and much of it is covered with forest growth.

In colonial Maryland agriculture was, of course, the principal commercial activity, but little attention was paid to the production of foodstuffs for the market. 'These Sot-weed Planters Crowd the Shoar,' wrote Ebenezer Cooke in his satirical poem 'The Sot-Weed Factor,' dealing with the customs of the Maryland colonists. Tobacco, raised with ease in soil especially suited to its growth, early became the staple crop of the province because of the active demand for it in the European markets. Hundreds of thousands of hogsheads of the tobacco cultivated by slave labor in the

Tidewater passed over rolling roads to shipping points. In return, the planters acquired rich profits that were not always honestly earned, as Ebenezer Cooke indicated:

> In Cask that should contain Compleat,
> Five hundred of Tobacco neat.
> The Contract thus betwixt us made,
> Not well acquainted with the Trade,
> My Goods I trusted to the Cheat,
> Whose crop was then aboard a Fleet.

Tobacco became the colony's medium of exchange for clothing and other manufactured articles; even taxes and tithes were levied in tobacco. Fines for violation of court orders and contributions for the construction of town halls were paid in the same currency. Mrs. William Beard produced 'to the Court of 1768 the best piece of white linen,' for which she was awarded 1,000 polls (pounds) of tobacco; at the same term, Catherine Kimball was awarded 900 polls of tobacco 'for the best piece of brown linen.' (The court in those days acted as judge in awarding prizes for the production of certain articles of general use.)

The constant cultivation of the one product gradually exhausted the soil, and consequently lowered the quality of the crops. This, together with excessive transportation rates to Europe, the exorbitant import duties levied by the crown, and the charges exacted by merchants in England for credits on manufactured goods, further lessened the profits from tobacco before the Revolution.

With the rapid growth of the population after the Revolution and the need for new sources of agricultural income, many newcomers settled in outlying sections of Maryland where they cultivated wheat as the money crop. Later they also planted other cereals and hay, and began the breeding of cattle. This was the only means, as Ebenezer Cooke wrote in *The Looking Glass*:

> The Common-Weal to Health restore;
> Consumptive is, and sickly grown;
> As shall in proper Place be shewn;
> Reduc'd to Penury indeed,
> By feeding on this Indian Weed.

The market for Maryland tobacco revived, however, after the first quarter of the nineteenth century, bringing about a continuous increase in the production of tobacco. In 1825 the crop amounted to 15,924 hogsheads, in 1846 to 41,029, and in 1860 production reached 51,247 hogsheads.

During the decade before the Civil War, crop and livestock farmers expanded their acreages of grain crops as fast as new land could be cleared and cultivated. England, its industry rapidly expanding, repealed its corn laws in 1845, and foodstuffs entered that country thereafter without the payment of duties. This enlarged the market for American breadstuffs, bringing about an expansion in wheat production in Maryland as elsewhere. Price increases boomed when the Crimean War shut off grain shipment from Russia through the Black Sea ports from 1854 to 1856. Even the Eastern Shore of Maryland began to grow wheat.

After the Civil War there was a general decline in the market value of agricultural lands and staple crops. The increase in farm debts and tenancy was due in part to overexpansion during the boom years and in part to the new control of markets and prices by produce exchanges. Prices were also lowered by competition from the vast acreages newly under cultivation in the Middle West. Many of the farmers, particularly in southern Maryland and on the Eastern Shore, suffered serious losses.

Prices of old staple crops such as wheat and corn fell below the cost of production in the 1870's and 1880's, yet farmers continued to plant these crops from habit and in the hope that prices would rise again. With the increasing construction of railroads, the cities were no longer dependent upon near-by areas for their food supplies. Products from distant parts of the Nation and the world could be bought more cheaply than on the farms near the older cities, where the farmers still thought in terms of boom prices. In addition, the cost of production had increased because the impoverished soil would not yield without application of fertilizers.

Before 1891 when crop rotation first became a subject of general serious discussion, most of the State's farmers had no systematic order of planting and were evidently governed in the selection of a field for corn, wheat, or potatoes by the success they had attained in growing grass and clover on it. Because of the difficulty frequently experienced in procuring good hay, Maryland farmers were at first opposed to plowing under any forage land as long as it remained productive. The value of rotation in the maintenance of soil fertility was gradually recognized, but adoption of the practice was slow.

With the extension of rapid transportation facilities on the Eastern Shore in the 1890's, and a reduction of transportation costs, farmers in this area took advantage of the rapidly increasing demand of seaboard cities for fresh fruits and vegetables. Good prices for peaches resulted in the transformation of much wheat, corn, and other farm land in Kent, Queen Annes, and Talbot counties into peach orchards. Diversified truck crops offered a chance for greater profits, and farmers on the lower Eastern Shore gradually turned to that type of production.

From 1896 to the beginning of the World War, prices of all farm products were fairly good. By 1900 dairying had rapidly expanded and, with the canning industry emerging from its infancy, Maryland had assumed a lead in the production of tomatoes for canning.

The legislature of 1916 completely reorganized the State's agricultural activities by placing under one board all the agencies then operating in the interests of the farmer. Since then Maryland agriculture has progressed through the Extension Service of the University of Maryland, through research work of the Agricultural Experiment Station of the university, through application of regulatory laws under the State Board of Agriculture, and through education of specialists in agriculture.

Except for the absence of the plantation and slave systems, tobacco cultivation in southern Maryland is carried on today much as it was in early colonial times in the same region. Although the planter who trundles tobacco hogsheads to market in oxcarts, as his forefathers did in 1690, is rare, many of them still follow routes to the same wharves. Much of the land, however, has been tragically misused through incompetent farming and tobacco cropping, and an alarming quantity of topsoil has been washed away.

In a report of the Manufacturers' Association for 1882 it was said: 'Today, wherever in Maryland . . . the wayfarer comes upon a piece of rustling brown sedge engirt by stunted and unsightly pines, he knows that here the broad, green leaf of the tobacco plant was tilled by the heavy hoe . . .' Nevertheless, tobacco survives as the principal money crop, some arable land in southern Maryland having been in tobacco continuously for almost three centuries by rotations of three or four years. The leaf is of the free-burning variety, suitable for cigarette manufacture. Until recent years the entire crop was exported to Europe.

In addition to the twenty or more million pounds of tobacco it produces annually, southern Maryland also raises corn and cereals, most of it for local consumption. Truck farming in this region is confined to the areas around Baltimore, Annapolis, and Washington.

Farming in the north-central section of the State is general, with dairying and cattle-feeding the most profitable activities. Frederick County leads the State in the production of wheat, hay, milk, and livestock; while the adjacent county of Carroll tops all others in corn, poultry, and eggs. Most of the land in this section is arable and fertile. Generally speaking, central Maryland is the State's outstanding horse-breeding region, with

Percherons and Belgians most in favor. Abundant pasture land, much of it unsuitable for other purposes, is largely responsible for this development. Horse breeding has been carried on in Maryland since colonial days and some of the Maryland racing stables are notable.

Washington County, occupying most of the region between the Blue Ridge and Allegheny Mountains, is western Maryland's chief agricultural producer. This county ranks third in the State in wheat and corn and high in other grains, hay, white potatoes, livestock, and dairying. The berries that grow profusely in the mountainous sections find a ready market. Fruit brings considerable revenue to the county; and while orchards are scattered throughout the section, the larger ones are in the vicinity of Smithsburg and Hancock. The fattening of cattle for market is also important in Washington County.

Allegany County consists of 414 square miles of mountainous country. But Garrett County near the Pennsylvania–West Virginia border is largely plateau where oats, rye, and white potatoes are grown. Garrett is the only county in the State that produces any considerable quantity of maple sugar. Its 57,000 trees from 1927 to 1937 produced an average of 24,000 pounds of sugar and 26,000 gallons of syrup annually.

The Eastern Shore is now mainly occupied with truck farming for the northeastern markets and the canneries. In Dorchester County alone 10,183 acres of tomatoes were grown in 1936, chiefly for Eastern Shore canneries.

In Somerset and Worcester counties are produced most of Maryland's white potatoes, and Somerset also leads the State in strawberries. Melons, too, are grown in large varieties and quantities in this section, as well as such greens as kale, broccoli, and spinach. Wicomico County produces as much as a half-million bushels of sweet potatoes yearly.

The soy bean, recently found satisfactory as a base for certain fabrics, has been a standard crop on the Eastern Shore, and in recent years it has been used successfully for manufacturing purposes, chiefly for the oil produced from it. It serves well as a livestock feed and works in with the crop rotation plan of the region.

In the northern part of the Eastern Shore, large acreages are used for wheat, barley, corn, and hay. This region is also well suited to the development of nurseries and orchards, owing to its proximity to the big eastern markets, its climate, and the abundance of cheap labor.

Livestock breeding and fattening also ranks high in this area. A steady improvement in beef and dairy cattle has been effected in recent years, and there has also been an active development of better dairy and poultry farming. This change has been brought about, in a measure, by the excellent management of the three co-operative associations serving Maryland dairymen.

The activities of gentlemen farmers, who were not compelled to make a profit on their land, have improved the quality and increased the quantity of beef cattle in the State. Finding the dairy market overcrowded, they revived the breeding of beef cattle to improve the various strains on the commercial farms. This increase in beef-cattle breeding is partly a result of Maryland's abundance of pasturage, an advantage over States with longer winters or dryer summers, and it is also partly the accomplishment of the University of Maryland College of Agriculture, which has helped to select stock, studied pastures and forage for the commercial feeders, and co-operated with breeders in shows and sales.

Annual fairs have helped rural communities to prosper. Organized as a means of providing social intercourse and entertainment, they gradually became media for the dissemination of new ideas on agriculture and for the sale of farm products. Livestock buyers soon learned that the best animals were found at the fairs.

Principal organizations of Maryland farmers are the American Farm Bureau Federation, with 2,500 members, and the Grange, their memberships largely overlapping. They co-operate closely with the farm demonstration agents, sponsor organizations of agriculturists, and study legislation affecting farm interests.

Through its Extension Service, the University of Maryland gives advice on the drainage of wet lands, disseminates market information, and maintains farm and home demonstration agents to each county to assist the farmers in their fight against plant and animal diseases. The Extension Service also supervises the Federal Government's farm aid program in Maryland, including crop curtailment and soil conservation projects.

The headquarters of the Maryland Agricultural Experiment Station, supported by the State and Federal Governments, is at College Park but there are approximately 1,000 acres of land under its supervision elsewhere in the State. Orchard, livestock, and field crop experiments, covering practically all the State's agricultural interests, are conducted at the station. The experiment station, in studying soil fertility problems, was among the first to use chemical tests in a practical way. The present 'rapid chemical tests,' which are at the service of farmers, are the result of years of painstaking laboratory research; they make possible quick detection of nutritional deficiencies.

The United States Department of Agriculture experimental plant at

History

CLIPPER SHIP ANN McKIM (1832)—THE FIRST AMERICAN SHIP IN CHINA TRADE

O say can you see, ~~through~~ by the dawn's early light,
What so proudly we hail'd at the twilight's last gleaming,
Whose broad stripes & bright stars through the perilous fight
O'er the ramparts we watch'd, were so gallantly streaming?
And the rocket's red glare, the bomb bursting in air,
Gave proof through the night that our flag was still there,
O say does that star-spangled banner yet wave
O'er the land of the free & the home of the brave?

On the shore dimly seen through the mists ~~of the deep,~~
Where the foe's haughty host in dread silence reposes,
What is that which the breeze, o'er the towering steep,
As it fitfully blows, half conceals, half discloses?
Now it catches the gleam of the morning's first beam,
In full glory reflected now shines in the stream,
'Tis the star-spangled banner — O long may it wave
O'er the land of the free & the home of the brave!

And where is that band who so vauntingly swore,
That the havoc of war & the battle's confusion
A home & a Country should leave us no more?
~~Their blood~~ Their blood has wash'd out their foul footsteps' pollution
No refuge could save the hireling & slave
From the terror of flight or the gloom of the grave,
And the star-spangled banner in triumph doth wave
O'er the land of the free & the home of the brave.

O thus be it ever when freemen shall stand
Between their lov'd home & the war's desolation,
Blest with vict'ry & peace may the heav'n rescued land
Praise the power that hath made & preserv'd us a nation.
Then conquer we must when our cause it is just,
And this be our motto — "In God is our trust,"
And the star-spangled banner in triumph shall wave
O'er the land of the free & the home of the brave.

FACSIMILE STAR SPANGLED BANNER (1814) AS WRITTEN BY FRANCIS SCOTT KEY

Lincoln Highton

FIREPLACE, FLAG HOUSE (1783), BALTIMORE

THE prefent American Poft-Office was firft fet up by a pri
Gentleman in one of the Southern Colonies, and the Miniftry
Great-Britain finding that a Revenue might arife from it, procu
an Act of Parliament in the 9th Year of the Reign of Q. An
to enable them to take it into their own Hands ; and fucceedi
Adminiftrations have, ever fince, taken upon them to regulat
—have committed the Management of it to whom they pleafed, and avai
themfelves of its Income, now faid to be at leaft £.3000 Sterling per Ann
clear. By this Means a Set of Officers, *Minifterial* indeed, in their C
ation, Direction and Dependance are maintained in the Colonies, into wh
Hands all the focial, commercial and political Intelligence of the Continent
neceffarily committed ; which, at this Time, every one muft confider as dan
rous in the extreme. It is not only our Letters that are liable to be ftopt a
opened by a Minifterial Mandate, and their Contents conftrued into treafonal
Confpiracies, but our News-Papers, thofe neceffary & important Alarms in Ti
of public Danger, may be rendered of little Confequence for want a Circulatio
Whenever it fhall be thought proper to reftrain the Liberty of the Prefs,
injure an Individual, how eafily may it be effected ! A Poftmafter-General m
difmifs a Rider, and fubftitute his Hoftler in his Place, who may tax the Nev
Papers to a Prohibition ; and when the Mafter is remonftrated to upon the He
he may deny he has any Concern in the Matter, and tell the Printer he m
make his Terms with the Poft.

As, therefore, the Maintenance of this dangerous and unconftitutional Prec
dent of Taxation without Confent—as the parting with very confiderable Su
of our Money to fupport Officers, of whom it feems to be expected that th
fhould be inimical to our Rights—as the great Danger of the Increafe
fuch Intereft and its Connexions, added to the Confiderations abovemention
muft be alarming to a People thoroughly convinced of the fatal Tenden
of this Parliamentary Eftablifhment, it is therefore propofed,

That Subfcriptions be opened for the Eftablifhment and Maintenance of
Poft-Office ; and for the neceffary Defence of Poft-Officers and Riders e
ployed in the fame.

That the Subfcribers, in each Colony, fhall annually appoint a Committ
from among themfelves, confifting of feven Perfons, whofe Bufinefs it fhall
to appoint Poft-Mafters in all Places within their refpective Provinces, where fu
Offices have hitherto been kept, or may hereafter be judged neceffary ; and

PROPOSAL FOR ESTABLISHING A POST OFFICE, APRIL 30, 1774

STATE HOUSE (1772), ANNAPOLIS

MARKET AND COURT HOUSE, PUBLIC SQUARE, HAGERSTOWN (1807)

BURNSIDE'S TROOPS IN BATTLE OF ANTIETAM

ANTIETAM BATTLEFIELD (1862)

McCLELLAN AND HIS ARMY PASSING THROUGH FREDERICK CITY (1862)

LINCOLN MEETS McCLELLAN AFTER THE BATTLE OF ANTIETAM

THE PLUG UGLIES (1854-6)—A POLITICAL ARGUMENT IN A RAILROAD TRAIN

Beltsville is becoming one of the largest and most comprehensive agricultural research centers in the world. Fourteen thousand acres are used for the study of farm problems of national interest by technicians of the bureaus of Animal Husbandry, Biological Survey, Dairy Industry, Entomology, Plant Quarantine, Plant Industry, and the insecticide testing section of the Food and Drug Administration. Particular attention is paid to the elimination of animal and plant diseases, and to parasites that ravage crops.

In recent years the Farm Security Administration has lent funds to tenant farmers for the purchase of the land they work. The farm tenancy ratio in Maryland is much lower, however, than the national average, being but 26.5 per cent in 1930 as compared with the national average of 42.4 per cent.

In 1937 the U.S.Department of Agriculture reported that Maryland ranked sixth in the country in early production of spinach and ninth in intermediate production; fourth in production of tomatoes, third in intermediate production of strawberries and seventh in annual; and ninth in production of tobacco. Most common products could be found on the 175,050 acres planted with commercial truck crops in the State in 1937; these with the noncommercial truck crops had a cash value of more than $9,500,000.

The program of the Agricultural Adjustment Administration has offered farmers the opportunity for co-operative organization to regulate crop production. In Maryland as elsewhere, the establishment of this program in 1932 helped to arrest the alarming increase in foreclosures and bankruptcies among farmers, and the cash income of farmers nearly doubled between 1932 and 1937.

Industry and Commerce

MARYLAND, in common with other American colonies, began primarily as an agricultural community with industry a necessary side line. In agriculture, tobacco became firmly intrenched as a ranking crop at an early date. The crop swiftly subordinated every other activity to it, shortly becoming the colony's medium of exchange; and it is recorded that more discerning citizens felt it was 'also our law, our religion and always our curse.'

The early commercial and industrial life of the colony—in addition to fur trading with the Indians—revolved around shipbuilding and the trade carried on with England; by 1680 the amount had reached considerable proportions. Though the grist mills on the larger plantations and those scattered among the smaller ones ground the limited amount of corn grown on the plantations, and some home industry was carried on to provide for the needs of the less affluent settlers and the slaves, nearly all manufactured stuff, largely from England—and even much foodstuff—was imported.

This situation, however, was not entirely satisfactory to the colonists, partly because the various British middlemen charged high prices for their services, and partly because the needs of the colonists exceeded production; everyone was building and furnishing a house in keeping with his desires or prospects and he wanted hardware, rugs, curtains, and other furnishings for it, in addition to the fine garments he and his family considered suitable to their prosperous station in life. Moreover, the plantations required tools and stock, and the slaves had to be clothed and some of them shod. When tobacco prices were low or the crop poor, the planters continued to import, pledging future crops to cover their indebtedness. This was the beginning of the planters' economic bondage to the British merchants that played such an important part in British-American relationships between 1763 and 1776.

While agriculture, shipping, and its attendant trade were the 'big' industries of the Colonial era, many smaller manufacturing enterprises were scattered throughout Maryland. British capital as early as 1715 financed what is thought to be the first furnace and forge in Maryland—the Principio in Cecil County. It was one of the first great ironworks in the American colonies and was operated largely by 'redemptionist' labor. Production gradually increased until the governor of Maryland was able to report to the Board of Trade and Plantations in England that 'there are 8 furnaces and 10 forges in the Province,' which made 2,500 tons of pig iron and 600 tons of bar iron yearly. One of these furnaces, built some time after 1723, was located in the section surrounding what is now Gwynn's Falls Park.

Another industry that had started in Colonial days in a minor way was ship and boatbuilding. By 1700 Maryland vessels were already in the coastal trade and a few were making trips to Europe and to the Azores and West Indies. The British Naval Office lists show 80 boats registered from Maryland between 1689 and 1701.

The first real stimulus to manufacturing in Maryland was the nonimportation agreement, which barred large numbers of articles for which the colonists had to find substitutes in America or do without. Later the Revolution, with its disruption of trade and credit, was a further goad to development. At this time iron foundries increased in number and output, particularly because of the demand for munitions; and, in addition, shipbuilding became a major industry in the port of Baltimore, primarily because of the demand created by privateering for larger and swifter boats which the town's shipbuilders were able to supply. Baltimore became a leading seaport shortly after the Revolution because of its geographical location, and because of the foresight of its businessmen who unknowingly saw eye to eye with George Alsop (*see Literature*), the early Colonial poet, who wrote in 1662 that:

> Trafique is earths atlas that supports
> The pay of armies and the heights of courts
> And makes mechanics live that else would die
> Meer starving martyrs in their penury
> None but the merchant of this can boast
> He, like the bee, comes laden from each coast
> And all to Kingdoms as within a hive
> Shows up those riches that doth make them thrive . . .

Naturally Baltimore's development as a port, to and from which ships from all over the world sailed, materially increased the wealth of the State. Its shipbuilders flourished, and during the Revolution some 250 privateers operated out of the city's harbor; stories of their exploits and the wealth they brought to Baltimore are legend.

Baltimoreans went into every conceivable kind of manufacture, and one of the earliest undertakings was the making of umbrellas in 1772, soon after the first one was brought to the city from India as a novelty. This industry continued to expand, and its volume of production inspired the slogan, 'Born in Baltimore, Raised Everywhere.'

Glassware, now eagerly sought as museum pieces, was made near Park Mills in Frederick County, where in 1785 John Frederick Amelung and 68 workmen from his home in Bremen were turning out glass rivaling in beauty and durability the work of the craftsmen of Venice and Bohemia. Lafayette on his visit to Frederick inspected the Amelung plant and village; and Charles Carroll of Carrollton, a neighbor, was a frequent visitor.

The beginnings of the factory system were evident between 1795 and 1815. Many Marylanders were stirred by the industrial revolution which followed the invention of the steam engine, and dozens of towns throughout the State have relics and stories of the varied enterprises begun hopefully but unsuccessfully by local mechanics and capitalists. Baltimoreans quickly seized the opportunities offered by the invention of the power loom and the cotton gin. Not long after Samuel Slater, the English immigrant to Rhode Island, outwitted English textile monopolists by constructing several of the Awkright cotton looms from memory, a cotton mill was built in Baltimore, and as early as 1820 this city had some 20,000 spindles humming in half a dozen cotton mills. However, neither in Baltimore nor elsewhere in the State had the factory system assumed the proportions which it had then reached in New England. The skilled worker and artisan were still the prime productive factors in Maryland industry.

Nevertheless, it was not until the 1820's that industry and commerce began to reach something of the stature of agriculture in the State. It was during this period and until about 1850 that the Baltimore Clippers were a major factor in the commercial field. Their sale and the trade they brought played an important part in lifting the city out of the depression caused by the War of 1812.

At about this same time Peter Cooper, who designed Tom Thumb, the first American-built steam locomotive, for the Baltimore & Ohio Railroad (*see Transportation*), helped to found the Canton Company on whose property a rolling mill and a series of small iron plants were operated. The Abbott Iron Works, of a slightly later period, was long the biggest steel mill south of Pittsburg.

The long depression that began in 1837 and lasted twelve years arrested the development of the State's industry and commerce. During the 50's prosperity returned, and for the next twenty years Baltimore's rapid expansion as an industrial and commercial center was interrupted only by Maryland's participation in the Civil War. As a matter of fact, the war brought a commercial and industrial decline, despite the fact that Maryland factories turned out large quantities of military supplies, and Maryland farmers, already profiting from the Crimean War, had found a good market for their wheat and other foodstuffs. The depression was followed by a boom in the postwar period, and speculation in Maryland, as in other parts of the country, reached dizzy heights. The disastrous panic of 1873 was partly the result of the unrestrained speculation and extravagance of this boom period.

Industry, after nearly two centuries of development, had finally surpassed agriculture in total wealth. Since then the manufacturing industries have continued their accelerated growth with only periodic interruptions, until today industry outranks farming—still the most important *single* economic enterprise—by four to one in the total money value of production.

During the prosperous periods preceding and following the Civil War, a number of firms still flourishing today were founded. Since 1856 a Baltimore firm has had a virtual monopoly on certain types of weather measure instruments and calculators in which a fine degree of accuracy is necessary. Its founder, Julien P. Friez, collaborated with Ottmar Mergenthaler in Baltimore in the invention of the linotype machine.

Chemical fertilizers, the artifical domestic substitute, were first prepared in Baltimore sometime during the 1850's. By the time the State's history was first seriously grappled with and put on paper in the 1880's, the historian Scharf—viewing forthrightly and in terms of the barnyard this industry which had begun in Baltimore in 1824 with the arrival of the first two barrels of guano brought to the United States—took its products in his stride and hymned them gently: 'In all respects,' he says, 'the manures of Baltimore houses have been found by long and thorough trial to be superior to those of any other city.' In the manufacture of fertilizer, Maryland is today the leader.

Maryland, and particularly Baltimore, experienced another war boom shortly after the outbreak of the war in Europe. By 1916 factories were expanding and working overtime, and the many service industries that had grown up around the great port were doing a business far in excess of their most sanguine dreams. Through the years commercial facilities and related activities of all kinds had been developing; these included wholesale and retail trade, insurance, banking, the packing and canning of agricultural products, transfer and warehouse services, and carrier construction, repair, and servicing.

The business collapse of 1929 hit Maryland less heavily than it did other parts of the country. However, recovery in the State has depended on recovery in the Nation, since Maryland until recently has been primarily a service state, as Federal statistics of 1930 indicated. At that time, only 12.5 per cent of the gainfully employed were dependent on agriculture and 38.2 per cent on manufacturing. The remaining 49.3 per cent of the workers were in service industries, including transportation. The proportion of service industries in Baltimore alone was much higher than in the rest of the State; there approximately three-fifths of the wage and salary earners were dependent on them. Since 1930, however, a rapid expansion of industry has taken place in Maryland, and it can no longer be called without qualification a service state.

Naturally, any account of the contemporary industrial and commercial life of Maryland must be centered largely around Baltimore. With the exception of the comparatively limited manufacturing enterprises of the Eastern Shore and western Maryland, and the sea food and coal mining industries, respectively, in those two sections, the industrial development of the State has been contingent upon that of its largest city, home of approximately half of Maryland's population.

The predominant productive industries of Maryland, based on the 1937 figures of the U.S. Bureau of the Census and ranked in the order of aggregate wages, were: iron and steel and their products, $41,538,000; textiles and their products, $15,997,000; food and kindred products, $15,083,000; transportation equipment, $12,978,000; paper, printing, publishing, and allied products, $8,652,000; machinery, other than transportation, $8,034,000; nonferrous metals and their products, $6,874,000; chemicals and allied products, $5,899,000; stone, clay, and glass products, $3,347,000; forest products, $2,725,000; and leather and its manufacture, $943,000. Miscellaneous industries paid out $2,554,000 in wages.

Steel and the conversion of steel into ships and other products have been intertwined with the industrial growth of the State. Maryland has now, in the plant of the Bethlehem Steel Company, the largest tidewater steel works in the country. The plant covers an area of 2,200 acres at Sparrows Point and employs an estimated 20,000 persons. It does much of the shipbuilding in the State, but there are other plants located at Baltimore, Fairfield, Cambridge, Annapolis, Solomons, Oxford, Honga, and Fishing Creek. In all, some 38,000 persons in 1930 found employment in the iron and steel industry in Maryland.

Wooden ship construction is still a source of considerable industrial revenue to Maryland manufacturers, and this type of vessel is turned out at several of the yards in the State. Oyster-dredging regulations, which provide that only sailing vessels may engage in certain phases of the operation, are mainly responsible for the survival of the wooden shipbuilding industry in the Chesapeake Bay waters. More than 15,000 vessels of one kind or another are registered in the Baltimore Customs District, the greater preponderance of these being of wooden construction.

Building and construction concerns employ more labor than any one industry in the city. There are more than 700 contracting concerns in Baltimore, and in good years their transactions involve as much as $108,075,431, with pay rolls totaling $20,834,193. One of them, the Arundel Corporation, performed what was regarded as an engineering feat by draining the Florida Everglades. In 1930, records show, 43,625 persons in the State were gainfully employed in the building industry.

The American Sugar Refining Company, with its annual output of 1,800,000 barrels, is the only sugar refinery in Baltimore. The plant at Locust Point covers an area of 21 acres. Among Baltimore's food industries is one of the largest spice businesses in the world. Founded in 1889, the concern imports spices from 33 countries and distributes its products nationally.

The largest of Baltimore's three oil refineries is the local plant of the Standard Oil Company of New Jersey, which has in recent years developed into one of the eastern seaboard's major refineries. These refineries, coupled with six companies which have facilities for bunkering oil-burning vessels, account for most of the city's oil business. The Standard Oil Company alone can store more than a million and a half barrels of oil and it bunkers both its own and other vessels.

Several factories that produce nonferrous metals are located in Baltimore. The local plant of the American Smelting and Refining Company, which has an annual capacity of 360,000 tons, is the largest copper refinery in the world; and it is Baltimore's second ranking establishment in value of products.

Maryland has a special natural resource in sea food, a three-to-five-million dollar industry, providing employment for approximately 10,000 persons. Some Eastern Shore communities, notably Crisfield and the Tangier Sound area, are largely dependent upon it. Several hundred persons in this section, however, find employment in local manufacturing, such as men's clothing and furnishings.

Oysters constitute 75 per cent of the 40,000,000 pounds of shell fish taken annually from the Chesapeake Bay, crabs 24 per cent, and clams a far smaller percentage. A majority of the more than 200 varieties of finfish native to the Chesapeake are in Maryland waters.

Constantly reduced catches of both fin and shell fish, due to lack of adequate conservation measures, have aroused considerable alarm. Different methods of conservation in 'working' and 'stocking' the bay are being studied. As in the case of certain agricultural regions of the State, this natural source of wealth has been so shamelessly exploited that the gravest fears are entertained for its future. Of the finfish, for example, the annual takings have dwindled to less than half the yields of fifty years ago; while the supply of oysters and crabs has been on the downgrade so long that most politicians promise 'to do something about it' as soon as elected.

In water up to ten or twelve feet, oysters are brought to the surface with hand-operated tongs—hence the name 'tonging.' Dredging, a process involving specially designed scoops that are drawn like a scraper over the bay floor, is legal only in deeper water. The law effects, to some extent, a double conservation, since it prohibits dredging save from sailboats, thus preserving this type of craft from extinction above the surface, while protecting (by proscribing boats faster than sail) the bivalve below.

The sea food industry has been largely responsible for the start of another industry—canning. 'Hermetical sealing' was first applied to the oyster, and when the result proved satisfactory the product found a ready market, largely in the West.

The preservation process was then extended to other foodstuffs and, because oyster, fruit, and vegetable canning were seasonal occupations which could be carried on with a single overhead, the Maryland industry enjoyed a favorable position in the competitive market.

Maryland's forests, 34 per cent of its total area of 12,327 square miles, have been another valuable source of industrial and commercial growth. They, too, present a problem in conservation, however. The 24 woods which grow in commercial quantities are being cut out at a rate one-tenth faster than new growth can replace. Fortunately, this cutting-out process has done nothing to mar the beauty of the woodlands. The hard woods have been replaced by second growth and the timberland scenery yearly draws many visitors. The State was the first to employ a forester and it has 600 wardens at its call, a fact which has enabled it to keep down fire losses.

Minerals in many varieties are found in the State. In some parts of Allegany and Garrett counties, coal mining is a major industry. Next in importance to coal are sand and gravel, clays, granite, marble, limestone, and slate. Other minerals include: feldspar, iron ore, copper, chromite, marl, soapstone, asbestos, and gold.

Cumberland, the seat of Allegany County, is also the site of a large Celanese textile factory, normally employing about 10,000 people, and a rubber factory employing approximately 800. The Celanese plant is the largest artificial silk plant of its type in the country.

The State has become an aircraft producer of national and international importance since the Glenn L. Martin Company plant was built at Middle River. This concern is known throughout the world for its 'China,' 'Philippine,' and 'Hawaiian' Clippers, among the world's largest flying boats. It has produced both military and commercial planes for a number of foreign countries and has built many bombers and patrol planes for the United States Navy. In 1939 it expanded its plant considerably and now employs 12,000 workers. The Fairchild Aircraft Corporation, near Hagerstown, builds both land and amphibian planes and has a large trade in craft designed for traffic over the Amazon River.

At Point Breeze, on the outskirts of Baltimore, the Western Electric Company makes lead covered, armored, and submarine cable and other equipment required by the Bell Telephone Companies. The latest large addition to Maryland factories is the Bat'a shoe factory, which was started in 1939 in Harford County.

Whisky manufacture on a commercial scale has been practiced in Maryland since early in the eighteenth century. Products of half a dozen of the local distilleries are sold in the national market while others serve a more restricted field. Through the years, Maryland whiskey has become almost as renowned as Maryland fried chicken.

Men's clothing made in Maryland is worn throughout the United States and is one of the most important industries in the State. In 1937 the industry provided employment for more than 8,000 persons. Women's garments, too, are made in sufficient quantity to make the industry important in the State's commerce.

Joseph Hiskey (who employed James Lick, later founder of Lick Observatory in California) was Baltimore's first piano manufacturer of note; William Knabe was another, founding his business in 1839. The House of Stieff (1842) is now the largest. At Hagerstown, the M.P.Möller Company builds organs on a large scale and for years after its founding in 1881 it was the western Maryland city's largest employer of labor. Perhaps the most unusual business, as well as a very profitable one, is the goldfish trade of Frederick County. Twelve 'farms' there turn out the greatest supply of any section in the country.

Horse breeding, commercial adjunct of horse racing, has for many years been an important industry in Maryland. There are currently 62 farms, with a total of more than 25,000 acres, which in whole or part are devoted to the business.

Among the more important manufactures are: tin and enameled ware; glass and glassware; bottle caps and seals; machine shop products; patent medicines and drugs; chemicals; printing and publishing house products; paper; paints and varnishes; cotton duck; cordage; meat products; and flour.

The 1937 census of manufacturers recorded 2,683 establishments engaged in some form of manufacture in the State, employing 145,932 men and women, and producing goods valued at $1,095,862,972. Wages paid the persons employed in manufacture amount to as much as $148,598,057 in busy years. Retail trade transactions in the city of Baltimore total an average of $400,000,000 annually.

A contributing factor in Baltimore's growth has been its harbor, through which 28,000,000 tons of water-borne commerce pass annually. The harbor has a channel deep enough for all save the superliners of the Atlantic service and there are 343 piers, wharves, and bulkheads. The municipality owns 41 of these; the railroads 99; the Federal Government 9; and private concerns the remaining 187.

Maryland, in taking stock of the industrial and commercial results of its 164 years of independence, can feel considerable pride. In 1776 it was an agricultural state with exhausted fields and a badly unbalanced economy; it was largely dependent on a single crop and had no great mineral resources. Through the years it has managed to achieve diversified agricultural production and, in a world where the farmer is generally in desperate straits, to place considerable numbers of its farms on a paying basis (*see Agriculture*). It has extricated itself from the plantation and slave system with less difficulty than other plantation States. By taking every possible advantage of its geographical position it has made its chief port the sixth most important in the world in import tonnage, and second in the New World. Through its key position in the national transportation system it has attracted industry. With its knowledge of what transportation has meant in its history it has already taken steps to assure itself an important place in international air transportation by developing a large air field by quiet water. A small State, Maryland has out-stripped many others that in 1776 seemed to have a great advantage over it.

Labor

THE laborers of colonial Maryland consisted mainly of Negro slaves and white indentured servants. The latter were imported under individual contracts setting forth the period of servitude, usually four or five years, and stipulating the 'freedom dues'—tools, clothing, provisions, and sometimes land—to be paid when this period terminated. The extent to which these rights of the indentured servant were protected is shown in the case of a certain Henry Spenk, who in 1648 sued the estate of his deceased master for recovery of 'freedom dues' and was awarded 'one cap or hatt, one cloak or frize suite, one shirt one pr shoes & stockins one broad and one narrow hoe 50 acres of land, and 3 barrells Corne.'

After 1683 white servants were seldom imported directly by their employers. Impecunious persons who wished to come to the colony were given a certain time after arrival to dispose of their services for a sum sufficient to repay the shipmaster for their passage; these people were 'redemptioners' or 'free-willers.' The first white indentured servants came from Great Britain and Ireland; the redemptioners were largely from Holland, Switzerland, and Germany; and in the two decades preceding the Revolution, England sent as seven-year servants large numbers of convicts. Many of the poor immigrants, who were skilled or educated, later became independent farmers or merchants; some even rose to wealth and prominence, and became in their turn employers of labor. The historian Scharf remarks that 'not a few of our "old Maryland families" are descended from indentured servants and apprentices.'

The cheapness of lands and the single-crop system of tobacco culture, however, encouraged the use of African slaves. As a result white servitude became so degraded that fewer and fewer servants could be induced to immigrate, whereas Negro slavery found a growing market in Maryland during the late seventeenth and the eighteenth centuries.

Toward the latter part of the eighteenth century, in addition to the Negro slaves, the indentured servants and apprentices, and a small number of free Negroes, the free white worker emerged as a new class in the ranks of labor. As factories were built, the need for semiskilled workers became acute and Maryland began to encourage immigration. As early as

1755 Charles Carroll of Annapolis, in connection with the extension and development of his iron works, planned 'to get Young Negro Lads to put under the Smiths Carpenter Founders Finers & Fillers as also to get a certain number of able Slaves to fill the Furnace Stock the Bridge Raise Ore & Cart and burn the same.' 'Wood cutters,' he continues, 'May for some time be hired. There should be Two master Colliers one at the Furnaces another at the Forge with a Suitable number of Slaves or Servts under Each who might coal in the Summer and Cut wood in winter . . .' Carroll added that he 'Can find Founders Keepers, Milwright and mason . . . who will work at Reasonable rates for erecting much works, and can likewise find some Forge men, altho if the matter should proceed Two finers from some part of Britain convenanted to serve a Time on proper Rates on the Tonnage will answer.' In the case of the 'finers' there appears to be an early example of 'piece-work.'

White servitude did not entirely disappear until after 1820, and as late as 1829 the Chesapeake and Ohio Canal Company invoked the fugitive slave and servant laws against some Irish laborers who had quit their employ.

The first Maryland labor organizations were founded in Baltimore. As far back as 1803 the printers' society was seeking to establish a uniform price list for the trade. The tailors had won three strikes for higher wages by 1807. This organizational activity of workers went on in the face of the repressive criminal conspiracy laws which declared all combinations of workmen for the purpose of raising wages illegal, but the militant cordwainers, who had sought in 1809 to obtain a closed shop, became involved in, and won, one of the first conspiracy cases tried in Maryland.

In 1833 several trades in Baltimore conducted a sympathetic strike against reduction in the wages of journeymen hatters. This action led to the formation of the Union Trade Society, one of the first central trades unions in the United States. Seventeen trades actively participated in it, and five days after its formation a movement was under way to form a 'mechanical ticket' for the ensuing election. Acting with the workingmen of Washington in that same year, the labor organizations of Baltimore had demanded a ten-hour day fully two years before the demand became general throughout the country. By 1834 Baltimore had become a leading trade union center with 3,500 members in numerous trades, including one of the first societies of women needleworkers in America.

But the growth of the labor movement was arrested by the long depression which began in 1837 and lasted for twelve years. With the return of prosperity in the 50's trade union activity revived to some extent. It was at this time that the first organization of cigar makers was formed in the factory of Tom Little in Baltimore.

The next 20 years were a period of comparative industrial peace. Baltimore expanded rapidly as an industrial and trade center during both the Civil War and the period of reconstruction which followed. In 1866 Baltimore was the host to the first convention of the National Labor Union, in which the Maryland delegates played a prominent though conservative role. Three years later, the first Negro state labor convention met in the city. As unemployment became widespread after the Panic of 1873, competition for jobs increased, resulting in a disintegration of union rules and organizations. By 1877 industry was beginning to make drastic cuts in costs of operation, among them the wages paid for labor. The years that followed were to usher in one of the most turbulent periods in the annals of labor. On July 16, 1877, the Baltimore & Ohio Railroad, following similar action by other major railroads, announced a 10 per cent wage cut for all men earning more than $1 a day. With an average daily wage of about $1.50 and with only four days work a week, the men would thus earn about $5 or $6 per week. The first strike on the road occurred at Martinsburg, W.Va. The company believed that with so many men out of work the strikers could easily be replaced; but the men displayed unexpected solidarity and militancy. The company then enlisted the co-operation of Governor Matthews of West Virginia, and the State militia was sent to Martinsburg. But so great was public sympathy for the workers that the militiamen were persuaded to lay down their arms and fraternize with the strikers. Unable to depend upon the State militia, the company next appealed to President Hayes, and for the first time in the history of the United States Federal troops engaged in strikebreaking activities. By this time the strike was in progress in Maryland, and the company persuaded Governor Carroll to send the Fifth and Sixth Regiments of the Maryland National Guard, stationed at Baltimore, to Cumberland. As the Fifth Regiment marched to Camden Station, it was met everywhere by groups of hostile strikers and their sympathizers, who mobbed the station and prevented the trains from moving. When the Sixth Regiment followed, near the very center of the city, it encountered a crowd of 2,000 infuriated citizens who pelted the troops with bricks and paving stones. Finding that the State troops were unable to cope with the situation, Governor Carroll appealed to the Federal government for aid, and the Federal troops were dispatched from New York to Baltimore. Seven hundred soldiers guarded the property at Camden Station with two Gatling guns and several field pieces. Furious rioting continued for three days, in the course of which 13 were killed and some 50 wounded. The railroad resumed operation through the combined efforts of the State and Federal troops and the Baltimore police.

The measures used against the strike, however, caused some repercussions, for soon afterward the Workingmen's Party of Baltimore emerged as part of a nation-wide political movement. In the fall of 1877 this party secured one-third of all the votes cast in the mayoralty election and might have won but for the unscrupulous manipulation of the election machinery by the political party then in power. A further result of this upsurge in the ranks of labor was the rapid and remarkable growth of trade unions and labor organizations between 1877 and 1890. It is, in fact, in this period that the modern trade union movement of the United States has its beginnings.

During the late 70's the Knights of Labor set out to organize the western Maryland coal fields and in the course of several years succeeded in recruiting a majority of the miners into their ranks. By 1882 the Knights of Labor had become strong enough to lead the miners in a strike against wage reductions. But the coal companies broke the strike by replacing the men with immigrants, and with this defeat the Knights of Labor began to decline in membership and influence. A district assembly of the Knights was organized in Baltimore about 1880; but although some 24 crafts became affiliated with it, the assembly did not make much progress. In 1883 a discontented section of the Baltimore Assembly set up a short-lived rival organization known as the 'Improved Order of Knights of Labor.' In the same year another group of 35 trade unions, organized along craft lines, banded together in the Building League, which was reorganized in 1889 under a charter from the American Federation of Labor as the Baltimore Federation of Labor, and so exists today.

The last two decades of the nineteenth century witnessed the growth and development of the eight-hour day movement. During the 80's working days of twelve and fourteen hours were general, and in some industries the hours were even longer. With the furniture and German-speaking unions in the vanguard, demonstrations, meetings, and strikes for the eight-hour and nine-hour day were frequent and persistent during the 80's. From this time on, in one industry after another, the working day was reduced, first to ten, then to nine, and finally to eight hours.

The struggles of labor in the decade which followed the Panic of 1873 culminated during 1884 in certain legislative reforms which established the legality of trade unions, invalidated the application of the conspiracy laws to labor disputes, and laid the foundation for legislation designed to protect the health and safety of workers. Further progress along these lines was made in 1888 with the passage of a law establishing a ten-hour day for women in factories manufacturing cotton and woolen goods.

Although it was declared unconstitutional two years after it was enacted, the first workmen's compensation law in the United States was passed by the Maryland legislature in 1902, thereby laying the foundation for a similar law passed in 1914.

Between 1900 and 1920 slow but steady progress characterized the growth of the trade union movement in Maryland. After a long series of unsuccessful strikes, the miners of western Maryland were brought into the United Mine Workers in 1900. Particularly rapid strides were made by the clothing workers of Baltimore between 1912 and 1917, when they succeeded in securing higher wages, better working conditions, and the elimination of many of the evils for which their industry was notorious.

The tremendous rise in the cost of living incident to the World War resulted during 1917 in numerous strikes throughout industry for higher wages. These strikes were largely successful because of the shortage of labor at the time and the necessity of arbitration imposed by the Government. At the end of the War business began to slump, and in 1920 the merchants and manufacturers of Baltimore waged a campaign for the open shop. Attempts to counter this campaign through strikes were unsuccessful because of the vast amount of unemployment resulting from the postwar depression. In 1922 the big railroad and coal strikes that swept the country reached the Allegany County coal fields. President Harding at this time called upon the various States in which strikes were in progress to mobilize the State militia to force the strikers back to work. The President's request met with only one refusal—that of Maryland's Governor Ritchie, who saw little use in moving against the coal miners so long as the railroad strike remained unsettled.

The general economic prosperity that prevailed after 1923 was reflected in wage increases and better working conditions. The Bethlehem Steel Company in 1923 adopted the eight-hour day for its Sparrows Point mills, and the building trades waged a successful strike for the closed shop. The International Ladies Garment Workers Union after a long struggle secured most of its demands for a 44-hour week, abolition of sub-contracting, weekly pay, and better shop conditions. The general and decided lowering of wages and the increasing employment of child labor during the years of depression after 1929 were checked to some extent by the provisions of the NRA in 1934 and 1935. Only the clothing workers, however, made important gains in trade union organization under the labor provisions of this act.

With the right to organize confirmed and implemented by passage of the National Labor Relations Act and the State anti-yellow dog bill, labor organizations in Maryland entered a period of unprecedented growth and expansion after 1935. It was in this period, also, that a number of unions withdrew from the American Federation of Labor and formed the Committee for Industrial Organization (CIO). With the increased organization of unskilled and semiskilled workers, chiefly in basic industries, came also the spread of union activities to sections outside Baltimore which had been largely untouched previously. Other recent labor developments in the State have been the increasing admission of Negro workers to unions, and the growth of many 'white collar' unions.

State laws provide for arbitration of labor disputes, prohibit factory labor by children under 14, regulate labor of children between 14 and 16, limit to 10 hours a day the work of women in all occupations, and give special protection to miners. Under the workmen's compensation law, which is compulsory for certain extra-hazardous occupations, a maximum benefit of $5,000 is provided in case of death or permanent disability and proportionate amounts for partial disability.

Under the Federal Social Security Act, Maryland established a State Unemployment Compensation Commission in 1937, greatly extended its Employment Service in co-operation with the U.S. Department of Labor, and authorized State contributions to the old-age pension system. These measures reflect to a large degree the philosophy and pressure of organized labor.

Transportation

MARYLAND'S first colonists, settling along the shores of the Chesapeake Bay and its tributaries, largely used boats for transportation. Roads for vehicular, horse, or foot travel gradually evolved; the first 'highwaies' were scarcely more than Indian trails leading from plantations to river landings and from river settlements to the little capital of St.Marys. The first public conveyance in Maryland, 'a ferry for the more safe and commodious passage of people to and from over St.George's River,' was established by act of assembly in 1639; one pound of tobacco was charged for each 'waftage.' A law of 1658 required each county to maintain at least one ferry; passengers were carried up, down, and across the rivers in canoes, barges, and shallops; and the Kent and Anne Arundel county delegates to the General Assembly received compensation for boat hire rather than for mileage. The first road law, passed in 1666, was entitled 'an act for making highwaies & making the heads of Rivers, Creeks, Branches and Swamps passable for horse and foote,' and with a few amendments it was continued until 1704.

The establishment in 1695 of a regular post route from the Potomac River to Philadelphia via Annapolis and the Eastern Shore was followed in 1704 by further legislation vesting road-making power in the several counties. This law called for the clearing and grubbing of all public and main roads, twenty feet wide, 'and all the roads that lead to any county courthouse shall have two notches on the trees on both sides of the road.' This law remained in effect for 50 years.

In 1716 the assembly ordered the construction of four 'rolling' roads for the transportation of tobacco casks from the plantations into Annapolis, the new capital. Soon nearly every county in the province had similar 'rolling' roads to landings.

The configuration of the Chesapeake Bay and its tributaries influenced the direction of the roads developed in the Tidewater. The main roads on each side of the Bay generally ran north and south, considerably inland to avoid crossing many streams. On the western shore, the roads from the interior usually connected with those leading into Baltimore, which was beginning to achieve eminence as a seaport. Shortly after Frederick Town was laid out in 1745, highways were laid out between it and Baltimore and Annapolis. In 1748 Maryland had 144 miles of post roads in comparison with 78 miles in Pennsylvania.

By 1765 Maryland had been transformed from a colony of scattered and isolated settlements into an integrated province. A stagecoach line, established that year between Philadelphia and Baltimore, was routed by water to Christiana, by stage to Frenchtown, and by water to Baltimore. Soon after, ferries and stage lines extended their services southward into Virginia.

The Revolution was hardly over before settlers, natives as well as Europeans, began to swarm across the mountains to the fertile lands of the Ohio Valley. Eastern businessmen were quick to realize the vast new market being created in the interior and were much concerned lest the commerce and trade of the region be diverted down the Mississippi. To facilitate the transportation of these settlers, the Monocacy Road was built and the Braddock military road improved. The latter, built in 1755, started at Wills Creek (Fort Cumberland) and was the first highway across the Allegheny Mountains.

The lack of good roads was then the subject of wide criticism. The public roads leading from Baltimore Town to the western part of the State were virtually impassable during the wet seasons and winter months because of the passage of heavy freight wagons. Passengers in stagecoaches had to lean out of the carriages, first on one side and then on the other, to keep the vehicles from upsetting; the worst ruts were usually filled in with saplings and covered with a layer of earth.

Meantime Baltimore's accessibility as an inland seaport enhanced its development as a market for trade with the West. Before the Revolution, goods destined for the West had been borne by pack horses along the narrow trails that led across the mountains. At the turn of the century, however, the volume of business had increased to such an extent that this form of freight transportation was supplanted by huge canvas-covered Conestoga wagons. These followed the old Braddock military road and later the turnpikes that led to the navigable rivers of the Middle and Far West.

The first improved roads in the State were the turnpikes constructed by incorporated road-building companies. Under an act of the 1804 assembly, the Frederick, Reisterstown, York, and Falls Road turnpike companies were formed and soon began to function. The game and Indian trails through the dense forests formed the basic routes of many of the highways of Maryland. One such pathway leading from Cumberland became the National Road, an artery important to the early growth and development of the country's resources.

The objections of opponents to road building by the Federal Government were drowned in the clamor of those trying to get this help for the advantage of their own States. That Maryland was successful resulted from one of those voting combinations so useful to Southern interests until the Civil War. In 1806 President Jefferson signed an enabling act for the road, the only one built entirely with Federal funds. About $3,000,000 was expended on it. Baltimore, Washington, and Georgetown later connected themselves with it by turnpike roads. Although the National Road reached Vandalia, Illinois, by 1840, and later extended to St.Louis, the way had been cleared and covered with crushed stone to the Ohio River at Wheeling, and was open to the public by 1818. It was recognized as the greatest wagon road in the world, two six-horse teams being able to race abreast on it.

Maryland, Virginia, Pennsylvania, Indiana, Ohio, and Illinois accepted responsibility for the National Road, established rates, and appointed officials to supervise maintenance under the jurisdiction of each State. The road was later macadamized, stone bridges were built, distances indicated by mileposts, and strong iron tollgates constructed. It continued in popular use until the middle of the nineteenth century when the expansion of passenger and freight railroad facilities resulted in slackened activity. (The development of the automobile industry in the twentieth century has restored much of its early prestige to this highway, now known as US 40.)

Another important thoroughfare, the Old Post Road between Philadelphia and Baltimore, is now US 1. Over this highway Washington's army marched to Philadelphia during the Revolution, and General Lafayette and his men used the same route when they traveled south to Yorktown. Spanning the Susquehanna River between Havre de Grace and Perryville on this highway is the Susquehanna Bridge, known for many years as the 'Gold Mine Bridge' because of the fortune in tolls collected while it was in operation.

With the new roads bringing in the products from the West, boatbuilding and shipbuilding boomed in Baltimore; merchants were soon making shipments in their own vessels, and the town's prominence as a seaport was assured. By 1810 the city had become the third largest in America, mainly because of its maritime business and the fact that its population had quadrupled since 1790. The harbor at Fells Point bristled with the tall masts of square-rigged vessels home from Santo Domingo, Buenos Aires, Cape Horn, Bengal, Calcutta, and Canton. Between 1810 and 1830 an active trade in American wheat and flour developed with Europe and the West Indies as a result of the interruption of normal agricultural pursuits in Europe by war. The superior sailing qualities of the Baltimore-built vessels had given them a world-wide reputation for speed and brought additional commerce to Baltimore.

Records in ocean crossings were made and broken by the later Baltimore Clippers, for no other type of ship was able to sail closer to the wind. They brought coffee from South America, tea and opium from China, and slaves from Africa; they also carried gold seekers around the Horn to California for some years after 1848.

The Baltimore Clipper had its origin in the small, speedy vessels used before the Revolution in the ocean trade, particularly with Bermuda. These vessels, noted for speed, were copied by the Chesapeake Bay builders, whose results were designated variously as 'Virginia-built,' 'pilot boat model,' and 'Virginia model.' As shipowners demanded greater speed to outsail and outpoint the ships of nations competing with them in trade, builders discarded the earlier brig type of rig in favor of the fore-and-aft-rigged 'rakish topsail schooner,' frequently mentioned in stories pertaining to the slave trade and the activities of the privateers. A number of these vessels were used as privateers and carried large crews. Sweeps were used for propulsion whenever the wind failed, thereby enabling them to out-maneuver or run from much larger enemy vessels, even in a flat calm.

When Congress sanctioned the use of privateers during the War of 1812, more of these vessels were built and commissioned in Baltimore than in any other port. The swift little craft darted among the ponderous, slow-moving vessels of the British fleet, doing immeasurable damage. The Britons captured a number of them and copied their lines and sail plans, as evidenced by the later English construction.

As the commercial relations with foreign countries were improved, domestic and inland water transportation advanced. Although James Rumsey of Cecil County had experimented with steam propulsion as early as 1784, the first commercial steamboat was not introduced into Maryland until 1813; it plied between Baltimore and Frenchtown. Numerous steamboat companies, which were to provide the principal means of transportation between Baltimore and points along the Bay until the end of the century, were formed shortly afterward, among them the Weems Line in 1817, which operated steamers between Baltimore and various points on the Patuxent River. This line later extended its service to landings on the Potomac and Rappahannock Rivers.

In spite of the introduction of steam the Clippers continued to improve in design and construction. In the 1820's the square rig had often been specified for new construction as better suited to long-distance ocean voyages, especially in the China trade, than the fore-and-aft rig, which could not withstand extended periods of extremely hazardous weather. None of the vessels of the true Baltimore Clipper type, built between 1830 and 1850, exceeded 800 tons. The *Ann McKim*, with a tonnage of 493 tons, was an extreme example of what Baltimore could build; sailing in the China trade from 1833 to 1847, this vessel made several record-breaking voyages. Very few Baltimore Clippers were built after 1850 and hardly any survived after 1860. The Baltimore Clippers were superseded by the much larger Yankee Clippers—a new type rather than a development of the older boat.

The introduction of steam soon affected the interstate commerce of Maryland. Steamboat communication between the Baltimore region and New York diverted enough trade from Baltimore to alarm local merchants so that they began to agitate for canals in 1823. Work had already been begun in 1804 on the Chesapeake and Delaware Canal between Chesapeake City, Maryland, and Delaware City, Delaware, and was completed in 1829. The Chesapeake and Ohio Canal Company, organized in 1823, flourished for about fifty years and was later taken over and discontinued by the Baltimore & Ohio Railroad.

One of the canal commissioners, representing Maryland, soon saw that the canal offered little advantage to Baltimore and resigned. He immediately set to work among Baltimore businessmen to urge construction of a railroad to compete with the Erie Canal. The charter received by the Baltimore & Ohio Railroad in 1827 was confirmed the same year by Virginia, and by Pennsylvania a year later. From that time on, Maryland's transportation facilities were rapidly extended, making possible the development of vast stretches of territory hitherto inaccessible and far removed from the waterways.

Although the company sent a commission to England to study that country's railways, particularly their steam locomotives, and despite the commission's favorable report on their practical value, the railroad at first used horsepower. In January 1830 the *Aeolus*, a carriage equipped with mast and a square canvas sail, made its maiden rail trip with a distinguished group of passengers.

The first section of track, six-and-a-half miles between a depot on Pratt Street and the Carrollton Viaduct (later called the Thomas Viaduct for Thomas Latrobe, its designer), was completed in December 1829. This viaduct, the first railroad bridge in Maryland, was built so solidly that heavy locomotives and long freight trains still cross it regularly. By May 1830 the railroad had reached Ellicott's Mills, more than 13 miles from

Baltimore. Point of Rocks, 69 miles from the city, became the terminus in 1832.

Meanwhile the Baltimore & Ohio was making valuable experiments in the construction of rolling stock and in the application of motive power. In 1829 Peter Cooper, a New Yorker who had settled in Baltimore, produced the *Tom Thumb*, a tiny locomotive weighing only a ton and traveling 80 miles on a ton of coal. Its efficiency was demonstrated after some difficulty, when Cooper raced it with a horse-drawn car on rails; although the horse-car came in first, the directors of the railroad were sufficiently convinced by Cooper's demonstration to advertise a competitive test for the most useful steam locomotive. In 1830 the *Tom Thumb* made its first run to Ellicott's Mills. The return run was made in 61 minutes.

In July 1831 the *York*, built by Davis & Gartner of York, Pa., was delivered to the Baltimore & Ohio and placed in service between Ellicott's Mills and Baltimore. It was shortly followed by the *Atlantic* and the *Traveller*. The first passenger cars were modeled after stagecoaches, with baggage space on top. In 1833 Ross Winans, who invented the camel-back engine, built special baggage cars and eight-wheeled coaches to carry 60 passengers; in the same year the Baltimore & Ohio erected works which later became the Mount Clare shops, and also extended a branch to Washington to tap the southern market.

Extending its rails westward, the B.& O. reached Cumberland in 1842 and Wheeling, W.Va (then Virginia) in 1852. By 1857 there was a through line from Baltimore to Cincinnati and St.Louis.

A legal battle for the right-of-way through the narrow passes of the river between Point of Rocks and Harpers Ferry had been fought between the canal and the railroad in 1831, resulting a year later in a decision in favor of the canal company. When the canal reached Cumberland in 1850, it helped the surrounding territory to prosper. Stores where farmers sold their produce to the boatmen dotted the courses of the waterway until the 1880's. Today the canal, lying obsolete and useless, is choked by vegetation, a mere reminder of its former economic importance. A portion of it, the section between Georgetown and Seneca, was marked off in 1938 for public recreational use, and the work of transforming it into a play area was supervised by the National Public Service.

In the 1850's the Pennsylvania Railroad entered Maryland. Competing with the B.& O for control, it absorbed a number of smaller roads that were caught in the struggle between the giants. Among them was the Northern Central, control of which gave the Pennsylvania Railroad the opportunity to enter Baltimore. Outwitting the Baltimore & Ohio, the

Pennsylvania then acquired another subsidiary, the Philadelphia, Wilmington & Baltimore Railroad, and still later acquired the Baltimore & Potomac Railroad, which had been organized in 1853 to give direct connection between Baltimore and Richmond through southern Maryland and across the Potomac below Washington.

The Western Maryland Railway (over which President Lincoln rode in 1863 to Gettysburg to make his famous speech) was formerly the Baltimore, Carroll & Frederick Railroad, incorporated in 1853 with the hope of recapturing the Cumberland Valley trade, which was being diverted to Philadelphia. With the consolidation of minor railroads, it extended its lines into West Virginia and Connellsville, Pa., reaching an agreement with the New York Central for interchange of traffic at that point with the Pittsburgh and Lake Erie. In 1927 it became a subsidiary of the Baltimore & Ohio.

The last railroad established in Maryland was the Maryland & Pennsylvania Railroad, incorporated in 1901. The B.& O., though suffering heavily from competition with motor vehicles, has continued as one of the most important adjuncts of the State. Entering 13 States, it continues to bring products from half of the United States to Baltimore for shipment and to carry Maryland products and imports on its return trips. Under Daniel Willard's leadership, it was one of the first of the eastern railroads to try to compete with motor vehicles by radical reductions in weight of equipment, increase in speed, and improvement in passenger service. Its rival, the Pennsylvania Railroad, has electrified its line between New York and Washington and increased the speed of its passenger trains until Baltimore is now within easy commuting distance of Washington and Philadelphia.

Since the organization of the State Roads Commission in 1908, a system of arterial highways has been built; old highways have been modernized and new ones built to serve automobiles and trucks. The State had spent $157,993,420 for roads alone up to September 30, 1938.

Before March 1935 when the Maryland State Planning Commission had issued its ten-year highway construction program, the State had pointed out with pride that 'no farm of Maryland is more than two miles from a hard-surfaced road, except in several swamp areas of the Eastern Shore and in some parts of Allegany and Garrett counties.' The State Planning Commission revealed, however, that Maryland's total road structure of 17,000 miles had become inverted, for although its secondary highway system had gained national prominence, its primary highway system was totally inadequate, its main-line traffic having been largely disregarded to extend unneeded aid to light rural traffic. Many of the hard-surfaced roads extended to sections where there was not even a tiny village at the end of the road, while narrow-curving, dangerous main highways, still following horse-and-buggy trails, were inadequate for the tremendous flow of modern traffic.

The roads program of the planning commission proposed to fit the roads to the traffic they were carrying, to make over a system in which 10,000 vehicles a day were being squeezed into 14 to 20 foot roadways. Some construction and improvements recommended in the report have since been realized, including the new widened Philadelphia and Annapolis roads. Much of the 906 miles of primary construction recommended is still to be done, however, and even dangerous curves on the Washington Boulevard have not yet been eliminated.

Forty bus lines carry passengers and freight to all parts of the State. The truck volume over the State system has been estimated at 316,487,000 vehicle miles, with an additional 353,295,000 vehicle miles over the county roads, or an aggregate of 669,782,000 vehicle miles.

Baltimore now has full and convenient air service to other parts of America and is the alternate to New York as a terminus in the new Bermuda and transatlantic air service. Planes to and from Europe can cross directly in the lower latitudes with a reasonable prospect of encountering mild weather, whereas planes making the crossing further north are not likely to be so fortunate. The city's new 360-acre airport, only 6 miles by highway from the center of the city, was near completion in 1939. Located at the water's edge, with commodious ramps leading from the wide expanse of the Patapsco River, it is free from ice in all but exceptionally severe winters, and is admirably suited to the requirements of the huge modern seaplane transports.

The State as a whole is fortunate in its transportation facilities. The Chesapeake Bay and its numerous tributaries make possible low freight rates for transportation of goods by water. During 1938 a total of 6,286 vessels of 15,660,459 net ship tons entered and cleared at the Baltimore Customs House. Statistics show that Baltimore is now second in importance in foreign trade among the seaports of the Atlantic Coast, and first in trade when reckoned in terms of shipping via the Panama Canal. Thirty-eight steamship lines engaged in foreign trade in 1938; 9 others carried products between the Atlantic and Pacific coasts by way of the Panama Canal; and 10 coastwise lines carried commodities to the ports along the east coast and the Gulf of Mexico.

Religion

RELIGIOUS toleration is a key to the history of Maryland. Great praise has been given to the early Lords Baltimore for granting freedom of worship in their feudal domain, but it is less than just to lift their action to the clouds of sheer idealism. The Calverts were devout Catholics but also practical businessmen. Like other intelligent men of their day who were interested in making money, they realized the waste and disruption caused by the religious wars and dissensions, and also by repressive measures. Catholics especially, and other dissenters from the Established Church almost equally, were subject to serious disabilities in England. Calvert wished to provide a haven for Catholics but any action favoring Catholicism would have endangered what promised to be a very lucrative colonial venture.

Thus the Lord Proprietary prohibited religious disputes among the *Ark* and *Dove* pilgrims, both on shipboard and after landing, and the governor promised when taking his oath of office to make no discrimination on religious grounds. Two laws passed by the assembly of 1638 assured that Holy Church within this province shall have all her rights and liberties'; these were ever afterward interpreted as applying to every church. These prohibitions and assurances were more than empty formulæ; even proselytizing was discouraged. In 1642 Thomas Gerard, a Catholic and a member of the council, was found guilty of a misdemeanor for taking away the key and books of a Protestant chapel on his land, and was fined 500 pounds of tobacco toward the support of the first Protestant minister who should arrive.

The first act of the settlers upon landing at St.Clements Island was to celebrate mass. Thereafter Catholic services were conducted with as little show as possible, and there is small mention of them in the records. The Jesuits were at first very discreet in their movements, and addressed themselves almost exclusively to the Catholics and the pagan Indians. The latter responded, and in 1640 the 'Emperor' of Piscataway was baptized with great formality. It was not long, however, before the Jesuits came into conflict with the Lord Proprietary by accepting large tracts of land directly from the Indians, although all purchases were supposed to be

made through the Lord Proprietary. This was not a matter that Ceci
could accept calmly. After repeated protests and complaints to their supe
riors, he threatened to replace the Jesuits by secular priests. The disput
was settled by patenting the same lands in the required way.

William Claiborne had already had a minister of the Church of Eng
land, the Reverend Richard James, at his Kent Island trading post since
1631. Several small chapels were built in early years among the settle
ments near St.Marys.

Nonconformists as well as Catholics were present from the beginning
but their number was considerably increased just before and during the
civil wars. In 1649 a body of Puritans from Virginia, where they were sub
ject to repressive laws, came to Maryland at Governor William Stone's in
vitation and settled near the Severn River. Stone, a Protestant, owed hi
commission to Lord Baltimore's efforts to solve the problems that then be
set him. Parliament had triumphed over the king, and there was increas
ing danger both to the charter and to religious freedom. Besides appoint
ing Protestants to the governorship and three of the six other council posi
tions, Lord Baltimore sent the draft of a law which, if passed, should make
plain that toleration was the will of the people.

The Act Concerning Religion was passed by the assembly on April 2
1649. Under penalty of fines and damages, or flogging in case of nonpay
ment, no believer in Christ might be molested for his religion, nor tende
consciences be outraged by *disorderly* recreation nor *unnecessary* work o
Sunday, nor might anyone be called in reproach a 'Heretick, Schismatick
Idolator, Puritan, Presbyterean, Independent, Popish Priest, Jesuit, Jes
uited Papist, Lutheran, Calvinist, Anabaptist, Brownist, Antinomian
Barrowist, Roundhead, Separatist.' But beliefs common to all were pro
tected by as severe penalties as elsewhere: 'reproachfull speeches, words
or language, concerning the Holy Trinity' were punishable by death, and
the same toward the saints, by fine or banishment.

Despite Lord Baltimore's efforts, he lost control of the province for a
time to the commissioners appointed by parliament. The Puritans were
temporarily in complete control, and in 1654 proceeded to enforce thei
own kind of toleration: freedom of conscience was guaranteed to all, 'Pro
vided such liberty be not extended to *Popery* or *prelacy*.'

After the Restoration there was no more united Puritanism; the dissent
ing bodies crystallized as Presbyterians, Friends, and minor sects. Ther
were a number of 'settled' meetings of the Society of Friends as early a
1661. George Fox, one of the founders of the society, visited the provinc
in 1672 and organized the Maryland Yearly Meeting, the second in Amer

ca. William Penn was more than once a visitor to the Quakers of both the Eastern and Western Shores. Among early meeting houses were one at Third Haven (Easton), built in 1684, and one near Calvert in Cecil County, built in 1709 on a spot that Penn (believing it to be part of his domain) had pointed out as 'a likely place to worship God.'

In response to a petition of the Presbyterians for a minister, the Reverend Francis Makemie came to the lower Eastern Shore in 1683. The congregations he founded at Snow Hill, Rehoboth, and Pitts Creek (Pocomoke City), the first regularly constituted Presbyterian congregations in America, still remain. Makemie was the leading spirit in the organization of the first American presbytery at Philadelphia in 1706, and became its first moderator.

In 1715 the Reverend Hugh Conn was called to the vicinity of North Point in Baltimore County, but the Presbyterian group there proved unable to support a pastor. It was not until 1761 that a congregation was organized by Scotch and Irish merchants of Baltimore.

Toleration had been secured by law, but the spirit of intolerance had not been eradicated. The hearty merrymakings of the population at large were an excruciating torment to narrow-minded folk, and loud protests were raised against the 'immorality' of the province. Catholicism was no less an abomination to them, and every adverse rumor was taken at face value. Time after time, the countryside was thrown into turmoil by reports that large forces of French and Indians were on their way to join the Catholics and massacre the Protestants. These tactics achieved success in 1692, when a local version of the Protestant Revolution was staged and the government was taken away from the Calverts.

Under the royal government, toleration was not wholly done away with; nevertheless the Catholics ceased to share in its benefits, owing to the belief that they were Stuart partisans. Priests were forbidden to say mass in public and to baptize. In 1718 all Catholics were disfranchised, and in 1740 they were required to pay double taxes. There were at the end of the seventeenth century less than 3,000 Catholics, with a half-dozen Jesuit priests to minister to them. The only brick chapels were on the Jesuits' land at St. Thomas Manor, their headquarters, and St. Inigoes Manor. Elsewhere there were a few rooms and wooden sheds fitted up for the purpose by private owners. The most pretentious of the private chapels was that of Doughoregan Manor (*see Tour 2b*). Toward the end of the Colonial period the restrictions were a little relaxed. In 1704 the Reverend Thomas Mansell had been sent to Bohemia Manor (*see Tour 4*), where land was gradually purchased with a view to establishing a school. The school did not become a reality until shortly after 1740. The first Catholic church on the lower Eastern Shore was St.Mary's, Star of the Sea, built in 1769. St.Peter's, Baltimore, was built in 1770.

The first assembly under the royal government, in 1692, passed an act for establishment of the Church of England. Thirty parishes were laid out, and the support of the church was assured by a poll tax of 40 pounds of tobacco, levied without regard to religious affiliation. Before 1694 there were only four Church of England clergymen in the province, much to the distress of persons who desired their guidance. The protests of the Reverend John Yeo and influential laymen were partly instrumental in bringing about the Establishment in the province. In 1699 the Reverend Thomas Bray was appointed commissary by the Bishop of London. Before sailing for America he collected books to form parish libraries and a central library in Annapolis. His efforts before leaving for Maryland also supplied more than twenty parishes with clergymen. Although he remained in the province only a year, he was instrumental in having the new Establishment Act of 1702 passed. Thereby the reading of the Book of Common Prayer in every church was made compulsory, and marriages by lay magistrates were forbidden; the latter provision is still the law of the State.

The dearth of ministers was remedied, but another evil soon made its appearance. The Lord Proprietary began to use parish livings as sinecures for needy friends without regard for the fitness of the appointees; many were pleasure-loving fellows with no urge to minister among the frontier settlements. But not all were of this type; the colonial clergy included several men of scholarly attainment and piety. The Reverend Thomas Cradock translated the Psalms of David into English verse. The Reverend Thomas Bacon founded a free school in Talbot County, was author of *Sermons to Masters and Servants*, and published (1765) an edition of the laws of Maryland.

A few Anabaptists had been present in early times, but it was not till the various Baptist sects had separated that they gained numerical importance in the colony. The first Baptist church in Maryland was built by Henry Sater of Baltimore County in 1742. Previously he had been content with holding meetings in his home whenever a wandering preacher arrived. This first congregation held to the general Baptist doctrine. A particular Baptist group seceded in 1754 and built its own church on Winters Run.

Germans began to arrive by way of Pennsylvania as early as 1729, bringing with them the Lutheran and Reformed faiths. A church was built near the site of Creagerstown in 1733. About 1747 both the Lutheran congregation under the Reverend Michael Schlatter and the Reformed congregaion under the Reverend Heinrich Melchior Mühlenberg were using this church. Shortly thereafter the latter changed their meeting place to Fredrick, which is still a Reformed center. In Baltimore there were two early Reformed congregations. The first, organized in 1756, worshipped in a building long known as the Town Clock Church. The other was organized by the Reverend Philip William Otterbein in 1774 (*see Baltimore*).

About 1760 Robert Strawbridge, after a few open-air sermons in Annaplis, preached in a small log chapel on Sams Creek, Carroll County. This was the first Methodist place of worship in Maryland. Methodism was well received in that vicinity, but did not at first have the same success in Baltimore. About 1770 a local convert named John King preached his first sermon unmolested, from the top of an anvil; his second, from a table top, was put to an end by tipping over the table. Later he was invited to preach from the pulpit of St.Paul's (Anglican) Church. The arrival of Francis Asbury in 1771 marks the beginning of organized Methodism in America. As a result of his efforts, a meeting house was built in 1773 at Fleet Street and Strawberry Alley. In 1774 construction of the Lovely Lane Meeting House was begun.

The Revolution resulted in the separation of American religious bodies from their English authorities. Among the first were the Methodists, who gathered in Lovely Lane Meeting House on Christmas Eve 1784 to organize their scattered churches into a single national body. Baltimore has continued to be the center of Methodism to the present day.

The problem of the Church of England was critical, for independence had resulted in disestablishment. A population suffering under forced levies to support an indifferent clergy had thrown off the yoke in the Declaration of Rights of 1776. Most of the Church of England clergy, either because they had taken oath of loyalty to the king or because they had to depend henceforth on voluntary support, had left the province soon after the Revolutionary War began. In 1780 the Reverend William Smith of Chestertown called a conference to find a means of reviving the church and overcoming the problem of ordination. Of the five other clergymen of the former Established Church left in the State, only two responded. The name Protestant Episcopal Church was first suggested at this meeting. In later years American bishops representing two opposing factions were consecrated in England. These united in 1792 in consecrating Dr.Thomas Clarett the first Protestant Episcopal Bishop of Maryland.

There was no more need to burden the Roman Catholic authorities in England, still subject to oppressive laws, with the management of a church across the ocean. In 1790 the Right Reverend John Carroll was conse-

crated Bishop of Baltimore with a diocese covering the whole United States
Growth of the church resulted in his being made Archbishop in 1808. On
of his first acts as bishop was the establishment of St.Mary's Seminary a
Baltimore, the first Catholic theological seminary in English-speakin
America.

Elizabeth Ann Seton (*see Tour* 15), founder of the community of nun
that in 1850 became the American branch of the Daughters of Charity o
Saint Vincent de Paul, received the title of Mother from Archbishop Car
roll on June 2, 1809. A movement for her canonization has been under wa
for many years.

As the center of Catholicism in the United States, Baltimore was th
scene of the three Plenary (national) Councils of 1852, 1866, and 1884, a
well as of a Laymen's Congress in 1889. The most notable of the Arch
bishops of Baltimore was James Cardinal Gibbons. Born in Baltimore i
1834, he was ordained priest in 1861 and became Vicar Apostolic of Nortl
Carolina in 1868, Bishop of Richmond in 1872, Archbishop of Baltimor
in 1877, Cardinal in 1886. His apologetic and devotional writings hav
great popularity, and have been translated into many languages.

The Baptists of Harford County established a mission in Baltimor
shortly before the Revolution, and in 1775 a piece of ground on Jones Fall
was acquired for baptisms. The First Baptist Church became a separat
congregation in 1785, with the Reverend Lewis Richards as pastor.

As early as 1779 the Baptists answered in the affirmative the question o
admitting slaves to membership, and ever since the Baptist faith has bee
exceedingly strong among the Negroes. The first Negro Baptist churcl
was organized in 1836; at present there are more than fifty in Baltimor
and its suburbs. Vaguely Baptist in belief are the numerous but ofte
short-lived mystical cults favored by the Negroes. Baltimore was the scen
of the early labors of two outstanding leaders in the cult field, Georg
Baker ('Father Divine') and Charles M. ('Daddy') Grace.

Methodist and Roman Catholic Negro congregations date from the be
ginning of the nineteenth century. The Sharp Street African Methodis
Episcopal Church was established in 1802. The influx of refugees from th
French West Indies in 1793 brought a number of Roman Catholic Ne
groes, both slave and free. These were accommodated in the basemen
chapel at St.Mary's Seminary, later in the lower church at St.Ignatius
and finally (1863) at St.Francis Xavier's Church, Calvert and Pleasan
Streets. The Reverend James Joubert,S.S., of St.Mary's Seminary, an
Elizabeth (Sister Mary) Lange, a Negress of Santiago, Cuba, founded i
1829 the Oblate Sisters of Providence, the first separate body of Negro nuns

The First Independent Unitarian Church was dedicated in 1818 as a Congregationalist church. At the ordination of Jared Sparks, its first minister, in 1819, Dr.William Ellery Channing of Boston preached a vigorous sermon that brought about the separation of the Unitarians from the more conservative Congregationalists. Dr.Sparks remained until 1823, when he gave up the ministry for literary pursuits; he is most widely known as the author of the *Life and Letters of George Washington*.

In course of time the Lutheran churches gave up the use of the German language. An exception is Zion Church, in the shadow of the City Hall, dedicated in 1808. The congregation of this church has never allied itself with the others, which were formed into a General Synod at Hagerstown in 1820.

The few Jews present in colonial times had enjoyed toleration by tacit consent, although it was not specifically secured to them by law. An exception to prove the rule is the case of Dr.Jacob Lumbrozo, who was charged with blasphemy during the Puritan regime after being inveigled into a theological argument; the case was never tried, and later Dr.Lumbrozo received a bill of naturalization. Under early State laws conscientious Jews were debarred from public office by the Christian formulæ of the oaths required; the 'Jew Bill' of 1825 removed this disability. In 1829 the Baltimore Hebrew Congregation received its charter from the assembly, to be followed in 1838 by the Fells Point Hebrew Friendship Congregation.

The Civil War period was one of division, occasioned in some cases by sectional feeling but in others by consideration of growth and convenience.

The question of lay representation had already led to the formation of the Methodist Protestant Church at a conference in Baltimore in 1830.

Still other congregations in the Baltimore Conference of the Methodist Episcopal Church seceded in 1861, and in 1866 announced their adherence to the Methodist Episcopal Church South, which had been formed in 1844 after a split in the main body of the church over the question of slavery. In 1939, all branches were re-united in Maryland, as was the case throughout the United States, under the one original name, the Methodist Church, and a new united Baltimore Conference was established.

Administrative convenience rather than sectional prejudice was responsible for the formation of the Roman Catholic Diocese of Wilmington in 1868 and the Protestant Episcopal Diocese of Easton in 1869.

No exact figures are available on church membership in Maryland or in any other part of the United States. Probably the best figures are those compiled by the United States Bureau of the Census with the aid of the heads of the congregations. Many denominations, however, frankly include in their numbers the people they consider within their spheres of influence—that is, people who have been baptized into the church even though they are not active, and people who occasionally attend or give support but do not formally join the organization. With these additions the church census shows that not quite half the population of the State has church affiliation; the 1926 census figures—no later figures were available in 1940—gave the membership of all denominations as 758,366. Of this number, 233,960 were listed as Roman Catholics, 179,530 as Methodists, 50,973 as Baptists, and 70,294 as Lutherans.

Education

FORMAL education in early colonial Maryland, with its widely scattered population, was limited to the sons of the landed gentry. Taught first by parish clergymen or by tutors imported from England, they were frequently sent to England for further knowledge and social finish. For the children of the poorer colonists virtually the only schooling was the meager knowledge handed down by their untutored parents. The few existing schools were largely for boys, and girls received scarcely any tutoring except in the household arts. The schools were staffed chiefly by indentured servants, often well-educated, or by transported convicts of some learning. Seldom adequately supplied with books and equipment, the pupils in most cases used fire-coal crayons to write on coarse, rough paper or white-painted lapboards.

As Annapolis developed into a cultural center, private schools for 'females' were opened, with emphasis placed on the practical requirements of woman's life in the home. Occasional concessions were made to such cultural studies as French—as indicated in an advertisement in 1754, in which Mary Salisbury proposed to keep school in Annapolis 'at the house where Mr. Sparrow lived . . . to teach young ladies French and all sorts of fine needlework, tapestry, embroidery with gold and silver . . . and all education fit for young ladies, except dancing.'

No general provisions were made for public education until 1694, in Governor Francis Nicholson's administration. Then the assembly passed an act for 'the encouragement of learning,' which imposed a tax on furs and skins exported from the colony to provide funds for the maintenance of schools.

In 1696 the assembly passed an act for the establishment at Annapolis of a school where 'Latin, Greek, writing, and the like' would be taught. The school was to be named King William's School in honor of the king, and the schoolmaster sent over by the Bishop of London was to be supported by the taxes voted in 1694. Through subscriptions of the leading men in the colony and the donation of a lot, construction of the school building was begun at once though it was not completed until 1701. This, the first 'free school' (*schola libera*) in Maryland, flourished for about 85 years.

Efforts in 1700 to raise funds for schools in each county 'for the purpose of instructing the youth of the said province in arithmetic, navigation and all useful learning' were futile. In 1723 schools were authorized in each of the twelve counties, with funds to be raised for their support by a *per capita* tobacco tax and by a tax of 20 shillings laid upon each Irish Catholic servant and each Negro imported into the province.

In spite of the interest in education shown by the legislature, many of the county schools existed for but short periods, partly because of lack of funds, but in the main because of a scarcity of teachers, who 'were to be members of the Church of England and of pious and exemplary lives and capable of teaching well the grammar, good writing and the mathematics.' Funds were not sufficient, however, to obtain teachers qualified to meet these varied requirements. In fact, the only schools of any value were conducted by clergymen. Typical of these was the one instituted in 1747 by the Reverend Thomas Cradock in his home in Baltimore County, where he taught young men Latin and Greek and furnished them board at $50 a year until his death in 1770. Of a different type was the charity school 'for orphans, other poor children and Negroes,' organized in 1750 by the Reverend Thomas Bacon in Talbot County. Besides the three 'R's,' this school devoted special attention to vocational training. It was abandoned in 1768, shortly after Dr.Bacon's death.

The census of pedagogues in 1745, made primarily for the purpose of preventing Roman Catholics from teaching, revealed some of the types of men engaged in teaching, such as 'Enoch Magruder's convict servant,' 'Thomas Harrison, a convict,' and 'Jeremiah Berry's indentured servant.' Teachers of the three 'R's' were in demand, however, as indicated by an advertisement in the *Maryland Gazette* of February 27, 1752, for 'a person of good sober character who understands teaching English, writing and arithmetic, and will undertake a school.' Frequently the educational attainments of indentured servants were responsible for their sale.

With the exception of two schools—the Baltimore Free School of 1766 and the grammar school opened in 1771 by William Dick of Philadelphia—educational facilities in Baltimore were meager. Schooling for poor children was left largely to charitable agencies. In 1799 the Benevolent Society of the City and County of Baltimore was incorporated for the purpose of educating poor female children; and in 1805 St.Peter's Episcopal School was also incorporated to educate poor children. The Female Humane Association Charity, the Baltimore Carpenters' Humane Society, and St.Patrick's Free School were soon established.

After the Revolution higher institutions of learning began to evolve.

The Kent County School at Chestertown was incorporated as Washington College in 1782 with the Reverend Dr. William Smith as president. A charter for St. John's College, with which the old King William's College was merged, was granted in 1785. This institution in recent years has inaugurated an advanced experiment in education (*see Annapolis*).

During the early part of the nineteenth century when public education was becoming general, the first colleges for professional training were established. Although the two liberal arts colleges, Washington and St. John's, had been functioning successfully, there were no accredited institutions giving special training to those who wanted to become lawyers and apothecaries. As in other parts of America, professional training was obtained by apprenticeship, and in the absence of a licensing system the 'barber-chirurgeon' and other varieties of medical quacks could practice without restraint.

A few progressive men sought to correct these evils, particularly in the field of medicine. One of these, Dr. John B. Davidge, boldly introduced a cadaver for dissection during one of his private medical lectures; when the news spread, the lecture hall was wrecked and Dr. Davidge was forced to abandon his demonstrations. But he persisted in his efforts to improve medical education and was instrumental in founding the College of Medicine of Maryland, which was incorporated in 1808. In 1812 the institution was granted a charter as the University of Maryland.

Training for the law was of the same amateurish character as for medicine. Almost any bright boy who attached himself to a lawyer's office for two years and put in a reasonable amount of time on *Blackstone* and *Coke* could hang out his own shingle, and his success thereafter was determined as much by his eloquence as by his learning. Recognizing the need for better legal education the University of Maryland began to offer instruction in the practice and theory of law in 1823. The director and principal instructor in the school was David Hoffman, author of *A Course of Legal Study*, adjudged by Justice Story to be the most perfect system for the study of law ever offered to the public. General Lafayette was awarded the school's first honorary law degree in 1824. Lack of students forced the law school to suspend its activities from 1836 until 1869. During its lifetime the university has absorbed several other institutions, notably the College of Physicians and Surgeons, founded in 1872; the Baltimore Medical College, founded in 1883; the Baltimore Law School, founded in 1900; and the Baltimore University School of Law, founded in 1890.

Another pioneer in professional education was Dr. Horace H. Hayden, founder of the first dental college in the United States. Established in 1840, the school achieved an enviable reputation, and during the following years had many imitators. As the Baltimore College of Dental Surgery it became a part of the reorganized University of Maryland in 1923.

Although numerous elementary and secondary schools of a religious or secular character—many of the latter supported in part by public funds—had sprung up in various parts of the State during the early part of the nineteenth century, the public-school system remained in a deplorable condition, unable to meet the needs of a rapidly-growing population. Little was done to remedy the defects until 1812, when a fund arising from a corporation tax on banking and turnpike companies was earmarked for use in establishing free schools throughout the State. Under an act of 1816 nine school commissioners were appointed in each county to distribute the funds raised by the act.

On February 28, 1826, an act was passed for the establishment of public schools throughout the State, and on the same day the Mayor and City Council of Baltimore were authorized by a further act to establish public schools in Baltimore. On January 27, 1827, the council approved and accepted the act of the assembly and in March 1828 created a board of commissioners of public schools with the power to establish schools in each of the six school districts. The ordinance was an idle gesture, as no money was appropriated. With $1,000 available from the State, it was decided to establish two schools in East Baltimore and two in the western section, with the hope that the city authorities would grant funds later. The first school was opened on September 21, 1829, followed by another a week later.

During the first year the schools were unable to accommodate all applicants and facilities had to be extended. The curriculum embraced spelling, reading, writing, arithmetic, grammar, geography, and history. One school is mentioned as giving instruction in bookkeeping; and the 'female' schools devoted part of two days each week to 'needlework.' The method of teaching followed the monitorial or Lancastrian system, in which the master imparted information to older pupils, who in turn repeated the information to the younger ones. By this method one master could, and generally did, instruct more than 400 pupils.

By 1839 it had become evident that the organization and management of the city schools needed a thorough overhauling. The new board of commissioners, which was appointed to bring about the necessary changes, concluded that the school system was incomplete and the system of instruction faulty. As a result they established the Male High School—which later became the Central High School and finally the Baltimore City College—and abolished the monitorial system, dividing the schools into classes and employing assistant teachers. Stimulated by the opportunity to enter high school, 675 pupils enrolled in all schools in 1838; by 1844, in which year two high schools for girls were opened, registration had increased to 3,366, and by 1850 to 7,093 from a population of 169,000.

In 1848 the division of the lower schools into primary and grammar grades was accomplished, and the necessary buildings and equipment were provided. In 1850 the studies in the Central High School were arranged in eight departments: ' 1. Belles Lettres and History; 2. Mathematics; 3. Natural Sciences; 4. Moral, Mental and Political Science; 5. Ancient Languages; 6. Modern Languages; 7. Graphics, including Drawing and Writing; and 8. Music.'

Although various measures dealing with public education throughout the State had been enacted during the first half of the century, no general and effective system was established until the creation of the State Board of Education and the appointment of a Superintendent of Public Instruction in 1864. The schools in each county were placed under the control and supervision of county school boards appointed by the governor. The Baltimore board consisted of one commissioner from each ward. The schools were supported by a state tax, supplemented by local taxation in each county.

The State Normal School for teachers was established in 1866 in Baltimore. The State School for Deaf and Dumb was founded in 1868 in Frederick to teach both the sign language and articulation to pupils between 9 and 21, who were to receive board and instruction without charge. The Manual Training School, founded in 1883 in response to a widespread demand for industrial training, was one of the first schools of its kind established in the United States as a part of the public school system. In 1893 it became the Baltimore Polytechnic Institute.

The first known effort to instruct Negro children in a group was made in 1818 when a school was opened by the Reverend Daniel Coker, a slave whose freedom had been purchased by Baltimore Negroes in appreciation of his efforts in the educational field. It was not until 1867, however, that the city acknowledged its educational responsibility toward its Negro population. Nevertheless, while the city council authorized schools for such pupils, it again failed to provide money for their support because of doubt as to legal authority to appropriate.

In 1868 the assembly passed an enabling act and the council voted sufficient funds to pay back bills and maintain the existing Negro schools for the current year. That these schools were inadequate for the first thirty years is evidenced by a survey of 1895 that showed 37 per cent of all Negroes over ten years old illiterate. In 1935, under improved conditions, literacy had been attained by 84 per cent of the same age group, and 23,140 Negro children were in the public schools.

Under the new charter for Baltimore City in 1900 the management of the public school system was fundamentally changed. With the rapid growth of population, over-crowded schools had become an insistent problem. Under the new charter a department of education was created on an equal footing with the other departments of the city government, with provisions for expansions to meet increased needs.

A compulsory school attendance law was enacted in 1911, to be enforced through attendance officers, the Juvenile Court, and the parental school. Teachers' salaries were increased, health inspection of school buildings was inaugurated, and provision was made for the instruction of handicapped children. The system inaugurated in 1900 has been modernized and improved at intervals until in September 1938, the city's public school system could receive approximately 125,000 children into 165 schools without difficulty.

Studies of the Department of Education show that enrollment is increasing in Negro elementary schools and decreasing in the white schools. This is owing to the increase in Baltimore's Negro population, which is fed by a steady movement of Negroes from Maryland counties and other parts of the country, and the decreasing white birth rate coupled with the limits set on immigration.

In 1937, outside of Baltimore City there were 149,319 pupils enrolled in the public schools of the State. Of this number 126,216 were white and 23,102 were Negro. In the State were 1,415 public elementary schools, junior and vocational high schools, junior-senior and regular senior high schools.

Baltimore had a considerable reputation as a medical center before 1889, but the founding of the Johns Hopkins Hospital in that year and the Johns Hopkins Medical School in 1893 gave it international renown. This medical school was the first in the United States to have a curriculum comparable with those of the finest medical schools of Europe. To Hopkins, President Daniel Coit Gilman had brought the greatest pathologist in America, Dr. William H. Welch, and he was soon joined by Doctors Kelly, Osler, and Halstead. The work of these four completely revolutionized the study and practice of medicine in America.

The university had already achieved eminence in the sciences and letters. The faculty at the opening of the school in 1876 included, in addition to President Gilman, the biologist, Newell A. Martin; the physicist, Henry

A. Rowland; the mathematician, J.J.Sylvester; the classical scholar, Basil L. Gildersleeve; and the chemist, Ira Remsen. Hopkins soon became one of the leading schools for graduate study in America, later attracting students from all over the world. The university added other departments as time went on, including an undergraduate school of arts and sciences, an engineering school, and college for teachers. The Walter Hines Page School of International Relations was added in 1930. The School of Hygiene and Public Health was established in 1918, through a grant from the Rockefeller Foundation.

The history of the present University of Maryland is the history of two institutions, the old University of Maryland in Baltimore and the Maryland State College in College Park. The Maryland State College was chartered in 1856 as a private institution called the Maryland Agricultural College, becoming one of the first institutions of its type. After passage of the Land Grant Act in 1862, which set aside land in each state for the support of a college where branches of learning related to agriculture and the mechanical arts were to be stressed, Maryland Agricultural College was designated as the Maryland beneficiary under this act. In 1914 the State assumed full control of the college, which two years later received a new charter as the Maryland State College of Agriculture. In 1920 the University of Maryland in Baltimore merged with this institution (*see Baltimore and Tour 1b*).

In the same year that the public schools were opened to Negroes (1867), the Central Bible Institute for training Negro candidates for the Methodist ministry had been founded. After twenty years of precarious existence, the struggling school received a considerable sum of money from the Reverend L.F.Morgan and was elevated to collegiate standing as Morgan College, becoming nonsectarian. With the aid of a grant from the Carnegie fund, matched by Baltimore contributions, the plant was enlarged and improved until today it can admit more than 600 students. In 1939 it became a State institution.

In Goucher College, Baltimore has a notable educational institution for women. Incorporated in 1886, it held its first session two years later. Land for the college was donated by the Reverend John F. Goucher, who for many years served as president without pay. Founded as the Woman's College of Baltimore, under the supervision of the Baltimore Conference of the Methodist Episcopal Church, it was technically a sectarian school. In 1910 it took its present name, and in 1914 an amendment to its charter freed it of sectarian influences.

Other institutions for higher learning in the State include the Maryland

College for Women at Lutherville, founded in 1853, and Western Maryland College, founded in Westminister in 1866. The Roman Catholic colleges are Loyola in Baltimore, founded 1852; Mt.St.Mary's, in Emmitsburg, founded 1808; Notre Dame of Maryland, in Baltimore, founded 1896; and St.Joseph's, in Emmitsburg, founded 1809.

There are about fourteen private preparatory schools for boys and thirteen for girls in the State, some of them established in the early part of the nineteenth century. Because of their smaller enrollments and other advantages, these schools are better equipped to give the individual attention and development stressed in modern educational theory. Also, there are a large number of Roman Catholic elementary and preparatory schools for boys and girls.

The educational facilities of Baltimore and the larger cities of Maryland include Americanization classes, night schools for adults, and vocational schools for boys and girls.

During the years following the economic collapse of 1929 many educational institutions, particularly those dependent on private funds, had difficulty in carrying on. The public institutions received much help, particularly in construction and modernization, through the various Federal agencies, notably the PWA and the WPA. Many rural schools were built in districts that would not have attempted to provide modern plants without such aid. Though there is still room for progress, Maryland can now offer fairly adequate educational facilities to most of her young people and to some of the older ones. The State's advance in education is indicated in the figures on literacy in the United States: in 1930 only 3.8 per cent of the State's population was illiterate against an average of 4.3 in the whole country. Part of the illiteracy counted against Maryland in these figures is the result of the migration from the far South in the World War and postwar years.

The Press

MARYLANDERS had their first journal in 1727 when William Parks, 'Public Printer,' began to issue his *Maryland Gazette* in Annapolis. The newspaper was not only Maryland's first, but was the first published in the South and the sixth in the colonies. After 1730 publication became irregular and about 1734 it was discontinued entirely.

In 1745 Jonas Green launched another *Maryland Gazette*, also in Annapolis, and members of his family continued its publication until 1839 except for one brief period of suspension. The *Gazette's* advertisements and 'Letters to the Printers,' which gave a more vivid picture of the life of the period than its scant news items, are of interest and value to the present-day reader and student. Excellent files of the periodical are in the Library of Congress, the Enoch Pratt Free Library, and the Maryland Historical Society.

It was not until 1773 that publishers felt Baltimore was big enough to support a newspaper; in that year William Goddard launched his *Maryland Journal and Baltimore Advertiser*. The young town had to wait 14 years more for its first daily paper. Goddard published his weekly with equipment purchased from Nicholas Hasselboct (or Hasselbach), who until then had been the town's only successful printer. An experienced journalist, Goddard had previously published a newspaper in Rhode Island and a journal in Philadelphia. An enterprising man, he adopted, among other modern practices, that of running a special post to Philadelphia to get news quickly; this became the nucleus of the national post office.

Goddard's life as an editor was stormy. He was suspected of Tory sympathies and suspicion was heightened by publication in the *Journal* of an ironic, unsigned letter discussing the British peace proposals. *Journal* readers missed the irony and construed the letter as an endorsement of the British course. Led by the Whig Club, they marched on the newspaper office. Goddard refused to reveal the identity of the letter's author and circumvented Whig plans to have him driven out of town.

Two years later, in 1779, the publisher again outraged his readers, this time by printing a letter from the court-martialed general, Charles Lee, criticizing Washington. Goddard was forced to make a public apology but retracted it after the Council of Safety at Annapolis had ordered Baltimore magistrates to assure his protection. In 1792 James Angell, Goddard's brother-in-law, purchased the *Journal*. In the meantime (since 1775) John Dunlap had been publishing Baltimore's second newspaper, the *Maryland Gazette*, first called the *Baltimore General Advertiser*.

Pennsylvania Germans brought the first printing presses to western Maryland. In 1786 Matthias Bartgis started publishing the *Maryland Chronicle* and the *Deutsche Zeitung* in Frederick Town. The *Washington Spy* followed in 1790 in Elizabeth-town (Hagerstown) and in 1795 the *Westliche Correspondent* in the same place.

The *Herald and Eastern Shore Intelligencer*, first issued in Easton in 1790, was the first paper on the Eastern Shore. Other papers of that region, some of them still owned by the families of their founders, include the *Kent News*, founded in Chestertown in 1823 and the *Marylander* and the *Herald*, published in Princess Anne in 1828.

Baltimore's first daily, the *Palladium of Freedom*, was issued August 2, 1787. Its history was brief and somewhat mysterious. Only one copy of the paper has been found; it is in the possession of the American Antiquarian Society, Worcester, Massachusetts. The copy bears the notation, believed to have been written by William Goddard: 'First Daily Paper at Baltimore, continued a few weeks. The Publishers abdicated under cover of Night.' Who the publishers were or why they abdicated research has not revealed.

Four years after the *Palladium* came Baltimore's second daily paper—the *Repository*, first issued on October 24, 1791, by David Graham. The daily *Baltimore Post* appeared in July of the following year. The *Sunday Monitor*, inaugurated in 1796 by Philip Edwards, who had established the *Post*, would seem to have been issued only once. For the next 50 years Baltimore had many competing newspapers, and there were the usual mergers, consolidations, and changes of name. Many papers appeared only to vanish after a brief struggle.

Maryland's earlier newspapers provided an outlet for much of the literary output of the time. They published efforts of innumerable embryo poets, and also short stories at frequent intervals. John H. Hewitt (1801-90), editor of the *Minerva* and *Saturday Post*, was also editing the Baltimore *Saturday Morning Visiter* in 1833, when it printed Edgar Allan Poe's 'Manuscript Found in a Bottle.' Poe was awarded a $100 prize for the tale, which he had entered in a contest sponsored by the *Visiter*. Hewitt's long newspaper career also included the editorship in 1839 of the Baltimore

Clipper, and in addition the production of many stories, operas, and ballads by his facile pen.

Hezekiah Niles, whose *Weekly Register* appeared in Baltimore in 1811, was probably the most painstaking of early Maryland publishers. His journal, which also appeared in Washington, was printed on book-size paper, and was a model of neatness and accuracy. In 1836 his son took over publication, renaming the paper *Niles Register*, and continued it until 1849.

Newspapers of the early nineteenth century were openly and bitterly partisan, Federalist or Democrat, and there was no middle ground between them. In 1808, with Jefferson ending his second term, five daily newspapers were being published in Baltimore: the *Federal Gazette* and the *North American* were strongly Federalist and the *Whig*, *Post*, and *American* were militantly Democratic.

Readers of the period also held strong views on other subjects of current interest and had an abrupt way with editors whose views did not coincide with their own. Two days after the War of 1812 was declared, one of the most dramatic episodes in Maryland newspaper history occurred. The *Federal Republican* published an article censuring the action of the Madison administration, arousing the fury of the Democratic majority of Baltimore's population. A mob forced entrance into the paper's plant at Gay and Second Streets, threw the presses, type, and paper into the street, and finally destroyed the building. Continuing its rampage, the mob dismantled several vessels, which, it was reported, were preparing to sail under British licenses.

The editors of the paper fled to the country for safety. On July 28, led by Alexander Contee Hanson, they returned to Baltimore, bringing with them for support a party of more than twenty friends, including General 'Lighthorse' Harry Lee, all of whom had armed themselves. Re-establishing the *Federal Republican* in a house on Charles Street near Mercer, the hardy group released an issue in which the actions of the citizenry and the authorities were roundly castigated. Again a mob surrounded the newspaper office, showering the house with stones. Undaunted by the firing of blank cartridges, the irate citizens stormed the building and did not retreat until one member of the attacking party was killed and several were wounded.

By this time the entire town was aroused, and a genuine siege developed when the throng returned with a nine-pounder. Major William Barney with a troop of cavalry intervened to halt the violence, and Hanson's party finally surrendered to Mayor Johnson and General Stricker.

Taken to jail for safekeeping, the group was left unguarded, and under cover of night the still simmering mob forced its way into the building. Deciding to go down fighting, the defenders of the 'freedom of the press' sallied forth to meet the attacking party. About half of the group managed to escape, but General Lingan, one of Hanson's friends, was killed, and General Lee, as well as the rest of the party, was badly beaten.

Scharf in his *History of Baltimore City and County* declared:

'A general feeling of horror and indignation was aroused throughout the State and the whole country by this atrocious affair. A political revolution placed the Federal party in power in Maryland, and Mr. Hanson became a member of Congress and in 1816–19 a United States Senator. Baltimore for many a year felt the consequences of the shameful deed, which fixed upon her an enduring reproach and the opprobrious name of "Mobtown".'

The partisan flavor of newspapers was not singular to Baltimore, the county editors vying with each other to defend their champions and decry their foes. In 1832 publication of the Hagerstown *Mail* was begun as the mouthpiece of the Democrats, opposing the Whig forerunner of the present *Morning Herald*. The *Torchlight* accused the Jackson stalwarts of resorting to physical violence, made much of the fact that congressmen were forced to carry dirks and daggers, and on occasion reported sarcastically: 'No new outrage has been committed on members of Congress during the past week—no attempts at murder.'

Surviving are several county newspapers whose titles indicate their origin in this period. Among them are the *Cecil Whig*, published at Elkton since 1841, and the *Westminster Democratic Advocate*, founded in 1838.

Arunah S. Abell found six dailies in Baltimore when he came from Philadelphia in 1837 to establish the *Sun*. All sold for 6¢ a copy. Abell offered his paper for a penny and devoted his attention to bringing out-of-town news quickly to the city. He organized a horseback express to rush news from Boston and used carrier pigeons between that city, Washington, New York, and Philadelphia. The *Sun* was prompt in availing itself of the newly invented telegraph, and its printing of the first presidential message transmitted by wire was hailed as an outstanding journalistic feat. During the Mexican War, 1846–7, the *Sun* again resorted to courier service and received war dispatches so rapidly that government officials read of events in the Baltimore papers as much as 24 hours before they obtained the same news through government mails.

The Civil War period was a trying one for Maryland newspapers, which differed widely on the issues of the conflict. Of the Baltimore papers, the *American* and the *Clipper* were loyal to the Union. The *South*, which first appeared on April 21, 1861, three days after the Massachusetts Volunteers had been attacked in the city, was the Confederacy's most sincere advocate. With its interests and sympathies largely allied with the Confederacy, the *Sun* realized, nevertheless, the danger of open opposition to the Federal Government. The paper played safe in the crisis and, according to Gerald Johnson in the *Sunpapers of Baltimore*, simply ignored the war. Throughout the war period, the *Sun* gave scant space, if any, to news of the conflict.

The *South* made a special appeal to the commercial interests of the city, contending that by an alliance with the Southern cause Baltimore would soon become the most important of American cities and thus replace New York as the banking and business capital. So obvious was the strength of Southern sentiment in Baltimore that the Confederate government advertised in the *South*, asking for bids on stamps and other postal supplies.

The *South*, the *Southern Herald*, the *Evening Loyalist*, and the *Gazette*, all of which openly espoused the Southern cause, were suppressed during the war. Only the *Gazette* resumed publication at the end of hostilities, and then for but a short time.

Immediately following Emancipation, several newspapers published by Negroes and carrying news of interest to Negro readers, appeared in Baltimore. Well edited, they were important adjuncts to the enlightenment of the newly liberated Negroes. Among the most effective Negro papers were the *True Communicator*, the *Golden Enterprise*, both weeklies, and a daily, the *Public Ledger*. By 1880 Maryland had five Negro papers. This peaceful growth of the Negro press was in marked contrast to the tumult aroused by William Lloyd Garrison's abolitionist newspaper, the *Genius of Universal Emancipation*, published in Baltimore in 1829–30, which had played an important role in crystallizing antislavery agitation.

After the war, newspapers entered a period of expansion and consolidation, but until 1870 all the Baltimore papers were confined to one sheet, folded in two and printed on the four pages. About this time the surviving papers began to expand in size, circulation, and influence; and the *Sun*, the *Herald*, the *News*, and the *American* became the city's leading dailies. Founded in 1872 the *News* was purchased in 1908 by Frank A. Munsey, who in 1920 also bought the *American* and its afternoon edition, the *Star*, merging the latter paper with his own afternoon *News*. In 1923 the Munsey holdings in Baltimore became part of the Hearst chain.

Early in the present century the *Herald* ceased publication. In 1910 the *Sun* began publishing an afternoon paper, the *Evening Sun*. The *American* is now issued only on Sunday. The *Sunpapers* and the *News-Post* are the only dailies still published in Baltimore. (The *News* became the *News-Post* in 1934, when it absorbed the shortlived Scripps-Howard *Post*.

The *Sun* and the *Evening Sun* easily dominate the local field. In recent years they have given only passing attention to many departments that are usually considered essential features and services of metropolitan publications, such as art, music, and literature. The morning paper carries the dispatches of a number of distinguished foreign correspondents, and gives comprehensive coverage to national and international issues, while the afternoon paper concentrates its attention largely on local news and is known for its casual and even facetious editorial attitudes, also chiefly directed toward the local scene.

Supporters of the principles and policies of the Democratic party from the beginning of publication, the *Sunpapers* reversed their traditional stand in the presidential campaign of 1936. Chief spokesmen for the papers in their changed political attitude have been Frank R. Kent and Henry L. Mencken.

Mr. Kent, vice-president of the A.S. Abell Company, owners of the papers, writes for the *Sun* the widely syndicated column 'The Great Game of Politics,' and Mr. Mencken, 'the sage of Baltimore' (*see Literature*), for a number of years wrote a weekly signed article for the editorial page of the *Evening Sun*. His articles now appear in the morning paper. For a few months during 1938 Mr. Mencken served as editor of the afternoon paper. In 1939 he described his position with the *Sunpapers* to a staff writer of the *Nation* as 'prime-minister without portfolio.'

Among local staff writers on the *Sunpapers* are a number of men whose work has attracted national attention. John W. Owens, then editor of the *Sun* and now editor-in-chief of the papers, in 1937 won the Pulitzer award for distinguished editorial writing. Lee McCardell of the *Evening Sun* received honorable mention in the Pulitzer awards for his story of the 'bonus army' march on Washington, and Edmund Duffy, *Sun* cartoonist, was twice awarded a Pulitzer prize, in 1931 and 1934. In 1938 and 1939 Frank Hopkins of the *Sun* and Stephen Fitzgerald of the *Evening Sun* were awarded Niemann Scholarships to Harvard University. A number of other *Sun* and *Evening Sun* staff members have been successful in the field of literature (*see Literature*).

In the counties are seven dailies, the majority of them offspring of the early party weekly. Despite the improved news and photographic services, and the swifter means of transportation, which have enabled metropolitan dailies to invade the rural field, about 80 weeklies still flourish in Maryland. In Baltimore are issued several foreign language and religious papers, both dailies and weeklies, as well as the *Daily Record*, devoted to news of the legal profession, and a bi-weekly Negro paper, the *Afro-American*. In 1938 the *CIO. News* began publication of a Baltimore edition devoted almost exclusively to national and local labor news. A weekly, the paper serves as a source of information for groups interested in the problems and progress of labor.

Since 1896 a State law has fortified the 'freedom of the press,' in that it restrains a court from compelling any newspaper man to divulge the source of information he has received for publication.

Sports and Recreation

MARYLAND, because of its topography and its temperate though wide climatic range, offers a variety of sports and recreational possibilities. It has excellent facilities for boating, yachting, and other water sports and for fresh water and deep-sea fishing. It is also famous for its horse racing and fox hunting. The western end of the State, with its rugged contours and State parks and forests protecting special areas, affords a diversity of outdoor activities appropriate to such a region.

From the earliest days of the colony, Marylanders found sport in tilting tournaments, cockfights, fox hunts, and horse races. Cockfights, though illegal, are frequently held in the counties, largely for private parties of gentlemen-farmers or the hunting set.

Inherited from an era when jousting was a gaudier and deadlier form of diversion, tilting, once common in the southern colonies, survives spontaneously only in Maryland. Although the knight of today need only transfix with his lance a small metal ring, rather than an opponent's head, the sport requires a firm seat in the saddle. In the early part of the twentieth century, baseball and automobiles diverted rural sportsmen from this traditional riding sport, but in recent years the tournament has again come to the fore among county folk and is held in connection with horse shows and county fairs and also as an annual event of many parishes. Formerly Christmas and New Year events, the tournaments are now called for July 4th, for some time in August, or for Labor Day.

A local politician or a member of a prominent family usually serves as Master of Ceremonies, or Lord of the Tourney. Most of the competing knights dress in jockey or riding outfits, sometimes topped with a fancy plumed hat, though at the less spectacular tournaments contestants may merely wear knickers, white duck trousers, or similar comfortable attire. The horses' saddles and bridles are often decorated with gay rosettes or ribbons of varied colors.

Assembled in a semicircle before the platform or dais upon which the Lord of the Tourney is seated, the knights hear their 'charge,' which in all likelihood is a combination harangue on chivalry and current political themes; it usually reminds the knights that they 'ride for womanhood and

Christianity.' Before the tournament begins each knight is allowed a practice ride through the arches from which the metal rings are suspended. The first rings are about an inch and a quarter in diameter; smaller and smaller rings are provided as the contest continues.

Each knight must gallop the course three times, with a possible nine rings of a size on his lance as the objective. Prizes for the winner and his closest rivals, and a crown for the winner's Queen of Love and Beauty are received on the point of the spear. The Queen may be crowned immediately, but the ceremony is often postponed until the party or dance in the evening.

One of the outstanding tournaments in Maryland is held at Bradshaw, northeast of Baltimore. Here riders from every section of the State compete. Probably the most unusual tournament is the one on My Lady's Manor, where women riders compete; the winner is given the privilege of choosing the King of Love and Beauty.

The first organized effort in the State to promote scheduled yacht racing came with the formation of the Chesapeake Bay Yacht Club of Easton on June 10, 1885. The club sponsors an annual race for the Lipton Trophy for Star Boats, presented to the club by Sir Thomas Lipton. Further interest is lent to the competition by the award of the Johnson Cup to the high point winner of the first and third races in the Lipton Series. This trophy honors J.Graham Johnson; he and his brother were the pioneer Star boat racers on Chesapeake Bay. The Star is a one-design class of mainsail and jib racing boat with a waterline length of 15 feet, 6 inches, an extreme beam of 5 feet, $8\frac{1}{4}$ inches, and a sail area of $281\frac{1}{2}$ square feet. The Marconi rig is used.

Another interesting class of racing, begun in 1922 and since held annually by the same club, is the Championship Workboat Race. Schooners, skipjacks, bugeyes, and other types of work boats under sail compete for trophies in this event.

The skipjack is a small vessel with a single mast, which has a pronounced rake. The craft is also identified by a large jib, a triangular mainsail and a low freeboard. The bugeye is a two-masted, narrow-hulled vessel with a sharp stern, a large jib, large triangular foresail, and smaller triangular mainsail. The masts have considerable rake. The narrow stern has a grating platform extension.

One of the most popular of the Chesapeake Bay regattas is held by the Miles River Yacht Club annually at St.Michaels. Races are staged for sailboats, powerboats, and outboards, in addition to the famous Chesapeake Bay Log Canoe event. The canoes are modeled after those used by the Indians in Maryland waters; the original craft were cut from single huge trees, but the modern canoe may be built of several great logs. As early as 1840 there were organized log canoe races at St.Michaels, inspiring such rivalry that boat builders began to design special canoes for racing purposes.

The Gibson Island Yacht Club has the largest fleet of single design boats —Stars—in the country. The outstanding event for the Gibson Island Squadron is the New London to Gibson Island Race, held every four years under agreement with the Corinthian Yacht Club of Philadelphia. The course, a distance of approximately 475 miles, gives a fair taste of blue water sailing and has been covered in forty-eight hours.

The Maryland Yacht Club regattas feature a large fleet of Snipes, competing for the G.Porter Huston Trophy. Resembling the Stars, this class of small centerboard knockabout sloops is in competition throughout the world.

Although there are numerous devotees to boating among Marylanders and visitors to the State, they are far outnumbered by the thousands who cast their lines into the numerous rivers and small streams. Still other thousands fish from power and sail craft in Chesapeake Bay or off the seashore of the State.

The Chesapeake, essentially a submerged meadow, is one of the most productive fishing areas in the country; its waters fairly teem with the minute organic matter essential to fish life. The long and much-indented shoreline of the bay, the large areas of shallow water, and many tributary rivers and small streams provide a natural spawning and feeding ground. The production limit of the Chesapeake fishing grounds has not nearly been reached and it abounds with more than 200 different species of fish. The principal game fish are channel bass, black drum, bluefish, rock or striped bass, trout, hardhead, spot, and perch. Others caught are the oyster toad, bonito, skate, black sea bass, cod, mackerel, sheepshead, herring, gudgeon, flounder, sea robin, and in the upper reaches of the bay, the shad.

The Chesapeake Bay Fishing Fair Association, a nonprofit corporation, was organized in 1936 to acquaint the people of the eastern part of the United States with the sport opportunities of the Chesapeake Bay fishing grounds. The 'fair,' an annual fishing contest, is held each year at a different fishing center. In 1938 more than 4,000 people participated at Rock Hall. One of the most sought-after trophies is the bronze plaque awarded by the Sportsmen's Luncheon Club of Maryland to the Captain of the boat bringing in the largest fish.

No definite bay sport fishing area can be defined as the center. Different species of fish run at varying periods to the confluent waters, and leave when their spawning time is over. For that reason uninitiated sportsmen usually depend on guides and powerboats to reach the banks or areas frequented by particular species. Powerboats, guides, accommodations, and bait are available at Crisfield, Cambridge, Oxford, Tilghman's, Solomons, Annapolis, Love Point, Rock Hall, Chestertown, and Betterton. Generally speaking, the eastern shore of the bay provides the most satisfactory fishing spots; there the angler may be reasonably certain of good catches of rock or striped bass, gray sea trout, spots, hardheads, bluefish, croakers, and white perch. The top weight of many of these is approximately twenty pounds, and red drum weighing up to seventy pounds have also been caught.

Big game fish of kinds associated with the waters off the coast of Florida and other areas far removed from Maryland shores can now be caught off Ocean City. A storm in 1933 cut an inlet through the narrow strip of land that parallels the coast, thereby linking Sinepuxent Bay and the Atlantic. This section then became an important center for amateur and commercial deep-sea fishing. The white marlin (swordfish) caught there average about 100 pounds in weight, while the blue variety may be more than twice as heavy. Large tuna weighing from 500 to 1,000 pounds are also taken.

The big game fish are sought between fifteen and thirty miles out, as they follow the warm waters of the Gulf Stream, making sallies shoreward to feed on smaller fish. The great fishing banks, a natural feeding ground for trout, flounders, croakers, sea bass, bluefish, porgies, blackfish, and butterfish, are only a few miles beyond the inlet from Ocean City, and are but a short run by motor boat from the resort. Boats for swordfishing are available for those seeking this exciting sport.

The unusual topography of Maryland limits the grounds of fresh water fish, since there are but few lakes or ponds. One of these is Deep Creek Lake in Garrett County. It is an artificial lake twelve miles long, and is well stocked with large- and small-mouthed bass, rainbow and brown trout, and pike. Roads give access to nearly every part of Deep Creek Lake and to the headwaters of the tributaries, which are often preferred as fishing grounds by those who are fond of fly casting. Fishermen seeking bigger quarry troll the lake from rowboats or outboard motorboats. Another favorite fresh water fishing spot is the Conowingo Pool and the section below the dam, where bass, eel, catfish, carp, sunfish, crappie, shad, and pike are caught.

Bass are found in every county of the State; especially noteworthy for size and number of the bass are the small rivers in Dorchester County.

Horse racing, the sport for which Maryland is most widely known, had an early origin in the State, though the exact date of its introduction is not definitely known. A deed filed in 1695 says that a tract of land in Talbot County 'starts at the race course,' indicating that the colonial gentry followed the sport even before that date.

The colonial track at Annapolis was under the auspices of the Maryland Jockey Club. Although this organization dates from 1745, Francis Barnum Culver, in his *Blooded Horses of Colonial Days*, expressed the opinion that an organized racing association existed in Annapolis as early as 1740 or '43. The widespread interest in racing created an early demand for swifter strains of horses and the more common stock was soon replaced by pedigreed animals.

Among the history-making blooded stock were Spark, imported by Governor Ogle; Governor Horatio Sharpe's Othello; the brood Queen Mab (out of the royal stud at Hampton Court); Colonel Tasker's importation, Selima, and Samuel Galloways's famous Selim, son of Othello and Selima. Arriving from England in 1780, Selima was destined to be one of the most important sources of thoroughbred blood in the country. To Selima many great horses, such as Man of War, Seabiscuit, and War Admiral trace their pedigrees.

The Revolution brought horsebreeding and racing to a standstill in Maryland. Fully half a century later, when Baltimore had superseded Annapolis as the metropolis of Maryland, a new track, the Baltimore Central Course, was established on a plateau near the Old Frederick Road, not far from the present Franklintown. About sixty horses took part in the opening meet which was held late in October 1831.

Today there are four one-mile tracks in Maryland. Pimlico, the oldest (1870) and the most famous of the four, is one of the country's major tracks. 'Old Hilltop,' as it is known to the racing fraternity, is a semiannual rendezvous for famous horses and distinguished guests. The outstanding racing classic at Pimlico is the Preakness, second only to the Kentucky Derby in popularity and first in traditional background. The winner of the event is awarded the Woodlawn Vase in addition to a substantial purse. The trophy was created by Tiffany in 1860 on the order of Colonel R.A.Alexander of Woodlawn, Kentucky.

The other Maryland mile tracks are Havre de Grace, Bowie, and Laurel. In addition there are five half-mile courses—Marlboro, Timonium, Belair, Cumberland, and Hagerstown.

Most popular with Maryland's ardent steeplechase followers are the three spring classics: the Maryland Hunt Cup, run over the J.W.Y.Martin estate in beautiful Worthington Valley; the Grand National, raced over the Hereford estate of the Whittingham family, and the My Lady's Manor Point-to-Point races in Baltimore County. Only gentlemen riders may participate in these events. There are also junior cross-country races each April for youthful riders. Although all of Maryland's amateur racing events attract national attention, the Maryland Hunt Cup is the most widely known.

The Foxcatcher National Cup Steeplechase was founded by a group of American sportsmen who hoped it would duplicate the fame of the English Grand National. The race is run annually over a three-mile course at Fair Hill, Cecil County, the only course in America with jumps higher than those of the English course at Aintree. The steeplechase is the feature event of a four-race card arranged by the Foxcatcher Hounds Club.

Fox hunting has been a gentleman's popular sport since Maryland's earliest days. The first recorded fox hunt in America was held about 1650 in Queen Annes County. The gray fox was hunted prior to 1730, in which year eight pairs of imported English red foxes were liberated along the eastern shore of Chesapeake Bay. This marked the beginning in America of fox hunting in its present form.

Eleven years after the introduction of golf in America (1888), the United States Men's Open was held in Maryland on the Baltimore Country Club's greens. This club and its adjunct, Five Farms, have been the scenes of the National Professional (1928) and the National Amateur (1932) tournaments, respectively. There are numerous other courses, public and private, in all sections of Maryland.

The best small-game hunting is found in Allegany and Garrett counties. Here, in addition to squirrels, rabbits, 'coons, 'possums, groundhogs, foxes, skunks, pheasant, grouse, and partridges, are found turkeys and deer in sufficient numbers to provide good sport. Partridges are numerous in nearly all the counties of Maryland.

The name of Susquehanna Flats is synonymous with good duck hunting. To old-timers it brings to mind sink boats, sneakboxes, swivel guns, 'long tom' and pump guns. Among the fowl frequenting the flats are mallard, canvasbacks, red heads, swans, black brant, pin tails, black ducks, coots, teal, and several species of geese.

Other areas where ducks are successfully hunted in the Chesapeake Bay country are Tilghman's Island, Kent Island, St.Michaels, Chestertown, Oxford, Crisfield, Cambridge, Solomons Island, Annapolis, Point Lookout, and Sandy Point.

A special breed of retriever, widely used by duck hunters and considered a pure Maryland strain, is the Chesapeake Bay dog. The species is distinguished by good form, reliability, and undaunted courage in retrieving, even under bad ice conditions.

The United States Government has purchased 10,000 acres in Dorchester County and Hooper's and other islands to create a refuge for ducks and geese. The twelve-acre duck port and one hundred-acre bird sanctuary along Herring Run and on Bowley's Lane are valuable in conserving Maryland's resources. A sufficient number of ducks with clipped wings are kept at the lake and a feeding place has been established to attract migrating ducks to the hatcheries of the preserve.

The Maryland Outdoor Life Federation, composed of more than forty groups interested in conservation, sponsors in February an annual North American Sports, Garden, and Outdoor Life Show.

Maryland has five State parks, five forest reserves, and nine State forests, which during 1937 attracted nearly 300,000 visitors. The State forests are more extensive in area, but not so well known as the parks; tent sites, fireplaces, shelters, and tables have been provided.

The Chesapeake & Ohio Canal is being restored and converted into a recreation area between Georgetown and Seneca. Plans include restoration of the old inn at Great Falls, stocking of the canal with bass, provision of canoes, and improvement of the towpath for the benefit of hikers and cyclists.

Ocean City is the State's only seaside resort; it has facilities for surf bathing, sport fishing (both deep-sea and surf casting) and many other activities. Maryland also has hundreds of public and private bathing beaches and small summer resorts along the shores of the Chesapeake and the many rivers. A number of these resorts are for Negroes.

Pen Mar Park is a popular mountain resort. Its chief attraction is an unusually beautiful view over far reaches of Maryland and Pennsylvania.

Architecture

IN architecture as in the other arts Maryland for the past hundred years has been conservative. The waves of taste and style that have swept other sections of the country have been met here with a lack of interest and a corresponding lack of understanding. As a result the Marylander of today, unless he travels outside his State, is relatively unfamiliar with the excesses of Victorianism of the mid-nineteenth century, the Romantic Revival, and the confusion of styles that followed. But at the same time he can find at home none of the good work of these periods, nothing to compare with the public buildings of New England erected by H.H.Richardson, nothing that equals the imperial and grandiloquent neoclassicism of the great Northern and Middle Western cities.

Maryland always glanced over its shoulder at the past but it could adapt designs and also create them to meet local needs. Not only did the traditional Georgian Colonial style reach a high development here but the province and early State also produced new designs of importance. Within the limited area of Maryland there is an astonishing variety, from the spreading houses built by an almost feudal aristocracy in the mild climate of the Tidewater to stone cottages erected by mountain pioneers for shelter against winds and snows rivaling those of Vermont. The influences that created these buildings are as varied as the terrain and the climate.

The first colonists' immediate problem was shelter, not pleasing design, and they moved into the long wigwams of the departing Yaocomico Indians. The earliest account of the colony records that until a better chapel could be built mass was said in one of the Indian dwellings. But the construction of houses of the English type was at once begun and, soon after the settlers had landed, the friendly Piscataway Indian chief was asking the governor for a 'man that could build him a house like the English.'

Of these earliest houses none remains. St.Marys City was abandoned and its buildings quickly vanished. Two existing houses, Cross Manor in St.Marys County and Preston-on-Patuxent in Calvert, are said to have been built between 1640 and 1650, but proof of these dates is lacking. All the other buildings of the first decades of the colony have disappeared, probably because many of them must have been of frame construction.

The colonists, having left a country where all but the most elaborate and aristocratic dwellings were of frame, continued to build in the medieval tradition by constructing their houses of split logs and half-timber. The clearing of the forest provided a glut of this building material. Though Father Andrew White in his narrative, *Relation of Maryland*, published in London in 1635, relates that excellent bricks were made in the colony, masonry construction was greatly hampered by the lack of lime for mortar.

Before the founding of the Maryland colony, architecture in England had been passing through a transitional phase from the medieval style to that of the early English Renaissance during the reign of James I. Although a few buildings had been designed in the classic manner, this style was considered both extreme and radical, and it was yet another generation before it passed from the stage of fashionable fad to general acceptance.

Thus the settlers of the frontier with their immediate demand for four walls and a roof merely adapted the familiar Tudor and Jacobean styles to local needs and conditions; the structures they erected along the shores of the Chesapeake and its tributaries are of a design now called Tidewater Colonial, that has a sharpness of line suggesting the medieval. They show many slight variations and can be divided and subdivided into a confusing classification.

The general characteristics of the seventeenth-century Maryland house are its low walls and steep roofs. The plan, one room deep and two rooms wide, or two rooms and a passage in width, is arranged with casual symmetry, and is made still more informal by the introduction of large end chimneys. The addition of entrance bays in the medieval tradition, with vestibule on the first floor and hall-chamber above, and a stairway enclosed in a separate tower at the rear, produced a cruciform plan. Troth's Fortune in Talbot County, with its stair tower, and Cedar Hill near Prince Frederick, with its front and rear bays, admirably exemplify this type of plan. Further characteristics of the seventeenth-century house are its one-and-a-half or two-and-a-half story height, and its sweeping gable or gambrel roofs unbroken by dormers. Many structures, such as Cedar Park in Anne Arundel County and Melwood Park near Upper Marlboro, have gable roofs as steep as their European prototypes.

The gambrel roof of two slopes, popularly but falsely called 'Dutch Colonial,' was perhaps more widely used in Maryland than in any other colony. Though it is seen in all the Tidewater sections of the State, it is most frequently found on the Eastern Shore. The lines of the Maryland gambrel are distinctive in that the first slope above the eaves is only slightly out of the perpendicular, covering the house like a hood or saddle. This type of Tidewater Colonial house is one of the most distinctive forms of building in Maryland.

Massive outside end chimneys are a local characteristic of the Tidewater Colonial house. These dwellings have great variations of design and many look almost medieval. Only a lofty chimney with clustered stacks is needed to make one of the houses resemble a Tudor country place. Chimneys of more traditional form are often seen in the Tidewater counties of Virginia but without the elaborate development and in less numbers than in southern Maryland. Here the chimney is broad at the base, to receive the wide fireplace of the first floor. As it rises it is narrowed, like a Gothic buttress, by successive sloping hips or pents until at the roof line it is just large enough to accommodate the flues.

In houses two rooms deep are usually twin end chimneys, joined as a rule by a brick pent with a sloping roof. This space may be used for a closet and is often lighted by a small window, as at St. Peters Key (1650) near St. Marys City. There are even places where doors have been cut through the chimney, as at Society Hill. Yet elsewhere the masonry is extended over the entire gable end of a house with frame front and back walls, as Rose Hill near Port Tobacco and at Deep Falls near Chaptico, or the pent is carried up two floors, as at Spout Farm (1660) near Prince Frederick. The typical southern Maryland chimneys have persisted through changes in style and also reconstruction.

Another seventeenth-century characteristic of Maryland was in the use of decorative brickwork patterns by bonding. The Flemish bond, so universally used in the colonial period, was often laid with alternate stretchers of ordinary red brick and headers of dark glazed brick. Centuries of weathering have had but little effect on the checkerboard pattern of many old walls, and at certain angles the sunshine is reflected from the headers in thousands of points of light. In some houses glazed brick was set in diamond or chevron patterns as at Hampton Court, Compton Winyates, and elsewhere in England. Though work of this type is found all over the Tidewater, it was particularly popular on the lower Eastern Shore. The Fassitt House in Worcester County, with its pattern of interlocking diamonds, has the most elaborate brickwork in the State. Elsewhere the initials of the builder and the date of construction were set in glazed headers in the gable end.

Unmistakably decorative elements of the contemporary Jacobean style are evident in many of these early buildings. Brick pilasters ornament the chimneys of Cloverfields, Queen Annes County; the Captain's House at

Wye House, Talbot County; and Comegys Bight House in Kent County. But of all the examples of nostalgia for the England of the colonists' grandsires, Bachelor's Hope near Chaptico in St.Marys County is outstanding. The steep roofs are not unusual, but the porch, with its naïve use of decorative forms borrowed without academic understanding from the classic, might have been lifted from an English building of the days of James I. In the frieze, above columns that lack both capitals and bases, rude triglyphs alternate with simplified Tudor roses. Still more unusual is the full Tudor rose set in plaster in the ceiling of Wye almost a century and a half after the death of Queen Elizabeth.

At the beginning of the eighteenth century, when some measure of prosperity and stability had been established and men could think again of building as an art rather than a necessity, the colonists turned to England for the latest fashions. The Georgian style was flourishing in the mother country and soon examples of Georgian design began to appear in the province. The old Tidewater Colonial persisted, however, since the less affluent were slow in adopting the new styles and until about the time of the Revolution the exterior design of some of the smaller farmhouses showed little change.

Prosperity came early to Lord Baltimore's colony; the soil was fertile, the climate mild, the bay and its tributaries provided highways to market, and even the Indians were not troublesome. As wealth increased the change was reflected in the dwellings. The simplest early houses contained two rooms on the main floor, the 'greate room' and a kitchen. When there was a small attic the stairway in many cases went up beside the chimney, as in the Eltonhead Manor room now in the Baltimore Museum. The stairhall was soon developed and additions were made; few old houses in the State did not undergo some alteration or have some additions before the end of the colonial period. Old houses were incorporated in new ones and larger houses were built. Since the character of the early style was preserved, the additions of succeeding generations frequently blended into a homogeneous composition, as at Otwell in Talbot County. The need for space to house an increasing family, or a growing prosperity, also resulted in a type of building Marylanders call a 'telescope house.' These dwellings were extended at one end by an addition slightly higher and wider than its predecessor; third and sometimes fourth units were added, each one a little higher than the one before it. This custom, which has persisted to the present, was common at all levels of society; examples range from the simple cabin to the imposing brick plantation house, such as Hard Bargain near La Plata.

Of all the local influences that have affected architecture in Maryland, the first and most powerful was climate. The colonists, as their records show, were impressed by the change from the intensely hot summer to the short but frequently severe period in winter. It was the heat, not the cold, that immediately affected design. Even the earliest houses have high ceilings. The inside chimney of New England is almost unknown in early Maryland; chimneys were built outside the walls of the houses and were frequently free standing above the first floor. Wherever possible houses were faced towards the south to catch the prevailing summer winds. The buildings were shallow to permit cross ventilation—in the majority of cases only one room deep. Whitehall (1766) near Millersville, one of the most notable Georgian Colonial houses in the State, is an excellent example of this type. It is 200 feet long and for the most part only one room deep. During a few months these buildings were, of course, unpleasantly cold and draughty. Some present problems even with modern heating systems.

The earliest effects of the English Georgian mode are noted in the treatment of interior woodwork. Paneling, classic moldings, cornices, and simple pilasters replaced the bare walls, simple wainscoting, or vertical feather-edged boarding of the first period. So many interiors were renovated that examples of seventeenth-century interior finish are extremely rare. At first the paneling was simple almost to the point of crudeness. The moldings were vigorous and bold. Classic motives were executed by amateur craftsmen who handled them with pleasant disregard for academic rules of proportion. Though the interiors of this period lack the sophistication of mid-eighteenth-century ones, they have a freshness that evidences the character of the growing colony.

The Tidewater Georgian Colonial style continued to flourish during the eighteenth century. In a broad sense the houses exhibit but slight variations from the contemporary types found from North Carolina to New York. The differences are largely the result of climatic and social conditions.

When the fedual and aristocratic system Lord Baltimore had cherished for his colony at last came to life, it depended on slavery and tobacco. Self-sufficient and widely separated plantations dotted the Tidewater and the Piedmont. The families that lived on them, in contrast with their busy pioneer ancestors, had leisure for culture. Their sons were sent to school in England, their daughters were trained in the domestic graces, and their houses were ornamented with the newest thing in furniture and silver from England. The design of their houses displayed luxury and sophistication. The richly paneled interiors were further decorated with elaborately carved mantels of wood, marbles, wall niches, and spindled stair balustrades. The walls were often painted or papered; plaster or stucco ornament enriched the cornices and ceilings.

To this period belong many of the best known houses of Maryland: Rose Hill (*c.*1730) near Port Tobacco; Mulberry Fields (*c.*1760) near Leonardtown; Tulip Hill (1743) near Owensville; Poplar Hill (1735) not far from Upper Marboro; Montpelier (1760) near Laurel; the Brice, Chase, and Hammond-Harwood houses, all in Annapolis; Hampton (1783–90) on the outskirts of Towson; Doughoregan Manor (1727) near Ellicott City; Bohemia Manor in the vicinity of Elkton; Ratcliffe Manor near Easton; Wye House; Beverly near Princess Anne. Throughout the settled sections of the State lesser houses followed the same architectural trend.

As elsewhere in America, the professional architect was practically non-existent, but a knowledge of design was part of the cultural equipment of the wealthy, and libraries contained the books on architecture popular in England at the time. Although the Hammond-Harwood, Chase, and some other Annapolis houses were designed by the English architect, William Buckland, most of the other great Georgian houses of the State were designed by amateurs—itinerant carpenters, builders, and occasionally their owners.

At this time there developed the house with two balanced wings, locally called the 'five-part house.' The main or central unit of two or two-and-a-half stories contained the drawing room, dining room, and the main bedrooms. At each end this had low one-story passages or 'curtains' to connect it with balancing end pavilions. One of these pavilions generally contained the kitchen and service quarters, the other the library, bedrooms, a ballroom, or the plantation offices.

The plan for the five-part house was found in the English books and was used in other colonies. Whereas in Virginia and South Carolina the wings were usually free standing, in Maryland they were closely connected with the main building and became integral parts of the design.

The type, popular for many years, had many variations, from the vigorous bold masses of the Brice House (1740) in Annapolis to the delicacy of detail and studied balance of Homewood (1798–1800) in Baltimore. The type, fundamentally a country or plantation house, had such popularity that it was built in the city. The Hammond-Harwood House of Annapolis, both by virtue of exterior design and interior decoration, is generally considered not only one of the finest five-part Maryland houses but also an outstanding example of Georgian Colonial architecture.

The formal Georgian mode was likewise adapted for the important public and semipublic buildings of the colonies. Construction of the third statehouse in Annapolis was begun in 1772; the oldest section, with small east portico, spacious arcaded central hall, and white-painted octagonal dome and cupola, was designed by Joseph Clark. The interior of the dome is decorated with delicate plaster ornament in the Adam style; and the stately old senate chamber, with its fine woodwork and green plaster walls, is typical of late Georgian Colonial design.

The changes that took place in architecture throughout the country after the Revolution had their counterpart in Maryland. Houses of the early Federal period in the State show but slight differences from those of the Middle Atlantic seaboard. The forms developed in late colonial days were given greater delicacy of detail and attenuated proportions, following the contemporary Adam style in England and the late eighteenth-century Renaissance mode of France. A few local mannerisms developed. From the growing city of Baltimore spread the use of reeded elliptical pilasters and colonettes in the interiors.

As the western part of the State was settled, its earliest dwellings showed the influence of the older Tidewater structures, but later designs had adaptations to the cooler climate of higher elevations, being smaller and more compact. Everywhere west of Baltimore there was an abundance of good building stone, and gray masonry replaced the red brick of the Coastal Plain. But settlers from other colonies and the mainland of Europe were responsible for the radically different types of houses in the Piedmont. Many were Germans from Pennsylvania, largely peasants with traditions of large barns and small houses. Thus many of the old dwellings of the western counties resemble those of southeastern Pennsylvania, rather than those of Lord Baltimore's manors.

Maryland played a unique part during the Classical and Greek Revivals. Though the State led in the movement, the forms associated with other sections of the country are practically unknown here. The monumental two-story Jeffersonian porticoes, so familiar in Virginia and the far South, are seldom found in Maryland domestic architecture. One or two churches and public buildings followed designs of Grecian temples, but not one family attempted to model its dwelling on that difficult form. On the other hand, the Washington Monument designed by Robert Mills for Baltimore in 1809, with simple Doric shaft, set a style for similar monuments, not only in America but also in Europe.

Benjamin H. Latrobe, a leader of the Greek Revival, lived for many years in Baltimore and left on that city an influence that still persists. His domed Roman Catholic cathedral, whose construction started in 1806, was the first of the Classical Revival churches and remains one of the outstanding examples of the style in America.

Many Greek Revival houses were built in Baltimore in the 1830's and 1840's. Some of these were designed by Latrobe, others by his pupil Mills, and still more by their imitators. Though commercial advance has destroyed most of them, a few remain. Their striking classic features include an entrance vestibule sheltered by a shallow portico, usually of gleaming white marble with two Ionic or Doric columns, large floor-length windows with Hellenic trim, iron-grilled balconies, and tiny attic windows that usually pierce the frieze under the main cornice. The style eventually gave way to romantic Victorianism and brownstone, but the row house of Baltimore's upper classes long utilized this characteristic fenestration.

The history of Baltimore's domestic architecture is the history of the row house. Because the city's growth did not begin until after 1800 and because the fire destroyed so much of the old section, buildings of the colonial and early Federal periods are extremely rare. About 1850 Waterloo Row was built from designs by Robert Mills. Landlordism, bent on utilizing every inch of space, swept Baltimore along with other cities, cutting it into narrow deep lots. Block after block of row houses spread into the countryside. This process has continued, with the result that the first impression every visitor has of the city is of monotonous vistas of identical houses with white steps.

Baltimore's ground rent system was a contributing factor in the intensive development of this type of dwelling. The system, though evil, had one point in its favor; it has saved the city from the congested slum tenements of other large cities.

The row house tradition was not broken to any marked degree until the Federal Housing Administration set aside funds for a low-cost housing construction program on seven tracts in widely separated sections of the city selected by the Baltimore Housing Authority; four of the tracts were for Negro housing and in all cases save one were occupied by deteriorated structures that had to be removed before construction could be started.

The architectural movements that followed the Classical Revival were regarded with characteristic apathy by the Marylander, who does not adopt new ideas until he is thoroughly convinced of their value. The Gothic Revival of the 1830's and 40's never flourished here in spite of the fact that Maximillian Godefroy's chapel of St. Mary's Seminary in Baltimore was one of the country's first Gothic Revival buildings, and Glen Ellen, near Towson, designed by Alexander Jackson Davis, was the first dwelling designed in the English Perpendicular Gothic.

Architecture

incoln Highton

HAMMOND-HARWOOD HOUSE (1770) FROM CHASE HOUSE, ANNAPO

ROSE HILL (1730), PORT TOBACCO

HOMEWOOD (1809), JOHNS HOPKINS CAMPUS, BALTIMORE

MONTPELIER (c.1770), LAUREL

DOUGHOREGAN MANOR (1727), NEAR ELLICOTT CITY

CHASE HOUSE (1769), ANNAPOLIS

Pickering S

INTERIOR, HOMEWOOD (1809), BALTIMORE

TULIP HILL (c.1756), SOUTH OF ANNAPOLIS

TEACKLE MANSION (1801), PRINCESS ANNE

BEVERLY (1774), NEAR POCOMOKE

CEDAR PARK (c.1700), ON WEST RIVER, ANNE ARUNDEL COUNTY

HARD BARGAIN (1768), CHARLES COUNTY

The exuberant prosperity of the clipper ship days gave way to the more meager conditions of the post-Civil War period. The full splendor of the turreted and bracketed Victorian house of that era is unknown except in the vicinity of Baltimore. Later in the century, H.H.Richardson's Romanesque Revival left only a superficial imprint on a few buildings; the deep feeling for masonry construction and the love of craftsmanship that made the work of Richardson and his followers notable failed to stir the Maryland designers. The outstanding example of this style in the State, the First Methodist Church in Baltimore, was the work of a Pennsylvanian, Charles F. McKim, of the New York firm, McKim, Mead and White.

After the great fire of 1904 Baltimore was faced with the problem of rebuilding more than seventy city blocks. This it did in the confusion of styles that existed elsewhere in the country. Like New York, which erected Venice's St.Mark's campanile on Madison Square, Baltimore set up the tower of Florence's Palazzo Vecchio, but outdid New York by putting a medicine bottle on top of it. During the 1920's a more restrained eclecticism and a better knowledge of traditional forms resulted in many excellent buildings—Gothic churches, suburban houses ranging from Norman French to Spanish, public buildings in the neoclassic style. The Gothic lines of the Baltimore Trust Building tower above everything in the city as a monument to the short flurry of building that expired in 1929.

Meanwhile, the revival of the Georgian Colonial had been going on, as part of the trend to the traditional, and this style ended by sweeping all others aside in local affection. Once again the community had an architecture that was truly congenial. Jerry-built houses, hot-dog stands, filling stations, and characterless commercial buildings with motifs of this style exist here, as elsewhere, in country, village, and city. But designs that take architecture seriously into consideration are almost universally called 'Colonial.' Probably the best local examples of this type of present-day design are in Baltimore's suburban developments, Guilford and Homeland, where houses with the Georgian Colonial imprint are varied only occasionally with residences exhibiting the Tudor, Regency, or French Provincial motifs.

Greenbelt, completed in 1937, is a model suburban community in Prince Georges County constructed with Resettlement Administration funds. Here several thousand persons of the low-income group occupy modern apartments and cottages. The settlement has a school and community center, a theater, stores, and garages and on its outskirts are tracts that may be used by the residents as gardens (*see Tour 1b*).

Modern trends in design have scarcely been felt at all in Maryland. Only an occasional store or restaurant building shows a break with historical precedent. In the field of domestic architecture the feeble stirrings of the movement make small progress against a wave of Early Americanism given new impetus by the restoration of Williamsburg in Virginia. Functionalism shows up, perforce, in industrial plants and warehouses, but though it is appearing elsewhere in domestic design with use of steel construction and reinforced concrete, the Marylander still looks on it with distaste, unconvinced that it offers him any additional comfort or esthetic pleasure.

Literature

DURING the seventeenth and the early eighteenth centuries, life in pioneer Maryland was too busy for much literary activity. For many years, moreover, there was neither a sufficiently active town life nor a sufficiently high level of general literacy to stimulate local writing. Yet even among the first settlers were individuals of considerable culture; from the beginning the provincial governors, their administrative assistants, and some of the large landholders were men educated according to standards of seventeenth-century British classicism. Their reading matter, like their luxuries, was imported from Europe.

The westward passage of the first colonists and the happenings surrounding the settlement of the territory were eloquently recorded in the *Relatio Itineris in Marylandium* (1635) of Father Andrew White (1579–1656), a Jesuit who came to the New World with Leonard Calvert. Father White had been the author of a sort of advertising prospectus, published in London in 1633, before the sailing of the expedition; its title is suggestive of the variety of motives that led people to embark for the New World: *A Declaration of the Lord Baltimore's Plantation in Mary-land; Wherein is set forth how Englishmen may become Angels, the King's Dominions be extended and the adventurers attain Land and Gear; together with other advantages of that Sweet Land*. Later developments in the colony were also described by Father White in several manuscripts written in Latin or English.

Apparently the new country soon found itself in need of defenders. Maryland and Virginia were reported to be a 'nest of Rogues, whores, desolate and rooking persons: a place of intolerable labour, bad usage and hard Diet.' In 1656 John Hammond, in a tract bearing the allegorical title, *Leah and Rachel*, undertook to refute these charges 'Whereby many deceived souls chose rather to Beg, Steal, rot in Prison, and come to shameful deaths, than to better their being by going thither.' Hammond had lived in Maryland 21 years when his book describing the benefits of living in the province was issued, and his work remains a valuable source of seventeenth-century Maryland history.

A decade later George Alsop, who is believed to have come to the colony as an indentured servant, published *A Character of the Province of Maryland*, a vigorous and amusing series of sketches in verse and prose describing both whites and Indians. Probably the most entertaining literary item of the period, however, was Ebenezer Cooke's *The Sot-Weed Factor; or a Voyage to Maryland. A Satyr . . . in Burlesque Verse*. Published in London in 1708, this long poetic extravaganza, dealing with the adventures of an unlucky English merchant in Maryland, offered a shrewd, if somewhat fantastic, picture of life in the colony at the turn of the eighteenth century. Its title was based on the slang of the day, in which tobacco was referred to as an inebriating or 'sot-making' weed; a 'sot-weed factor' was a tobacco agent or supercargo. In 1730 *Sot-Weed Redivivus: or the Planters' Looking-Glass*, by 'E.C.Gent.,' appeared in Annapolis, and is thought to have been the work of the original Ebenezer Cooke. One of the characters in this poem is a Maryland squire who opposes the introduction of paper money into the colony,

> Alledging, *Planters*, when in drink,
> Wou'd light their Pipes with Paper Chink (money);
> And knowing not to read, might be
> Impos'd on, by such Currency.

In 1728 from a Maryland press came what was probably the colony's first purely literary production, a translation by Richard Lewis of a satiric poem in Latin by Edward Holdsworth (1684–1746). Entitled *Muscipula: the Mouse Trap, or the Battle of the Cambrians & the Mice*, the translation was published by William Parks at Annapolis. In 1756 the Reverend Thomas Cradock (1718–70), rector of St.Thomas', Baltimore, published at Annapolis *A New Version of the Psalms of David*, a translation of the psalms into heroic couplets.

During the late colonial period, Annapolis developed a notable social life, and from 1745 to 1755 its Tuesday Club was a center of literary conversation, criticism, and poetry. The Tuesday Club lawyers, physicians, and clergymen wrote satirical verses, anniversary odes, and essays; and recited their works or published them anonymously in the local journals. Charles Carroll and Benjamin Franklin were among the many distinguished guests of the club.

Much of the gay life of Annapolis prior to the Revolution is mirrored in the letters of William Eddis, Governor Robert Eden's secretary. Eddis' informative correspondence with friends in England was published in London in 1792 as *Letters from America*.

The literary and cultural awakening of Maryland came with political independence. In the decade following the Revolution printing presses were set up in many sections of the State and newspapers and magazines came into circulation. Parson Mason Locke Weems (1759–1825), native of Maryland, was one of the State's first book agents and became the first nationally popular author. Weems' *The Life and Memorable Activities of George Washington* swept the country and contributed many legends, including the cherry tree episode, to the tradition of Washington.

In this period the center of culture shifted from the stagnating capital of Annapolis to the bustling commercial town of Baltimore. Here in 1793 was published the first periodical south of Philadelphia, the *Free Universal Magazine*. In 1791 the town had a daily newspaper and in 1796 a semipublic library.

In 1792 Benjamin Banneker (1736–1806), Negro mathematician and native Marylander, published his first almanac. Banneker became known in Europe as the 'African Astronomer.'

William Wirt (1772–1834), one of the most prominent literary figures of early nineteenth-century America, was born in Bladensburg but had most of his career in Virginia. He won fame as a lawyer and orator, became Attorney-General of the United States, and was a candidate for the presidency in 1832 on the Anti-Masonic ticket. His first book, *The British Spy*, published in installments in 1803 in the *Virginia Argus*, a Richmond newspaper, attracted great attention and became a best seller. Wirt was also author of a biography of Patrick Henry in whose mouth he placed the phrase, 'Give me liberty, or give me death.'

The contributions of the numerous poets of the early decades of the nineteenth century were as ephemeral as the literary journals that printed them, and with which Baltimore teemed. A few works of Marylanders, dating from this period, can still be found, however, in the standard anthologies of southern poetry. The fame of Francis Scott Key rests solely on 'The Star-Spangled Banner.' Though Key wrote other verse as well, this was to him little more than an avocation. Edward Coote Pinkney (1802–26) is represented in many anthologies of American poetry by his lyrics 'A Health,' addressed as a toast to a Baltimore lady, and 'A Serenade.' Pinkney was a member of the Baltimore bar and edited *The Marylander*, which supported John Quincy Adams. Although he died at an early age Pinkney's little volume *Poems* (1825), containing only 21 pieces, marked him as one of the leading lyricists of his day, and caused Poe to praise him broadly in his 'Lecture on the Poetic Principle.' Frederick Pinkney (1804–73), brother of Edward and like him a Baltimore lawyer, won attention for his poems during the Civil War.

John Leeds Bozman (1757–1823), author of a two-volume *History of*

Maryland (1837), published after his death, was the first of a long list of State historians.

The center of literary activity in Baltimore between 1816 and 1825 was a group of physicians, lawyers, and journalists who made up the Delphian Club. The literary output of the 16 members of the Delphian Club is impressive more for its quantity than its literary merit, consisting of not less than 48 volumes of fiction, history, travel, letters, and biography, as well as 9 volumes of poetry, one drama, and 19 speeches. Members of the Delphian Club were editors of 12 newspapers or magazines.

Associated with the Delphians was that remarkably versatile, picaresque figure, John Neal (1793–1876), writer, lecturer, and controversialist on every conceivable subject, rival of Cooper with his Indian novels, poet, critic, historian, editor, businessman, lawyer—challenged to a duel by Edward Coote Pinkney (he ignored the challenge), expelled from the Society of Friends for his writings and other doings, sponsor in America of the philosophy of Jeremy Bentham, and to whom Poe credited 'the very first words of encouragement I ever remember to have heard.' Neal came to Baltimore to conduct a retail drygoods business with John Pierpont (1785–1866), a grandfather of J.P.Morgan, the banker; the business collapsed, but Pierpont issued a volume of verse in Baltimore, *Airs of Palestine* (1816), and later published two more collections. In his Maryland period, Neal edited the *Baltimore Telegraph*, and the Delphians' magazine, *The Portico*, wrote the narrative poems, 'Battle of Niagara, a Poem, without Notes,' and 'Goldau, or, The Maniac Harper,' both published in 1818, a poetic tragedy, *Otho* (1819), and five novels that had wide sale. In 1823 he left Maryland and after a sojourn in England spent the remainder of his long and exceedingly prolific life in his native city, Portland, Maine. Lowell, in his *Fable for Critics*, wrote of him:

> There swaggers John Neal,
> In letters, too soon is as bad as too late,
> Could he only have waited, he might have been great.

John Pendleton Kennedy (1795–1870), whom V.L.Parrington called 'one of the most attractive figures of his generation,' was the son of a Baltimore merchant. In his youth he fought the British as a member of a Baltimore regiment, collaborated in the series of sketches entitled *The Red Book*, was active in Maryland politics, and served as president of the board of directors of the Baltimore & Ohio Railroad. The Baltimore of his day had become a busy commercial port whose intellectual life was dominated by new ideals of industrialism and progress. Kennedy is outstanding in American literature for his light satirical sketches, which show some influence of Washington Irving, and for his romantic picturesque novels and descriptive pieces—among them *Swallow Barn*, which deals with plantation life in Virginia, *Horseshoe Robinson*, a historical romance, and *Rob of the Bowl*, a tale set in bygone days. He was also author of a memorable life of William Wirt, whose political disciple he remained for many years.

The grandfather of Edgar Allan Poe (1809–49) had been a furniture-maker in Baltimore, where he had taken part in the Revolution, and the poet's father was born in that city and studied law there before he turned to the stage. Poe arrived in Baltimore for the first time in 1829 and stayed with his brother and his aunt, Mrs.Maria Clemm, whose daughter Virginia he later married. He called on William Wirt, and arranged with a local firm for the publication of his second volume of poems, which was highly lauded by John Neal. From Baltimore Poe went to West Point, but returned to the city in 1831 and remained there for about four years. During this period he wrote short stories and poems for the literary journals of Philadelphia and Baltimore. In 1832 Poe submitted a number of these stories and poems to the Baltimore *Saturday Morning Visitor* in a prize competition. His 'Ms. Found in a Bottle' received the prose award of $50, and he was denied the poetry prize solely because the judges were reluctant to give both prizes to the same author. (The poetry prize was bestowed upon John H. Hewitt (1801–90), editor of the *Visitor*, who competed under a *nom de plume*, for his 'Song of the Winds.' Hewitt was the author of the 'Minstrel's Return from the War' and many other popular ballads.)

One of the judges in the contest was John Pendleton Kennedy, and he befriended Poe and even supplied him with money. It was through Kennedy's influence that Poe in 1835 obtained the position of editor on the *Southern Literary Messenger* in Richmond.

Poe had many friends and relatives in Baltimore; yet, except for one or two brief visits, he remained away from the city until 1849, when he met his death there under mysterious circumstances during the election campaign. One of many stories regarding the event is that the poet, either drunken or drugged, was kidnaped by a gang of political hoodlums and taken from one polling place to another as a repeater. He was in poor health and the strain of this experience led to a collapse to which he soon succumbed. Thus Baltimore, which saw the beginning of this great poet's career, was also the site of its unhappy end.

Other Maryland writers of the first half of the nineteenth century include: 'The grandma of the muckrakers,' Anne Newport Royall (1769–1854), whose career as a writer and editor involved her in many bitter contests with prominent Washington personages; the poetess Amelia B.C. Welby (1819–52), whose *Poems by Amelia* (1844) ran into many editions and of whom Poe said: 'Very few American poets are at all comparable with her in the true poetical qualities'; Frances E. Watkins Harper (1825–1911), Negro poetess, novelist, lecturer, and abolitionist leader, whose *Poems*, published in 1854, ran into several editions; and Frederick Douglass (1817–95), the Negro abolitionist, born a slave on an Eastern Shore plantation, whose *My Bondage and My Freedom* appeared a year after Mrs.Harper's book of poems, and whose many vivid orations were also published and widely circulated.

In the popular romantic literature characteristic of the pre-Civil War era, Maryland produced several writers of bright but transitory reputation. The novels, plays, and verse of George Henry Miles (1824–71), born and educated in Maryland, and for most of his adult life professor of English literature at Mount Saint Mary's College, were charged with an exotic and religious flavor the taste of the 1850's found very gratifying. And in 1864 there appeared an anonymous novel, *Emily Chester*, which was soon eagerly read both in England and America, was translated into several foreign languages, and dramatized by Miles. The author was a twenty-year old Baltimore girl, Anne Moncure Crane (1838–72), who later published two more novels, *Opportunity* (1867) and *Reginald Archer* (1871).

On the outbreak of the Civil War the population of Maryland was sharply divided in its allegiance. Although Maryland finally stayed with the Union, numerous Confederate sympathizers remained in the State. Their ardor is revealed in the work of three Maryland poets, of whom the best known is James Ryder Randall. Randall, whose early youth was spent in Maryland, was teaching English at Poydras College in Louisiana when reports reached him of the death of a friend in an encounter between street crowds and the Massachusetts Volunteers in Baltimore in 1861. This incident was the inspiration for 'My Maryland,' a poem that was soon published in nearly every Southern journal. Set to the tune of 'O, Tannenbaum,' it became the 'Marseillaise' of the Confederacy and is now the State anthem of Maryland.

Abram Joseph Ryan (1838–86), called the 'poet of the Lost Cause,' was born in Hagerstown; and at 18 was ordained as a Roman Catholic priest. In 1862 he became chaplain of the Confederate Army. Father Ryan is the author of a number of songs and poems that became very popular in the South after the Civil War. The best known are 'The Conquered Banner' and 'The Sword of Robert E. Lee.'

Like so many other Southern poets John Williamson Palmer is remembered for a single poem, 'Stonewall Jackson's Way,' written on the death of the popular general.

The unusual poet and critic, Sidney Lanier (1846–81), first reached Maryland as a prisoner of war, being confined at Point Lookout prison camp; his experiences there were described in his novel, *Tiger-Lilies*. It was in Baltimore, to which he came in 1873, that Lanier's literary career began in earnest. It was while living in Baltimore that his first poems were published, and that he played the flute in the Peabody Orchestra and lectured in English literature at Johns Hopkins University. Some of his outstanding critical works came out of these Baltimore lectures.

John Banister (Father) Tabb (1845–1909), a Virginian by birth, spent the greater part of his adult life in Baltimore where he did most of his writing. While serving as a Confederate blockade runner he was seized and thrown into the same prison with Lanier, and the poets became fast friends. Father Tabb never forgot the 'Lost Cause.' His poetry gained a wide reception during the last two decades of the nineteenth century.

Richard Malcolm Johnston (1822–98), friend of Lanier, was another Southern writer who came to make his home in Baltimore. His *Dukesborough Tales* (1871), nostalgic stories of the South, and his *The Primes and Their Neighbors* were among the early collections appearing in the rising tide of short story writing which marked the latter decades of the nineteenth century. Francis Hopkinson Smith (1836–1915), Baltimore novelist, also contributed to the short story movement with his *A Day at Laguerre's and Other Days*. Smith is probably best known for his *Colonel Carter of Cartersville* and *Kennedy Square*. Charles Heber Clarke, who used the pen name of Max Adeler, was a popular humorous writer of the late nineteenth century. Eugene Lemoine Didier (1838–1913) wrote a popular life of Poe in 1879. William Hand Browne (1836–1915) is remembered chiefly for his work on thirty-two volumes of the *Archives of Maryland*, a compilation continued by Bernard C. Steiner (1867–1926). Henry Calvert (1803–89), a member of the family that founded the colony, was born at Bladensburg. His essays, travel books, poems, and literary biographies were once widely known, and he pioneered in the study of German literature. Daniel Kirkwood (1814–95), who was born in Harford County, became one of the eminent astronomers of his day, and wrote a well-received work, *Comets and Meteors*. *The Entailed Hat* and *Katy of Catoctin*, by George Alfred ('Gath') Townsend (1841–1914), who had a country house at South Mountain, give a pre-Civil War picture of life on the Eastern Shore that is still the best introduction to the region.

Probably the most popular books for juveniles in the latter part of the nineteenth century were those written in Maryland by Martha Farquharson Finley (1828–1907). Born in Ohio Miss Finley came to Elkton in 1876. *Elsie Dinsmore* (1867), the first of two dozen Elsie books, won the immediate approval of parents and Sunday School teachers. The Mildred series was also quite popular. In the present generation Miss Finley's youthful heroines are considered dull and unpleasantly priggish.

The works of J.Thomas Scharf (1843–98), historian and chronicler, are still used extensively by students and research workers. Sometimes inaccurate, somewhat provincial or sectional in his point of view, he nevertheless produced a valuable *History of Maryland from the Earliest Period to the Present Day*, as well as several other detailed volumes on particular sections of the State. Basil Lannean Gildersleeve (1831–1924), of Johns Hopkins University, was a leading American teacher and scholar of the classics and founded the *American Journal of Philology* in 1880.

Lizette Woodworth Reese (1856–1935) was born in Baltimore and for most of her life taught in the city's public schools. Several lyrics from the six volumes she published during her lifetime have found what seems to be an enduring place in American literature. *White April*, *Pastures*, *A Branch of May*, and *Spicewood* are her best known collections. Miss Reese was an integral part of the life of her native city, whose atmosphere she recreated in two prose works, *A Victorian Village* and *The Old York Road*.

Upton Sinclair, novelist, critic, crusader, and publicist, was born in Baltimore in 1878. At the age of ten, however, his family left the State and his variegated pilgrimage in search of justice in America was undertaken elsewhere. It is generally considered that Sinclair's major literary work is his novel *The Jungle*, which made a sensation in the early part of the twentieth century with its description of the Chicago stockyards and was a herald of what is commonly called the muckraking era in American literature.

Born in Baltimore in 1880, Henry L. Mencken, modern Maryland's most important literary figure, began his career there as a journalist in 1899. From 1914 to 1923 he collaborated with George Jean Nathan, dramatic critic, in editing the *Smart Set*, a monthly magazine of the 'sophisticates' of that era. During these years he distinguished himself among those writers who had set out to attack provincial Puritanism and middle-class smugness as an obstacle to the development of American culture. This campaign he continued as editor of *The American Mercury* from 1924 to 1933. Among his critical works, *In Defense of Women* and his nine volumes of articles collected under the title of *Prejudices*—the first volume in 1919—received widespread critical attention, as did his later and more substantial study, *The American Language*. In general, two strains dominate Mencken's work—a progressive tendency, manifesting itself in his hostility to academic deadness and his support of native expression, and a reactionary, naïve-Nietzchean philosophy of 'the Aristocrat,' which has led him to bluster against the democratic tradition. Since 1933 Mencken has restricted his activities largely to the *Sunpapers* and his labors on the American language studies. A volume of reminiscences of his boyhood in Baltimore, *Happy Days*, 1880–92, was published in 1940.

Among native Marylanders who have won recognition in contemporary American writing are the novelists James W. Cain, William B. Seabrook, Fulton Oursler, Sidney L. Nyburg, Holmes Alexander, and Frederic Arnold Kummer. Mr.Kummer has also been successful as a playwright and film scenario writer, and has written several successful books for children. V.F.Calverton (pen name of George Goetz, of Baltimore) is a critic well known as an editor and social commentator. Waters Edward Turpin, young Maryland Negro, has won praise for his two novels, *These Low Grounds* and *O Canaan*. His first novel is the record of several generations of Negroes on the author's native Eastern Shore. An early 1940 volume, *Men of Marque*, by two Baltimoreans, John Philips Cranwell and William B. Crane, achieved considerable success, and was widely praised as a noteworthy contribution to the history of Baltimore privateers.

Other contemporary Maryland writers include Dr.Wardlaw Miles, professor of English at the Johns Hopkins University, who is the author of *The Tender Realist and Other Essays*; Swepson Earle, who has written a popular volume on *The Chesapeake Bay Country*; Frederick P. Stieff, who dealt with his native city and State in *The Government of a Great American City* and *Eat, Drink and Be Merry in Maryland*; Miss Letitia Stockett, compiler of *Baltimore: A Not Too Serious History*. Another Baltimorean who wrote of the city in which he was a well-known and popular figure for many years was Meredith Janvier, author of *Baltimore in the Eighties and Nineties* and *Baltimore Yesterdays*.

Among books for children by contemporary Marylanders are: *Little Heiskell* by Isabella B. Hurlburt; *Turkey Tale* by Frances Bacon; and *Young Fu of the Upper Yangtze* by Elizabeth Forman Lewis. Mrs.Lewis was awarded the Newberry Medal in 1936 for 'the most distinguished contribution to American literature for children.' *Young Fu* has been printed in seven languages.

A number of writers from other sections of the United States have moved to Maryland during the past two or three decades. Among them are Mauritz A. Hallgren, political writer and economist; Gerald W. Johnson, Neil Swanson, and R.P.Harriss, all of the *Evening Sun*; the historians Matthew Page Andrews and William Cabell Bruce; Sophie Kerr; Hervey Allen, author of *Anthony Adverse* and *Israfel*, a biography of E.A.Poe; Ogden Nash, author of several 'best-selling' volumes of satirical verse; John Rathbone Oliver; Pat O'Mara; and Sara Hardt (who died in 1935), wife of Henry L. Mencken.

In the field of detective fiction the State is represented by Norman Stanley Bortner, Hulbert Footner, Mrs.Ford K. Brown (known in America as Leslie Ford and in England as David Frome), Francis Van Wyck Mason, Katherine S. Daiger, and many others.

Writers as varied as Gertrude Stein, Winston Churchill, and Emily Post are associated with Maryland. Miss Stein, a curious figure of the Paris 'left bank' and author of the *Autobiography of Alice B. Toklas*, studied at Johns Hopkins University and continues to visit members of her family in Baltimore. Churchill was a graduate of the Naval Academy at Annapolis, the scene of his very successful novel, *Richard Carvel*, and Mrs.Post, author of the standard volume on etiquette, was born in Baltimore.

Technical and scientific works by members of the faculties of the Johns Hopkins University, the University of Maryland, and other educational institutions in the State, many of them outstanding contributions to the cultural, social, and scientific development of the Nation, are far too numerous to mention here.

The Theater

THE first entertainers in Maryland—traveling troupes and individual performers with varied repertoires of tricks, recitations, and acts—were heartily welcomed, but it was not until June 1752 that the curtain rose in Annapolis upon a genuine theatrical performance, *The Beggar's Opera*, by Gay. It was presented by the Murray-Kean troupe, which called itself the Company of Comedians from Virginia, and shortly afterward gave several other productions, including *The Beaux' Strategem*, by Farquhar, and *The Merchant of Venice*. The troupe also visited Upper Marlboro, Piscataway, and Port Tobacco.

The theater in which the company appeared, while formal enough in plan with stage, boxes, pit, and gallery, was actually little more than a flimsy wooden barn. Its unsightliness inspired a writer of the period to bemoan 'the horrid ruggedness of the roof and the untoward construction of the whole,' though an item in the *Maryland Gazette* gives a more flattering description: 'The house is entirely lined throughout for the reception of Ladies and Gentlemen; and they have also raised a Porch at the Door that will keep out the inclemency of the weather.'

While some of the other colonies, controlled by groups that frowned upon the 'prophane' world of grease paint and make-believe, were passing acts forbidding dramatic presentations, the more tolerant Marylanders welcomed worldly diversions. Annapolis, then the largest town in the province, home of the leading officials, and social center of the wealthy planters of the province, was the logical birthplace of the Maryland theater.

Eight years after the production of *The Beggar's Opera*, David Douglass and his American Company gave a number of plays in Annapolis and in several other towns. Local interest in the stage increased and in 1771 Douglass returned to dedicate a theater, the first especially designed for such use in Maryland. It was constructed of brick, was commodious and charmingly decorated with scenes by Doll of London. It was, indeed, so magnificent that it quite overshadowed St. Anne's Church, on part of whose grounds it stood, moving a nameless poet of the period to protest:

I would not, if I could, restrain
A moral stage; yet, I would fain
Of your indulgence and esteem
At least an equal portion claim.

. . .

Here in Annapolis alone
God has the meanest house in town.

Baltimore's only dramatic fare until the 1770's consisted of performances by strolling players and private theatricals by 'ladies and gentlemen for their own amusement.' But in 1773 a large warehouse at the corner of Baltimore and Frederick Streets was converted into a temporary theater for the presentation of a series of plays by the Douglass and Hallam Company. The production was so well received by the town's six thousand inhabitants that the company built its own theater at Water and Albermarle Streets, and continued to perform there until anti-British sentiment compelled the group to leave the country.

The prohibition by Congress of 'shews and plays' suspended theatrical performances in a number of the Northern cities from 1775 to 1783, but it was not sufficient to prevent altogether the production of plays in Maryland, and in 1781 the Messrs. Wall and Lindsay remodeled a stable in Baltimore for performances by their company. It had such immediate success that they then erected a brick structure at the corner of Milk Lane (now East Street) and Great York Street (now East Baltimore Street). The *Maryland Journal* of January 15, 1782, carried an advertisement of the opening production: 'The New Theatre in Baltimore will open with an Historical Tragedy called *Richard III*, containing the distress and death of Henry IV, the contention between the houses of York and Lancaster, etc. and an occasional prologue by Mr. Wall, to which a farce will be added, called *Miss in Her Teens* or *A Medley of Lovers*. Boxes One Dollar —Pit Five Shillings—Gallery 9 D—Doors open at 4.30—Will begin at 6.'

The company of the New Theater was the first resident stock company of professional actors in America, and for several seasons the country's outstanding theatrical group. It brought the leading English plays of the period across the Atlantic, among its productions being *School for Scandal*, *Grecian Daughter*, and *Gustavus Vasa*. Twenty-two plays were presented the first season; although pantomime, comic opera, and even tragedy enjoyed a fair amount of popularity, it was the Restoration farce that particularly pleased Baltimore audiences. The company frequently used local talent; the amateurs' names, however, were not printed on the program, but were indicated merely as 'performances by gentlemen for their own amusement.'

In 1783 the theater was taken over by Dennis Ryan, a capable manager and a pleasing actor, who for three years presented the usual program of plays, hornpipe solos, and songs, though performances were often postponed because of inclement weather; the unpaved streets were impassable during parts of spring and autumn, and bridges over the numerous streams were always in need of repair. An advertisement appearing in the *Maryland Journal* of February 18, 1783, reads: 'D.Ryan's most respectful Compliments await the Ladies and Gentlemen of Baltimore. He begs leave to inform them that the Bridge is repaired so as to make it passable for Foot Passengers and Carriages; and that he intends to have proper lights for the Bridge and Theatre.'

The popularity of the first theater is attested by the fact that in 1786 another theater was erected by Hallam and Henry at Pratt and Albermarle Streets, with *School for Scandal* as the initial production, and that on September 25, 1794, Thomas Wignell and Alexander Reinagle opened still another New Theater with *Every One Has His Faults* and a comic opera, *The Flitch of Bacon.*

These early performances were true social events. A chronicler vividly described the femine theatergoers of this era as 'grave matrons and stirring damsels moving erect in stately transit, like the wooden and pasteboard figures of a puppet show . . . arrayed in gorgeous brocade and taffeta, luxuriantly displayed over hoops, with comely bodices, laced around that ancient piece of armor, the stay, disclosing most ample breasts. And such faces . . . so rosy, so spirited and sharp!' He was also amused by their mincing gait in shoes of many colors and high and tottering heels, their towering hats garnished with tall feathers that waved aristocratically backward at each step 'as if they took pride in the slow paces of the wearer.'

During the early part of the nineteenth century Baltimore rivaled New York as a theatrical center. Until nearly the end of the century the repertory system prevailed, for inter-city travel was slow, uncertain, and even hazardous, and the transportation of theatrical troupes and productions was both expensive and cumbersome. It was not until the improvement of travel facilities, and the control of theaters throughout the country by New York syndicates led to the development of touring companies and road shows that Baltimore was without its own producing group or groups.

The Baltimore theater was particularly gay during the seasons of 1810 and 1811. Shows began at half-past six and always included a 'celebrated' tragedy, melodrama, or comedy in five acts, as well as a two-act musical farce or 'buretta,' with sometimes a song and dance specialty presented between the two major parts of the program. For these lengthy entertainments, 'A box is One Dollar, the Pit is the Fourth of a Dollar.'

A cosmopolitan flavor was lent to resident stock companies by the frequent appearances of stars from New York or England. Among the actors of the short-lived Baltimore Theater were John Howard Payne, composer of 'Home, Sweet Home,' who appeared in *Hamlet* and three other productions; and a 'Mr. Jefferson,' grandfather of Joseph Jefferson, later famous as Rip Van Winkle.

The Holliday Street Theater began its long and illustrious career on May 10, 1813. Its first wooden structure was replaced by one of brick, in September 1813, to house a stock company managed by William Warren and William Wood. The outstanding actors of the day appeared in this building, including George Frederick Cooke, Edmund Kean, Macready, the elder Wallack, and Charles Kean. The theater achieved distinction on October 19, 1814, when a 'Mr. Hardinge' publicly rendered for the first time 'a much admired new song—"The Star Spangled Banner."' Frequently repeated, it was sung again during November of the same year at a performance 'commemorating the repulse of the enemy from Baltimore,' according to the *Federal Gazette*. Wood's *Recollections of the Stage* is a valuable record of the early nineteenth-century drama.

In 1846 the Holliday Street Theater became involved in financial difficulties and was closed until the autumn of 1854, when an association of wealthy men purchased the building and refitted it on an elaborate scale. Though brilliant actors were engaged and generous salaries were paid, the season closed with a loss of $15,000. John T. Ford then took charge of the theater, and through his shrewd showmanship, judgment, and diplomacy inaugurated a new era in the city's dramatic history. To Baltimoreans of the older generation, the name of the theater conjures up glowing memories of a stage peopled with the dramatic stars of the period. Destroyed by fire and rebuilt in the 1870's, the theater began to wane in popularity, and Victorian melodramas of the most lurid type replaced the classics. Used only infrequently after the turn of the century, the building was razed in 1917 to make room for the Civic Center.

Other Baltimore theaters that flourished during the nineteenth century were the Adelphia, the Front Street, the Baltimore Museum, and the Howard Athenaeum. The high points in the Adelphia's history came with the appearance of Junius Booth in *Richard III* in 1827 and his return to manage the theater in 1830. Under various names, the building housed productions of many kinds until 1876, when it was destroyed by fire.

First called the New Theater and Circus, the Front Street had an auspicious opening on September 10, 1829, when approximately three thousand persons attended the initial performance. The elder Booth played here, also, but the greatest event was the appearance of Jenny Lind in December 1850 in a series of four concerts, for which she received $60,000. Fires, hurricanes, and other disasters marked the theater's history, climaxed by a panic on December 27, 1895, when twenty-three persons were killed and more than a score of others injured. Frequent political conventions were held at the Front Street Theater, including those nominating Stephen A. Douglas and Abraham Lincoln for the presidency. The building was condemned and razed in 1904.

The Baltimore Museum, which had housed Rembrandt Peale's collection of theatrical portraits, was first opened as a theater by Edmund Peale in 1844; it was later known as Kunkel's Ethiopian Opera House. Though visited by many of the ranking actors of its day, the theater became rather disreputable in its last years; it was destroyed by fire in 1873. Peale was also the owner of the Howard Athenaeum, where John Wilkes Booth made his debut as Richmond in *Richard III*. The building was torn down in 1880. In the last two decades of the nineteenth century the Monumental Theater was popular, presenting such plays as *The Ticket of Leave Man* and *The Black Crook*. Here Denman Thompson appeared in *Joshua Whitcomb, or The Female Brothers*, a characterization that he later developed into his perennial, *The Old Homestead*. Comedies and melodramas and finally burlesque filled the Monumental's last years, when its name had been changed to the Folly. Sharing the fate of many of Baltimore's playhouses, it burned in 1928.

The Lyceum, built in 1884 and first called the Alliston, operated with varying success, but was distinguished by the appearance of such stars as Sarah Bernhardt, Fanny Davenport, and Marie Tempest. For four prosperous years it housed a stock company headed by George Fawcett. It was destroyed by fire in 1925.

To the Academy of Music, built in 1875 and razed a half-century later to make room for a modern motion picture house, and to Ford's Grand Opera House, which opened its doors in 1871, came all the great actors of that period. Among them were Sir Henry Irving, Ellen Terry, Eleanora Duse, Lily Langtry, Helena Modjeska, Beerbohm Tree, Otis Skinner, J. Forbes Robertson, Henrietta Crossman, John Drew and the Barrymores, Sothern and Marlowe, Richard Mansfield, Joseph Jefferson, Ada Rehan, Minnie Maddern Fiske, and Bertha Kalisch.

In 1939 only three legitimate theaters remained in Baltimore: Ford's, the Maryland, and the Auditorium. The Auditorium opened as a music hall in 1866. Though Weber and Fields and the Four Cohans appeared here in the early part of the present century, the theater's history has been unimportant since the 1920's. The Maryland was the home of Keith Vaudeville in the more prosperous days of that form of entertainment. In 1931–2, the theater housed the University Players, a group of young actors and actresses who have since achieved fame on both the legitimate stage and the screen. Among them were Margaret Sullavan, Henry Fonda, Myron McCormick, and Kent Smith. Financial difficulties and lack of public support forced them to leave Baltimore.

Several theaters in Baltimore have featured burlesque but only one, the Gayety, built in 1905, was still operating regularly in 1939.

As has been the case in most large cities except New York, theatrical fare in Baltimore in the 1930's was scarce and of uneven quality. The city still has openings at infrequent intervals, but too many of the productions are second or third road companies. Owing to competition from the motion pictures, only a few outstanding actors and actresses, such as Katherine Cornell, Lunt and Fontanne, and Helen Hayes, can be sure of S.R.O. signs.

Partly offsetting the scarcity of professional presentations are those of the numerous little theaters that have sprung up in the State. The best known of these is the Vagabond Players, organized in Baltimore in 1916 and counted one of the oldest amateur groups in the United States. In its first years the Vagabond Players experimented with productions ignored by the commercial theater, and consequently provided thought-provoking theatrical fare; but since about 1930 it has concentrated largely on revivals of one-time Broadway successes. The theater has, however, served as a training school for a number of actors who moved on to professional groups.

For almost a score of years the Johns Hopkins Playhouse, on the University Campus, has been active, generally presenting the works of such playwrights as Moliere, Ibsen, Chekhov, and Strindberg. The Guild Theater group, also in Baltimore, for some years has devoted itself almost exclusively to Gilbert and Sullivan operas.

The Negro community of Baltimore has its own little theater, founded in 1930. This group in 1937 set up a children's department, which produces two plays a year suitable for very young audiences. The Negro Intercollegiate Dramatic Association was organized in Baltimore in 1930 by Randolph Edmunds, then professor of English and director of dramatics at Morgan College. The association holds annual tournaments at which students from Negro colleges present one-act plays dealing with Negro life and problems. The Morgan College Dramatic Club won several of the tournaments with plays written by Mr. Edmunds.

There are about half-a-dozen other little theater groups in the State, limiting themselves to revivals.

In the winter, towns and cities of Maryland outside Baltimore see few professional theatrical performances, except vaudeville and occasional minor road shows. However, the summer theater movement, which began to develop in Maryland in the late 1930's, has brought popular plays to many of the rural areas, with amateur organizations sometimes supported by players of note from Broadway.

Although he was born in England, Junius Brutus Booth was closely associated with Maryland, for he served as director and actor in Baltimore theaters and built a house near Belair. Here his sons Edwin and John Wilkes Booth were born. Both, of course, took their places among the ranking stars of their period, though the younger brother's career ended in tragedy and disgrace. According to some accounts Ira Aldridge, the Negro tragedian, was born in Belair about 1810. Other sources give New York as his birthplace, but in any case Aldridge spent part of his youth in Maryland. He won honors in Europe in Shakespearian roles and was considered one of the greatest Othellos. He died in Poland in 1867. Stuart Robson (1836–1903) was born in Annapolis and played his first role in *Uncle Tom's Cabin* in Baltimore. He was well known as a comedian, particularly as a team mate with William H. Crane.

In musical comedy, older theatergoers recall Irene Bentley, a popular star at the turn of the twentieth century. Gertrude Vanderbilt, also a Baltimorean, was prominent in musical shows in the first decades of the present century. Rida Johnson Young, born in Baltimore, was one of the most successful librettists in the light-opera field, with *Glorious Betsy*, *Brown of Harvard*, and the perennially popular *Maytime* to her credit. James Young, her husband, was well known as a Shakespearian actor. George Bronson Howard (1884–1922), born in Howard County, was a prolific writer of stories, plays, and photoplays. His best known play is *The Only Law*. S. Broughton Tall, chiefly known as a dramatic critic, wrote *Madame Bonaparte*. In another branch of the show business, Raymond Sovey and Isaac Benesch, of Baltimore, are successful scene designers.

On the whole, Maryland has had an unusually solid part in America's dramatic history. It never suffered from the blighting effects of Puritanism and its chief city was well established as a dramatic center when the drama was still struggling for a foothold in other States. The local decline merely paralleled the general trend in the country.

Music

THE province's first recorded public musical performance for which admission was charged took place in 1752, when the Kean and Murray Company with an orchestra gave a production of *The Beggar's Opera* in Annapolis. Documents, however, broadly hint of the singing of boisterous songs of English origin in the ordinaries. Unfortunately the bawdy lyrics—which aroused the displeasure of the church fathers and led to the passage of laws against the 'Prophaning of the Sabbath' by swearing or by drinking—and their accompanying melodies are buried in obscurity.

Public musical performances until the latter part of the eighteenth century were primarily an adjunct of religion. When Hugh Maguire opened a singing school in St.Anne's Church, Annapolis, in July 1765, he taught 'the new version of the psalms with all the tunes, both of particular and common measure,' charging a one dollar entrance fee and fifteen shillings a quarter. In addition he gave lessons to young ladies in their homes, where 'such as play on the spinet may in a short time and with the greatest ease learn the different psalm tunes.'

In an advertisement of November 1789, Ishmael Spicer offered his services to Baltimoreans as a teacher of psalmody at a fee of $2.50 a quarter for tuition, firewood, and candles. The emergence in Baltimore of an interest in music is indicated by several similar items of the period, including the announcement of a harpsichord instructor and the performance of a concert at John Starck's tavern on April 9, 1789, by Boyer, music master to the town's gentry.

Among the early musicians in Annapolis, then the rallying point for all the arts in the Maryland province, were George James L'Argeau, a specialist on 'musical glasses,' and Raynor Taylor (1747–1825), who settled in Annapolis during October 1792. Taylor, the organist of St.Anne's Church, sought to establish himself as a 'music professor, organist and teacher of music in general,' but affairs in Annapolis did not run smoothly for him. His salary guarantors failed to respect their pledges and he departed for Philadelphia.

The appreciation of music became more widespread with the expansion of industry and the consequent development of a prosperous and educated society in Baltimore. As a result, a number of composers of sacred music, sentimental ballads, and operatic scores were attracted to that city. One of the earliest, Alexander Reinagle (1756–1809), an Englishman of Austrian origin, studied with Raynor Taylor, and spent his later years in Baltimore composing musical scores and managing a theater. Settling in Baltimore in the period between 1800 and 1830 were Christopher Meinecke, who arrived in 1800 and became a leading influence in musical circles both as an organist at St.Paul's Church and as a composer of religious and secular music; Phillip Anthony Corri, better known as Arthur Clifton, who composed a number of popular marches; Samuel Dyer, an English conductor of singing classes, who wrote religious music of a high order; and Frederick Crouch, a prolific ballad writer. Crouch, composer of 'Kathleen Mavourneen,' taught music in Baltimore for a number of years.

At about this time Baltimore began to publish sheet music in large quantities, owing largely to the increase in the number of music teachers settling in the town. The first known Maryland publisher of music was Joseph Carr, an organist at St.Paul's Church. Together with his son Thomas, he opened a music store on Gay Street in 1796. Carr's *Musical Miscellany* and *Journal* were standard publications for a number of years.

The peak years of sheet music publication were between 1820 and 1840. Among those who particularly prospered in this field were John Cole, who published several editions of psalms and anthems that had wide circulation; F.D.Benteen, who was particularly successful; and Samuel Carusi, who published the song, 'Long, Long Ago,' in 1837.

Most of the popular music during the first quarter of the nineteenth century was of the sentimental ballad type such as 'The Old Maid' and 'The Old Bachelor' of 1824, or was patriotic—'Yankee Doodle' and 'The Star Spangled Banner' are examples of the latter. Few songs have had such a dramatic birth as the anthem conceived by Francis Scott Key, and set to the strains of an old drinking song, 'Anacreon in Heaven.'

Many songs and marches were written for special Maryland institutions or occasions; one praised the *Baltimore Sun*, others commemorated Lafayette's visit to the city, the Baltimore & Ohio Railroad, and the Whig Convention of 1844.

The Maryland Historical Society is the custodian of the Dielman collection of 7,000 items of sheet music, composed mostly by Baltimoreans between 1796 and 1898. The collection is important for its reflection of the popular musical tastes of the nineteenth century, rather than for the quality of the compositions. No neglected masterpieces await discovery by the student; he will find much of the collection consisting of such trivia as 'Do Not Slight This Faithful Heart,' 'Moonlight, Music, Love and Flowers,' 'The Indian Captive, or The Absent Lover,' and 'No, My Love, No, or The Wife's Farewell.'

But not all Maryland composers of the period belonged to the popular ballad school. Henry Dielman (1811–82) was a composer of considerable merit as well as the first musician in the country to receive the degree of Doctor of Music, bestowed on him by Georgetown University.

Public interest in religious music led David Creamer (1812–87), a Baltimorean, to investigate the history of Methodist hymns. He instructed his agents in Europe to purchase copies of all editions of Wesley's poems and hymns that could be found, and his *Methodist Hymnology* (1849) was the result of this compilation.

Nonetheless, this period in the musical history of the State is distinguished not so much by composition as by important local developments of the pianoforte; some of the most noted piano builders of the first half of the nineteenth century lived in Baltimore, among them Thomas Stewart, Joseph Hiskey, Conrad Meyer, William Knabe, and Charles Stieff.

During the second decade of the century the small chamber groups of the gentry began to make way for choral societies capable of interpreting the works of Mozart, Beethoven, Haydn, and Handel. The poorly equipped, early music masters were replaced by teachers whose knowledge supplemented good taste and judgment.

In 1819 the Harmonic Society of Baltimore gave its first concert of vocal and instrumental music, and two years later presented Haydn's *Creation* in the new Roman Catholic Cathedral in Baltimore, 'assisted by music professors and more than one hundred and twenty ladies and gentlemen amateurs.' Despite a heavy rain a large audience 'of beauty and fashion' overflowed the orchestra section at an early hour.

Several progressive musical movements followed in quick succession. The formation of the Musical Association in May 1827 was followed a year later by the organization of the Baltimore Choral Society. These organizations jointly presented a series of concerts for the benefit of the city's poor. Baltimore's taste in music was still far from mature, however, to judge by the comments of John F. Petri, a Leipzig-educated musician. Speaking of the popular musical taste when he arrived in Baltimore in 1831, Petri said, '. . . Music was yet in its infancy—Even in good society and among well-educated people nothing was appreciated beyond waltzes, marches and variations on some familiar theme, or simple airs from Rossini's operas. There were few educated musicians . . . among them

H.Gilles, C.Meinecke, John Nenninger, Henry Dielman and your humble servant.'

With the formation of the Liederkranz in 1836, however, the city's interest in music increased, with Germans dominating the scene. The Liederkranz was the second German singing club in the United States and grew out of Pastor Scheib's choir at Zion Church. Making its debut in March 1837, the group presented a grand concert program that included a Beethoven symphony, two quartets, and several other selections. After the influx of well-educated Germans following the 1848 revolts in their country, musical standards of Baltimoreans were raised appreciably.

Jenny Lind's Baltimore appearance in 1850 brought overflowing crowds that gladly paid as much as $10 a seat to hear her. Her visit materially fostered the appreciation of vocal music in the city, and during the same year a number of famous tenors and prima donnas, including Sontag, Albonie, Patti, Grisi, Mario, Adelaide Phillips, Brignoli, and Parepa Rosa, appeared in Baltimore.

In 1859 the Grand National Saengerbund assembled in the city, and presented a series of concerts in which large choruses participated. In the following year a number of celebrated musicians performed in Baltimore, including the pianists Gottschalk and Careno, and the violinists Vieuxtemps, Sivori, Wieniawski, and Sauret.

At first pianos were luxuries, the annual Baltimore production reaching only 200. But by 1861 eight companies were making them, in all turning out 1,400 pianos a year, most of which went to the Southern States. Makers of wood-wind instruments were not far behind the piano makers. One of the first concerns in this field was the C.H.Hildebrandt & Sons company, founded in 1814. The firm now specializes in making violins.

The Civil War inspired a number of songs, dedicated, since the State was divided in its sympathies, to one or the other side in the conflict. One song, for example, was addressed to the Volunteers of the United States and another to Jefferson Davis. The lyric 'Maryland, My Maryland' was written by James Ryder Randall in 1861 while he was teaching at Poydras College in Louisiana, and was set to the music of the German song 'O Tannenbaum'; it has become the State anthem. The most prolific writer of Southern war songs was John H. Hewitt of Baltimore, author of 'You are Going to the Wars, Willie Boy,' 'The Soldier's Farewell,' 'Who Will Care for Mother Now?,' 'All Quiet Along the Potomac Tonight,' and twenty-five or thirty others, practically all of them published in the Confederacy.

After the war Otto Sutro, an accomplished musician, published a few pieces of sheet music but most of the local music houses were soon absorbed by publishing houses elsewhere.

The opening in 1868 of the Peabody Conservatory of Music, first endowed music school in the United States, was the most important event of the local music world in the early postwar period. The work of the conservatory, in the words of George Peabody, its founder, was to be 'adapted in the most effective manner to diffuse and cultivate a taste for music, the most refining of all the arts, by providing a means of studying its principles and practicing its compositions, and by periodical concerts, aided by the best talent and most eminent skill within the means of the trustees to procure.'

While Baltimore history of the 1870's was not marked by any outstanding creative achievement in music, the city's progress in appreciation of music continued. To the Academy of Music in a single year, 1870, came Thomas' Orchestra, Wachtel's German Opera Company, the Italian Opera with Pappenheim, and the Grand Lyric Constellation of Strakosch. Kellog's Opera Company sang at Ford's and the Germania Maennerchor produced Mozart's *Magic Flute*. These were not one-night stands, but full-week engagements. The Richtings Opera Company, a local organization, made extensive tours, presenting programs whose range included Offenbach, Lecocq, Mozart, and Wagner.

The site selected for the Academy of Music caused numerous protests, for freight trains were then running on Howard Street, and bellowing cattle were often driven through the adjacent streets. The Academy was opened in January 1875, with footlights that were individually lighted from an oil torch. The housewarming was a 'grand ball,' attended by foreign ambassadors, delegations from Washington, and prominent civil and military dignitaries. The institution had a long and important part in Baltimore's cultural history.

In 1870 the Reverend John Sebastian Bach Hodges organized the first choir school for boys in the United States at St.Paul's (P.E.) Church in Baltimore. In the meantime the Peabody Symphony Orchestra under Asger Hamerik had begun its Saturday evening concerts, which were to become a vital part of local musical activities. Hamerik, a native of Copenhagen, had studied with Gade, Matthison-Hensen, Haberbier, and Von Bulow. He came to Baltimore after sojourns in Vienna (with Berlioz), in Paris, and in Italy. From 1871 to 1898, as director of the Peabody Conservatory of Music, he took a leading part in the musical affairs of the city. His compositions included a number of operas, choral works, symphonies, and orchestral suites. In 1898 he returned to Copenhagen where he remained until his death in 1923.

Commemorating the fiftieth anniversary of Beethoven's death, a 'Monumental Beethoven Festival' was held in 1877, at which the great composer's Fifth Symphony was played. A number of other events of musical importance took place during this decade, among them Rubinstein's first concert in Baltimore, in 1872, and Sullivan's appearance in 1880. Concerts were also given by Rudolph Green and H.Jungnickel, cellists; Roswald Zech, Allen, Fitz Gaul, and Gustave Bornshein, violinists; and B.Courlander, Nanette Falk-Auerbach, and Cecilia Gaul, pianists.

Popular compositions written by Baltimoreans at this period included 'Angel Music, or The Voice of My Mother' and 'The Little Blonde in Blue.' The latter was a representative jazz number of the day, with its lines:

> Whenever I go down the street,
> The gents all stop and stare,
> They say, there goes our little blonde,
> The girl with the golden hair.

The following decade began with the formation of another important group. Predecessor of the present-day Handel Choir, the Oratorio Society of Baltimore was established in 1880 by Otto Sutro, and two years later its chorus of 300 sang at Theodore Thomas' May Festival in New York. For more than 40 years the society presented great choral works in Baltimore. Joseph Pache, who had studied at the Munich Conservatory and with Max Bruch in Breslau, succeeded Sutro as conductor of the Oratorio Society in 1894. He later founded the Women's Philharmonic Chorus, and also composed a number of choruses and songs.

In the 1890's Sutro's two daughters, Rose and Ottilie, made a joint debut with the famous Joachim, playing the Bach concerto for two pianos. They became probably the best-known duo-pianists of their day.

In recent years the centers of musical culture in Baltimore have been the Lyric Theater, the Municipal Department of Music, and the Peabody Conservatory.

The Lyric Theater, since its opening in 1892, has been the scene of concerts by leading artists and orchestras. Each spring the Metropolitan Opera Company under the auspices of the Baltimore Opera Club, which guarantees it against loss, presents a brief series of operas in the theater.

Baltimore has a notable record in the field of municipally sponsored music. The man chiefly responsible for this development is Frederick Huber, who was born in Baltimore and studied at the Peabody Conservatory of

Music. Although the city's park concerts began in 1865, its municipal music program was really inaugurated in 1914, when the city appropriated $8,000 for a band to give concerts in the various neighborhoods. In 1915, at the suggestion of Huber, then manager of the Summer School of the Peabody Conservatory, Mayor James H. Preston sanctioned community singing concerts on summer evenings in Mount Vernon Place. Words were thrown upon a screen and the municipal band played accompaniments.

Meantime Baltimore, in a wave of civic pride, had adopted a city flag and was considering the idea of finding a municipal anthem. In 1916 six hundred poems were submitted in competition for the prize of $250. Folger McKinsey, the popular Bentztown Bard of the *Baltimore Sun*, won the lyric contest with his poem, 'Baltimore, Our Baltimore,' and Mrs. Theodore Hemberger, wife of the conductor of the Germania Maennerchor, won the contest for a musical setting. The anthem was sung for the first time at the Lyric Theater on February 22, 1916, by a chorus of girls from the high schools, assisted by the United Singers, a male chorus from the German singing societies in the city.

Eleven days earlier the Baltimore Symphony Orchestra had made its debut at the Lyric under municipal auspices. A Baltimore soprano, Mabel Garrison of the Metropolitan Opera Company, was the guest soloist. The national publicity obtained for the city by the orchestra led to the establishment of a department of music under the direction of Huber.

Many notable artists have since appeared with the Baltimore Symphony. During the season of 1923-4 the policy of having occasional guest conductors was inaugurated. The first of these was Siegfried Wagner, who in 1924 conducted a program consisting of his own works, as well as compositions of his father, Richard, and of his grandfather, Franz Liszt. Other guest conductors have been Henry Hadley, Albert Stoessel, Richard Ageman, Chalmers Clifton, and Eugene Goosens.

Gustave Strube, composer of a number of operas, symphonies, and instrumental works, wielded the baton from the orchestra's inception until 1930, when he retired. His successors included George Siemonn, Ernest Schelling, Werner Janssen, and, in 1940, Howard Barlow.

Local composers have been encouraged by frequent inclusion of their works in the orchestra's programs. Compositions by the two conductors, Strube and Siemonn, have been introduced as well as the works of George F. Boyle, Franz C. Bornschein, Howard R. Thatcher, Charles H. Bochau, Louis Cheslock, Eugene Bonner, Emma and Theodore Hemberger, David S. Melamet, and John Itzel. The orchestra has also given recognition to Baltimore singers, such as Hilda Burke. Following her concert with the local orchestra, Miss Burke appeared successfully with the Chicago Civic Opera Company and is now a member of the Metropolitan.

Harold Randolph (1861–1927), a Peabody graduate, became director of the conservatory in 1898 when it had only 200 students. Under his supervision the conservatory grew, and within 20 years the student body had increased to 1,400. Since Randolph's death in 1927 the present director, Otto Ortmann, also a Peabody graduate, has greatly broadened the curriculum. Mr.Ortmann is well known for his studies in music education. A research department, the first of its kind in a conservatory, has done extensive work in a systematic analysis of problems in this field. For 20 weeks of the winter season there are regular Friday afternoon recitals by visiting artists of high rank, and a free series of summer concerts at the Peabody constitutes the only serious music in Baltimore during that season. The Peabody concerts are the nucleus of practically all concert activities in Baltimore.

The reputation of the Peabody faculty and graduates is widespread, many working all over the country as teachers, directors, and performers. Among them are Emanuel Wad, Danish composer and pianist, who joined the Peabody faculty under Asger Hamerik and remained there until 1919; Charles H. Bochau, who has written many anthems and other songs, and works for violin and piano; Frank Gittelson, a member of the Peabody faculty, one of the few local violinists to have achieved a degree of international success; J.C.Van Hulsteyn, Dutch violinist, who came to the Peabody in 1892; Louis Robert, who taught the organ and led the chorus at the conservatory from 1924 until his death in 1938; Howard R. Thatcher, Baltimore organist and composer who has taught at Peabody for 24 years; Franz C. Bornschein, also Baltimore-born, a violinist and composer of orchestral and choral works, conductor of the Baltimore Chorus and Glee Club, and member of the Advisory Board of the National Academy of Music; Austin Conradi, pianist, born in Baltimore, who studied with Ernest Hutcheson when the latter was teaching at Peabody from 1900 to 1912; Pasquale Tallarico, Italian-born pianist; and Alexander Sklarevski, pianist from Russia.

Among those who studied in the voice department of the conservatory are the distinguished Metropolitan Opera baritone, John Charles Thomas, who has taken his place as one of the leading baritones of the present generation; the soprano, Mabel Garrison; Robert Weede, baritone, who in 1927 won the contests sponsored by the National Federation of Music Clubs in Chicago; and Elizabeth Gutman, soprano, who has sung successfully with several European companies. Another Peabody graduate is Virgil Fox, who has won international praise as a concert organist.

Other local singers include Harriet Zell Colston, a lyric soprano who has sung star roles with visiting opera companies; and Emma Redell, soprano, who made her concert debut at Budapest in 1923 and her operatic debut in *Tosca* at Altenburg, Germany, in 1925.

Since its formation in 1932 the Bach Club has occupied a very special place in the more erudite musical life of Baltimore. Devoting its attention entirely to 'musicians' music,' the club brings to the city in half-a-dozen concerts each season such distinguished chamber music groups as the Budapest String Quartette, the London String Quartette, the Compinsky Trio, and the Roth Quartette, as well as individual concert artists of the caliber of Myra Hess, Joseph Szigeti, and Harold Bauer. All of these musicians were first brought to Baltimore by the Peabody for its concert series.

Baltimoreans have followed the career of Shura Cherkassky with more than casual interest, because it was in Baltimore that the child pianist made his American debut. He had already won attention at the age of five in Odessa, Russia, and he was only eleven when he astounded his first formal Baltimore audience with his impressive performance.

Appreciation of good music is fostered in the public schools of the State. Through the use of the phonograph and the radio, students become accustomed to hearing classics, and interest is fostered by the production of operettas and by participation in the activities of choral and orchestral groups. An all-Maryland High School Orchestra has won considerable praise for its annual concerts under the auspices of the Maryland State Teachers' Association.

The Work Projects Administration Orchestra has played before thousands of people who would otherwise be denied the pleasures of orchestral music. Made up of unemployed musicians under the direction of Emil Odend'hal, the orchestra has presented regular concerts in Baltimore and has also played frequently in other Maryland cities.

The Baltimore Civic Opera Company, founded in 1932 by Eugene Martinet, is made up of a number of ambitious singers, who each year present three popular operas carefully staged and competently sung.

The Baltimore & Ohio Railroad Glee Club of 90 men, organized in 1913, has sung in Maryland and 12 other States. In 1929 this organization was awarded first prize in the male chorus competition held in New York City under the auspices of the Associated Glee Clubs of America. In 1934 it won first prize in the Chicago Music Festival. The club gives an annual concert in May at the Lyric Theater. The Associated Glee Clubs of Baltimore, organized in 1938, gave its first concert that year under the leadership of Ivan Servais.

In the field of jazz many native Baltimoreans have won ranking positions. Eubie Blake, a Negro composer, wrote 'Daddy, Won't You Please Come Home?' and 'Lovin' You the Way I Do' for the shows *Shuffle Along* and *Folies Bergère Revue*, respectively. Cab Calloway's showmanship has led his band to international fame. The late Chick Webb's band was equally popular and one of his performers, Ella Fitzgerald, has made her swing contribution, 'Tisket a' Tasket,' to the nursery-rhyme school of jazz. Other popular songs written in recent years by Baltimoreans include Raymond Klages' 'Who Do You Love?' (1926), Abel Baer's 'I Ain't Got Nobody' (1926), Edward Claypoole's 'Raggin' the Scales' (1923), and Billy Mayhew's 'It's a Sin to Tell a Lie' (1936).

In the summer of 1922 the city began providing its Negro community with special concerts by Negro musicians. The Baltimore City Colored Orchestra first performed publicly in 1931, and its initial concert with the Baltimore City Colored Chorus took place a year later. The same season the Negro Symphony inaugurated its performances for Negro children, replacing the Baltimore Symphony Orchestra in this field.

Hagerstown, settled by Germans and producing pipe organs, is a music-loving community, supporting a municipal band and a symphony orchestra. The municipal band, organized in 1915 and financed by the city, now consists of about 50 pieces. The organization of the Hagerstown Symphony Orchestra in 1935 marked a definite forward step in small-town music. Made up of 80 pieces, its first conductor was Stephen Déak, a Hungarian 'cellist, composer, and instructor in 'cello and chamber music at the Peabody. A series of concerts, with programs ranging from Berlioz to Wagner, is given annually during the spring and summer. Gerrit Smith (1859–1912), first president of the Manuscript Society and the American Guild of Organists, was born in Hagerstown. He studied at the Stuttgart Conservatory, and was a pupil of S.P.Warren, Eugene Thayer, Sherwood, and Haupt. His compositions include *King David*, a cantata; and a hundred songs, anthems, and choruses.

Of interest also are the Cumberland Valley Choristers, with members from Hagerstown, Williamsport, and Clearspring, Maryland, and from Waynesboro and Greencastle, Pennsylvania. Under the direction of Charles M. Cassel, its concerts have aroused interest in choral group music throughout the region.

Arts and Crafts

MARYLAND'S earliest settlers had little time for making articles of more than utilitarian value. Of necessity the first pieces they fabricated were tables, stools, beds, and chests, all from wood abundant in near-by forests. This furniture tended to be rectangular in form and rather heavily built, with ornamentation subordinated to sturdiness. Tables were hewn of plank; rough three-legged stools, benches, and beds were made of soft pine. To be sure, the handsome manor houses of the baronial planters soon began to fill with furnishings brought back from France, England, and Holland on the ships that had carried their tobacco to market, but the average farmer continued to make and use his home-made articles until well into the eighteenth century.

Gradually, as the number of craftsmen increased, furnishings made in the colony became more refined in workmanship, and imported pieces were duplicated in American woods. By about 1780, when Heppelwhite styles came into vogue, boxwood, holly, and satinwood were being used for inlaying, sometimes for veneer. Native American walnut was worked by Maryland cabinetmakers from the earliest times—its dark color, fine grain, and susceptibility to wax finishes making it a favorite. Mahogany was introduced before 1759. Hard yellow pine was serviceable for the frames of tables, beds, desks, and the like, but only for invisible parts.

It was the practice to paint furniture black and brick-red, and color played an important part in the interiors of the period, mainly owing to the skill and industry of the women. The embroideries, used for upholstering as well as for wearing apparel, were highly valued, as frequent mention of them in the wills of the period indicates. Hangings, cushions, and rugs were often richly embroidered in a variety of stitches, including turkey-work made by drawing gay-colored yarns through a coarse fabric, knotting and cutting them in imitation of Oriental rugs.

With the growth of a local aristocracy, portraits by visiting European artists were occasionally commissioned in the colony and paintings executed abroad were brought over by wealthier settlers. The dominant influence was the British style of portraiture—stiff, dignified, and with elaborate treatment of the textures and patterns of the sitter's costume.

Industry and Commerce

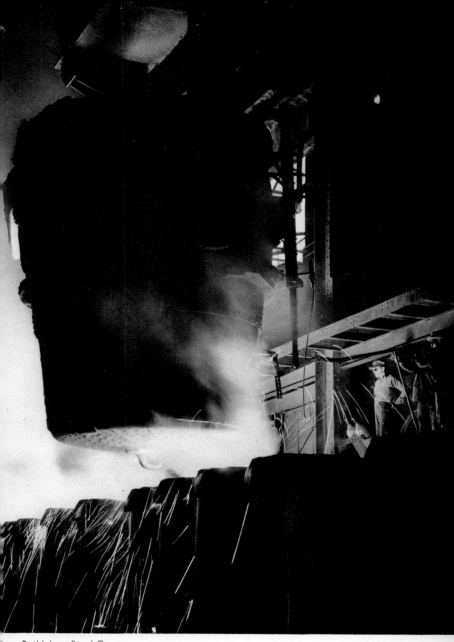

STEEL MILL

Holmes I. M

GIRL TESTING TELEPHONE WIRE, WESTERN ELECTRIC CO., BALTIMORE

CANNING FACTORY

WIRE MILL

CLIPPER SHIP

Kramer-Ba

nes I. Mettee

BALTIMORE SKYLINE

AIRVIEW, BALTIMORE HARBOR, WITH FORT McHENRY IN FOREGROUND

OYSTERING SKIPJACK, CHESAPEAKE BAY

OYSTER DREDGERS

DIAMONDBACK TERRAPIN

HAUL OF ROCK FISH, PATUXENT

IN A BALTIMORE CLOTHING FACTORY

Local portraiture may be said to begin with the arrival of Justus Engel-hart Kühn, who came to Annapolis during the year that it was granted a municipal charter by Governor Seymour in the name of Queen Anne. He was active as a painter there from 1708 to 1717, a period in which Annap-olis attracted wealthy planters from all parts of the province for the meet-ings of the General Assembly and the courts, and for the races and the social gaieties that centered around the governor and other officials.

Kühn's three large canvases of children, with baroque formal garden backgrounds, are very expressive; the figures have a primness that is not without charm, and the costumes and draperies in soft reds, terra cottas, browns, and blues are well painted. Besides accessory objects of interest— a parrot, a bobwhite, and a dog—in each of the three canvases, there is also in one the earliest example in American portraiture of a Negro slave— part of the background of the portrait of Henry Darnall III. The remain-ing seven of the ten extant portraits by Kühn are studies of local gentry, with costumes and backgrounds in somber dark browns and grays.

It might seem that such a painter would do well in a prosperous and cultured atmosphere, yet probate records reveal that Kühn died with more liabilities than assets. The latter included, in addition to his flute and 39 books, '14 pictures & Landskips' valued at £2.8.0 and several 'parcells of paint & all other things belonging to painting' at £7. No doubt the 'brass mortar & Pestle,' valued at 5s., was used for grinding the painter's colors.

About 1717, the Swedish painter and organ builder, Gustavus Hesselius (1682–1755), moved from Philadelphia to Maryland, receiving from the parish church of St.Barnabas in Queen Anne Parish 'the first commission on record for a work of art for a public building in America,' that of deco-rating the church. Of his Maryland period, covering the years between 1717 and 1735, little is known except what is gleaned from the church rec-ords and from the thirty or more Maryland and Virginia portraits extant. The satisfactory execution of several small commissions led the St.Barna-bas vestry to re-engage him in 1721 'to draw ye History of our Blessed Saviour and ye Twelve Apostles at ye last supper . . . Proportioned to ye space over the Altar piece . . .'

Hesselius received £17 for this elaborate commission. A work of consid-erable distinction, it is suggestive of early Italian paintings of the same subject.

In the 1750's John Hesselius (1728–78), son and pupil of Gustavus, came on painting expeditions to Maryland and finally settled in Annapolis, painting a number of portraits, including one of John Hanson, president

of the Continental Congress. It was here that he became the first teacher
of Charles Willson Peale (1741–1827), one of the outstanding artists of
early republican America.

Peale was born in Queen Annes County, Maryland, where his father
taught school, and the early part of his life is associated with this State.
Commissions he procured in Annapolis launched him on his artistic career,
and it was there that he received the financial support that enabled him to
go to London and attend the school of Benjamin West. Upon his return
from abroad he settled once more in Annapolis and painted many portraits in this city and in the outlying Maryland districts. His canvases of
Maryland dignitaries and prominent families represent the late Colonial
epoch at the height of its wealth and stability. During the 1760's Peale
gave instruction in painting to his younger brother, James (1749–1831),
who was born in Chestertown, Maryland, encouraging him to give up his
trade as a cabinetmaker and undertake miniature painting. Although he
achieved some successful large portraits and did many landscapes and
still-life compositions, the Maryland work of the younger Peale was almost exclusively in the miniature field.

Besides the school-trained artists of early Maryland, coach and sign
painters often turned to 'limning' and the painting of 'likenesses.' Some of
these craftsmen traveled in the outlying districts, especially in spring and
summer, and for a small fee or even for a night's lodging made portraits
of the farmers and their wives. To expedite their work, the itinerant artists carried with them canvases on which figures and backgrounds were
already painted, and the customer could choose the setting and costume
in which he wished his face to appear.

Caesar Ghiselin, flourishing in Annapolis from about 1715 until 1728,
was perhaps the first Maryland silversmith to devote himself exclusively
to this craft. The earliest silverware of established Maryland origin is,
however, a fine punch bowl made by John Inch of Annapolis for a prize in
a three-mile horse race run at Annapolis on May 4, 1743. Inch, to judge by
an advertisement in the *Maryland Gazette* of March 11, 1762, was a tavern-
keeper as well as a silversmith. Contemporary with Inch was Samuel
Soumaien, who also combined silversmithing with innkeeping; and William Faris (1728–1805), best of all Maryland colonial silversmiths, who
was a watch and clockmaker as well as an innkeeper in Annapolis.

Other prominent silversmiths who flourished in Annapolis between 1750
and 1775, during the period when the town had developed into a wealthy
and luxurious center with a pleasure-loving aristocracy patronizing its
taverns and buying silver spoons, ladles, plates, and goblets, were John

Patterson, James Chalmers, William Woodward, Thomas Sparrow, William Whetcroft, and Abraham Claude.

After the Revolution, painting in Maryland followed the general trend toward historical subjects led by artists who owed some part of their training to Benjamin West. One of James Peale's earliest works was a Revolutionary scene depicting the *Death of General Mercer at Princeton*. Painting in this transitional era continued to follow the English tradition, neither the political break of the Revolution nor the economic cleavage of the War of 1812 producing a corresponding separation in the cultural relations of the two countries. Outstanding artists of this period in Maryland were Robert Edge Pine (1742–90), an English historical painter and 'artist to the King,' and Rembrandt Peale (1778–1860), portraitist and allegorical and historical painter.

Pine came to this country in 1784 to do a series of pictures portraying the outstanding events of the Revolutionary struggle, but his activities were diverted primarily to portrait painting. Many of his portraits were painted in Baltimore and Annapolis, including one of General Smallwood, a distinguished officer in the Continental Army who afterwards became governor of Maryland. He later painted the *Carroll Family* in Annapolis.

Rembrandt Peale, who studied with West, was the outstanding Maryland portrait painter of the early part of the nineteenth century. Among his historical canvases are *Commander Warrington*, a hero of the War of 1812, and a painting of the American frigate *Constitution*. His allegorical *Court of Death*, exhibited in traveling shows, grossed almost $9,000 in admission fees. Like his father, Charles Willson Peale, Rembrandt Peale was extremely versatile and upon his return from Paris established a museum in Baltimore, opened in 1814 as 'an elegant rendezvous of taste, curiosity and leisure.' This museum, called the Gallery of Fine Arts, had on its walls no less than 64 portraits of illustrious men distinguished in the Revolutionary War, painted by Peale himself. The gallery, recently restored, is now the Municipal Museum. Raphael Peale (1774–1825), brother of Rembrandt, was born at Annapolis and did some work in Maryland, though most of his life was spent in Philadelphia. Recently there has been some revival of interest in his still-life paintings.

The Maryland Institute for the Promotion of the Mechanic Arts and the School of Fine and Practical Arts was organized in 1825 to provide instruction in various branches of art. It has continued to function until the present day, and its contribution to the arts of Maryland has been of incalculable value.

During the years between 1760 and 1820 the household crafts grew both in quantity and quality, and Maryland can boast of distinguished Colonial and early Republican cabinetmakers, silversmiths, potters, glass blowers, and cloth makers. This progress in local handiwork was stimulated mainly by the fact that Maryland planters were forced by prohibitive duties on British-made goods to turn their attention to native wares. Soon Maryland shops offered the well-to-do furniture, silver, glass, ceramics, metal work, and textiles with which to adorn themselves and their homes.

After the Revolution Annapolis declined as a commercial and shipping center, and many of its silversmiths moved to Baltimore. Patrick Sinnott, a Philadelphia jeweler, and watch and clockmaker, seems to have been the first silversmith in Baltimore; and by 1830 more than 200 silversmiths were practicing their craft in the city. Even small country towns had their silversmiths by the middle of the nineteenth century, for there were nearly 300 practitioners of the craft who are known to have worked in Maryland before 1830, including 10 in Easton, 4 in Chestertown, 4 in Frederick, and 9 in Hagerstown.

Baltimore is unique among American communities in requiring, under the law of 1814, the stamping of silver made in the city to ensure its purity. The term 'Baltimore hallmarks' has, however, been found erroneous, as the town never harbored any guild of silversmiths or 'hall' authorized to stamp silver as in England. This was entrusted to a public official called the Assayer of Silver Plate. Marking by the Assay Office was discontinued in 1830, after which silversmiths were required by law to stamp their own creations with numerals showing the proportion of pure silver.

The most prominent glassmaker in Maryland was John Frederick Amelung, who came from Germany and founded the New Bremen Glass Works in the latter part of the eighteenth century. Amelung, with his manufacture of 'all kinds of glassware, window glass from the lowest to the finest sorts, white and green bottles, wine and other drinking glasses, as also optical glasses and looking glasses finished complete,' achieved some national distinction as an artist and a merchant. In a letter to Thomas Jefferson, George Washington referred to the New Bremen works: 'A factory of glass is established upon a large scale . . . near Frederick in Maryland . . . that . . . will produce this year glass of various kinds to the amount of ten thousand pounds.' In March 1789 Amelung, garbed in full court costume, presented the President with the most excellent example of his art, 'two capacious goblets of flint glass, exhibiting the General's coat of arms.'

Collectors of early American glass compare and often confuse the products of Amelung with those of Stiegel of Pennsylvania, although Amelung's special pieces are judged superior to any glass produced by his competitor and predecessor. One of the most valuable pieces of glass in America today is the early engraved chalice made by Amelung during his first years at New Bremen and now on exhibition at the Metropolitan Museum in New York.

Numbered among the leading pioneers in American pottery, Edwin and William Bennett were the first to introduce the manufacture of Rockingham ware into this country. A yellow ware with a mottled glaze of brown and yellow, it was at the time (1846) considered a great advance in the art of pottery. Perhaps the most widely known single design produced in the country was the 'Rebecca at the Well' teapot, which the Bennetts originated. Made in rich, dark mottled glaze with figures in high relief, this design struck the popular fancy and was still a staple after more than 75 years, and potters all over the world copied it.

Shipwrights of Baltimore in colonial times adorned their clippers, barques, and smaller sailing vessels with elaborately-carved, painted and gilded figureheads. The carvers, nameless and forgotten, lavished painstaking care in the design and execution of these figureheads. Fancy nameboards were carved, painted, and gilded under the bowsprits, the letters and decorative scrolls being covered with gold leaf. With the termination of the sailing vessel era, shipwrights' carving became a craft of the past, except for the nameboard work, which is still produced in one or two Bay towns.

Private collections in the homes of wealthy men were an important factor in the progress of art in Maryland. One of the earliest of importance in the United States was that of Robert Gilmor, Jr. who died in 1848. Gilmor not only collected the works of the old masters but also gave orders to the prominent American artists of his day. Later patrons of art in Baltimore were Dr. Thomas Edmondson, Granville S. Oldfield, J. Collins Lee, and John H.B. Latrobe. Charles Eaton (1803–93) as a collector and patron purchased many pictures and other works of art in the course of frequent trips to Europe and bequeathed the greater part of his collection to the Peabody Institute.

Sculpture of the neoclassic (Italianate) school flourished in Baltimore during the period of national expansion (1820–60). Because it was the first American city where such imposing structures as the Washington and Battle monuments were erected, young Baltimore earned for itself the name of the Monumental City. The huge statue of Washington was executed by Henrico Causici, an Italian sculptor who had settled in Baltimore. The Battle Monument, commemorating the War of 1812, was dedicated in 1825. Antonio Cappellano, a pupil of Canova's living in Baltimore, was the sculptor.

National expansion and the development of industry and commerce turned the attention of American culture to the American scene. Artistic dependence upon England, which had continued long after the political ties were severed, slowly began to disappear with the rapid extension of the frontier. Landscape and genre painting commenced to take their place beside portraiture and historical painting and finally to displace them as a major trend. The influence of the romantic school of Düsseldorf gained the ascendency over the stolid neoclassicism of the British school.

In Maryland Alfred J. Miller (1810–74) might be said to represent this transition. Although he painted portraits and historical and allegorical themes, the new interest in landscape and genre manifest themselves in his best work. He made sketches in the Rocky Mountains for his interesting series of studies of the life of American Indians. Another painter of both historical subjects and genre was Frank B. Mayer (1827–99), who produced canvases picturing the many phases of life in Annapolis when that city was characterized as the Athens of America. The best-known of these, *My Lady's Visit*, is in the Maryland Historical Society gallery. His two historical paintings, *The Burning of the Peggy Stewart* and *The Founding of Maryland* are, however, considered his best works.

Other painters prominent in this movement were Charles Volkmar, Jr., John R. Tait (1834–1908), and Richard Caton Woodville (1820–55). Many of Volkmar's canvases were landscape paintings of considerable dimensions. A number of Tait's landscapes were bought by the German government during his twelve-year sojourn there and placed in art museums; Woodville, born in Baltimore, was a prolific painter of genre who studied the works of the Gilmor collection and later continued his education at Düsseldorf.

The disruption of national life at the close of the Civil War was followed by a tremendous advance in trade and communication with Europe. During the latter decades of the nineteenth century many artists left for Europe—some expatriating themselves temporarily, others permanently. On the other hand, the importation of works of art from abroad and the establishment of art organizations and public and private collections served as a stimulus to native artists. The Walters Art Gallery, founded in 1858, displayed to many for the first time the masterpieces of the French Barbizon School, which became a dominating influence in landscape painting during this period. Instruction to artists was furnished at the

Maryland Institute, and proximity to the art museums and schools of New York helped to broaden the vision and scope of Maryland artists.

The new turning to Europe resulted in a wide diversification of American painting and sculpture. In addition to the Barbizon style, the methods of Impressionism and the broad free-stroke technique of the Munich School were absorbed by American students abroad.

The Maryland artists of this period are recorded by Andrew John Henry Way (1826–88), who himself established a reputation for his portraiture and still-life pieces. Among the artists mentioned by Way were A.J.Volck, Louis Dieterich, and the landscapists, Hugh Newall and F.Hopkinson Smith (1838–1915). Hugh Bolton Jones (1848–1927), born in Baltimore, did landscapes in France, Spain, and North Africa and later in several New England States. Reuben Legrand Johnston belonged to the Barbizon school, painting in the 'polished, orderly and logical language' of Millet and Corot, and choosing as subjects the landscapes of Normandy and Brittany. Another Marylander, Harper Pennington, formed an undying admiration for Whistler's art and attached himself to the group of expatriates sojourning in London and Paris.

Among the portrait painters of more recent years Thomas C. Corner (1865–1937) was considered the dean. There is hardly a public building in Baltimore and other cities of the State that does not have a Corner portrait of some favorite son. He is also represented in the Virginia State Library at Richmond by the portrait of Governor F.W.Mackay Holliday.

Contemporary with Corner is George Bernhard Meyer, who, born in Germany in 1873 and educated at the Royal Academy in Dresden, has lived for more than thirty years in Baltimore. While listed in *Who's Who in American Art* as a miniature painter, he also excels in portraits and included among his subjects many of the leading doctors at the Johns Hopkins Hospital. Camelia Whitehurst (1875–1936) was well known for her portraits of children. Charles Yardley Turner (1850–1919) was an outstanding mural painter who was born in Baltimore and studied in New York at the National Academy and in Paris under Laurens, Munkacy, and Bonnat. His murals, *Calvert's Treaty with the Indians* and *The Burning of the Peggy Stewart*, are in the Baltimore Court House. Turner also assisted Francis D. Millet in the decoration of the World's Fair in Chicago in 1893. Here enormous spaces had to be covered in such a short time that the artists made use of a method of spraying paint invented by Thomas Turner, a brother of Charles.

R.McGill Mackall, muralist and portrait painter, was born in Baltimore in 1889. His murals in the Baltimore War Memorial and the Baltimore Trust Building are well executed. Another of his larger works is the chancel decoration in the First English Lutheran Church at Baltimore and Pulaski streets.

The Maryland Institute has been a major factor in the development of sculpture in the State, for it was there that William H. Rinehart (1825–74), 'the father of Maryland sculpture,' whose works are exhibited in the Metropolitan Museum in New York and other leading institutions, received the beginnings of his training. After him came a distinguished group of local sculptors including Ephraim Keyser, who was born in Baltimore in 1850 and studied in Munich and Berlin; Hans Schuler (b.1874), director of the Institute and sculptor of many Baltimore monuments; J.Maxwell Miller, born in Baltimore in 1877, and student at the Institute and at the Rinehart School as well as in Europe; Edward Berge (1876–1924), creator of the Watson and Armistead Monuments, Baltimore; Ben Kurtz, born in Baltimore in 1899, who has contributed busts and sculptural groups to many public buildings; and William Simpson (b.1903) now head of the Rinehart School.

Since early in the twentieth century, a new realism and various experimental strains imported from abroad have dominated American painting. These tendencies are reflected in the work of the younger Maryland artists. Abstraction and simplified design have become typical of an important branch of recent sculpture, while on the representational side the emphasis is on an increased fidelity to character and detail. In painting, scenes from local life executed in a variety of styles provide the most favored themes, with minor tendencies toward abstraction and social subjects. In connection with modern art, it is worth noting that Baltimore is the home of the Etta Cone collection, renowned among students of vanguard art; it includes a profusion of works by Matisse, Cezanne, Picasso, Renoir, Degas, Manet, and many others, as well as textiles, jewelry, and craft work. The collection, housed in Miss Cone's apartments, may be seen only by special permission.

An interesting development of recent years in which Maryland has shared is the Government sponsorship of art through the Fine Arts Division of the U.S.Treasury Department and the Arts Project of the Work Projects Administration. The Fine Arts Division awards commissions for murals and sculptures that are placed in post offices and other public buildings. The Art Project has been giving work to unemployed artists in a variety of fields, including sculpture, mural and easel painting, and the graphic arts. One of the most interesting of the Art Project departments is the Index of Design Division, which is reproducing in a series of documented drawings, watercolors, and photographs the work of early American folk artists and craftsmen.

Baltimore was one of the first American cities to establish art in its public schools, instruction in geometric drawing and design having been introduced into a high school course as early as 1845. As the result of an ever-growing demand, instruction in drawing and design had earned a place in the public elementary schools by 1872.

In the art galleries of Baltimore, much of the history of the arts and crafts in the State may be traced. The Maryland Historical Society houses a fine collection of early American portraits and many fine examples of old masters. Among the Colonial portraits of note are a Gilbert Stuart of George Washington, a number of portraits of Revolutionary generals by Charles Willson Peale, and the best examples of Rembrandt Peale's art.

One of the oldest and best private collections in the United States is in the Walters Art Gallery. This museum, which was bequeathed to Baltimore City in 1931, contains works of art of almost every period and country, including the paintings of the French Barbizon and American schools. Outstanding paintings by Millet, Corot, Rousseau, and Troyon adorn its walls, while other rooms are dedicated to the bronzes of Barye, other sculpture, priceless ceramics, and ivories.

The Baltimore Museum of Art, a municipally owned art gallery, contains valuable collections of old furniture, miniatures, silver, cut glass, old laces, the Antioch mosaics, the Jacob Epstein collection of paintings, the Rosenthal bronzes, and an outstanding collection of over 40,000 prints. It also has on display throughout the year a number of interesting exhibitions of the work of local, national, and international artists.

The Enoch Pratt Free Library houses (but does not own) early portraits of five of the Lords Baltimore, and of one Calvert who served as Colonial Governor of Maryland. Purchased privately in London, the portraits were brought to Maryland in November 1933—the 300th anniversary of the sailing of Cecil Calvert's ships from England.

Cookery

APPRECIATION of good food and the art of cooking it are traditional in Maryland, harking back to provincial days. Except for slight modifications and additions from Pennsylvania (chiefly of German origin), the predominating character of Maryland cooking is Southern.

F.Hopkinson Smith in his *Kennedy Square* (1911) sang the praise of a Maryland dinner in pre-Civil War days:

'. . . the soup as an advance guard—of gumbo or clams—or both if you chose; then a sheepshead caught off Cobb's Island the day before, just arrived by the dayboat, with potatoes that would melt in your mouth—in grey jackets these; then soft-shell crabs—big, crisp fellows, with fixed bayonets for legs, and orderlies of cucumbers . . . then the woodcock and green peas—and green corn—their teeth in a broad grin; then an olio of pineapple, and a wonderful Cheshire cheese, just arrived in a late invoice—and marvelous crackers—and coffee—and fruit (cantaloupes and peaches that would make your mouth water), then nuts . . .'

And this was the menu, not for a festive occasion, but of an average meal in a well-to-do Maryland home. No wonder Oliver Wendell Holmes praised Baltimore in his *Professor at the Breakfast Table* (1860) as 'the gastronomic metropolis of the Union.' 'Why,' he asks, 'don't you put a canvasback duck on top of the Washington column? Why don't you get the lady off from the Battle Monument and plant a terrapin in her place? Why will you ask for other glories when you have soft crabs . . . ?'

Those, of course, were the days when a simple buffet supper at a private dance would consist of terrapin, wild duck, olio (a salad), cold joints, and oysters in every conceivable style—all to be washed down with apple toddy, eggnog, and punch. The patriotic Maryland gourmet has reason for bemoaning the decay that has overtaken the cookery of his State. But that the former glory has not wholly passed away is shown by the presence of the names Baltimore, Chesapeake, and Maryland on menus from one end of the continent to another.

The variety as well as the local character of the culinary repertoire of the State is easily explained. The waters of the Chesapeake supply crabs, clams, and the famed oysters; and salt-water and fresh-water fish are plentiful. The tidewater regions produce a variety of wild fowl—duck, geese, swan, and brant. The mountain regions in western Maryland still yield an occasional deer, as well as wild turkey, ruffed grouse, and game fish. Throughout the State partridges, doves, rabbits, and even an occasional pheasant are found. Most sacred to epicures, however, is the diamondback terrapin, a land tortoise caught in the tidewater marshes and kept in the cellar against the day of his sacrifice. With such a wealth of native produce to draw upon, it is not surprising that Maryland should have made cooking her principal art.

Old-fashioned fried chicken, Maryland Style, has attained nation-wide fame, though discriminating Free Staters often have difficulty in recognizing the concoction of that name foisted on a gullible public outside the State. The standard recipe calls for a young chicken, cut into pieces, floured, and fried in deep fat. According to the oldest custom it is served on a layer of fried cornmeal mush or a crisp johnnycake with cream gravy poured over the cornbread but not over the chicken.

Another Maryland masterpiece, stuffed ham, is popular at Easter. A stuffing of greens and minced spring onions is inserted into openings half an inch apart in a parboiled ham, which is then sewed up in a clean white linen cloth, boiled a second time, and allowed to cool overnight. On being sliced, it reveals alternate stripes of pink and variegated green.

The choicest Maryland foodstuff, the diamondback terrapin, is no longer as plentiful as it once was. In 1797 the Maryland Assembly, fearing that slave owners would try to economize by serving terrapin to the exclusion of other meat, passed a law forbidding the feeding of terrapin to slaves more than once a week. Today the smallest count sells for $3 (counts are terrapin not less than five inches from end to end of the under shell), and genuine Maryland terrapin brings at least $2.50 a portion.

The ritual of preparing terrapin is subject only to minor variations. Authorities agree that a recipe is impossible and that judgment and taste rule every step of the operation. The terrapin, after being carefully washed, are dropped into boiling water and cooked until the expert decides they can be removed from the pot; the test is the ease with which the toenails can be pulled out. The terrapin are then laid on their backs (so that the shell holds the juices) and when cool enough to handle the front shell is removed. The meat and eggs are taken out and the liver is cut into small pieces. If the shell does not contain sufficient juice more is obtained by reducing to a jelly the water in which the terrapin was boiled. Butter is added in large quantities and a slight seasoning of salt, pepper, and a dash of cayenne. All other seasonings are taboo. The subtle and delicate flavor of the terrapin must not be smothered. The terrapin connoisseur is as horrified by terrapin seasoned with sherry as he is by an overdone canvasback duck. Sherry, or preferably dry madeira, should be served with the course.

Of equal merit with the chicken, ham, and terrapin are the sea foods from the waters that bound much of the State. Numerous 'raw bars' in the towns proffer Maryland oysters in a natural state and most restaurants and hotels serve fish daily.

Planked shad is a delicacy obtainable only during the spring runs. A whiteoak plank, about an inch and a quarter thick, with an indention in the shape of a fish, is used for the cooking. The shad is opened, cleaned, stuffed with bread, butter, salt, pepper, and sage, sewed up, placed on the preheated plank, and baked in a hot oven for about 40 minutes, before it is served on hot plates. A modern—and inferior—method of cooking is to bake the fish in a pan containing a cup of water. When the shad is taken from the pan, a half cup of milk, two tablespoons of tomato juice, and one teaspoonful of butter are added to the remaining water, all of which is brought to a boil and used as a sauce on the fish.

The crab is another staple among the sea foods of the State. Soft-shell crabs are very lightly sprinkled with salt and flour, then fried for about 20 minutes in butter and served with tartar sauce or gravy. Hard-shell crabs are steamed, made into crab cakes or soup, or deviled.

According to one time-honored recipe for deviled crabs, two tablespoonfuls of flour are rubbed into one of butter and put into two cups of hot milk. When the mixture comes to a boil, two pounds of crab meat are added and a well-beaten egg is stirred in. The shells of the crabs are then rubbed with onion, filled with the mixture, covered with bread crumbs, and browned in a moderate oven.

Striped bass, butterfish, sea trout, herring, hardheads (or croakers), white and yellow perch, eels, catfish, and carp are also among Maryland's more common food fish.

Strangers are often shocked by the Maryland custom (imported long ago from Pennsylvania) of serving sauerkraut with roast turkey, goose, duck, or chicken. One Thanksgiving or Christmas dinner, however, is usually enough to win even the most recalcitrant New Englander to the custom.

A discussion of Maryland cooking would not be complete without mention of beaten biscuit, produced by generations of cooks who would have considered that a recipe degraded their art into a trade. One and all of these *virtuosi* would have assured the reader that Maryland biscuit made by rule is an impossibility and a sacrilege. But for the benefit of the curious the following instructions are included: Rub ⅓ tablespoonful of lard thoroughly into ½ pint of flour, into which ⅓ teaspoonful of salt has been sifted. Moisten with enough milk and water, half and half, to make a very stiff dough. Knead for 5 minutes and beat wholeheartedly with a hatchet (or paddle) for 30 minutes. Make into small biscuits and prick on top with a fork. Bake in a moderate oven for 20 minutes.

Another illustration of the methods that placed emphasis upon quality rather than speed is the recipe for Maryland apple toddy as it *should* be made. About Thanksgiving a dozen large red apples are baked until their skins burst. While still piping hot, they are covered with a mixture of spirits, usually in the proportions of 1 quart brandy, ½ pint rum, and ½ pint peach brandy. After being sweetened to taste and, according to some recipes seasoned with nutmeg, allspice, and clove, they are sealed in a stone jar. And woe unto him who opens it before Christmas Day!

Though the best Maryland cooking is found in private homes, hotels and other public eating places have had their share in making Maryland food famous. Among the better-known of the old inns were the Fountain, the Indian Queen, and the General Wayne inns, Guy's Hotel and Barnum's Hotel, several of which were along old Market Street (now Baltimore Street) in Baltimore. In addition there were numerous oyster 'bays' or bars, usually in cellars, each with its distinctive clientele. Most famous of these was one on South Street near Lovely Lane, run by a Scotsman named Boyd, and frequented by many of the actors of its day.

After the presidential election of 1936, Maryland hospitality was sampled by the Republican candidate, Alfred M. Landon, at a dinner given by H.L.Mencken. The menu included:

Chesapeake Bay Oysters
Olives   Stuffed Celery   Nuts
Terrapin a la Maryland
Maryland Beaten Biscuits
Fried Chicken a la Maryland
Cream Sauce
Grilled Bacon
Corn Fritters   Potato Croquettes
Maryland Ham
Maryland Hearts of Lettuce
Maryland Water Ice

And good Maryland rye whiskey was used in the cocktails.

It is Maryland's belief that Mr.Landon was somewhat consoled for the loss of the election.

PART II
Cities

Annapolis

Railroad Stations: Bladen St. Station, Bladen St. near Armory Place, for Baltimore & Annapolis R.R. (electric interurban).
Busses: Interurban to Washington from Bladen St. Station; Arundel Bus Co., 8 Creek View Ave., Eastport, to Eastport and Bay Ridge with city stops.
Taxis: Fare 25¢ within city limits.
Traffic Regulations: Speed limit 25 m.p.h.; one hour parking in business district; one-way traffic around State Circle and Church Circle.

Information Service: Chamber of Commerce, State Circle at East St.; A.A.A., Carvel Hall Hotel, Prince George St.; Baltimore & Ohio R.R. Ticket Office, 54 Maryland Ave.; Pennsylvania R.R. Ticket Office, 51 Maryland Ave.; Travel Service Bureau, 68 Maryland Ave.

Accommodations: 2 large hotels, 10 small hotels and inns; tourist camps in environs.

Motion Picture Houses: 3.
Ferries: Annapolis-Matapeake Ferry, foot of King George St., hourly, 50¢ one-way, 85¢ round trip; automobiles $1.50 and up.
Libraries: The Public Library of Annapolis and Anne Arundel County, Church Circle at Franklin St., 9–5 weekdays, 9–12:30 Saturdays; State Library, Court of Appeals Building, Bladen St. at State Circle, 9–2 weekdays; St.John's College Library; and Naval Academy Library (for research only).
Tennis: St.John's College courts, College Ave., under supervision of Annapolis Tennis Club during summer, permits to public, small fee.
Golf: Annapolis Roads Golf Club (semiprivate), Bay Ridge Road, 9 holes, greens fee 50¢.
Riding: Mary Helen's Riding Academy, Central Ave., near Parole, $1 an hour.
Fishing: Boats, bait, equipment, and guides for hire at water front by hour or day.

Annual Events: U.S.Naval Academy June Week; Annapolis Yacht Club Regatta, latter part of August; Garden Club Tour of Historic Houses, May; St.Margaret's Horse Show (St.Margaret's, near Annapolis), May; West Annapolis Firemen's Fair, July; Waterwitch Fire Department Fair, June.

ANNAPOLIS (20 alt.,12,531 pop.) is neutral ground where Baltimore and the counties of Maryland meet every other January in legislative session and try to iron out their conflicting interests. The only capital deliberately laid out in colonial times primarily as the seat of government, Annapolis by a peculiar combination of circumstances has retained much of its pre-Revolutionary flavor. Here no filling stations and garages are hidden behind Georgian façades and no tourist hostesses in sprigged and ruffled skirts give a carefully studied atmosphere of quaintness; yet the city has that air of age and gracious dignity found only where old centers of wealth and culture have kept their importance but have not been overwhelmed by industry and commerce. Its tree-shaded streets are too narrow for modern traffic; otherwise the town has easily adapted itself to its modern role of capital of a commercial and industrial State and seat of the Nation's naval academy.

Annapolis is on the south bank of the wide Severn, near its mouth. The first settlers of the region were Puritans who arrived by invitation in 1648 from Virginia, where their militant dogmatism had made them unwelcome. Within seven years, however, Maryland was greatly to regret its hospitable gesture, for the Puritans of the Severn area—then called Providence—took advantage of victories in England and tried to seize the provincial government. Governor William Stone came up the Chesapeake to establish order but his unarmed vessels were no match for the armed merchantman *Golden Lion*, whose master had turned it to the service of the Puritans. The governor was defeated at Herring Bay, just below the Severn's mouth, on March 25, 1655. But shortly after the Restoration in England the Puritans began to lose power in Maryland, though they continued to exercise a disturbing role.

A tiny community gradually developed on the peninsula here, and was known as Anne Arundel Town, taking its name from the county, which had been named for the wife of the second Lord Baltimore.

As settlement progressed in the province (there was a population of nearly 25,000) increasing objection was made to remote St.Marys as the capital. In 1683 the experiment had been made of moving the courts and assembly to 'the ridge in Anne Arundel County' but lack of accommodations had forced the government's return to the old town.

Soon after Sir Francis Nicholson arrived as second royal governor he determined to establish a more central capital and selected the site by the Severn. The decision caused much anguish in St.Marys County where, as protesting landowners pointed out, many had invested in less fertile lands because of their proximity to the seat of government. Their long memorial pointed out the cost of removing courts and records, the cost of new buildings, the advantages of a defensible harbor by the capital. To offset the disadvantage of remoteness from large parts of the province they offered to provide 'a coach or caravan or both' to go daily during all courts and assemblies, and once a week at all other times, between St.Marys and the Patuxent; they also offered to 'keep constantly a dozen horses at least with suitable furniture for any person or persons having occasion to ride post or otherwise with or without a guide' to any part of the Western Shore. These frantic offers were made in vain; the assembly pointed out that the new site had the advantage of being nearer New York 'and other Governments,' and the first meeting in the new capital was held in the house of Edward Dorsey on February 28, 1695.

Nicholson was a progressive administrator. In laying out the new capital he kept convenience and vistas in mind. Streets radiated from State Circle, where the capitol was to be built; a second circle was designed for an Anglican church; shipping and trade districts were zoned; lots were measured off in a residential district for the prosperous and influential, and smaller ones for the artisans and working men—in another part of town. These smaller lots were also provided with a common, Bloomsbury Square, where the lower classes could have their games and frolics. The new capital was named for Princess Anne—later Queen of England. Nicholson had been transferred to Maryland from Virginia, where as lieutenant governor he had been very helpful to the Virginians in the founding of the college they had long wanted—William and Mary at Williamsburg. In 1696 he persuaded the assembly to grant a charter to King William's School, to be opened at Annapolis.

Nicholson's new capital was laid out at a time when the province had passed its frontier stage, when fertile soil and slavery had begun to stock the houses with European luxuries, and plantation owners could spend much more time on social activities. But though Annapolis very soon became the chief center of business and political life in the colony, it was nearly half a century before leaders of provincial affairs began to build the houses that are the city's pride today. From the earliest time there was a lively male social life during the meetings of the assembly and on the occasions when the planters came to town on business or brought their wives and daughters in to inspect the latest importations of the factors. Eventually the assemblymen brought their wives and daughters with them to enjoy the social events held during the legislative sessions; in 1744 visitors were commenting on the elegance of the clothing worn by the young ladies attending the 'Assembly balls,' which were held in a house with 'a back room for wines, punch and sweetmeats, and the playing of cards, dice and backgammon.' These balls lasted until one in the morning and it was customary for the gentlemen to escort their partners home—Annapolis was no stiff-backed Boston.

Yet as late as 1762 the Philadelphian Benjamin Mifflin reported that 'altho there are several Large Buildings with Capacious Gardens, I did not See One with any Degree of Elegance or Taste.' But Annapolis was evolving from 'a parcel of wooden houses' into a city of stately residences and public buildings, where the gaieties and elegances of eighteenth-century London were cultivated with all the exaggerated enthusiasm of a provincial capital. Opulent tobacco planters were building elaborate town houses in which they wined and dined away the time between fox hunts and racing meets. The Tuesday Club, the Homony Club, the South River Club, administered the 'gelastic law' to offenders and celebrated every possible event with 'toasts loyal and amorous, our stomachs keen to relish our fare and our punch-bowls always replete with nectarious liquor.'

The French and Indian War did not greatly disturb most of the inhabitants, though Governor Sharpe, acting under orders from England, had a bad time of it and little opportunity to give the grand parties at White Hall that were his delight. Even the early events of the Revolution did not disturb the city. Racing, dancing, and gaming went on more briskly than ever. When George Washington came over for a few days in September 1771 he lost £8 at the races, went four times to the theater, and danced at three balls. A year later between Sunday and Friday he again managed to go four times to the theater and to one ball, to lose five pounds sixpence at cards but win thirteen and seven at the races.

The golden age gradually gave way to the turmoil of the American Revolution, with Charles Carroll and Daniel Dulany at loggerheads over the question of loyalty or rebellion and all colonists beginning to take sides. When the Stamp Act was passed in 1765 Zachariah Hood, stamp agent sent from England, was not permitted to land and was hanged and burned in effigy. After Hood had landed secretly, he met with such a warm reception that he fled to Long Island and resigned his office. The brig *Peggy Stewart* arrived on October 14, 1774, with a cargo of tea, after the colonists had signed their nonimportation agreements. Andrew Stewart, part owner, had already offended the townspeople by attempting to evade their regulations. After several days of discussion, he was made to set fire to the vessel as well as to the cargo. Local tension increased rapidly but tempers were kept well in hand. When it became clear that war was unavoidable, the Maryland Convention suggested with polite attestations of friendship that it would be better if Governor Robert Eden should leave. In an equally friendly manner he acceded and sailed on June 24, 1776— though he was to return in 1783 as a visitor.

Fortifications were erected at the mouth of the Severn but though British vessels passed up and down the Bay there were no attacks; American troops passed through on their way from one field of operations to another; Annapolis watched the war without being unduly excited by it. The last years frequently were enlivened by the presence of the French under Rochambeau and Lafayette. The French officers and the Annapolis ladies, even those of Tory sympathies, were charmed with one another.

The new Congress of the United States met here from November 26, 1783, to June 3, 1784.

After the Revolution Baltimore began to forge ahead with the opening up of the western routes; the Tories of the old aristocracy had either fled or been impoverished; and other men of wealth were drawn to the rising city of the north.

In 1808 after *H.M.S.Leopard* had attacked the *U.S.S.Chesapeake* and war seemed imminent, the government built Fort Severn on Windmill Point. This stronghold apparently prevented the British from attacking the city during the War of 1812, for, though squadrons more than once anchored near the mouth of the river, they sailed away without attempting to capture the little capital.

Fort Severn was garrisoned by the army until 1845, when the post was transferred to the navy. In 1850 it became the United States Naval Academy, the source of much of the city's present vitality.

During the Civil War Annapolitans were predominantly Southern in sympathy but engaged in no acts of violence. General Benjamin F. Butler, on his way to Washington with Massachusetts troops, heard of the Baltimore riot of April 19, 1861, and sailed past that city to Annapolis on the Perryville-Havre de Grace ferryboat. After remaining for about a month and sending several regiments to Washington, he moved to Baltimore. Annapolis was out of the way of military operations and saw the effects of war only in the multitude of wounded, who were hospitalized at St.John's College and the Naval Academy, and the prisoners concentrated there and later removed to Camp Parole on the outskirts.

Since the Civil War Annapolis has prospered by the expansion of the Naval Academy; but its population has only a little more than trebled. Life is organized around two institutions—the State government and the

Academy. During the first months of every other year, while the assembly is in session, Annapolis is host to the thousands who have business to transact for or with the State of Maryland, and during June Week of every year, commencement time at the Academy, the town is thronged with relatives, friends, and sweethearts of the middies. Caring for visitors is an important activity, but Annapolis also transacts business for the farmers of southern Maryland, packs sea food, and builds log canoes, pungies, and other small craft.

Annapolis has had just enough prosperity to save itself from dinginess and decay; the tendency has been, particularly in recent years, to restore the old buildings and design new ones to harmonize with them. Thus, although it is not the oldest of the American cities, it has earned and is determined to keep its appellation, 'the Ancient City.'

POINTS OF INTEREST

1. The STATE HOUSE, in State Circle, a severe brick building surmounted by a tall, white-painted octagonal dome and cupola, contains the legislative chambers and the governor's and adjutant general's offices. The first statehouse on the site, called the Stadt House in deference to King William's Dutch origin, was completed in 1697. Its successor, completed in 1706, was reduced to such condition by 65 years of use that it came to be looked upon as 'the emblem of public poverty,' and was torn down. Construction of the present structure, designed by Joseph Clark, was begun in 1772. Its roof was sheathed with copper until a fierce gale tore the copper off and rolled it up 'like a scroll.'

The main entrance, facing the east, is protected by a one-story pedimented Corinthian portico with marble floor, wooden columns, iron capitals, and cast-iron railing; it is obviously a later addition. The portal opens into a wide arcaded hall of similar classic order under the central dome, which has arched and oval windows and delicate plaster interior ornament in the Adam style, completed in 1793. It is the work of Thomas Dance

---

KEY FOR ANNAPOLIS MAP

1.State House 2.Old Treasury 3.Calvary M.E. Church 4.Court of Appeals Building 5.Executive Mansion 6.St.Anne's (P.E.) Church 7.Anne Arundel County Court House 8.Public Library of Annapolis and Anne Arundel County 9.Postoffice 10.State Office Building 11.Pinkney House 12.St.John's College 13.Ogle House 14.Chase Home 15.Hammond-Harwood House 16.Bordley-Randall House 17.Dorsey House 18.Jennings House 19.Carvel Hall Hotel 20.Brice House 21.Aunt Lucy's Bake Shop 22.Sands House 23.Market Space 24.Masonic Temple 25.City Hall 26.Ridout House 27.St.Mary's (R.C.) Church 28.Scott House 29.Jonas Green House 30.Maryland Avenue Gate of the U.S. Naval Academy 31.Naval Academy Museum 32.Herndon Monument 33.Japanese Bell 34.Naval Academy Chapel 35.Dahlgren Hall 36.Thompson Stadium 37.Bancroft Hall 38.Tecumseh Statue 39.MacDonough Hall 40.Luce Hall 41.Mexican Monument 42.Mahan Hall 43.Macedonian Monument 44.Maury Hall 45.Sampson Hall 46.Tripoli Monument 47.Isherwood Hall

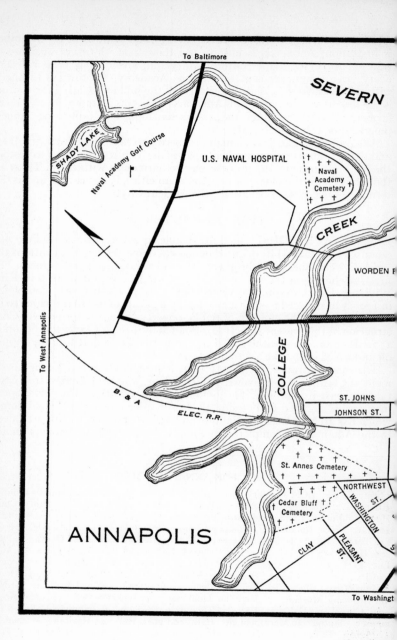

To Baltimore

SEVERN

SHADY LAKE

Naval Academy Golf Course

U.S. NAVAL HOSPITAL

Naval Academy Cemetery

CREEK

WORDEN F

To West Annapolis

COLLEGE

B. & A.

ELEC. R.R.

ST. JOHNS

JOHNSON ST.

St. Annes Cemetery

NORTHWEST ST.

WASHINGTON ST.

Cedar Bluff Cemetery

ANNAPOLIS

CLAY

PLEASANT ST.

To Washingt

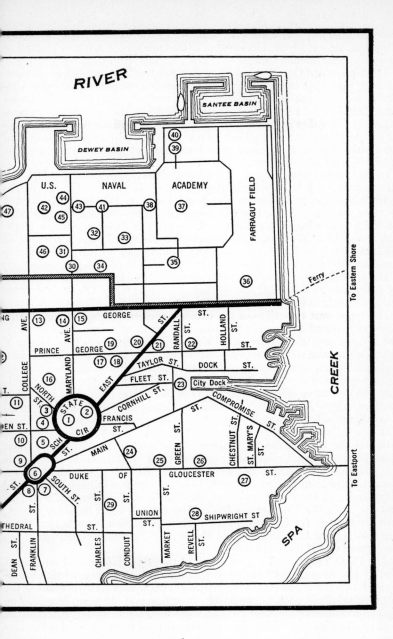

RIVER

SANTEE BASIN

DEWEY BASIN

40
39

U.S.   NAVAL   ACADEMY   FARRAGUT FIELD

47

44
42
45

43   41   38

37

32   33

46   31

30   34

35

36

To Eastern Shore

Ferry

CREEK

NG   13   14   15   GEORGE   ST.   ST.   HOLLAND

PRINCE   GEORGE   19   20   21   RANDALL   22   ST.

17   18   TAYLOR   ST.   DOCK   ST.

16   FLEET   ST.   23   City Dock

11   CORNHILL   ST.   COMPROMISE   ST.

3   1   2   FRANCIS   ST.

EN ST.   4   ST.

10   5   MAIN   24   GREEN   CHESTNUT   ST.

9   25   26   ST. MARY'S

6   DUKE   OF   GLOUCESTER   27   ST.

8   7   SOUTH ST.   ST.

29   UNION   28   SHIPWRIGHT ST

THEDRAL   ST.   ST.

DEAN   ST.   CHARLES   CONDUIT   MARKET   REVELL   SPA

FRANKLIN   ST.   ST.   ST.   ST.

To Eastport

who was killed by a fall from the scaffold. In the hall are portraits of two Maryland signers of the Declaration of Independence, Charles Carroll of Carrollton and Samuel Chase.

The high-ceiled OLD SENATE CHAMBER has brightly painted green plaster walls and white trim. Over the entrance is a curved balustraded visitors' gallery, supported by fluted Ionic columns. Spectators also sit under the gallery behind a low paneled screen. Opposite the entrance is a circular, stepped speaker's platform with its chair in a pedimented niche. Typical of late Georgian Colonial design are the twenty-four-paned sash windows with deep paneled reveals, window seats and inner shutters, and the classically trimmed fireplace.

In this room the new Congress of the United States met from November 16, 1783, to June 3, 1784; on December 23, it received George Washington's resignation as commander in chief and on January 14 it ratified the treaty of peace signed in Paris the preceding September. Charles Willson Peale's painting of Washington, Lafayette, and Colonel Tench Tilghman (an aide of Washington's) is over the fireplace. Peale's portrait of William Pitt is in the Senate Retiring Room; also portraits of Thomas Stone and William Paca, signers of the Declaration of Independence.

The OLD HALL OF DELEGATES is opposite the Old Senate Chamber. In the retiring room adjoining are old flags, including United States flags carried by Maryland troops during the Revolution.

The large west extension of the capitol, approached by a deep Corinthian portico and designed in the neoclassic style, was completed in 1905. The present Senate chamber on the north and the chamber of the House of Delegates on the south are almost identical—square and decorated in a modified Italian Renaissance style with marble columns and vaulted arcades; both have skylighted ceilings of stained glass. In the marble corridors and executive offices are portraits of Maryland governors and other notables. Above the landing of the main stairway is a large painting (1859) of Washington tendering his resignation as commander in chief, by Edwin White.

Before the east entrance is a bronze statue of Roger Brooke Taney, Chief Justice of the United States; the work of William H. Rinehart, it is a duplicate of a bronze in Mt. Vernon Place, Baltimore. To the left is a statue by Ephraim Keyser of Baron de Kalb, who was killed while leading Maryland and Delaware troops at the Battle of Camden, S.C., on August 16, 1780. To the right is one of the cannon from St. Mary's Fort, brought by the *Ark* in 1634. Father White's *Relation* records that these *tormenta majora* held the Indians thunderstruck because they were 'so much more vocal' than bowstrings.

2. The OLD TREASURY, just south of the State House and now occupied by the Annapolis Chamber of Commerce, is a one-story brick building with two low wings giving it a cruciform plan. Especially notable is the entrance vestibule with heavy batten door hung on old strap hinges. The vaulted rooms of the interior have modern metal ceilings decorated in the Adam style with bell-and-flower festoons around the walls and delicately carved mantelpieces. It was built about 1695 and used in early days as a

council chamber. Its later use (1837–1903) accounts for the iron doors and massive locks and hinges.

3. CALVARY METHODIST CHURCH (1923), corner State Circle and North Street, is an impressive square brick building of Georgian Colonial design with hip roof and octagonal cupola. The windowless façade is relieved only by a slightly projecting central pavilion, accented with corner quoins and eave pediment. The paneled doorway, framed by wooden pilasters cut with beveled joints to simulate rusticated stone, is topped with a segmental pediment. The galleried interior is less traditional in style.

4. The COURT OF APPEALS BUILDING (1900), behind the State House, is a neoclassic structure of brick and white limestone, with a tall Ionic colonnade facing the Executive Mansion. Three stained-glass windows over the main stair show the ancient and modern Great Seals of Maryland. The central window represents the seal of 1648 (preserved in the Land Office, Hall of Records Building), which Lord Baltimore described as '. . . our Figure in Compleat Armour on Horse Back with our Sword drawn and our Helmett on and a Great Plume of Feathers affixed to it the Horsetrappings furniture and Caparisons being adorn'd with the figure of our Paternal Coat of Arms and underneath the Horse a Sea Shoar engraven with Certain Flowers and Grass Growing upon it . . .' To the left is the reverse of the old seal, showing the full Baltimore arms; to the right is the modern version, adopted in 1876. Besides the Court of Appeals, the supreme court of the State, the building houses the State comptroller's and the treasurer's offices.

The STATE LIBRARY (*open daily* 9–3), at the west end of the second floor, contains a large legal collection, a complete file of the *Maryland Gazette*, and the four volumes of Audubon's *Birds of America*.

5. The EXECUTIVE MANSION, between State and Church Circles, was built in 1866 and remodeled in 1936, when the mansard roof and other mid-Victorian features were replaced by broad gables, Palladian windows, and end chimneys more in harmony with the older buildings of the town. Additions made at this time include the one-story flanking wings. The governor's offices in the right wing are approached by a separate entrance facing State Circle. The broad semicircular lawn, enclosed by an iron picket fence, is crossed by a long tile-paved walk bordered with low boxwood.

6. ST.ANNE'S CHURCH, in Church Circle, erected in 1859, is architecturally undistinguished. It has a square clock tower, octagonal steeple, and circular apse. This is the third church built here for St.Anne's or Middle Neck Parish since it was established in 1692. Governor Nicholson contracted with Edward Dorsey in 1696 for construction of the first, and when not even a foundation had been laid by 1699, Dorsey was fined £200 and required to repay the £333. 6. 8 advanced to him. The church was finished by others before 1704. But the parishioners were so little interested in the building that by the 1770's it was in such condition that a poet complained:

> Here in Annapolis alone
> God has the meanest house in town.

The second church, on which construction began soon after this lament, was completed in 1792 and destroyed by fire in 1858. The silver communion service, made by Francis Garthorne of London in 1695, bears the arms of King William.

7. The ANNE ARUNDEL COUNTY COURTHOUSE, Church Circle and Franklin St., is a large brick block with domed cupola and two-story arcaded entrance porch. Built in 1824, it was enlarged in 1892 and again in 1925. The Will Office served the whole province, and testamentary papers dating from 1634 were here until the new Hall of Records was opened.

8. The PUBLIC LIBRARY OF ANNAPOLIS AND ANNE ARUNDEL COUNTY, Church Circle and Franklin St., is in the Reynolds Tavern, built in 1737. The two-story building has a dormered gambrel roof and end chimneys. The most notable features are the brickwork, laid in all-header bond, the unusual arched stringcourse between the first and second stories, and the arched and gabled portico with its delicate wooden railing. The latter detail is seen also on the portico of the Ogle House at the corner of King George Street and College Avenue.

9. The POST OFFICE (1910), Church Circle and Northwest St., is a dignified two-story brick building with wood and sandstone trim designed in the late Georgian style. The rectangular structure is crowned with a dormered hip roof surrounded by a balustrade. On the roof is a beautiful octagonal cupola with gilded dome and weather-vane.

10. The H-shaped STATE OFFICE BUILDING, College Ave. and Bladen St., completed in 1939, is designed in a neo-Georgian style with crowning cupola. The three-and-one-half-story structure houses State offices previously quartered in Baltimore.

11. The PINKNEY HOUSE, 5 St. John St., a two-and-one-half-story brick structure with pedimented doorway, is said to have been built on designs by John Callahan in 1750. Here was born William Pinkney, who became attorney general of the State in 1805, minister extraordinary to Great Britain in 1806, and Attorney General of the United States in 1811. The house, moved from its first site on Bladen Street and College Avenue, is now the infirmary of St. John's College. The stuccoed wing at the rear is a later addition.

12. ST. JOHN'S COLLEGE, housed in a group of ivy-covered brick buildings on College Avenue, is nonsectarian and uncompromisingly non-coeducational; a president who urged coeducation was obliged to resign. St. John's was chartered in 1784 and in 1785 the college acquired the funds of King William's School, to which it is usually regarded as a successor. The latter institution, which was not a college, was established by the assembly in 1696. Like its predecessor, St. John's enjoyed eminent patronage, numbering all the Maryland signers of the Declaration of Independence among the petitioners for its establishment. George Washington sent his nephews, Fairfax and Lawrence Washington, to St. John's in 1794 and his wife's grandson, George Washington Parke Custis, in 1798. Other early alumni were Francis Scott Key and Reverdy Johnson. St. John's was taken over for camp and hospital purposes during the Civil War.

In 1937 a new educational program was introduced, designed to give a broad and integrated command of the accumulated intellectual resources of western civilization. A hundred great and representative books from every age were selected as a nucleus, and the whole curriculum made to revolve around them.

McDOWELL HALL, the administration building, was named for the first president of the college. The large square brick building, with its broad hip roof and octagonal cupola, has an air of complacent dignity. Its history goes back to 1742 when the assembly authorized Governor Thomas Bladen to buy four acres of land and build 'a Dwelling House and other Conveniences for the Residence of the Governor of *Maryland* for the Time being,' the cost not to exceed £4,000. Bladen employed Simon Duff, a Scot, to build the house. Two years later a request for £2,000 more to complete the mansion turned the assembly against the project and the building was left unroofed. Benjamin Mifflin, a Philadelphian visiting Annapolis in 1762, 'Viewd Bladens Folly as the Inhabitants Call it, the ruins of a Spacious Building began by Govr Bladen but carried no further than the Brick Work & Joists 2 Stories High but if Finished would have been a Beautifull Edifice.' After forty years of neglect the building was turned over to the college and completed. When Lafayette visited Annapolis in 1824 it was the scene of two banquets and a ball in his honor. After the old building was burned in 1909 it was reconstructed along the orginal lines. The projecting one-story entrance portico leads into a large two-story central hall, now used for assemblies, with a continuous open gallery. The hall is furnished in keeping with the Colonial period and holds some old manuscripts of interest.

The library in WOODWARD HALL, at the eastern end of the campus, contains 34,000 volumes, among them some 400 from the collection brought by Thomas Bray in 1696 to found the first public library in Maryland (*see Religion*). Among the documentary oddities preserved here are a citizen's application for permission to keep his cow on the campus, and State lottery tickets of 1830, including one on which the college president won a cask of wine. The façade is embellished by a two-story Corinthian colonnade.

The LIBERTY TREE, in front of Woodward Hall, is a tulip poplar 29 feet in circumference, festooned with trumpet creeper and ivy, and believed to be more than 600 years old. The treaty of 1652 with the Susquehannock is said to have been signed beneath it. Revolutionary meetings held in its shade earned it its present name. In 1840 boys ignited gunpowder in its hollow trunk, setting it afire; citizens rushed out with as much zeal as though a public building were threatened and succeeded in saving the tree. The next spring, having been freed of parasites by the heat, it burst into leaf with exceptional vigor.

13. The OGLE HOUSE, College Ave. and King George St., was built in 1742 by Samuel Ogle, three times provincial governor. The gray-painted brick dwelling has a steep gable roof and wide built-in end chimneys. The main entrance on King George Street opens on a modern open porch, is flanked by engaged Doric columns and topped with a triglyphed entablature. The windows of the five-bay façade have double-hung sashes set

back from the face of the wall without the usual trim. A later wing with a porch forms an L at the rear. An entrance on the right side is protected by a hooded and pedimented portico with two slender columns. The narrow doorway opening from a corner bedroom onto a small wooden balcony is probably of later construction.

14. The CHASE HOME (25¢ *expected for endowment fund*), 22 Maryland Ave., is a hip roofed, three-story dwelling of late Georgian Colonial design on a shaded lawn surrounded by a white picket fence. At the left side is a three-story, white-columned portico, the upper stories of which have been added recently. The broad façade has three windows closely spaced in the pedimented central pavilion. The brick walls laid in Flemish bond are accented with window headings, belt courses, and base mold of hand-rubbed brick. The entrance with its Ionic columns and pilasters, crowning fanlight and pediment is flanked by two windows under a heavy dentiled and modillioned cornice. The interior is rich in ornamental plaster and woodwork, and in the parlor and dining room are two fine marble mantels. Opposite the entrance in the wide central hall is an Ionic colonnaded screen and beyond it an impressive staircase rising in a single flight to a landing and dividing into two flights to the upper floor. Above the landing is a large Palladian window. The most notable feature of this open-string stairway is the serpentine surface of the under side of the steps. The upper hall has arched and pedimented doorways and two large wall niches. Other notable features of the interior include a fine Adam coffered ceiling in the parlor (L) and unusually elaborate trim in the dining room (R)—heavy molded architraves with the dog-eared corners and heavy rope twists, and doorways topped with broken pediments—all painted white against Nile-green plaster walls. The paneled doors in this room, of dark mahogany, have handles of silver. The paneled window shutters, with octagonal medallions and rosettes, are of similar pattern to those in the Hammond-Harwood House and in the front parlor of the Paca House—probably the work of the same craftsman.

Construction of the house was begun by Samuel Chase, the signer, in 1769; it was sold in 1771 to Edward Lloyd, later governor of the State, who completed it in 1774. Its last owner, Mrs. Hester Ann Chase Ridout, bequeathed it to the Protestant Episcopal Church as 'a home for destitute, aged and infirm ladies,' which was opened in 1897.

15. The HAMMOND–HARWOOD HOUSE (*adm.* 25¢), opposite the Chase Home, was built in 1770–74 by Matthias Hammond, a close friend of Colonel Lloyd. One story lower than the Chase dwelling, according to tradition, it was kept at this height so that Lloyd's view of the harbor would not be obstructed. The symmetrical building, typical of the Georgian manor houses in this area, consists of a five-bay central section with two-story flankers connected by covered passages. The fronts of these flankers have octagonal bays; the one at the left formerly contained the house office. The main entrance flanked by low boxwood is framed with engaged Ionic columns and pediment. The second-story window above is trimmed with a wide architrave and ornamented with sill brackets and crowning cornice. A small bull's eye window in the central eave pediment is framed

with a somewhat rococo trim. The plan of the main block of the house is not symmetrical, having a short central hall with classically trimmed doors opening into a large dining room (L) in the rear, an enclosed stair-hall (R), and two front parlors. The kitchen, in the right flanker, with brick paved floor and huge fireplace, is at a lower level.

The interior woodwork is in general more delicately and intricately carved than that of the Chase House. The windows have unusually high sills permitting a wide wainscot of matched boarding and heavy chair rail and base mold. The most elaborate rooms are the dining room and the large ballroom directly above. Their woodwork is richly carved with beads, acanthus leaves, scrolls, interlaces, and gauge work. Especially notable are the headings of the dining room doors and the over-mantel panel in that room. The frieze of the ballroom is embellished with Adam urns and festoons.

Hammond's interest in his new house, for which William Buckland was the architect, was so intense that his fiancee jilted him on the plea that he cared more for the house than for her. The Harwood whose name is attached to the house was a schoolteacher of Civil War days whose sympathy with the South was so strong that he walked to Baltimore twice weekly rather than take the oath of allegiance required of railroad passengers. The house is now owned by St. John's College.

16. The rambling BORDLEY-RANDALL HOUSE, a two-story brick structure painted yellow, stands amid magnolias and evergreens in the center of Randall Place, between the State House and St. John's College. Construction of the oldest wing (R), one story high, was begun by Thomas Bordley, one of the petitioners for the incorporation of Annapolis, shortly before his death in 1726. A two-story columned porch on the main unit was replaced in 1860 by a smaller enclosed porch floored with marble from the State House, which was undergoing repairs at that time. At the left, connected by a low passage, is an L-shaped gambrel-roofed wing. Stephen Bordley (1709–64), son of the builder, was one of the foremost lawyers in colonial America and a much-detested rival of arrogant Daniel Dulany II. Thomas Johnson and William Paca received their legal training in his office. While still in his twenties he became involved in a lawsuit with the lord proprietary, who sought to revoke a grant to Thomas Bordley that included the whole site of Annapolis. The house was bought in 1804 by John Randall, whose descendants owned it for about 125 years. Randall's son, Alexander (1803–81), was a representative in the twenty-seventh Congress; another son, Richard (1796–1829), was appointed governor of Liberia, where he died of a malignant fever. Reverdy Johnson (1796–1876), born here and a playmate of the young Randalls, was one of the defense lawyers in the Dred Scott case, United States Senator in 1845 and again in 1863, and Attorney General of the United States in 1849.

17. The DORSEY HOUSE (*private*), 211 Prince George St., consists of a two-story structure believed to date from about 1685 and a three-story addition on the left, built when the dwelling was remodeled after the Civil War. The house, with its curved double flight of iron steps, is of brick painted gray. Edward Dorsey, its builder, was a member of the provincial

council, the ranking officer of the militia, and a man unusually competent in handling Indian affairs. Governor Francis Nicholson lived here from 1694 to 1709, and the assembly is believed to have met in the house in 1695 and after the burning of the State House in 1704.

18. The JENNINGS HOUSE (*private*), 195 Prince George St., one-and-a-half stories high, with dormered gambrel roof and four tall chimneys, stands back among trees in a small garden. The house may have been built for Edmund Jennings; it was bought by Amos Garrett, first mayor of Annapolis, and sold in 1737 to John Brice II.

19. The CARVEL HALL HOTEL, 192 Prince George St., has for its nucleus the WILLIAM PACA HOUSE, built in 1763. Paca was a signer of the Declaration of Independence and governor of the State from 1782 to 1785. The house, a hotel since 1899, has been enlarged by the addition of rear wings, and otherwise greatly altered. High above a terraced lawn, the Prince George Street façade still reveals its stately plan—a two-and-a-half-story central section with connected flankers. Arched and pedimented dormers project from the roofs of the main building and lower wings. A room (L) by the entrance, painted a rich blue with white trim, has its original woodwork, and the stairway in the main section of the house has its old Chinese Chippendale balustrade.

20. The BRICE HOUSE (*private*), Prince George and East Sts., was built in 1740 by Edmund Jennings for his daughter Juliana upon her marriage to Colonel James Brice. The massive two-story brick dwelling with its steep gable roof, wide end chimneys, and low wings is similar in plan to the old Paca House. The main entrance, unprotected by hood or portico, is approached by a flight of wooden steps at one side of a high rail-enclosed stoop; the doorway is simple. The most unusual features of the exterior are the triple pedimented window above the entrance, with slender colonnettes and modillioned cornice, and the heavy main cornice with a fret and arch-traceried frieze. After being an annex to Carvel Hall Hotel for some years, the house was acquired by St. John's College as a residence for faculty members.

The ghosts accredited to the house are said to be those of Mrs. Brice's son Thomas and a servant who clubbed him to death in the night.

21. AUNT LUCY'S BAKE SHOP, 160 Prince George St., is a low one-and-a-half-story house with a Dutch gambrel roof, a single end chimney, and shed dormers. Its low brick walls are painted yellow with white trim. In front of the house is a narrow strip filled with plants and enclosed by a knee-high picket fence. The small entrance door with its tiny wood stoop is flanked by shuttered windows, two at the left and three at the right.

22. The gambrel-roofed SANDS HOUSE (*private*), 130 Prince George St., a small frame clapboarded structure, was built about 1680 for Edward Carter 'with saw, adze and hatchet.' The trim white-painted clapboarded dwelling, with a low 'salt-box' addition at the left, has a small pedimented entrance portico that projects onto the brick-paved sidewalk. A low gabled wing has been added at the rear.

The Sands family has owned the house since before the Revolution and many old furnishings are still in use. Among the family treasures are cop-

lum was revised; a department of steam engineering was an innovation signalizing the revolution from the traditional sails to engines. The Spanish-American War, the first foreign war engaged in by the United States since the Mexican War to demonstrate the importance of the navy, brought about another revision of the curriculum and considerable expansion of facilities. An entirely new layout of buildings was planned, and construction of the first new units was begun in 1899. Fort Severn, the old chapel, and most of the other mellow red brick landmarks were swept away. Meanwhile the student body increased from a few dozen to hundreds; a peak enrollment of 2,499 was attained in 1923.

Undergraduate students, termed midshipmen, gain admittance to the Academy in various ways; while all must pass academic examinations or have certificates of credit from schools or colleges whose standing is recognized by the Academy, their appointments must go through one of several channels. Five places in the Academy belong to appointees of the vice president of the United States, four to each senator and representative in Congress; fifteen can be appointed at large annually by the president and a few others by Government officials for the territories and so on. In addition, special regulations make place for the sons of military and naval men who have died as a result of wounds or disease contracted in service. All candidates must be more than 16 years old and not more than 20, must be at least five feet five and a half inches tall, and must have a specified weight according to age, beginning with 112 pounds at 16. Many candidates who have passed the other hurdles to appointment meet trouble in the physical requirements; some of the most popular Academy lore is connected with the ingenious—and sometimes heroic—ways candidates have overcome physical handicaps. These range from the drinking of quarts of water to increase weight to almost incredible exercises to increase height; it is insisted that one lad met the height requirement by having a friend sandbag the top of his head—thereby raising a bump—not long before he was to be measured.

The Academy is primarily a technical school; some critics believe it should give a more rounded education or should demand that candidates have more academic training before entering. Defenders of the present curriculum point out that graduates who are commissioned must do further academic as well as technical work for promotion.

From the time a candidate is accepted, his personal as well as his school life is under Academy control; he may not marry until he has been graduated and spent two years in the service, his first and third year vacation periods are spent at sea, his social life must conform to certain patterns. The graduate receives a commission as ensign. Between periods of active duty he is expected to do graduate work in some special field that he selects. There is a postgraduate school at the Academy but certain civil universities as well as other naval institutions also give advanced technical training.

The great event of the Academy year is June Week, when the fourth-year men who have successfully invoked the 'God of 2.5' (the passing mark) receive their commissions, an event signalized by the tossing away of midshipman caps. Newsreel men haunt the Academy grounds to get pictures of the pretty girl guests from all parts of the United States, and to witness 'the colorful ceremony of the presentation of colors by the color girl.' This consists of the transfer of the National and regimental flags from the Sixth to the Fifth company of midshipmen, and it is the one occasion of the year when the superintendent of the Academy and his officers step aside to permit a girl to review the middies.

One of the features of June Week near the turn of the century was the march composed for each graduating class by the bandmaster, Lieutenant Charles A. Zimmerman. In 1907, collaborating with Midshipman Alfred H. Miles, he composed the march that has become the anthem of the Navy as well as the Naval Academy—'Anchors Aweigh.'

30. Bronze grilles of the MARYLAND AVENUE GATE, main entrance to the quadrangle called The Yard, were presented by the Class of 1907.

31. The NAVAL ACADEMY MUSEUM (L), just inside the entrance, contains a large collection of ship models covering three centuries of naval history, also swords and decorations of distinguished naval officers, and American and captured foreign battle flags.

To the right along Lovers' Lane, the promenade of romantic middies and their guests, is the HERNDON MONUMENT, a granite obelisk commemorating W.L.Herndon, who in 1857 helped save passengers of the *S.S. Central America*, which he commanded and on which he went down. A little farther is the JAPANESE BELL presented to Perry on his voyage to Japan in 1853–54, now sounded only when Navy beats Army in the annual football match.

32. Also right from the gate, along Blake Road, is the huge NAVAL ACADEMY CHAPEL, flanked by the small ivy-covered Administration Building and Superintendent's House. The Chapel was originally in the form of a Greek cross, but a long nave was added in 1939–40. The dome over the crossing, with its glittering gilded cupola, rises more than two hundred feet above the ground. Its former terra-cotta decorative work— drums, flags, and festoons—has been replaced with plain sheet copper; the coffered ceiling is ornamented with symbolic designs in plaster. Stained glass windows in the apse and transepts commemorate naval heroes— Sampson, Mason, Porter, Farragut—and Academy men who served in the World War. Under the crossing is the crypt, a round colonnaded chamber containing the bronze and marble sarcophagus holding the dust of John Paul Jones, who on his death in 1792 was buried in Paris. In 1905 the coffin was ceremoniously transferred to America. The sarcophagus somewhat resembles Napoleon's in the Hôtel des Invalides, Paris.

33. Near the front of DAHLGREN HALL, named for Rear Admiral John A.Dahlgren, are the offices of the department of ordnance and gunnery. The rest of the building is a huge hall used for drill, musters, also for 'hops' of the three upper classes and for the June Week farewell ball and graduation exercises.

34. All of Navy's home football games are played in THOMPSON STADIUM, behind Dahlgren Hall, which was named for Colonel Robert M. Thompson, an alumnus who left the navy but became a member of the

Board of Visitors and was active in promoting the expansion of academy facilities.

FARRAGUT FIELD, between the stadium and the water front, is used for drill and parades. Gunnery sheds are along the water.

35. BANCROFT HALL, to the left of Dahlgren Hall, was named for George Bancroft, who promoted establishment of the Academy.

TECUMSEH, facing the entrance, is a bronze copy (1930) of the *U.S.S. Delaware's* figurehead which represented the Delaware chief, Tamenend, but was renamed by the midshipmen. The figure, set up shortly after the Civil War, became a sort of totem, the 'God of 2.5.' Students toss pennies —ultimately salvaged by the small boys of Annapolis—for good grades, athletic victories, and other help.

This impressive U-shaped dormitory, which has three miles of corridors, is approached by a broad flight of steps and has a large forecourt before its three arched doorways flanked by gray granite columns. Under the mansard roof broken by numerous dormers is an elaborate cornice and frieze. From a lofty colonnaded hall with domed and vaulted ceiling and an inlaid polished marble floor rises a grand staircase turned at a central landing. A monumental doorway on the landing leads into spacious Memorial Hall, where relics and memorials of naval heroes are displayed. Notable is Perry's battle flag with its rather crudely lettered motto, 'Don't give up the ship.' New midshipmen face this flag when taking their oath of allegiance. In the lunettes at the ends of the hall are paintings of the battles between the frigate *Constitution* and *H.M.* frigate *Java* on December 29, 1812, and between the frigate *Constellation* and the French frigate *Insurgents* on February 9, 1799.

36. MACDONOUGH HALL, beyond Bancroft, is the gymnasium. Commodore Thomas MacDonough, for whom it is named, was victor in the Battle of Lake Champlain on September 11, 1814. Its trophy room memorializes Navy's athletic victories. Over the indoor running track is a model, more than 35 feet long, of the steam sloop *Antietam*, whose construction, begun in 1864, was never completed. The hull of the model was made at Washington, the spars and sails at Philadelphia, and it was assembled at Annapolis in 1872–3. A huge indoor pool is in the Natatorium.

37. LUCE HALL, beyond MacDonough, houses the departments of seamanship and navigation, economics and government, and languages. It is named for Stephen B. Luce, who was head of the seamanship department during the Civil War and in 1881 became first president of the Naval War College of Newport. On the landward wall is a tablet commemorating the burning of the *Peggy Stewart* while anchored near this point.

DEWEY BASIN (L) and SANTEE BASIN (R) are enclosed harbors for craft assigned to the Academy. In Dewey Basin, opposite the entrance to Luce Hall, is the schooner *America*, which in 1851 won the Royal Yacht Club cup that England has not yet been able to regain. She became a Confederate blockade runner, and after capture was made a Union training ship. General Ben Butler bought her at auction in 1874, and she remained in private hands until 1921. In Santee Basin is the old *U.S.S.Cumberland*, used to quarter mess attendants. At the same wharf is the Spanish cruiser

Reina Mercedes, captured at the battle of Santiago and now used as en listed men's quarters and 'brig.'

In the center of The Yard is the MEXICAN MONUMENT, a small marble memorial to Midshipmen Clemson, Hynson, Pillsbury, and Shubrick killed at Vera Cruz during the Mexican War.

Across The Yard from Bancroft Hall are three connected granite build ings holding class and lecture rooms, library, and auditorium.

38. MAHAN HALL, the central unit, was named for Alfred T. Mahan naval historian and president of the Naval War College in 1886–9 and 1892–3. It contains an auditorium and a library of more than 80,000 books mostly on naval subjects. Old battle flags are in the auditorium and corri dors. The clock in the tower strikes the traditional bells instead of hours

Opposite the entrance is the MACEDONIAN MONUMENT, a marble copy of the figurehead of *H.M.S.Macedonian*, captured by Decatur near Ma deira on October 12, 1812.

39. MAURY HALL, the left wing, named for the oceanographer Mat thew F. Maury, houses the departments of English, history, and mathe matics.

40. SAMPSON HALL, the right wing, devoted to electrical engineering and physics, was named for William T. Sampson, head of the physics de partment 1874–8, superintendent of the Academy 1886–90, and com mander in chief at the battle of Santiago in 1898.

Between the museum and the dispensary building is the TRIPOLI MON UMENT, an eagle-surmounted marble shaft surrounded by symbolic figures and standing on a broad high base. It commemorates six young American officers killed in the war with Tripoli. Made in Italy, the shaft was brought to America on the *Constitution* and erected in the Washington Navy Yard in 1808; it stood on the capitol grounds after the War of 1812 and was brought here in 1860.

41. ISHERWOOD HALL, the engineering building, behind the academic group, bears the name of Benjamin F. Isherwood (1822–1915), an early authority in steam engineering.

In autumn and spring, dress parades are held on Wednesday afternoons on WORDEN FIELD behind Isherwood Hall. Infantry and boat drills take place on other week-day afternoons and Saturday mornings.

42. Across College or Dorsey Creek are the NAVAL HOSPITAL and the NAVAL CEMETERY. The JEANNETTE MONUMENT in the cemetery is a cairn similar to that raised in Siberia over the bodies of Lieutenant George W. De Long and part of the *Jeannette* crew, who died with him In 1879 De Long set out for the North Pole by way of Bering Strait, but his ship was icebound for 21 months and finally crushed. A boatload under Chief Engineer Melville and another under De Long himself reached land at different points. When Melville found his superior's party, all were dead. De Long had kept up his notes while freezing to death.

POINTS OF INTEREST IN ENVIRONS

Naval Experiment Station and Radio Station, 2 *m.*; Whitehall, 7 *m.* (see Tour 8a). All Hallows Church, 8 *m.*; South River Club, 9 *m.* (see Tour 8b).

Baltimore

Railroad Stations: Pennsylvania Station, N.Charles St. near Lanvale St. for Pennsylvania R.R. and Western Maryland Ry.; Mt.Royal Station, Mt.Royal Ave. at Cathedral St. and Camden Station, 311 W.Camden St. for Baltimore & Ohio R.R. and Baltimore & Annapolis R.R.; Falls Road Station, North Ave. and Howard St. for Maryland & Pennsylvania R.R.

Bus Stations: 217 W.Baltimore St. for Blue Ridge, Pennsylvania Greyhound, and Peninsula Lines (to Southern Maryland and Norfolk,Va.); 100 S.Howard St. for Safeway Trails, Lake Shore (to Gibson Island), Maryland Coach (to Hanover,Pa.), and West Shore Transit Lines (to Solomons Island); 7 N.Liberty St. for Red Star Bus Line (to Eastern Shore) and Pan-American.

Airports: (New) Municipal Airport, 2800 Broening Highway (foot of Willow Springs Road), Pan-American Airways for alternate route to Europe and Bermuda; Logan Field (municipal), Sollers Point Road and Broening Highway, for American Airlines, Inc., Eastern Air Lines, Pennsylvania Central Airlines Corporation, and Logan Flying Service, Inc.; Curtiss-Wright Field, Greenspring and Smith Aves., for Thompson Airways, Inc., and Airlines Charter Service.

Taxis: 25¢ first 2½ miles, 5¢ each additional half mile.

Streetcars and Busses: Fares 10¢, children 5¢; special trip tickets 10 to 4 weekdays and all day Sun. first ride 10¢, return 5¢; free transfer.

Ferries: Pier 5, Light St. for Love Point Ferry, pedestrians 50¢, one-day round trip 65¢, 4-day round trip 85¢, car and driver $2 one way; Pier 16 Light St. for Tolchester Ferry, 50¢ round trip, no autos carried.

Excursion boats: Steamer Dixie (Wilson Line, Pier 8 Light St.) makes daylight excursions to Seaside Park and daily 'moonlight trips' down the bay from May to Oct.

Piers: Light St., Pratt St. and Key Highway for various bay and river steamers. Light St., Pier 10, Balto. Steam Packet Co. daily to Norfolk,Va.; Pratt St., Pier 3, Merchants & Miners Transp. Co.; Pier 5, Bull Steamship Line (merchant); Canton, Pier 11, Roosevelt Lines to West Coast. For additional information on coastwise, intercoastal, and transoceanic steamships consult telephone directory or travel bureaus.

Traffic Regulations: 20 m.p.h. in downtown areas; 25 m.p.h. in residential districts; turns on green light only; two hour downtown parking; no all-night parking.

Accommodations: 119 hotels and many tourist homes, auto and trailer camps in environs.

Information Service: Baltimore Association of Commerce, 404 St.Paul St.; A.A.A., Mt.Royal Ave. and Cathedral St.; Keystone Automobile Club, 810 N.Charles St.

Radio Stations: WCAO (600 kc.), WBAL (1060 kc.), WFBR (1270 kc.), WCBM (1370 kc.).

Theaters and Motion Picture Houses: 3 legitimate theaters open at irregular intervals; 3 little theaters; 1 burlesque theater; 100 motion picture houses.

Concert Halls: Lyric Theater (used for Metropolitan Opera Company short season), Mt.Royal Ave. near Maryland Ave.; Peabody Conservatory of Music, 1 E.Mt.Vernon Place.

Athletics: Municipal Stadium, 33rd St. between Ellerslie Ave. and Ednor Rd. (football); Fifth Regiment Armory, Hoffman and Bolton Sts. (indoor track meets); Oriole Park, 29th and Barclay Sts. (International League baseball); Sports Center, North Ave. near Charles St. (ice hockey); Carlin's Arena, Reisterstown Rd. and Park Heights Ave. (wrestling); Homewood Field, Charles St. and University Parkway (Hopkins University athletic field); Coliseum, 2201 N.Monroe St. (boxing, basketball).

Golf Courses: Hillsdale Golf Course, Forest Park Ave. and Hillsdale Rd., 9 holes, 15¢ weekdays, 25¢ Sun., holidays; Mt.Pleasant Golf Course, Hillen Rd. north of Hamilton Ave., 18 holes, 50¢ daily; Herring Run Golf Course, Harford Rd. near Clifton Park, practice course; Clifton Park Municipal Golf Course, Harford Ave. and Old Hillen Rd., 18 holes, 25¢ weekdays, 50¢ Sat., Sun., holidays; Baltimore Country Club, Club Rd., Roland Park, 18 holes, private.

Tennis: 110 municipal courts (14 illuminated) in 11 parks, free during day, after 6 P.M. 25¢ for 2 hours; Baltimore Country Club (private), Club Rd., Roland Park, 25 grass and 4 clay courts; several other private clubs.

Swimming: Lakewood Pool (outdoor) Charles and 26th Sts.; Meadowbrook Pool (outdoor) Falls Rd. and Kelly Ave.; Bay Shore Park (bathhouses) with beach on Chesapeake Bay, trolley 26; municipal swimming pools in Druid Hill Park (one white, one Negro), Clifton Park and Patterson Park.

Riding: 7 miles of bridle paths in Druid Hill Park.

Horse Racing: Pimlico, 2900 W.Rogers Ave., one-mile track, also steeplechase course. Spring meet May 2–14; Fall meet Nov. 1–15, under auspices of the Maryland Jockey Club.

Polo: Maryland Polo Club (outdoor) near Stevenson, 3 miles from city limits on Park Heights Ave.; 110th Field artillery (indoors), Pikesville, Reisterstown Rd. at city limits.

Yachting: Maryland Yacht Club, Broening Park, Hanover St. Bridge.

Fishing: Curtis Bay and Creek; Colgate Creek; Fort Armistead; Patapsco River (Hanover St. Bridge).

Annual Events: Second Bachelors' Cotillon, Lyric Theater, 1st Mon. Jan.; Maryland Day Celebration (state-wide), Mar. 25; Spring Concert, United German Singers, Alcazar, Mar.; Metropolitan Opera Co., Lyric Theater, Mar. or Apr.; Tenebrae services, Roman Catholic Cathedral, Holy Thurs. and Good Fri.; Maryland Artists' Exhibition, Baltimore Museum of Art, April 1–30; Pimlico Spring Race Meet, May 2–14 incl.; Concert, Peabody Conservatory Chorus, Mount Vernon Place, last wk. May; Maryland Yacht Club Spring Regatta, 1st Sat. & Sun. in June; Flag Day Celebration, Flag House, June 14; State Women's and State Men's Golf Tournaments, June–July; Maryland Yacht Club Annual Cruise, July 30; Old Defenders' Day (fireworks at Fort McHenry) Sept. 12; Baltimore Live Stock Show, Union Stock Yards, Oct.; Pimlico Fall Race Meet, Nov. 1–15; First Bachelors' Cotillon (most important social event, estab. 1796) 1st Mon. in Dec.; Empty Stocking Club, Fifth Regiment Armory Dec. 23.

BALTIMORE (20 alt., 804,874 pop.), proud, self-sufficient, sits beside the Patapsco River, looking nostalgically to the South but turning to the North for what it takes to make a bank account grow. Midway between North and South, a seething cauldron of dissension during the Civil War, it is even today a city of violent contradictions. It is gentle and blatant, wanton and prudish, cosmopolitan and insular. Baltimore embraces within its capacious borders the grave of Edgar Allan Poe and the center of the straw hat industry; it manufactures steel ships, and steel rings to protect their wearers from rheumatism; it cans more food than any other city in America, and it is proud of the grave of Betsy Bonaparte, of the former home of the Duchess of Windsor, of the present home of H.L.Mencken, and of Johns Hopkins University. City of rarefied aristocrats and often rowdy intellectuals, of dismal slums and spacious mansions, of the insistent odor of fertilizer and the delicate bouquet of the Cardinal's crocuses, of cobblestones and gas lights and monuments; gazing wistfully upon the old, suspiciously upon the new, and benevolently upon the rest of the country.

Baltimore may be an ugly city; nevertheless it is charmingly picturesque in its ugliness. Red brick houses, row on row, with scrubbed white steps, line the narrow streets of the old town; yellow brick houses, miles of them, run uphill and down through the purgatories of the twentieth century realtors; crooked alleys with odd names meander behind old red brick fronts; lordly mansions of the rich preen themselves in groves and parks in the smart suburbs to the north along Charles Street Avenue Extended. The city suffers, though not in silence, the periodic 'trade winds' laden with the odors of industry from the factory suburbs down river.

But it is not Baltimore streets, Baltimore architecture, Baltimore monuments, Baltimore factories that eventually charm the newcomer and make him wish to spend here the remainder of his days. Rather is it the essence of lusty, cantankerous life that this sprawling city distills, under the placid surface of its neo-British aristocracy, which causes people from Kalamazoo and Mauch Chunk and Yazoo City and Walla Walla to label themselves, sooner rather than later, Baltimoreans. Baltimoreans, secure in a sense of unimpeachable superiority, comport themselves with a glowing pride, glad to be citizens of Maryland's metropolis, happy in the thought that the Bachelors' Cotillon is more exclusive than Charleston's Saint Cecilia Society. Resentful of alien criticism, they reserve to themselves the right to curse the city's shortcomings with might and main.

It is the people who live here and their lineage of independence—those who trace their line back to the original Maryland pilgrims and those who have no pride of ancestry nor hope of distinguished posterity—that make Baltimore. Outwardly an old city gone industrial, inwardly it is one of the last refuges of a way of living and a mode of thinking long since engulfed in commercialism almost everywhere else in the United States. Almost any idea, any statement, is permissible in Baltimore, if it is urbanely presented.

For more than a century Baltimore was rough and boisterous. The first blood of the Civil War was shed here when a mob attacked Massachusetts militia, although the State never seceded from the Union. Rioting was the rule and longer than most American cities, Baltimore, like ancient European metropolises, had its 'mob,' which the gentlemen of the town were sometimes hard put to quell.

Today Baltimoreans no longer stage riots but they give vent to the same ungovernable individualism in unusual and delightful outbursts. It was a Baltimorean who, failing in a perennial campaign to have corrected an inaccurate quotation on a monument to Poe, took hammer and chisel and altered it himself; and it was a Baltimore magistrate who appreciated the provocation and gave him a suspended sentence. It was another Baltimore magistrate who, on Christmas and New Year's mornings, convicted left-over merrymakers of drunkenness only if they could not lie on the floor without falling off. It was a Baltimorean who, in an excess of Anglophobia, knocked off the tails of the lions on the Calvert Street Bridge. It was a Baltimore politician who lost the mayoralty election because, among other things, he would not promise to put Mary Ann, the baby elephant, in the zoo over the veto of the Park Board. It was in Baltimore that possible disorder during a parade of radicals was averted when a shrewd policeman arranged an official permit for the demonstration in the name of one Alexander Turnipseed. Had the parade been held without a permit, as the protestants would have preferred it, police would have felt called upon to break it up; under official auspices, it moved peacefully to its designation. 'Turnipseed,' who applied for the permit, has never been discovered. And it was the tough old gentry of Baltimore who would consent to street cars only on condition that the tracks be the precise width of their carriage wheels.

Baltimore—rich in memories and the smell of good food; where the leading advertising man has a portrait of Mencken enshrined over his desk; where the oyster is bigger and more succulent than elsewhere; where the professional booster thrives amid the jibes of the intelligentsia; where the soft-shell crab and the terrapin delight the palate of the epicure, and a man is arrested for mowing his lawn on Sunday!

Baltimore's rise to sixth among the ports of the world has not been an accident. Conservative or not, its citizens have never hesitated in seizing every opportunity to take advantage of its strategic position. Its initial lead over the older town of Annapolis came because it was slightly more accessible as a port and trade center when settlement first spread westward and the center of western shore population shifted. Its merchants and businessmen promoted Federal construction of the Cumberland Road across the mountains to tap the new producing area and then improved the road between Baltimore and Cumberland to make sure that trade was not diverted to Philadelphia. Again, when New York with the single water route that could be improved to reach the western market threatened to divert much of the coveted trade, Baltimore businessmen hastily put through plans for building the first railroad across the mountains. This last move so far secured the city's position as a port that other railroad builders were driven to send competing roads to the city. The automobile era has in no way disturbed the city's lead; Baltimore is midway on the main highway along the Atlantic Coast.

The city's natural advantages are the result of geological structure. Here the fall line—the point where the harder rocks of the Piedmont meet the softer rocks of the coastal plain—moves close to the coast and the wide estuary of the Patapsco River affords a large sheltered harbor. North and south of Baltimore most centers of population developed along this fall line, where streams had the velocity to provide power; roads and railroads connecting these centers with one another were bound to pass through Baltimore. Thus the city early became the commercial center of gravity to which industry was inevitably attracted.

When Baltimore County was laid out in 1659—to embrace a much larger area than the present county—the uninhabited land here was partly meadow and partly marsh at the foot of irregular wooded bluffs divided by the brawling creek later called Jones Falls. Below the bluff the Falls meandered sharply westward then eastward before turning south to the broad cove later named the North West Branch of the Patapsco River. Patapsco Falls came in from the west, emptying into the cove later named the Middle Branch. Between the two bodies of water lay a low peninsula called Whetstone Neck.

In June 1661 land on the west side of Jones Falls near the water was surveyed for David Jones, who soon came here to live. Shortly before this Charles Gorsuch, a Quaker, had patented a tract out on the toe of the little peninsula. During the next sixty years numerous tracts were patented in what is now the city of Baltimore; and these were exchanged, broken up, and repatented without, however, producing much settlement. Among the names distinguishing the holdings were Haphazard, Hale's Folly, Luns Lot, Ridgeley's Delight, Fell's Prospect, Gallow Bar, David's Fancy, and The Choice.

Settlement progressed in the region but the possibilities of this site for a town were ignored; the county seat was not even in the present Baltimore County. In 1696 Charles and Daniel Carroll resurveyed and patented a thousand acres on the west side of Jones Falls, including part of an earlier patent called Cole's Harbor. By 1726 there was a gristmill on the east bank of the Falls and near it were three dwellings, a store, and some tobacco 'houses'—whether barns or storehouses for shippers is not clear. Tobacco growers to the north were becoming desirous of a customhouse here to enable them to ship without having to roll their tobacco needless miles to some duly constituted port. Local landholders therefore united, with Daniel and Charles Carroll in the lead, to 'pray' the assembly for establishment of a town on the north side of the Patapsco. They had first chosen a site on the Middle Branch but the owner, an English merchant named John Moale, was one of many who had speculated in warrants along the Patapsco in the hope of uncovering rich deposits of iron ore, and he refused to sell. The land selected for the new town was that held by the Carrolls. The bill was passed and was signed by Governor Benedict Leonard Calvert on August 8, 1729.

Many of the early characteristics of the terrain have now disappeared; creeks have been diverted, marshes filled in, bluffs graded. Even the ravine of Jones Falls is hardly noticeable.

One of Baltimore's peculiarities is that only one approach—the river—reveals the city's metropolitan character. Railroad trains entering plunge underground at the edge of the residential district. Highways entering from the northeast, the west, and the south run through minor industrial areas and endless rows of small identical houses. To the north are the more elegant residential districts, with estates of notable beauty and country clubs of more than local fame.

But approached from the harbor—as relatively few strangers do approach it—Baltimore appears as a modern city. Fort McHenry is the only anachronism among the steel mills, sugar refinery, piers, warehouses, and fertilizer plants on the shores of the North West Branch of the Patapsco. Bay and river boats, railroad barges, tugs and ocean freighters make it clear that this is a great modern port. Behind the active water front are areas with dismal old stores, their fronts boarded up, and cobblestoned rat-infested streets. Also on the old flats near the Basin is the chief business section, rebuilt since the fire of 1904 and dominated by a small group of postwar skyscrapers; it has little to distinguish it from similar sections of other American cities. Some few buildings have been given ultramodern fronts of colored porcelain tile, structural glass, or chromium and bakelite. Window displays of the larger establishments are modeled on those of New York.

The shopping district of Baltimore that is probably most familiar to visitors, however, is that centered on or around Charles Street. Here the shopper may, and does, move in leisurely fashion, avoiding the more crowded streets of the department store area. It is traditional that on Charles Street a Baltimorean will always meet people 'one knows'; here the larger and more expensive motor cars park in the narrow thoroughfare (already cluttered with trolley cars), while elderly ladies shop and gossip with Miss Sally, Miss Mamie, or some equally friendly and familiar salesperson. Probably in no other city of its size is the buying public so accustomed to dealing with favorite salespeople, known and asked for by name.

Baltimore's stores, large and small, are known for the seemingly endless good nature of their owners or operators. A customer with a charge account in a Baltimore shop thinks nothing of returning a purchase after an indefinite period of consideration. Efforts have been made to promote a 'one-way shopping' system, but it has not met with notable success.

Yet only a few blocks beyond the busy center, outside the area destroyed by the 'great fire,' nineteenth-century Baltimore is seen; early post-Revolutionary houses, their wrought-iron handrails topped by polished, urn-shaped finials; Classic Revival houses with severely paneled doors flanked by Ionic columns; Classic Revival monuments and a cathedral; Victorian row houses with white marble steps and with white arched vestibules; cast-iron grillwork with interlacing scrolls and grapevine motifs, reminiscent of New Orleans and Charleston; gas street lamps. Some of the houses are in slum areas that were once fashionable residential sections.

The city is not a blend of the new and old. Largely because of the fire, Baltimore is an old city with a single modern district reached by modernized lanes. Relatively few large new buildings have been erected outside the burned area; only the irrepressible filling stations appear everywhere.

Not so old nor so grand as the Victorian row houses are the row houses built near the turn of the century in a band around the older core and housing a considerable part of the city's inhabitants. Their number is so great as to make them the most characteristic sight seen by the hurried visitor. Even in an era of standarized construction, the uniformity of these houses from block to block is amazing.

From one street to the next is a solid line of two-story houses of yellow brick; the next may be of red. Some rows are blank and severe, others are cluttered with fussy gables, but within each block there is no variation, so that even the owner must recognize his own door by the number. The most striking feature of these uniform houses is their uniform white steps, which are always just scrubbed or being scrubbed. In some blocks the steps are of white stone, in others they are of wood painted white. The people scrubbing them may be Negro servants—male or female—or they may be housewives, or schoolgirls wearing silk stockings, but the pattern is the same—gleaming white steps and kneeling scrubbers—for mile after mile around the city.

Only to the west and north is the pattern broken. There in suburbs, most of them inhabited by the moderately well to do, but some—Roland Park, Homeland, Guilford—notable for the wealth and prestige of their citizens, are the neo-Colonial separate houses designed by realtors, and the mansions of Georgian, Tudor, Regency, French Provincial, and a few of the modern international types.

Because of the topography of the older sections and because through a couple of centuries the town has been so often enlarged, the streets are tangled, changing direction sometimes at an angle of forty-five degrees. They also change their character from business to slum to faded grandeur within a few blocks and change their names for reasons that have long been forgotten. A Baltimorean might explain to a visitor that 'Cathedral Street is Mount Royal Avenue north of Mount Royal Avenue'; Mount Royal Avenue makes such a sharp turn that its upper section seems to be a continuation of Cathedral Street. Baltimore has an East North Avenue, and a West North Avenue, an East West Street and a West West Street. However, the street naming system has been improved in recent times. Older residents remember when various sections of what is now Charles Street were called Charles Street Avenue Extended, Charles Street Avenue Boulevard, and Charles Street Avenue Boulevard Road. The Baltimore telephone directory still recognizes Charles Street Avenue.

But the visiting motorist has other reasons for complaint besides streets that turn corners or change their names. Downtown traffic is heavy and many of the streets are narrow. Traffic signals may be overhead, or on the corner, or on the roof of a 'pillbox' kiosk in the middle of the street. (Baltimore has tenderly protected many of its traffic officers from sun and cold in these odd structures, the last few of which were being removed in 1940.) The rugged individualism of Baltimoreans is particularly noticeable in traffic. Cars are parked on both sides of streets no matter how narrow; pedestrians jaywalk and dodge; boys equip their bicycles with sirens; children with roller skates have free range.

No other great port of the world gives so little the impression of being a port city. Here again the terrain is accountable. The twenty-five mile water front does not encircle the city or even part of it; rather it is indented into one corner that is off all lines of through traffic. Moreover, most of the city is on ground much higher than the water front and the twisting streets provide no vistas. To view the harbor visitors must make a special trip to it. Perhaps because it is so far out of the ordinary paths of city life, the inhabitants have never made any attempt to recapture part of it from business; only Fort McHenry and Federal Hill Park provide a detached vantage point from which to watch the busy and ever fascinating life of the Basin.

Nonetheless, some of the streets near the water front have a teeming life quite different from that of other parts of the city. The section of town centering around South Broadway is the haunt of the thousands of seamen—ashore between trips or 'on the beach' [unemployed]—who man the ships constantly moving between Baltimore and the remotest parts of the world.

This has been the haunt of seamen since Baltimore became a port. Along the shore of this point were the yards in which the Baltimore clippers were built. Having escaped improvement as well as the fires so common in most districts where the inhabitants have little responsibility of ownership, South Broadway remains early Baltimore. Narrow streets, many of them still cobblestoned, are lined with brick houses, close together, whose age is clear in their shuttered windows, dormered roofs, and paneled doors.

Seamen seldom go far from the foot of Broadway. Here and on the narrow intersecting streets—Shakespeare, Aliceanna, Thames—are the stores, saloons, restaurants, and dine-and-dance taverns they patronize. Here also are the Seamen's Mission and the Anchorage (a branch of the Y.M.C.A.). At the union hall, Fleet Street and Broadway, the seamen stand by for assignments, and on summer days when the Broadway market is not used for sales they gather in the lower section to swap yarns.

Greeks, Italians, Scandinavians, South Americans are here—representatives of virtually every maritime nation on the globe. Workers on Bay and river boats are also here, though the blue-water men feel quite superior to the green-water men. There is trouble at times, but at worst these visitors settle their arguments with fists, or with a leather glove holding ball bearings or other metallic bits. Many of them see nothing wrong in smuggling and get past the customs officers when they can, with dope, perfume, surgical instruments, foreign-made pistols, and other articles. As a whole, however, they give the police little trouble; in fact they are more often victims than criminals, being preyed upon by all manner of land sharks and 'con' men.

The South Broadway area is not occupied exclusively by seamen. Most of its permanent residents are of Polish extraction with a social life centering around St.Stanislaus Church at Ann and Aliceanna Streets. Houses are brightly painted and the neighborhood churches ornate. More than 10,000 people of Polish birth live in southeastern Baltimore. The Polish National Alliance, a settlement, maintains a library of several thousand volumes in the mother tongue and has its own Boy Scout troop, students' society, choir, and ballet group. Many of the names on the windows of the stores and offices end in -*ski* or -*wicz*, and Polish is commonly heard on the streets.

Baltimore's compact Little Italy lies mainly south of Pratt Street, east of Jones Falls and between Central Avenue and the old President Street railroad yards. The most picturesque and self-contained of all Baltimore's foreign sections, it consists of many small colonies, since the Italian is homesick unless he is living among people from his native parish. The Italian restaurants around Fawn and High Streets attract customers from all sections of Baltimore with their spaghetti, ravioli, and scaloppino. The stores have attractive displays of Italian wines and cheeses and the finest vegetables available can always be found in this district.

There is a larger, though not so picturesque, Italian colony in Highlandtown, centering at Claremont and Pratt Streets. Many of the men of this section work in the steel mills at Sparrows Point. There are also many families of Italian extraction living around Lexington Market.

The city has a half a dozen other districts inhabited largely by people of

European birth and their descendants. The more than 7,000 people of British and Irish birth are scattered, but the 14,000 Germans tend to live in neighborhoods where they may use their native tongue frequently. The 17,000 people of Russian birth counted in the census of 1930 live mostly in southeast Baltimore.

The 142,000 Negroes are scattered all over the city, but Pennsylvania Avenue is the Main Street of a large 'black belt' in the northwest section. Here is a duplicate of the life of the white city—from bottom to top— though a few somewhat exotic touches catch the eye of foreign visitors; on Saturday unusual numbers of smartly dressed girls are seen, as well as elderly houseworkers using their off time to have their hair straightened. Young men in gaudy clothes shoot by on their way to the swing spots, and broadshouldered acidmakers, burnermen, and chambermen from the fertilizer plants stand about on street corners and near pool halls, taking their enjoyment in watching other people having a good time.

On the Avenue are all the usual stores, five-and-dime, small groceries where two cigarettes can be had for a cent, expensive restaurants with the best of everything, and little eating places where two hot dogs cost a nickel or free soup is given with all meals costing more than ten cents. It is still possible to purchase 'charms' here, but the old folkways are rapidly disappearing.

Baltimore's Negroes (*see The Negro*) publish one of the leading Negro newspapers of the country, have their own city-supported symphony orchestra and choral group of some 300 voices, and a little theater organization.

It is hard to think of any kind of social life that can not be found in the city; in addition to the entertainments and groups found in the average cities, northern as well as southern, Baltimore has a few peculiarly its own. It is the only city in America—with the possible exception of Cambridge, Massachusetts—where medical men play a prominent part in society and civic affairs and are seen quite as often with men of other professions as with those of their own.

No other city presents such a barrier to the girl with social aspirations as does Baltimore with its Bachelors' Cotillon. Founded in 1796, the cotillon is controlled by a board of governors that deals summarily with the lists of girls who each year hope to 'come out.' Not to be invited to the Monday Germans (the name is derived from the old dance, the German) means not to be a debutante; there is no other way of making a debut. Birth alone will guarantee an invitation to the cotillon, even though the family is penniless. A girl may be a debutante in Baltimore at the cost of one white dress for the first German. Frequently, however, balls of considerable size and cost are arranged by wealthy families who may not belong to the limited circle or by non-Baltimoreans who are anxious to put the halo of a Baltimore debut on their daughters' heads. Many girls with the proper credentials come to the Bachelors' Cotillon from far parts of the country in the belief that their social careers are better launched here than anywhere else, even in New York. Baltimore women who have married into European peerages have brought their daughters home for debuts.

A Baltimorean calls his town 'Bawlemer,' otherwise he does not betray his origin by peculiarities or pronunciation. Most Baltimoreans speak a border dialect that in the Deep South would be regarded as Yankee and in New England as a 'Southern drawl.' But many native Baltimoreans treat the letter 'r' as did their grandfathers or great grandfathers—men from the North and the Middle West, who came here during the period of industrial development. Baltimore has one word peculiarly its own, *espantoon*, meaning a policeman's club or nightstick. It apparently originated during the Revolutionary period when officers of the British infantry carried *spontoons* (Fr. *sponton, esponton*)—short pikes. An espantoon (sometimes *spantoon*) is a symbol of a policeman's office and dignity.

Baltimore is a sporting town. All the usual sports are popular and Baltimoreans do not have to travel far for fox hunting, duck hunting, salt- and fresh-water fishing. Any citizen with $5 can get on a streetcar, go to the famous Preakness, place a minimum bet on the wrong horse, invest heavily in beer and hot dogs, and return with some change. But Baltimore is not a sinful city. Sailors who have taken their fun in many seaports call it a graveyard. There are two or three gambling houses where a $1,000 note may be handled, and the number of small bookmakers accepting 50¢ bets is countless. The most important organized racket is the numbers, which takes pennies, dimes and quarters, particularly from the Negroes. Many restaurants and taverns have elaborate 'pin-ball machines' near the cash registers and in giving change include unnecessary quantities of nickels, apparently to encourage customers to play the machines. The town has one theater visited by traveling burlesque shows and a number of night clubs ranging from the smart to the gin-mill. But neither is Baltimore a crusading town. Vice crusades are started from time to time, but no very large part of the population can be stirred to synthetic indignation. There was a time when Billy Sunday came to town and persuaded whole squads of police, among others, to hit the sawdust trail. Another time a prominent surgeon led a crusade against the 'red light district' and succeeded in scattering it for a time; this crusade, however, aroused some criticism among citizens of prominence and high morality—being Baltimoreans they branded some of the tactics as ungentlemanly. However Baltimore's relative purity is owing not to indignation but to indifference. Sin does not flourish because there is little demand for it.

Maryland cooking was developed on the plantations, but Baltimore has shared the State's reputation for good food and continued to share it long after the distinctive local cuisines of most other cities had disappeared. It is still possible in some of the better hotels and restaurants to get terrapin, snapper soup, hot biscuits, spoon bread, or boned duck. In most expensive eating places, however, French or Italian food is offered and the cheaper places serve the usual Virginia baked ham, chile con carne, Boston baked beans, chicken chow mein, Maryland fried chicken, and anomalous 'salads.'

Although Baltimore has never had the reputation of being a cultural center, it compares favorably in its general cultural development with other cities (*see The Arts*). The Johns Hopkins University, the Peabody Conservatory of Music, the Enoch Pratt Free Library, and the Walters

Art Gallery are evidence of strong noncommercial interests during the last quarter of the nineteenth century. The men who established these institutions shared with tens of thousands of their fellow citizens the conviction that humanity can and must be educated, that it is the special responsibility of the man of wealth to provide money for such enterprises.

There are no songs entitled 'Way Down upon the Patapsco,' nor 'The Baltimore Blues'; the city has inspired no outstanding novels; it is not planning a world's fair; it does not boast of the biggest, the newest, or the fastest anything. This does not indicate lack of city pride; it merely means that Baltimoreans are too sure of themselves and their city to feel the need of advertising its virtues.

It was largely an accident that the future metropolis of the State was given the name of Lord Baltimore's titular seat in Ireland. Most early Maryland county names honored the Calverts, and 'Charles,' 'Calvert,' and 'Anne Arundel' had already been assigned when the county at the head of the Chesapeake was erected. It was natural for the town founders to attempt to establish their real estate development as *the* town of Baltimore County, though little Joppa to the north seemed to have a head start in the race for prominence.

By 1730 the town established a year before had been laid out roughly in the shape of an arrowhead with the tip near the present intersection of Hopkins Place and Redwood Street. This original townsite of sixty acres, for which the Carrolls were paid the equivalent of about £600, is now bounded by Gay Street on the east, Saratoga Street on the north, Liberty Street and Hopkins Place on the west, and Pratt Street on the south. At that the town grew so slowly that some of the lots were not taken up for years. The Basin then curved up to what is now Water Street. Harrison's Marsh was a good place for snipe and woodcock and not a business street. John Flemming, a tenant of the Carrolls, was probably the only man then living in the vicinity. Soon after the first lots were taken up a causeway across Harrison's Marsh and a bridge across Jones Falls, where Gay Street now crosses the Fallsway, were constructed to link the new town with Jones Town, the older settlement east of the Falls.

In 1732 the residents of Jones Town, watching what was happening on the other side of the stream, persuaded the assembly to pass a bill erecting their settlement into 'a town on a Creek Divided on the East from the Town lately laid out in Baltimore County called Baltimore Town on the Land whereon Edward Fell keeps Store.' The town on a creek was to occupy twenty acres, the area now roughly bounded by the Fallsway on the west, Hillen Street on the north, Exeter Street on the east, and Lexington Street on the south. This section, older in point of settlement than Baltimore Town, is still called Old Town.

Perhaps there was some rivalry for a time but in 1745 the assembly, on a joint petition of the citizens of both towns, united the two, making them 'one entire Town, and for the future called and known by the Name Baltimore Town, and by no other Name.' Commissioners were appointed and empowered to employ a clerk and to 'levy, assess, and take by Way of Distress if needful, from the Inhabitants of the said Town, by even and equal

Proportion, the Sum of three Pounds yearly for the Encouragement of their Clerk, to be paid to him.' Two annual fairs were permitted, during which every person within the bounds of the town was to be free from arrest, except for felony or breach of the peace. The commissioners must also require each citizen to keep a ladder tall enough to reach the top of his chimney.

From a picture attributed to John Moale, son of the man who did not want the town on his land, and from other sources, it has been learned that Baltimore Town in 1752 had twenty-five houses, one church, and two taverns; four of these buildings were of brick; the streets were crooked and irregular; there was one patch of tobacco within the town limits; the parish church of St.Pauls stood far off up the hill, near what is now the corner of Charles and Lexington streets. About two hundred persons, among them Englishmen, Scots, and Germans, lived here at the time.

In 1755 a boatload of French Acadian exiles from Nova Scotia arrived and were received with great hospitality, even though they had been expelled from their homeland by England because of their unwillingness to give up their French allegiance. In time the Acadians were able to construct small houses along South Charles Street; for a century this section of Baltimore was called French Town.

The port grew slowly but steadily. In 1756 a Baltimore bottom cleared for the British West Indies with a diversity of cargo consisting of Indian corn, flour—ground in mills along the Patapsco and Jones Falls—beans, hams, bread, iron, staves and heading, peas, and of course tobacco. The vessel returned with the usual sugar, rum, and slaves. This event marked the end of Baltimore Town's dependence on tobacco and the beginning of an era of diversified shipping. Two years later a cargo of wheat from upland farms was shipped to New York.

In a few years Baltimore had a pottery and a distillery. An educator from London was teaching young men 'writing, arithmetic (both vulgar and decimal), merchants' accounts, geometry, etc.,' was teaching young ladies the 'Italian hand,' and was selling 'choice West India rum by the hogshead, loaf-sugar, coffee, chocolate, Madeira wine, and cedar desks.'

In July 1762 a visitor, Benjamin Mifflin, noted in his diary that the town had about one hundred and fifty houses, mostly of brick, and thirty or forty under construction. '. . . it seems to Encrease very Fast. There are 2 Bridges over the creek which Joyns the 2 Parts of the Town together the Creek so shoal that only Boats or Flats can go up, & runs such a short distance in the Country that there is but very Little Currant to keep it clear so that its my Oppinion both that & the Bason to the S. of the Town must in a Few Years be Choak'd up Except a small Stream that the Creek which they call the Falls will keep open sufficient perhaps for Flat Bottom Craft & in that case the Sea Trade will draw down to a point Call'd Fells Point where the Shipping now Lye there being at this time 3 Ships & a Snow from London Loading with Tobacco. for other Sea Trade there is very Little now the bent of the Inhabitants not being as yet that way but I think a very considerable one might be carried on here there being Two Merch^t Mills now Building on the above Creek contiguous to the Town and another ab^t 2 Mile off the First by Willm Moore the second by John Burgess & co & the Third by ———the Back Country will amply supply them with wheat & Indian Corn in very Plenty. as to Lumber altho there seem to be very good Timber about the Country the people has not fell Into making Staves, & as to Fells Point about a Mile below the Town the Owner has such a High notion of it, has Laid it out into such small Lotts proposing a perpetual Ground rent of £3 Ster^g for the water & 30/Ster^g for the Inner Lotts that he has Let but 2 or 3 & I believe in his time will not Let many, without he Lowers his Terms or Inlarges his Lotts . . .'

William Fell, nephew of the storekeeper, had laid out these lots on Fell's Point, and in spite of Mifflin's prophecy a wharf, warehouse, and shipyard had been established within a few years. For a time there was intense rivalry between the Point and Baltimore Town, but in 1773 the assembly added eighty acres, including Fell's Point, to the town.

Baltimore had been made the county seat in 1768 and a courthouse was built near the site of the Battle Monument, on a bluff that was then some 30 or 40 feet above the present street level. By this time the town had three or four thousand inhabitants, but it was still possible to catch crabs with a stick at what is now the intersection of Charles and Lombard Streets, or to drown, as one citizen did, at the place where Calvert now crosses Lexington Street.

It was natural that Mifflin, a Philadelphian, should have surveyed Baltimore's business possibilities with a sharp eye, for the little city was beginning to divert some trade from his own home, which with its suburbs had about 30,000 people at the time. Baltimore's importance by 1769 is attested by the fact that the Merchants' Committee of Philadelphia believed it necessary to get the co-operation of Baltimore merchants to strengthen their own nonimportation agreement made to force repeal of the Townshend Acts. The temper of Baltimoreans was vigorous; they not only responded promptly to the appeal but took the lead in getting agreement throughout Maryland.

In 1765 citizens hanged in effigy the man appointed stamp distributor for Maryland. When in 1770 two sloops with contraband arrived they were forced to leave the port; and Baltimoreans passed a resolution not to trade with Rhode Island when the New England colony violated the intercolonial nonimportation agreement. In 1774 a Committee of Correspondence was appointed and resolutions were passed recommending that all trade with Great Britain and the West Indies cease—even though the trade with the West Indies was then the most profitable carried on by Baltimore citizens. Only four days after the Virginia House of Burgesses made a similar recommendation and before the news had been brought up the Bay, Baltimore citizens in a general meeting went on record as favoring a convention of representatives from all the colonies.

In December 1774 a company of militia was formed and Mordecai Gist was elected captain. These 'Baltimore Independent Cadets' were 'impress'd with a sense of the unhappy [state] of our Suffering Bretheren in Boston,' and they firmly resolved 'to Procure at our own Expense a

Uniform Suit of Cloths, (vizt) [a Coat] turned up with Buff, and trim'd with Yellow Metal, or Gold Buttons, White Stockings and black Cloth half Boots; likewise a good Gun with Cartouch Pouch, a pair of Pistolls Belt and Cutlass, with 4 pounds of powder and 16 pounds of lead.' Six months later, after the news of Lexington and Concord had reached the town, there were seven companies drilling in Baltimore.

Many of these boys, and others later recruited by Lafayette and Pulaski, became dependable soldiers in the Revolutionary Army, distinguishing themselves in many battles. In July 1783 the veterans returned from the war, 'penniless and in rags,' under the command of Mordecai Gist, then a brigadier general.

Meanwhile the folks at home had had their adventures. Several times the town had with good reason been thrown into a state of excitement by the approach of British men-of-war. General Greene, passing through the town in 1780, reported that Baltimore was in 'so defenseless a state' that 'a twenty-gun ship might lay the town under contribution.' But perhaps the most gloomy period of the war had been December 1776, when Baltimore was host to Congress, which had fled southward before the British advance, and there seemed little hope for the cause of independence. The representatives of the new States had met in a three-story building at Sharp (then correctly spelled Sharpe) and Baltimore Streets. And to add to Baltimore's problems, not all of the distinguished guests had been polite. A Virginia delegate had written, 'If you desire to keep out of the damnedest hole on earth come not here!' But the Congress had accomplished much during its brief stay. A New Hampshire delegate wrote, 'Congress is now doing business with more spirit than they have for some time past. I hope the air of this place, which is much finer than Philadelphia, will brace up the weak nerves.'

Baltimore, however, had made her greatest contribution on the sea. In October 1775 the Continental Congress had passed an act for the formation of a navy, and in the same month the Continental Marine Committee at Baltimore had fitted out two of the first cruisers of the American Navy. A new flag had been sent down from Philadelphia to be used on one of these vessels, the *Hornet*, and Joshua Barney, the recruiting officer of the ship, had unfurled this flag to the music of fifes and drums. 'The heart-stirring sounds of the Martial instruments, then a novel incident in Baltimore,' wrote Barney's wife, 'and the still more novel sight of the *Rebel colors* gracefully waving in the breeze, attracted crowds of all ranks and eyes to the gay scene of the rendezvous, and before the setting of the same day's sun, the young recruiting-officer had enlisted a full crew of jolly "rebels" for the *Hornet*.'

There was also a Maryland navy which did good service in keeping down plunderers in the bay and at times in suppressing Tory uprisings. Many of these vessels were built and equipped at Baltimore. They ranged in size from tiny barges carrying six or a dozen 'jolly rebels' with perhaps as many muskets, to cruisers of twenty-two guns. The larger vessels might have such mild names as *Defense, Friendship*, or *Amelia*, but the barges carried such mighty names as *Revenge, Terrible, Intrepid*, or *Fearnaught*.

In March 1776 Congress had authorized the fitting out of 'private armed vessels,' and this act, in the words of a nineteenth-century historian, 'offered to the enterprise and patriotism of the citizens of Baltimore an opportunity of acquiring wealth, while defending their commerce and protecting the people from the depredations of the common enemy. Under this act *privateering* became a business as well of fortune as of patriotism.' Here indeed was a business exactly to the taste of Revolutionary Baltimore.

Between April 1, 1777, and March 14, 1783, 248 vessels, most of them owned by Baltimoreans, sailed from the Patapsco to capture what they could from the British and they succeeded so well that British merchants for more than 30 years referred to Baltimore as a 'nest of pirates.' When a prize was captured it might be manned by a skeleton crew and sent to the nearest American port, or if this was impossible it was burned or sunk. The damage done to English shipping during this period has been estimated at £1,000,000.

Baltimore Town had contributed perhaps more than its share of the money needed to carry on the war and, like all other American towns of the period, had suffered from the disruption of business. But Baltimoreans had learned to build fast ships and were to profit much by this knowledge during the succeeding period of privateering and slave running.

In 1776 the town had some 6,700 inhabitants; the Federal census of 1810 showed a population of 45,000. From the outbreak of the French Revolution to the close of the Napoleonic Wars there was a good European market for foodstuffs. Land to the south and west of Baltimore supplied grain and other necessities; the citizens of Baltimore loaded this merchandise on their fast ships and profited; and profited again when the ships returned with manufactured goods to be auctioned on the wharves.

There was of course great building activity within the town. In 1784 Baltimore underpinned the courthouse, leaving it standing upon stone stilts, and carted away the hill to open up Calvert Street beneath it. 'At that time,' says a historian, 'the arch under the court house was supplied with stocks, pillory, and whipping post, and Justice straddled over the city's center like Gulliver in Lilliput.'

A writer described the Baltimore of the 1780's as 'so conceited, so bustling and *debonnaire*, growing up like a saucy, chubby boy, with his dumpling cheeks and short, grinning face, fat and mischievous, and bursting incontinently out of his clothes in spite of all the allowance of tucks and broad selvages. Market Street had shot, like a Nuremberg snake out of its toy box, as far as Congress Hall, with its line of low-browed, hipped-roof wooden houses in disorderly array, standing forward and back, after the manner of a regiment of militia with many an interval between the files. Some of these structures were painted blue and white and some yellow, and here and there sprang up a more magnificent mansion of brick, with windows like a multiplication table and great wastes of wall between the stories, with occasional courtyards before them, and reverential locust trees, under whose shade bevies of truant schoolboys, ragged little Negroes, and grotesque chimney-sweeps "skyed coppers" and disported themselves at marbles.'

About this time Noah Webster was so pleased by Baltimore that he decided to open a school here 'for the instruction of young gentlemen and ladies in reading, speaking, and writing the English language with propriety and correctness.' Also he was prepared to teach 'vocal music in as great perfection as it is taught in America.' Whether or not he actually established such a school is uncertain.

For a decade there was a spirited battle between the conservative and well-to-do citizens on the one hand and the 'mechanical, Republican, and carpenters' societies' on the other over the problem of incorporation, the latter groups objecting strenuously to provisions in the proposed act of incorporation 'contrary to reason and good policy, to the spirit of equal liberty and our free constitution.' Finally in 1796 the assembly passed the act 'to erect Baltimore Town . . . into a city, and to incorporate the inhabitants thereof.' The new act had many, though not all, of the provisions to which the mechanics and carpenters had objected.

The following year the newly elected mayor approved an ordinance to prepare 'a scheme of lottery, to raise a sum of money for the use of the city of Baltimore.' For a long time Baltimore enjoyed lotteries. They were held to raise money for churches, schools, colleges, and all manner of civic improvements, including the Washington Monument. One winter a lottery was held for its own sake, the money to be used for any suitable enterprise in the spring.

Baltimore continued to hate the British. In 1808, after passage of the Embargo Act, in a huge ceremony attended by all citizens, 1,200 of them on horseback, the city burned 720 gallons of gin because the master of a vessel had paid duty on it in an English port. After the declaration of the War of 1812 patriotism ran so high that the office of a Federalist newspaper, which was opposed to the war, was raided. During the ensuing riot there was loss of life on both sides. The editor and his friends were tortured. One of the latter, General James M. Lingan, died. Another, General 'Light-Horse Harry' Lee, father of Robert E. Lee, remained a cripple for life.

Besides contributing to the Federal Navy, Baltimore enthusiastically resumed its old business of privateering. Four months after the declaration of war 42 privateers, carrying 330 guns and about 3,000 men, had put out from Baltimore, and some of them preyed on English shipping within a few miles of the British coast.

A British statesman called Baltimore 'the great depository of the hostile spirit of the United States against England.' A British admiral said, 'Baltimore is a doomed town,' and a London paper declared that 'the truculent inhabitants of Baltimore must be tamed.'

The 'truculent inhabitants' were worried. Fort McHenry had been neglected. Big guns were scarce. The Federal Government had sent many of Baltimore's fighting men on the disastrous Canadian expedition and besides was in no condition to aid the city. Baltimore would have to fight its own battle. Fort McHenry was repaired as soon as possible and the guns of an abandoned French frigate were borrowed from the consul. Furnaces were built to make the 42-pound balls. Forty pieces of artillery were stationed on elevated ground east of the city (now Patterson Park) and every man and boy was assigned to the military duty. A Baltimore seamstress made a big flag for Fort McHenry.

Then the news came that Washington had been captured and partly burned. The British army landed on North Point under the command of General Ross, and the British fleet came up the Patapsco. 'The citizen-soldiery of Baltimore on that gloomy Sunday bade a tearful adieu to their wives and children, put on the harness of battle, and went forth to meet the insolent invader.' But General Ross, who was going to eat dinner 'in Baltimore or in hell,' was knocked off his horse by a Baltimore marksman and died a few hours later. The British, who had just defeated Napoleon's army, found to their dismay not only that the citizen soldiers were good shots but that they loaded their cannon with 'grape and canister, shot, old locks, pieces of broken muskets, and everything which they could cram into their guns.'

After a preliminary skirmish the British spent a miserable 24 hours in a cold rain without even blankets to protect them, and contemplated the earthworks behind which Baltimoreans and soldiers from Pennsylvania and western Maryland waited to shoot their metallic scrap. Meanwhile the British fleet fired more than 1,500 bombs at Fort McHenry and the garrison could not reply because the fleet was out of range of the borrowed French guns.

But by dawn's early light it appeared that the flag made by the seamstress was still there, and the English army had sneaked off in the middle of the night. The 'truculent' citizens were greatly relieved and within a few days were attempting to learn the difficult tune to which Francis Scott Key had written some new words.

The Peace of Ghent put an end to privateering, and the Baltimore vessels became once more the carriers of a vigorous foreign trade. The principal export was flour. With abundant water power and easy access to large wheat-growing areas, Baltimore became one of the largest milling centers in the country. By 1825, when the population had grown to about 72,000, there were some 60 mills within a few miles of the city. The soft flour produced was found especially well suited to tropical conditions; this advantage combined with its advantages of position made Baltimore the largest exporter of flour to Antillean and South American ports. Returning vessels brought coffee from Brazil and guano from Peru. The latter commodity was first introduced to the country through Baltimore in 1824; the demand for it was greatest in the Southern States, and until the Civil War Baltimore enjoyed a monopoly in its importation and distribution.

Baltimoreans had played a vigorous part in obtaining Federal funds to build the Cumberland Road (the first across the mountains to the west) and had also improved the road between Baltimore and Cumberland to draw the trade to and from the new settlements beyond the mountains. Conestoga wagons were bringing wheat, corn, and pork, and leaving with manufactured wares for the Ohio Valley. Then the Erie Canal, completed in 1825, cut deeply into this western trade, and local merchants were much concerned to find a means of recovering their advantage. At a meeting in February 1827, at the home of the banker George Brown, a committee was appointed to determine whether a railroad would be practicable. The committee reported favorably, and a charter incorporating the Baltimore and Ohio Railroad Company was obtained from the assembly on February 28. This was probably the most decisive event in the city's history. The railroad, completed to Ellicott's Mills in 1830, to Cumberland in 1842, and to Chicago in 1874, enabled the city to retain its hold on its western market.

Baltimore in the 1820's and 30's was a center for the domestic slave trade. Slaves were brought across the Atlantic in the fast Baltimore clippers and transshipped to Southern ports, and great numbers of escaped slaves captured in Pennsylvania and New York were returned to their owners by way of Baltimore.

During the nineteenth century Baltimore acquired several nicknames of characterizations, each of which reflected some phase of the city's life or growth. The Washington Monument, the cornerstone of which was laid in 1815, the Battle Monument, and others gave it the name of 'Monumental City,' a title it still proudly retains.

Baltimore also became known as the 'convention city.' Because of its central position on the Atlantic seaboard and its accessibility by train from the west and because it was a border State with mixed agricultural and business interests, political parties frequently chose it for their National conventions. Presidents Jackson, Van Buren, Tyler, Polk, Pierce, Lincoln (for his second term), and Wilson were nominated in Baltimore; as were several unsuccessful candidates including Stephen A. Douglas, Horace Greeley, and Henry Clay.

A less enviable title was 'Mobtown.' The streets of Baltimore had seen violence, at long intervals, since Revolutionary days, but about the middle of the century violence and fraud became a part of the regular political technique of various groups and finally the sole means of winning an election. Edgar Allan Poe was accidentally and tragically involved in one of Baltimore's roughhouse elections (*see Literature*).

During the 1850's the 'Know-Nothing' party gained control of the city. Although it began as a reform movement it soon degenerated into a corrupt political machine. Clubs bearing such names as Plug-Uglies, Rip-Raps, and Blood-Tubs seized the polling places and beat or stabbed with shoemakers' awls anyone who attempted to cast an opposition ballot. During the presidential election of 1856 there was a street battle between the Know-Nothings and the Democrats, each side using brass cannon. Reform was finally accomplished by the more responsible citizens of the town, aided by voters of the State; an assembly was elected which in 1860 made the needed changes in the election laws and put the police under direct State control.

The outbreak of the Civil War found Baltimore citizens divided in their sympathies but willing to postpone action until the people of the State had an opportunity to vote on the question of secession. The palmetto flag was not permitted in the harbor of Baltimore, and persons displaying emblems denoting sympathy with the seceding States were attacked on the streets.

There were, however, few who favored military action against neighboring States.

On April 19, 1861, four soldiers and eleven citizens were killed in a riot that occured as the Sixth Massachusetts Regiment was marching across town from one railroad station to another. News of this event moved the Baltimorean James Ryder Randall, then in New Orleans, to write the stirring song, *Maryland, My Maryland*.

This and other events brought military rule to the State and throughout the war the city was subject to strict supervision. Some of its officials were deprived of office and even of liberty, and their constitutional rights were suspended. A ring of forts encircled the city with guns trained not outward but toward its heart.

In April 1864, shortly before the Republican National Convention and while there was still some doubt of his nomination, Abraham Lincoln made a speech in Baltimore which, though seldom quoted, rivals his Gettysburg address in clarity.

'The world,' he said, 'has never had a good definition of the word liberty, and the American people, just now, are much in want of one. We all declare for liberty, but in using the same word we do not all mean the same thing. With some the word liberty may mean for each man to do as he pleases with himself and the product of his labor, while with others the same word may mean for some men to do as they please with other men and the product of other men's labor. Here are two, not only different, but incompatible things, called by the same name, liberty. And it follows that each of the things is, by the respective parties, called by two different and incompatible names—liberty and tyranny.

'The shepherd drives the wolf from the sheep's throat, for which the sheep thanks the shepherd as his liberator, while the wolf denounces him for the same act, as the destroyer of liberty, especially as the sheep was a black one.

'Plainly the sheep and the wolf are not agreed upon a definition of the word liberty, and precisely the same difference prevails today among the human creatures, even in the North, and all professing to love liberty. Hence we behold the process by which thousands are daily passing from under the yoke of bondage hailed by some as the advance of liberty and bewailed by others as the destruction of all liberty.'

In July 1864, after the defeat of General Lew Wallace on the Monocacy, a Confederate force under Generál Bradley T. Johnson, composed largely of Baltimoreans and other Marylanders, passed close to the city. Bridges were burned and trains captured. Northern sympathizers in Baltimore were in terror while Southern sympathizers prepared to greet an 'army of deliverance.' But Baltimore was not the objective of the movement, and the Confederates moved on towards Washington.

The war disrupted the city's normal commerce and deprived it of its extensive market in the South. But as the nearest large city to the scene of operations it became an important military depot and profited by the traffic in army supplies. When demobilization at the end of the war put an end to this business, Baltimore was faced with a problem of reconstruction almost as great as that of any city of the Confederacy. Among new-comers of this period were many members of leading Southern families, seeking to recoup their fortunes.

After several years of stagnation the city began to recover. New industries were established, new markets were found in Europe and elsewhere, and great improvements were made in port and railroad facilities.

The depression that began in 1873 led to cuts in the wage scale of the Baltimore & Ohio Railroad in 1877 with resultant strikes and riots (*see Labor*).

Throughout the remainder of the nineteenth century Baltimore continued to grow as a trade center, but the manufacture of clothing, chemical fertilizer, and iron and steel products gained in importance. Flour milling declined because of competition from the Middle West, though the city still handled much flour and grain. Oyster packing has always been prominent in the city's economy; in 1880 Baltimore was the chief packing center in the world, but since that time the industry has steadily declined owing to a depletion of the beds in Chesapeake Bay.

During the 90's Baltimore became a leader in the corporate bonding business, which was then something of a financial novelty. Of the five surety companies founded in the city during that decade, three are still in existence, having absorbed the other two and gained control of a large number of the seventy or more similiar institutions in the United States.

On February 7, 1904, a fire that started in a warehouse, near what is now the corner of Liberty and Redwood Streets, was soon out of control. Embers were blown from block to block by a strong southwest wind until even the buildings of the civic center were endangered. Fire companies came from as far as New York City and Richmond and buildings were dynamited, but the flames were not checked until the wind shifted and drove them to the water front. The area over which the flames swept was almost the same as the arrowhead tract upon which the town was laid out in 1730—plus what was once Harrison's Marsh and a filled-in section between Water Street and the Basin. More than a thousand buildings were destroyed and the damage was estimated at $125,000,000, of which only $50,000,000 was covered by insurance.

The city was faced with an enormous task of rehabilitation. A Burnt District Commission was appointed and reconstruction began at once. Some changes were made in the city plan but, unfortunately, the automobile era was not far enough advanced for the commission to understand how imperative it would soon be to have wider streets. Baltimore's economic vitality was such that recovery was rapid and within a few years the 'great fire' was little more than a chronological marker in the community memory—a point in time before which or after which all recent events have occurred.

Meanwhile the city's economic activity continued its slow and steady development. Manufacturing came to rival commerce in importance and also to change the nature of the commerce. Exports of industrial products increased while those of agricultural products, except wheat, decreased. Raw materials, especially petroleum and ores, began to dominate the imports in place of manufactured goods. The change was accelerated by the outbreak of the World War, and continued with increasing speed until well after the war was over. From eleventh place in manufacturing in 1914 the city rose to seventh by 1919, and held that position for several years. By 1929 it had sunk to twelfth place, but during the depression years it returned to eleventh place. Most of the increase has occurred in the metal-lurgical and chemical industries; with clothing, meat packing, and the canning of sea food, vegetables, fruit, and spices next in importance. Since 1922 the city has had one of the largest sugar refineries on the Atlantic coast.

Nearly 30,000 Baltimore citizens are making straw hats, suits, dresses, pajamas, and shirts, and 20,000 are working in metal, principally steel. Other industries employing from 1,000 to 3,000 workers include publishing, canning, slaughtering, baking, sugar refining, the making of fertilizer, glass jars and bottles, bottle caps, electrical equipment, paper and wood containers, industrial alcohol, liquor, and the building of airplanes and ships.

POINTS OF INTEREST

Mount Vernon Place and downtown Baltimore

MOUNT VERNON PLACE on Monument St. and WASHINGTON PLACE on Charles St., which form a cross radiating from the base of Washington Monument, have been the center of a favored residential section for more than a century. Large and luxurious dwellings overlook the four squares, covered in summer with grass and flowering shrubs and trees. There are fountains in all but the northern square and a number of bronze statues, including duplicates of several by Antoine Barye (1795–1875), which are now in the Louvre.

This area is the scene of the annual Flower Mart, a one-day affair held early in May, directed by the Women's Civic League, assisted by garden clubs, art groups, and similar organizations. Then the area in the vicinity of the monument is a blaze of spring flowers, and the normally sedate neighborhood relaxes in holiday mood. Salespeople are dressed in bright smocks. Flowers, bulbs, plants; home-made cakes, pies and preserves and many other articles are sold. 'Independent' artists have an opportunity to display and sell work which in some instances may have been too 'independent' for exhibition in museums. Traffic is re-routed for the day, so that children may ride through the square on ponies and the sounds of a merry-go-round add to the general festivity of the occasion.

Mt. Vernon Place (few Baltimoreans know that part of the square is officially Washington Place) means a great deal to the city and its people. It is an island of dignity and graciousness in a section now largely commercial, and mournful are the predictions as to its chances of continuing indefinitely its fight against encroachment. So determined have the city fathers been to maintain the slightly severe quality of its charm that it was only very recently that benches were placed in the square. 'Old' families die out, or don't care to continue the upkeep of a large town house as well as a suburban residence in Guilford, Roland Park, or Homeland. Some of the homes have already been converted into apartments and the threat of shops or parking lots is a specter frequently discussed. For the present, however, Mt.Vernon Place nestles quietly in the heart of a city that has grown away from it; and spring regularly transforms it into aisles of fluffy white cherry blossoms, flaming azaleas, all contributed by an 'anonymous' citizen who loves gardens and who has included them among his countless philanthropies to Baltimore.

1. The WASHINGTON MONUMENT (*interior open 7 a.m. to 5 p.m., adm. 15¢*), Mt.Vernon and Washington Places, 204 feet high, was the first Washington Monument to be begun and except for the rough stone tower near Boonsboro (*see Tour 2c*) the first of importance to be completed. John Eager Howard contributed the site and prominent Baltimoreans were active in raising funds for construction. They obtained permission of the General Assembly to conduct a lottery and in this way obtained $40,000. The remainder of the necessary $150,000 was contributed by the State with the understanding that the monument become State property. Plans were made in 1809, but the project was delayed by the War of 1812. On July 4, 1815, the cornerstone was laid and in 1829 the figure of Washington was placed on the top.

The base, 50 feet square and 28 feet high, supports an unfluted Doric column with cap block forming an observatory. Surmounting the column is a stepped dome supporting a 16-foot statue of Washington carved by Henrico Caucici, Italian sculptor. Robert Mills is generally credited with designing the monument, but Rembrandt Peale claimed credit for many of its features.

In the base is a collection of relics of Washington. The Washington marble bust is the work of Joseph Carrachi (1740–1801), Italian sculptor. Weapons on exhibition include naval cutlasses and British sidearms of the Revolutionary War period, a hand-forged sword and guns and bayonets used in the War of 1812. Also on display is a fire engine built in 1764 and given by Washington to the Volunteer Firemen of Alexandria, Virginia.

2. The LAFAYETTE MONUMENT in Washington Place just south of the Washington Monument, an unusually animated bronze equestrian figure of Lafayette as a young man, is the work of Andrew O'Connor; the marble pedestal is by Thomas Hastings. Ground for the monument was broken in 1917 by Field Marshall Joseph Joffre.

3. The GEORGE PEABODY MONUMENT (1890), in Mt.Vernon Place just east of the Washington Monument, is a copy of a portrait study by W.W.Story.

4. The SEVERN TEACKLE WALLIS MONUMENT, at the east end of Mt.Vernon Place, an eight-foot bronze statue on a granite base of the same height, is the work of Laurent Marqueste of Toulouse. Severn Teackle Wallis (1816–94), a noted lawyer, poet, and wit, was a leader of the campaign for civil service reform. During the Civil War he was imprisoned because of his criticism of arbitrary orders issued by the Federal Government.

5. The TANEY MONUMENT in Washington Place just north of the Washington Monument is a figure of Roger Brooke Taney (*see Frederick*)

in judicial robes, by William Henry Rinehart. It is a duplicate of the monument in front of the State House at Annapolis.

6. The HOWARD MONUMENT (1904), at the north end of Washington Place, is an equestrian statue of John Eager Howard (1752–1827) (*see Tour* 14), by Emmanuel Fremiet. On the granite pedestal is a copy of the medal given to Howard at the order of Congress for valor at the Battle of Cowpens, and a panel showing a Continental officer riding down a British soldier. Howard led the bayonet charge which is credited with bringing victory to the American forces in the battle.

7. The MT.VERNON PLACE METHODIST CHURCH, NE. Corner Charles and Mt.Vernon and Washington Places, is constructed of green Maryland sandstone with red sandstone trim. Built in 1870, it is a notable example of Victorian Gothic design. Its two rose windows, one on the front and the other in the left transept, are among the finest in the State. The flamboyant structure is notable for its lofty corner spire and turrets. The church is on the site of the building in which Francis Scott Key died, January 11, 1843. Key became ill while visiting his daughter, Mrs.Charles Howard.

8. The PEABODY INSTITUTE (*open weekdays 9 a.m. to 10 p.m. in winter, 9 a.m. to 5 p.m. daily in summer; 2 to 6 p.m. Sun. Oct. to May*), East Mt.Vernon Place, is a two-story marble building in Italian Renaissance style with columned portico, flat roof and balustrade parapet, housing a conservatory of music, a library, and an art gallery.

George Peabody, who lived in Baltimore as a young man and later amassed a fortune as a London banker, offered to give the city a conservatory in 1857. His offer was accepted in the following year, but because of the Civil War the building was not opened until 1868. In all, Peabody gave $1,400,000 to establish and maintain the conservatory. J.Wilson Leakin, a Baltimorean, left the Institute a substantial sum which was used for erection of the annex on the east. The Conservatory of Music, with a faculty of 104, offers instruction in 40 departments.

9. NUMBER ONE W.MT.VERNON PLACE is a three-story, gray-painted brick house with a Corinthian flat-roofed portico and double flight of steps. The window headings and bracketed cornice are topped with floral cresting. The bracketed cornice has cresting along the roof. The shutters are latticed and the central bay has a triple window; first and second floor windows have iron balconies. This house was built about 1848 and is believed to have been designed by a Swedish architect visiting in this country.

10. The WALTERS ART GALLERY (*open 11 a.m. to 5 p.m. daily; 2 p.m. to 6 p.m. Sun. and holidays*), Charles and Centre Sts., is a white marble building of Italian Renaissance design. Above the sloping base the first-story walls are finished with rusticated stonework and the upper story with fluted Corinthian pilasters supporting an elaborately carved frieze. The entrance on the Charles Street side, framed by a graceful arch, is flanked by bracketed balconies at the first-story windows. Above the entrance is an elaborate oval niche containing a bust of the elder Walters. The heavy bronze doors lead into a marble-lined vaulted foyer, enclosed

at the first floor level by an arcaded gallery supported on coupled Tuscan columns. The galleries on the first and second floors are symmetrically disposed around a two-story arcaded court lighted by a skylight. A monumental double flight of steps at the rear of the court leads to the exhibits on the upper floors. The gallery was built by Henry Walters (1848–1931) to house art treasures which he and his father, William Thompson Walters, collected over a period of 80 years.

William Thompson Walters (1820–94) was born in Pennsylvania, the son of Scotch-Irish parents. He was educated as a civil engineer and came to Baltimore in 1841. Here he became associated with Johns Hopkins in the organization of railroads and amassed a fortune while still a young man. He became a patron of arts and artists and each year brought from Europe some object of art. These he exhibited to friends at his mansion at 5 W. Mt.Vernon Place.

Henry Walters shared his father's interest in both railroads and art, engaged in the development of railroads in the South and Southwest, and was for a time reputed the wealthiest man in the South. Henry Walters accumulated so many works of art that he built a museum in which to store them. In 1920 he bought the Marcello Massaranti collection of Italian art for $1,000,000 and chartered a ship to bring it from Europe. In 1909 Walters opened his museum to the public and charged a small admission which he gave to charity. He died in 1931 and left to the city his museum, its contents, and his Mt.Vernon Place mansion.

In the foyer of the museum in an illuminated case is the original manuscript of the *Star Spangled Banner*. Henry Walters owned the manuscript but did not leave it to the city; trustees of the museum bought it for $24,000 when the Walters' estate was settled in New York. It is one of 641 manuscripts on display. Bronze figures of Henry Walters by Hans Schuler and of William Walters by W.H.Rinehart are in the main room.

More than 22,000 items have been catalogued; outstanding are the collections of medieval and Byzantine art, the manuscripts, enamels, and stained glass. Also here are objects representative of Egyptian and classical antiquities. Among the many special collections for which there is no permanent display space are ancient church vestments, locks, doorknobs, clocks, small arms, Daumier watercolors, minor masterpieces of the Middle Ages, court portraits of the Second Empire, and crayon sketches for some of Millet's paintings.

A bridge at the rear leads to the Walters residence (*not open*), which faces on Mount Vernon Place. The house is built of gray-painted brick, three stories in height, with small Corinthian portico and floor-length windows opening onto a delicate wrought-iron balcony at the first story, designed in the Greek Revival style in keeping with many other stately mansions of the same period in this vicinity. It is used to store and repair art objects not on display in the museum. A light which once burned day and night in the vestibule was the basis of a romantic legend which neither Henry nor William Walters ever troubled to deny. The elder Walters is supposed to have quarreled with his daughter when she returned from a ball at a late hour; the daughter left home, and Walters kept the light burning so that she might know of his forgiveness and return. A less romantic explanation is that the light was part of a burglar alarm system.

11. The HENRY BARTON JACOBS HOUSE, 11 W.Mt.Vernon Place, is reputed to be the largest private dwelling in the city. Designed by Stanford White in Italian Renaissance style, it is built of rose-colored brownstone. It is 100 feet long, three stories high, and has a projecting entrance vestibule and a rounded bay extending to the highly decorated cornice and frieze. The roof is hidden by a balustrade; windows on the second and third stories are of leaded glass.

12. The RANDALL HOUSE, 8 W.Mt.Vernon Place, is of Greek Revival design with a Doric portico. The yellow-painted brick house, built about 1834, is three stories in height, and has an English basement and roof balustrade.

13. The THIRD CHURCH OF CHRIST SCIENTIST, 702 Cathedral St., once a dwelling, is a noteworthy example of the late Victorian style of architecture. It is three stories high, with a projecting cornice, gable roof, and square cupola. A flight of steps with brownstone abutments leads to a deep vestibule. Flanking this entrance is a brownstone, balustraded balcony across two floor-length windows. The exact date of construction and the name of the architect are unknown. In 1923 it was purchased and remodeled for its present use.

14. 800–806 CATHEDRAL ST., a row of four houses built about 1850, are four stories high with attic, the first story of rusticated brownstone. A second-story cast-iron gallery porch, reminiscent of those seen in Charleston and New Orleans, extends along the fronts of all four houses and projects in more elaborate style on the Madison Street side of No. 800.

15. EMMANUEL PROTESTANT EPISCOPAL CHURCH (1854), Cathedral and Read Sts., is of neo-Gothic style, constructed of small irregular granite blocks trimmed with dressed limestone. The church is cruciform, with apse supported by buttressed piers. The richly carved tower on the front, 137 feet high, was added in 1920 when the building was remodeled by Woldemar H. Ritter of Boston.

The lofty interior with its graceful nave arcades and slender clustered piers has a fine arched-truss ceiling and a stained-glass window above the carved reredos in the small east chancel.

16. The FIRST PRESBYTERIAN CHURCH, Park Ave. and Madison St., was designed in 1854 by N.G.Starkweather and dedicated October 2, 1859; the spires were completed in 1874. It is a notable example of flamboyant Gothic architecture. This brownstone edifice is dominated by an impressive 273-foot tower in the center of the façade; the tower, with its pinnacles, crockets and finials, has an unusually vertical silhouette. A stone from the Argonne Forest has been set up in the church in memory of members of the congregation who died in the World War. Six silver collection plates made by Tiffany are among the church's treasures; they were presented by the rector, wardens, and vestry of Christ Protestant Episcopal Church who used Presbyterian churches while their own was being rebuilt in 1865.

17. The MARYLAND HISTORICAL SOCIETY HEADQUARTERS (*open 9 to 5 weekdays; Saturdays 9 to 12*), SW. corner Monument St. and Park Ave., was once the city home of Enoch Pratt. The main building, a square four-story brick structure, has a mansard roof and an Ionic portico approached by a flight of marble steps. There is a wall-enclosed side garden and at the rear a three-story brick addition designed in a modified Italian Renaissance style.

The society, organized in 1888, has a library of 30,000 volumes. Among the rare books are the Eliot *Indian Bible* and Audubon's *Birds of America*. The newspaper files include copies of some of the earliest Maryland periodicals. Among the 200,000 manuscripts are 1,000 Calvert papers, many Carroll papers, and 2,000 letters written by Maryland leaders in the Revolution. Also on display are a copy of Gilbert Stuart's portrait of Washington by Stuart himself, and other portraits of prominent Americans.

The Noel Wyatt Collection includes Empire furniture, miniatures, glass, jewelry, and lace.

On the main floor, east corner, is the BONAPARTE ROOM, which contains pictures of the Bonapartes, clothes and many other possessions of Madame Bonaparte, the former Betsy Patterson. In her last years Betsy saved fragments of lace from her dresses when they became too shabby for use. Bits of silk whose color has been mellowed by the years are wrapped just as she left them in a large piece of cotton material. A game box contains an ivory chess set; poker chips made of mother-of-pearl; ivory dominoes, a pair of ivory castanets, and two sets of carved jigsaw puzzles, one of mother-of-pearl and the other of ivory. There are also several decks of cards.

Elizabeth Patterson (1785-1879) was the daughter of William Dorcas Patterson, one of the wealthiest men in Baltimore. In 1803 she met Jerome Bonaparte, aged nineteen and youngest brother of Napoleon; they were married on Christmas Eve of the same year by Bishop John Carroll.

Napoleon directed the French Consul in New York to cut off his brother's allowance and ordered Jerome to come home at once, and alone. The couple made several attempts to sail for France, but each time French gunboats turned them back. Finally, aboard one of William Patterson's vessels, the *Erin*, they sailed for Portugal. At Lisbon Jerome landed and went to France to plead with his brother. Betsy landed in England where she learned a short time later that Napoleon had prevailed upon Jerome to give her up. Jerome later became King of Westphalia. Betsy's son, Jerome Napoleon, was born in 1805 at Camberwell, England. Pope Pius VII refused Napoleon's demand to dissolve the marriage, but the Maryland General Assembly, urged by Betsy's relatives, declared the marriage annulled. Betsy had meantime refused a pension offered in Jerome's name, also Napoleon's offer of $12,000 to refrain from signing her name as Madame Bonaparte. Later, however, she accepted an annual pension of 60,000 francs. Betsy returned to Baltimore in 1834. She spent the last years of her life in a miserly fashion, saving her money with the thought always in mind that her descendants would one day occupy the throne of France. She died at the age of 94 in a rooming house on Cathedral Street, es of the *London Gentleman*, the earliest dating from 1743, and the sword and epaulets of a Sands who was a Revolutionary officer.

23. The MARKET SPACE at the foot of Main St. is the ancient center of the city's commercial life and still a busy place on market days when farmers, fishermen, merchants, and housewives buy, sell, and inspect one another's wares. The City Dock, by the Market Space, is too small for large modern steamers, but accommodates every type of smaller craft from fishing schooners and power boats to dories with crooked peeled-pole masts.

24. The MASONIC TEMPLE, 162 Conduit St., is in the old City Hotel, part of which was built on Main Street before 1770 as the residence of Lloyd Dulany. After the Dulanys became very active in the Tory cause, the house was confiscated by the State, and sold to Colonel William Mann, who made it an inn. The building now standing, part of a later addition, is a three-story five-bay brick structure with broad gable roof above a fine dentiled cornice. In front of its pedimented Georgian doorway is a low brick stoop with twin flight of steps and delicate iron railing. George Washington stopped several times at Mann's. On his last visit here in March 1791, the boat in which he crossed from Chestertown ran aground twice within a mile of the city, 'the night being immensely dark with heavy and variable squals of wind—constant lightning and tremendous thunder.' In the morning 'Having lain all night in my Great Coat & Boots, in a birth not long enough for me by the head, and much cramped,' he was rescued by a small boat amid the roar of a fifteen-gun artillery salute.

25. The CITY HALL, Duke of Gloucester and Market Sts., is a two-story brick building with cupola on the site of the old Assembly Rooms. This center for social gatherings is said to have been built in 1764 with the proceeds of a lottery. The building burned during the Civil War, when it was the provost marshal's headquarters. Three of the original walls have been incorporated into the more recent structure.

26. The RIDOUT HOUSE (*private*), 120 Duke of Gloucester St., was built about the middle of the eighteenth century by John Ridout, secretary and lifelong friend of Governor Horatio Sharpe. The rectangular, two-story, gable-roofed mansion has two massive projecting end chimneys. The brick work on the main façade, similar to that of the Reynold's Tavern, is laid in all-header bond; brick arches over the narrow sash windows are of smooth hand-rubbed brick, and the high basement wall is covered with stucco tooled to simulate stone. A wide flight of stone steps with simple wrought-iron hand-rail leads to the pedimented Doric entrance. The regular spacing of the windows, the wide overhanging dentiled cornice which returns slightly at the corners, and the slightly projecting window trim are all characteristic of the period of construction. The garden façade is more elaborate than the front, having a wide, flat-roofed Doric portico under a Palladian window that breaks through the cornice line and is topped with a pediment. The flankers are separate from the main building.

27. ST. MARY'S CHURCH, Duke of Gloucester and Chestnut Sts., is on the grounds of the CARROLL MANSION (*private*), the birthplace and early home of Charles Carroll of Carrollton. The massive gabled house, three-and-one-half stories in height, was built in 1735 by Dr. Charles Carroll,

father of the signer. A chapel on the upper floor, 40 feet long, was the firs Roman Catholic place of worship in Annapolis. A small church was buil in 1825 on the site of the present parish school. In 1852 the property wa presented to the Congregation of the Most Holy Redeemer (Redemp torists) by Carroll's grandchildren. The present church, a brick Victoria Gothic edifice, was dedicated in 1860. The mansion is now the House o Second Novitiate.

28. The SCOTT HOUSE (*private*), 4 Shipwright St., described in Winstor Churchill's *Carvel Hall*, was built for Dr. Upton Scott, a physician attend ing Governor Horatio Sharpe. Robert Eden, the last provincial governor died here in 1784 after his return from England, and Francis Scott Key lived here while a student at St. John's. The front of the square, hip-roofec structure, which has two tall chimneys and pedimented doorway, i broken by a projecting central pavilion. The heavy bracketed cornice i obviously of later date. The building is now occupied by the Sisters o Notre Dame.

29. The JONAS GREEN HOUSE, 124 Charles St., is a gambrel-roofec building of brick, one story high to the eaves but with two attic stories There are two outside chimneys at each end, with windows between. Th house, believed to have been built about 1680, was occupied for a time by Jonas Green, publisher of the *Maryland Gazette* (*see The Press*). Benjamin Mifflin, the Philadelphia visitor of 1762, 'Went with Jonas Green to View his p[r]inting office which is all below Capacious Airy & Convenient took a Walk in his garden . . .' Green was the official 'Poet, Printer, Punster, Purveyor and Punch-Maker' of the Tuesday Club, and contributed largely to the hilarity of its uproarious proceedings.

The UNITED STATES NAVAL ACADEMY (*open to visitors sunrise to sunset; no picnicking*), whose main entrance is at Maryland Ave. and Hanover St., occupies a tract of approximately 80 acres along the Severn River, and a much larger tract north of College Creek. The buildings, forming an imposing group, were designed by Ernest Flagg of New York City, in the late French Renaissance style. The decorations throughout are symbolical of the sea and of naval warfare—sails, parts of ships, cannon, Father Neptune's trident appear on every side.

Largely through the influence of Secretary of the Navy George Bancroft, the Naval School, as it was called until 1850, was opened here at Fort Severn on October 10, 1845, with Franklin Buchanan, who was later to become the ranking admiral of the Confederate Navy, as superintendent.

The Civil War disrupted the school, midshipmen from the seceding States resigning. As preparations were being made to transfer the remaining students to Newport in the old frigate *Constitution*, Union General Butler appeared on the ferryboat he had commandeered at Perryville; Commodore G. S. Blake, the Superintendent, at first mistook him for a Confederate raider. The Academy buildings and grounds became a military hospital and camp until the end of the war.

When the school was brought back to Annapolis in September of 1865 with Rear Admiral David Dixon Porter as superintendent, traditional rigor was relaxed to permit athletics and more recreation and the curricu-

Education and Religion

er-Bodine

JOHNS HOPKINS HOSPITAL, BALTIMORE

AIRVIEW, U. S. NAVAL ACADEMY, ANNAPOLIS

SCHOOL OF MEDICINE (1808), UNIVERSITY OF MARYLAND, BALTIMORE

RANDALL HALL, ST. JOHNS COLLEGE, ANNAPOLIS

ART CLASS (c.1890), GOUCHER COLLEGE, BALTIMORE

CHEMISTRY LABORATORY, GOUCHER COLLEGE

GRADUATING CLASS, U. S. NAVAL ACADEMY

THIRD HAVEN FRIENDS MEETING HOUSE (c.1684), TALBOT COUNTY

W. Lincoln Hight

WYE CHURCH (1700), TALBOT COUNTY

CATHEDRAL OF THE ASSUMPTION (1806), BALTIMORE

olmes I. Mettee

TRINITY CHURCH (BEFORE 1680), CHURCH CREEK

W. Lincoln Hight

now destroyed. Her tombstone in Greenmount Cemetery bears the words, ' After life's fitful fever, she sleeps well.'

18. The WILLIAM McKIM HOUSE (1832), 522 Park Ave., of Greek Revival design, is of the double type and has a marble base to the top of the cellar windows and red brick above. Marble pilasters and entablature frame a deep vestibule.

19. The FRANKLIN STREET PRESBYTERIAN CHURCH, NW. corner of Franklin and Cathedral Sts., is constructed of red brick with gray limestone trim in Gothic Revival style. The deeply-recessed entrance is covered by a two-centered arch, and the large window above it is flanked by two octagonal battlemented towers. At either side of the towers are smaller, arched aisle doors. The low-pitched gable roof is hidden by battlements. The side walls are lined with narrow stepped buttresses.

The interior furnishings and paneling are of oiled, carved walnut. The stained-glass windows were the gift of the daughters of Dr.W.S.Plumer, first pastor of the church. The congregation was organized in 1844 and the dedication ceremonies took place three years later.

20. The FIRST UNITARIAN CHURCH (1819), NW. corner Charles and Franklin Sts., designed by Maximilian Godefroy, is a square stucco Graeco-Roman structure, with a heavy cornice and attic parapet. The entrance is under an arcaded loggia with four Tuscan columns, topped with a pediment bearing a terra-cotta relief figure of the Angel of Truth. Behind the high parapet is a huge dome, hidden from interior view by a barrel-vaulted ceiling.

21. FRANKLIN 'FARMS,' 3 W.Franklin St., is a three-bay, three-and-a-half-story Greek Revival house of brick covered with buff stucco. The entrance, in a deep vestibule at one side, is sheltered by a small Doric portico. Especially notable are the windows and the delicate but widely-projecting cornice. The floor-length windows of the first story have delicate wrought-iron balconies, and the low-pitched gable roof is pierced on the front by a single dormer.

In 1922 the property was occupied by Congressman John Philip Clayton Boynton Hill, a bitter foe of the Eighteenth Amendment who constantly attacked the law on the ground that it permitted the farmer to manufacture wines and ciders while denying the city men beer. In the yard behind the house he planted a few apple saplings and some grape vines. Then he hung fruit on the fence, gathered it a short time later, pressed it and permitted it to ferment, and telephoned prohibition agents that 'his wine and cider were breaking the law.' They arrested him and he was tried before a Federal jury. The juice was found to contain twelve per cent alcohol but the jury tasted it and stated that it was not 'intoxicating in fact' and released Hill.

22. The ENOCH PRATT FREE LIBRARY (*open 9–9 p.m. weekdays; newspaper-and-magazine and reference rooms 2–9 Sun. and holidays*), Franklin and Cathedral Sts., is a three-story limestone building of neoclassic design. Twelve display windows at street level flank a monumental arched entrance on the Cathedral Street side. The walls, adorned with fluted pilasters, are pierced by long rows of casement windows. The building was

erected in 1933 to replace an older one on Mulberry Street near Cathedral.

In the central hall are two murals by George Novikoff, one showing Gutenberg and his press and the other Caxton presenting his first book to his patroness, the Duchess Marguerite. The history of printing is illustrated by the devices of seventeen publishers in a frieze below the second-floor windows. On the walls are portraits of the Lords Baltimore.

In the Maryland room, second floor, are early records of the province and State and books and pamphlets on contemporary Maryland, also a Maryland picture collection of 1,500 subjects and 200 engravings of Maryland scenes from 1752 to 1931, the gift of George Cator. The Hester Dorsey Richardson collection of Maryland coats of arms is in this room.

In the EDGAR ALLAN POE ROOM, second floor, are manuscripts and letters of the poet and a lithograph of his wife, Virginia Clemm, by an unknown artist. The Edgar Allan Poe Society meets here and from time to time there are lectures on Poe and other poets. The music section in the FINE ARTS ROOM, in addition to books, periodicals and scores, supplies phonograph records and is equipped with booths in which they may be played. More than 400,000 volumes are in this building; the entire system, including 27 branches, has nearly 700,000 volumes.

Enoch Pratt (1808–96) came to Baltimore from Massachusetts in 1831 and founded an ironware business at 23 South Charles Street. His business prospered and in 1882 he offered the city a library to cost $225,000, if the city would provide a site. This offer was accepted and he agreed to give an additional $833,333 provided the city created a $50,000 annuity for the use of the library. The central building and four branches were completed in 1884 and opened a short time later. Pratt served as president of the board of trustees and visited the central building daily.

23. The CATHEDRAL OF THE ASSUMPTION OF THE BLESSED VIRGIN MARY (*open 6 a.m. to 9 p.m.*), Cathedral and Mulberry Sts., was the first Roman Catholic cathedral in the United States. Its cornerstone was laid in 1806 by Bishop John Carroll at a time when more than half of the Catholics in the United States lived in Maryland. Construction was delayed by the War of 1812 and it was not until 1821 that the building was dedicated by Archbishop Ambrose Marechal. Baltimore became the primatial see of the Catholic Church in America, and seven provincial and three plenary or national councils have been held here. In 1936 Pope Pius XI gave the Cathedral the rank of minor basilica, a title bestowed on churches notable for historic associations. It confers the right of precedence and special insignia.

The Cathedral, designed by Henry Latrobe, is one of the most notable ecclesiastical edifices of the early Republic, with a design based upon the traditional temple-rotunda plan. The mass of the granite structure is Roman with cruciform plan and low central dome. The hexastyle Ionic portico (of later date) is flanked by two large square towers with round arcaded cupolas crowned by small onion-shaped domes.

The interior is lined with large paneled piers; the nave and apse are almost of equal length, each crowned with a dome smaller than that over the rotunda-like drossing. The domed and vaulted ceiling has deep coffered panels, painted in gold, gray-green, and blue, and carved with rosettes. The high altar, a gift of the priests of Marseilles to Archbishop Marechal, is of marble with a red damask screen that forms an effective background for the gold altar fixtures. Paintings in the church include Baron Charles de Steuben's picture of Louis IX burying his plague-stricken soldiers before Tunis in 1270 and *The Descent from the Cross* by Baron Pierre Narcisse Guerin; the first is the gift of Louis XVIII, the other of Charles X of France.

On the north side near the entrance is a shrine to the Sacred Heart, and on the south side a shrine to St.Therese of Lisieux.

The church has a monstrance given by Pope Leo XIII to the late James Cardinal Gibbons, and a gold chalice made in Rome, the gift of a member of the congregation. The two tower bells, given to Archbishop Marechal by French Catholics, were cast in Lyons, France, in 1830.

In the crypt (*obtain permission to visit at* 408 *N.Charles St.*) under the main altar are the remains of six of the nine prelates who have presided at the Cathedral: John Carroll, 1808–15; Leonard Neale, 1815–17; Ambrose Marechal, 1817–28; James Whitfield, 1828–34; Samuel Eccleston, 1834–51; Francis Patrick Kendrick, 1851–63; John Spaulding, 1864–72; James Roosevelt Bayley, 1872–77, and James Cardinal Gibbons, 1877–1921.

John Carroll (1735–1815) was born at Upper Marlboro. His earlier education was received at home and after a year in the Jesuit school at Bohemia Manor he was sent to the English Jesuit college at St.Omer's, France. From the college he passed to the novitiate of the order at Watten, and was ordained priest in 1767. The Jesuits were suppressed by the Pope in 1773, and after a year in England, Carroll returned to America.

After the Revolution the American church was removed from the jurisdiction of the vicar apostolic of London and Father Carroll was made Prefect Apostolic in 1784–85 and consecrated as a bishop August 15, 1790 at Lulworth Castle, England. One of his first acts as bishop was to accept the Sulpicians' offer to establish a seminary in America; he had already been instrumental in founding Georgetown University, which he put in charge of the Jesuits upon the revival of their order. Besides welcoming several orders to this country, such as the Trappists and the Carmelite and Visitation nuns, he aided in the founding of the Sisters of Charity by Mother Seton. In 1808 he was made an archbishop, and the country was divided into four dioceses.

James Gibbons (1834–1921) was born in Baltimore of Irish parents. Educated at St.Charles College and St.Mary's Seminary, he was ordained priest on June 30, 1861. After only five years as a priest he was chosen as bishop of the new vicariate apostolic of North Carolina and consecrated two years later, August 16, 1868. In 1872 he was made Bishop of Richmond, but not relieved of his former see. Chosen as coadjutor by Archbishop Bayley in 1877, he succeeded to the archbishopric upon the latter's death a few months later. Pope Leo XIII selected him to preside over the Third Plenary Council of Baltimore (1884) and raised him to the cardinalate in 1886.

Cardinal Gibbons was an equally vigorous defender of the doctrines of his church and of the principles of American democracy. While in Rome to be made cardinal, he prevented the condemnation of the Knights of Labor, an early labor union organized as a secret order, and kept Henry George's *Progress and Poverty* off the index of forbidden books although he was opposed to its theories. The foreign control of immigrant groups which was then prevalent, especially in church matters, aroused his determined opposition. His long advocacy of a Catholic university met with success when the Catholic University of America was established at Washington he became its chancellor and president of its board of trustees. A voluminous writer whose work is scattered through many periodicals, he is best known by his books, *The Faith of Our Fathers* (over 100 editions in many languages), *Our Christian Heritage*, and *The Ambassador of Christ*.

The SEXTON'S HOUSE, an oblong gray brick structure of two stories, is entered through a vestibule broken by latticed windows.

The Archbishop's House, connected with the Cathedral by an ambulatory but facing on Charles St., is a large and solid but unpretentious building of gray-painted brick and stone, completed before the Cathedral. Its garden was a source of joy to Cardinal Gibbons, who is said to have planted some of the crocuses which according to Baltimore tradition herald the coming of spring. A large elm at the corner is believed to have been standing when Rochambeau camped near by.

24. CALVERT HALL COLLEGE, Cathedral and Mulberry Sts., conducted by the Brothers of the Christian Schools, is on the site of the encampment of Rochambeau and his troops after their victorious return from the campaign at Yorktown.

The school, which offers academic and business courses, was named for Cecil Calvert, second Lord Baltimore, and a marble statue of him stands in a niche at the corner of the building.

25. The FRIENDS OF ART BUILDING (*open 10 a.m. to 6 p.m.*), 8 E Pleasant St., a two-and-a-half-story brick house of modified Georgian architecture, is a meeting place for those interested in art and the aim of the organization is to bring together the artist and the collector. The collection of art publications here is the largest in the city.

26. ST.PAUL'S PROTESTANT EPISCOPAL CHURCH (1856) Charles and Saratoga Sts., the fourth church on the site, is a brick structure painted yellow with dark brown trim. Its three entrance portals are set behind a sidewalk arcade flanked by a low square tower and a baptistery. Though the parish was organized in 1692, the first church on this site was completed in 1739. The walls of the church that stood here from 1814 to 1854 are included in the present structure.

27. ST.PAUL'S RECTORY, 24 W.Saratoga St., on a terraced knoll overlooking the busy downtown intersection of Liberty and Saratoga Streets was built in 1791 with funds raised by lottery. The land on which it stands was deeded by Governor John Eager Howard, who stipulated in the conveyance that it must forever be the site of St.Paul's Rectory.

The yellow-painted late Georgian brick house is two-and-one-half stories high with lower and narrower wings. Three short flights of stone steps lead up to the transomed doorway under a triangular pediment

Above are a Palladian window and a classic eave pediment framing a graceful circular window. The high gable roof is pierced by small dormers and turn end chimneys.

28. The MASONIC TEMPLE, 225 N.Charles St. (*open except Saturdays and Sundays*), is a marble structure in the style of the Second French Empire, with a mansard roof. A ballroom, assembly hall, and offices are on the first floor and the second floor is used for lodge rooms.

The oldest Masonic lodge in Baltimore, at Fells Point, was chartered by the Grand Lodge of London June 28, 1770, and came under the jurisdiction of the Grand Lodge of Maryland when the latter was organized April 17, 1787. The cornerstone of a hall on St.Paul St. was laid May 16, 1814. That of the first building on the present site was laid November 20, 1866, with President Andrew Johnson attending. This building burned on Christmas Day, 1890, and another completed in 1893 burned in 1908. The present building, erected at a cost of $350,000, was dedicated November 16, 1909.

29. The BALTIMORE CITY COURT HOUSE (*open daily 9 to 4:30*), St.Paul and Fayette Sts., was built in 1899. The building, in the French Renaissance style, is four stories high and faced with white Baltimore County marble. It is topped with a balustrade behind heavy classic cornice. The corniced and pedimented windows in the projecting corner pavilions, the Ionic colonnades rising from the second to the fourth story on the Calvert street façade, and the smaller colonnades on the other three sides are predominating architectural features.

The bronze 'Cecilius' Calvert statue is on the steps of the building.

Charles Yardley Turner's *Barter with the Indians for Land in Southern Maryland in* 1634 is in the Criminal Court corridor on the east side of the main floor, and in the vestibule of the Criminal Court is his *Burning of the Peggy Stewart*. *Religious Toleration*, by Edwin Blashfield, is on the walls of the Court of Equity, third floor, south, and depicts Lord Baltimore recommending Wisdom, Justice and Mercy to the colonists. *Washington Surrendering His Commission*, by the same artist, is in the Court of Common Pleas, main floor, north.

In the Orphans Court, four panels done by Jean Paul Laurens, the French artist, when he was seventy-two, depict the *Surrender of Cornwallis at Yorktown*.

John La Farge's *Lawgivers*, four murals inside the St.Paul Street entrance, depict Justinian, Moses, Mohammed, Lycurgus, and Confucius.

30. The BATTLE MONUMENT, Calvert and Fayette Sts., a memorial to the heroes of the Battle of North Point and the Defense of Fort McHenry, September 12–14, 1814, is a white marble shaft on a square base in 'Egyptian' style with rusticated walls laid in eighteen courses, a course for each State in the Union in 1814. The cavetto cornice is ornamented with a winged globe and four griffins. The shaft is a Roman fasces, its fillets bearing the names of those killed in the battle. Above is a Victory wearing a mural crown and holding a rudder and a laurel wreath.

The Committee of Vigilance and Safety, which undertook the protection of the city in 1814, ordered the monument which was designed by

Maximilian Godefroy. The cornerstone was laid on the first anniversary of the battle.

31. The SITE OF BARNUM'S CITY HOTEL, Calvert and Fayette Sts. is occupied by the Equitable Building, an office building of 1894 in 'Venetian' style.

The hotel, opened in 1825 by David Barnum and others and under Barnum's complete control in 1826, was one of the noted hostelries of the mid-nineteenth century. Charles Dickens wrote from Barnum's, March 23, 1842, to William Guy of Philadelphia: 'I am truly obliged to you for the beautiful and delicious mint julep which you so kindly sent me. I have looked at it but await further proceedings until the arrival of Washington Irving, whom I expect to dine with me "tete-a-tete," and who will help me to drink to your health.' Dickens also wrote in *American Notes*: 'The most comfortable of all the hotels of which I had any experience in the United States, and they were not a few, is Barnum's in that city; where the English traveler will find curtains to his bed, for the first and probably the last time, in America; and where he will be likely to have enough water for washing himself, which is not at all a common case.'

The hotel began to decline after the Civil War, was sold at auction in 1870 and finally closed in 1889.

32. The UNITED STATES POST OFFICE AND FEDERAL BUILD-ING, Fayette and Calvert Sts., is a white sandstone building of severe neoclassic design. The fourth story is set back from the projecting cornice. At each corner is a square pavilion with Corinthian columns. Bronze busts, each weighing a ton and a quarter, of former Presidents McKinley and Harding, postal employees' gifts, formerly in the old Post Office, are now in the parcel post station on St. Paul Street.

33. The CITY HALL, Fayette and Holliday Sts., faced with Baltimore County marble, is an arcaded three-story Second Empire structure with a steep mansard roof pierced by bulls-eye dormers and an elaborate cast-iron cresting. The main front on Holliday Street has a composite-columned portico. A high narrow drum supports a central dome with a four-dial clock and belfry.

34. The MUNICIPAL BUILDING, Guilford Ave. and Lexington St., faced with Indiana limestone, is an impressive set-back mass with fluted pilasters and wide grilled windows.

35. ZION LUTHERAN CHURCH, Gay and Lexington Sts., a rectangular brick structure fronting on Gay Street, is entered through a rounded arch in a battlemented brick bay which rises to the gable roof level. At the right is a lofty gabled tower. The building is a reconstruction on the remains of an earlier edifice destroyed by fire in 1840.

The adjoining parish house in German Gothic style faces on Holliday Street. In it are a carillon given to the congregation by the former Kaiser, and a German Bible presented by von Hindenburg. An arcaded gallery opens onto a small churchyard. For years the church was the center of German cultural activities, and a nondenominational school was conducted on the grounds until 1895.

36. The MUNICIPAL MUSEUM (*open daily* 9–5; *Sun.* 2–6), 226 N.Holliday St., was founded in 1813 as Peale's Museum and Gallery of Fine Arts and was in its early days 'an elegant rendezvous of taste, curiosity and leisure.'

Rembrandt Peale, its founder, was a son of Charles Willson Peale (1741–1827), one of the most talented of early American painters. George Washington gave the elder Peale one sitting, and at least 14 portraits of Washington are credited to him. Rembrandt Peale, the son (1778–1860), was also a painter of considerable talent. Both father and son were men of wide and varied interests. Already in 1796 Rembrandt, with a brother, had opened in Baltimore a gallery of their paintings, accompanied by a 'cabinet of natural history.' In 1813 he determined 'to establish a Scientific Institution, such as the population and wealth of this city demand,' and bought out an older museum which advertised 'a Leopard, 70 Snakes, a Shark, 10 and an Alligator, 7 feet length—The Mocow, Bird of the Rock and Eagle alive—Electrical Machines hired out—Visitors operated on gratis.' In 1814 he opened the present building, designed by Robert Carey Long,Sr. This was one of the first buildings to be 'elegantly illuminated, except during the hot weather,' by gas. The fixtures which provided the gas light have been adjusted to serve for electric lighting. The younger Peale headed the first commercial gas-lighting company in the country. In 1830 the museum was sold to the City of Baltimore and the building served as a City Hall from that time until 1875. In 1930 the city restored the building as nearly as possible to its original appearance and made it a museum once more.

Typically early Republic in style, this three-story, seven-bay brick building has a limestone base, belt course and sills, a low-pitched gable roof, and twin end chimneys. Above the Doric loggia which forms the entrance are three closely spaced windows framed by pilasters and arches. Especially notable is the long dining room at the rear with its corner cabinets and octagonal end.

One of the canvases displayed here is *The Court of Death*, a large mural painting by Rembrandt Peale in 1820. *The Exhuming of the First American Mastodon*, by Charles Willson Peale, depicts workmen exhuming a mastodon near Newburg,N.Y., in 1801. A mural of Rembrandt Peale demonstrating the use of illuminating gas is the work of R.MacGill Mackall, local artist.

37. The WORLD WAR MEMORIAL (*open* 10 *a.m. to* 4 *p.m.*) is on Memorial Plaza which covers two city blocks at the east end of the civic center. Ground for the memorial was broken in 1921 by Marshal Ferdinand Foch, and it was opened to the public in 1925. The building, designed by Laurence Hall Fowler in neoclassic style, has a portico of six Doric columns. The entrance is approached by a broad flight of steps flanked by sea horses and tripods. In the trophy room on the first floor are captured machine guns, helmets, breastplates, sabers and lances. Two vases of black Belgian marble at the head of the stairs are inscribed with the names of the battles in which Maryland soldiers took part. On the wall at the south end of the second floor is the *Sacrifice to Patriotism*, a mural by

R.MacGill Mackall of Baltimore, showing Victory standing over the tomb of the Unknown Soldier.

38. The BALTIMORE POLICE HEADQUARTERS, 200 Fallsway, is a five-story brick and limestone building, erected in 1924. Trophies won by department athletes are displayed in the corridor.

39. ST.VINCENT'S ROMAN CATHOLIC CHURCH, Front St. between Fayette and Lexington Sts., is a rectangular, gray-painted brick building of modified Greek Revival architecture; its octagonal tower, with red painted trim, is topped by a silvered dome. The pedimented façade shelters a niched figure of St.Vincent de Paul. The interior is decorated in the usual manner with painted wall panels and religious figures.

40. The SHOT TOWER, Fayette and Front Sts., a tapering, cylindrical brick structure, 234 feet high, was once used in the manufacture of shot. Molten lead poured through a sieve at the top hardened into round pellets as it fell.

41. The CARROLL HOUSE (*open*), Lombard and Front Sts., owned by the city since 1914 and now a recreational center, is a three-and-one-half-story, five-bay mansion of red brick. The wide paneled door is flanked by Ionic pilasters and crowned with a paneled frieze and cornice. Other notable features are the square, thin, mullioned casement windows, the panels between the second and third story windows, and the fine dentil cornice. The low gable roof is pierced by three pedimented dormers, a central chimney, and two chimneys at each end. One semicircular window admits light at an end of the attic story. The interior still retains much of the original trim and a spiral stairway with an open well extending through three stories.

The house was built in 1823 on land Charles Carroll of Carrollton deeded to his daughter Mary and her husband, Richard Caton. Lafayette was a guest in 1824; Carroll spent most of his last years in this house and died here in 1832.

42. In the FLAG HOUSE (*open 10 a.m. to 5 p.m. weekdays*), Albemarle and Pratt Sts., Mrs.Mary Pickersgill made the huge Star Spangled Banner that inspired Key on the morning of September 14, 1814. The house is a two-and-one-half-story red brick structure built in 1793. The flag, an 'American Ensign 30 by 42 feet first quality bunting' with fifteen stars and fifteen stripes, was too large to finish in this small house and its maker found more adequate working quarters in a near-by brewery. She was assisted in this work by her mother, Rebecca Young, who had made the Great Union flag of 1775 and had been a professional flag maker until 1813. The original flag is now in the Smithsonian Museum.

The house, now a museum, contains numerous items pertaining to the War of 1812, including a receipt for $405.90, the price of the flag. A recent painting by L.Rodda depicts Mary Pickersgill, her mother, and her daughter at work on the flag.

The PRATT STREET WATER FRONT, from Jones Falls to Light St., is a wide, roughly-paved thoroughfare between the Basin and a row of three- and four-story red brick buildings, almost identical in design, erected immediately after the fire of 1904—wholesale coffee houses, dingy lunch rooms, sailors' rooming houses, taverns, sailmakers' lofts, ship chandlers' stores. Here may be purchased a foghorn or an anchor, a revolver or a pair of brass knuckles, a catfish sandwich or a can of grapefruit juice, an outboard motor, or a sail for a schooner.

Bay craft, both power and sail, are tied up sometimes three or four deep. Cargoes are sold to retail customers and through commission men. The dock is busiest during watermelon season. All unloading is done by hand. A human chain is formed from the deck or hold of the vessel to the buyer's vehicle, sometimes across one or more intervening craft, and the watermelons, one by one, are thrown from man to man and inspected in transit by the buyers, who usually form part of the chain.

The oyster business, which used to be a big industry in Baltimore, has reached such a low ebb that now only buy-boats and a few tongers, skipjacks, or bugeyes occupy the space once crowded by dredgers and runboats. Many of the men employed on these boats are oyster tongers or dredgers during the *r* months and farmers and cannery workers during the summer.

This section of Pratt Street was once under water and vessels could reach what is now the corner of Calvert and Water Streets. In the early years of the nineteenth century the area was filled in and the street was named to honor Charles Pratt, first Earl of Camden, an English statesman who had been friendly to the American cause during the Revolution.

Before and during the Civil War passenger cars were drawn by horses between the President Street Station of the Philadelphia, Washington and Baltimore Railroad and the Camden Station of the Baltimore and Ohio Railroad, a distance of about a mile, mostly along Pratt Street. On April 19, 1861, when Baltimoreans were greatly excited, Federal troops from Massachusetts and Pennsylvania arrived at the President Street Station. Their officers anticipated trouble and the Massachusetts men were ordered to load their arms. As the cars began to move through the city, crowds gathered and there was considerable jeering and booing. About half of the Massachusetts soldiers had been safely transported when the crowd began to throw stones and forced one of the cars to return to the President Street Station. Soon the tracks were obstructed with cobbles and ships' anchors, and it was decided that the remainder of the Massachusetts soldiers, numbering about 220, should march to the Camden Station accompanied by Baltimore police while the Pennsylvania men remained in the President Street Station. With some difficulty they were formed in double file and the march began. At the Pratt Street bridge soldiers were struck by missiles. One of them was knocked down and had to be rescued by the police. A group of men appeared with a Confederate flag, and there was a fight in the crowd when a Union sympathizer attempted to destroy this flag. Police interfered and probably saved the life of the Union man. Soldiers began firing and from this point to Light Street there was a running fight, in which four soldiers were killed and thirty-five wounded, and eleven citizens were killed and a great many wounded. George William Brown, mayor of Baltimore, appeared and at great personal risk put himself at the head of the troops, and George P. Kane, marshal of police, came from the

Camden Street Station with forty picked men and formed a line in the rear. Thus the troops were able to reach the station and board a Washington train. As the train was pulling out of the city, soldiers fired from the train windows and killed a prominent citizen of Baltimore who knew nothing of the riot that had just occurred.

43. The WHOLESALE FISH MARKET, Market Place at Water St., is most interesting at six o'clock on Thursday and Friday mornings when wholesalers, armed with bale hooks and scoop shovels, serve their first customers, the pushcart peddlers. Later the more leisurely trade, the restaurant and hotel owners and a few housewives, will come down. The present market is the central unit of three red brick buildings put up soon after the fire of 1904 to replace old Marsh Market. It is still called the Marsh or 'Mash' Market.

44. GODFREY SAILMAKER'S LOFT, 116 S.Frederick St., is the largest of several such concerns on or near the Pratt Street water front. Two steep flights of steps with rope banisters lead to the loft, which is stocked with coils of rope of special quality, bolts of canvas of various weights, metal fittings ranging from small brass eyelets or grommets to heavy galvanized iron thimbles and cringles, a hand windlass used to stretch the rope before it is sewed to the edge of a sail, and an electrically operated sewing machine. The old hand method of sewing is still employed in small patching and for certain other operations. The sailmaker sits on a wooden bench and uses a hook, fastened to the end of the bench by a heavy cord, to hold the sail cloth in place across his knees as he stitches. Usually most of the floor space is occupied by a large new sail in process of having its rope edges fitted to it (bolt-roping), its reef points sewed in place, and other fittings attached.

45. The UNITED STATES APPRAISERS' STORES BUILDING, 103 S.Gay St., built in 1932, is a nine-story brick and limestone structure of modified classic design, embellished with giant eagles on the four corners at the eighth-story setback and an impressive bronze framed entrance set between classic piers. The architects were Taylor and Fisher, and William F. Stone,Jr., of Baltimore.

46. The UNITED STATES CUSTOMS HOUSE, Gay and Lombard Sts., is a four-story building with high rusticated base and huge Ionic colonnades.

In the basement are located an out-patients clinic of the U.S. Public Health Service, the office of the U.S. Shipping Commissioner, a branch of the U.S. Hydrographic Office in which charts of domestic as well as foreign waters may be inspected, and a branch of the U.S. Lighthouse Service.

47 The SITE OF THE LOVELY LANE MEETING HOUSE (*visited by permission*), 206 E.Redwood St., is a four-story red brick building occupied by the Merchants' Club, a lunching and lounging quarters for Baltimore business men.

The meeting house was built in 1774 and destroyed by fire in 1796. The Methodist Conference held here in May 1776 was the fourth such conference in America. In December 1784 representatives of the Methodist Societies met here and organized the Methodist Episcopal Church of the United States of America. The Reverend Francis Asbury and Dr.Thomas

Cook, who had been appointed superintendents by Wesley, were re-chosen at this meeting, where Asbury was ordained deacon and elder, and consecrated as superintendent. Henceforth he started calling himself bishop, a title accepted by later conferences.

48. The OBER BUILDING, 110 E.Lombard St., is a splendid example of neo-Federal architecture. Three stories in height with a wood-corbeled cornice and crowning parapet, the cream-colored brick house has a fine triple window at the second story, crowned with an elliptical fan arch of Adam design. The main entrance on Lombard Street, with its fine, traceried arched transom, is flanked by engaged Doric columns which support a late Georgian pediment. There is a similar doorway at the side. The windows of the two upper stories have solid paneled green shutters; between them are square surface panels. The building, originally of two stories, was erected in 1905. It was purchased and remodeled in 1916 by the Ober Fertilizer Co. and is now owned by several doctors who maintain offices there.

49. The SITE OF THE FOUNTAIN INN, Light and Redwood Sts., is now occupied by the Southern Hotel, a fourteen-story brick building. The old inn, named for a fountain in the courtyard, was completed about 1775 and for nearly a century had a wide reputation among travelers. Public and private balls held here often disturbed the gatherings at the Methodist church that stood across the street. In 1781 Washington and Rochambeau made plans here for the Virginia campaign, and on April 11, 1789, when Washington passed through Baltimore on his way to New York to take oath as first president, he was met by 'a large body of respectable citizens on horseback, and . . . escorted to the Fountain Inn, his favorite lodging place in Baltimore . . .' There he was then presented with a testimonial address, suitably engraved, to which he replied 'in his usual gracious speech.'

According to tradition, Francis Scott Key came to this Inn on the morning of September 14, 1814. In his pocket was a rough draft of his poem, the 'Star Spangled Banner,' and here he is supposed to have revised and completed the poem and to have made the notation that it was to be sung to the tune of 'Anacreon in Heaven.'

50. The BALTIMORE TRUST BUILDING, Baltimore and Light Sts., 34 stories high, is the tallest building in the city. The brick façade rises above an Indiana limestone base extending to the fifth floor and is decorated with a projecting cornice around the entire structure. Beyond the 20th floor the setbacks terminate in a tower of capped arches and winged buttresses, topped by a steep ribbed roof of copper and gold leaf. The huge arched entrances on Baltimore and Light Streets have massive bronze doors.

51. The SITE OF CONGRESS HALL, SE. corner Baltimore and Liberty Sts., is now occupied by a retail clothing store. The square stone structure here was the headquarters, from December 1776 until February 1777, of the Continental Congress that voted Washington full military powers.

52. The EMERSON TOWER, also known as the Bromo-Seltzer Building, Lombard and Eutaw Sts., rises 357 feet above a five-story brick

office building. The tower, with its large clock under a corbeled gallery crowned with battlements, resembles the Palazzo Vecchi in Florence, Italy. Until 1937 it carried a huge Bromo-Seltzer bottle with a gilded crown.

53. The UNIVERSITY OF MARYLAND SCHOOL OF MEDICINE, NE. corner of Lombard and Greene Sts., was established in 1813. The red brick structure, modeled after the Pantheon in Rome, was designed by Richard Carey Long, and houses the anatomical and chemical laboratories, offices, and lecture rooms. Several Baltimore physicians, notably Dr.John Beale Davidge, began teaching medicine to applicants as early as 1792. In 1808 the assembly on the recommendation of these physicians and other prominent citizens provided for a lottery by which $40,000 was raised to found the College of Medicine of Maryland. This college was included in 1812 in the charter of the University of Maryland.

54. DAVIDGE HALL, SE. corner of Lombard and Greene Sts., named in honor of Dr.Davidge, houses the libraries of the medical and law schools. The one-story red brick building, with corner pilasters and gable pediment, was erected in 1842 by the West Baltimore Methodist Protestant Church. In 1881 it was sold to the Calvary Methodist Episcopal Church, South, and in 1905 the university took it over.

55. The SCHOOLS OF PHARMACY AND DENTISTRY, NW. corner of Lombard and Greene Sts., are in a five-story red brick and limestone building erected in 1928. The School of Pharmacy was opened as the Maryland College of Pharmacy in 1841, and the School of Dentistry as a department of the University in 1882. The dental clinic is fitted with the latest scientific equipment.

56. The UNIVERSITY OF MARYLAND HOSPITAL, SW. corner of Greene and Redwood Sts. (main entrance on Greene St.), is a 12-story brick and limestone structure erected in 1934. The modern set-back building, in the form of a Greek cross, is topped with an octagonal tower, and a high brick wall encloses the grounds. Herbert G. Crisp and James R. Edmonds,Jr. were the architects. The hospital has a school of nursing, an X-ray department devoted to five special branches of the treatment, and a clinic theater for student instruction.

57. The FRANK C. BRESSLER RESEARCH LABORATORY, Greene between Lombard and Redwood Sts., is a six-story building erected in 1939 in the same severe style as the hospital. The laboratory, founded by a bequest of a local physician, conducts a broad and generalized program of medical research.

58. The UNIVERSITY OF MARYLAND SCHOOL OF LAW, NE. corner of Greene and Redwood Sts., occupies a three-story brick and limestone building erected in 1928. The school was organized in 1813, opened in 1823, and closed in 1836. It was reorganized in 1869 and now is the largest law school in the State.

59. SAINT PAUL'S CEMETERY, Lombard St. and Fremont Ave., was opened about 1692 as the burial ground of St.Paul's Protestant Episcopal Church. Colonel Tench Tilghman, John Eager Howard, Daniel Dulaney, and Colonel George Armistead are buried here.

60. The EDGAR ALLAN POE GRAVE, in WESTMINSTER CHURCHYARD (*open* 9 *to* 5), SE. corner of Fayette and Greene Sts., is marked by a low stone with Poe's likeness on one side and a bronze plaque, given by French admirers, on the other. Poe first was buried in the rear of the church but in 1875 Baltimore school teachers, aroused by the neglect of the poet's grave, collected pennies from their pupils and with these had the body removed to the present spot near the entrance. At the time of his death here in 1849 (*see Literature*), he was so little known that the mourners at his funeral 'filled a single carriage.'

The graveyard, established by Baltimore Presbyterians early in the nineteenth century, contains the graves of David Poe, grandfather of the poet, Colonel James McHenry, Washington's Secretary of War; James Calhoun, first Baltimore mayor; Isaac McKim, founder of the McKim Free School, among others.

61. ONE HUNDRED AND FOURTH MEDICAL REGIMENT ARMORY, Fayette St. between Paca and Greene Sts., is a two-story brick building with granite base, flanked by a three-story square brick tower, the entire structure surmounted by a battlement. It is now used by a medical unit and as headquarters for the Maryland National Guard. From 1897 until 1917 the building was the headquarters of the 'Fighting Fourth,' an infantry regiment organized in 1885 by the younger members of the Protestant Episcopal Church of the Ascension, Lafayette and Arlington Avenues. The regiment served during the Spanish-American War, on the Mexican border in 1916, and overseas in the World War.

62. FORD'S THEATER, 318 W.Fayette St., is a three-story red brick building of mid-Victorian architecture, built in 1871 with James T. Gifford as architect. Joseph Jefferson, Edwin Booth, George Holland, and John E. Owens have played here. Horace Greeley was nominated for the presidency by the short-lived Radical Republican Party at Ford's in 1872.

63. LEXINGTON MARKET, Lexington St. from Eutaw St. to Pearl St., is one of the oldest and most picturesque markets in the nation. It has been operating since 1803. Flowers, vegetables, fish, poultry, homemade candy, cake, pickles, and preserves are displayed on open counters or modern display cases. Stores lining the street have merchandise ranging from cheap liquor to socks at five cents a pair. Sidewalk 'competitors' overflow the surrounding curbs to the dismay of motorists and traffic police.

The market is part of the pre-Revolutionary estate of John Eager Howard, who presented the land to the city in 1782. In spite of congestion, any effort to replace the old market is apt to raise a storm of protest.

64. ST.MARY'S SEMINARY, Paca St. and Druid Hill Ave., built in 1806–8 by Maximilian Godefroy, is one of the first examples of Gothic Revival architecture in America. It is a two-story brick structure trimmed in gray limestone, with lancet windows and doors and a decorated roof curtain backed by flying buttresses. The building is used by two lower classes of candidates for the Catholic priesthood.

The new St.Mary's Seminary, Belvedere near Roland Ave., was dedicated in 1929 and houses the upper classes of students.

EAST AND NORTHEAST BALTIMORE

65. WATERLOO ROW (1815), 606–628 N.Calvert St., was the first row of houses with identical exteriors built in the city. These three-story brick buildings originally had gable dormers and entrance steps paralleling the plane of the house; only one, 612, now is in its original state. Robert Mills, architect of the Washington Monument, designed the row which was finished about the time of the Battle of Waterloo and its name probably commemorates that battle.

66. The BALTIMORE CITY JAIL (1850), 801 Van Buren St., is a granite three-part building on the site of the first city prison, built in 1768. The five-story central portion is flanked by two long three-story wings. The whipping post, a relic of former days, is kept in storage except when used to punish wife beaters. The last public whipping, in March 1938, raised such adverse criticism that attempts have been made to repeal the statute, and the rare whippings are now carried out in an isolated wing of the jail hospital. Maryland and Delaware are the only States still retaining this old method of punishment.

67. The MARYLAND PENITENTIARY, Forrest and Eager Sts., adjoins the city jail. The State's principal prison, it was erected in 1899, contains 940 cells, and covers a six-acre area surrounded by a high wall.

68. The WELLS–McCOMAS MONUMENT, Gay, Monument, and Aisquith Sts., an obelisk of Baltimore County marble, was erected in 1871 as a memorial to Daniel Wells and Henry McComas who, so tradition says, shot General Robert Ross during the Battle of North Point, September 12, 1814. The British forces landed at North Point (now Fort Howard) and marched toward Baltimore. They were met by a small force of Maryland Volunteers near Bear Creek and a sharp skirmish ensued. Wells and McComas, two Baltimore youths, were in the American front ranks when the British general spurred forward. In the first volley, Ross fell, mortally wounded. Wells and McComas both were killed by a British volley a few minutes later.

69. BELAIR MARKET, Gay and Forrest Sts., built in 1813, was remodeled in 1939 when near-by streets were relocated. On November 4, 1856, a bloody fight between the Know-Nothings and Democrats broke out during the presidential elections. Both factions were heavily armed and the riot waged for several hours until darkness halted hostilities with a Democratic victory.

70. NUMBER SIX FIRE ENGINE HOUSE, Gay and Ensor Sts., a two-story gray brick building with a 103 foot campanile tower, is a Baltimore landmark. Organized in 1799 as the Federal Fire Company and renamed the Independent Fire Company in 1802, this volunteer organization wielded considerable influence in its heyday. The present fire house was erected in 1853 and was purchased by the city in 1858 when a paid fire department was organized. Quite a number of houses still standing in Baltimore bear the metal symbols—crossed hands, and the like—identifying them as having been under the protection of this or that fire company. If a company appeared by mistake at a building whose owner was giving support to a rival the members would stand by placidly while the

structure burned. This rivalry between companies resulted in acts that helped bring the companies into disrepute; fist and stone fights were frequent and more than one company was accused of incendiarism for one cause or another.

71. The FRIENDS MEETING HOUSE (*opened on request to caretaker*), Fayette and Aisquith Sts., is a plain two-story building with a squat, square chimney at each end. Built in 1781, it is used now by the city as a storehouse for playground equipment. When the city purchased the property in 1920 for a playground, the remains of some 300 members were removed from the church burying ground to other cemeteries.

72. The McKIM FREE SCHOOL, Baltimore and Aisquith Sts., a one-story granite building with a façade copied from the Temple of Theseus in Athens, is one of the best architectural examples of Greek Revival in the country. The Doric hexastyle portico is topped with triglyphed frieze and pediment, with a lioness' head at the roof corners. The interior resembles an old farm house. Designed by Dr.William Howard, the school was opened in 1822 by the Society of Friends with a $600 donation from Isaac McKim to provide free education. It now houses a kindergarten in the morning, a community center in the afternoon, and the Church of Our Saviour Italian Presbyterian congregation on Sundays.

73. BELFORT, NW. corner Baltimore St. and Central Ave., was built in 1870 by Julien Friez who modeled the house after buildings of Belfort, in his native France. Here Ottmar Mergenthaler, aided by Friez, worked from 1876 to 1885 perfecting his linotype machine. The linotype used today in setting newspaper type and headlines replaced old hand typesetting by casting a solid type line.

The elder Friez developed the disc phonograph and the Rowland multiflex machine. His son, Julien P. Friez, now manufactures precision and weather instruments for the United States Weather Bureau, altitude recorders for aviators, and power dam level recorders at Belfort.

74. A modern tombstone in the yard of 1607 Shakespeare St. marks the FELL GRAVES. Edward Fell operated a store in the 1720's near the present corner of Hillen Street and the Fallsway. His brother William owned a tract of land south of the store, and his nephew Edward laid out Fells Point in 1763. A fourth member of the family is also buried here.

75. ST.STANISLAUS KOSTKA CHURCH (1896), Aliceanna and Ann Sts., is a large modified Romanesque brick structure with gable roof and square central tower. Its three-arched portals have large wooden doors with decorative strap hinges. On the front of the tower is the stone figure of the patron saint set in a semicircular niche. The main auditorium is on the second floor. Here the elaborate high altar, sparkling with numerous votive candles, is screened in front by a mural. The interior decorations reflect a striking Byzantine and early Romanesque influence. Directly below on the ground floor is a low-ceiled crypt chapel. The church and the parish hall, a two-story brick building on Aliceanna St., form the center of Polish life in Baltimore. Here on Easter morning can be seen a colorful procession of uniformed members of the 16 Polish societies, the veterans of the World War who served in the Polish army, and gaily clad boys and

girls. On feast days throughout the year Poles parade through the section around the church. St.Stanislaus is one of six Catholic churches serving the 50,000 Poles of Baltimore.

76. A can manufacturing plant now occupies the SITE OF STERRETT'S SHIPYARD, Boston and Hudson Sts., where the *Constellation* was launched in September 1797. This famous 36-gun frigate defeated two of the finest vessels in the French Navy in 1799 and 1800 and captured an Algerian frigate in 1815. The *Constellation* is now America's oldest fighting ship and is docked at Newport, Rhode Island. An effort is being made to return the vessel to Baltimore.

PATTERSON PARK, Eastern and Patterson Park Aves., was a pasture owned by William Dorcas Patterson, father of Betsy Patterson, when the British attacked Baltimore, September 14, 1814. A hastily constructed breastworks along the hilltop protected about 12,000 volunteers armed with 100 cannon. 'It would be absurd to suppose,' a British soldier wrote, 'that the sight of preparations so warlike did not in some degree damp the ardor of our leaders.' The British withdrew in the face of these preparations, and Baltimore was saved. Patterson gave five acres to the city in 1827, and later additional land was acquired until 1853 when the park was formally opened. The park site was the scene of military operations again in 1861 when Colonel George I. Beal and his regiment, the Tenth Maine, took it over and called it Fort Washburn. Throughout the Civil War Federal troops occupied the place and for a time a government hospital was maintained there.

Athletic facilities include football, baseball, and soccer grounds, tennis and indoor croquet courts, a swimming pool and a boat lake. The park contains also a music pavilion, a casino, and a conservatory.

77. The BREASTWORKS, known as Rogers Bastion, overlook the harbor near the Lombard Street entrance; seven old cannon are near by.

78. The STAR–SPANGLED BANNER MONUMENT, near the bastion, is a life-size figure of a boy and girl, carrying books and a slate and holding a scroll between them. It is the work of J.Maxwell Miller, is mounted on a granite boulder, and was erected during the 1914 Centennial with funds contributed by Baltimore school children.

79. The PAGODA, a four-story frame building resembling a Chinese sacred tower, affords an excellent view of East and South Baltimore from the highest point in the park.

80. The bronze CONRADIN KREUTZER BUST, near the Gough Street entrance, was won by the United Singers of Baltimore at the 24th National Saengerfest in Brooklyn, New York.

81. 1701 E.BALTIMORE STREET, corner Broadway, is a three-story brick house of modified Georgian design. A two-story extension at the rear has an intricate wrought-iron grill on the porches.

82. CHURCH HOME AND INFIRMARY, Broadway and Fairmount Ave., is a six-story L-shaped brick building, with balustraded porches on the Broadway side at the four upper stories. At right angles to the main building is a brick three-story addition where Edgar Allan Poe died in 1849.

83. The WILDEY MONUMENT, Broadway at Fayette St., erected by the Fraternal Order of Odd Fellows, honors their founder in America. Edward F. Durang designed the shaft supporting a figure of Charity protecting orphans. The dedication ceremonies, September 20, 1865, reunited members from all sections of the country.

JOHNS HOPKINS HOSPITAL (1889), Broadway and Monument St., occupies more than four city blocks. The three buildings on Broadway are of dark red brick trimmed with sandstone, the central and largest setting back from the flanking ones. This central building is rectangular, gable-roofed, and topped with an octagonal dome and cupola. The buildings on each side are of three stories, topped with large octagonal cupolas. The buildings at the rear face two sides of a rectangular plot and are of similar but plainer design.

The hospital is operated in conjunction with the Medical School of Johns Hopkins University and shares with the school a world-wide reputation for work in the medical sciences (*see Johns Hopkins University*). It began operation in 1889, four years before the Medical School was opened.

84. The ADMINISTRATION BUILDING and 21 auxiliary buildings linked to it by corridors are on a 13-acre plot bounded by Broadway, Wolfe, Monument, and Jefferson Streets. Inside the Administration building is the heroic figure of Christ. The statue is of Carrara marble and is a copy of the work of Bertel Thorvaldsen.

85. The BRADY UROLOGICAL INSTITUTE, a seven-story red brick building facing Monument St., was the first clinic in the United States devoted entirely to the treatment of urological ailments and, with its dispensary, cares for 10,000 patients annually. Brady urologists engage extensively in research and publish the *Journal of Urology*. In 1912, soon after he had received treatment at the hospital, James Buchanan (Diamond Jim) Brady contributed $600,000 for the erection and maintenance of the clinic.

86. The OSLER CLINIC, a nine-story red brick building, east of the Brady Institute building, accommodates 1,400 patients annually.

87. The HALSTED CLINIC adjoins the Osler Clinic building and contains surgical wards.

88. The HOPKINS WOMAN'S CLINIC, Wolfe and Monument Sts., is housed in two six-story red brick structures.

89. The HARRIET LANE HOME for invalid children, Jefferson and Wolfe Sts., specializes in the treatment of child malnutrition and cooperates with the pediatric department of the hospital.

90. The PHIPPS PSYCHIATRIC CLINIC (1915), Jefferson St. side, is a four-story U-shaped building endowed by Henry Phipps, steel magnate, the Rockefeller Foundation, and Edward Harkness. Research reports issued by the clinic are eagerly awaited by psychiatrists everywhere.

91. The WILMER OPHTHALMOLOGICAL INSTITUTE and LIBRARY, Broadway near Jefferson St., has an endowment of $3,000,000 largely contributed by former patients of Dr. William Henry Wilmer.

At the DISPENSARY, Monument St. east of Broadway, 1,000 patients are given free treatment every day.

92. The JOHNS HOPKINS MEDICAL SCHOOL occupies three brick buildings in which is housed the anatomy department, the department of physiology, and the Hunterian Laboratory.

93. The WELCH LIBRARY, 1900 E.Monument St., contains John Singer Sargent's oil painting *Four Doctors*, showing Drs.William Osler, William S. Halsted, William H. Welch, and Howard A. Kelly.

The 'big four,' as these physicians were known, were entrusted with the task of carrying out Hopkins' desire that the hospital advance the cause of medicine. Osler, born in Canada in 1849, was at the hospital as physician in chief and at the University as professor of medicine from 1889 until 1905, when he left to become regius professor of medicine at Oxford. He was raised to the baronetcy in England and died at Oxford in 1919.

Halsted, born in 1852, was surgeon in chief at the hospital and professor of surgery at the university from 1889 until his death at the Hopkins in 1922. Dr.Welch was professor of pathology and hospital pathologist from 1889 until 1930. He died in 1934.

Dr.Howard A. Kelly was born in Camden, New Jersey, in 1858. He was associated with the hospital from 1889 until 1919, when he resigned his professorship in gynecology for which he has since been consultant. Dr.Kelly was a pioneer in experimenting with radium as a cure for cancer and invented the cystoscope that introduces light into the human body, disclosing the diseased parts.

Among the early associates of the 'big four' were two physicians who gave their lives attempting to advance the cause of medicine. They were Dr.Jesse Lazear, fatally stricken seeking the cause of yellow fever, and Dr.Frederick H. Baetjer, who died as the result of his experiments with the X-ray.

94. HAMPTON HOUSE, 624 N.Broadway, is the modern five-story Hopkins nurses' home.

95. The COLUMBUS MONUMENT, North Ave. and Bond St., is a graceful obelisk built of English brick cemented on the outside. Dedicated October 12, 1792, it was the first to be erected to Columbus in the New World.

96. The old SITE OF THE SAMUEL READY SCHOOL, North and Harford Aves., has been occupied since 1938 by the Sears-Roebuck & Co. store, a glistening three-story building in the modern functional style. One of the school buildings is used by the company as a restaurant.

The Samuel Ready School is an elementary and preparatory school, founded on a $370,000 bequest of Samuel Ready, a local merchant, for the education of orphan girls. It opened in 1887 with seven pupils. In two years it reached its capacity enrollment of 45; later improvements enabled it to enroll 72 girls. When the old site came to be surrounded by a business district it was sold, and the school reopened in 1938 at 5100 Old Frederick Road. It is maintained entirely by its endowment and receives no State aid.

CLIFTON PARK, main entrance Harford Rd., was once the property of Johns Hopkins. It consists of 263 acres and was acquired by the city in 1893.

97. CLIFTON MANSION HOUSE, built by Hopkins, is of Italian Renaissance design and was the summer home of the Hopkins family. Clifton is a three-story house with hip roof and two-story wings. The first story has an arcaded porch on the front and north sides. At the end of the wing on the south side is a large square tower, six stories high, with projecting string courses; the sixth story is a glassed-in observatory with an outside balcony on each face. The pyramid roof at its apex has a square, wooden, railed-in platform. The rear of the house is irregular. The building is now occupied by park administration offices. There is also a confectionery shop here.

HERRING RUN PARK, main entrance Harford Rd., is 572 acres of meadow and woodland on which are located the city's filtration plant and the Sydenham Hospital, a municipal institution. Portions of this park are particularly well-adapted for picnic and camping purposes; several 'natural swimming holes' and an old millrace are in this area. It has a free public practice golf course of five holes, a lake for racing model yachts, and athletic fields. The park can also be entered from Belair Road, Hillen Road, and Hamilton Avenue.

98. BALTIMORE CITY COLLEGE, in Venable Park at 33rd St., is a three-story gray stone building of Collegiate Gothic design with a buttressed and traceried tower rising above the main entrance. This school, opened by the City of Baltimore in 1839 as the Male High School, offers academic and commercial courses.

99. The BALTIMORE MUNICIPAL STADIUM, E.33rd St., between Ellerslie Ave. and Ednor Rd., the largest structure of its kind in the State, is used for outstanding athletic events. It has a Doric colonnaded entrance formed by a pedimented central pavilion and flanking arched gateways and was designed by municipal engineers. When it was erected in 1922 it had a seating capacity of 40,000, but it has since been enlarged so that with the addition of temporary seats it can accommodate 100,000.

NORTH BALTIMORE

100. LOYOLA COLLEGE, 4501 N.Charles St., has a wooded campus with faculty residence of stone and half-timber in Tudor style. Other buildings are rough gray stone of Collegiate Gothic design. Loyola is a college of the arts and sciences conducted for day students by members of the Society of Jesus.

101. The SCOTTISH RITE TEMPLE, Charles and 39th Sts., designed by Clyde and Nelson Friez, won for this Masonic order the prize offered by the Baltimore *Evening Sun* for the most beautiful building erected in the city in 1932. It is an imposing neoclassic structure in the form of a Greek cross with a Corinthian entrance portico fronting a wide, terraced lawn. The central mass of the building, rising in the form of a traditional Roman attic, is topped with a ribbed metal roof. Ground for the structure was broken with a spade used by John Carroll in a similar ceremony when the Mt.Clare Station of the Baltimore & Ohio Railroad was built in 1830. The building contains a banquet hall with a seating capacity of 1,500;

a large, square auditorium with terraced seats and a lofty dome; lounges, reading rooms, degree rooms, and a stage.

102. The CONFEDERATE WOMEN'S MONUMENT, University Parkway and Charles St., was erected in 1913. The bronze figures of a fallen fighter, clutching a tattered banner as a nurse supports him, and a girl, her fists clenched, representing the spirit of rebellion, are the work of J.Maxwell Miller.

JOHNS HOPKINS UNIVERSITY (*open to visitors 9 to 4, free guide service*), Charles and 34th Sts., comprises a group of modern buildings of Georgian design constructed of red brick with white trim to harmonize with Homewood, built for the son of Charles Carroll of Carrollton, which is on the campus. Johns Hopkins University was incorporated in 1867 on the promise of Johns Hopkins, a wealthy Baltimore merchant, to endow the institution. No further action was taken until the founder's death in 1873, when his bequest of $7,000,000 was divided equally between the university itself and a hospital projected as an adjunct to its medical school.

Two dwellings on Howard Street near Centre were purchased and remodeled, and the university was opened on October 3, 1876, with a faculty that included Daniel Coit Gilman, president; and James Joseph Sylvester, mathematics; Ira Remsen, chemistry; Henry Augustus Rowland, physics; Henry Newell Martin, biology; Basil L. Gildersleeve, Greek; and Charles D. Morris, Latin. The poet Sidney Lanier was a lecturer in English literature from 1879 until shortly before his death in 1881.

This school was established primarily as a postgraduate university, emphasizing mature scholarship and academic freedom and using seminar methods, new in America at that time. In 1902 a group headed by William Wyman donated a tract of land including most of the Homewood tract, then owned by Mr.Wyman, but removal to the new site was not completed until 1916.

The medical school was established in 1893, under the direction of William H. Welch, William Osler, William S. Halsted, Howard A. Kelly, and others. In 1918 the School of Hygiene and Public Health was opened.

The university as a whole was distinguished even in its early days by important contributions to experimental science. In the physical laboratory Rowland perfected a method of ruling extremely fine diffraction gratings, with some 50,000 lines to an inch. The preparation of these Rowland gratings, which have made possible the rapid development of stellar spectroscopy in the past fifty years, is still a specialty of the Hopkins laboratory, the Rowland process having been developed and refined by Dr.Robert W. Wood. Ira Remsen, who became president of the university in 1901, was the discoverer of 'Remsen's law' relating to the nonoxidation of methyl and other groups under certain conditions. Research suggested and supervised by Remsen led C.Fahlberg to his discovery of saccharin in 1879.

Innovations adopted early by 'the Hopkins' were summer courses in 1911 and evening courses in 1916, both undergraduate. The School of

Business Economics conferring the degree of Bachelor of Science in Economics was established in 1922.

103. Inside the entrance of GILMAN HALL, the largest of the eight buildings on the campus, is a full length plaster statue of Johns Hopkins, the work of the late Herman D.A. Henning, one of Baltimore's first sculptors, which for 60 years remained forgotten in the cellar of the Henning home. The Gilman Memorial Room in Gilman Hall exhibits the manuscripts, books, medals, degrees, and other possessions of the late Dr.Daniel Coit Gilman, first president of the university. A bronze plaque of Dr.Gilman by J.Maxwell Miller is on the wall, as are bronze figures holding aloft the torch of knowledge, and portraits of various faculty members. The second bronze is also Miller's work. An Archeological Museum, containing 1,000 specimens, mostly from ancient Greece and Rome, is in Gilman Hall. The main Library of 400,000 volumes is in the same building.

104. HOMEWOOD, a stately mansion standing on a knoll among tall trees, was erected by Charles Carroll for his son in 1809 on part of a tract surveyed in 1670 for John Homewood. The house has been carefully restored with funds supplied by Mr. and Mrs.Francis P. Garvan of New York. Its symmetrical mass and slender proportions are in keeping with the architectural traditions of the early Republic. A square, story-and-a-half central section is flanked by low one-story wings and outbuildings, the latter back of the larger mass. The outer walls, laid in Flemish bond brick, are trimmed with white-painted wood and brick and decorated with plaster panels and facings. A low-pitched hip roof rises above a thin modillioned cornice. The roof of the main block has pierced tiny barrel dormers, and at the center ridge is a small square cupola; chimneys of the central mass and the flankers are broad.

The exterior shows the popular taste for the Louis XVI and contemporary Adam styles typical of the period of construction. The delicately transomed entrance, approached by a broad flight of stone steps, is protected by a deep, four-columned portico in whose pediment is a window draped with scrolls and ribbon swags. Two elliptical engaged fluted columns frame the arched, eight-panel door. Other notable features of the exterior are the long narrow shuttered windows and the narrow transomed doors, flanked by modified Palladian windows on the wings.

The high-ceiled interior is planned with ease and balance. A wide central passage is crossed by a narrow transverse corridor leading to the wings, which are at slightly lower level. On each side of the front hall are two spacious chambers—the living room (now the office of the president of Johns Hopkins University) on the left, and the main parlor on the right. Overlooking the garden at the rear is the dining room, and opposite it is the master bedroom. The east flanker, formerly a kitchen and service wing, now houses various administrative offices. A narrow enclosed stairway opening off the rear hall leads to a suite of low attic chambers. The large transomed doorway in the rear hall opens onto a Doric portico.

The interior decorations are executed with delicacy, variety, and sophistication—plain plaster walls painted in light shades of green, gray, and beige; thin molded trim with delicate flutings, leaves, beads, and inter-laces; and doorways framed with engaged elliptical columns and paneled pilasters. Perhaps the most notable features of the interior are the im-pressive arch dividing the front and rear hall with its paneled door framed by leaded tracery in both transom and side lights, and the ribbed, vaulted ceilings in the transverse corridors.

The interior has been refurnished in the style which prevailed when the house was built. Nearly all of it is a loan from the Mabel Brady Garvan Institute of American Arts and Crafts of Yale University. Most pieces are of American make, but patterned after the Directoire and early Empire styles. Hangings and upholstery are in original fabrics of the period. On the walls are portraits of Charles Carroll, by Vanderlyn; of Washington as president, by Savage; and of Lafayette in his old age, by Jouett.

Among the porcelains are a blue and white service portraying Lafay-ette's arrival at New York in 1824, and a Chinese Lowestoft set with views of Mount Vernon. The house also contains rare Heppelwhite and Sheraton pieces.

105. ROWLAND HALL, named in honor of Henry A. Rowland, first pro-fessor of physics, contains the departments of physics and mathematics as well as the laboratory in which fine diffraction gratings are made.

106. REMSEN HALL, a memorial to Dr. Ira Remsen, first professor of chemistry, has classrooms and the usual laboratories, and also a low tem-perature laboratory in which temperatures approaching absolute zero are attained. There is also a powerful apparatus for the disruption of atoms and the investigation of their subatomic components.

107. MARYLAND HALL houses the departments of electrical, mechan-ical, and chemical engineering.

108. LATROBE HALL houses the departments of civil and sanitary en-gineering and the department of geology and its libraries.

109. LEVERING HALL is the headquarters of a branch of the Young Men's Christian Association and the center of student activities.

110. The JOHNS HOPKINS CLUB, for members of the faculty, alumni, and graduate students, has dining rooms, reading rooms, and facilities for indoor games.

111. The BOTANICAL LABORATORY adjoins the BOTANICAL GAR-DENS (*open 3 to 7 p.m.*); both are used for the study of botany and related subjects. Plants and trees in the gardens are selected more with a view to assisting the students than as a means of bringing together rare or beauti-ful plants.

112. ALUMNI MEMORIAL HALL, a domitory for 150 students and faculty members, has its own dining rooms and lounging quarters.

113. The JOHNS HOPKINS MEMORIAL MONUMENT, Charles and 34th Sts., east of the campus, was erected in 1934 by the Municipal Art Society. Hans Schuler, a Baltimorean, was the sculptor and William Gordon Beecher the architect.

114. The UNIVERSITY BAPTIST CHURCH (1927), Charles and 34th Sts., is designed in the Palladian style of the Italian Renaissance. The white limestone structure, designed by John Russell Pope, forms a Greek

cross with the main entrance through a hexastyle Ionic portico. The bays are also pedimented. Over the crossing a low segmental dome, raised on a polygonal drum with circular windows, is surmounted by a cupola.

115. The BALTIMORE MUSEUM OF ART (*open daily* 10 *to* 5 *p.m.;* *Sun.,* 2–5 *p.m.*), Art Museum Drive and 31st St., was opened April 18, 1929. The building, designed by John Russell Pope and Howard Sill, is an impressive neoclassic structure of Indiana limestone with a six-columned Ionic portico. The end walls of the building repeat the classic order of the front portico with deep loggias. Behind a colonnaded atrium is an arcaded quadrangle with formally landscaped court. The small stucco-covered and porticoed dairy house adjoining the garden is notable. The museum, municipally owned, holds current loan exhibitions and has a permanent collection of great interest.

The *Thinker*, a copy of Auguste Rodin's work, on the steps before the building, was purchased in Paris in 1928 by Jacob Epstein, Baltimore philanthropist and art collector, who gave it to the museum.

The Epstein Collection, in the gallery on the west of the main hall, contains paintings by Raphael, Titian, Tintoretto, Veronese, Rubens, Botticelli, Romano, Van Dyck, Rembrandt, Hals, Reynolds, Gainsborough, Goya, and Susterman. Bronzes in this collection are by Rodin, Barye, Isenstein, and Jacob Epstein, the English sculptor (not the donor).

In the George A. Lucas Collection, loaned by the Maryland Institute, are paintings and prints by Breton, Constable, Corot, Daumier, Greuze, Millet, and others. The Ernest de Weerth Collection contains paintings by Dutch and German artists of the seventeenth century. The Antioch Mosaics, on the walls of the arcade leading to the new wing, include some made in the first century,A.D.

In the new wing is the Jacobs Collection of paintings, tapestries, crystals, jades, and furniture, representing artists of the English, Flemish-Dutch, French, and Italian schools; it is the gift of Mary Frick Jacobs.

The Maryland Wing, on the west side of the building, contains the woodwork from three colonial houses. In the Stone Room, from the Habre de Benture home of Thomas Stone, are the portraits of Robert Edge, another signer, and of Dr. and Mrs.Gustavus Brown, Stone's parents-in-law, by John Hesselius. The Eltonhead Manor Room is from the mansion built in Calvert County in 1700. The Chestertown Room is from the older section of the Carroll Mansion, built by Nathanial Palmer in Chestertown in 1740. The paneling is pine, painted white. All these rooms are furnished with changing loan collections of furniture and accessories of the colonial period. The White Collection of colonial silver is outside the Chestertown Room in a gallery overlooking the Guilford Garden Court. Other collections include the Francis R. Harvey ceramics and watches; the George C. Jenkins blue and white china; the Ellen H. Bayard Irish glass, china, American silver, jewelry, and laces; and the Saidie A. May and Blanche Adler prints and textiles.

116. The UNITED STATES MARINE HOSPITAL, Remington Ave. and Wyman's Park Drive, is considered the most handsome structure of the U.S. Public Health Service and one of the most modern hospitals in

the country. Erected in 1936, after designs by Ernest R.E. Litzan, a Baltimorean, this seven-story structure is of stone to the second floor and of red brick, trimmed with stone, above. The style is modified Georgian Colonial. It has nearly 500 beds and cares for men of the merchant marine coast guard, and lighthouse service, as well as civil employees injured in the line of duty, and others. A tumor clinic, with facilities for in- as well as out-patients, has been added to the numerous other special departments.

117. The POE MONUMENT, 29th St. between Maryland Ave. and Oak St., a bronze figure of Edgar Allan Poe, clad in a dressing gown, listening to the muses, is by Moses J. Ezekiel. In 1930 Edmund Fontaine, a Poe enthusiast, demanded that the Park Board remove the *s* from 'mortals in the quotation from 'The Raven' on this monument which read 'Dreaming Dreams no Mortals Ever Dared to Dream Before.' When the board ignored his demand he announced that on the night of May 30 he would remove the offending letter himself. Police prepared to guard the monument that night, but Fontaine outwitted them by chiseling the *s* from 'mortals' on the night of the 29th. He was arrested, but admirers defended him and the case was dropped.

118. The heroic bronze SAMUEL SMITH MONUMENT, Charles and 29th Sts., unveiled July 4, 1918, commemorates Major General Samuel Smith, a distinguished soldier of the Revolutionary War who strengthened the defenses of Baltimore against the British attack in 1814.

119. SAINTS PHILIP AND JAMES ROMAN CATHOLIC CHURCH (1930), Charles and 28th Sts., of Italian Renaissance design with a Corinthian portico and a low dome, was designed by Theodore Wells Pietsch.

120. The MARYLAND ACADEMY OF SCIENCES (*open 10:30 a.m.- 4:30 p.m.; Thurs. 7:30–10 p.m.: adm. free*), 2724 N.Charles St., which had its inception in 1797, has occupied the present building since 1927. The Academy conducts research in varied scientific fields, and offers the general public a year round series of weekly lectures and moving pictures in its own building and a winter series of monthly lectures at the Lyric Theater. Its museum contains extensive collections in anthropology mineralogy, and zoology, also a noteworthy arms collection. The astronomical observatory is open every clear Thursday evening.

121. GOUCHER COLLEGE, St.Paul and 23rd Sts., is housed in a group of 26 gray granite buildings designed by Stanford White in Romanesque Revival style with dark red tile roofs. The school was opened in 1888 as the Woman's College of Baltimore, a Methodist institution, on land given by Dr.John F. Goucher, pastor of the First Methodist Episcopal Church. From 1890 to 1907 he served as president of the college without pay. In 1914 the institution became a nonsectarian school and the name was changed to Goucher College. It has purchased a large tract of land near Towson and will in time be moved to that site. Goucher has about 800 students and confers the degree of bachelor of arts.

122. The FIRST METHODIST CHURCH, St.Paul and 22nd Sts., on the Goucher campus and also designed by Stanford White, is constructed

of roughhewn granite blocks in the Romanesque style. The church is square with hip roof and a circular bay on the front. A low-arched portico gives entrance from both streets. A lofty tower at the corner rises 165 feet with tapering setbacks to a conical roof. The pulpit is from Sant' Appolinare in Ravenna, and on the windows are copies of mosaics from the mausoleum of Galla Placida. The ceiling is painted to resemble the sky.

123. The GREENMOUNT CEMETERY GATEHOUSE, Greenmount and Oliver Sts., is a battlemented one-story structure of the same dark gray stone which forms the high boundary wall. A Gothic stained-glass window on each side of the gateway softens the military rigor of the general design.

The cemetery, bounded by Greenmount and North Aves. and Ensor and Hoffman Sts., was founded on the estate of Robert Oliver in 1838. Local tradition ascribes its foundation to Oliver himself as a measure of atonement for a tragic error. Oliver, a landed aristocrat of the old school, had threatened to shoot a young man who was trespassing on his property to meet his daughter. One evening the daughter, hoping thus to escape notice, crept to the meeting in man's attire and the father, mistaking her for the lover, shot her dead. Among prominent Marylanders buried here are Betsy Patterson Bonaparte, wife of Napoleon's brother Jerome; Johns Hopkins, philanthropist; Joseph E. Johnston, Confederate general; Sidney Lanier, poet; Albert Cabell Ritchie, four times governor of Maryland; Junius Booth, tragedian; and in an unmarked grave, John Wilkes Booth.

124. The GREENMOUNT CEMETERY CHAPEL, on a knoll a short distance from the gatehouse, is a brownstone building of remarkable pure and graceful Gothic design. Both buildings were designed by Robert Carey Long, Jr.

125. WALLIS WARFIELD HOME (*closed*), 212 East Biddle Street. The house in which the central figure of the modern world's most dramatic romance lived for a number of years is a simple, three-story brick building. For a short time after her marriage in 1937 to the former Edward VIII, the house was opened as a museum, and tourists paid to see the room in which the duchess-to-be had slept. Later the house was operated as a rooming house, and more recently it has been closed. Born Bessie Wallis Warfield, daughter of Teackle Wallis Warfield and Alys Montague Warfield, she was brought as an infant to Baltimore from Monterey, Pennsylvania, where she was born on July 19, 1896. At 12 she took part in her mother's marriage to I. Freeman Rasin, Maryland political leader. She attended the Arundell School in Mt. Vernon Place and was later enrolled as a pupil of Madame le Fevre, instructor for children of the city's most prominent families. She also was a student at the fashionable Oldfields School near Baltimore. Presented to Baltimore society at the Bachelors' Cotillon in 1914, she was married in this house two years later to Lieutenant Earl Winfield Spencer, U.S.N. The house, during its brief period as a museum, was filled with displays of newspaper clippings from every part of the world, photographs of Wallis as a young girl, and similar items. The one thing in the house most certainly there when Wallis was a child is a built-in stove of the type popular in the early years of the twentieth century; on

the front of the stove is a metal plate, marked with the name *Windsor*. Tourists broke the heart of the museum owner by scorning it as an unromantic 'prop.'

NORTHWEST BALTIMORE

126. The FIFTH REGIMENT ARMORY, whose main entrance is at Hoffman and Bolton Sts., is on the site of the hall in which Woodrow Wilson received the Democratic nomination for the presidency in 1912. The massive, three-story, fortresslike building of rough gray stone occupies a city block. Wide arched windows are between projecting V-shaped bastions and the impressive arched portal on Hoffman Street has large bronze doors and symbolic sculptures. The great drill hall has seats for more than one thousand in its galleries. The armory was erected in 1901, burned in 1933, and rebuilt in 1934. It is the headquarters of the Fifth Maryland Regiment, organized in 1775 and later part of the Maryland Line. It was nicknamed the 'Dandy Fifth' for its splendid uniforms: one of its companies, under Captain Mordecai Gist, wore scarlet coats trimmed in buff. In 1814 the Fifth, with other Maryland troops, was routed by the British at Bladensburg (*see Tour 1a*) and participated in the Battle of North Point (*see Tour 2a*). The Civil War found members of the Fifth divided in their allegiance and the regiment was disbanded, most of its members fighting for the Confederacy. After the war the regiment was reorganized and in 1875 went to Boston to participate in a celebration there, the first time that a 'Rebel Regiment' had 'invaded' the North since the war. Many Northerners protested its visit. In 1877 the regiment was attacked on the way to Camden Station.

127. The GREEK ORTHODOX CHURCH, Preston St. and Maryland Ave., is a low, gray granite structure of Byzantine design with a circular plan and cone-shaped tile roof. The entrance is through a projecting circular portico supported on coupled marble columns with an elaborately carved and pedimented central arcade. The front portico is flanked by two massive bays. A two-story Sunday school building, erected in 1894, adjoins the main structure. In it are icons from Mt.Athos and relics from monasteries and holy places of the Near East.

128. The MARYLAND LINE MONUMENT, Mt.Royal Ave. and Cathedral St., was erected in 1901 by the Maryland Society of the Sons of the American Revolution in honor of Maryland troops in the Revolutionary War. A high Ionic shaft bears a bronze figure of the Goddess of Liberty holding a scroll representing the Declaration of Independence.

129. The MARYLAND INSTITUTE, Mt.Royal Ave. and Lanvale St., is a rectangular white marble structure of Italian Renaissance design with monumental arched windows and elaborately carved frieze. The Institute is the home of the Rinehart School of Sculpture. The first charter of 'the Maryland Institute for the promotion of the Mechanic Arts' was granted January 10, 1826. A new charter granted February 18, 1850, added to the industrial curriculum 'a school of design, adapted to mechanical and manufacturing purposes'—an appendage that has evolved into a notable school of fine arts. After the old building on Marsh Market Space was

burned in the great fire of 1904, it was rebuilt to house only the classes in mechanical arts, and the school of fine arts was transferred to the Mount Royal Avenue site.

130. The FRANCIS SCOTT KEY MONUMENT, Eutaw Place and Lanvale St., shows Key offering the manuscript of the *Star Spangled Banner* to Columbia. The monument, unveiled in 1911, is the work of Jean Marius Antonin, French sculptor.

DRUID HILL PARK is a wooded, hilly tract of 675 acres extending westward from the deep rocky valley of Jones Falls. The land was formerly owned by Nicholas Rogers, aide de camp to Baron de Kalb. It was bought by the city from his son Nicholas Lloyd Rogers and opened as a park in 1860. Much of its present beauty is the result of planning and landscaping by the former owners in imitation of English private parks. More recent are the eight lakes formed by earthen embankments—Druid Lake, 1.5 miles in circumference, a boat lake, and ponds used for fly-casting, model-yacht sailing, and the like. Recreational facilities include two swimming pools (white and colored), tennis and quoit courts, baseball, football, and soccer fields, bridle paths and hurdles, and ten picnic groves equipped with shelters. A conservatory and an elaborate 'Moorish' bandstand are in the western part of the park.

131. The MARTIN LUTHER STATUE, at the Mt. Royal Ave. entrance, was unveiled on Reformation Day, October 31, 1936, the gift of the late Arthur Wallenhorst, a Baltimore jeweler. Hans Schuler, a local sculptor, executed the 18-foot bronze figure of Martin Luther, which rests on a high curved granite base.

132. The central bronze figure of the UNION SOLDIERS AND SAILORS MONUMENT, at the foot of the steep embankment of Druid Lake, is a soldier turning from the plow and anvil to the sword. Unveiled in 1909, it is the work of A.A. Weinman.

133. The LIVING TULIP CATALOG (*blooms April to June*) is just inside the Madison Ave. entrance, and has more than 3,000 bulbs in 1,600 shades, colors, and combinations. The bulbs are arranged in lettered sections and numbered rows so that a fancier can identify plants he likes and order them by number from his dealer.

134. The REPEAL STATUE, near the tulip beds, is believed to be the only monument in the country commemorating the repeal of the eighteenth amendment. It is a rough stone in which has been carved cherubs operating a distillery with corn and grapes in the background. The stone was carved by John Monroe, English sculptor, and was placed in the old post office in 1894. William H. Parker, who had helped erect the post office, bought it when the building was razed in 1932 and presented it to the Park Board with the understanding that it be erected when the 'country went wet again.' It was brought here in 1933.

135. The WALLENHORST CLOCK, in the front of the administration building at the Madison Ave. entrance, was given to the park, according to tradition, by Arthur Wallenhorst because children kept asking him the time in order to see his watch, an old-time repeater, and hear it chime the hours.

136. The WILLIAM WALLACE MONUMENT, overlooking Druid Lake, is a heroic bronze figure of the Scottish hero and was given to the city by one of his descendants, William Wallace Spence, a Baltimorean, in 1893. Spence saw the original statue, by D.W.Stevenson, at Abbey Craig, Scotland, and had a copy made.

137. The COLUMBUS MONUMENT, on Swann Drive, is a life-size stone figure of Columbus, copied by Albert Weinert from one by Achille Canessa in Genoa. It was presented to the city by Baltimore Italians on Columbus Day, October 12, 1892.

138. The MARYLAND HOUSE (10 *to* 5 *weekdays, except Mon.;* 9 *to* 5 *Sun.*), a one-story frame building, has a central gable-roofed section flanked by wings at right angles to that on the central part. Each wing has a four-posted porch at ground level, and a front and rear porch covered with a continuation of the roof. The building housed the Maryland exhibit at the Philadelphia Centennial Exposition in 1876 and afterward was torn down and reconstructed in the park. It contains geological specimens, minerals, shell and fin fish, birds and reptiles, all native to Maryland. The west wing holds Indian relics. A large part of the collection belongs to the Natural History Society of Maryland.

139. The MANSION HOUSE (*open* 9 *to* 9 *in summer;* 9 *to* 4 *other seasons*), on a hilltop south of Memorial Grove in the center of the park, was formerly the home of the Rogers family. It is Georgian with Roman treatment. An outside stairway to the second story peristyle gives the arcaded first floor the appearance of a basement. The house is topped with a pyramid roof at the apex of which is a square cupola. Its first floor houses a restaurant and its basement, the park police headquarters. A rumor that Captain Kidd had buried treasure on this hill brought so much digging by treasure seekers that the house was in danger of being undermined and they had to be restrained. No treasure was discovered.

140. The ZOO is in a valley north of the Maryland and Mansion Houses.

141. North and west of the pavilion is MEMORIAL GROVE, nine groups of trees representing the Maryland chapters of the Daughters of the American Revolution. Services are held there on Memorial Day.

142. The AQUARIUM is in an old pumping station near the northwest corner. Fifty tanks contain about 150 varieties of fish, including most native fresh-water species and a number of exotic species from tropical America and Asia. The aquarium, under the joint supervision of the Park Board, the State Conservation Commission, and the Federal Government, was remodeled by W.P.A. labor.

143. The ETTING CEMETERY, North Ave. between Woodbrook and Pennsylvania Aves., is hidden in the shadow of a large moving picture theater and surrounded by the backs of business buildings. The first interment was made in 1799 when the area was far beyond the city limits. Among the 25 graves is that of Solomon Etting (d.1847), a Jewish merchant, who became president of the city council shortly after passage of the ' Jew Bill' and was one of the founders of the Baltimore & Ohio Railroad. Zalma Rehine (d.1842), also buried here, was leader of a Jewish

group that met at his house before the Baltimore Hebrew Congregation was organized.

144. The PIMLICO RACETRACK, Belvedere and Park Heights Aves., is an 80-acre racing plant with a grandstand seating 20,000, stables for 1,200 horses, a large clubhouse, and jockey and groom quarters. Pimlico was the name of the original land grant, which was named for a district in London. Fifteen-day meets are held at Pimlico each spring and autumn. The more important races are the Preakness, Dixie, Bowie, Pimlico Cup, Riggs, Futurity, Walden, and Manley Memorial. A steeplechase is run in the infield each day of both meets. The Preakness, for three-year olds, its most-advertised race, has drawn crowds of as many as 60,000 and is named for a famous horse of the 1870's. It was first run in 1873, was discontinued for many years, and revived in 1909. It is now run at every May meeting at a mile and three-sixteenths and has a value of $50,000 and added money.

Pimlico is operated by the Maryland Jockey Club, which was founded in 1830 and numbered Andrew Jackson among its members. Accepting membership, Jackson said he would not be able to attend the races because 'I experience in the advance of old age that change in the relish of amusements which would lead me as a matter of course not to partake of those of the turf . . . ' In 1877 Congress adjourned so that its members might come here to witness the 'Great Sweepstakes,' a test of speed between the horses of the East and West. Ten Broeck of Kentucky had broken records in the West, Parole and Tom Ochiltree had been raced successfully in the East, but neither was considered a match for the Kentucky horse. The Pimlico race was for two and one-half miles and Parole finished first after a grueling contest, Ten Broeck was second and Tom Ochiltree third. Contemporary newspapers reported that 'the grandstand bloomed with the fair daughters of Baltimore and the field in front was brilliant with gay equipages and rich costumes and handsome women.'

Pimlico was one of the first tracks to adopt the pari-mutuel system of betting, the totalisator, and the starting gate. Under the pari-mutuel plan the money wagered on horses to take first, second, and third places is placed in three separate pools. From each pool is deducted a State tax and the track's 'take' or percentage of the play. The remainder of the money in each pool is divided among the holders of winning tickets.

The totalisator is a recently invented device that records each bet the moment it is placed and calculates the odds each horse in the race will pay if he wins. It is placed in front of the grandstand so that betters do not have to depend upon approximate odds in making their betting calculations.

The starting gate is a metal framework of padded stalls. It is drawn onto the track and each horse is led into a stall. It prevents jostling and crowding, and perfect starts are frequently possible.

WEST BALTIMORE

145. The FIRST Y.M.C.A. BUILDING, Pierce and Schroeder Sts., a two-story brick structure erected in 1859, is now occupied by the Christ Methodist Church for the Deaf.

The Young Men's Christian Association of Baltimore was organized in Baltimore in 1852 by a group of men belonging to various denominations and headed by the Reverend Franklin Wilson. Johns Hopkins was a member of the committee to raise funds. At that time there was only one other such organization in the United States, and the Baltimore association was the first to erect its own building.

146. The EDGAR ALLAN POE HOUSE (*private*), 203 Amity St., is just north of Lexington Market. Here the melancholy poet spent what his biographers term his 'dark and mysterious years.' It was here that he wrote his only play, *Politan*, and here that he courted his cousin Virginia Clemm, who later became his wife. The house is a narrow two-story brick building; its steeply-pitched gable roof holds one dormer. As the house is in a slum area, the Federal Housing Authority was preparing to tear it down in 1938 when Poe admirers protested so vigorously that it was agreed to preserve the house.

147. The old MOUNT CLARE STATION (*open to visitors daily 9 to 4*), Pratt St. between Poppleton and Schroeder, is now a printing shop and freight office of the Baltimore & Ohio Railroad, and adjoins the group of buildings that comprise the railroad's shops. The building was erected in 1830 on land deeded to the railroad by Charles Carroll of Carrollton, and was the first passenger and freight station in the United States. In May 1830 the railroad was completed to Ellicott's Mills, a distance of about 13 miles. On the first trip with passengers, including Charles Carroll, made on May 24, the passenger car *Pioneer* was horse-drawn; it covered the distance from Ellicott's Mills to Baltimore in one hour and five minutes. On the same day the 'official annunciation' of regular passenger service was published. A 'brigade, or train of coaches,' said this first American timetable, 'will leave the Company's Depot on Pratt Street, and return, making three trips each day . . . The price for the 26 miles will be 75 cents for each person. Tickets to be had at the Depot. Should the demand be found to exceed the present means of accommodation, passengers will be under the necessity of going and returning in the same coach until a sufficient additional number of coaches can be furnished . . .'

Tom Thumb, the first American built steam locomotive, was constructed in a shop near the station by Peter Cooper, one of the founders of Canton; he built it of scrap iron, using the barrels of 69 muskrat guns for tubing in the boilers. Cooper, accompanied by officials of the road, made a trial trip with his locomotive to Ellicott's Mills on August 28, 1830. The journey out took an hour and fifteen minutes, ten minutes longer than the horse had needed. Coming back, Cooper did better, making the downgrade trip in sixty-one minutes, including a four minute stop for water.

On May 24, 1844, the world's first official telegraph message was received at Mount Clare when Samuel F.B.Morse sent 'What hath God wrought' from the chambers of the Supreme Court in Washington,D.C.

CARROLL PARK, its main entrance on Washington Blvd. at Carey St., was once a part of Georgia, the plantation of Charles Carroll, 'chyrurgeon,' father of Charles Carroll, the barrister.

148. MOUNT CLARE, near the center of the park, was built by the elder Carroll in 1754. Ivy from Mount Vernon covers its walls.

The park has a wading pool (*free*), athletic fields, a golf course, and a bandstand.

149. The UNION STOCKYARDS, at the southern end of Brunswick St., is one of the largest livestock markets in the East. Thousands of cattle, swine, and sheep pass through the hands of commission merchants, and in the spring and fall horses from as far as Oklahoma and the State of Washington, as well as from Maryland, are sold. The yards were opened in the early nineteenth century when the assembly commissioned John Eager Howard to establish a market for Maryland farmers and dealers.

The Claremont Hotel is a two-and-one-half-story brick building in the center of the yards. For generations it has been the headquarters of farmers and drovers and its dining room and lobby retain the appearance they had half a century ago.

150. The SHIPLEY–LYDECKER HOUSE, McHenry St. and Franklin-town Rd., is a pretentious three-story, square, brick structure built by Charles Shipley in 1803. It has a two-story addition at the rear and a flat hipped roof surmounted by a cupola with a gilded weathervane and three round-arch windows. The tympanum of the two-story columned portico is decorated with rays radiating from a half sun. The elaborate cast-iron grillwork of the two-story gallery porches, extending around three sides of the house, is notable.

SOUTH BALTIMORE

151. CAMDEN STATION, Howard and Camden Sts., a two-story stuccoed building showing a mid-Victorian influence, is the principal passenger and freight depot of the Baltimore and Ohio Railroad. When it was built in 1852 it was proclaimed the largest railroad station in the world. Camden was Lincoln's only stop on his trip from Philadelphia to Washington on February 22, 1861. The car bearing the president-elect was transferred to the station from President Street, then coupled to a special locomotive to take him to Washington. The movement was carried out with a special secrecy because of the tenseness of the time. Allan Pinkerton, then employed as a detective by the Philadelphia, Wilmington & Baltimore Railroad, had uncovered, he reported, an elaborate plot to assassinate the president-elect. If Lincoln were taken in a carriage from the Calvert Street Station to the Camden Station, he would be killed at the time; if he came by the Northern Central, a fight would be started as he emerged from a narrow doorway to give opportunity to the assassins. Lincoln refused to take the report seriously but when agents of the Federal Government, working independently, made a similar report, he permitted a change of plans. He passed through Baltimore at 3:30 a.m., several hours before he was supposed to reach the city.

Two months later 220 Union soldiers reached safety in this station, after a running fight with Southern sympathizers on the Pratt Street water front.

On July 20, 1877, during the Baltimore & Ohio Railroad strike, the

Fifth and Sixth Regiments, Maryland National Guard, also found refuge here after they had been attacked by strikers and sympathizers. The Sixth Regiment, called out to control rioting along the right of way, was attacked the moment it left the armory at Fayette and Front Streets. Only 50 of the 120 men in the detachment reached Camden, and they were bleeding from stone and club blows. Police barricaded the station doors but the troops were prevented from leaving by the crowd, which circled the station, set fire to the dispatchers' shed, and tore up hundreds of feet of track. The crowd dispersed the following day when a detachment of Marines arrived.

152. OTTERBEIN UNITED BRETHREN CHURCH, 124 W. Conway St., is a rectangular structure with mellowed brick walls and a simplicity of design that lends it charm. Built in 1785, it has suffered few changes, though the main portal is now closed off by another building and a small gabled side vestibule must be used in entering. The long walls are broken by two tiers of many paned sash windows with shutters and arched heads. A low square tower in four stages further breaks the severity of the lines; above the octagonal belfry rises a lantern supporting a weathervane. In the interior is a gallery over the main entrance and the ceiling is vaulted. Four years after the church was completed, its German Evangelical Reformed Congregation was presented with two bells that had been cast in Bremen and are still in use. Much of the old churchyard remains.

In the parsonage, erected in 1815, hangs a portrait of Philip William Otterbein, first pastor of the congregation. Born at Dillenburg, Germany, on June 3, 1726, Otterbein was ordained in June 1749. Michael Schlatter interested him in missionary work among the Pennsylvania Germans and persuaded him to come to America in 1752. Five of the following eighteen years he spent in work near Frederick and in 1774 he took charge of the Baltimore congregation that built this church. With Martin Boehm, a former Mennonite bishop, Otterbein formed a new church in 1789, but continued to serve as a Reformed minister. At the first annual conference of the new group held near Frederick in 1800, the name United Brethren in Christ was adopted and both founders were elected bishops. This congregation is the Mother Church of the United Brethren in Christ.

153. The STATE TOBACCO WAREHOUSE, Charles and Conway Sts., built in 1846, is a four-story rectangular building with brick walls four feet thick below a low-sloping hip roof. Tobacco from this State and sections of Ohio is sold here under a system almost as old as Maryland. Samplers go through the storehouse selecting from each hogshead six handfuls of the leaf typical of the entire hogshead. The bundles are bound and marked with the name of the owner. The buyers inspect the bundles, write their offers on pieces of paper, and place the bids in a locked box. When the box is opened each noon, the owner or factor accepts or rejects the bid. Until 1933 the sampler was required to tie the bundles with red string and place on them the seal of Maryland.

154. FEDERAL HILL PARK, bounded by Key Highway, Covington St., Warren Ave., and Battery Ave. to a point just south of the Upper Basin of the harbor, has terraces that afford a good view of Baltimore's skyline.

In May 1788, to celebrate Maryland's ratification of the Constitution, 3,000 marchers accompanied Commodore Joshua Barney and his *Federalist*, a 15-foot model of a full-rigged ship, in a triumphant parade up this hill. Later the *Federalist* was presented to George Washington.

The Maritime Exchange, organization of Baltimore shipping interests, built a lookout tower on Federal Hill in 1797 and from it received advance news of the approach of their vessels.

In May 1861, soon after an unsuccessful attempt by Southern sympathizers to raise a Confederate flag on the hill, Major General Benjamin Butler with 3,000 Federal troops seized the hill, and manned it with 50 guns which he trained on Baltimore.

The Government abandoned the hill after the Civil War and in 1875 the city purchased it for a park.

The ARMISTEAD MONUMENT honors Colonel George Armistead, commander of Fort McHenry when the British attacked Baltimore on September 13, 1814.

155. BAILEY'S ROUNDHOUSE (*open* 8:30 *a.m.*–5 *p.m. daily;* 8:30 *a.m.*–1 *p.m. Saturdays*), Howard and Ostend Sts., is a one-story red brick building in which is stored an exhibit showing the part played by steam in the development of land transportation. These were housed in the Hall of Transportation at Halethorpe, Md., built in 1927 for the Fair of the Iron Horse, until a sudden storm destroyed the structure in 1936.

In the collection are an oxcart of the time of Ptolemy III (225 B.C.); a full-scale model of Brunton's 'horse-leg' English locomotive, built in 1813; a duplicate of *Tom Thumb*, built by Cooper in 1830; a wooden model of the *York*, built in 1831 by Phineas Davis at York, Pa.; the *Atlantic*, also by Davis, built in 1832; a reproduction of the *William Galloway*, built by Ross Winans in 1848; and many others.

156. ST. MARY'S STAR OF THE SEA, Gittings St. and Riverside Ave., is a Roman Catholic Church of Victorian Gothic design built in 1869. A square corner tower of this rectangular structure supports a belfry and a tapering octagonal spire surmounted with an electrically lighted cross. The latter formerly served as a beacon to mariners; in 1870, after a mariner confused it with the north star and steered his vessel off his course, the Government indicated the light on its charts.

157. FERRY BAR, Foot of Light St., jutting out into the Patapsco River, is a sand bar, now included within the Port Covington yards of the Western Maryland Railway. In 1858 the 'cigar ship,' designed by Ross Winans and his brother Thomas, was launched here. Expected to cross the ocean in four days, it was propelled by the turning of a huge iron wheel around the middle. On its maiden trip it made fair speed but did not come up to expectations. Later it was enlarged and made several short trips but was not particularly successful.

In 1897 the cigar-shaped *Argonaut*—most successful of the early submarines—was launched here. In the *Argonaut*, driven by a gasoline motor attached to a screw propeller, its inventor, Simon Lake, made a 200-mile trip, part of it under water, from Baltimore to Norfolk, Virginia. It is said that when the vessel came to the surface several miles down the Patapsco

River a lone fisherman, sitting on the bank, took one look at the mechanical marvel and ran for his life.

158. FORT McHENRY (*open 7 a.m. to 5:30 p.m., adm. 10¢*), in the park of the same name at the foot of Fort Ave., is on Whetstone Point overlooking the North West and Middle Branches of the Patapsco River. The star-shaped fort has brick walls 20 feet high. Outside the entrance, or sally port, is a detached bastion protecting the approach. This bastion, with a drawbridge on each side, was formerly an island in the moat that surrounded the fort. Underground on both sides of the sally port are dungeons entered through narrow wooden doors battened with iron supports. They housed some of the 6,000 prisoners held at McHenry during the Civil War. Other Civil War prisoners were kept in the guardhouses where cells are entered through low, heavy iron-grated doors.

In BUILDING A, once the commanding officers' quarters, nineteenth-century furniture and cooking utensils are displayed.

BUILDING B, formerly a powder magazine, has walls ten feet thick. A squat building, it stands over deep pits in which ammunition was stored.

BUILDING C, the junior officers' quarters, is now the office of the National Park Service which has charge of the reservation.

BUILDING D, once a barracks for enlisted men, now houses the E. BERKLEY BOWIE COLLECTION OF WEAPONS, which has 500 items; including a match-lock pistol of the early sixteenth century, a Boone—or Kentucky—rifle, Enfield rifles used in the World War, and swords and knives from all parts of the world.

BUILDING E, also a former barracks, houses the Maritime Collection small tools used by shipbuilders of the nineteenth century and pictures of early fighting vessels, also a relief model of the fort as it looked during the bombardment.

Between the fort and the Fort Avenue entrance to the reservation are parade grounds. On either side of the road through the parade grounds are plaques bearing the names of the States with the dates of their admission into the Union. Behind them are oaks, one for each State.

The FRANCIS SCOTT KEY MONUMENT, near the Fort Avenue entrance is a heroic bronze figure of Orpheus, legendary Thracian musician and hero, mounted on a granite base. Its sculptor was Charles H. Niehaus.

In 1776 Baltimoreans hurriedly threw up a crude fort of mud and logs on Whetstone Point to protect the town against a British vessel. It was called Fort Whetstone and was closer to the river than is McHenry During the last decade of the eighteenth century the Federal Government appropriated $20,000 and Baltimoreans raised additional funds to build the present strong defense which was named Fort McHenry, honoring Colonel James McHenry of Baltimore, who had been an aide to General Washington during the Revolution and was Secretary of War from 1790 to 1800. At the outbreak of the War of 1812 the citizens of Baltimore strengthened the armament of the fort.

When two fleets of British warships entered Chesapeake Bay in 1814 convoying transports carrying 7,000 troops commanded by General Ross the force at Fort McHenry was increased to 1,000 men by the addition of militia, under the leadership of Judge Nicholson, related by marriage to Francis Scott Key. One of the British fleets, under Rear Admiral Cockburn, operated for a time in the Patuxent River and formed a base for the army divisions that marched on Washington and destroyed the principal buildings in August 1814. This done, General Ross re-embarked his troops at Benedict, Maryland, and Rear Admiral Cockburn set sail for Baltimore, to join forces with the fleet operating in the Patapsco under command of Vice Admiral Cochrane. An unwilling passenger on the flagship that sailed from Benedict was Dr. William Beanes, a wealthy physician of Upper Marlboro. Because of a supposed insult to the British troops, Dr. Beanes had been arrested in his home at midnight and, clad only in his night shirt, had been compelled to ride a horse bareback all the way to Benedict. Word of Dr. Beanes' plight was carried to Francis Scott Key in Georgetown, and Key, equipped with a letter from President Madison, set forth to aid his friend. While Key and the cartel officer of Baltimore were on board Admiral Cockburn's flagship negotiating for Beanes' release, Cockburn's fleet joined Cochrane's and Key was ordered to remain on the cartel sloop *Minden* under guard of marines, as important events were pending. These events materialized on September 13, when the combined British fleets commenced a bombardment of Fort McHenry that continued throughout the day and into the night. The attack did little damage although the sky was illuminated by bursting bombs and the red light from Congreve rockets, used for the first time in warfare. Near midnight Vice Admiral Cochrane ordered all boats out for a landing party and an attempt was made to storm the fort. Lieutenant Colonel Armistead, in command of the fort, had reserved his fire, but on the approach of boats carrying sailors and marines he began a vigorous defense. Practically every attacking boat was sunk and for some time British sailors were seen swimming in the Patapsco, awaiting rescue from their ships.

All this was witnessed by the lawyer, Francis Scott Key, from the deck of the *Minden*, and that night the words of *The Star Spangled Banner* were born.

On the morning of the 14th, with the flag still waving above Fort McHenry, word came to the British commander that General Ross had been killed (*see Tour 2a*); Vice Admiral Cochrane ordered a retreat. Key was put on shore, and the British fleet sailed down the Chesapeake to sea. Dr. Beanes' fate is not certain; there is evidence that he was taken to Halifax and imprisoned there for a year.

On April 19, 1861, after the clash with Federal troops, citizens paraded through the town shouting 'Capture Fort McHenry.' The small garrison at the fort was worried. On the following day a vessel, the *Spaulding*, came from Fortress Monroe for coal and anchored under the fort. Army officers spread the word that this ship had brought 800 troops, and to give color to the story, they ordered tents pitched. This hoax probably saved the fort from attack and, in the opinion of some, prevented Maryland from seceding. Exactly 47 years from the day Key wrote *The Star Spangled Banner*, his grandson, Francis Key Howard, was arrested and imprisoned in this fort with others, including the mayor of Baltimore and members of the assembly, suspected of sympathizing with the South. Howard was taken to Fortress Monroe, where he was kept a prisoner for a long time.

From 1861 to 1900 the fort was an infantry post, but modern artillery made it useless and the Government abandoned it. In 1915 the fort and the grounds were leased to the city of Baltimore for a park but were reclaimed by the Government during the World War and converted into a hospital. In 1925 the area was made a National park.

POINTS OF INTEREST IN THE ENVIRONS

Patapsco State Park, 9.9 *m.* (*see Tour 1b*); Hampton, 10 *m.*, Maryland Whippet Club Track, 10.5 *m.*, Brooklandwood, 10.9 *m.*, Loch Raven Dam, 13.2 *m.* (*see Tour 1A*); Folly Quarter, 16.6 *m.* (*see Tour 1B*); North Point Battlefield, 7.7 *m.*, Bay Shore Amusement Park, 16.7 *m.* (*see Tour 2a*); Doughoregan Manor, 16.3 *m.* (*see Tour 2b*); Timonium Fair Grounds, 11.3 *m.* (*see Tour 13*); Trentham, 11.3 *m.*, State Game Farm, 12 *m.*; Maryland Polo Club, 12.7 *m.*, St. Thomas Church, Garrison Forest, 13.2 *m.* (*see Tour 14*).

Cambridge

Bus Stations: Hotel Cambridge and Oakley Beach Hotel for Red Star Busses; Muir Street for Kirwan's local busses.

Traffic Regulations: No **U** turns, all turns on green; parking meters in business section, 5¢ an hour.

Accommodations: Hotels and tourist homes.

Information Service: Town Hall, and larger hotels.

Motion Picture Houses: 2. Opera House open for occasional shows and concerts.

Baseball: Eastern Shore League (Class D) Park on Fair Grounds, S. end of Race St.

Fishing and Crabbing: From bridge or from rented boats.

Annual Events: Cambridge Yacht Club Regatta, 1st week in Aug.; Cambridge Yacht Club Dinner and Fireworks Display, July 4; Muskrat Skinning Contest, 1st week in Feb.; American Legion Basketball Tournament, no fixed date; Annual Spring Flower Show, Dorchester Garden Club, no fixed date.

CAMBRIDGE (20 alt.,8,544 pop.), seat of Dorchester County, is along the south shore of the two-mile-wide Choptank River and is second on the Eastern Shore in size and business activity. Cambridge Creek, which divides the town into East and West Cambridge, is lined with fish wharves, crab plants, canneries, and warehouses; but the Choptank River is bordered with fine homes, large shade trees, and lawns ornamented with magnolia, mimosa, and crepe myrtle trees.

The Choptank had never been bridged here until 1935 when the Governor Harrington Bridge, then the longest concrete span in Maryland, was opened. The presidential yacht, bearing President Franklin D. Roosevelt, was the first vessel to pass through the draw.

Most of the stores and offices are crowded on narrow Race and Poplar Streets; in this section, on Gay Street, are the new municipal building and the public library. In the High Street section, the older part of Cambridge, are many interesting old houses and the Victorian courthouse. Although there is a quickening movement to the town, the pace is still moderate and the mood sociable. 'Hello, Cap'n!' is a frequent form of address; nautical caps sit rakishly above tanned faces. In the crowded yacht basin on the Choptank at the foot of Mill Street are pleasure boats of every description; in contrast, Cambridge Creek is the harbor for commercial fish, oyster, and crab vessels that supply the packing houses. In addition to their vegetable- and seafood-packing plants, Cambridge has a fertilizer plant, lumber, flour, and textile mills, and shipyards. Great numbers of diamondback terrapin (*see Tour 6B*) and black muskrat pelts are shipped each year.

Four newspapers, one a daily, are published in this town. It has modern schools, a new library, a hospital that serves a wide area, a $375,000-sewage treatment plant, four banks (with assets of $15,000,000), three hotels, and a new country club and a yacht club, both by the Choptank River.

Cambridge is governed by a mayor and five commissioners, one from each of the five wards. The new municipal building houses all civic departments, including an ultramodern volunteer fire department. This is a particular pet of the citizens since they have had several disastrous fires; one in 1910 damaged the business section to the extent of $250,000. The firemen conduct an annual festival at which they stoke up the boiler of the old horse-drawn steam engine and roast bushels of oysters to be dipped into vinegar or melted butter and eaten by the crowd.

Cambridge was founded in 1684 on 'Daniel Jones's Plantation on the South Side of the *Great Choptank*.' It was one of the towns provided for in a supplement to the 1683 Act for Advancement of Trade. To facilitate the collection of revenue, this act called for the establishment of 31 towns where '. . . All Ships and Vessels Trading into this Province, after the last Day of *August*, 1685, shall unlade their respective Goods [and where] All Goods, Wares & of the Growth, Production, or Manufacture of this Province . . . to be exported, shall first be brought . . .' The penalty designated for trading outside the established ports was confiscation of all such goods 'one Third to his Lordship, one Third to the benefit of the next adjacent Town in the County where such offence shall be committed, and one Third to the Informer.' Instructions for purchasing and laying out the towns were detailed, including the surveyor's fee of '80 lb. of Tobacco for each Lot, to be paid by the Taker-up.' Nevertheless shipping from planters' private wharves continued and a supplement to the act was passed by the assembly the following year, giving more instructions and listing additional sites. The new settlement on Jones's Plantation was called Cambridge for the English town, and in 1686 the assembly ordered a courthouse to be built on the site. Two streets laid out at that time, High and Poplar, retain those names today.

At first Cambridge was the home chiefly of court and county officials and of lawyers, but when tobacco raising had brought prosperity to the planters, some moved to the county seat. In 1745 the town was incorporated by act of assembly. Slave labor, both in the early days and in the first half of the nineteenth century, formed much of the basis for the luxury and ease that characterized the village. By 1770 the population was between three and five hundred.

Following the Revolution, in which the residents took a prominent part, the town was resurveyed (1799) and new town lots laid out. Growth, however, was slight and by 1860 the population had reached only about 1,200. In 1869 the first large factory was established, and sawmills and flour mills were erected. Fruit and vegetable canneries and large oyster- and crab-packing plants came later.

In 1899 a Dorchester historian described Cambridge as 'a charming city of flower-gardens, shaded streets, and modern buildings that collectively decorate a well-selected town location; a spot of the red men's choice where they built their wigwams centuries ago.' In many ways this describes the Cambridge of today.

POINTS OF INTEREST

THE POINT, at the confluence of Cambridge Creek and the river, a large white frame mansion with a portico, is reputedly the oldest dwelling in Cambridge; the main part was erected 1706–10 by Colonel John Kirk, agent of Lord Baltimore for Dorchester County.

The SITE OF DORCHESTER HOUSE, corner of Race and Gay Sts., now covered by business houses, garages, and a parking lot, was occupied until 1939 by a splendid eighteenth-century house with spacious lawns. It was owned by Thomas Nevitt, later by Gustavus Scott of the Continental Congress, and by Dr. Thomas White who converted it into a hotel. On the hotel lawn was held in 1850 a week-long discussion between Democrats and Whigs over the convention called that year to change the State constitution. Race Street, which began at this point and extended an exact mile to the town limits, was long used for races between the owners of sleighs and buggies.

LA GRANGE or Muse House, N. end of Maryland Ave., a three-story red brick dwelling erected in the 1760's, presumably by the Woolford family, is distinguished by its tall, wide chimneys and thick walls. The estate, purchased from the Indians in 1686, was conveyed by deed bearing the mark of Ababco, 'king of the natives,' and confirmed in 1702 by 'Winacaco, otherwise Onocknateon, ruler and king,' the consideration being '42 matchcoats.' When Dr. William Muse was the owner, it is said, he played a lyre at a third-floor window to please his brother listening in the near-by cupola of the Muse Mansion, later Cambridge Seminary.

The HILL or WALLACE MANSION, Gay and Spring Sts., one block east of the courthouse, a large two-and-a-half-story brick building with a small front porch and a large wing extending west, is now used as an annex to the Hotel Dixon. A magnolia tree, said to be the largest and oldest on the Eastern Shore, stands in the garden of boxwood and spring jonquils. This was formerly the home of Sir Roger Woolford, Lord Baltimore's Commissioner for this section of Maryland; tradition says that the commissioner and his wife are buried on the grounds, although the only marked graves today are those of John Woolford (1703–70) and his wife, Margaret (1705–72). Colonel James Wallace, who acquired the house about 1838, was the first to raise peaches on a commercial scale in Dorchester County and was a pioneer in this section in canning oysters and vegetables.

DORCHESTER COURTHOUSE, Spring, High, and Court Place, a three-story cream-colored brick building completed in 1853, is the third courthouse on this site. The first was built in 1687, when Captain Anthony Dawson contracted with Major Thomas Taylor, steward of Dorchester County, to build for 26,000 pounds of tobacco, 'a house 40 feet in length and 24 feet in breadth, of two floors, four large windows below and one small closet window, with two large casements to each window. . . . Chambers to be sealed; one large pair of stairs with rails and balusters, a large porch at ye end of the house . . .'

On October 17, 1695, the assembly ordered that the 'Courthouse at Cambridge be used for holding Episcopal Church services, as it stood convenient for church purposes in the parish.' This building was replaced in 1770 by the second courthouse that served till 1851 when it was destroyed by fire.

At the rear of the present courthouse is the three-story granite MUNICIPAL AND COUNTY JAIL. Upon the courthouse lawn a small pavilion faces a fountain, fed by a spring whose waters had cut into the earth and formed a creek deep enough to float vessels of light draft. Spring Street was named for this spring, and the indentation in the lawn is called Spring Valley.

CHRIST PROTESTANT EPISCOPAL CHURCH, NE. corner High and Spring Sts., a Gothic building of green serpentine stone, has three memorial windows including a representation of the Sermon on the Mount done in stained glass. Among those buried in the churchyard are Revolutionary and other war heroes, as well as statesmen and jurists.

In 1692 the colony was divided into thirty Anglican parishes, two of which, Old Dorchester and Great Choptank, were in Dorchester County. Shortly after 1695 the first church on this site was built, and one has stood here ever since.

The CAMBRIDGE YACHT CLUB, foot of Mill Street, resembles the bridge and deck house of a large modern yacht. An electrically-operated panel board indicates, by the push of a button, the daily temperature, wind velocity and direction. A basin extending from Mill Street to High Street provides mooring space for eighty yachts. The Club sponsors an annual regatta.

MEMORIAL PARK, foot of High Street, honoring World War heroes, has an illuminated fountain that nightly throws streams of water 25 feet in the air.

GLASGOW, on Hambrook Boulevard, at the city line, a two-and-a-half-story brick mansion painted white, was built in 1760 by William Murray on Lockerman's Manor, a tract granted to a William Murray who was a ward and cousin of the chief of the Clan Murray in Scotland, and who came to America late in the seventeenth century.

The high-ceilinged house has carved mantels, mahogany stair rails, walnut floors, and deep window seats.

The JORDAN HOUSE, SW. corner of High and Glasgow Sts., is a U-shaped two-and-a-half-story white frame Georgian house. The oldest section of the house was erected before the Revolution, it is believed, by a member of the Vans Murray clan. The spacious entrance hall, wide stairway, beautiful paneling, and attractive mantels with fluted columns form suitable background for its old furnishings which had been stored in the attic until recently. A twelve-foot square frame building near the house was formerly used as a smokehouse and is believed to be one of the oldest structures in Cambridge.

The gardens of the estate contain a formal arrangement of old boxwood and a flower garden blooming from early spring to late fall. Here, near a goldfish pool and rock garden, an enormous old mill wheel forms a garden seat, and a huge wistaria spreads its branches along the rear of the house.

SYCAMORE COTTAGE, 217 High Street, so-named for the large trees that surround it, is a two-story white building with green hip roof, at present the home of the Cambridge Woman's Club. It was erected by Daniel and Mary Maynadier, the latter a granddaughter of William Vans Murray who, having embraced the cause of the Pretender in the Scottish Rebellion of 1715, was forced to flee and settled in Cambridge. Maynadier was the son of the Reverend Daniel Maynadier, a French Huguenot who left France following the revocation of the Edict of Nantes and came to Talbot County. Sycamore Cottage was the home, after the Revolution, of Henry Page, a distinguished lawyer and State Senator.

The PHILLIPS PACKING COMPANY PLANT, in East Cambridge, houses the company's largest branch factory, principal offices, and experimental kitchens and laboratories. The company, founded in 1902 by Colonel Albanus Phillips, packs forty varieties of vegetables, meat, and fish, including sixteen kinds of soup, in this and fifteen other large plants in New Jersey, Delaware, and Maryland. During the peak of seasonal production more than 4,000 persons are employed here. About 700 workers are employed at the plant the year round. Adjoining the Cambridge plant is a large company-owned recreation park containing sports facilities for the employes.

POINTS OF INTEREST IN ENVIRONS

Compton, 8.8 *m.*; Crosiadore, 8.1 *m.* (*see Tour 3E*). Horns Point, du Pont house, 3.8 *m.*; Windmere, old house, 5.3 *m.*; Spocot, old house, 5.7 *m.*; Pokety Lodge, 7.8 *m.* (*see Tour 3F*). Old Trinity P.E. Church, 7.2 *m.*; Busick House, 7.5 *m.* (*see Tour 3G*).

Cumberland

Railroad Stations: Queen City Station, S.Front St. near Harrison St., for Baltimore and Ohio R.R. and Cumberland and Pennsylvania R.R.; Western Maryland Station, Canal St. near Harrison St., for Pennsylvania R.R. (freight only) and Western Maryland Ry.
Bus Stations: 4 Frederick St. for Albright Bus Terminal; 20 S.Mechanic St. for Cumberland & Westernport Transit Co., Somerset Bus Co., and Blue Ridge Transportation Co. (the Blue Ridge operates into Western Pennsylvania, Baltimore, and Washington); 10 N.George St. for Franklin Cumberland Transit Co., L.& A. Bus Lines, Mt.Savage Bus Line and Ridgley Bus Co.Inc.; 59 Baltimore St. for The Potomac-Edison Co.
City Busses: Fare 10¢, 15 tickets for $1.
Taxis: Zone system, fares 25¢ to 50¢.
Traffic Regulations: Speed limit 20 and 25 m.p.h. in city; parking meters in downtown section, one hour 5¢.

Information Service: Cumberland A.A.A., 229 Baltimore Ave.; Chamber of Commerce, Liberty Trust Building, 7 S.Centre St.; Central Y.M.C.A., 219 Baltimore Ave.; Traveller's Aid Society, 217 Glenn St.

Accommodations: 15 hotels; tourist homes, camps, and trailer camps in environs, especially along US 40.

Airfield: 2 m. S.; no regular service.
Motion Picture Houses: Five.
Radio Station: WTBO (800 kc.).
Swimming: Ali Ghan Shrine Club pool, 111 Baltimore St., invitation and 20¢; Y.M.C.A., indoor swimming pool, 219 Baltimore Ave., 50¢ for nonmembers.
Tennis: Dingle Courts, Ridgedale near Lake Ave., season ticket $5, 25¢ an hour; Fort Hill High School courts, Greenway and Warwick Aves.
Golf: Fort Cumberland Golf Course, 5 m. E. on Old Town Road, 18 holes, 50¢ one round or 75¢ entire day.

Annual Events: Agricultural Fair, third week in August; 10-day racing card during 2nd and 3rd weeks in August, parimutuel system; free summer outdoor concerts by Eagles' Band and American Legion Band at South End Fire Department Park, Constitution Park and Riverside Park; City and County Tennis Tournaments, August; Fort Cumberland Golf Tournaments, August.

CUMBERLAND (641 alt.,37,747 pop.), Maryland's second city in size, is in a cuplike valley formed by the Potomac, southern boundary of Maryland, at one of two places where it bends so far north it almost reaches the Pennsylvania Line. The river forms an abrupt loop northward within the city limits to its junction with Will's Creek. The narrow finger within this loop belongs to West Virginia and the community occupying it is called Ridgley; its interests are almost completely centered in Cumberland.

East of Will's Creek is the old business district where dark, solidly built Victorian and Romanesque Revival structures give evidence of the city's prosperous development during the last half of the nineteenth century, and some modern shops west of Will's Creek give testimony to continuing expansion.

Cumberland's appearance of newness in the business district is due largely to its ancient enemy—floods. No other city in Maryland has suffered from flood conditions as has Cumberland. Normally a quiet, shallow, narrow stream, Will's Creek occasionally becomes a raging torrent, carrying destruction in its path. To add to local discomfort, the Potomac usually rises simultaneously, flooding most of the city's business and industrial district to depths varying from five to ten feet. So far, flood control measures have not been entirely satisfactory.

The latest recorded flood occurred October 27, 1937, when the low-lying streets along the river were inundated, causing damage amounting to more than $100,000. The most serious flood in recent years occurred March 17, 1936. Rising to 29.1 feet, Will's Creek swirled over nearly five square miles of the city, backing the muddy, debris-strewn waters over the entire downtown area. One life was lost, scores were injured, property damages totaled $2,000,000, and railroad communication was interrupted. After this flood subsided, new store fronts were installed on Baltimore, Greene, Washington, and other downtown streets. The highest recorded flood stage occurred on May 30–31, 1889 (coinciding with the Johnstown,Pa., flood), when a stage of 29.2 feet was recorded.

Though downtown Cumberland has the appearance of an industrial city, there are unusual numbers of country people on the streets, since this is the metropolis of a very large rural area, and many of the cars parked along the streets are filmed with the dust and mud of country roads. Hill farmers, railroad and factory workers, western Maryland politicians, and businessmen drink Cumberland beer in the same popular barroom, a place with modern tubular furniture.

Southwest of the commercial district is the Kelly-Springfield Tire Company plant, one of the major factories of the region. Eastward, across the loop of the Potomac, are the shops and yards of the Baltimore & Ohio Railroad, foundation of industrial Cumberland. Scores of other manufacturing plants, producing glass, steel and tin plate, and beer, crowd between the river and foothills. A huge plant manufacturing artificial silk is located about 5 miles southwest of the city.

The tangle of railroad tracks following the bends of the river, cutting across the Ridgley peninsula, sending spurs in this and that direction, carry much coal and limestone from the surrounding mountains, as well as raw materials for local plants and wholesale lots of goods for the region. Day and night the hills echo the whistling of locomotives, the clank of freight car wheels crossing switches, and the bump of cars being coupled.

While the settlers of Cumberland were largely of British and German stock, and the hill people who came in to work in the first decades of the twentieth century were also of British descent, the town has a large number of workers whose ancestors lived in eastern Europe. Just as the Irish came to build the railroad, Slavs and Magyars came with later industrial development. Many of the merchants and business leaders live in new, hillside residential developments overlooking the business and industrial districts, their houses clinging to steep slopes and fronting on winding streets. Some century-old houses are occupied by the poorer element in narrow streets paralleling the old business district. There are even cultivated plots within the city limits.

Before the arrival of the white settlers in the eighteenth century, the lowlands near Will's Creek, then known as Caicuctuck Creek, were occupied by Shawnee Indians. For a long time after they moved away the only inhabitant was Indian Will, whose name has been given to the creek and the near-by mountain.

In 1750 the Ohio Company, formed by English merchants and Virginia planters to exploit a half million acres granted north of the Ohio, established a trading post and a small storehouse here. Two years later a larger storehouse was built. The activities of the Ohio Company stirred the French to move southward and Governor Dinwiddie of Virginia, protecting the interests of his Virginians as well as those of the king, sent George Washington with a small company to tell the French that their advance would be opposed. Washington arrived at this post in November 1753 and met Christopher Gist, the trapper, who joined him on his expedition westward. By January of 1754 Washington was back in Williamsburg with the news that the French were unmoved by Dinwiddie's message. In the meantime Captain William Trent had started to build a fortification for the Ohio Company at the head of the Ohio River; because of delay by the colonial legislatures in sending troops to protect him he was forced to leave, and Washington, returning to the frontier in the spring, met him at Will's Creek. Washington continued westward and met the bands of French and Indians, who forced him to surrender at the little post grimly called Fort Necessity. On July 4, 1754, he returned to Will's Creek and began to build Fort Mount Pleasant here. This work was taken over by the militia commander, Colonel James Inness, who expanded the plans and renamed the post Fort Cumberland, honoring the third son of George II. By this time the Colonial conflict between the French and British was becoming acute and the Crown determined to send General Edward Braddock with some regular troops to America to take charge of the campaign. As soon as he arrived Braddock gave orders to gather here in early April for the advance westward. But the time allowed for recruiting militia and for travel was far too short, the date having been set in complete ignorance of the lack of roads and of the conditions of an American spring; Braddock even planned to ride to the rendezvous in his 'Chariot.' His understanding of the foes he was facing was equally limited. He estimated that the French fort on the Ohio would 'detain' him only three or four days and added: 'These savages may, indeed, be a formidable enemy to your raw American militia but upon the King's regular and disciplined troops it is impossible they should make any impression.'

He finally assembled 2,000 men, half regulars and half 'raw American militia,' after delays and difficulties he had not dreamed could exist; they left Fort Cumberland for that slow struggle through the wilderness that ended with Braddock's defeat and death. The surviving troops straggled back to Fort Cumberland, and Governor Sharpe, anxiously visiting the post to learn the true frontier situation, found that the regulars had suffered most, partly because of their ignorance of Indian fighting technique and partly because they were unaccustomed to American climate and diet.

For a time there was quiet in this neighborhood, then the attacks by the Indian allies of the French increased in violence and the hardy but terrified settlers of the border filled Fort Cumberland with their families and possessions. By the spring of 1756 Washington, who had been made a colonel and placed in command of the post, was greatly disturbed by the difficulties of caring for the refugees. The post was strengthened and the defenders waited anxiously, fearing attack. But none came, though there were raids on scattered settlements in the region. Washington made his last appearance on the old parade ground on October 19, 1794, when he reviewed troops called out to suppress the Whisky Rebellion.

Washington's sojourn here and his trips westward from this point were momentous in the town's history because they convinced him that the important route from Virginia to the West came through this valley. He continued to acquire title to lands beyond the mountains and as soon as peace was declared began to promote the opening of the Potomac for navigation. In the fall of 1783 the two men appointed by Maryland to survey the Potomac reported that it could be made navigable between Great Falls and Cumberland—both men held lands in the region. Washington became president of the company that was to carry out the work, and it was not until after his death that the futile enterprise was abandoned —to be superseded by construction of the Chesapeake and Ohio Canal.

In the meantime Thomas Beall of Samuel had laid out Washington Town here; two years later—in 1787—the assembly had erected the town under its present name and in 1789 had made it the seat of the newly formed Allegany County.

As the country west of the mountain received large numbers of settlers there were many demands on Congress to build a road that would connect the seaboard with the country drained by the Ohio. With the strong interest of Virginians in the western lands it is not surprising that this first road built with Federal funds should have followed the route early advocated by Washington. For various reasons construction of the National Road was not authorized until 1807 and work on it did not begin until 1811; it was at first called the Cumberland Road because the western terminus was here.

Thus Cumberland began to grow as a transfer and supply town on the first great artery overland. Wagons rolled in from Baltimore and from Pennsylvania in a steady stream. Year by year the road was extended toward the Mississippi; and the longer the road the more business there was for Cumberland. The building of the Chesapeake and Ohio Canal—to compete with the Erie which was drawing freight from the National Road —gave new hopes to Cumberland. Fortunately for Cumberland, construction of the Baltimore & Ohio Railroad, which made the canal an obsolete project, did not injure the town; so slow was canal construction that the first train reached the town in 1842, eight years before the canal was opened. Cumberland had the good fortune to be made a division point for the railroad.

The discovery of large quantities of soft coal in the Alleghenies also favored Cumberland. Between 1842 and 1872 the State's production of coal rose from 2,000 tons to 2,000,000, and all of it was concentrated here for shipment by canal and railroad. Eventually various manufacturing plants were established because of the city's key position on a transportation route between the interior and the seaboard and its proximity to sources of fuel and raw materials.

Civic development did not always keep pace with industry; in the election of 1826 the citizens voted 1,031 to 249 against the establishment of a primary school.

For several years Cumberland suffered from time to time the visits of a demented Virginian named Harris, who would walk naked through the streets prophesying the wrath of heaven. On one occasion he paraded up the aisle of a church. At last his relatives were prevailed upon to keep him home. Shortly afterwards, however, the city met with a visitation that some regarded as a fulfilment of Harris' prophecies. On April 14, 1833, a fire destroyed seventy-five buildings in the heart of town, including every store but one. Fears of celestial wrath had begun to abate by November when they were roused to fever pitch by the unusually splendid showers of Leonids of that year.

During most of the Civil War, Union soldiers were here in large numbers and the city remained, in appearance, entirely loyal. A local flurry came June 16, 1862, the day after all troops had been ordered temporarily to the vicinity of Keyser, West Virginia. About 300 of Imboden's Confederate cavalry galloped in, cut the telegraph wires, spent some hours making purchases with Confederate money, then disappeared as speedily as they had come.

Cumberland was one of the centers of the railroad strike of 1877. Many workers in other industries had recently suffered pay cuts because of the acute collapse of national business and there was much sympathy in the town for the striking railroad workers; the strike was broken after Federal troops arrived.

Through the years Cumberland has served as a barometer of the national economic situation; as production and carloadings go down nationally this city is one of the first to tighten its belt. Long before other parts of the country have evidence of returning good times, Cumberland has heard the increasing volume of clinking wheels and tooting whistles and is again hard at work.

POINTS OF INTEREST

1. The probable SITE OF FORT CUMBERLAND is on the hill above the intersection of Washington and Green Sts. near Emmanuel Episcopal Church. The square fort had star bastions at its corners, each manned with four cannon. The walls were of stone, mud, and logs. Barracks and a company parade ground were inclosed by a stockade. West of the fort was a grand parade ground, unstockaded; this is now Prospect Square.

After the fort was abandoned it rapidly disappeared. Settlers of the growing town found its unguarded walls and houses cheap source of cut timber.

That the settlers feared and hated the Indians after the raids instigated by the French had begun is understandable; but the average frontiersman's attitude toward the natives of the land would have made for conflict without French interference. The Calvert policy of placating the natives and treating them equably was maintained with difficulty in the western part of the State. Away from the area where the proprietary's representatives enforced the long-sighted policy in the interest of peace, settlers treated the Indians with dangerous contempt. One incident that took place at the fort was typical; one day a local chief, Killbuck, arrived professing friendship and was admitted, only to be seized, disarmed, dressed in petticoats, and chased out into the forest amid the hoots and ribald yells of the militiamen. How many later attacks on settlers could be traced to this insult is not known.

2. EMMANUEL CHURCH (P.E.), Washington and Green Sts., is a cruciform stone building of the Gothic type. Above its square buttressed tower rises a slender spire. The church was erected in 1850. Protestant Episcopal services were being held in Cumberland in 1804.

3. The FIRST PRESBYTERIAN CHURCH, 15 Washington St., was built in 1872 of Allegany County limestone. It is of modified Gothic design and has a tower and a spire.

4. In RIVERSIDE PARK, Green and Water Sts., which is on the point of land where Will's Creek flows into the Potomac, is a log cabin used, according to local tradition, by George Washington during the French and Indian War. It formerly stood on the spot now occupied by the Allegany County Courthouse. In 1921 it was presented to the city by James W. Thomas, a local historian.

The rough granite THOMAS CRESAP MONUMENT was erected to the memory of the 'Pathfinder, Pioneer, and Patriot'—called Big Spoon by the Indians because of his tactful hospitality to them—who was one of Maryland's most notable Indian traders. Cresap was the father of Daniel Cresap for whom Dan's Mountain is named; of Thomas Cresap, Jr., killed on Savage Mountain by Indians; and of Michael Cresap, Revolutionary hero.

5. The DENT HOUSE, 118 Green St., is a small, two-story brick building, with a low gable roof and flush end chimneys; it is notable as the home of George and Susanna Dent, whose son Frederick (1786–1876) was the first white child born in Cumberland and became the father-in-law of U.S. Grant. Dent died in the White House.

KEY FOR CUMBERLAND MAP

1. Fort Cumberland   2. Emmanuel P.E. Church   3. First Presbyterian Church   4. Riverside Park   5. Dent House   6. Rose Hill   7. Kelly-Springfield Plant   8. Gephart House   9. St. Peter & Paul Roman Catholic Church   10. First Methodist Protestant Church   11. Site of Revere House   12. B. & O. Shops   13. Memorial Hospital

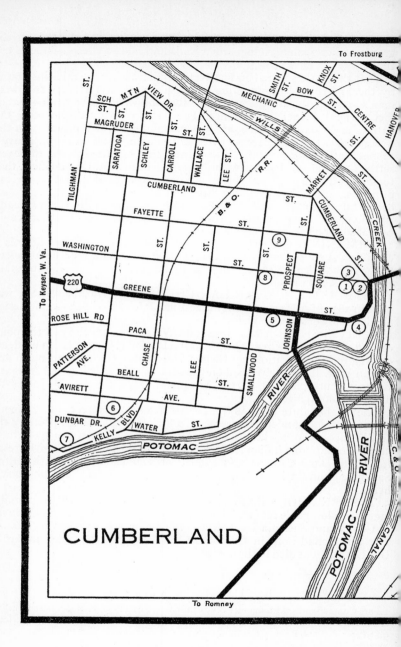

CUMBERLAND

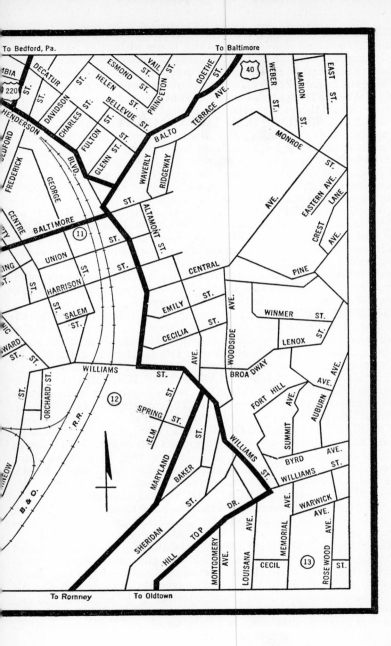

6. ROSE HILL, 512 Dunbar Dr., is on a high hill that drops sharply to the Potomac. The two-and-a-half-story brick house with gable roof and galleried wing was erected in 1801. Porches of recent construction quite obscure the original lines. This hill was occupied by Colonel Lew Wallace and his 11th Indiana Zouaves, when the troops came to the city on June 8, 1861. Wallace brought those suspected of Southern sympathies to his camp and forced them to take the oath of allegiance.

7. The KELLY–SPRINGFIELD TIRE COMPANY PLANT (*visited by arrangement*) is at the foot of Kelly Blvd. and consists of eight buildings. The main structure of brick and steel has a sawtooth roof. The plant, completed in 1920 at a cost of approximately $17,500,000, was at that time proclaimed the best equipped tire factory in the world. It can produce 15,000 tires and tubes each day, but the plant has been operating in recent years at less than half capacity. In addition a large modern laboratory is maintained. Here a staff of chemists and engineers continually are carrying on secret experimental and research work. Daily analysis of material and the development of specially constructed testing machinery permits continual improvement in the company's product. Simulating actual operating conditions, test tires are placed on passenger cars and trucks which are driven by day and night over all types of roads in the surrounding countryside and under all kinds of weather conditions. Any weaknesses discovered are corrected in the laboratory.

8. The GEPHART HOUSE, 104 Washington St., is a two-and-a-half-story brick house with gable roof and brick cornice. It has an imposing central recessed Doric portico and a small Doric side portico. The house was built about 1840 by Thomas Perry. It was later the home of John Gephart, organizer of the First Methodist Protestant Church.

9. STS. PETER AND PAUL ROMAN CATHOLIC CHURCH, Fayette St. between Johnson and Smallwood Sts., is a brick structure with a square tower surmounted by an octagonal spire. The corner stone of the building, which has been remodeled at intervals, was laid in 1818.

10. The FIRST METHODIST CHURCH (1897), Bedford and Center Sts., is a brick structure with arched windows and an entrance through a square tower. The congregation, organized in 1837 by John Gephart, erected a frame structure—which came to be called the Cumberland Station—on Bedford Street near Henderson Boulevard.

11. The SITE OF THE REVERE HOUSE, 184 Baltimore St., is now occupied by a grocery warehouse. From the hotel General George Crook was abducted by a troop of about 60 Confederate cavalrymen on February 21, 1865.

12. The SITE OF BARNUM HOTEL, 154 Baltimore St., is now occupied by the Windsor House. On the same night that General George Crook was abducted from the Revere House, part of the Confederate cavalry troop entered the Barnum Hotel and seized Brevet Major General Kelly. Although there were 6,000 Union troops stationed in the town, the raid and capture of these commanders were executed so rapidly and daringly that the raiders escaped without firing a shot. Crook and Kelly were sent to Richmond where they were imprisoned.

13. BALTIMORE & OHIO RAILROAD SHOPS (*guides furnished*), Virginia Avenue and Queen Street, are a group of seven brick and steel structures and several smaller buildings. The largest was erected in 1919 and the others, considerably older, were modernized in 1916. Repairs are made by the progressive spot system under which locomotives and freight cars, stripped, sandblasted, and inspected before they are taken into the shops, pass from one spot to another, reaching each point at a scheduled time. At each spot workmen complete a single repair operation. These shops are the third largest on the Baltimore and Ohio system. Overhead electric cranes, traveling jibs, and a pipe line that supplies acetylene and oxygen gases to 16 operators simultaneously, are among the equipment. Normally 1300 workers are employed.

The railroad's bolt and forge plant, rolling mill, and fabricating shops are reached from Front and Williams Sts. The main structure, frame, is T-shaped; in it car parts are made for shipment to various points on the railroad's system and brake beam and air valve repairs are made. North of the main buildings is a brick and corrugated iron structure housing a machine shop, tool room, and general offices. In another building power is generated for the operation of the plant. Scrap metal from points along the system is classified by this yard and reworked. About 200 men are normally employed here.

14. The MEMORIAL HOSPITAL, 325 Memorial Ave., is a severely plain four-story brick building with three-story wing terminating in brick sun porches. The city dedicated its hospital to Cumberland soldiers killed in the World War.

POINTS OF INTEREST IN ENVIRONS

Martin Mountain, 8.9 *m.* (*see Tour 2d*); Allegany County Fair grounds, 3.8 *m.* (*see Tour* 18); Pinto apple orchards, 8.4 *m.* and Celanese Corporation of America plant, 5.5 *m.* (*see Tour* 18).

Frederick

Railroad Stations: East and Patrick Sts. for Pennsylvania R.R.; 100 S.Market St. for Baltimore & Ohio R.R.; Patrick and Carroll Sts. for Hagerstown & Frederick Electric Ry.
Bus Stations: 22 W.Patrick St. for Blue Ridge Lines and Potomac Motor Lines; 100 S.Market St. for Crawford Line.
Airport: Detrick Field, municipal, W.4th St.Ext., one mile NW. of business district.
Taxis: 20¢ within city limits, fixed rates to outside points.
Traffic Regulations: 15 m.p.h. in business district; 20 and 25 m.p.h. in residential district; 2-hour parking in business section; no all-night parking.

Accommodations: 5 hotels; tourist camps in environs.

Information Service: Automobile Club of Maryland (AAA) and Chamber of Commerce, Patrick and Court Sts.

Guide Service: Uniformed guides for points of interest available at the Francis Scott Key Hotel and Barbara Fritchie Home (West Patrick St.) from 8 to 5; $1 for one-hour tour.
Radio Station: WFMD (900 kc.).
Motion Picture Houses: 3.
Tennis: Baker Park (municipal), west side N.Bentz St. between Carroll Parkway and W.Second St., free.
Swimming: Baker Park Municipal Pool, Fleming Ave., 9 to 9, Sun. 1 to 9, adults 15¢, children 10¢, no suits rented; Y.M.C.A. pool, Church and Court Sts.
Golf: Catoctin Country Club, 3 m. west on US 40, 9 holes, greens fee, $1.50, Sun. $2. Municipal Miniature Golf Course, N.Bentz St. and Carroll Parkway.

Annual Events: Frederick County Agricultural Fair end of Patrick St. (US 40), usually 4 days in 2nd week of October.

FREDERICK (296 alt.,14,434 pop.), the seat of Frederick County, is primarily a trading and shipping point for the prosperous farmers and dairymen of the Piedmont; it is also a small manufacturing center, producing brushes, hosiery, clothing, and cooking utensils. Its growth has been steady but not spectacular since the time, about thirty years before the Revolutionary War, when Palatine Germans began to take up farms in the Monocacy Valley below the blue-hazed Catoctin Mountain.

Approached from east or west, Frederick is fringed with neglected frame and brick houses, but approached from the north it presents a more prosperous appearance with comfortable homes on broad lawns shaded by beautiful old oaks and maples. The conservative character of Frederick is seen in its unshaded narrow downtown streets; while there are some modern buildings, much of the local business is carried on in structures, including remodeled dwellings, erected around or before the turn of the century.

Benjamin Tasker surveyed a 30,000-acre tract in this vicinity in 1725; two years later he was granted a patent to his tract, which he named Tasker's Chance. In 1744 Daniel Dulany the elder purchased 7,700 acres of the original tract from Tasker's heirs. Dulany, aided by his brother Patrick, laid a townsite in 1745 and advertised for settlers among the Palatine Germans of Pennsylvania. Among the first hundred families to accept the invitation was John Thomas Schley, who took up land here, built the first house, and opened a school. Dulany named his settlement Frederick Town, probably for Frederick Calvert, sixth Lord Baltimore. By 1748 when Frederick County was erected and this became the county seat, the town had several taverns, an indication of the amount of traffic that had developed on the route between Pennsylvania and Virginia.

In 1755 General Braddock stopped here on his way to Cumberland where he expected Colonial militia to aid him in the campaign against the French and Indians at Fort Duquesne. Angry over delays in carrying out orders he had given in ignorance of frontier conditions, he 'showered curses upon the Colonies and especially upon Maryland' for failing to provide horses and wagons to transport the equipment of his regulars. Benjamin Franklin hurried down to assist him in getting wagons and horses, and endeavored to explain the conditions under which he was to operate, but had no success.

After Braddock's defeat there was considerable apprehension among the older citizens of Frederick Town, who feared French and Indian raids; the younger men, however, apparently admired the redskins who had defeated the regulars and killed the British commander. At any rate, according to a chronicler of the day, they disturbed their elders by adopting Indian costumes.

The Frederick County Court in November 1765 responded to popular feeling and declared that the Stamp Act was not in force in the county. Feeling continued high against the high-handed British Parliament and ten years later men from Frederick County, painted like Indians and armed with tomahawks and rifles, made a record-breaking march to the aid of Boston, where they astonished New Englanders by shooting down the British 'even at more than double the distance of common musket shot.'

By 1808 the road from Baltimore through Frederick Town was being improved to meet the Cumberland Road, and local prosperity increased steadily in this important supply point on the way to the frontier.

During the War of 1812 companies of militia were organized here, British prisoners were kept in the county jail, and many loads of specie and Government documents were deposited here for safekeeping.

Incorporated in 1817, the population of the settlement had increased from 3,640 in 1820 to 8,143 in 1860; when the Civil War came it was a small city of some importance, serving the farmers of this wheat-growing area, and dominated by wealthy planters and their families.

The Civil War brought a boom to Frederick because of the demand for grain. But in September 1862 troops under Lee and Jackson occupied the town; a few days later the roar of cannon from South Mountain and Antietam could be heard here. Women of opposing sympathies united to care for the thousands of wounded brought from the battlefields. During the following summer troop movements were around the town rather than through it but there were cavalry skirmishes in the streets. When in July 1864 General Jubal Early's army crossed into Maryland, there was an engagement on the outskirts of town as General Lew Wallace's men resisted the Confederate advance. But by this time Frederick citizens had become accustomed to war and astonished Wallace by climbing on fences and house tops to watch the skirmish. He wrote later that even battle had apparently ceased to have horrors for the people of Frederick.

On July 9 the Confederate forces occupied the town and General Early, by threatening destruction, forced town officials to raise $200,000 for them. Frederick again heard the roar of cannon when the Battle of Monocacy was fought a few miles to the south. Afterward it again had to care for the wounded.

After the war the town grew slowly, though by 1890 there was a canning factory and a fertilizer plant, and knit goods were being manufactured here. At the turn of the century an electric interurban carline was constructed to connect Frederick with the Middletown Valley and this road, eventually extended to Hagerstown, helped to increase retail trade and give the town a more urban character. Cobblestones in time were replaced by asphalt, parks were developed, and by the time of the World War a strong booster campaign was on to bring in factories and at the same time develop tourist attractions. Brushes, hosiery, clothing, cooking utensils, brick, pumps, and stokers are now manufactured and farm products are canned in large quantities.

POINTS OF INTEREST

1. The FREDERICK COUNTY COURTHOUSE, Record and Church Sts., built during the Civil War, is a two-story, red brick structure surmounted by a wooden cupola.

Construction of a courthouse on this site, begun in 1752, was interrupted in 1755 when General Braddock took all available wagons to transport equipment for his troops. The courthouse was in use by 1765 but the judges who decided to repudiate the Stamp Act made their decision in a smaller building across the street, where they had gone into secret session.

A second courthouse was erected in 1785. In this building in May 1861 the Maryland General Assembly met to consider the question of secession, but later moved to another building. The conferences were still going on when the courthouse burned. Construction of the present building began at once.

2. In the RAMSEY HOUSE, 119 Record St., a plain three-story brick structure now divided into apartments, General George L. Hartsuff recovered from a wound received in the Battle of Antietam. He was visited by Abraham Lincoln during his convalescence.

3. The C.BURR ARTZ FREE LIBRARY, Record and Council Sts., a one-story red brick building erected in 1936, has documents bearing the signatures of George Washington, Thomas Jefferson, John Hanson, and John Jay. It is on the site of the Frederick Academy, established as the Frederick County School in the last decade of the eighteenth century, and

granted a charter as a college in 1829. When Roger Brooke Taney was a member of the governing board of the academy, Salmon P. Chase applied for a position in it but was refused appointment. Chase later succeeded Taney as Chief Justice of the United States.

4. ALL SAINTS PARISH HOUSE, 21–25 N.Court St., with stuccoed brick walls, was erected as a Protestant Episcopal church in 1813. Here worshiped Thomas Johnson, first governor of Maryland, and other prominent citizens of the day. It was abandoned as a church in 1856 but was converted into a parish house in 1892.

5. The EVANGELICAL REFORMED CHURCH, 9–13 W.Church St., was built in 1848. It is of gray brick trimmed with granite and has an Ionic portico in the Greek Revival style and two open towers. While in Frederick in September 1862 General Jackson learned that the Reverend Daniel Zacharias, pastor of the church, intended to pray at the Sunday evening service for the success of the Union troops. Jackson, fearing some of his force might disturb the service, came to the service to prevent trouble. The minister stuck to his intention but Jackson did not hear him. He had slept through most of the service.

6. TRINITY CHAPEL, W.Church St. near Market St., is a two-story building with a square stone tower carrying a high octagonal spire. In 1745 Daniel Dulany gave the plot of ground for the structure to the German Reformed congregation, which erected a log building that was used as both church and courthouse until the building whose construction was interrupted by the French and Indian War levies could be completed.

In 1764 the present church was built and the congregation soon boasted 'we are the only church in the Province that has a steeple.' In 1807 the tower clock was installed, and the old steeple replaced by the present cupola and spire. Since the German Reformed congregation merged with the Evangelical Reformed in 1881, the building has been used for the Sunday school.

7. KEMP HALL, North Market and East Church Sts., a three-story brick structure now occupied by business firms and lodges, was erected in 1860 and named for a local resident. The assembly meeting in it in April 1861 decided it had no authority to vote Maryland out of the Union.

8. The SITE OF TORY JAIL, 6 E.Second St., is now occupied by an apartment house. Of seven leading Tories lodged in this jail in 1780, three were hanged, drawn, and quartered; probably in the space behind the jail where the Market House now stands.

9. WINCHESTER HALL, 14 E.Church Street, consists of two notable buildings of Classic Revival design connected by a corridor. The doorways

---

KEY FOR FREDERICK MAP

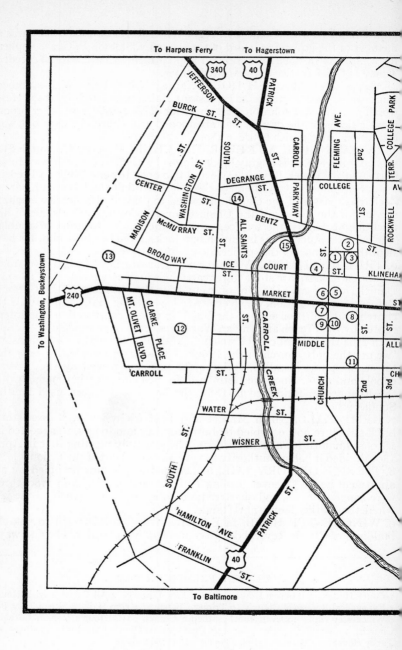

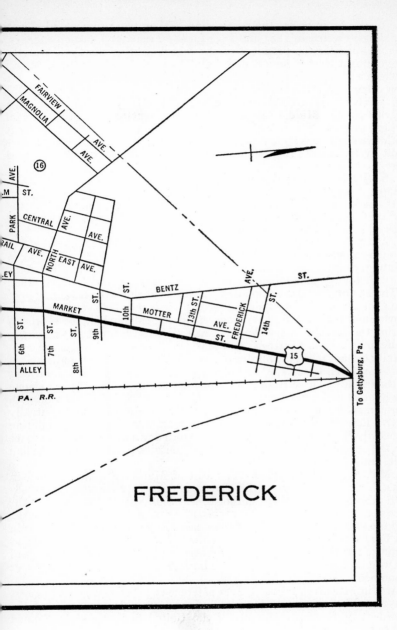

FREDERICK

are of the Ionic order, the porticos are elaborately ornamented. These buildings, erected in 1843 and 1844 for the Frederick Female Seminary, were named for the president of the school. During the Civil War the Government used them as a hospital. The seminary, later the Woman's College and now Hood College, used the buildings until 1915. They are now occupied by county offices.

10. The EVANGELICAL LUTHERAN CHURCH, Church St. between Market St. and Middle Alley, is a two-story structure of Gothic Revival design, with twin spires. To a structure built about 1753, the present front with two spires was added in 1854. During the Civil War a false floor was built over the pews so that sick and wounded soldiers could be housed here.

11. ST.JOHN'S ROMAN CATHOLIC CHURCH, Second St. and Chapel Alley, is a cruciform building of stuccoed masonry ornamented with quoins and Ionic pilasters. It has an open tower somewhat in the style of Christopher Wren. Work on this church was begun about 1800 but the corner stone was not laid until 1828.

12. At the MARYLAND SCHOOL FOR THE DEAF, 242 S.Market St., about 180 pupils receive free training in academic subjects as well as in printing, cabinetmaking, shoe repairing, and domestic science. The four-story Victorian main building, constructed in 1870, has walls of red brick.

The FREDERICK BARRACKS (*apply at school*), behind the main building, is one of two gray stone buildings erected, it is now believed, during the French and Indian War. They were repaired or enlarged for use as prisons during the Revolutionary War. Hessian soldiers captured at the battles of Bennington and Saratoga were quartered here for a time. As the community did not relish the burden of supporting them, those who wished to were permitted to 'escape' and bind themselves over to German farmers in the vicinity. These Hessians, trained marksmen recruited from among the hunters and gamekeepers of Germany, found much in common with German-speaking people of this region, and many of them eventually settled here on their own farms. The Barracks became hospitals during the Civil War. One of the structures was torn down in 1870 to make space for the school building; the other now contains a collection of Indian relics and minerals.

13. MT.OLIVET CEMETERY, S.end of Market St., was opened in 1852. Near the entrance is the FRANCIS SCOTT KEY MONUMENT (1898) with a bronze statue of the author of *The Star Spangled Banner*. At the base is a group of three figures representing patriotism, war, and music, and the seal of Maryland is on the pedestal. Key (1779–1843) was born in old Frederick County and practiced law in Frederick in 1801–2. Citizens organized as the Key Monument Association had the bodies of Key and his wife brought from Baltimore for burial here and in 1898 erected this monument.

Also in Mt.Olivet are the graves of Thomas Johnson (1732–1819) first governor of the State of Maryland; Jane Contee Hanson, wife of the president of the first Congress of the United States; and Dr.Samuel Hansen, a Revolutionary Army surgeon.

The CONFEDERATE MONUMENT, a 16-foot granite shaft, commemorates 404 Confederate soldiers killed at South Mountain, Monocacy, and Antietam and buried in the cemetery.

On the granite BARBARA FRITCHIE MONUMENT has been carved Whittier's poem describing her defiance of invading troops. Her body and that of her husband, John Caspar Fritchie, were removed from the old Episcopal Churchyard and brought here about 1914.

14. The ROGER BROOKE TANEY HOME (*open 9–5, adm. 35¢*), 123 S.Bentz St., is a two-story brick house built in 1815. In it are the table on which Taney wrote the Dred Scott decision, the robe he wore as Chief Justice of the United States, and portraits and articles that belonged to members of his family. A second-floor room contains articles owned by Francis Scott Key, Taney's friend and brother-in-law. The slave quarters in the rear are furnished as they presumably were about 1812.

Born in Calvert County in 1777, Taney was admitted to the bar in 1799. In 1801 he came here with Francis Scott Key to practice law and in 1806 married Key's sister Anne. His practice prospered and he became very influential in State politics. He was elected to the State Senate in 1816 and seven years later moved to Baltimore. He was appointed attorney general of Maryland in 1827 and attorney general of the United States in 1831. President Jackson in 1835 appointed Taney to fill the vacancy in the United States Supreme Court created by the death of John Marshall.

Taney had two great legal interests—laws to control unsound currency and banking, and laws protecting the Negro. Nonetheless he is best known for his decision in the Dred Scott case, which aroused much resentment among liberals because of its failure to protect a Negro. Taney died in 1864 and was buried in St.John's Roman Catholic Cemetery, Fourth and East Streets.

15. The BARBARA FRITCHIE HOME (*open 8 a.m.–9 p.m., April to Oct., adm. 35¢*), 154 W.Patrick St., a story-and-a-half brick building with two dormers and a steeply pitched gable roof, is supposedly a reproduction of the dwelling occupied by the heroine of John Greenleaf Whittier's poem. It contains clothing said to have been made by Barbara Fritchie, a spinning wheel, china, and a Bible that belonged to her. Barbara, described as plain and sharp-tongued, was the wife of John Caspar Fritchie, a prosperous glovemaker.

Whether she really defied General Stonewall Jackson and his 'rebel hordes' is a question still much debated. Whittier, himself, was noncommittal on the subject. He once wrote: 'There has been a great deal of dispute about my little poem, but if there is any mistake in the details, there was none in my estimate of her noble character, her loyalty and her patriotism.' Northerners of the period treasured the 'Shoot if you must this old gray head' which gave wide publicity to the incident. Years after the war when Frederick veterans marched through Philadelphia with a flag reputed to have been Barbara's, they were given enthusiastic cheers. Sentiment greatly increased the value of the simple clothes once worn by the craftsman's wife. One of the cashmeres she wore to church was recently sold for $1,000.

16. HOOD COLLEGE, Dill Ave. and N.College St., has 14 brick buildings designed in the modern Georgian Colonial style. The college, the successor to the Frederick Female Seminary, is supported by the Potomac and Pittsburg Synods of the Evangelical Reformed Church. It has about 400 students and confers degrees of bachelor of arts and sciences.

POINTS OF INTEREST IN THE ENVIRONS

Jug Bridge, 2.7 *m.* (*see Tour 2b*). Prospect Hall, 1.7 *m.* (*see Tour 2B*). Richfield, 4 *m.*; Peter Kemp House, 6.9 *m.*; Lilypons, 7 *m.* (*see Tour 15*). Monocacy Battlefield Park, 2.2 *m.*; Old Fort Furnace, 3.4 *m.*; Thomas House, 4.5 *m.*; (*see Tour 16*).

Hagerstown

Railroad Stations: Washington and Walnut Sts. for Pennsylvania R.R. and Norfolk & Western R.R.; Washington and McPherson Sts. for Western Maryland Ry.; Antietam St. and Summit Ave. for Baltimore & Ohio R.R.
Bus Station: 55 E. Washington St. for Blue Ridge Lines.
Airport: Municipal Airport 5 m. north on US 11.
Busses, local: Fare 8¢, book of 10 tickets 50¢, free transfers.
Taxis: Fares, 15¢ and 20¢ in city limits.

Accommodations: Several modern hotels, also tourist homes and camps.

Traffic Regulations: 25 m.p.h.; Mulberry St. one-way going north and Locust St. going south; parking meters in business section, 5¢ an hr.

Information Service: 5 E. Washington St. in the Alexander Hotel Building; A.A.A. in Hotel Hamilton, 92 W. Washington St.

Radio Station: WJEJ (1210 kc.).
Motion Picture Houses: 4.
Athletics: City Park, Virginia Ave. near Reynolds Ave.; Y.M.C.A., corner North Potomac St. and East Ave.; Wheaton Park (Negro), Charles St. between Pennsylvania Ave. and North Prospect St.; Hager Park, Frederick St. and the Parkway, children's playground and facilities for picnicking.
Swimming Pools: Municipal (outdoor), 730 Frederick St. at B.& O. R.R., open May 30 to Labor Day, 15¢ and 25¢; Y.M.C.A., North Potomac St. and East Ave.
Baseball Fields: Municipal Stadium, Washington County League Field, Parkway near Hager Park.
Tennis Courts, public: 2, free, in City Park, Reynolds and Virginia Aves.
Golf Courses: Municipal, East Washington St. and Cleveland Ave., 9 holes, greens fee 50¢; Fountain Head Country Club, 18 holes, Middleburg Pike, near city.
Washington County Free Library: 21 Summit Ave., daily 9 to 9.

Annual Events: 10-day race meet, Fairgrounds (half-mile track), May; annual agricultural exhibit, Fairgrounds, 4 days following Labor Day; Mummers' Parade, Halloween.

HAGERSTOWN (560 alt., 30,861 pop.), seat of Washington County, lies almost in the center of the Hagerstown Valley near the entrances to the Shenandoah and Cumberland valleys.

Two of the most modern buildings from the point of architectural design are the new City Hall, a five-story brick and stone structure of neoclassic design, built in 1938 on the site of the old Town Hall, which had served the city as municipal headquarters and market since 1822, and the Municipal Market House, whose simplicity of line and careful balance of mass give pleasure to the functionalist.

The offices of the Mayor and City Council, the Police Department and various city boards are housed in the City Hall.

The town is an architectural composite. Around the Public Square and near it are business buildings and hotels of solid late nineteenth-century design and construction, and a sprinkling of modern buildings and metal-trimmed shop fronts. Less than a block from the square on narrow tree-lined Antietam Street are squat brick and stone houses of the early German-speaking inhabitants. Close to the town's newest hotel rise the low steeples of severely plain red brick or white frame churches, used by Dunkards and United Brethren for their religious services. In the older sections of town, particularly along South Prospect and North Potomac Streets and Summit Avenue, are houses of Georgian Colonial and Classic Revival design, set far back on spacious lawns behind the trees for which the city is notable. Even the smaller new houses have gardens and many of them also are shaded by trees. All have the trim well-cared-for look seen only in places where the majority of the inhabitants own their own homes and are proud of them. This appreciation of growing things and of the natural beauty of the valley stems back to Jonathan Hager, who even stipulated in the deeds to some of the lots on the lower side of hilly South Prospect Street that houses built there should not be more than a story and a half high—thus preserving the view of the distant Blue Ridge for the fortunate owners of lots on the upper side. (Land along that street is now too valuable for such restrictions and the clause has been allowed to lapse by common consent.) The school buildings also have the appearance of having been planned primarily for use, rather than to exhibit the architects' skill with ornament. The churches, for the most part, are of the types popular about 1900 and the decades before it.

The pleasant residential character of the city has not been destroyed by the presence of factories—largely on the outskirts—producing organs, furniture, flour, sandblasting equipment, cement, airplanes, shoes, paper boxes, and other products. Indeed, the factories are in part responsible for many of the city's most admirable characteristics; such products as organs require craftsmen with skills that place them close to the professional class. Certainly it is the presence of the organ makers that has helped to produce the Hagerstown Symphony Orchestra, an organization whose sixty-eight members are not professional musicians, in the usual sense of the term, but whose concerts attract audiences of a thousand. Not all members of the orchestra live in Hagerstown; some come from Frederick and from Pennsylvania towns. But the nucleus is here and the rehearsals, held twice a week, take place in Hagerstown. The first concerts of the group as now organized were given in 1935.

A key to the character of Hagerstown is found in the advertising pamphlets of the Chamber of Commerce, where as much stress is placed on the possession of a fine library and museum, of a full-time health officer, of paid welfare work, of the publicly owned power plant, the modern schools, and the musical and dramatic clubs as on the advantages the city can offer as a site for factories.

Quite as important as manufacturing to local prosperity are banking, shipping, distributing, and other services for the farmers, orchardists, and dairymen of the prosperous valley. Hagerstown's relations to the county of which it is the seat are unusual. County and city officials work closely

Baltimore

nes I. Mettee

SNOW SCENE, MOUNT VERNON PLACE

Holmes I. Mettee

BALTIMORE TRUST BUILDING

SHOT TOWER (1828)

Kramer-Bodine

mer-Bodine

BATTLE MONUMENT (1815)

PEALE MUSEUM (1814)

WAR MEMORIAL AND PLAZA

ENOCH PRATT FREE LIBRARY

SUNDAY AFTERNOON

Maryland Stu

MULLIKIN STREET

ROW HOUSES

UNIVERSITY HOSPITAL

together in making various public utilities as available to country as to Hagerstown folk. A traveling library service is only one of the far-sighted devices for welding the prosperous countryside to the city that depends on it.

Hagerstown boasts two active dramatic groups. The *Potomac Playmakers* is a little theater group which presents on the average of four full-length plays annually, a number of one-act plays and a 'frolic.' The plays are presented on a season-ticket basis. The group is sponsored by the Women's Club of Hagerstown, and the plays are presented on a stage built by members of the cast in the auditorium of the club. Officers of the theater group, with the exception of the president who is appointed, are elected by the membership. All profits are shared.

The Alsatia Club, a men's social organization, gives a three-evening performance annually of the Alsatia Minstrels. Club members manage the business end of the production but draw upon the community for talent. The club also stages the annual 'Mummers' Parade,' a Halloween frolic which draws thousands of spectators from Hagerstown and the surrounding country.

Jonathan Hager, a German, came to this place in 1737 and was granted a tract of land that he named Hager's Delight. Here he built a log house with an arched stone cellar. 'Capt. Hager,' wrote a historian, 'was frequently assailed by the savages, and his family found the cellar a most useful asylum. It was often necessary to protect the dairy-maids with armed men while engaged in milking the cows.'

Gradually other settlers arrived and in 1762 Elizabeth Town—named for Hager's wife—was laid out. Within a decade there were a hundred dwellings and the place was an important trading post.

Life at this period was hard but the settlers in this region, as elsewhere in Maryland, displayed the hearty levity in naming their tracts that was a characteristic of people in the far western frontier camps of later days. Among the farms of this vicinity in Hager's day were: Agreed to Have it Shared, All that's Left, Discontent, I am Glad it is no Worse, Love in a Village, Near the Navel, Scared from Home, Search Well and You Will Find, The Third Time of Asking, Trouble Enough, The Widow's Last Shift.

By January 1814 the population of the village was about 2,500 and the assembly passed 'an act to change the name of Elizabeth Town in Washington County, to Hager's Town, and incorporate the same.'

One of the most serious calamities in the history of the city was an outbreak of Asiatic cholera in 1832. The disease had been brought from Europe, largely by immigrants coming to take up lands in the West, and it spread far inland along important travel routes. Medical science of that day was ignorant of the cause of the disease and the manner of its transmission, but William D. Bell, the Hagerstown moderator, saw a connection between the disease and filth and instituted a vigorous cleanup campaign in the town. Householders were exhorted to tidy-up cellars, yards, gutters, and vacant lots, and Bell's inspectors ranged everywhere to see that the orders were carried out. How much this activity helped to check the spread of the epidemic can only be surmised, but Bell's theory was sound.

Hagerstown was not in a plantation district with many slaves, so in 1861 a majority of its citizens voted against secession. The first year of the war brought a local boom because of the demand for foodstuffs, but the town's position as a supply point later had disadvantages; in July 1863 General John McCausland appeared with 1,500 Confederate troops and demanded $20,000 and 20,000 complete sets of clothing. The town raised the money and in part filled the demand for clothing. After the Confederate forces were defeated at Gettysburg, Hagerstown was for a time between the Confederate and the Union forces and the inhabitants hourly expected to have their homes destroyed. But the only incident was a cavalry skirmish in the streets.

The close of the war found both city and county impoverished, and it was not until completion (1867) of the 24-mile spur connecting Hagerstown with the main line of the Baltimore & Ohio Railroad at Weverton that there was any real business revival. This road decreased the hauling distance to Baltimore by about 63 miles. In June 1872 the first train from Baltimore on the Western Maryland Railroad track reached Hagerstown, cutting the distance by another 20 miles. On September 4, 1880, the first passenger train from the South arrived over the Shenandoah Valley Railroad. The Western Maryland made this a division point and established offices here. The railroads, giving the town transportation routes into important agricultural areas and outlets to one of the chief ports on the Atlantic Coast, started it on its way to becoming the third city of Maryland. Between 1890 and 1900 the population increased more rapidly than it had in the entire preceding century; and the increase continued in the following decade.

POINTS OF INTEREST

1. The GRUBER ALMANAC COMPANY OFFICE is at 9 N.Potomac St. Here is published the *Hagers-Town Town and Country Almanack*. John Gruber, born in Pennsylvania in 1768, settled in Hagers-Town, as it was then spelled, and in 1797 put out the first issue of the *Almanack*—in German. From 1798 to 1918 the publication appeared in both German and English. Until shortly before his death in 1857 Gruber did both the editing and typesetting.

The style and general format of the *Almanack* has changed little in fourteen decades; old style woodcuts are still used. Its 'conjectures of the weather' for each month—which have proved about 60 per cent accurate through the years—have been used by generations of farmers in many States. There is always a 'Large Multiplication Table' and a rhyme that lists the presidents. A century ago the *Almanack* contained essays on 'Female Virtue and Pursuits,' 'Faithless Husbands,' and similar popular topics; recent issues give scientific advice on farm problems. The average annual circulation is approximately 150,000. It is said that William T. Hamilton, while he was Governor of Maryland, always consulted the

Almanack before setting the date for a hanging in an attempt to insure good weather for the popular event.

The original printing office, torn down years ago, stood on North Potomac Street not far from the present headquarters.

2. The HAGERSTOWN DAY NURSERY AND KINDERGARTEN (*open* 10–11:30 *and* 2:30–4 *daily*), Washington and Locusts Sts., is in a two-story brick building erected in 1842. The institution had its beginning in 1815, when it was known as the Charity School and provided an elementary education for children whose parents could not pay for it. When free education became general it undertook its present work of providing nursing care and kindergarten instruction for children whose mothers are employed.

3. ZION REFORMED CHURCH, Potomac and Church Sts., was built in 1774 as the German Reformed Church; successive alterations have greatly changed its early appearance. While dressing logs for this early church, Jonathan Hager, founder of Hagerstown, was accidentally killed in his sawmill. The present gray limestone building has tall narrow windows and a square tower with an open belfry. During the Civil War General George Custer one day climbed to the bell tower to take observations. Suddenly becoming a mark for sharpshooters, he abandoned his position with more haste than dignity. In the graveyard back of the church are buried Jonathan Hager (1719–75); John Gruber (1768–1857), founder of *The Hagerstown Almanac*; and Peter Humrichouse, who by his timely dash from Philadelphia supplied Washington's troops with much needed ammunition for the siege of Yorktown.

4. In CANNON PARK, Potomac St. and North Ave., stands a bronze cannon made in 1757 at Douai, France, by Beranger, leading French ordnance manufacturer. The story is that it was used by Napoleon's army during the Peninsular Wars, later captured by the Spanish at Cordova, and eventually sent to Fort Morro, Cuba. After the American forces captured this stronghold during the Battle of Santiago (1898), the cannon was given to Hagerstown because Washington County had more volunteers for service in the Spanish-American War than had any other county in the State. By the cannon is a pyramid of cannon balls, some of them specially manufactured to replace those carried off by souvenir collectors.

5. OAK HILL (*private*), 921 The Terrace, a rambling three-story frame house of the ornate Victorian Gothic style, was the home of William T. Hamilton who, after several years in both houses of Congress, became the Governor of Maryland (1879). Sunk in the driveway is the old slave block that formerly stood where the Antietam St. entrance to the Hotel Hamilton now is. Around this block planters made their bids for slaves; standing

---

KEY FOR HAGERSTOWN MAP

1.Gruber Almanac Co.   2.Day Nursery   3.Zion Reformed Church   4.Cannon Park 5.Oak Hall   6.Fairchild Aircraft Co.   7.Moller Organ Co.   8.Mt.Prospect   9.Washington County Library   10.Millstone Circle   11.Washington County Museum of Fine Arts   12.Rose Hill Cemetery   13.Hager Mill

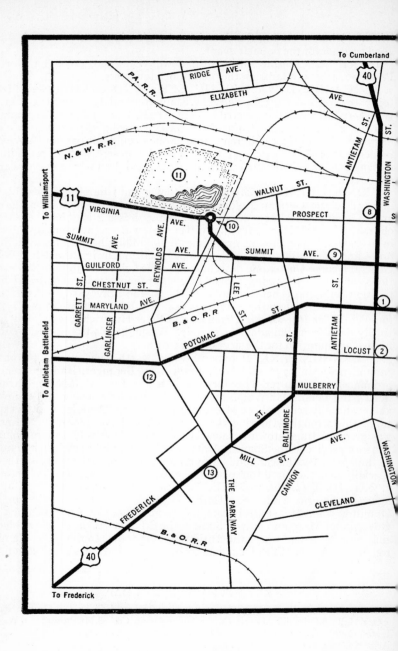

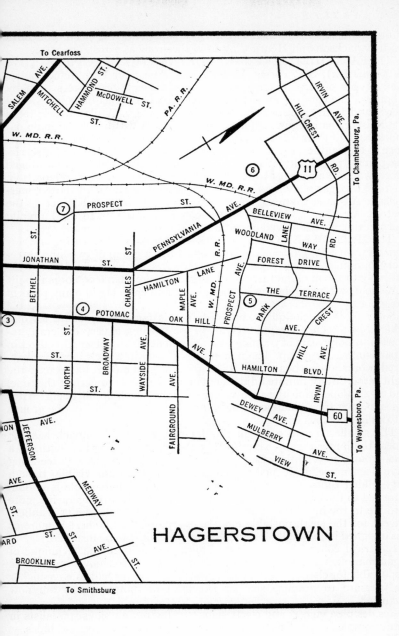

on it, politicians made their bids for the support of the electorate. Both Andrew Jackson and Henry Clay used the stone as a rostrum in 1830.

6. The FAIRCHILD AIRCRAFT CORPORATION FACTORY (*visited by permission*), SW. corner Pennsylvania Ave. and Park Lane, builds many types of airplanes ranging from swift single-seat racers to Baby Clippers. The company's first manufacturing plant was built in 1926 by Lewis and Henry Reisner and Ammon H. Kreider. While in their teens the Reisners had begun to build and experiment with airplanes in an old shack back of their home at 449 Salem Avenue. With the financial assistance of their father, they soon had a completely equipped shop for servicing planes, principally Wacos. The first plane they built, a low-winged racer, won the air meet at the Philadelphia Sesquicentennial celebration. In 1928 a larger plant was opened by the firm, then called the Kreider-Reisner Airplane Company. After the death of Ammon Kreider at the Detroit Air Meet in April 1929, the company was sold to the Fairchild Corporation, which moved operations to this place at the end of 1934.

7. The M.P.MÖLLER ORGAN WORKS (*open to visitors during business hours, except Sat.; guides*), 403 N.Prospect St., a group of two- and three-story buildings, is one of the largest factories in the world devoted exclusively to the manufacture of pipe organs. More than 6,000 organs built here are now in use in homes, schools, halls, and churches in many parts of the globe.

Some of the techniques employed in this factory are centuries old; others have been perfected recently. Pipe voicing, a very old craft, requires not only years of training but high talent. Each voicer specializes in a particular tone group. The new pipe is placed in a rack behind a battered, workshop keyboard, and its length is altered until it has exactly the right pitch. Many minute adjustments must be made to perfect the tone, and in this operation the pipe voicer displays his skill and talent. After pipes in each tone group are voiced, another specialist blends the groups into an harmonious whole.

The smallest organ made in this factory, a portable model, has 197 pipes; the larger organs have up to 5,000 pipes, varying in length, as a rule, from three-eighths of an inch to 16 feet, though pipes 32 feet long have been made. In a modern organ real pipes are not visible, though large gilded tubes are often used as decorations. The console is seldom attached to the organ, since electrical control permits arrangements more suitable to the interior of the auditorium in which the organ is installed. Except for the small portable models, every organ made here is more or less designed individually for the place in which it is to be installed.

Electrical control has brought many innovations in the technique of organ manufacture. The demand during the 1920's for movie organs was responsible for changes in the wind chest; these organs had to have higher air pressure to produce sharper effects. Few movie organs are now produced.

Besides pipe voicers and electricians, the factory employs specialists in many complex operations, including a special curing of wood and hides.

Mathias Peter Möller (1855–1937), who came to America from Denmark in 1872, constructed a pipe organ for the Philadelphia Centennial Exposition of 1876 and in 1880 opened this factory. A constant experimenter, he had just developed a new type of wind chest that improved the tonal quality of the instrument. Möller's experimental work and his philanthropic activities won him such wide recognition that in 1926 he was made a Knight of the Ancient Order of Dannebrog.

8. MT.PROSPECT, 201 W.Washington St., is a long two-and-a-half-story house built in 1789 by the Virginian, Nathaniel Rochester (1751–1831), a colonel in the Revolutionary Army. Rochester first operated a nail factory here and later became the town's first banker. In 1811 Rochester moved to New York State where he established a settlement on land now occupied by the city bearing his name.

In 1850 Mt.Prospect was purchased by Dr.Howard Kennedy, son of Thomas Kennedy, author of the 'Jew Bill.' About three days after the Battle of Antietam (September 17-18, 1862) as Mrs.Kennedy and her small daughter Annie were watching the dreary procession of wounded pass by, a badly wounded Union officer collapsed before their door. Mrs.Kennedy had the young man brought into the house and cared for him. The officer was Oliver Wendell Holmes,Jr., later a Justice of the U.S. Supreme Court. His father, after a frantic search of the battlefield, finally found his son whom he had given up for dead. He commemorated the event in the poem *My Search for the Captain*.

9. The WASHINGTON COUNTY FREE LIBRARY (*hours 9-9 weekdays*), 21 Summit Ave., is a two-story concrete structure with limestone front and trim, and an entrance loggia flanked by Ionic columns. The building houses an institution established in 1901 through the efforts of a clergyman, a banker, a papermaker, two lawyers, a farmer, and a storekeeper—public-spirited men who had already been impressed by the success of other county institutions. Its sound and progressive development was largely the work of the first librarian, Miss Mary L. Titcomb. One of the first county libraries in the United States, it began service in a section where bookstores were unknown, where there was only one small private high school, and where reading was looked upon as the privilege of the idle and the rich. But as soon as the doors were opened, everybody wanted to 'join the Library.' A countrywoman with her first book wrapped in her starched gingham apron remarked as she left the building, 'It's a great day when poor folks like us can take home such handsome books.' And a rural boy who had happened to draw one of Shakespeare's plays, returned it with the request: 'Give me another by that same man; I think he's a right good writer.'

Service to outlying districts was first initiated by placing cases of books in general stores, schools, and private homes. After a few years direct delivery to borrowers was begun; a two-horse wagon equipped with outside bookshelves began to make tours even in remote country districts. Eventually the plan was widely copied abroad as well as in America. The institution now possesses more than 37,000 volumes, employs three trucks in their distribution, and has several permanent branches. The work is supported by endowments and gifts, as well as by city and county funds.

10. MILLSTONE CIRCLE, usually called Park Circle, is just north of City Park at the intersection of Virginia and Summit Avenues and Prospect Street. Stones, some dating back as far as 1791, from various old mills of Washington County, form the circle.

The principal entrance of City Park, formerly the Heyser estate, is at the corner of Virginia and Reynolds Aves.; the park covers 50 acres of rolling woodland, and has a lake, several springs, and a number of natural streams. Swans, Canada geese, Chinese geese, and mallard ducks nest on the island in the lake on the shores of which are Japanese azaleas and rock gardens. Recreational facilities include baseball diamonds, two tennis courts, a playground, a bandstand, and a small zoo housing a number of small native animals.

11. The WASHINGTON COUNTY MUSEUM OF FINE ARTS (*open 10–5 weekdays, except Monday; 1–6 Sundays and holidays*) in the City Park at the edge of the lake was opened to the public in September 1931, the gift to Hagerstown and Washington County of Anna Brugh Singer, a native of Hagerstown and wife of the American painter, William H. Singer, Jr. The museum receives $5,000 annually from the city of Hagerstown and $2,500 annually from Washington County. The staff does extensive educational work, which includes gallery talks, lectures, special loan exhibitions, educational lectures for children, and loans of art reference material to schools and clubs. The permanent collection of the museum includes 204 examples of sculpture, painting, and the graphic arts. Among the artists represented in the collection are: Gutzon Borglum, Paul Gauguin, Constantin Meunier, Auguste Rodin, Gustave Courbet, Childe Hassam, Charles W. Hawthorne, J.B. Jongkind, Jonas Lie, Adolphe Monticelli, John Noble, Alfred Stevens, John H. Twachtmen, André Derain, and Max Liebermann.

Also on display are Jonathan Hager's furniture, silver, and glassware.

12. In ROSE HILL CEMETERY, main entrance near the corner of Potomac St. and Willow Lane, are the graves of 5,000 Confederates killed in the battles of Antietam and South Mountain, and the CONFEDERATE MONUMENT erected in 1877, seven years after the General Assembly had appropriated $5,000 to bring the bodies to Hagerstown. The principal figure is of marble and represents Hope leaning upon an anchor. It stands on a shaft of dappled brown Scottish granite with a base of American granite.

In the same cemetery is buried Percy Hiram Maxim (1869–1936), inventor of the Maxim gun silencer. He was the son of Hudson Maxim, inventor of the machine gun bearing his name and of other devices.

The KENNEDY MONUMENT in the SE. corner of the cemetery marks the grave of Thomas Kennedy, merchant, lawyer, and poet who spent years fighting for the passage of legislation that would grant Jews the civil rights enjoyed by gentiles. Kennedy won his fight in 1826. This monument was erected in 1919 by prominent Maryland Jews. Its tall white marble shaft bears a history of Kennedy's life.

13. The three-story stone HAGER MILL (*open to visitors*), in Hager Park, Frederick and Hager Sts., was built in 1791. Most of it is now a furniture

storehouse, but it still looks much as it did in early days and the water wheel has been preserved.

POINTS OF INTEREST IN ENVIRONS

Old Conococheague Bridge, 7.1 *m.*; Stafford Hall, 10.4 *m.* (*see Tour 2d*). Pangborn Corporation Plant (*see Tour 2C*). St. James School, 5.9 *m.*; Antietam battlefield, 12.8 *m.* (*see Tour 2D*). Fiddlersburg, old-fashioned village, 2.4 *m.*; Jacob's Lutheran Church, 10.7 *m.* (*see Tour 17*).

Salisbury

Railroad Station: Pennsylvania R.R., W.Railroad and Wilson Aves.
Taxis: Fare for one or more persons within city limits, 20¢.
Traffic Regulations: Speed limit 20 m.p.h. in commercial sections, 25 m.p.h. in residential sections; parking in commercial sections 5¢ by meter for one or two hours according to position.

Accommodations: 5 hotels, many tourist lodges and boarding houses.

Information Service: Salisbury Chamber of Commerce, NW. cor. S.Division and Camden Sts.; Keystone Automobile Club, same building; Automobile Club of Maryland, 104 N.Division St.
Radio Station: WSAL (1,200 kc.)
Motion Picture Theaters: 4.
Golf: Elks Golf Course at city limits on Snow Hill road, greens fee 50¢; Green Hill Country Club by Wicomico River, 10 m.SW., greens fee $1.
Swimming, tennis, picnicking facilities: Municipal Park, S. of E.Main St.

Annual Events: Presentation of the Salisbury Award, Arcade Theater, 1st Sun. afternoon in March; Wicomico Horse Show, a Sat. in May.

SALISBURY (23 alt.,10,997 pop.), an industrial and shipping point at the head of Wicomico River, is the largest town on the Eastern Shore and the second largest port in Maryland. Its rapid growth is a contradiction of the traditional quiet and gentle pace of the Eastern Shore. The population increase in the last ten years has been estimated at 877.

During the 1920's the population increased 46 per cent. Streets and stores have become more and more crowded through depression times. From year to year, even month to month, new private and public construction has continued to change the aspect of the place. The business blocks of Main Street resemble those of a large city. The air is charged with business deals and real-estate promotion as well as with exhaust gas from the dense motor traffic. Banks and stores gleam with colored neon signs and bright metal façades. The well-equipped eight-story hotel serves 'businessmen's luncheons' and for dinner offers terrapin à la Maryland to local epicures and tourists on their way north or south on US 13.

Comfortable Victorian dwellings line narrow shady streets in the older residential section. Modern homes on parklike lawns are rising in the newer, outlying real-estate developments. A Federal slum clearance project, pending in 1940, is planned to eliminate the present unsightly shacks near the railroad now occupied by 'poor whites' and Negroes. The Negro population in 1930 amounted to 17 per cent of the city's total. Institutions include a large hospital serving a wide area, a State teachers' college, two homes for the aged administered by private endowment, a children's home, a new public library and many churches. The powerful influence of the Methodist ministry is largely responsible for county laws forbidding the serving of hard liquor at restaurants and the holding of Sunday entertainments for paid admission. These prohibitions have little effect, however, on the social life of most of the wealthy citizens, busy with their horse shows, fox hunts, and contests and entertainments at the country clubs.

Most of Salisbury's industries depend on products from the surrounding countryside. Large mills manufacture construction woodwork as well as crates, baskets, and barrels for farm produce shipped from the region. Two meat-packing houses process hogs, cattle, and sheep. Two plants supply hundreds of tons of ice to refrigerate cars of fresh fruits and vegetables. Long lines of trucks and wagons pass through auction blocks on the outskirts where auctioneers chant and commission buyers lift lids of crates and nod acceptance of prices. Canneries pack many tons of fruit and vegetables. A half-dozen factories turn out skirts, hosiery, and other apparel, taking advantage of minimum-wage scales for women workers, and low tax and power rates. Other plants include an iron furnace and foundry, bakeries, a brickyard, and a shipyard where work boats and yachts are built, repaired, and painted.

In addition to the railroad and the motor-truck fleets, small Diesel-powered freighters load here with the region's products. Other vessels bring in material for the fish-fertilizer plants, as well as large quantities of gasoline, fuel oil, and coal for distribution by truck through the Delmarva peninsula.

In 1732 the Provincial Assembly of Maryland authorized the purchase from William Winder, a minor, of 15 acres of Pemberton's Good Will at Handy's Landing in the forks of the Wicomico in Somerset County. Commissioners were ordered to 'cause the same to be surveyed and laid out into 20 lots . . . the town to be called Salisbury-Town.'

In 1932 the city of Salisbury held a five-day jubilee to celebrate its bicentennial, climaxed by a parade 'by far the longest and most elaborate ever attempted on the Eastern Shore.' Floodlights and a public-address system were installed for the benefit of crowds in Municipal Park, which used to be the bottom of a lake. Though this was the worst year of the depression elsewhere, Salisbury was prosperous and had reason to rejoice.

After the railroad reached Salisbury in 1860 no great change came over Peninsula farming; the revolution came when refrigerator cars enabled growers to send fresh fruits and vegetables to cities 100 to 1,000 miles away. Then the countryside prospered and basket making and other activities allied with commercial farming sprang up here. There was still no great increase in the town's population or business enterprises, however, because farmers continued to deal in the smaller towns and crossroads stores. The waterways and railroads merely tapped the lower Peninsula resources. Then came the great social and economic change; motor vehicles appeared and paved highways became an important means of transportation. As the villages lost, Salisbury (and Cambridge) gained. Farmers came here for supplies they formerly ordered from mail-order catalogues. Salisbury has since been extending its domain year after year until now it derives trade from three States.

There have been some stirring times here. During the Revolution Tories and riffraff pirates masking as Tories plundered the river settlements and farms. Of these Ben Allen survives in legend. Tory or plain thug, Allen was big as an ox, strong as a mule, and mean as the devil. It is said he was finally executed by a patriot firing squad. The hero of that era was a Scot named Alexander Roxburgh, who rallied the Maryland line in the celebrated Long Island retreat. After the war Major Roxburgh eloped with Frances Handy, granddaughter of Colonel Isaac Handy of Pemberton Hall (*see Tour 3H*). In 1794 Roxburgh was made brigadier general of Somerset and Worcester militia, and in 1801 Congress granted him a soldier's bonus of 400 acres in Ohio in appreciation of his services.

The great Whitsuntide Fair of Salisbury drew country people for several days of celebration, fun, and shopping among the wares of Baltimore merchants who set up booths. In wagons, oxcarts, boats, on horseback, and afoot the crowds came from miles around to handle the silks and linsey-woolseys, the guns and necklaces. Revivalists exhorted and young people made love. Bishop Francis Asbury thought his exhortations did little good here. In 1786 he recorded in his journal: 'Thursday 10. Rode to Salisbury, where, as it was court-time, I had but few hearers; and some of these made their escape when I began to insist on the necessity of holiness; a subject this which the Antinomians do not like to hear pressed too closely.'

During the Civil War Salisbury and its country side were badly split; most of the slave owners were Confederate sympathizers and the rest of the population favored the Union. Federal troops, Maryland and Delaware volunteers, were stationed here from 1861. They made occasional forays through Maryland, Delaware, and Virginia disarming 'secessionists' but there was no actual fighting. At elections troops were posted at every polling place, officially to 'preserve order' but actually, Southern sympathizers charged, to intimidate voters into voting Republican.

Until 1867 Salisbury was partly in Somerset and partly in Worcester County. After a bitter contest the petition to set up Wicomico County carried and this became the county seat. When fire devastated the town in 1860 and again in 1886, hardly an old building escaped; but the bell of St. Peter's Episcopal Church, which rang out the first alarm in 1886, now sounds the hours from the courthouse tower.

POINTS OF INTEREST

POPLAR HILL MANSION, head of Poplar Hill Ave., somehow escaped the fires of 1860 and 1886. The large, squarish house, weather-boarded and painted white, with its Adam decorations, is a good example of the postcolonial style. It was erected in 1795 by Major Levin Landy, who married the daughter of Captain John Winder, then owner of the land on which the house stands. Above the porch, a later addition, is a Palladian window that overlooked fields of the former estate. The interior paneling is of old-growth heart pine. Especially fine are the wainscoted drawing room and the delicate stairway. The hallway, 12 feet wide, is spanned by a hall arch resting on fluted pilasters.

The STATE TEACHERS' COLLEGE OF SALISBURY, E. side of Camden Ave. at College Ave., was established in 1925 and occupies a very large and imposing brick building of Georgian style erected between 1925 and 1932. The main central section with cupola and tall portico is flanked by colonnaded lower sections and large wings. Faculty residences and other buildings also stand on the 29-acre campus.

Two-thirds of its more than 200 students are women. The degree of Bachelor of Science is conferred after two years of academic college work and two years of an intensive teacher-training course.

BETHESDA METHODIST CHURCH, NW. cor. Division and William Sts., is a stone structure of the neo-Gothic type completed in 1923. Above the pulpit is a large mural of Christ holding a lamb. The foreground and landscape are a careful rendering of the sandy soil, the cacti, and other vegetation of the Holy Land studied there by the artist, Edwin Howland Blashfield (1848–1936) of New York.

POINTS OF INTEREST IN ENVIRONS

Wicomico State Game Farm, 1.4 *m.*; Spring Hill Church, 7.1 *m.* (*see Tour 3b*). Pemberton Hall, old house, 2.2 *m.*; Upper Ferry, hand-operated scow, 6.2 *m.*; Tonytank Manor, 2.4 *m.*; Cherry Hill, old house, 4.5 *m.* (*see Tour 6c*).

PART III
Touring the State

Tour 1

(Philadelphia,Pa.)—Belair—Baltimore—Hyattsville (Washington,D.C.); US 1. Pennsylvania Line to District of Columbia Line, 82.6 m.

Chiefly concrete-paved roadbed, some asphalt; 2 lanes wide north of Belair, 3 between Belair and Baltimore, 4 between Baltimore and the District of Columbia.
Baltimore & Ohio R.R. and the Pennsylvania R.R. roughly parallel route.
Accommodations of all kinds.

This section of US 1, which is the lifeline of the seaboard States, is in Maryland, but not of it. Although north of Baltimore it affords occasional views of pleasant countryside, the road reveals practically nothing of a State that has some of the most charming lands on the eastern coast. Except in the neighborhood of the Susquehanna, it offers no hint of the great expanse of shore that has helped to make Baltimore one of the leading ports of the world and is also making the State one of the prized residential areas of eastern America. Although the traveler sees rolling fields from US 1, he does not see the beautiful and fertile Piedmont where farming is still successfully carried on by families who have worked the land since they first cleared the forest.

This unrepresentative character of US 1 is not peculiar to Maryland. From northern Maine to southern Florida, US 1 began as Indian trails that in time became wagon and cattle roads between settlements, then were paved and repaved as motor transportation was introduced and expanded. From Maine to Florida the worst of the curves have gradually been eliminated, roadbeds widened and rewidened, but the route remains essentially a relic of horse and buggy days, lacking the expert engineering that has reduced hazards and annoyances on newer sections of Maryland's US 40. On the 3,000-mile highway Baltimore and Washington are the only important cities still lacking by-passes for through travelers, but plans are now under way for construction of boulevards that will save motorists from the present annoyances.

Section a. PENNSYLVANIA LINE to BALTIMORE; 48.8 m.

This section of US 1 had little importance before 1774, when the assembly voted several thousand dollars for improving three roads north of Baltimore. The first survey of this road, a trail between Baltimore and Belair, is believed to have been made in 1787 by John Eager Howard. During most of the nineteenth century the road was controlled by a turnpike company.

US 1 crosses the Pennsylvania Line, 0 m., in SYLMAR, (470 alt., 50 pop.), about 53 miles southwest of Philadelphia. Here a granite shaft (L) marks the Mason and Dixon Line.

At 1.5 *m.* is the junction with State 273.

Left on State 273 to CALVERT, 2.5 *m.* (441 alt.,75 pop.), founded in 1701 on one of the Nottingham Lots (*see below*) and first called Brick Meeting House. Here in colonial times lived Benjamin Chandlee, whose brass-dialed clocks and scientific instruments are now prized by collectors.

One end of the EAST NOTTINGHAM FRIENDS MEETING HOUSE (*visited by application to sexton*) is of brick, the other of stone. There is a movable partition which can be used to divide the structure into two rooms. Plain benches, some of them without backs, bespeak the spirit of the small society still meeting here four times a year. The brick end was built in 1724 to replace a log structure erected in 1709. After a fire destroyed the woodwork in 1751, the building was repaired and the stone end added. The records of the society since 1730 have been preserved.

In 1778 a detachment of General Smallwood's Continentals used the meeting house to shelter their wounded and some of the soldiers are buried in the graveyard. On April 11, 1781, Lafayette's army encamped near here on their march to Yorktown. During the Revolution several members of the Brick Meeting House Society took up arms in defiance of Quaker principles and were read out of the group.

In BLUE BALL, 5.3 *m.* (375 alt.,15 pop.), is (L) the BLUE BALL TAVERN, a long two-and-a-half-story stone inn operated until about 1866, but now housing only a country store. An inn was established here about 1710 by Andrew Job on the Nottingham Lots. While visiting in Philadelphia, Job acquired as a bond servant Elizabeth Maxwell, 16-year-old niece of Daniel Defoe. This girl, thwarted by relatives in a love affair, had run away and indentured herself in return for passage to America. Shortly after 1725, when she married Thomas Job, son of Andrew, her mother died and left Elizabeth considerable property, including some furniture her uncle had used while writing *Robinson Crusoe*.

In FAIR HILL, 8.7 *m.* (385 alt.,30 pop.), on the northeastern corner of the junction with State 280, is the MITCHELL HOUSE, a two-and-a-half-story stone building with a frame addition. On one of the firebacks is the date 1764. The front door of wide boards has two long strap hinges.

Opposite the Mitchell House is the FOXCATCHER HOUNDS HUNT CLUB (*grounds visited by permission*). Hunts are held here over the old Fair Hill Course, part of the 7,000-acre estate of William duPont,Jr. As an event of the annual Cecil County Breeders' Fair (*September*), the Foxcatcher National Cup Steeplechase for four-year-olds is run here for a cup and a $5,260 purse. The three-mile brush course is patterned after the Aintree course in England.

Near Fair Hill along Big Elk Creek was NEW MUNSTER, a 6,000-acre tract only about two miles wide. It was patented in 1683 by George Talbot for Edwin O'Dwire and 15 other Irishmen.

The wood-and-steel overpass spanning the road at 11.3 *m.* is one of six between this point and Fair Hill, constructed by the Foxcatcher Hounds Hunt Club to keep the fox hunters out of plebeian traffic.

The only house in APPLETON, 11.6 *m.* (337 alt.), is the SEVEN STARS TAVERN (L), a long two-and-a-half-story stone building erected about 1714. At one time the innkeeper was Katie Dysart, who according to recorded tradition, 'bore an unsavory reputation and came to a violent end.'

State 273 crosses the Delaware Line, 13 *m.*, 2 miles west of Newark, Del.

US 1 continues through the Nottingham Lots, which figured prominently in the boundary dispute between Lord Baltimore and William Penn. In 1702 during the period after the accession of William and Mary in England when Lord Baltimore fell into disfavor, Penn pushed his settlements southward into George Talbot's Susquehanna Manor grant (*see Tour 2a*), and here laid out the 37 lots of 500 acres each under the name Nottingham. Not until the Mason and Dixon Line was run in 1765 was most of this territory restored to Maryland.

RISING SUN, 3.2 *m.* (387 alt.,565 pop.), is a banking and trading center of grain growing farmers. A large well-equipped dairy is here. Founded as Summer Hill, the town in 1816 took its present name from a tavern whose shingle depicted the sun peeping over the horizon.

Left from Rising Sun on State 276, concrete and asphalt paved, to asphalt-paved State 269, 1.6 *m.*; R. here 1 *m.* to WEST NOTTINGHAM ACADEMY, established about 1741 on a large tract of rolling land. The founder of the academy was the Reverend Samuel Finley who, when the Whitefield revival caused a split in the Presbyterian ranks in 1741, headed the New Light party in this district. In 1761 Dr.Finley left to become president of Princeton College.

In a grove at the entrance to the academy is (L) the WEST NOTTINGHAM PRESBYTERIAN CHURCH, built in 1804 after the Old Light and New Light congregations had reunited. On the grounds is a memorial arch for Richard Stockton of New Jersey and Benjamin Rush of Pennsylvania, alumni who signed the Declaration of Independence.

State 269 continues southwestward to the junction, 6.3 *m.*, with US 222 near Port Deposit (*see below*).

By State 276 south of the junction with State 269 is the former BATTLE SWAMP TAVERN (R), 4.6 *m.* The stone building, now a residence, is two-and-a-half stories high with gable roof and small dormers and it has a frame addition. There is a fireplace in every room and some of the mantels are hand-carved. The old bar has recently been set up again. Rochambeau's heavy artillery and baggage train camped near here on September 9, 1781, before fording the Susquehanna River at Bald Friar.

On State 276 is the entrance (R), 7.5 *m.*, to ANCHOR AND HOPE FARM (*open*). The estate, which formerly included the site of the upper part of Port Deposit, was acquired by a member of the Creswell family before 1700. Anchor and Hope farmhouse, a long stone structure, substantial but rather crude, was probably built early in the seventeenth century and became the first inn in the neighborhood. The old taproom, now the living room, with a large stone fireplace at each end, has a closet with a sliding panel that was once the ticket office for the stagecoaches and ferry. George Washington used this ferry on May 8, 1775, on his way to Philadelphia for the session of the Continental Congress that chose him commander in chief of the American forces.

State 276 continues to PORT DEPOSIT (*see below*), 8.2 *m.*, at the junction with US 222.

The LAFAYETTE OAK (R), 6.1 *m.*, around which Lafayette and his troops camped on April 12, 1781, is also called the Richards Oak for a family who once owned this land. The tree, estimated to be more than 500 years old, has a trunk circumference of 21 feet, 8 inches, a height of 70 feet, and a spread of 105.

US 1 crosses Octoraro Creek, 6.8 *m.*, whose Indian name means 'rushing waters.' These waters formerly turned numerous grist and paper mills but are now chiefly important to bass fishermen.

At 8.9 *m.* are junctions with macadamized State 338 and with US 222, which unites briefly southward with US 1.

1. Right 0.2 *m.* on US 222 to the entrance (L) of SUCCESS, one of two tracts surveyed in 1683 for Thomas Lightfoot. At one time this estate belonged to a member of the Cromwell family. The dwelling, reputedly built in 1734, is a two-story, gambrel-roofed structure of squared logs covered with weatherboarding. It was evidently built in two sections, each with its own entrance and without communication between them on the second floor. A stone addition that replaced a log kitchen in 1849 still contains a fireplace spacious enough for eight-foot logs. It is said that a horse was used to drag in the fuel by means of a rope passed in one door of the kitchen and out another on the opposite side.

In the main house is the so-called Betsy Ross room. Local tradition insists that the shape of this room, rendered pentagonal by a chimney cutting diagonally across the corner, suggested the five-pointed star of the American flag to Betsy Claypoole'(Ross), the Philadelphia upholsterer who was a frequent visitor here; however, in spite of tradition, Betsy did not design the flag or the star.

At 3.2 *m.* on US 222 is the junction with a dirt road; L. here 0.8 *m.* to LINE PITS, an abandoned chrome mine, whose two shafts extended downward 250 feet. Isaac Tyson,Jr., who early acquired a virtual monopoly of chrome mining in Maryland, opened the pits in 1828 to reach one of the richest chrome deposits in Maryland. Between 1828 and 1850 the State furnished most of the world's chrome ore supply. The mine was closed about 1880, but attracted national attention in 1890 when prospectors asserted that the serpentine formation containing the chromite deposits also carried large pockets of gold. A gold rush created by the Klondike Mining Company resulted in much reckless speculation but found no gold.

US 222 crosses the Pennsylvania Line, 3.7 *m.*, at a point about 30 miles south of Lancaster,Pa. (*see Pennsylvania Guide*).

2. Left from US 1 on State 338 to the tree-bordered entrance lane (L) of beautiful OCTORARA (*private*), 0.4 *m.*, whose stone house, built in the late seventeenth century, forms part of the present mansion on an elevation commanding a view of the Susquehanna River and Conowingo Lake. Two wings, one frame and the other brick, are later additions.

Octorara, once part of Mount Welcome (*see below*), a tract granted to Richard Hall in the early days of the province, was first called Mount Independence. In 1807 the property was sold to the Physick family of Philadelphia and in 1823 passed into the hands of Dr.Philip Syng Physick (1768–1837), who had studied medicine in London under John Hunter, a great English surgeon. After a brilliant career as surgeon and teacher in Philadelphia, he retired to Octorara. In 1831, six years before his death, he successfully performed a difficult operation on the 73-year-old Chief Justice Marshall.

In the general store and post office at ROWLANDSVILLE, 1.3 *m.* (60 alt.,110 pop.), which stands on the bank of the deep Octoraro Creek gorge, are account books dating back to 1810. Opposite the store are ruins of an old iron foundry, whose industrial successor is a small flour mill on the opposite bank.

MOUNT WELCOME (R), 9.1 *m.* (*open*), a two-and-a-half-story plastered brick house with gable roof, dormers, and a stone wing, stands on one of the oldest grants in this section (*see above*). Although preceded by another manor house, the present building is itself quite old. The handrail of its stairway is of bird's-eye maple, floorboards are a foot wide, and the doors, only three-quarters of an inch thick, still hang perfectly true.

In CONOWINGO, 9.4 *m.* (77 alt.,300 pop.), a hamlet of filling stations and roadside restaurants, US 222 branches south along the east bank of the Susquehanna.

Left on US 222 to the PORT DEPOSIT QUARRIES (L), 4 *m.*, in operation since 1808. This source of Everlasting Granite, used extensively in Maryland buildings, extends 200 feet up the face of the cliff.

Opposite the quarries in the river are SMITH'S FALLS, so named since 1606 when Captain John Smith ascended the Susquehanna until the rocks at this spot blocked further passage. On his map he named the place Smyth's Fales and marked it with a cross, a symbol he explained as meaning '. . . to the crosses hath bin discovered what beyond is by relation.'

His *General Historie of Virginia* in reporting this expedition noted 'that abundance of fish, lying so thick with their heads above the water, as for want of nets (our barge driving amongst them) we attempted to catch them with a frying pan; but we found it a bad instrumente to catch fish with: neither better fish, more plentyous nor more varietie for small fish had any of us ever seen in any place so swimming in the water, but they are not to be catched with frying pans.' The river still provides excellent fishing, with pike and rock abundant in the spring, bass in the fall.

At 4.6 *m.* is the junction (L) with concrete-paved State 269 (*see above*). On the northeastern corner of the junction is the old stone ROCK RUN MILL, now a sausage factory. In 1731 a petition for a road to this point mentioned this structure as 'the merchants' mill.'

PORT DEPOSIT, 6. *m.* (16 alt.,963 pop.), is a town interesting both for its setting and its history. Here the Susquehanna River is flanked by steep cliffs that rise more than 200 feet, and leave space along the shore for little but mile-long Main Street and railroad tracks. High Street, somewhat shorter, runs parallel with Main Street on the cliffside. In three places where the steep wall to the northeast is broken by hollows, the town has also reached out with a few houses. In spite of its situation, Port Deposit, like most industrial communities, is not particularly attractive.

As early as 1729 Thomas Cresap (*see Tour 2E*) operated a ferry near here; and in the early nineteenth century the place was called Creswell's Ferry. In 1812 when completion of the Maryland Canal brought a boom along the river, Philip Thomas established the town and the next year the assembly gave the settlement its present name, doubtless with the idea that the town would be a port of deposit for products coming down the Susquehanna. Local belief in the town's importance was high by the spring of 1813 when the British entered the Susquehanna, and the inhabitants threw up a little fort to defend their city. They were grossly insulted when the enemy, after burning a warehouse at Bell's Ferry across the river, passed on without so much as deigning to notice their existence.

Port Deposit grew rapidly, however; by 1822 it handled $1,337,925 worth of merchandise in one year. Nearly a thousand arks and rafts came down the river and canal, and 126 vessels entered and cleared. Lumber was the main article of commerce, but large quantities of wheat, flour, whisky, and iron were also transported. Herring and shad fishing added to the prosperity of the town; the quarries in their heyday employed several hundred men; lumber mills turned out various products; and an iron foundry was established and later began to produce the popular Armstrong stoves. In spite of the railroad competition the town in 1880 had a population of 1,950, more than twice the present figure. The decline, which had already set in, was induced by depletion of timber up-river, the effect of dams upon commercial fishing, as well as by the railroads and the use of deeper harbors. The only important industry that has survived is quarrying.

WASHINGTON HALL (L), on Main St., is a large brick building that houses the Town Schools of the Jacob Tome Institute. In the center of the front façade, carved in the brownstone caps at the base of two engaged columns, are reliefs of Tome and his wife. Opposite the hall are three granite buildings also belonging to the school. Jacob Tome (1810–98), born in York County, Pennsylvania of German Lutheran parentage, was compelled by the death of his father to go to work before he had received much schooling. In 1833 he arrived here on a raft. Though practically penniless, he found a partner with capital and entered the lumber business. Feeling the need of a knowledge of bookkeeping, he managed to acquire it after the day's work by riding horseback to Perryville, taking the train to Philadelphia, attending night school there, then returning to this place by train and horseback in time for breakfast. For three months he slept only on the train to and from Philadelphia. The business prospered so well that Tome became one of the leading financiers of the State and extended his investments to the timber lands of Michigan. Most important of his many philanthropical ventures was the Jacob Tome Institute, an educational foundation incorporated in 1829 to provide not only book learning but manual training; the Town Schools in Port Deposit were opened in 1894. Before his death Tome had given $1,650,000 to the Institute and he left to it his residuary estate, valued at $3,500,000. The Town Schools, with classes from kindergarten through high school, now take the place of a public school in the community. The enrollment of nearly 600, reached in 1898, has been halved by the development of the county school system.

At the NE. corner of Main St. and Woodlawn Rd. is the ANGLER'S INN, occupying the Heald House, an old dressed-stone building formerly on the Creswell estate, which embraced the northern end of the town and the heights above. Although commercial fishing has disappeared from Port Deposit (*boats and guides available*), sport fishing is still popular, especially above the first rapids.

At the southern end of town is the main entrance (L) to TOME SCHOOL, which is in the cliffs. This boys' boarding school was opened in 1900 by the Jacob Tome Institute, but in 1938 the trustees had to offer the school for sale because of depreciation in the Institute's holdings. A company organized by its alumni bought it.

In Port Deposit is the junction with State 276 (*see above*).

At 7.2 *m.* on US 222 is the junction with a gravel road; L. here 0.2 *m.* to the old Perryville-Port Deposit road; straight ahead at the junction on a high elevation is the PHYSICK HOUSE, built in 1812. The two-and-a-half-story stone structure, now covered with plaster, has a hip roof with twin dormers and a deck. Both the drive and garden fronts have entrance porticoes. In the large, well-proportioned rooms is delicate woodwork. The house is on a tract that was called Mount Ararat when it was surveyed in 1664 for Thomas Griffith. The present name was acquired when this was the residence of a son of Dr.Philip Syng Physick (*see above*).

At 11.6 *m* is the junction with US 40 in PERRYVILLE (*see Tour 2a*).

US 1 crosses the Susquehanna River along the top of CONOWINGO DAM, 9.5 *m.*, which is 4,648 feet long, 105 feet high, and was completed in 1927. The Susquehanna backs up north of the dam for more than 14 miles, forming CONOWINGO LAKE.

On land now submerged once stood rocks bearing Indian pictographs, known in William Penn's time. Some of these are now in the Maryland Academy of Sciences' museum.

STATE POLICE SUBSTATION F (*information and first aid*) is at 11.5 *m.*, beyond the western end of the dam.

At HOPKINS CORNER, 12.8 *m.*, is the junction with macadam State 162.

Right on State 162 to the NATHAN RIGBIE HOUSE (*open*), 2 *m.*, overlooking Conowingo Lake. The stone dwelling, built in 1732 and enlarged in 1750 by a frame addition, contains elaborately paneled interior walls, carved walnut banisters, and a huge fireplace. On April 13, 1781, while Lafayette was stopping here with Colonel James Rigbie on his way to Yorktown, a mutiny broke out among his troops. After the trouble was quelled, the ringleader was tried and executed on the spot.

In POOLE, 16.2 *m.* (400 alt.,50 pop.), is the junction with macadamized State 136, the Whiteford-Churchville Road.

Left on State 136, crossing Deer Creek Bridge, to PRIEST NEALE'S MASS HOUSE (R), 2.9 *m.*, a one-story stone building where a Jesuit mission was established in 1747. The adjoining graveyard contains stones dated 1750. In 1764 Thomas Shea deeded the tract called 'Paradice' to Father Bennett Neale, who probably erected the mass house. Since Catholic churches were banned by law at this time, the building took the form of a dwelling with a large hall for use as a chapel. The place resembles a blockhouse. Since 1800 the building has been a dwelling, and the old chapel hall is now a living room. State 136 meets State 22 at 5.8 *m.*, in CHURCHVILLE (*see Tour 2a*).

At 22.6 *m.* on US 1 is the junction with State 23.

Right on State 23 to FOREST HILL, 2.1 *m.* (544 alt.,400 pop.), a trading and banking center on the Maryland and Pennsylvania Railroad. Canning, fruit packing, and the nursery business add to local income.

BELAIR, 25.8 *m.* (396 alt.,1,650 pop.), seat of Harford County, is the trading and banking town of a fertile farming country. When Harford was formed out of Baltimore County in 1773, the county seat was established at Old Harford Town on Bush River. In 1782 it was moved to Aquila Scott's Old Field, which eventually became Belair, though the place was not incorporated until 1901. Today the town has a leisurely, settled air and the comfortable looking houses—many of them spacious—along the tree-lined streets give it a certain charm.

On Bond Street, one block R. of Main Street, is the COUNTRY CLUB INN, formerly the Eagle Hotel. The first building was erected in 1718, and the principal addition in 1790. Surrounded by attractive grounds, this inn contains a number of old furnishings and other relics of its two centuries of service.

Belair is at a junction with State 22 (see Tour 2a).

The HARFORD COUNTY FAIRGROUNDS, 26.5 m., are the scene of the county fair in October. The Harford County Pony Show is held here in June, and a ten-day race meet occupies the last week of July and the first week of August.

At 28.4 m. is the junction with State 147, the Harford Road, an alternate route to Baltimore, which is only two lanes wide and has many curves.

Right on State 147 to the junction with macadamized State 152, 1 m.; R. here 0.8 m. to FALLSTON, (442 alt., 150 pop.), at the western end of which is the LITTLE FALLS MEETING HOUSE (R), belonging to the Society of Friends. The stone building in 1773 replaced a log structure built in 1738. Friendly Senecas helped build the first meeting house and attended services upon its completion. In the adjoining graveyard are stones marked with the names of many families prominent in the early history of Maryland. Across the road from Little Falls Church, set back about fifty yards from the highway, is ST.MARK'S CHURCH. Here each August a tilting tournament is held (see Sports and Recreation).

In Fallston at 0.9 m. is the junction with a dirt road; L. 0.4 m. to BONAIR (L), whose old stone farmhouse is about 200 yards from the road. Built in 1795 by Francis de la Forte, an officer in Rochambeau's army, this whitewashed dwelling, with its graceful curved roof surmounted by tall brick chimneys, is reminiscent of a Norman farmhouse. Near the house is a tomb in which are buried the builder of the house, his wife, and his mother.

At 4.7 m. on State 147 is the junction with a macadamized road; L. on this road to FORK METHODIST CHURCH (L), 0.4 m. The first church here was built of logs in 1773 on land donated by James Baker. It is said that Baker was converted to the Methodist faith by a wandering preacher while walking on what is now Hillen Street in Baltimore, and returned to his home near here determined to organize a Methodist society. The log building was used until 1852 when it was replaced by the present structure, which has twice been remodeled.

MT.VISTA (L), 5.4 m. on State 147, is a modern residence on the site of the house of the same name occupied by Charles J. Bonaparte, Attorney General of the United States in Theodore Roosevelt's cabinet. The Bonaparte house burned in 1933.

For several miles the Harford Road passes through a narrow valley dotted with the rambling red buildings of extensive farms divided one from another by neat white picket fences. The road skirts the Gunpowder Falls, a noisy stream, for more than half a mile.

The SITE OF GUNPOWDER COPPER MILL (L) is at 8.5 m. The establishment, built about 1812 by Levi Hollingsworth, was the second of its kind in this country. The plant employed about twenty men, who lived in houses built by the mill company. One of the houses, formerly occupied by an overseer, stands (R) by the road. The property was sold in 1883, when competition from the West had made operation unprofitable, and abandoned a short time later. The former mill race (L) parallels the road, and the old blacksmith's forge is between the river and the highway.

The road crosses the picturesque Gunpowder Falls at 9.6 m.

CUB HILL, 10.6 m. (382 alt.,300 pop.), is at the junction with a macadamized road.

Right on this road 1.4 *m.* to (R) the MARYLAND TRAINING SCHOOL FOR BOYS (*open to visitors* 9–5), situated on a 365-acre tract overlooking Loch Raven. This State institution for the physical and mental education of white boys who have been committed by the courts and justices of the peace, represents an investment of $1,000,000. It has 40 buildings, with accommodations for a staff of 47 and for 300 boys. When founded in 1830 the institution was called the Baltimore House of Refuge and was administered by a board of managers and maintained by private subscriptions and State appropriations. In 1918 its entire support was assumed by the State.

CARNEY, 11.9 *m.* (358 alt.,1,993 pop.), a commuters' village, is the terminus of an extension of a Baltimore streetcar line. At Carney is the junction with Joppa Road (*see Tour 1A*).

State 147 continues to a junction with US 1, 18.8 *m.* on North Avenue in BALTI-MORE.

On US 1 at BENSON, 28.9 *m.* (400 alt.,40 pop.), is the junction with a dirt road.

Left here to the FRESH AIR FARM, 0.5 *m.*, covering about 40 acres of land. This camp, operated by the Children's Fresh Air Society of Baltimore City, provides ten-day summer vacations for underprivileged boys and girls between five and twelve years of age. Since its establishment in 1891, it has cared for nearly a quarter of a million children.

An old stone (L) at 32.5 *m.* is known as the HOODOO MARKER, because of its inscription: 'Cursed be he who removeth his neighbor's landmark, and all the people shall say amen. *Deuteronomy Chap. 27, Verse 17.*' It is further inscribed: 'This stone is in place of a double poplar tree, a boundary of Onion's Prospect Hills, the latter owned by Edward Day.' The rough stone, probably set up in the early seventeenth century, is about nine feet high. The story is that this is a relic of a lifetime quarrel between two brothers—so bitter that when clergymen attempted to reconcile them before the expected death of one, even the supposedly dying man gave only a qualified response. He was willing to be reconciled if he were dying —not otherwise.

KINGSVILLE, 33.2 *m.* (271 alt.,50 pop.), is a crossroads trading center at the junction with asphalt-paved Jerusalem Road.

1. Left on Jerusalem Road 2 *m.* to JERUSALEM (145 alt.,50 pop.). By the bridge over the Little Gunpowder Falls are (R) the JERUSALEM MILLS, whose construction was begun in 1772 by David Lee, a Quaker from Bucks County, Pennsylvania. The unusual building has a first story of stone, a second of frame construction, and two half stories under a steep gable roof. Two tiers of alternating dormer windows light the third story and the loft. The low ceilings of the building are supported by hand-hewn white oak beams, two feet square, which show no signs of decay. The mill, with its ponderous stone grinders, is still operated. During the Revolution, Lee, though a Quaker, manufactured guns in a two-story stone building, now a dwelling back of the mill.

2. Right on Jerusalem Road to the SITE OF ISHMAEL DAY'S HOUSE (R), 1.1 *m.* When a member of Sergeant Fields' division of the Second Maryland Cavalry, C.S.A., attempted to pull down a Union flag during Harry Gilmor's raid, Day filled the raider with buckshot and escaped to the woods. The Confederates burned Day's house and barn.

KINGSVILLE INN (R), 33.4 *m.*, dating from 1753, has become a long, three-story stone building with central gable and six dormers. The first unit was two stories high and had but ten rooms. There is the usual tradition of visits by George Washington and by Lafayette. John Paul, who operated the hotel at the time of the War of 1812, was arrested for giving flour to British troops. Convicted and sentenced to death, he escaped, hid in a cave near Franklinville, and finally managed to board a ship for England. In 1924 Henry Ford bought an old stagecoach from the inn for his Greenfield Village in Michigan.

At 36.6 m. is the junction with a dirt lane. Right on this to PERRY HALL MANSION (R), 0.6 m., a very large stone structure commanding a wide view. When first erected, probably about 1750, it was twice its present size; the remaining half was rebuilt after a fire in 1824.

The present house has no great interest, but before the fire it was a showplace with magnificent gardens and even a Roman bath. Harry Dorsey Gough, the first owner, was converted to Methodism and erected a chapel on this land. His home became a center of hospitality for itinerant Methodist preachers, notably for Asbury and Coke. Here in December 1784 assembled the group that rode into Baltimore for the Christmas conference at Lovely Lane Meeting House to organize the Methodist Church in America. It was at this meeting that Francis Asbury was elected first superintendent of the united Methodists.

At 38.1 m. is a junction with Joppa Road (see Tour 1A) and at 46.8 m. on North Avenue in Baltimore is the junction with the Harford Road (see above), alternate to US 1.

BALTIMORE, 48.8 m. (20 alt.,804,874 pop.) (see Baltimore).

Points of Interest: Fort McHenry, Shot Tower, Flag House, Washington Monument, Johns Hopkins University, Roman Catholic Cathedral, Druid Hill Park, and many others.

Baltimore is at junctions with US 40 (see Tour 2) US 111 (see Tour 13), State 26 (see Tour 2A), US 140 (see Tour 14), State 2 (see Tour 8), and State 3 (see Tour 9).

Section b. BALTIMORE to DISTRICT OF COLUMBIA LINE; 33.8 m.

This section of US 1 is one of the busiest roads in the nation because traffic shared north of Baltimore and south of Washington by various routes converges on this 30-mile stretch. Added to the hordes of trucks, busses, and private motorcars bound for places far north and south are the cars of commuters to the two large cities, and the small trucks of farmers living in the intracity area. Owing to its unplanned development US 1 is a highly dangerous route in spite of its width and the elimination of the worst curves. One hazard being fought by motoring associations, newspapers of Baltimore and Washington, and clubwomen, partly from an esthetic point of view, is the intensive commercialization that has lined the 30 miles of highway with more than 5,000 signboards and innumerable filling stations, hot dog stands, junk heaps, tourist cabins, and the like. Every known device is used to induce tourists to stop and buy sandwiches, hot drinks, cold drinks, liquor, cans of jam, used cars, and even tombstones. Clotheslines hung with gaudy tufted bedspreads vie with the neon lights for attention.

Natives often express the belief that their fellow-Marylander, Ogden Nash, had this route in mind when he wrote:

> I think that I shall never see
> A billboard lovely as a tree.
> Perhaps unless the billboards fall
> I'll never see a tree at all.

US 1 has a night life of its own. In addition to the patrons of dancing and drinking resorts along the way, there are many nighttime truck drivers—from farmers with ancient and rickety flivvers to professionals with mammoth 15-ton cab and trailers. Those with regular schedules come to know each other well in the eating places.

South of BALTIMORE, 0 m., is HALETHORPE (R), 6.9 m. (78 alt., 1,831 pop.), inhabited largely by commuters who work in Baltimore.

In a large field (L), 7 m., was held the Fair of the Iron Horse, the centennial celebration by the Baltimore and Ohio Railroad in 1929 to commemorate its founding. Many of the exhibits that attracted 1,250,000 people are now at the Old Bailey Roundhouse in Baltimore.

In 1910 the first major airplane meet in the United States was held on this same field. At this time Hubert Latham piloted a 50-horsepower monoplane over Baltimore in the first successful flight over a large American city.

At 8.2 m. is the junction with Rolling Road (State 166), one of the many thoroughfares over which, in colonial times, huge hogsheads of tobacco were trundled toward shipping points in the Tidewater (*see Tour 1A*).

Right on Rolling Road to RELAY, 1.4 m. (200 alt.,2,016 pop.). In the brief period before the introduction of steam, Baltimore & Ohio Railroad trains stopped here at the Relay House for a change of horses. This two-story combination hotel, ticket office, and waiting room, the first 'mealing-station' erected by a railroad for the comfort of its patrons, burned in 1897. On its foundations, about a block east of the present station, stands a boarding house.

On May 4, 1861, Butler's Sixth Massachusetts Regiment, which had been attacked in the Pratt Street Riot (*see Baltimore*), took possession of Relay House and fortified the heights above the Thomas Viaduct with two cannon. On May 13 they boarded a train in Relay for Baltimore where that same night they 'captured' Federal Hill.

State 166 continues to junction in CATONSVILLE (*see Tour 2b*), 5 m., on US 40 and a northern section of Rolling Road (*see Tour 1A*).

At 8.7 m. on US 1 is the junction with the River Road.

Right on this macadam road 0.3 m. to the THOMAS VIADUCT, which carries the Baltimore & Ohio Railroad over the Patapsco River. Supported on eight elliptical arches of granite, the structure forms a sweeping curve 612 feet long. Although built in 1835 for the tiny locomotives and wooden coaches of that time, it stands up perfectly under the modern trains. Beneath the viaduct is one of the favorite spots in the State for gudgeon fishing.

The River Road continues along the gorge of the Patapsco to PATAPSCO STATE PARK (R), 1.2 m. (*Permits for a single night's camping from park superintendent at Ilchester; permits for longer periods from Department of Forestry, Baltimore, Md.*) This 1,116-acre tract of wooded hills rises to an elevation of 250 feet on each side of the river, and from the plateau above flow small streams that break into cascades over rocky ledges. Foot and bridle trails thread the park. At ORANGE GROVE, 2.9 m., is the junction (L) with the Cascade Trail, one of the most beautiful byways in the park.

ILCHESTER, 4.6 *m.* (102 alt.,270 pop.), on the south side of the Patapsco, is largely dependent upon the mill at Thistle. At Ilchester are the TRINITY COLLEGE PREPARATORY SCHOOL (1934) and ST.MARY'S COLLEGE (1867), a Redemptorist noviate and mission house. An old bridge abutment (R), 0.4 *m.*, is the remains of the Baltimore & Ohio's first bridge, built about 1829 and destroyed by a flood in July 1868.

In THISTLE, 4.8 *m.* (130 alt.,25 pop.), by the north bank of the Patapsco, is a fiber boxboard mill on the SITE OF THE THISTLE FACTORY, erected in 1821 for the manufacture of cotton print.

Along the rocky, wooded bank of the river are the ruins of PATAPSCO FACTORY (L), 5.8 *m.*, built in 1820 by Edward Gray and nearly destroyed in the flood of 1868. It was repaired and operated by Gray's daughter until wrecked in another flood 20 years later. Adjacent is (L) the remodeled PATAPSCO HOUSE, built about 1812 by Edward Gray. The floods greatly damaged the house, as well as the mill, swept away the gardens and outbuildings, and destroyed books, prints, and other valuable objects. John Pendleton Kennedy, Baltimore man-of-letters (*see Literature*), married one of Gray's daughters and lived here for many summers. Washington Irving visited Kennedy in 1854 and described the countryside here as 'Mahomet's Paradise'; he wrote that he would have liked to destroy the mills and the railroad and build chateaux along the river. To make his medieval picture complete, Irving said, 'All the cotton lords should live in baronial castles on the cliff; and the cotton spinners should be virtuous peasantry of both sexes, in silk shirts and smallclothes and straw hats with long ribbons and should do nothing but sing songs and choruses and dance on the margin of the river.'

The River Road continues to the junction with US 40 (*see Tour 2b*) and US 29 (*see Tour 1B*) in ELLICOTT CITY, 6.2 *m.*

ELKRIDGE, 8.9 *m.* (78 alt.,800 pop.), is a residential and trading center for farmers. As colonial Elk Ridge Landing, the town shipped large quantities of tobacco, grain, and timber. Agents were stationed here to assess the tobacco and to carry on other port functions. In 1765 the inhabitants hanged in effigy Zachariah Hood, Stamp Act agent for Maryland. Although the tobacco trade decreased considerably during the Revolutionary War, forges and furnaces were busy here producing arms for the Continental Army. In 1781 Lafayette's troops camped at the landing for two days on their way to engage Cornwallis in Virginia in the final campaign of the war.

At 9.9 *m.* is the junction with Montgomery Road (State 103).

Right on this concrete-paved road 0.7 *m.* to another concrete road; L. here 1 *m.* to BELMONT (L), whose rambling five-part, two-story house of brick now covered with yellow plaster was built by Caleb Dorsey, operator of near-by iron mines, for his bride, Priscilla Hill. On the main door is an iron plate inscribed 'C & P 1738,' and other doors are reinforced by huge iron straps of the type called witch crosses in early New England. The old box hedge in some places is now 15 feet high.

Behind SPRING HILL, 5.8 *m.* on State 103, a two-and-a-half-story house on terraced grounds at the end of a long lane, are stone slave quarters built before the Revolution.

State 103 continues to the junction with US 29 (*see Tour 1B*), 6.8 *m.*, at a point 1.5 *m.* southwest of Ellicott City.

LAUREL RACE TRACK (L), 19.6 *m.*, with its seating capacity of 10,000, is one of the most popular tracks in the State (*see Sports and Recreation*).

In 1887 David J. Weems formed a company for rapid transportation of mail and express matter between Boston and Washington by remote-controlled electric trains. After the plan had been approved by the physicist Rowland, the company built a banked circular track here several miles in circumference, with an overhead rail to serve both for support and power feed. The six-ton electric locomotive was equipped with three sets of 40-inch drivers run by a powerful motor without the intervention of gears. At the trial of its utility the engine reached a speed of 120 miles an hour and maintained it for 22 minutes, but the superstructure collapsed under the tremendous strain. After the destruction of their equipment the company was forced to suspend the experiments for lack of funds.

LAUREL, 20.4 m. (150 alt.,2,532 pop.), is on land patented late in the seventeenth century to Richard Snowden, who had been an officer in Cromwell's army. The region was still subject to incursions of the Susquehannock who terrified the settlers by 'hollowing around their Plantations and attempting their dwellings chiefly Mr.Duval and Richard Snowden.' Industrial development was several times attempted here; discovery of iron ore led Snowden's heirs to form the Patuxent Iron Ore Company in 1736. A grist mill, built in 1811, gave way to a cotton mill in 1824. Several other cotton factories were established during the nineteenth century, but all had been abandoned by 1911.

Left from Laurel on State 197 to MONTPELIER (R), 2.1 m., built in the latter half of the eighteenth century by Thomas Snowden and his son, Major Thomas Snowden. The knoll on which this large brick house stands slopes so abruptly that the floor level of the wings is several feet lower than that of the main house.

The five-bay main section with its twelve-light double hung windows, steep hip roof, two lofty chimneys, and central eave pediments (front and rear) has been ably restored. Its central portals are of similar design, with deeply recessed, eight-paneled front door framed by fluted Doric pilasters and triglyphed frieze, under a pediment; the garden doorway has an additional traceried fanlight breaking into its pediment. Perhaps the most distinctive feature of the exterior is the octagonal treatment of the garden façade of each flanker.

Most of the interior woodwork is hand-carved. Especially notable is the detail of the stair railing between the north hyphen and the library; it has turned balusters—three on each step, and each of different pattern.

State 197 continues to BOWIE, 9 m. (see Tour 10).

At 22 m. on US 1 is the junction with a dirt road.

Left on this to OAKLAND (L), 0.2 m., a sturdy brick house on an elevated site. Built in 1798 by Richard Snowden, son of Major Thomas Snowden of Montpelier, it is distinguished by fine doorways and excellent brickwork varied by heavy glazed headers. From the terraced garden in the rear is an exceptional view of the rolling countryside. The living room was long the scene of uproarious and spirits-drenched card games for immense stakes. Legend has it that one night when a player was called away, the host swore in exasperation, 'I would play with the devil if he took your place'—whereupon a lean, dark stranger walked in, asked to be let into the game, and after an uncanny streak of luck departed with all the money in sight.

MUIRKIRK, 23.4 m. (170 alt.,200 pop.), was named for Muirkirk, Scotland, by the Scots who in 1747 built an iron furnace here. Six of the beehive-shaped brick charcoal ovens are still standing. Because Muirkirk iron had greater tensile strength, the plant outlasted most of the others that utilized Maryland ore and it supplied cannon and cannon balls to the Federal Army during the Civil War and later began the production of gun carriages and car wheels. Razed by an explosion in 1880, the plant was immediately rebuilt. About the time of the World War Muirkirk turned to the production of ochre from local ores but since 1924 has produced dry pigments from higher grade foreign ores.

AMMENDALE NORMAL INSTITUTE (R), 24.6 *m.*, is the provincial house and novitiate of the Brothers of the Christian Schools for the District of Baltimore. Established in 1880 it prepares young men for the teaching brotherhood and is a retreat for aged or invalid members.

At 25.8 *m.* is the junction with a concrete-paved road.

Left on this road 0.5 *m.* to the NATIONAL AGRICULTURAL RESEARCH CENTER (*visitors 9–4 weekdays, 9–1 Sat.*), the 14,000-acre experimental farm of the Department of Agriculture. Here in some 20 modern stucco buildings, 500 trained technicians and workmen do plant, livestock, and poultry research. Scientists develop new plant and livestock strains, experiment in the elimination of poultry and cattle diseases, and study marketing methods, soil conservation, and crop rotation. The center costs approximately $1,000,000 annually but has more than repaid this sum by increased farm production. Pamphlets reporting the results of these experiments have wide distribution.

In the administration building (R), 0.9 *m.*, is a basement laboratory used for nutrition experiments on white mice. Back of this building are the dairy barns and silos where experiments in artificial insemination are carried on. Beside these barns is a bull exerciser resembling a huge, rimless wheel. The nutrition laboratory of the Bureau of Animal Husbandry (L), 1.3 *m.*, is housed in a red brick building; here diets are planned to increase the milk supply of cows and produce hogs with firm flesh. In the sheep barn (L), a two-story brick building with one-story stucco wings, experimental breeding of black-faced Corriedale and Highland ewes to Karakul rams produces a karakul wool suitable for commercial purposes. Beyond the sheep barn is (L) the poultry section; scattered over several acres are small chicken houses containing from a dozen to several score hens each. Separated by wire fences, these houses shelter flocks ranging from week-old chicks to pullets scientifically fed to produce the most eggs or the best fryers or broilers. Similar pens contain turkeys, guinea hens, ducks, and pigeons.

In the poultry laboratories, 1.8 *m.*, four large stucco buildings, poultry experimental work is carried on. Here several hundred chickens confined in cages are infected with parasites and bacteria, then treated in various ways in an effort to discover the best methods of curing the costly poultry diseases. In other rooms hens are fed on various diets to find which gives the best egg production. These experiments are said to have increased egg production throughout the country by several million dollars annually. A log recreation building (R) contains a kitchen and recreation hall for employees. Near this building are (L) the dog houses where Hungarian Pulis are crossbred to produce a superior sheep dog. The goat barn (R), 2.7 *m.*, houses a Toggenberg and Saanen herd bred to high-grade milk producers; the kids are bottle-fed so that an accurate milk production record can be kept.

The HORTICULTURAL STATION of the Bureau of Plant Industry (R), 26.7 *m.*, is part of the National Agricultural Research Center. Behind the two large laboratories are greenhouses in which seedlings are nourished in various soils and experiments are conducted in budding and crossing.

In stagecoach days RHODES TAVERN (R), 27 *m.*, still in operation, was the first station for feeding and watering the horses on the trip from Washington to Baltimore. The large beams of the three-story building are of oak; only six of the 17 rooms are without fireplaces, and the kitchen fireplace with its brick oven occupies the entire end of a room.

At 29 *m.* is the junction with a concrete-paved road.

Left on this road to Edmonson Road, 1.4 *m.*; L. here to GREENBELT, 3.7 *m.*, (109 alt.,1,500 pop.), a village built by the Resettlement Administration. Begun in 1935 and completed in 1938 at a cost of about $9,000,000, it provides low-priced housing for families of moderate income, for the most part government workers in Washington. The village is landscaped to utilize the small stream winding through town and to relieve the monotony of two basic types of structure. A central heating plant serves the community, underpasses have been built at highway crossings, and house construction and equipment meet modern standards. Garden and farm space is provided on the outskirts of the settlement.

COLLEGE PARK, 29.5 *m*. (60 alt.,316 pop.), is the seat of the UNIVERSITY OF MARYLAND (*see Education*), whose dignified buildings of modern Georgian Colonial design overlook the boulevard and the countryside from a hilly campus. A rebuilding program, still under way in 1940, gives an air of newness to the old university. Outstanding among the 26 buildings is the two-story red brick LIBRARY, trimmed in limestone, surmounted by a white cupola, and occupying the center of the campus; it has about 58,000 volumes. The administrative offices are on the ground floor. Two new buildings near the Library house the College of Arts and Sciences and the Department of Mines. On the crest of the hill is the Agriculture Building, while other units, visible from the highway, include the Engineering Building and two new dormitories. The Student Center houses the offices of *Old Line* and *The Terrapin*, student publications, and the Religious Work Council and the Maryland Christian Association. The gymnasium and outdoor tennis field provide facilities for athletics and recreation.

The Maryland Agricultural Experiment Station, operated in connection with the university and adjoining the boulevard, has done some noteworthy work in the field of plant and tree culture, especially in the standardization and increase of tobacco yields and in the eradication of Oriental fruit moths. About one-third of the university campus is used for experimental purposes by the station; here in orchards and vineyards students get practical experience in coping with agricultural problems. A large poultry house has recently been added and experiments are conducted similar to those carried on at the National Agricultural Research Center (*see above*). Another recent addition to the station's activities is the horticultural research section, which is about two miles north of the university and back from the highway. Under the presidency of Dr.H.C.Byrd, the university has undergone its period of greatest expansion and development.

RITCHIE STADIUM (L), 29.6 *m*., the athletic bowl of the university, is opposite the ROSSBURG INN (R), now occupied by Agricultural Experiment Station offices. A mansard roof of 1888 replaces the original gable of this three-story structure which has had numerous alterations. The keystone of the doorway bears the name T.Coad, the date 1798, and a figure of Silenus, preceptor of Bacchus, god of wine.

RIVERDALE, 30.9 *m*. (37 alt.,1,533 pop.), is a residential suburb of Washington. On Arthur Ave. two blocks from Madison, is the CALVERT MANSION (R), built in the mid-eighteenth century by Baron von Stier for his daughter, who married George, son of Benedict Calvert. The stuccoed Georgian Colonial building is of brick. Behind the house in the garden stands a cannon, said to be one of the four brought to Maryland on the *Ark*. Tradition has it that Henry Clay wrote the Missouri Compromise while he was a visitor here.

HYATTSVILLE, 31.7 *m.* (46 alt.,4,264 pop.), another community largely composed of commuters to Washington, is also a banking and commercial center for a considerable area. The town, incorporated in 1880, was named for its first postmaster.

In Hyattsville is a junction with US 50 (*see Tour* 10).

US 1 crosses the DISTRICT OF COLUMBIA LINE, 33.8 *m.*, at a point about 5.5 miles northeast of the Zero Stone behind the White House.

Tour 1A

Northern Junction with US 1—Carney—Towson—Rockland—Pikesville —Southern Junction with US 1, 31.8 *m.*; Joppa Road, Old Court Road, and Rolling Road.

Narrow concrete or asphalt paving.
Accommodations limited.

This route, roughly paralleling the northern and western boundaries of Baltimore and longer than a direct route through the city, has relatively light traffic and few billboards to obstruct pleasant views. Joppa Road and Old Court Road roughly follow Indian trails that became highways leading to Joppa Town and Towson when these were towns of importance in Baltimore County.

Joppa Road branches west from US 1 (*see Tour* 1a), 0 *m.*, at a point 2.3 miles southwest of Perry Hall (*see Tour* 1a).

CARNEY, 2.4 *m.* (358 alt.,100 pop.), is at the junction with State 147 (*see Tour* 1a), an alternate to US 1.

At 4.7 *m.* is the junction with Loch Raven Boulevard, a concrete-paved dual highway.

1. Left on Loch Raven Boulevard to Taylor Avenue, 1.1 *m.* At the southeastern corner of the junction is the HILLENDALE COUNTRY CLUB, opened in 1924. The club has one of the most difficult golf courses in the State, a stone clubhouse, tennis courts, and swimming pool. Near this course is the MT. PLEASANT MUNICIPAL GOLF COURSE.
Loch Raven Boulevard continues into Baltimore.

2. Right 0.6 *m.* on Loch Raven Boulevard to Cromwell Bridge Road and R. on this to Loch Raven Road, 2.5 *m.*; L. here to LOCH RAVEN DAM, 2.9 *m.* This dam, completed in 1922, forms a lake ten miles long which, together with the lake formed by Pretty Boy Dam (*see Tour* 13), supplies water for Baltimore. The dam, 75 feet high and 650 feet wide, is built across a narrow valley whose heavily wooded hillsides are a popular picnicking ground.
On Loch Raven Road is the entrance (L) to GLEN ELLEN, 3.2 *m.*, birthplace of Harry Gilmor, the Confederate raider. Now deserted and roofless, the house, romantically decorated with battlemented towers and high mullioned windows, was

built by Robert Gilmor in 1834. It was designed by A.J.Davis of Newburgh,N.Y., as suitable for the Hudson Valley.

At 5.4 *m*. is the junction with Dulany Valley Road; L. here at 7.1 *m*. on Dulany Valley Road is the junction with the concrete-paved Jarrettsville Road; R. here 0.5 *m*. to MARCHMONT (*open*), a three-part house with additions stepped down. It is believed that the smallest section was built in the last decade of the seventeenth century, the central part shortly afterwards; the large two-and-a-half-story stone section about 1790.

On the Jarrettsville Road is (L) KING'S TAVERN, 2.5 *m*., a two-and-a-half-story frame building with a two-story annex. The main house was built about 1780. The raider Harry Gilmor made this place his headquarters for several expeditions into Baltimore County. Local farmers hid their livestock in a ravine near by when warned of his approach.

On Dulany Valley Road at 10.9 *m*. is (R) HAMPTON (*visited by written permission from John Ridgely,Jr., Keyser Building, Baltimore*). Perhaps no other large house in Maryland so nearly retains its early atmosphere. It has always been inhabited by members of the same family, people of wealth who were able to preserve both the house and its elaborate furnishings. Through the years its terraced gardens have been enriched until notable for their beauty.

The builder of Hampton was Charles Ridgely, whose forebears were early settlers of Maryland and quickly piled up fortunes. Charles Ridgely patented a large tract here in 1758 and later added to his holdings. By 1783, at the end of the Revolution, he was able to start construction of the fine house he had long contemplated with the assistance of John Howell, an amateur architect—apparently a sound builder. The design is basically Georgian Colonial—with central hall, simple treatment of windows, simple deep cornice, and low flankers. Ivy covers part of the stuccoed stone walls and fills in much of the space under the large two-story pedimented portico which has a Palladian window in the tympanum and shelters a balcony having a Chinese Chippendale balustrade. The simplicity of the basic design is obscured by the elaborately framed dormers on the low-pitched roof, by urns at the corners of the roof, and on the portico's pediment and, above all, by the large domed octagonal cupola surmounting the roof. While there is a tradition that this ornamentation was done at the time the house was built there is reason for believing that it was added later. Within is a family portrait gallery that provides examples of work by most of the leading artists in Maryland from the days of the second Hesselius, who painted the builder and his wife, Rebecca Dorsey. Charles and Rebecca Ridgely were an ill-assorted pair; he was the typical jovial country squire and she a convert to Methodism, torn by concern for her soul. She bitterly opposed his plans for a grand housewarming; and when he persisted in these, she called a housewarming of her own—a prayer meeting in the upper rooms. Ridgely died within a short period and, having no children, willed the estate to his nephew on condition that he take the name of Ridgely; he offered his wife a choice of life interest in an older near-by house with land, or in the new house without land, apparently hoping to place his cherished mansion in the hands of one who appreciated it. The widow perversely chose the mansion, so the nephew had to devote his attention to developing the terraced gardens while waiting for her death.

TOWSON, 6.9 *m*. (465 alt.,2,074 pop.) (*see Tour 13*), is at the junction with US 111 (*see Tour 13*) and Dulany Valley Road (*see above*).

At 11.1 *m*. is the junction with State 25 (Falls Road).

Right here to Valley Road, 0.3 *m*.; L. on Valley Road is entrance to BROOKLAND-WOOD (R), the Emerson estate, until 1924 the scene of the annual Grand National Steeplechase. The rambling stone mansion, on a hill overlooking Jones Falls and Green Spring Valley, is one of the show places of the State.

ROCKLAND, 12.5 *m*., (255 alt.,25 pop.), is a hamlet of one-story stone houses around a cotton bleaching mill. Here in 1810 the English immigrant Robert Wright erected a mill in which he bleached cotton by a secret process. Some descendants of the workers whom he taught work in the present mill which was built on the foundations of the original structure burned in 1857.

In Rockland is the junction with State 133 (the Old Court Road), which becomes the main route.

At 15.8 *m.* is the junction with asphalt-paved Stevenson Road.

Right here to DUMBARTON (R), 0.3 *m.*, a two-and-a-half-story stuccoed stone house, built in 1853 by Noah Walker, a wealthy merchant. It is said to have been the first house in Maryland with a bathroom having running hot and cold water. Below the house is the OLD WALKER HOUSE, a two-story, seven-room structure in which Noah Walker lived while Dumbarton was being built. Near by are many stables and out-buildings in which he kept fine trotting horses and about 800 head of cattle.

During the Civil War, Walker equipped the entire 44th Virginia Regiment of Confederates with uniforms made at his clothing factory. Walker later provided the first horse-drawn streetcar service between Baltimore and Pikesville and was the first merchant to offer men's ready-to-wear suits for sale.

By Stevenson Road is GARRISON FORT (R), 1.3 *m.*, on Fort Garrison Farm. The blockhouse, a one-story, rectangular structure of gray granite, is pierced with small rifle embrasures on each side. Originally it had a stone roof and was protected by a log stockade. The structure is known to have been in existence in 1698.

At 15.9 *m.* on Old Court Road is the junction with Park Heights Avenue (*see Tour* 14). At the northwest corner of this junction is DRUID RIDGE CEMETERY (*see Tour* 14).

In 1835 the little stone METTAM MEMORIAL BAPTIST CHURCH (R), 16.1 *m.*, was dedicated by the Reverend Joseph Mettam. Some time before this the clergyman had been jogging along in this vicinity when his horse shied and bolted, unseating the rider. Mettam's foot had been caught in the stirrup and he had been dragged and painfully bruised. While being nursed in a house near by by a woman who conducted a little school in Pikesville, he had become acquainted with the neighbors and determined to establish a church and school here.

PIKESVILLE, 16.3 *m.* (516 alt.,2,000 pop.) (*see Tour* 14), is at the junction with US 140.

In Pikesville the route turns R. on US 140 to Naylor's Lane, 16.8 *m.*; L. here to State 26 (*see Tour* 2A), 20.3 *m.*; L. on State 26 to Rolling Road, 20.8 *m.*; R. on Rolling Road to US 40–29 (*see Tour* 2b and Tour 1B), 27.3 *m.*; with which Rolling Road unites (L) to CATONSVILLE, 28.3 *m.* Here Rolling Road turns R. to a southern junction with US 1, 31.8 *m.* (*See Tour* 1b).

Tour 1B

Baltimore—Ellicott City—Ashton—Silver Spring—(Washington,D.C.); US 29.

Baltimore to District of Columbia Line, 39 *m.*
Alternate concrete or asphalt roadbed, two lanes wide.
Limited accommodations.

The Maryland section of US 29, locally called the Columbia Pike, traverses pleasant rolling country used chiefly for truck and dairy farming. It is an alternate route to US 1 between Baltimore and Washington, somewhat longer but much less crowded than the other route.

Between BALTIMORE, 0 *m.* (20 alt.,804,874 pop.) (*see Baltimore*), and ELLICOTT CITY, 10.5 *m.*, US 29 is united with US 40 (*see Tour 2b*). On the eastern outskirts of Ellicott City is the junction with River Road (*see Tour 1b*). US 29 turns L. from Main St., to wind steeply up a narrow street flanked by picturesque old stone houses. It soon reaches prosperous-looking dairy farms, whose Guernseys and Holsteins supply much milk for Baltimore and Washington.

At 12 *m.* is the junction with State 103 (*see Tour 1b*).

In COLUMBIA, 13.5 *m.* (402 alt.,20 pop.), a crossroads with a few houses and a general store, is the junction with the Old Columbia Pike.

Left (straight ahead) on this road 0.3 *m.* to ARLINGTON (R) whose three-and-a-half-story stone house has a one-and-a-half-story ell. The house was built in the early nineteenth century on land patented in the 1680's to John Dorsey. There is a tradition that all the stone used for the structure was pushed up a circular scaffold around the walls by a slave who was given his freedom when the job was completed. It is now the quarters of the All View Golf Club (18-*hole course open to public; greens fee* 50¢ *except on Sat., Sun., and holidays* $1).

At 1.3 *m.* is the junction with Guilford Road; L. on this road 0.9 *m.* to (L) BLAND AIR (*open*), with a large two-and-a-half-story brick house having a two-story annex. Built in the early 1800's it was for a time the home of Theodorick Bland (1776–1846), Chancellor of Maryland (1824–46).

On Guilford Road is (L) WAVELAND (*open*), 2.1 *m.* The two-and-a-half-story T-shaped brick house on a stone foundation was built in the early nineteenth century by Larkin Dorsey on the New Year's Gift tract, so named when patented in 1706 to Edward Dorsey and Charles Carroll because they received the 1,300 acres as a New Year's gift from the proprietary.

CHRIST CHURCH (P.E.), 3.4 *m.*, is a small rectangular brick building (R) built in 1809. The first church here, erected in 1729, was burned.

A few hundred yards west of the church is ATHOL. The house, erected in 1746 by the Reverend James Macgill, first rector of Christ Church, has gray stone walls, high massive chimneys, and a steep-pitched roof.

OAK HALL (*open*), 3.7 *m.*, a large three-story brick house painted white, also is on the New Year's Gift tract and was built early in the nineteenth century by Richard Dorsey, who practiced law in Baltimore.

316

A few hundred yards on the Oak Hall entrance lane is ELK HORN FARMHOUSE, a three-part house. The two-and-a-half-story main segment of dressed granite blocks was built about 1840 by Hammond Dorsey I. The two-story weatherboarded south wing stands on the stone foundations of a house built in 1728. Behind it are two log cabins formerly used for slaves.

Near CLARKSVILLE, 20 m. (484 alt.,65 pop.), rural crossroads settlement, limestone was once quarried in considerable quantities.

Between Clarksville and Ashton are many apple orchards and in the late fall farmers market cider and apples at roadside stands.

In ASHTON, 25.9 m. (498 alt.,194 pop.), is the junction with concrete-paved State 28.

Right (straight ahead) on State 28 to SANDY SPRING, 0.9 m. (490 alt.,80 pop.), a village settled by Quakers in 1650. The red brick Friends Meeting House (L) on Meeting House Road, built in 1817, and a few early houses still stand.

Probably the oldest building in OLNEY, 3.4 m. (544 alt.,82 pop.), is the pre-Revolutionary FAIR HILL (R), a rambling, three-part white plastered structure built by Richard Brooke but now housing a kennel. East of Fair Hill, near the outskirts of the village, is (R) the modern MONTGOMERY COUNTY HOSPITAL. This crossroads community which clusters about a combination post office and general store at a point where State 28 turns L., uniting with State 97, has assumed an air of importance since Harold Ickes, Secretary of the Interior (1933–), has become its leading citizen. The secretary's home, a two-and-a-half-story red brick farmhouse, faces State 28 (R) from a slight elevation in the southwestern section of the village. Nearly opposite the Ickes home is (L) the OLNEY INN, a converted farm building that has become a fashionable dining place for the Capital's social and government set. The inn has many old furnishings gathered from Montgomery County homes and also murals of colonial Maryland events, painted by Oskar Hausenstein (1883–), the Vienna artist.

State 97 continues to SILVER SPRING, 15.4 m. (see below). In the various modern settlements developed between Olney and Washington live many government executives.

Us 29 turns L. in Ashton to (L) CLIFTON (open), 27.1 m. The two-and-a-half-story brick house is recognized by the three dormers in its gambrel roof and its two tall chimneys. The main part of the dwelling was built in 1742 by Richard Thomas of Sandy Spring, and the one-and-a-half-story left wing was rebuilt in 1846. The house has no second-floor hall; steps branch out fanwise into all bedrooms.

COLESVILLE, 31.8 m. (430 alt.,56 pop.), is at the junction with State 183.

Right 0.4 m. on this tar-and-gravel road to (L) MOUNT RADNOR. Part of the two-and-a-half-story stone house belongs to a structure built early in the nineteenth century and burned in 1853. It is the birthplace of Philip E. Thomas (1776–1861), first president of the Baltimore & Ohio Railroad. Thomas had been appointed a member of the commission to study the question of reviving the Chesapeake and Ohio Canal as a means of capturing the western traffic being diverted to the Erie Canal in New York. Before long he resigned because the project offered no benefits to Baltimore. In February 1827 he called businessmen of Baltimore together to urge that they unite to build a railroad to save the city's trade; the Baltimore & Ohio Railroad was chartered in the following month and Thomas became the president, a position he held until 1836. Had it not been for his foresight and initiative it is probable that Maryland would have lost the lead that established Baltimore among world ports.

SILVER SPRING, 38.3 m. (340 alt.,7,500 pop.), takes its name from the mica flakes that gleamed on the bottom of a near-by spring. A suburb of Washington, most of its residents are Government workers. It has a modern shopping district and a few small manufacturing concerns, as well as the plant, classrooms, and laboratory of the National Association of Cleaners and Dyers of the United States and Canada. In the laboratory, studies and tests of cleaning and dyeing methods and of the effects of solvents on fabrics are made.

At 38.7 *m.* is a junction with Philadelphia Ave.

Left here to TAKOMA PARK, 1 *m.* (280 alt.,6,415 pop.), chartered in 1890. Much of the activity of the town is centered around headquarters of the Seventh Day Adventists who operate a sanitarium, a missionary college, and a junior college here.

US 29 becomes Georgia Avenue, which crosses the DISTRICT OF COLUMBIA LINE, 39 *m.*, about 5.5 miles north of the Zero Milestone behind the White House.

Tour 2

(New Castle,Del.)—Elkton—Baltimore—Frederick—Hagerstown—Cumberland—(Uniontown,Pa.); US 40.

Delaware Line to Pennsylvania Line, 225 *m.*
Dual highway, concrete-paved, Delaware Line to Elkton, and Havre de Grace to Baltimore; elsewhere concrete or asphalt of varying widths; western end of route impassable following heavy snowfall and occasionally dangerous from fogs. Pennsylvania and Baltimore & Ohio Railroads parallel route between Delaware Line and Baltimore; Western Maryland and Baltimore & Ohio Railroads roughly parallel route between Baltimore and Cumberland.
Accommodations ample throughout.

The Maryland section of US 40 links the State's four largest cities and serves as an outlet to and from the West. Northeast of Baltimore the route roughly parallels the old Post Road, where Revolutionary troops marched on their way to Yorktown. After the Revolution regular stages operated over the road to Philadelphia, and traffic increased rapidly until 1838 when completion of the railroad lessened the highway's importance. Recently, increased truck and automobile traffic has overtaxed the old Post Road and a modern dual-lane highway is under construction.

West of Baltimore US 40 follows the old pioneer route to the Ohio Valley. The section between Cumberland and Wheeling, West Virginia, completed in 1818, was the first nationally improved highway in the country. Known first as the Cumberland Road and later as the National Road, it was the main travel artery across the Allegheny Mountains till 1852. Blacksmith shops along the route did a thriving business; inns and taverns were crowded with travelers and homeseekers pushing westward in mounting numbers, and with teamsters transporting goods between the growing port of Baltimore and the Ohio Valley. Many of these taverns were the nuclei around which present-day villages and towns have risen.

Section a.   DELAWARE LINE to BALTIMORE; 53 m.

A modern dual-lane superhighway, by-passing most of the towns along its route, is now (1940) in course of construction from the Delaware Line to Baltimore. The sections from the State Line to Elkton and from two miles south of Havre de Grace to Baltimore have been completed (1940). Work is progressing on the remaining sections to be finished in 1941. This new highway, now officially designated as US 40, replaces the old outworn US 40 and cuts across the countryside in an almost straight line. Local garden clubs are co-operating with State and Federal officials in beautifying this new road and in conducting a vigorous campaign to eliminate unsightly roadside signs.

Between Elkton and Baltimore distant Chesapeake Bay vistas are seen to the left as the highway crosses the rivers or skirts smaller streams which abound in this part of the State.

US 40 crosses the DELAWARE LINE, 0 m., 13.5 miles west of New Castle, Delaware.

CRESWELL HALL (R), 1.7 m., is a two-and-a-half-story yellow brick house with hooded roof and ornamented balconies. It was built about 1840 and was the home of A.J.Creswell who, as Postmaster General during the Grant administration, is credited with introducing penny postcards.

At 2.3 m. is the junction with US 213 (see Tour 3), principal route (L) to the Eastern Shore.

Right on US 213 is ELKTON, 0.3 m. (29 alt.,3,331 pop.), seat of Cecil County and Gretna Green of the East until 1938. A number of clergymen, aided by taxicab drivers and court clerks, formerly did a flourishing business marrying couples who had eloped. Until the 48-hour marriage law stopped this lucrative practice, Main Street was lined with signs advertising these 'marrying parsons.' An occasional manse still displays a weatherbeaten sign, but most of the preachers now devote their efforts to the gospel. The town now depends on the manufacture of pulp and paper, flour, fertilizer, and shirts.

Patented as Friendship in 1681 and later called Head of Elk, the town became the county seat in 1786 and by 1807 was one of the leading American wheat markets, handling 250,000 bushels annually.

In August 1777 General Howe landed an army on Elk Neck in his attack on Philadelphia. Lafayette's troops embarked here for Annapolis in March 1781, and Washington's troops passed here on their way to Yorktown the following September. In April 1813 Admiral Cockburn's British fleet attacked the town because of its commercial importance, but was repulsed.

Substantial houses, many of them decorated with iron grillwork and railings, are set back on large lawns.

The HERMITAGE (open), 259 E.Main St., a two-and-a-half-story stone house with dormers, was built about 1735 and enlarged in later years. Robert Alexander, a Tory, entertained officers of the British fleet here in 1777. Local patriots later confiscated his estate, which embraced most of the area of the present town, and disposed of it in lots.

The FINLEY HOUSE, 255 E.Main St., a remodeled three-story frame structure, was the home of Martha Finley (1828–1909), author of the popular Elsie books.

The MITCHELL HOUSE (L), E.Main St. west of Church St., a stuccoed two-story structure with a side garden, was built in 1769 by Dr.Abraham Mitchell, scholar and physician from Lancaster County, Pennsylvania. Mitchell opened it as a hospital during the Revolution, and the Maryland apse in the chapel at Valley Forge is dedicated to him. His son, Dr.George E. Mitchell, who was born here, led the Pike expedition into Canada during the War of 1812.

PARTRIDGE HILL (*open*), NW. corner of Bow and E.Main Sts., a two-story stone house with gable roof, dormers, and large end chimneys, was built in 1768. The interior has cornices, mantels, built-in cupboards, and fine paneling in good condition.

The old HOLLINGSWORTH TAVERN (*open*), W.Main St. west of Bridge St., was built about 1750. General Washington spent the night here on August 27, 1777, while reconnoitering British movements up the bay. Two nights later British General Howe occupied the same room and was served by the same Negro servant.

1. Right on East Main Street, which becomes a rough dirt road leading 1.8 *m.* to GRAYMOUNT (R), perched on the summit of Gray's Hill. The rear section of the house was built about 1769; the present main part added about 1810. Washington is said to have watched Howe's army from this hill as they disembarked for their march on Philadelphia. Along this road are excavations (R) made in 1804 when an attempt was made to dig a canal from the Chesapeake to Delaware Bay. It was not until 1830 that the Chesapeake and Delaware Canal was opened, 5 miles south of Elkton.

2. Right from Elkton on North Street (State 279) to GILPIN MANOR (L), 1.1 *m.*, a wide, two-story brick structure that has remained in the Gilpin family since the east section with its gable roof and small dormers was erected in 1760 by Joseph Gilpin. The west section and the vestibule were added a century later. The arched doorway of the main entrance is patterned after the English home of the Gilpins. Charm and distinction are revealed in the spacious rooms, scrolled ceilings, generous fireplaces, and huge double doors.

The 'Ghost of Gilpin Manor' is said to be Dr.John Gilpin who still walks about the farm with gun on shoulder, the same gun with which he shot a prowling Negro in the shrubbery during the Civil War. For years before his death it is said that Negroes passing between house and barn at night would whistle to let the doctor know their intentions were good.

At 1.6 *m.* on State 279 is the junction with a graveled road; L. here 0.3 *m.* to the old RICKETTS HOMESTEAD (R) built about 1700. The two-story gabled house is back from the roadside in a tree-shaded yard with slave quarters on the north side.

At 2.1 *m.* is the junction with a macadam road.

Left (*straight ahead*) 1.6 *m.* to the Elk Mills Road; L. here, crossing Big Elk Creek, 2.1 *m.*, to a feeder road; L. here, 0.4 *m.*, to a lane (R) leading 100 yards to the ELK FORGE. This large one-story stone building is thought to be the one constructed about 1761 for utilization of Lancaster County (Pennsylvania) pig iron. Guns were manufactured here for the Continental Army and the place was damaged by British raiders in August 1777.

On the Elk Mills Road, near the Elk Mills factory at the far end of the bridge over Big Elk Creek, a big stone burr marks the site of an old gristmill. When the British raided Elk Forge they compelled the miller here to grind flour for them; tradition has it that he mixed in some ground glass.

Part way up a steep grade on the Elk Mills Road is the BALDWIN HOUSE (R), a large two-and-a-half-story stone dwelling with gable roof and large A windows, built about 1769. A stone burr from the gristmill is used as a lawn table on this estate.

On top of the hill, strung along the road for half a mile is ELK MILLS, 2.3 *m.* (144 alt.,500 pop.). The BALDWIN MANUFACTURING COMPANY PLANT (R) here makes velours.

At 3.9 *m.* a road leads (L) to IRON HILL, 0.5 *m.* (125 alt.,47 pop.), where iron ore was mined from 1661 to 1891. The settlement is on a portion of a 30,000-acre tract, granted by William Penn in 1701 and settled by Welsh Baptists.

At 4.1 *m.* is a lane leading (R) a short distance to the MASON AND DIXON TANGENT STONE in a pasture back of a farmhouse. Beside a weathered marker set by Mason and Dixon in 1765, and still bearing the Baltimore and Penn arms, is a stone inscribed 'Tangent,' placed in 1849 by the Graham Resurvey. Both mark the point at which the straight line between Maryland and Delaware intersects the twelve-mile-radius arc around New Castle—boundaries agreed upon in 1732 by the contesting heirs of William Penn and Charles Calvert.

State 279 crosses the DELAWARE LINE, 4.2 *m.*, at a point about three miles southwest of Newark, Delaware.

3. Right from Elkton on macadam State 280 (Bridge St.) to concrete-paved Childs Road, 0.5 *m.*; L. on this 3.2 *m.* to the HARVEY HOUSE (R) on a hill in a grove of trees. This two-and-a-half-story L-shaped stone house was erected about 1740; on the locks of the main house are small seals bearing the lion and unicorn of Great Britain.

CHILDS, 3.7 *m.* (137 alt.,61 pop.), was named for George W. Childs, onetime editor of the *Philadelphia Ledger*, who also owned and operated the Marley paper mills here. The old stone Marley building has been enlarged to house the ELK PAPER MANUFACTURING COMPANY PLANT. Close by, on Little Elk Creek, in 1794 was the Cecil Manufacturing Company Plant, which wove linen, woolen, and cotton goods. Cloth for the suit Thomas Jefferson wore at his inauguration was made here.

The 24 low gray stone buildings at 4.4 *m.* on State 280 belong to the SPRINGDALE MUSHROOM FARM (*visited on application*), the largest producer of mushrooms in the State. In rooms, kept at an average temperature of 55 degrees, mushrooms are grown in shallow trays containing a layer of fertilizer and a layer of black loam.

State 280 continues to FAIR HILL, 7 *m.*, on State 273 (*see Tour 1a*).

4. Left from Elkton on Landing Road to Elk Neck Road, 0.4 *m.*; R. here to the SITE OF FORT DEFIANCE, (L) 1.5 *m.*, on a high bluff overlooking Elk River. Here on August 29, 1813, a local infantry company repulsed a landing party from the British fleet that burned Frenchtown.

West of Elkton US 40 skirts the 4,000-acre ELK NECK STATE FOR–EST (L) for several miles.

BEACON HILL (L), 5.6 *m.*, had signal flares on its summit, probably as early as the 1680's, when George Talbot organized volunteers for defense against hostile Indians and established a system of signals as warnings against raids.

At 8.2 *m.* the new US 40 crosses State 272.

1. Right on State 272 to CALVERT, 7 *m.* (*see Tour 1a*).

2. Left on State 272 to NORTH EAST, 0.6 *m.* (20 alt.,1,412 pop.). Once a shipping point with regular boat service to Baltimore, it is now the banking and trading center for a hay and grain district. The older residential and business sections are on Main Street (State 272); farm supply stores, a stove brick foundry, and a small basket factory are located near the railroad.

The BRYSON HOUSE (R) on old US 40, 200 yards W. of Main Street, was built about 1740 in three sections, the front of frame construction and the two rear parts of sheathed logs.

At the western end of the bridge across Northeast Creek, GREEN HILL (R) was built about 1780 by Thomas Russell of the Principio Company (*see below*). The rambling house is on a knoll overlooking the road.

ST.MARY'S PROTESTANT EPISCOPAL CHURCH (R) on S.Main St. was built in 1700. This brick building has a gambrel roof of the Dutch type, round-arched windows, and a bulls-eye window high in the west wall. The square tower topped with a cupola was added in 1904. In the churchyard are graves of Susquehannock Indians.

Main Street becomes a graveled road at 2.5 *m.*; R. 0.3 *m.* to the NORTH EAST YACHT CLUB, which annually sponsors a sail and motorboat regatta.

At 4.6 *m.* on State 272 is another graveled road; R. on this road 1.1 *m.* to SANDY COVE, a summer resort for business and professional women. The SANDY COVE YACHT CLUB, organized in 1936, is the only yacht club in the country exclusively for women.

ELK NECK STATE PARK, 9.6 *m.*, was the 650-acre estate of Dr.William Louis Abbott, traveler and naturalist, whose will bequeathed the property to the State.

The cliffs that form the shore line south of Elk Neck State Park are called WHITE BANKS and have guided mariners since the time of Captain John Smith.

The road ends at TURKEY POINT LIGHTHOUSE (1834), 13 m. (*open June–July–Aug.*), a 35-foot tower on a 100-foot bluff.

At 11 m., on US 40 is the junction with Charlestown Beach Road.

Left on this road is CHARLESTOWN, 1.5 m. (35 alt.,286 pop.), on the Northeast River. Founded in 1742, it was the seat of Cecil County until the courthouse was moved to Elkton in 1786. In colonial days Charlestown rivaled Baltimore as a port and boat building center. The old two-story brick TAVERN on Market Street has a gable roof and large end chimneys.

At 13.5 m. new US 40 crosses Principio Creek. Here (L) is the probable site of the PRINCIPIO IRON WORKS established about 1715 by Stephen Onion and Thomas Russell. For nearly a century the Principio Company operated a furnace on the west bank of the creek, making bar iron and supplying cannon balls during the Revolution. British raiders burned the plant in May 1813 and it was not until 1836 that another company started operations near the original site. A pig iron furnace operated on the new site until about 1910, and a charcoal iron forge until 1936. Ruins of the old brick-lined furnace and a turbine waterwheel are visible in the tangled undergrowth of the millrace between the Pennsylvania Railroad and old US 40. The present village of Principio is about five miles north.

The road passes through Susquehanna Manor, a 32,000-acre tract granted to George Talbot in 1680. Talbot brought over a hundred Irish settlers, built block houses and signal towers for protection against hostile Indians, and was named deputy governor in 1684. In the same year he fatally stabbed Christopher Rousby, Collector of the District of Patuxent, in a quarrel aboard the ketch *Quaker*. Talbot was captured and tried in Jamestown, Virginia. Escaping with the aid of his wife and relatives, he hid in a cave on the Susquehanna River near Perryville. Here, according to legend, two trained falcons brought him food, until he surrendered in July 1685. A royal pardon later freed him from a death sentence and he left the colonies in 1687.

In PERRYVILLE, 16 m. (20 alt.,704 pop.), near the mouth of the Susquehanna River, the Pennsylvania Railroad maintains division repair shops. The town also depends on a small stove factory, a fertilizer plant, and a veterans' hospital.

RODGERS TAVERN (R), a two-and-one-half-story stone house near the bridge, was opened about 1780 by the father of Commodore John Rodgers (1771–1838), acting Secretary of the Navy in 1823.

PERRY POINT HOSPITAL (*driving through park 9–4; no parking; pass required to visit patients*), officially known as the Veterans' Administration Facility, overlooks the mouth of the river on land patented to John Bateman in 1658.

Perryville is at the junction with US 222 (*see Tour 1a*).

The SUSQUEHANNA, 16.5 m., one of the longest rivers on the Atlantic seaboard, is navigable for only five miles. Attempts to construct canals in 1797 and again in 1840 were partly successful and brought temporary activity along the stream, but railroad competition caused abandonment of the project.

GARRETT ISLAND, in the middle of the river, is named for John W. Garrett (1820–84), president of the Baltimore & Ohio Railroad during the Civil War period. In 1622 Edward Palmer, an Englishman, attempted to establish a trading post here but the venture failed. At his death in 1625 Palmer willed the island to Oxford University.

Right in Havre de Grace at the end of the Susquehanna Bridge on paved State 155 to SION HILL, 2.7 *m.*, a two-and-one-half-story brick house with dormers, gable roof, and unusually wide end chimneys. John Ireland built it in 1775 for a boys' school, which did not prosper. State 155 continues to the junction, 7.6 *m.*, with State 22 in CHURCHVILLE (*see below*).

HAVRE DE GRACE (*pron. haverdegrass*), 17.5 *m.* (35 alt.,3,985 pop.), is the banking, trading, and railroad center for a wide area. It is a quiet, rather old-fashioned town, with tree-lined streets, and substantial frame houses on wide lawns, a few modern industrial plants, including a distillery, and a modernized shopping center on Washington Street. The drab older section is scattered along the river. Stone quarrying provides considerable employment in this section. This site, settled in 1658, developed as a stop on the old Post Road and was known as Susquehanna Lower Ferry. The town was incorporated in 1785 and the present name first was used in a letter written that year by Lafayette to Washington.

During the Revolution Rochambeau's troops camped twice on the present Havre de Grace race track. On May 3, 1813, a British fleet attacked the town, routed local militia under Lieutenant John O'Neill, and plundered and burned most of the buildings.

The FERRY HOUSE, now the Lafayette Hotel at the end of the old Susquehanna bridge, is a wide two-and-one-half-story brick structure built in 1760. The stucco surface, front porch, and rear sections are later additions.

The RODGERS HOUSE, 226 W.Washington St., built in 1774, was the home of Colonel John Rodgers, first American member of a family distinguished in the naval history of the United States. Colonel Rodgers commanded a militia company in the Revolution. During the British attack in 1813 the house was damaged by fire, but was restored later, and the street floor has recently been altered by installing a modern store front.

ST. JOHN'S PROTESTANT EPISCOPAL CHURCH, NW. corner Union and Congress Aves., in 1832 replaced an earlier church. The bricks are laid in Flemish bond, and roundheaded windows now have stained glass. The belfry was added some time after the church was built.

CITY PARK, also called Bayside Park, foot of S.Union Ave., is a seven-acre bay-front area with yacht anchorage.

ST.FRANCIS VILLA, east end of City Park, formerly the Hotel Bayou, is the home for retired Sisters of St.Francis.

The HAVRE DE GRACE LIGHTHOUSE, built in 1827, stands on Concord Point. Lieutenant John O'Neill, its first keeper, commanded the town militia during the War of 1812. In appreciation of the gallant stand made by O'Neill during the British raid in May 1813, the lighthouse keepers appointed here have always been his descendants.

Members of the HAVRE DE GRACE YACHT CLUB, near the lighthouse, sponsor an annual regatta on the third Friday and Saturday in July.

PENN'S BEACH (*bath house, picnic tables*), adjoining the Yacht Club, is municipally owned.

The HAVRE DE GRACE RACE TRACK (L), 19.2 *m.*, a mile course opened in 1912, has an unusually beautiful setting near Chesapeake Bay. During the spring and fall meets a number of rich stake races attract the country's greatest thoroughbreds and special trains are run from Philadelphia, Baltimore, and Washington. Man O'War outran Wildair and Blazes here in 1920, and Sir Barton, Chance Play, Rose of Sharon, and Sun Beau have all captured substantial purses. Rochambeau's army camped on this spot in September 1781 on its way to Yorktown, Virginia and again on their way north after Cornwallis' surrender.

At 21 *m.* is the junction with a macadamized road.

Left on this road over a narrow wooden bridge to OAKINGTON FARMS, 1.5 *m.* (*visited during Garden Clubs pilgrimage and on application*), the 550-acre estate of Millard E. Tydings, U.S.Senator from Maryland (1932–   ). The two-and-one-half-story mansion is on a wooded knoll, overlooking the Chesapeake Bay; boxwood on the landscaped grounds is very old.

ABERDEEN, 22.5 *m.* (80 alt.,1,240 pop.), is the home of a third of the civilian employees in the near-by proving grounds (*see below*). On the side streets intersecting US 40 are pleasant, well-kept residences. The town has modern public facilities, as well as a number of restaurants catering to the heavy through tourist traffic, and a canning factory that ships hundreds of carloads annually.

1. Right from Aberdeen on State 22 to macadamized Paradise Road, 0.7.*m*; R. 3 *m.* here to the old WESLEYAN CHAPEL (R), a yellow brick church erected in 1826.

At 8.3 *m.* on State 22 is macadamized State 154; R. here 2.7 *m.* to MEDICAL HALL, a stuccoed brick house with a large central hall. It is the birthplace of Dr.John Archer (1741–1810), who in 1768 received from the Philadelphia Medical College the first medical diploma issued in America. Dr.Archer was a signer in 1775 of the Bush Declaration of Independence, in which men of Harford County indicated their readiness to fight for independence. Dr.Archer became a member of Congress in 1802 and was a founder of the Medical and Chirurgical Faculty of Maryland.

TUDOR HALL (R), 9.2 *m.*, is a brick, two-story house surrounded by fine shade trees including a sycamore 18 feet in circumference. The house was built in 1822 by Junius Brutus Booth, the actor, who came to America in 1821. His sons, Edwin Booth, leading Shakespearean actor of the nineteenth century, and John Wilkes Booth, also an actor and the assassin of Abraham Lincoln, were born here in 1833 and 1839, respectively. Among Booth relics are spurs said to have been worn by John Wilkes Booth the night he shot Lincoln.

State 22 continues to the junction, 11.9 *m.*, with US 1 in BELAIR (*see Tour 1a*).

2. Left on State 22 to a macadamized road, 0.9 *m.*, which continues into the ABER–DEEN PROVING GROUNDS (*obtain pass at sentry box*), 3.2 *m.* This Federal reservation, including Edgewood Arsenal (*see below*), covers 35,000 acres along Chesapeake Bay. In addition to many civilian employes, 350 officers and men are employed. Ordnance, shells, air bombs, mines, and other military material are tested under conditions simulating actual combat. Some of the Nation's largest disappearing rifles are fired here over guarded Chesapeake Bay areas. Phillips Field, part of the reservation, is named for an army pilot who lost his life here. A shed opposite the Administration Building houses a collection of French, German, English, Spanish, and American ordnance, tanks, and shells used in past wars.

At 23.2 *m.* old US 40, now designated State 7, branches left; the dual highway, US 40, continues straight ahead.

Left on State 7, 1.5 *m.* to Perryman Road; 1.2 *m.* to the old SPESUTIE CHURCH (R), a stone structure with roundheaded windows, pentagonal apse, stone entrance portico, and a belfry. The silver communion service presented to the church in 1722 is still in use.

At 25 *m.* US 40, the dual highway, crosses State 7 (old US 40).

Right on State 7 to BUSH, 3.9 *m.* (150 alt.,70 pop.), the first seat of Harford County; it was originally called Harford Town for Henry Harford, son of the last Lord Baltimore. The BUSH TAVERN (R), one of Maryland's old landmarks, is a whitewashed two-and-one-half-story unoccupied stone structure with gabled roof and dormers, erected about 1750. It is reputed to have sheltered George Washington, Thomas Jefferson, James Madison, and James Monroe.

ABINGDON, 5.1 *m.* (160 alt.,1,000 pop.), was founded in 1779 by William Paca (1740–99), a signer of the Declaration of Independence and later governor of the State.

Cokesbury College, first Methodist college in the western hemisphere, was established here in June 1785 by Bishop Thomas Coke and Francis Asbury. Discipline was 'of the sternest and most ample "boy killing" character.' One rule stated: 'The students shall be indulged with nothing which the world calls play. Let this rule be observed with the strictest nicety: for those who play when they are young will play when they are old.' The curriculum included seven hours of daily study, a manual training course, and gardening. When the college building burned in 1795 Francis Asbury recorded: ' . . . a sacrifice of £10,000 in about ten years! . . . Its enemies may rejoice, and its friends need not mourn. Would any man give me £10,000 per year to do and suffer again what I have done for that house, I would not do it. The Lord called not Mr. Whitefield nor the Methodists to build colleges. I wished only for schools—Doctor Coke wanted a college. I feel distressed at the loss of the library.' The school was later re-established in Baltimore as Asbury College.

In VAN BIBBER, 6.9 *m.* (22 alt.,31 pop.), is the concrete-paved Emmorton Road; R. 0.6 *m.* to CONSTANT FRIENDSHIP (R), a 1,000-acre manor acquired in 1761 by Colonel Thomas White, father of William White, the first Episcopal bishop ordained in America. Robert Morris, the Revolutionary financier, married Colonel White's daughter. The two-and-one-half-story brick farmhouse, built in 1790, has flush end chimneys and a gable roof. On the tract of land is a lane known as Ha-Ha Road. A laughing ghost is said to haunt this path at night.

BRADSHAW, 11.9 *m.* (40 alt.,100 pop.) on State 7, was originally called Crook's Mill. When Lafayette passed through here in 1781 he ordered the arrest of John Paul, a wealthy Baltimore County landowner, Walter Pickett (or Pigot), the miller, Jesse Dunning, and John Warner. All were charged with piloting raiding parties from a British fleet anchored at the mouth of Gunpowder River. Warner was seriously wounded in attempting to escape, and records fail to note what became of Dunning. Paul and Pickett were said to have been imprisoned in a storehouse adjoining the mill. Pickett was hanged at Joppa for his treason but Paul escaped, some say with the aid of a generous lady of Joppa who hid him under her hoop skirts.

At 22.1 *m.* is the southern junction with new US 40 (*see below*).

At 27.3 *m.*, on new US 40 is SOPHIA'S DAIRY, a two-story-and-basement brick house built in 1768 by Captain Aquilla Hall and presented as a dowry to his daughter Sophia. The name is probably a corruption of Sophia's Dowry. The walls, foundation, flooring, and wainscoting show few signs of age and retain much of the original appearance. It is now used as a club for Bat'a employees.

BELCAMP, 27.8 *m.* (35 alt.), was a flag station on the Baltimore & Ohio Railroad in 1939, when Jan Bat'a, head of Europe's largest shoe company, built a five-story factory here. After the Nazi occupation of Czecho-Slovakia, Bat'a started operations in this country. The plant and model village at Belcamp is patterned after the Zlin, Czecho-Slovakia plant. Eventually a town housing 10,000 Bat'a workers with hospitals, schools, newspapers, stores, and theaters may grow around the shoe factories, tanneries, dye works, and other auxiliary plants which the Bat'a interests plan. Labor leaders who protested admission to this country of 74 Czech instructors and foremen sent here to train workers in Bat'a factory methods were assured these instructors would remain only until 1941 when American employees would take charge of the plant.

At 32.3 *m.* is the junction with concrete-paved Edgewood Road.

Left on this to EDGEWOOD ARSENAL (*admission on pass*), 1.8 *m.*, the U.S. Army chemical warfare station, where various types of gases are developed for military use and training is carried on in offensive and defensive chemical warfare. FORT HOYLE, on the same reservation, is a field artillery and ordnance battery headquarters, as well as the summer camp of the U.S. Army Field Artillery Reserve.

At 35.8 *m.* is the junction with a graveled road just north of Gunpowder River.

Left on this road, which forks immediately; R. at fork 1.8 *m.* to the site of JOPPA TOWN on the Gunpowder River, seat of Baltimore County from 1712 to 1768. Before the Revolution Joppa Town became a major tobacco exporting point where ships from New England, the West Indies, and Europe made regular calls. In an effort to foster this trade, planters were allowed 10 per cent discount for bills paid in tobacco. Roads were widened to provide easy access from all parts of the county, and rolling roads were improved to permit horses to pull tobacco casks to the town's wharves. A local law required chimneys to be built of brick and a minimum of 400 square feet of floor space to each house. Joppa developed a gay social life as merchants and travelers visited friends here and attended the local race track.

After 1750 Joppa suffered from competition with Baltimore. Timber cutting along the Gunpowder had caused the harbor here to fill with silt, and a smallpox epidemic decimated the population. In 1768 Baltimore became the county seat. From then until the first decade of the nineteenth century, the town declined. The inhabitants began to move to the more prosperous Baltimore. Storehouses and wharves fell into ruin, the prison and courthouse finally were sold, and old Joppa became a ghost town. All that remain are some gravestones and the RUMSEY MANSION, a two-and-a-half-story brick house with a gambrel roof, flush chimneys, and three dormers each on the north and south roof slopes. It is believed this was built about 1720, and enlarged about 1771 when it was acquired by Colonel Benjamin Rumsey, a member of the Continental Congress, who died here in 1808.

The present hamlet of Joppa is a flag stop on the railroad about two miles northeast of the Gunpowder River.

At 42.5 *m.* is the junction with concrete-paved Middle River Road.

Left 2.4 *m.* to the GLENN L. MARTIN COMPANY PLANT (*visitors 9–4; apply at main office*), a 1,200-acre tract on Middle River, where military and commercial planes as well as private aircraft are built. Four Pacific Clippers, used between the West Coast and the Orient, were constructed at this plant.

At 47.3 *m.* is the southern junction with State 7, 0.4 miles east of Baltimore City Line.

At 48.3 *m.* is the junction with macadamized State 20, the North Point Road.

Left to NORTH POINT, 3.3 *m.* (20 alt.,1,000 district pop.), a Baltimore suburban settlement of small truck farms; on September 12, 1814, the decisive Battle of North Point took place in this neighborhood. At the head of Bear Creek (R) 3,100 Maryland militia, under General John Stricker, awaited a British attack. Early in the morning

5,000 British under General Robert Ross disembarked at the tip of the peninsula where Fort Howard is now, and began their northward march. Stricker sent a small force to meet the invaders, and the battle began. General Ross was killed by the opening volley and Colonel Brooke, who replaced Ross as commanding officer, spurred his troops onward. The American skirmishers fell back to their breastworks near the city. When word reached Brooke of the failure of the British fleet to force the harbor defenses, he ordered a retreat in the night.

The first deed in Baltimore County was filed in 1664 for Todd's Inheritance, 5.5 *m.* The first will recorded in the county was also Todd's, in which he devised 'one brood mare and a feather-bed to each of my daughters.' The house was burned by the British during the Battle of North Point.

A lane at 6.1 *m.* leads (R) to Gorsuch Farm. In the farmhouse that was here Ross breakfasted before the Battle of North Point and here, according to tradition, he boasted he would eat dinner 'in Baltimore or in hell.' The house was burned that day and the present two-and-one-half-story frame structure was erected shortly afterwards.

At 8 *m.* is the junction with State 151, macadam; R. here 2.5 *m.* to Sparrows Point Plant, 2.9 *m.* (*open* 10–4 *workdays; guides*), where the Bethlehem Steel Company operates the largest tidewater steel mill in the United States. At full capacity the plant employs 21,000 men and can produce 1,800,000 tons of steel annually.

At 10.5 *m.* is the macadamized Fort Howard Road; R. here 2.1 *m.* to Fort Howard (*obtain pass at sentry box*), established in 1900 as the chief coast artillery defense for Baltimore and named for Colonel John Eager Howard of Revolutionary fame (*see Baltimore*). A marker indicates the spot where the British landed.

Bay Shore Amusement Park (*bathing, dancing, dining, and picnic grounds*), 12.3 *m.*, is open in the summer.

BALTIMORE, 53 *m.* (20 alt.,804,874 pop.) (*see Baltimore*).

Points of Interest: Fort McHenry, the Shot Tower, Homewood, Washington Monument, Johns Hopkins University, the Cathedral, Druid Hill Park, and many others.

Baltimore is at junctions with US 1 (*see Tour 1*), US 111 (*see Tour 13*), State 26 (*see Tour 2A*), US 140 (*see Tour 14*), State 2 (*see Tour 8*), and State 3 (*see Tour 9*).

Section b. BALTIMORE to FREDERICK; 46.3 m.

Before 1765 a road—not much more than a trail—had been cut from Baltimore to Frederick Town. About 1774 the Ellicotts at their own expense opened a superior wagon road from their mills to Baltimore, a distance of twelve miles; they extended it to join the older road toward Frederick Town at a point four miles north of their mills. This became the main route and is now US 40.

Generations before the initiation of the 'Convict-Leasing System,' the road was kept in repair by 'wheelbarrow men,' bands of prisoners in charge of armed overseers. At night the road workers were housed and fed in log cabins set up several miles apart.

An alternate US 40, 9.1 miles long, was opened to traffic in 1939. This concrete extension of Edmondson Avenue, Baltimore, by-passes Catonsville and Ellicott City and rejoins old US 40 3.7 miles west of the latter town.

Between Baltimore and Catonsville is a suburban area of small homes, with a few larger houses that were built late in the nineteenth century when this section was a fashionable summer settlement. West of Ellicott City is slightly rolling wheat and dairy-farming country. A number of the large estates still belong to descendants of their colonial owners. Tidy, well-cared-for farms indicate the section's prosperity.

West of BALTIMORE, 0. *m.*, old US 40 follows Frederick Avenue.

CATONSVILLE, 7.1 *m.* (500 alt.,7,647 pop.), a suburb of comfortable homes and modern stores, extends about two miles along the highway. It is older than Baltimore and was first called Johnnycake for an inn here on the old road that was famed for its cornbread. About 1800 the town was renamed in honor of Richard Caton, a son-in-law of Charles Carroll of Carrollton. An estate that included the site was Carroll's gift to the young couple.

The MOUNT DE SALES ACADEMY, Nunnery Lane and Edmondson Ave., a Roman Catholic secondary and college preparatory school for girls, was established in 1852. The yellow brick buildings stand in a grove on an elevation overlooking the surrounding countryside. The library contains 142 plates of Audubon's *Quadrupeds of North America* and some 50 plates of Rex Brasher's *Birds and Trees of North America*.

ST.CHARLES COLLEGE (L), on Maiden's Choice Lane, prepares candidates for the Roman Catholic priesthood to enter St.Mary's Seminary. The school, founded in 1830 in Howard County, was moved here in 1911 when the original buildings burned. Faience, terra cotta, and colored marble in the chapel form an effective setting for *The Coronation of the Virgin*, a somber mosaic against a gold background. St.Charles alumni include 16 bishops, 7 archbishops, and James Cardinal Gibbons (1834–1921). John Banister (Father) Tabb, musician and lyric poet, studied here (1872–75) and later was instructor in English literature. The Convent of the Dominican Nuns of the Perpetual Rosary, erected in 1880, is opposite the college.

ST.TIMOTHY'S PROTESTANT EPISCOPAL CHURCH, St.Timothy's Lane, is a rectangular stone building of Gothic design erected in 1844. The frame building (R) of St.Timothy's School for girls is on the site of the old Catonsville Military Academy, founded in 1845 and believed to be the first church military school in the United States. John Wilkes Booth, assassin of Abraham Lincoln, was a student here (1851–52). The academy burned in 1862. The present girl's school was opened in 1889.

At 8 *m.* (L) and at 8.5 *m.* (R) are junctions with State 165 (*see Tour 1A*).

The business section of ELLICOTT CITY, 10.5 *m.* (144 alt.,1,216 pop.), seat and principal banking and trading center of Howard County, lies along narrow congested Main Street. The houses, built of dark local granite, appear to be wedged in the rocky hillside. Some of the buildings on the south side of Main Street straddle the narrow Tiber Creek which flows into the Patapsco at this point. The town developed around the Ellicotts' grist and flour mills established in 1774 on the east bank of the river. Following the building of the Cumberland Road westward and the coming of the railroad in 1830, the town grew rapidly. In 1864 many wounded in the Battle of the Monocacy (*see Tour 16*) were cared for here until they could be sent to Baltimore.

At the east end of the bridge over the Patapsco is the DOUGHNUT CORPORATION OF AMERICA PLANT (*visited 2 p.m. Tuesdays and Thursdays*), an eight-story concrete building that was formerly a flour mill. Its bins have a storage capacity of 500,000 bushels of wheat.

The main building is on the SITE OF ELLICOTTS' MILLS, founded by John, Joseph, and Andrew Ellicott, sons of Andrew Ellicott, a Quaker who had emigrated in 1730 from England to Bucks County, Pennsylvania. They bought land and water rights here in 1774 and brought machinery of their own invention by boat from Philadelphia to Elkridge Landing and thence overland to the mill site, where they built comfortable dwellings for themselves and their workers. Two of Joseph Ellicott's sons, who grew up here, became noted surveyors. Andrew (1754–1820) redrew L'Enfant's plans of Washington, D.C. for Jefferson, surveyed several State boundaries and in 1796 the frontier between the United States and Florida. Joseph (1760–1826) was the surveyor and the western land agent for the Holland Land Company. He founded Buffalo, advocated and later directed early surveys for the Erie Canal. He spent his last years in an asylum suffering from melancholia. For 60 years Ellicotts operated the mill here successfully and Patapsco Flour became widely known. During the panic of 1837, however, the plant was turned over to Charles Gambrill and Charles Carroll, son of Charles Carroll of Carrollton. Thirty-one years later the mill, bridge, dam, and several houses were washed away in a flood, and 42 persons were drowned.

Across the road from the doughnut plant and facing the former mill-race are (R) the GEORGE ELLICOTT HOUSE (1789), the JONATHAN ELLICOTT HOUSE (1782), and the JOHN ELLICOTT HOUSE (1772), two-and-a-half-story stone structures with dormers. About 200 yards west is the JOHN ELLICOTT STORE, a long three-story yellow stone building erected before 1790.

The first building (R) on Main Street west of the bridge over the Patapsco is the old PATAPSCO HOTEL, a two-story granite structure, now an apartment house. Tradition has it that on a Sunday morning during his presidential campaign Henry Clay appeared on the balcony that extended across the front of this building. A crowd quickly gathered and shouted for a speech. Clay held up his arms for silence. But before he could begin, the sound of a church bell was heard, whereupon Clay called out: 'My friends and fellow citizens, the notes of yonder church bell remind me that this is a day for prayer and not for public speaking.' Once more he raised his hands, this time in benediction, and retired to his room.

The exterior of the stone BALTIMORE & OHIO RAILROAD DEPOT, directly opposite, is little changed since the first horsecars were hauled here from Baltimore over strap-iron rails on May 24, 1830. The rounded stone wall, extending south from the station and now part of the platform, was the foundation of a turntable.

The old TOWN HALL, two doors west of the hotel, is (R) a five-story building with a series of cellars dug out of the rocky hillside behind each of the first four stories.

The Ellicott City High School on College Ave. is on the site of Sam's Academy built in 1827, and of Rock Hill Academy, a boys' school erected here by the Brothers of the Christian Schools 30 years later. In 1865 the academy was chartered as Rock Hill College. After fire destroyed the building in 1922, Rock Hill was merged with Calvert Hall College in Baltimore.

In the ELLICOTT BURIAL GROUND (*key to gate at cottage next door*), a few hundred yards L. on steep Columbia Pike, are the graves of Andrew and John Ellicott and some of their descendants. Beyond the cemetery a private lane leads to the FRIENDS MEETING HOUSE (*closed*), a plain rectangular brick building with low gables, built in 1798; it has served as a meeting house, a war hospital, and a school.

Facing Court House Lane (R) is the HOWARD COUNTY COURTHOUSE (L) on Capitoline Hill. Like most buildings in Ellicott City it is a Classic-Revival structure of local granite. The battered old British cannon on the lawn, captured at the Battle of Bladensburg in the War of 1812 by 'Bachelor' John Dorsey, was one of the few souvenirs the Americans got out of that encounter.

The ANGELO COTTAGE (R), Institute Road, is a Gothic-Revival house built in 1831 by Samuel Vaughn, a French artist. The octagonal-turreted structure, overlooking a ravine from the rim of Tarpeian Rock aroused such curiosity that the Baltimore & Ohio R.R. ran excursion trains from Baltimore in 1831.

On Institute Road, at the top of the hill, is the PATAPSCO FEMALE INSTITUTE (L), a large granite Greek-Revival structure, overlooking the Patapsco River valley. Established on seven acres of land donated in 1829 by the Ellicott family, the school was supported by private contributions and annual grants by the State. For 15 years before the Civil War, the headmistress was Mrs. Almira Hart Lincoln Phelps, a pioneer in education for women. Winnie Davis, daughter of Jefferson Davis, and Alice Montague of Virginia, mother of Wallis Duchess of Windsor, were pupils here. After the war the fortunes of the school declined and it finally closed its doors in 1890.

In Ellicott City is the junction with US 29 (*see Tour 1B*).

At 12.7 *m.* is the junction with macadamized St. John's Lane.

Right on this to a concrete-paved road, 2.4 *m.*; and R. to MOUNT HEBRON (L), 3.4 *m.*, a two-and-a-half-story stone structure built about 1780. The 15-room house has a fireplace in each room and overlooks Dorsey's Search, later called Dorsey's Run, one of the oldest grants in this section.

The new Ellicott City by-pass joins old US 40 at 14.2 *m.*

At 14.7 *m.* is the junction with a macadam road.

Left on this road is (R) BURLEIGH MANOR (*private*), 1.2 *m.*, a yellow brick house built about 1785 by Colonel Rezin Hammond. The main two-and-a-half-story structure is connected with a wing of the same height by a short gallery. The late Georgian Colonial structure is notable for its beautifully carved marble mantels. An unusual feature is the wide L-shaped hall. Near the road and behind the house are old outbuildings and slave quarters. The 2,300-acre estate has been held intact by descendants of the first owners.

An old house (L), 16.3 *m.*, formerly the gate house of Doughoregan Manor and a good example of Gothic-Revival architecture, marks the junction with Carroll Lane.

Left on Carroll Lane to the tree-lined entrance (R) to DOUGHOREGAN MANOR (*open for Howard Co. Horse Show end of April*), 0.7 *m.*, the home of Charles Carroll of Carrollton, who survived all other signers of the Declaration of Independence. The two-story manor house, built about 1727, is 300 feet long with two ells; the whole exemplifies the eighteenth-century passion for axial symmetry. The south ell contains servants' quarters; the north ell is a richly furnished Roman Catholic chapel, a reminder of the days when Roman Catholic services were conducted privately. The chapel has been remodeled several times but still retains the same general lines as the manor house. The central section is surmounted by a railed roof platform and octagonal cupola. From the roof promenade could be seen a great part of the original estate of more than 13,000 acres with beautiful lawns shaded by great elms, and farm buildings and quarters that housed almost a thousand slaves. A Doric portico with chamber above has been added to the front. The interior is paneled with oak and decorated with hunting scenes and family portraits by Kühn, Sully, and other early American painters.

Charles Carroll of Carrollton, the third of his name in America, was born in Annapolis, September 19, 1737. His grandfather, land agent for Lord Baltimore, had acquired thousands of desirable acres in the colony including the manor of Carrollton near Frederick. Young Carroll spent several years in France and completed his education with the study of law in London. Returning to America when he was twenty-eight, he found himself barred from practicing his profession because of the restrictions surrounding Roman Catholics. In 1768 he married his cousin Mary Darnall.

With the growth of unrest in the colonies, Carroll began to play an increasingly important role in politics. A delegate to the Maryland convention in 1776, Carroll was instrumental in effecting the resolution of separation from England and on July 4th of the same year, as a member of the Continental Congress, signed the Declaration of Independence. After the Revolution he was Senator from Maryland in the first Federal Congress.

A brilliant lawyer and a shrewd business man, Carroll was involved in many of the major commercial and industrial enterprises of the young nation. He was a member of the Potomac Company and of its successor, the Chesapeake and Ohio Canal Company, and a director of the Baltimore & Ohio Railroad. With his vast land holdings and the fortune he had accumulated, Carroll was known as the wealthiest man in America at the time of his death in 1832. He was buried in the chapel here.

A subsequent occupant of the manor, John Lee Carroll, was governor of Maryland (1876-80). The estate, held intact until about 1870, now contains about 3,000 acres—farmed by tenants. On Thanksgiving Day members of the Howard County Hunt Club attend pre-hunt services here, perpetuating an English custom of blessing the hounds.

At 16.6 *m.* on US 40 is the junction with graveled Folly Quarters Road.

Left on this 3.3 *m.*, to Rolling Road which becomes the main side route.

Left (straight ahead) 1.8 *m.* on Folly Quarters Road to WALNUT GROVE, a two-and-a-half-story gray stone house with gables and dormers built about 1740 on a knoll some distance from the road. It was the home of Captain Gassaway Watkins, commander of the Fifth Maryland Regiment at the battle of Cowpens during the Revolution and of troops at Annapolis during the War of 1812.

Right on Rolling Road 3.8 *m.* to the NOVITIATE OF THE FRANCISCAN FATHERS, a large marble structure with two ells facing an open court. It was erected in 1930 and patterned after the Convent of St. Francis at Assisi, Italy. The FOLLY QUARTER MANSION, a two-and-a-half-story house built in 1832 with matching front and rear porticoes, is used now as a recreation hall. Large granite blocks laid in coursed ashlar, and portico columns carved from single granite blocks, give the house solid dignity. The name of the estate is said to be derived from Charles Carroll of Carrollton's disgusted remark, 'Folly!,' when he learned that his son had bought still more land.

The house was planned by the elder Carroll for his daughter at a cost, it is said, of more than $100,000. Long neglected, it was finally bought by Van Lear Black (1875-1930), Baltimore newspaper publisher, who staged rodeos and other spectacular entertainments for guests prominent in journalistic, governmental, and diplomatic circles.

At 4.9 *m.* is the entrance lane (L) of GLENELG MANOR, now called the Governor

George Lowndes Estate. The large ivy-covered Gothic-Revival house is surrounded by giant hemlock and locust trees and overlooks rolling farmlands. The main two-story U-shaped house has a three-story crenelated tower at the left wing. Behind it is a remodeled house, built about 1700. There are several gray stone outbuildings, one of which is a Gothic-Revival 'prospect tower.'

At 6.3 *m.* R. on the macadamized Triadelphia Road to the HOWARD COUNTY HUNT CLUB (L), 6.4 *m.* a two-story frame clubhouse on 50 acres of land.

The Triadelphia Road continues to a junction with US 40 at 9.5 *m.*

At 17.3 *m.* on US 40 is the junction with a dirt road.

Right on this road to WAVERLY (R), 1.4 *m.*, whose two-story, L-shaped stone house has a one-story curtain connecting it with a two-story wing. The house, built about 1750, is still surrounded by more than 200 acres of the original 1,300-acre estate. It was formerly the home of Governor George Howard, son of John Eager Howard of Revolutionary fame. A neighborhood story tells of Howard's frustrated ambition to own 1,000 slaves; death always kept the number down to 999. Although some outbuildings have been torn down, the overseer's house and the slave jail still stand. The latter has barred windows and iron fetters. In the yard is the gravestone of the governor's son, John Eager Howard the Younger, whose body was removed to Frederick.

At 19.7 *m.* is the junction with Triadelphia Road (*see above*).

At 26.2 *m.* is the junction with graveled Daisy Road, State 96.

Left on this to the hamlet of DAISY, 2.9 *m.* (553 alt.,25 pop.); R. from Daisy on a macadamized road to the entrance lane (L) to OAKDALE (*private*) 3.4 *m.* The massive three-and-a-half-story brick structure with Classic portico was built in 1838 and over-looks the 1,300 acres that remain of a vast tract patented to Captain Richard War-field in 1763. Oakdale was the home of Edwin Warfield, governor of Maryland from 1904 to 1908. The interior is richly paneled and ancestral portraits decorate most of the downstairs rooms. Wide lawns are shaded by old maples, hemlocks, and oaks. To the right of the house is an artificial lake on the north bank of which stands the kiln where the bricks for the house were made.

In NEW MARKET, 38.4 *m.* (575 alt.,274 pop.), trading center for a farming area, is the junction with State 75 (*see Tour* 15).

JUG BRIDGE, 43.6 *m.*, spanning the Monocacy River was so named because of a huge stone jug (R) at the eastern end. This is said to contain a demijohn of whisky sealed up with loving care by the trowel master. The bridge was constructed in 1807 for the turnpike company building the Frederick road. Lafayette was met here in 1824 by a delegation from Frederick and escorted into the city.

FREDERICK, 46.3 *m.* (300 alt.,14,434 pop.)(*see Frederick*).

Points of Interest: The Barbara Fritchie House, the Roger Taney House, Hood College, Rose Hill Manor, the Maryland State School for Deaf, and others.

Frederick is at a junction with US 15 (*see Tour* 15) and US 340 (*see Tour* 2B).

Section c.   FREDERICK to HAGERSTOWN; 26.5 m.

Between Frederick and Hagerstown US 40 traverses rolling, fertile countryside and crosses Catoctin and South Mountains. From Braddock Heights the Middletown Valley spreads south to the Potomac and west to South Mountain, the highest point on this route east of Hagerstown. This section was largely settled by Germans from the Palatine, whose descendants are successful wheat and dairy farmers and horse-breeders. Their thrift and industry are evident in their great red barns, visible from the road, that are often more impressive than their farmhouses. In the vicinity of Hagerstown the farm buildings are decorated with 'hex' signs to ward off evil spirits. Braddock's troops and later the armies of the North and South marched along this route, and these peaceful fields were the scenes of numerous conflicts.

A dual highway, now being built (1940) north of the present narrow winding macadam road, will shorten the route between Frederick and Hagerstown by several miles and eliminate dangerous curves.

West of FREDERICK, 0 *m.*, US 40 follows an eastern extension of the old Cumberland Road.

At 1.8 *m.* is the eastern junction (R) with the new National Road (*under construction* 1940).

BRADDOCK, 3.5 *m.* (720 alt.,150 pop.), called Old Braddock to distinguish it from Braddock Heights, was a stagecoach stop where teamsters deemed it their right and privilege to celebrate with uproarious drinking bouts.

An early nineteenth-century inn, HAGAN'S TAVERN (R), 4.6 *m.*, is now a tourist home. In 1830, according to neighborhood legend, a guest buried a chest of jewels on a near-by mountainside. Two years later he returned and while attempting to recover his cache was fatally injured in a mountain storm. As he was dying the stranger confessed the jewels had been stolen from a grand duchess in France. The landlord dug fruitlessly, but residents of the vicinity insist the treasure awaits the persistent or lucky prospector.

During the Antietam campaign in September 1862 a detachment of Confederate cavalry stopped at the tavern for refreshments and was captured by Federal troops.

BRADDOCK'S SPRING (L), 4.8 *m.*, said to have been used during the French and Indian War by Braddock's troops, is now covered and provides its water through a small pump.

BRADDOCK HEIGHTS, 5.3 *m.* (950 alt.,150 pop.) (*swimming pool, other recreational facilities*), is a summer resort founded in 1896 on the peak of Catoctin Mountain, which is only 250 feet wide here. From the observation tower, parts of Pennsylvania, West Virginia, and Virginia are visible.

MIDDLETOWN, 8 *m.* (575 alt.,818 pop.), settled in the eighteenth century by people of English and German stock, was incorporated in 1834. Although it has no factories, the town has an air of modest wealth and comfort, founded chiefly on the prosperity of the agricultural region it serves. It is immaculately clean and has solidly built and well-appointed houses. The *Valley Register*, a weekly newspaper, has been published here since 1844 by four generations of the same family.

Several Civil War skirmishes took place in the vicinity and Middletown homes and churches were crowded with wounded after the battles of South Mountain and Antietam. Colonel Rutherford B. Hayes, commander of the 23rd Ohio Volunteers and later President of the United States, was among those injured at South Mountain.

ZION LUTHERAN CHURCH (R), Main Street, was built in 1860 to replace an earlier church building erected about 1783. A 12-foot marble shaft in the yard is a memorial to 31 Lutheran ministers born in the Middletown Valley.

The NANCY CROUSE HOUSE (L), Main Street, is a small brick dwelling with a low front porch. Here, according to Middletown historians, seventeen-year old Nancy Crouse stood with the Union flag wrapped around her when Confederate cavalrymen galloped into town. Nancy, unfortunately, overestimated Southern gallantry, for the flag was wrested from her and destroyed.

In the Lutheran Cemetery is a 12-foot marble shaft marking the GRAVE OF SERGEANT EVERHART, a local hero credited with having saved the lives of General Lafayette and Colonel William Augustine Washington. Lafayette was wounded at the Battle of the Brandywine on September 11, 1777, and was carried to safety by Everhart. On July 17, 1781, at the Battle of Cowpens, Everhart came to the aid of his commander, Colonel Washington, who was engaged in a personal encounter with a British officer. The cemetery is on the site of the Martenbox Church where Everhart, a Methodist minister, preached after the Revolutionary War.

CHRIST REFORMED CHURCH, built in 1819 and enlarged in 1897, is the third church on this site. It is a brick building with a tall, graceful spire. This church conducted a school here from 1847 until the present public school was opened.

In Middletown is a junction with State 33 (see Tour 2B).

US 40 crosses Catoctin Creek, 9.1 m. At the western end of the bridge is a macadam road.

Left on this road to FOX'S TAVERN (L), 1.9 m., a stone building erected shortly after the Revolutionary War. During the War of 1812, it is said, soldiers came to the tavern seeking shelter from the rain and 'all got Galory and engaged in a free fight, laying aside Captain Smith's commission, while King Whiskey took command.'

The RENO MONUMENT (L), 2.8 m., marks the spot where Major General Jesse Lee Reno, commander of the 9th Army Corps, U.S.Volunteers, was killed during the Battle of South Mountain.

A few yards from the monument are foundation stones and part of the fences of OLD WISE'S CABIN. 'Old Wise' was paid by the Government $5 each for burying soldiers but is said to have unceremoniously tossed 50 bodies into a near-by well. As a result disgruntled ghosts haunted the mountain, demanding decent burial, and one threatened to haunt him forever unless its body was turned over. After dark the old man reburied the body and the ghost disappeared.

US 40 crosses SOUTH MOUNTAIN (1,100 alt.) at 13.3 m. On the crest is the MOUNTAIN HOUSE (L), an old tavern that included among its guests several presidents and many statesmen traveling this route between the West and Washington,D.C. In 1876 the building was remodeled as a summer residence but is again being operated as an inn.

The LITTLE STONE CHURCH (R) was built in 1881 by Mrs.Madeleine Dahlgren, widow of Admiral John A.B. Dahlgren, expert on naval ordnance. The admiral's grave is inside the church, which is no longer used.

The Battle of South Mountain was fought here and at Fox's Gap, one mile south, on September 14, 1862, during Lee's first invasion of Maryland. Opposed to Lee's forces were Federal troops under General George B. McClellan. The battle began at Fox's Gap and continued there and along South Mountain throughout the day. Lee and General Longstreet were at Hagerstown when they received word of the desperate straits of the Confederates on South Mountain. Longstreet's men reached the scene about four o'clock in the afternoon, but the Confederates were outflanked and at nightfall were forced to retire toward Sharpsburg. Federal losses in killed, wounded, and missing totaled 1,831, and Confederate losses were approximately the same; however, the heroic defense of their position by General D.H.Hill's forces probably saved the Confederate army from destruction as it gave Lee time to concentrate his forces at Sharpsburg.

South Mountain has been the subject of many legends and superstitions. As late as 1859 many residents of the section believed that bands of Indians still passed over the mountain secretly. Lights moving at night along the mountainside long were known in the vicinity as 'the Saxon's fire.' According to the tale, a youthful Saxon among troops marching through here on his way to the Seminole War, stopped at the Mountain House Tavern and fell in love with the innkeeper's daughter. He deserted and hid on the mountain until the troops moved on, so he could marry the girl.

At 13.9 *m.*, about half-way down the mountainside, is the junction with the Zittlestown Road.

Right on this macadam road through ZITTLESTOWN, 0.2 *m.*, so named for the large Zittle family here, to WASHINGTON MONUMENT STATE PARK (*free picnic grounds*), 1.3 *m.* A monument erected here on July 4, 1827, was completed in one day by citizens of Boonsboro. During the Antietam and Gettysburg campaigns in the Civil War this mound, which had almost fallen to pieces, was patched with logs and used as a Union signal station. In 1934 ten acres of land, including the monument, were deeded to the State, and additional land was subsequently acquired for a State park. A copy of the earlier monument was built of local stone by the Civilian Conservation Corps and rededicated July 4, 1936.

From the tower, reached by an interior stairway, the Hagerstown, Potomac, Cumberland, and Middletown Valleys, and parts of neighboring States are visible.

At 15 *m.* is the junction with State 67, the Weverton Road (*see Tour 2B*).

BOONSBORO, 15.8 *m.* (530 alt.,824 pop.), a closely built residential town, is the home of retired farmers. The solid brick and stone houses have low front porches close to the sidewalks. Boonsboro has not always been a quiet town. It was settled in 1774 by George and William Boone, whom legend has related to the more famous Daniel. The town was prosperous in the 1830's when the pike was alive with westward-moving traffic; its blacksmith shops and stores were busy and its inns and taverns were filled with travelers and teamsters.

'Stonewall' Jackson narrowly escaped capture on the outskirts of Boonsboro on September 11, 1862. Colonel Henry Kyd Douglas, one of his staff officers, was advancing into town with a few cavalrymen when a detachment of Federal cavalry dashed out of the Sharpsburg road and drove the Confederates back toward their main column. On the way back they met General Jackson, unmounted and leading his horse, far ahead of his troops. The Confederate detail wheeled about, called to imaginary reinforcements, and charged the Federals. The ruse succeeded and the Federal cavalry withdrew before what they believed to be a superior force.

Four days after the Battle of South Mountain, Fitzhugh Lee's cavalry, while protecting the rear of Lee's army as it moved toward Sharpsburg, had a skirmish in the streets of Boonsboro with advancing Federal troops. After the battle of Antietam Boonsboro's churches and many of its private homes were used for the care of the wounded.

On July 8, 1863, Federal cavalry holding Boonsboro had an all-day engagement here with General J.E.B.Stuart's cavalry.

ROSE HILL (R), Main Street, a two-story house constructed of heavy timbers encased with mortar, was built in 1814. Rows of lilac bushes and boxwood and a number of fine old maple trees surround the house. This was one of the settings for David Belasco's play, *The Heart of Maryland*, first produced in 1895. Several scenes of the film version were photographed here.

MT.NEBO CHURCH (R), Main Street, was built in 1868 to replace a log structure erected by the United Brethren in 1832. Before that date the congregation worshiped in Shonk's Church, the site of which is marked by a graveyard on the outskirts of Boonsboro. Bishop Philip W. Otterbein (1726–1813), who with Martin Boehm founded the United Brethren in Christ, frequently preached at Shonk's.

At Main and Church Streets is (R) the former UNITED STATES HOTEL (1811) where many celebrities stopped. Little changed, the old place is still operated as a hotel.

TRINITY REFORMED CHURCH (R), Church Street near Main, occupies the site of the Salem Union Church in which Lutheran and Reformed congregations jointly worshiped from 1810 to 1870, when the present building was erected. The earlier church served as a military hospital during the Civil War. The Salem Church became the center of a town controversy. The Lutherans advocated round-topped windows, while the Reformed members of the congregation insisted on square windows, contending that the other type was 'sinful.' A compromise resulted in square windows on one side of the building and round on the other. Toleration again was necessary when dispute arose concerning heat in the church. Some brethren demanded comfort, others felt heat would be 'sacrilege and gross impiety.' In order that both body and spirit might be satisfied, the elders installed a stove on one side of the church. It is said that the body finally won out completely in the conflict when the more rigid members scuttled one by one to the warmer side of the building.

In the adjoining graveyard a monument to William Boone, one of the town's founders, was erected in 1935 to replace the simple stone that had marked the grave for 137 years.

On Main Street near Church Street is an old cannon (R) that was cast in a local furnace for use in the War of 1812. For many years it was used in political celebrations here.

WELDON, two blocks R. from the corner of Main and St.Paul Sts., was built about 1741 by Moses Chapline. The brick mansion is surrounded by fine trees, and its garden is noted for its boxwood hedges. In the rear of the house is a log cabin said to have been used as a church and later as slave quarters. Weldon was a hospital base after the battles at South Mountain and Antietam. This old mansion was another of the settings used by David Belasco in *The Heart of Maryland*.

Records indicate that members of the Chapline family had a flair for giving odd names to their estates. Among the family grants were Hunting the Hare, Loss and Gain, Strife, Tuckett, Tweedle, Little Thought, and Badham's Refuse. To Moses Chapline, in addition to his original tract, Well Done, there were grants of Resurvey of Well Done, and Jonah's Last Bit.

In Boonsboro are junctions with State 66 (*see Tour 2C*) and with State 34 (*see Tour 2D*).

At 16.8 *m.* is the junction with macadamized State 68.

Left on this road, which follows the route said to have been cut through the forest by General Braddock's army and used by 'Stonewall' Jackson's troops on their march to Harper's Ferry in 1862.

The DELEMERE BRIDGE, 3.3 *m.*, a three-arched limestone structure, was built over Antietam Creek in 1833. At the west end of the bridge is the entrance lane (R) of DELEMERE, a house built about 1776 by the Reverend Bartholomew Booth, who had come from England a few years before. The large rambling structure of bricks and logs was weatherboarded in later years and is still occupied. Many distinguished figures of the Revolutionary period were guests at Delemere. Here General Horatio Gates, then a widower, met and courted Mary Valence, wealthy daughter of a Liverpool merchant. The fortune of nearly half a million dollars that she brought to the general was generously spent in aiding his indigent comrades in arms during the Revolution. Near the house is the site of the school operated by Booth. Among his pupils were the son of Robert Morris, financier of the Revolution; Bushrod Washington, nephew of General Washington and later a justice of the United States Court; and the two young sons of Benedict Arnold. When he entered his sons in the school, Arnold wrote to Booth: 'I wish their education to be useful rather than learned. Life is too uncertain to throw away in studies that perhaps one man in ten thousand has the genius to make a figure in. You will pardon my dictating to you, Sir, but as the fortune of every man in this country is uncertain, I wish my sons to be educated in such a manner that with prudence and industry they may acquire a fortune; as well as become useful members of society . . . I will expect them to write to me frequently—of this they will doubtless want reminding.' In their first year here the boys gloried in their father's exploits, but the following year brought the news of his treason and disgrace. Shortly afterward the boys were sent to relatives in Philadelphia.

In BENEVOLA, 18.8 *m.* (410 alt.,50 pop.), is an old limestone building with a first-floor store. A tale is told that the proprietor of this store at the beginning of the Civil War painted a large American flag on his building. When, however, he heard that the Confederates were advancing on the town discretion overcame his valor, and he quickly whitewashed his painting.

A few hundred yards north of US 40, on the outskirts of Benevola beside Beaver Creek, was an ARMY OF THE POTOMAC HEADQUARTERS, where on July 9–14, 1863, General Meade held several councils of war with his corps commanders, deliberating over President Lincoln's orders to attack Lee before the latter could retire south of the Potomac.

At 22.5 *m.* is the junction with Garris Shop Road.

Left on this narrow macadamized road is ROSE'S MILL BRIDGE, 0.6 *m.*, a three-arch limestone structure built in 1839 over Antietam Creek. Near the bridge is a stone mill house (R) of about 1800. Opposite this is the site of CLAGGETT'S MILL, erected in Revolutionary times when it was one of the largest in this section of the country. The point where the water wheels were attached is still readily seen.

On a hill (R) is VALENTIA (*visited on written application to E.R.Roulette, Hagerstown, Md.*), a well-preserved two-and-one-half-story limestone house, with a high-pillared porch. The rooms are large and high-ceiled, and the hand-carved mantels, hand-fashioned window and door frames are in excellent condition. In the rear are white-washed stone slave quarters. On the estate is also a giant sycamore tree more than 100 feet tall, the largest in Maryland according to records of the State Forester.

FUNKSTOWN, 23.8 *m.* (524 alt.,700 pop.), is named for Henry Funk, to whom in 1754 Frederick Calvert granted a tract of land on which this town was laid out. First called Jerusalem, Funkstown missed its opportunity to grow when in 1776 shrewd Jonathan Hager, proprietor of Hagers-Town, rode to Annapolis and had his settlement named the county seat. Hardly more than a suburb of Hagerstown, it now has an appearance of modest prosperity, and its sturdy old brick and stone houses are tidy and well kept. Most of the residents of Funkstown bear names indicative of their German descent.

On US 40, near the center of town, is a house (R) that was SOUTH'S HOTEL in the turnpike era. John Brown stopped here in June 1859 when he was transporting pikes to arm the slaves in preparation for the great projected uprising.

Between Funkstown and Hagerstown Confederate cavalry and troops held back Federal forces from July 7 to 10, 1863, then withdrew to Hagerstown.

US 40 crosses Antietam Creek at 24 *m.* The bridge here, though widened and repaired, still rests solidly on limestone arches constructed in 1823. Within sight is another bridge (L) of approximately the same age. Both were scenes of conflict during the Civil War and withstood frequent efforts to destroy them.

US 40 crosses the line of battle of General Meade's Army of the Potomac at 24.2 *m.*, where on July 10–14, 1863, the Confederates held the heights while awaiting recession of the flooded waters of the Potomac before crossing into Virginia. Both armies threw up breastworks; the Confederates hoped to avenge their Gettysburg defeat, and the Union command hoped to hold the advantages already gained. By July 14 the Potomac had receded enough to permit Lee's army to withdraw.

HAGERSTOWN, 26.3 *m.* (552 alt.,30,861 pop.) (*see Hagerstown*).

Points of Interest: Washington County Museum of Fine Arts, Rose Hill Cemetery, Washington County Free Library, Möller Organ Works, and others.

Hagerstown is at junctions with US 11 (*see Tour 17*), State 65 (*Tour 2D*) and State 64 (*Tour 2C*), and the western junction with the new National Road (*under construction 1940*).

Section d. HAGERSTOWN to CUMBERLAND; 64.8 m.

West of HAGERSTOWN, 0 *m.*, US 40 passes through fertile hill country, much of it under cultivation though fields are small and some of them on steep slopes. There are many peach and apple orchards along the highway, and in season the fruit is sold at roadside stands.

This section of road, built between 1816 and 1821, was called the 'Bank Road' because the banks of Maryland financed its construction by purchase of stock.

Moonshine whisky and applejack have been manufactured for generations in western Maryland mountains. Actually very few of the hill people are engaged in this illicit manufacture; nor do they carry on feuds nor believe that the world is flat, as some outsiders like to think. In general they are as well read as the people of other sections; and many hear world events and the latest fad in swing music over small radio sets—assembled and kept in operation by the most ingenious methods.

OLD CONOCOCHEAGUE BRIDGE (R), 7.1 *m.*, by a modern concrete structure, was built of limestone in 1819 and served as a model for more than a score of similar bridges in Washington County.

At 8.4 *m.* is the junction with a macadamized road.

Right on this road to the CUSHWA TROUT REARING STATION (R), 2 *m.*, operated by the Conservation Department of Maryland.

At 10 *m.* is the junction with a macadam road.

Right here to STAFFORD HALL (R), 0.4 *m.*, a large, two-story brick and stone structure with nine double chimneys. It was built probably about 1835 by Judge John Thompson (1815–73), descendant of Colonel George Mason who came from Staffordshire, England, about 1651. Natives of the countryside have believed for years that there is a secret room in the house and that anyone who attempts to find the room will die. It is told that a prominent citizen of Hagerstown searched for the room in 1924 and died within the year; that two years later a nine-year-old child, who had spent many afternoons seeking the room, was taken ill and on her deathbed told what she had done and begged members of her family never to look for the room.

CLEARSPRING, 11.5 *m.* (566 alt.,539 pop.), a banking and trading town, was named for a spring so large that at one time it turned a mill wheel. The spring is behind the hotel.

1. Right from Clearspring on a macadamized road to MONTPELIER (R), 2.2 *m.*, whose two-story brick manor house was built about 1770 by Colonel Richard Barnes. John Thompson Mason, father of the builder of Stafford Hall, owned Montpelier for many years and is buried on the estate. He was a brilliant lawyer but because of ill health could not accept public offices frequently proffered him. President Jefferson once visited Montpelier to urge Mason to accept an appointment as Attorney General of the United States.

2. Left from Clearspring on the macadamized Ft.Frederick Road to a graveled road, 4.2 *m.*, which forks a few yards beyond the macadam.

a. Right on this graveled road (bear R.) about 100 yards to the SITE OF GREEN SPRING FURNACE (R), identified by a millrace and part of the stack of a later furnace (1848). The Green Spring Furnace, built about 1768 by Lancelot Jacques, a Frenchman, manufactured cannon for the Continental Army. Thomas Johnson was a partner in this enterprise until 1776 when he became the first governor of the State of Maryland.

b. Left on the graveled road, which is rough and narrow, to the SITE OF McCOY's FERRY, 1.2 *m.*, where the first Civil War skirmish in Maryland occurred in May 1861 as a party of Confederates attempted to take the ferryboat.

The macadamized road becomes State 56 and continues westward.

The JACQUES HOUSE (R), 4.3 *m.* (*visited by written application to A.B.Perrott, Hagerstown,Md.*), is a two-story, weatherboarded structure with a hip roof, built about

1766. In front of the house is a log cabin, possibly built about 1755 by Denton Jacques, nephew of Lancelot. It is strongly constructed, with doors and shutters thickly studded with large-headed nails.

At 5.9 m. is the junction with a macadamized road.

Left on this 0.6 m. to FORT FREDERICK (L) in the State park of the same name. The fort, now restored, was erected in 1756 for defense against the French and Indians and was named for Frederick Calvert, sixth Lord Baltimore. It is square with large bastions at the corner of the walls (which are 17 feet high) and as a whole is typical of contemporary fortifications. The stone for its heavy walls was brought from the mountains. The fort was garrisoned during both the Revolution and the Civil War but never suffered attack.

The park is a 188-acre tract extending to the Potomac River (free campsites; permits for overnight parking from superintendent). The administration building, near the fort, contains relics and watercolor paintings relating to the history of the post.

State 56 continues northward to a junction with US 40 at INDIAN SPRINGS (see below), 8.7 m.

On FAIRVIEW MOUNTAIN, 14 m. (975 alt.), at a point approximately one mile north of US 40, was a Union signal station from which messages could be relayed during the Civil War to Washington, D.C.

In INDIAN SPRING, 15.8 m. (500 alt., 75 pop.), is the junction with State 56 (see above).

The PARKHEAD EVANGELICAL CHURCH (R), 18.4 m., erected in 1833, was used during the Civil War by the Federals on picket duty along the Potomac. The gallery formerly used by the slaves has been preserved.

The stretch of country along the river west of this church is known as Parkhead Level. Below the highway is the abandoned bed of the old Chesapeake and Ohio Canal, fringed with trees and bushes and choked with weeds.

Somewhere in the hills, approximately a mile north of the highway, a small log outpost was erected in 1756 and named Fort Mills for an early settler. It was one of a chain built to protect Fort Frederick.

HANCOCK, 27 m. (450 alt., 947 pop.), is the center of a sand-mining and fruit-growing region. This section of the State, less than two miles wide in the vicinity of Hancock, is called Maryland's Neck. In 1755, after Braddock's defeat, a stockaded block house, called Fort Tonoloway, was erected on the Potomac not far from this point but was abandoned after Fort Frederick had been completed. As early as 1790 three-day race meets were being held at Hancock, and after the construction of the Cumberland Road the town was a stop-over point for travelers. The Chesapeake and Ohio Canal, completed to Hancock in 1839, further stimulated the growth of the town.

ST. THOMAS EPISCOPAL CHURCH, Church and High Sts., a brick structure with a square belfry, was built in 1835. In 1861 and 1862 the church was used to shelter Federal wounded, and batteries were placed near it as a defense against Stonewall Jackson's guns across the river.

OLD MR. FLINT'S HOME (R), 28.4 m., a two-story house about 200 yards from the highway, was constructed of heavy logs, now covered with white stucco. The exact date of its erection is unknown but a cast-iron fireback dated 1762 was discovered when a large chimney was being repaired. 'Old Mr. Flint' was an Indian trader, several times visited here by George Washington.

At 30.8 *m.* is the junction with a macadamized road.

Left on this to the WOODMONT ROD AND GUN CLUB (L), 6.7 *m.* (*visited by permission; apply at clubhouse*). The club was founded in 1870 by Grover Cleveland and Admiral Robley D. ('Fighting Bob') Evans. Several presidents have been members or guests of the club. The new clubhouse, built in 1930, is of stone and has a wide veranda overlooking the Potomac. Wild fowl are bred here; there are several hundred deer on the 5,000-acre preserve; and the lakes are stocked with trout and bass.

Right from the club entrance on a graveled road 1.8 *m.* to the WASHINGTON COUNTY GAME PRESERVE, a 3,000-acre tract owned by the State. Hunting is permitted from November 10 to December 31 on a part of this refuge.

From the summit of SIDELING HILL MOUNTAIN (1,595 alt.), 33.9 *m.*, is a view of the Potomac and the Hagerstown and Shenandoah valleys. To the west the Alleghenies are seen.

On US 40 at 43.7 *m.* is the entrance (L) to the 606-acre BILL MEYER GAME REFUGE, and the contiguous 50-acre PERRY BARNES GAME REFUGE.

Between Fifteen Mile Creek, 45.8 *m.*, and the summit of POLISH MOUNTAIN, 49.4 *m.* (1,340 alt.), the highway traverses the northern tip of the GREEN RIDGE STATE FOREST (*roads good in summer; hunting in season; inquire at State Forestry office, Cumberland Court House*). Most of this 16,888-acre tract lies between US 40 and the Potomac and takes in parts of Town Hill, Green Ridge, and Polish Mountains. It is stocked with wild turkeys, deer, and small game.

The houses of FLINTSTONE, 52.1 *m.* (828 alt.,150 pop.), line the road for about three-quarters of a mile in the fertile valley between Polish and Martin Mountains. Most of the townspeople are descendents of the early Scotch, German, and French settlers.

US 40 ascends to the summit of MARTIN MOUNTAIN (1,675 alt.), 55.9 *m.*

EVITT'S CREEK, 62 *m.*, was named for Evart, an Englishman who fled from civilization to this wild region in the early part of the eighteenth century. In hermit-like seclusion he died in 1750 on EVITT'S MOUNTAIN, the shaggy 2,300-foot range to the northeast.

HOYE'S CROSSROADS, 62.1 *m.*, is the junction with a mile-long road (R) connecting with US 220 (*see Tour* 18) north of Cumberland.

At 63.7 *m.* is the junction with Henderson Boulevard, which by-passes the business center of Cumberland and reunites with US 40 at Mechanic Street.

CUMBERLAND, 64.8 *m.* (641 alt.,37,747 pop.) (*see Cumberland*).

Points of Interest: Rose Hill, Site of Fort Cumberland, Washington's Headquarters, the Dent House, and others.

Cumberland is at junctions with State 51 (*see Tour* 2*E*) and State 220 (*see Tour* 18).

Section e. CUMBERLAND to PENNSYLVANIA LINE; 34.4 *m.*

Between Cumberland and the Pennsylvania Line is a wooded mountain region producing coal, some corn, wheat, fruit, and maple sugar. Some of the farms are submarginal, but others are very fertile. There are many rail fences along the steep hillsides.

In 1808, two years after Congress had voted to build a road connecting the East Coast with the Mississippi River, construction was begun westward from Cumberland, but it was nine years before the road reached Ohio. Named for its starting point, the entire route was originally called the Cumberland Road. This old route, which this section of US 40 follows, parallels the Braddock Road, an Indian trail Braddock's army tried to follow in 1755.

West of CUMBERLAND, 0 *m.*, US 40 passes through the Narrows, a mountain gorge, discovered in 1755 by Lieutenant Spendelow of Braddock's army. In the Narrows US 40 crosses Will's Creek at 1.2 *m.* OLD WILL'S CREEK BRIDGE (L), constructed in 1834, was used for nearly 100 years.

On WILL'S MOUNTAIN, 1.5 *m.*, is (R) the lover's leap of this vicinity, a limestone cliff rising more than 1,000 feet. The legendary lovers were, as usual, Indians. It was named for Will, an Indian who lived near here late in the eighteenth century.

At 2.2 *m.* is the junction with State 35 (*see Tour* 18*A*).

The old road over the mountain meets US 40 at 6.1 *m.* It follows the trail used in 1754 by Washington on leaving the place that became Fort Cumberland. A year later Braddock started west over it with his troops, hacking down trees as they went. When they had advanced only five miles in two days and had wrecked three wagons, another route was sought. It was then that Lieutenant Spendelow discovered the Narrows.

The six-sided TOLL HOUSE (L), 6.5 *m.*, a two-room, two-story whitewashed building, bears a sign showing what the rates of toll for vehicles and livestock were a century ago. By the house, which was built about 1833, are the old tollgate posts.

CLARYSVILLE INN (L), 8.5 *m.*, called Eight Mile House, was built in 1807. The two-and-a-half-story structure of brick and stone painted white is little changed externally. During the Civil War it was used as headquarters for a large Federal hospital camp.

In ECKHART MINES, 9.2 *m.* (1,720 alt.,1,500 pop.), a high-grade bituminous coal has been mined for more than a century. Coal was first mined in this vicinity about 1804 but extensive operations did not begin until the 1830's. Some of the houses lining the highway are of stone or logs and were evidently built before the Civil War.

FROSTBURG, 11.5 *m.* (1,929 alt.,5,588 pop.), is a trading point for a coal-mining and firebrick making area. Most of its inhabitants are descendants of English, Scotch, Irish, and Welsh immigrants.

After Meshach Frost established a tavern here in 1812, a settlement grew up that Frost called Mount Pleasant and everyone else called Frost's Town. In 1820 the Post Office Department decided to call it Frostburg.

The BRADDOCK ROAD MILESTONE, in a field off Midlothian Road about 100 yards from Park Ave., is a sandstone slab about three feet high. On one side the inscription, now very difficult to read, gives the distances to 'Ft. Cumberland' and 'Captn Smyth's Inn & Bridge,' and also 'Red Stone Old Fort'; on the opposite side is 'Our Country's Rights we will defend.' Many years ago this stone was split; half was used as a doorstep and the other half as a foundation stone. The halves have been cemented together.

In FROSTBURG is the junction with State 36 (*see Tour 18A*).

BIG SAVAGE MOUNTAIN (2,850 alt.), 13.8 *m.*, was named for an early surveyor, John Savage. In 1755 Braddock's soldiers 'intirely demolished three wagons and shattered several descending Savage Mountain.'

For 35 years the STONE HOUSE INN (R), 22.2 *m.*, a large, two-story structure built in 1818, was a popular tavern on the National Road. It stands on or near the site of Red House Tavern, built after the French and Indian War.

At 22.4 *m.* are junctions with US 219 (*see Tour 19*), which unites westward with US 40 for about 9 miles, and with a dirt and graveled road.

> Left on this into SAVAGE RIVER STATE FOREST, 3 *m.* (*free camping; permits issued by resident warden at New Germany*), a 17,000-acre tract of great natural beauty. From NEW GERMANY, 4.7 *m.* (2,471 alt.,10 pop.), roads branch to all parts of the preserve.

STANTON'S MILL (R), 24.6 *m.*, a three-story, white structure about 50 yards from the highway is on a stone foundation, now partly encased in cement. This foundation was probably built in 1797 when a saw and grist mill was erected here. The old mill was rebuilt in 1856 and enlarged in 1900. Old burr stones are used as steps to the door.

US 40 crosses the Castleman River, 24.7 *m.* OLD CASTLEMAN RIVER BRIDGE (R), still used for a side road, was considered the largest of its kind in the country when it was built in 1816. Many persons doubted that the masonry would stand up when the supporting framework was removed. According to local tradition even the contractor was worried and on the night before the formal opening he had his workmen remove the framework to see if it would collapse.

GRANTSVILLE, 25.5 *m.* (2,351 alt.,400 pop.), serving miners and farmers, was settled by Daniel Grant, a Baltimorean, during the last decade of the eighteenth century. Much of the maple syrup and sugar produced in the region immediately south of the town is purchased by northern dealers and marketed under a Vermont label.

> Left from Grantsville on macadamized State 495 to BITTINGER, 8.5 *m.* (2,660 alt.,150 pop.), a mountain village named for Henry Bittinger or Bedinger who acquired land here in 1814 and of whom it was said that 'he mostly raised a large family.'
>
> This section was settled by Pennsylvania Germans, including many Amish who still cling to peculiarities of dress adopted by their ancestors in Switzerland as protests against taxes on buttons and mustaches. The men wear dark gray or black suits and wide-brimmed black felt hats; the women wear black bonnets and long black dresses fastened only with hooks and eyes. The men have beards but no mustaches. They abstain from worldly vanities and maintain their own schools, lest their children come too much in contact with the world. They are noted for their well-kept farms, great red barns, and spotless homes. Shelves of flowering plants serve as a substitute for window curtains and shades in their homes.

On NEGRO MOUNTAIN, 28.6 *m.* (2,908 alt.), is the highest point on US 40 in Maryland. During the French and Indian War a force under Colonel Thomas Cresap had a skirmish with a band of Indians on this mountain and one of Cresap's men, a giant Negro, was killed and buried here; hence the name.

At the summit of KEYSER'S RIDGE, 31 m. (2,881 alt.), US 219 (see Tour 19) branches south. US 40 continues to the Pennsylvania Line, 34.4 m., which it crosses at a point about 29 miles southeast of Uniontown, Pa. (see Pennsylvania Guide).

Tour 2A

Baltimore—Eldersburg—Libertytown—Junction with US 15; 46.7 m., State 26.

Macadam and concrete-paved roadbed, two lanes wide.
Accommodations ample.

Because of its much lighter traffic State 26 (Liberty Road) is a desirable alternate to US 40 between Baltimore and Frederick. It traverses rolling farm country that produces wheat, corn, vegetables, and fruit as well as quantities of poultry and milk.

In BALTIMORE, 0 m., State 26 branches northwest from US 40 (see Tour 2b) on Liberty Heights Avenue.

At 7.5 m. is the junction with macadamized Campfield Road.

Right on this to the AUGSBURG HOME FOR CHILDREN AND AGED (L), 0.6 m., an institution supported by the Lutheran Synod.

At 10.7 m. is the junction with macadamized Old Court Road (see Tour 1A).

Left on this to the WALTERSVILLE GRANITE QUARRIES (R), 4.2 m., opened in 1830 by Captain Alexander Walters and operated till 1925. Stone quarried here was used in the construction of many of the bridges built for the Baltimore & Ohio Railroad and in the public buildings and monuments of Baltimore and Washington.

GRANITE, 4.4 m. (461 alt.,500 pop.), called Waltersville when it was established with the opening of the quarries, received its present name in 1873.

The COLLEGE OF THE SACRED HEART (R), 5.6 m., better known as Woodstock College, a Jesuit Seminary, was opened in 1869. The buildings on the tract of 700 acres include a four-story main structure of brick and stone, whose construction was begun in 1866, an observatory, a science building, and a library containing a number of rare theological works and parchment manuscripts. In the school's mineral collection are some 800 specimens of Italian marbles.

WOODSTOCK, 6.4 m. (276 alt.,210 pop.), founded in the late 1860's, is dependent on near-by granite quarries.

RANDALLSTOWN, 11.4 m. (585 alt.,133 pop.), was founded early in the eighteenth century by Thomas and Christopher Randall, Jr. James Ryder Randall (1839–1908) of this family was the author of Maryland, My Maryland.

Sports and Recreation

Rowan

BOARDWALK, OCEAN CITY

YACHT BASIN, OCEAN CITY

Robins Hollyday

LOG CANOE—*FLYING CLOUD*

MILES RIVER REGATTA

Robins Hollyday

CROSS-COUNTRY POINT-TO-POINT RACE

PREAKNESS DAY AT PIMLICO RACE TRACK, BALTIMORE

A MARYLAND TROUT STREAM

BLESSING OF THE HOUNDS—ST. THOMAS'S CHURCH, BALTIMORE COUNTY

ner-Bodine

SURF CASTING, OCEAN CITY

DUCK HUNTING

Robins Hollyday

WILD GEESE FEEDING

DUCK SHOOTING FROM BLIND

mer-Bodine

WATERFRONT, CHESTERTOWN

YACHT RACING, OFF OXFORD SHORE

At 14.8 *m.* is the junction with macadamized Lyons Mills Road.

Right on this to MT.PARAN CHURCH (R), 0.3 *m.*, believed to be the second oldest Presbyterian church in Maryland. The first congregation meeting on this site was organized about 1715 as the Patapsco Church. The present small frame building, which replaced several earlier log churches, was probably built in the early part of the eighteenth century.

Part of WOODLAWN (L), 0.4 *m.*, a one-and-a-half-story stone house with high gable roof, was probably built before Mt.Paran Church. Additions have increased its original three rooms to seven. The first patent in the estate was made to a Worthington whose descendants still own it. Members of this family played conspicuous roles in the Revolution and the War of 1812.

In the colonial period this was part of the political subdivision, Soldier's Delight Hundred. Troops stationed in an outpost near here (*see Tour 14*) are said to have been responsible for this name because of their pleasure in hunting the section's abundant and varied game.

ELDERSBURG (642 alt.,90 pop.) is at 20.8 *m.*

1. Right from Eldersburg on macadamized State 32 to the STRAWBRIDGE HOME FOR BOYS (L), 0.8 *m.*, which was opened in 1924 and named for Robert Strawbridge, one of the founders of Methodism in America. The stone buildings have accommodations for about 50 boys. Although under Methodist supervision, boys of other denominations are admitted, the principal requirements being 'poverty and good health.'

State 32 continues to a junction with US 140 in WESTMINSTER, 14.6 *m.*

2. Left from Eldersburg on State 32 to SPRINGFIELD STATE HOSPITAL FOR THE INSANE (L), 1 *m.*, established in 1894 and supported by the counties, the cities, and the State. The brick buildings have beds for about 2,500 patients. The 1,200-acre grounds were part of Springfield, the estate of William Patterson, father of Betsy Patterson (*see Tour 14A*).

State 32 continues 8 *m.* to a junction with US 40 (*see Tour 2b*).

TAYLORSVILLE, 28 *m.* (820 alt.,75 pop.), is the trade center of Carroll County's wormseed oil industry, in which Maryland leads the rest of the nation. The plant has been used to eliminate intestinal parasites since colonial times but large scale cultivation began only in 1916, when the oil was found to be a substitute for thymol. The seeds, a profitable by-product, are ground and sold as vermifuge for poultry and livestock. The distillery at 29.4 *m.* manufactures the oil during the plant harvest season, September and October.

A lane (L) 37.2 *m.* leads to the OLD DOLLYHIDE MINE on the eastern side of Dollyhide Creek. Copper workings were opened here in 1760 and operated till about 1900. On the west side of the creek is one of the original stone buildings and on the east side are traces of the old shafts and pits. The creek was named for Dolly Hyde, daughter of a settler whose lands in this section were patented as Hide and Seek and I Spy.

At 37.2 *m.* is the junction with State 31 (*see Tour 15*).

LIBERTYTOWN, 37.6 *m.* (524 alt.,425 pop.), was laid out in 1782 on part of 6,000 acres patented as Duke's Woods. There were enough settlers in the neighborhood before that, however, to enable a physician to practice here in 1775. A Civil War yarn concerns a local newspaper editor who excitedly marched away with a body of Confederate troops who were passing through the village, in the belief that it was a Union detachment. In Libertytown is the junction with State 75 (*see Tour 15*).

CERESVILLE, 45.7 *m.* (300 alt.,75 pop.), on the eastern bank of the Monocacy River, is on a tract of land originally considered as the site of

Frederick. The settlement was laid out in 1785 on land owned by General Otho Holland Williams, a Revolutionary War officer (*see Tour* 17). The CERESVILLE MILLS (L) have been in operation since 1790. The present four-story stone building was erected in 1812.

The bridge across the Monocacy at 46 *m.* replaced the Williams Ferry, used by Mad Anthony Wayne's army on May 13, 1781, in their march to Virginia for the closing campaign of the Revolution.

In September 1862 a part of Lee's army camped by WORMAN'S MILL (R), 46.6 *m.*, which is believed to have been built before the Revolutionary War.

At 46.7 *m.* is the junction with US 15 (*see Tour* 15), about 2 miles northeast of Frederick (*see Frederick*).

Tour 2B

Frederick—Jefferson—Knoxville—Brunswick—(Harpers Ferry,W.Va.); US 340. Frederick to West Virginia Line, 19.2 *m.*

Macadamized roadbed, two lanes wide.
Baltimore and Ohio Railroad roughly parallels route.
Hotels in Frederick; limited accommodations elsewhere.

US 340 passes through farming country chiefly used for pasture and for growing wheat, corn, and rye.

US 340 branches southwest from US 40 (*see Tour 2b*) in FREDERICK, 0 *m.*, on Jefferson Street.

A five-foot granite block (R), 1.6 *m.*, designates the spot where Major General George Meade took command of the Army of the Potomac on June 28, 1863, three days before the Battle of Gettysburg. Meade's Army and the Army of Northern Virginia under General Robert E. Lee followed approximately parallel routes through Maryland into Pennsylvania.

PROSPECT HALL (R), 1.7 *m.*, a two-story brick house built shortly before the Revolution is on a tract patented as Dickson's Struggle. This place was the country home of Benjamin Tasker Dulany, clerk of the Frederick County Court and son of Daniel Dulany the younger. This Dulany, unlike his father, espoused the American cause and became one of Washington's aides. Washington's favorite horse, Blueskin, was a present from Dulany. After the Revolution, Washington returned the horse to Mrs.Dulany, and in writing of the incident said: 'marks of antiquity have supplanted the place of those beauties with which the horse abounded in his better days, nothing but the recollections of which and of his having been the favorite of Mr.Dulany in the days of his courtship, can reconcile her to the meager appearance he now makes.' There is a legend that Blueskin is buried somewhere on the grounds.

At 1.7 *m.* is the junction with Butterfly Lane, part of the route Braddock's troops followed in marching from Frederick to Fort Cumberland in 1755.

Right on this asphalt-paved road to RADIO TRANSMITTING STATION WFMD (L), 0.5 *m.*

The first settlers of JEFFERSON, 7.7 *m.* (610 alt.,275 pop.), arrived in 1779. In the days when highway robbers had headquarters here it became known as The Trap. The present name was given in 1832 within six years of Thomas Jefferson's death.

The EVANGELICAL REFORMED CHURCH and ST.PAUL'S LUTHERAN CHURCH belong to congregations organized about the time the town was formally named. In the cemetery adjoining the Reformed Church is the grave of William Cost Johnson.

The JOHNSON HOUSE (R), 8.4 *m.*, a two-story **L**-shaped brick dwelling, was the home of William Cost Johnson, who served in Congress from 1833 to 1843 and attained some notoriety by fighting a pistol duel in 1836 with William Schley, a prominent lawyer. Both Johnson and Schley were wounded, but recovered and buried their quarrel.

US 340 crosses what was once the Merryland Tract granted to Captain John Colville in 1732 and enlarged in 1753. George Washington was one of the executors who sold the land in smaller parcels after Colville's death.

In PETERSVILLE, 12.2 *m.* (475 alt.,150 pop.), is ST.MARY'S CHURCH, built in 1826 with money contributed by Governor Thomas Sim Lee. For nearly 70 years this was the only Roman Catholic Church between Frederick and Harpers Ferry, West Virginia. The brick church has a portico with four Doric columns.

At 12.4 *m.* is the junction with a stone road.

Right on this to the THOMAS SIM LEE HOUSE, 2.3 *m.*, a two-story stuccoed log house built in 1775 for the Reverend Bartholomew Booth, who had come to America from England a few years earlier. When his neighbors suspected that the clergyman was using his house for Tory gatherings they threatened to destroy it. Alarmed, Booth fled to Washington County, where he established a school at Delamere (*see Tour 2c*). Shortly afterward the house was acquired by Lee, governor of Maryland from 1779 to 1782 and from 1792 to 1794 and earlier a member of the Continental Congress. He also served in the Maryland convention that ratified the Constitution of the United States. Elected United States Senator in 1794 and governor of Maryland for a third term in 1798, he declined both honors.

MT.O'DONNELL (L), 12.7 *m.*, a two-and-one-half-story brick house first called Montevue, was built in 1819 by Colonel John Thomas. For several years this was the home of his son, Francis Thomas, governor of Maryland 1841–44, and known as one of the State's strongest and most courageous political figures. At 23 he was elected to the State legislature, and from 1831 until he became governor he was a member of Congress. As a man from the Piedmont where slaves were few, he frequently denounced Maryland's system of representation, whereby the slaveholding counties of the eastern and southern sections exercised more power in the legislature than the western counties.

BARLEYWOOD (*open*), 13.2 *m.*, is a two-story log house built about 1800. The Reverend R.H.Phillips, rector of St.Mark's Protestant Episcopal Church, conducted an Episcopal school for girls here.

At 13.9 *m.* is the junction with State 33.

1. Right on State 33 to the SITE OF THE HORSEY DISTILLERY (R), 2.8 *m.*, established in 1850. In the beginning whisky manufactured at this plant was loaded on slow-sailing vessels, shipped around Cape Horn to California, and then shipped back to the plant, because the rocking of the ship was believed to age the whisky more rapidly. The plant continued in operation until the prohibition amendment went into force.

Residents of a Negro settlement near the distillery are firm in their belief that the neighborhood has a 'Snallygaster'—a fabulous reptilian bird of vast size that preys on poultry and Negro children after nightfall. (The name, as well as the monster, was probably acquired from German settlers who had their *Schnelle geist*.)

BURKITTSVILLE, 4.3 *m.* (550 alt.,173 pop.), at the foot of South Mountain, was called Harley's Postoffice until it was laid out as a town and named for a settler, Henry Burkitt, in 1829.

The CHURCH OF THE RESURRECTION, built in 1829, was used by both the Reformed and Lutheran congregations until the Lutherans built ST.PAUL'S CHURCH in 1859. The Reformed group then enlarged and remodeled the earlier brick building but retained the original front section with its two Ionic columns. After the engagement at Crampton's Gap in the Battle of South Mountain in 1862 (*see Tour 2c*), wounded soldiers were brought here for treatment and shelter.

Left 1.1 *m.* from Burkittsville on an asphalt-paved road to the WAR CORRESPONDENTS MEMORIAL, erected by George Alfred Townsend (Gath), Civil War correspondent and novelist, in honor of his fellow newspapermen who covered the Civil War. This strange structure, designed by Townsend to include the most bizarre features of a Moorish arch at a railroad station and a tower on a firehouse—both of which had aroused his admiration—was dedicated on October 16, 1896, with much publicity. The arch is of local stone trimmed with brown sandstone, blue limestone, and brick. The front is decorated with red brick panels into which the words 'War Correspondents' have been cut. In a niche near the top of the arch is a six-foot figure of Orpheus sheathing a sword and playing a pipe. Tablets on one side of the arch bear the names of 147 correspondents and artists of the war and other tablets include a description of the engagement that occurred in the pass. The grounds and memorial were given to the Government by Townsend in 1904.

Opposite the arch are the ruins of Gapland, a group of buildings in which Townsend lived during his most successful years as a writer. Born in Delaware in 1841, Townsend spent most of his life in Maryland. After the Civil War when royalties from *Katy of Catoctin* and *The Entailed Hat* began to pour in, he began to build his retreat in this pass. In all he built five houses here, one for his own use, one for his wife, and the others for his children, their nurses, and his servants. He entertained extravagantly and invitations to parties at Gapland were welcomed by outstanding people of the period. Each of the five houses was a fantastic architectural conception—with entrances and exits placed at the whim of the owner, and numerous spires, arches, and turrets jutting from the roofs. Set in marble in the walls were quotations from the classics.

When his fortunes began to decline, he had to move from his elaborate establishment, on which he had spent half a million dollars, to simpler quarters in Washington. Gath died in 1914, and in 1922 his heirs sold this estate for $9,500. An effort was made to convert the place into a summer hotel, but the plan was abandoned and Gapland was left to the mercy of vandals and the elements. In 1938 it was sold at auction for $750.

State 33 continues to US 40, 8 *m.* (*see Tour 2c*).

2. Left on State 33 to BRUNSWICK, 2.4 *m.* (248 alt.,3,671 pop.), a community of frame houses whose residents are almost entirely dependent on the repair shops estab-

lished here in 1890 by the Baltimore & Ohio Railroad. The town is on part of the large tract patented as Hawkins' Merry Peep o' Day by John Hawkins in 1753. In 1787 the tract was laid out as the town of Berlin, but the name was changed in 1890 to avoid confusion with Berlin on Maryland's Eastern Shore.

The POTOMAC RIVER BRIDGE was built in 1894 on the piers of a covered wooden span burned by the Confederates. The old bridge had been used by the Confederate troops for frequent dashes into Maryland to cut the Baltimore and Ohio Railroad or the telegraph lines. Following the Battles of Antietam and Gettysburg, the Federal armies under General McClellan and General Meade, respectively, crossed the Potomac here for their advances into Virginia.

The BALTIMORE & OHIO RAILROAD YARDS AND SHOPS do only light repairs, major rebuilding being done in Baltimore and Cumberland.

PERI-LAND (L) 14.9 m. on US 340, was built in 1852 on part of the Merryland Tract. The two-story-and-attic brick building has wide front and rear porches.

KNOXVILLE, 15.5 m. (261 alt.,425 pop.), like Brunswick is chiefly dependent on Baltimore & Ohio Railroad shops. Laid out in 1772 on several lots of the Merryland Tract, the town prospered in the days of the Chesapeake and Ohio Canal. Small industries developed, including iron smelting which continued until about 1890.

Just west of Knoxville in 1835 Casper W. Wever, a civil engineer who built the first bridge at Harpers Ferry, tried to establish a manufacturing town to be called Weverton. Wever drew plans for factory and home sites here, constructed a power dam across the river, and built several mills that were never used. One factory, manufacturing files, operated from 1846 until the beginning of the Civil War, and a marble works also did business for a brief period. The entire plan collapsed after Wever's death and the town today is marked only by the crumbling walls of stone houses.

At modern WEVERTON, 16.4 m. (260 alt.,50 pop.), is the junction with State 67 (see Tour 2c).

From POTOMAC VIEW, 17.6 m., the river is visible, flowing through Harpers Ferry gap, between the steep and craggy slopes of Maryland Heights and Loudon Heights, Virginia. These hills on both sides of the river were occupied by Union and Confederate troops at various times.

SANDY HOOK, 18.2 m. (200 alt.,300 pop.), came into existence about 1832, with the completion of the Chesapeake and Ohio Canal. First known as Keep Tryst, its present name is said to refer to a near-by quicksand pool in which a teamster lost his horses.

At 19 m. is the junction with an asphalt-bound road.

Right on this to a graveled road, 4.2 m.; R. on it 0.6 m. to the JOHN BROWN HOUSE (L). Early in June 1859 Brown, under an assumed name, with two of his sons and a follower, Jerry Anderson, rented this farmhouse and 260 acres, allegedly for farming purposes. Brown's daughter and a daughter-in-law soon joined him. For about three months the group received from Northern abolitionists packages of arms and ammunition, which were stored in a log cabin; in the attic of the farmhouse Brown gathered about a thousand pikes that had been sent to him from Connecticut.

On the night of October 16, after attending services at a Dunkard church, Brown with less than a score of followers surprised the little garrison at Harpers Ferry and captured the arsenal. The anticipated uprising of slaves throughout the South failed to materialize and a day later the arsenal was recaptured under the leadership of Robert E. Lee. Another detachment under J.E.B.Stuart seized the house in which Brown had been living, confiscated the firearms and pikes, and found among his papers the constitution of the revolutionary government Brown had intended to set up. Brown was tried, sentenced, and hanged on December 2, 1859, at Charlestown, West Virginia. Though many of the abolitionists had disapproved Brown's action, his dignified conduct at his trial and his execution made him a martyr in their eyes and the incident widened the breach between the North and South.

US 340 crosses the WEST VIRGINIA LINE, 19.2 *m.*, on a bridge spanning the Potomac River to Harpers Ferry,W.Va.

Tour 2C

Boonsboro—Cavetown—Hagerstown; 17.7 *m.*, State 66 and State 64.

Asphalt and concrete roadbed, two lanes wide.
Western Maryland R.R. roughly parallels route between Cavetown and Hagerstown.
Limited accommodations except in Hagerstown.

State 66 and State 64 traverse part of the fertile wheat-raising Hagerstown Valley. Between the route and the slopes of South Mountain is much land used for truck farming, and raspberry, cantaloupe, and peach growing.

This section of Maryland is peopled by descendants of the Palatine Germans who came here early in the eighteenth century.

State 66 branches northeast from the junction with US 40 (*see Tour 2c*) in BOONSBORO, 0 *m.*

At 0.4 *m.* is the junction with a dirt lane.

Left on this to SHANK'S CHURCH, 0.5 *m.*, a small log building erected in 1750 by a United Brethren congregation and abandoned in 1832. Philip William Otterbein, co-founder of the denomination, frequently preached here.

MAPLEVILLE, 2 *m.* (679 alt.,93 pop.), originally called Mt.Pleasant, is a trading point for an area where strawberries, blackberries, raspberries, and cantaloupes are intensively cultivated.

The PETER GRAY HOME FOR ORPHAN CHILDREN (L), 2.6 *m.*, is largely supported by the county.

In WAGNER'S CROSSROADS, 4.4 *m.*, is the junction with the asphalt-paved Funkstown Road.

Left on this to the ALBINO FROG FARM (L), 0.5 *m.*, probably the only place in the world where only albino frogs are bred. In 1933 C.C.Moler, an electrical engineer of Hagerstown, discovered a few tadpoles of a pale saffron color in the fish pools at Lilypons (*see Tour 15*). From these he succeeded in breeding and raising albino frogs and had converted several discarded trolley cars into frog hatcheries. The frogs are in some demand by biologists.

Opposite the frog farm is DOUB'S MILL, a three-story stone structure in continuous use since it was built about 1800. Since 1930 it has ground grain only for neighborhood farmers. Close by are five stone houses built before 1800.

BEAVER CREEK, 5.1 *m.* (534 alt.,250 pop.), on the banks of the stream for which it was named, was a milling center early in the nineteenth century. A few of the stone mills are still in operation with power supplied by the original water wheels. Some of the few dwellings here, built shortly after 1800, have been acquired by Hagerstown people and are being modernized.

Right from Beaver Creek on a dirt road to BAGTOWN, 2 *m.*, a village of about a dozen houses, from which a rough, steep foot path leads past the BLACK ROCK CLIFFS, 0.7 *m.*, to the summit of SOUTH MOUNTAIN (1,700 alt.), 3.6 *m.*

MT.AETNA CAVERNS (R), 6.6 *m.* (*June to Sept.*, 50¢; *free parking and picnic grounds*), are the largest limestone caverns in Maryland and are lighted for a distance of 650 feet. The numerous formations bear the usual names, ranging from the Great Wall of China to Jefferson Davis, because of fancied resemblances. The caverns were discovered by Boy Scouts in 1928 and opened to the public in 1933.

Site of the MT.AETNA FURNACE (R) is at 6.8 *m.* Here ordnance for the Continental Army was made during the Revolutionary War. Despite an advertisement in 1786 that stated: 'The ore is of excellent quality, either for bar-iron or castings . . . The buildings, bellows, gears, etc. are in good repair, and the stream of water constant. Pot stove and other patterns may be had with the furnace, and also meadow ground and land for farming,' the furnace was abandoned in 1815.

THE MAPLES (L), 8.5 *m.*, a three-story house with limestone walls, was built in 1815 by Ludwig Huyett on part of a tract granted to his grandfather, Lodwick Huyett, in 1761. Handcarved paneling and trim and a spiral staircase leading from the central hall to the third story are noteworthy. At the entrance to the house is a pair of carved lions.

At CAVETOWN, 10.4 *m.* (750 alt.,285 pop.), named for a large cave that has been destroyed, farmers and townspeople find seasonal employment in a large fruit and vegetable cannery.

CHRIST EVANGELICAL CHURCH still uses the brick building erected in 1826 by a Reformed Lutheran congregation.

In Cavetown is the junction with State 64, which (L) becomes the main route.

Right on State 64 to the SMITHSBURG CEMETERY (L), 0.9 *m.*, and the grave of the Maryland sculptor, Emily Clayton Bishop, marked by a flat limestone tablet.
At 1 *m.* is a dirt road; R. here 0.5 *m.* to INGRAM'S MILL (L), a three-story stone structure probably built in the first decade of the nineteenth century and still owned and operated by the Ingram family, who erected it.
SMITHSBURG, 1.1. *m.* (792 alt.,598 pop.), founded about 1806 on an elevation at the base of South Mountain, is the banking and trading center of fruit growers. After the battle of Gettysburg, when Union Cavalry occupied the town, General J.E.B.Stuart's Confederate batteries shelled it from the top of South Mountain. There was also a hospital base here after the battles of Antietam and South Mountain.
TRINITY LUTHERAN CHURCH, Main St., is a brick building dedicated in 1824, two years after its congregation had been organized.

The SMITHSBURG PUBLIC LIBRARY (*open Tues. only*, 3–6), built about 1813, was formerly a dwelling. About 1865 the town bought it for a jail, and in 1921 the local Women's Club presented it to the town for its present use.

The BISHOP HOUSE is a two-and-a-half-story brick house on a limestone foundation. Its exterior is much the same as when it was built in 1813 by Dr. Elijah Bishop. This was the birthplace and lifelong home of Emily Clayton Bishop (1883–1912), sculptor, whose work is seen in the Pennsylvania Academy of Fine Arts.

Right from Smithsburg on State 92 to EDGEMONT, 3.8 *m.* (960 alt.,135 pop.), are fields producing apples, peaches, and raspberries. In summer the population is increased by vacationists whose cottages are in the surrounding hills. The village, on the western slope of South Mountain, commands an excellent view.

State 64 continues to RINGGOLD, 4 *m.*, and crosses the Pennsylvania Line, 4.7 *m.*, about 3 miles south of Waynesboro, Pennsylvania.

In Cavetown the other section of State 64 becomes the main route and swings L.

In CHEWSVILLE, 13 *m.* (625 alt.,208 pop.), which is strung along the highway for half a mile, most of the houses are of stone and were built before the Civil War. The village occupies part of a tract granted to Samuel Chew, Jr. in 1736.

Left from Chewsville on macadamized Beaver Creek Road to WHITE HALL (L), 1.8 *m.*, a two-and-a-half-story brick house built in 1813. On the second floor is a large ballroom and each bedroom has a large fireplace. The interior woodwork and paneling is considered a fine example of early Federal work.

On this road at 2.5 *m.* is a dirt road.

Left 0.8 *m.* to the JOHNNIE GEORGE HOME (R), another two-and-a-half-story brick house, built in 1815. Bricks forming the arch over the main entrance are more than a foot long. In the yard are slave quarters and a smokehouse.

At 13.7 *m.* is the junction with macadamized State 62.

Right on this 1 *m.* to THE HIVE (R), a two-story rectangular brick house built in 1790 by Colonel William Fitzhugh, Revolutionary War veteran. Colonel Fitzhugh was the son of William Fitzhugh, an officer in the British Army who came to Maryland during the French and Indian War, and a brother of Captain Peregrine Fitzhugh. Parts of The Hive have been altered, but 13 of the original rooms are unchanged. The high-ceiled rooms are decorated with handcarved woodwork.

At 14.9 *m.* is the junction with a dirt road.

Right on this road is TROVINGER'S MILL (L), 0.8 *m.*, a long two-story stone structure with a second floor gallery. It was built in 1771 and operated as a mill until 1917.

At 16.4 *m.* is the junction with Pangborn Boulevard; R. here 0.6 *m.* to the PANGBORN CORPORATION PLANT (*open to visitors*), one of the largest factories manufacturing sandblast-cleaning and dust-control equipment. The plant includes 11 modern brick buildings on a 15-acre landscaped tract of much beauty. Machines have been developed here for cleaning articles as small as dental drills and as large as castings for locomotives or ship's parts.

Directly across the street from the factory is PANGBORN PARK, a public recreational area donated by Thomas Pangborn, head of the corporation, and developed with WPA labor. A lake in the center has been stocked with fish.

HAGERSTOWN, 17.7 *m.* (552 alt.,30,861 pop.) (*see Hagerstown*).

Points of Interest: Washington County Museum of Fine Arts, Rose Hill Cemetery, Washington County Free Library, Möller Organ Plant, Mt.Prospect, and others.

Hagerstown is at junctions of US 40 (*see Tour 2*), US 11 (*see Tour 17*), and State 34 (*see Tour 2D*).

Tour 2D

Boonsboro—Sharpsburg—Antietam Battlefield—Hagerstown; 20.1 *m.*, State 34, State 65.

Concrete or asphalt-paved roadbed, three and four lanes wide.
B.& O. and Norfolk & Western Railroads parallel route between Sharpsburg and Hagerstown.
Inns and tourist camps in battlefield area.

State 34 traverses the lower end of the fertile Hagerstown Valley and passes through a noted battle area of the Civil War. Limestone rock is everywhere; limestone fences surround the farms and limestone springhouses, barns, garages, houses, and bridges are seen constantly.

In BOONSBORO, 0 *m.*, State 34 branches southwest from US 40 (*see Tour 2c*).

CRYSTAL GROTTOES (*Admission* 50¢) are L. at 1.4 *m*.

War scars have remained in KEEDYSVILLE, 2.8 *m.* (350 alt.,393 pop.), since the days when Confederate and Union troops surged through it and across Little Antietam. The settlement was called Centerville until residents requested a new name because of confusion with the Queen Annes county seat on the Eastern Shore. On the petition were so many Keedy signatures that Keedysville was decided upon. The Church of the United Brethren, an offshoot of the Reformed Church in Frederick, was established here in 1770 by George Adam Geeting. A native of Keedysville, Geeting was converted by Philip William Otterbein (*see Baltimore*) and later became a bishop of the church.

State 34 crosses Antietam Creek, 5 *m.*, on a concrete bridge.

At 5.6 *m.* is the junction with Richardson Avenue.

Right on this asphalt-paved road 0.8 *m.* to an observation tower overlooking AN-TIETAM BATTLEFIELD, on which the most sanguinary one-day fight in the history of the United States took place September 17, 1862. More than 23,000 Confederate and Union soldiers were killed or wounded. Along Bloody Lane, then known as Sunken Road, dead and wounded lay piled two to five deep. The battlefield is now a National park but farmers cultivate the land and cattle graze almost to the base of the monuments, markers, and plaques that tell of attacks, ambushes, assaults, counter-assaults, and defeat.

At 5.7 *m.* on State 34 is the junction with a paved road.

Left here 1.1 *m.* to BURNSIDE BRIDGE, in much the same condition today as when it formed a key to the Confederate right flank. Burnside and his troops effected a crossing only after several assaults were repulsed by the 2nd and 20th Georgia Regiments.

The NATIONAL PARK SERVICE OFFICE (L), 6 *m.*, containing a museum and library is at the entrance to the NATIONAL CEMETERY. In the cemetery is a monument erected to honor the Civil War dead of both Confederate and Union armies.

At 6.4 *m.* is the junction with State 65, now the main route (R), which continues north from here.

Straight ahead 0.1 *m.* on State 34 to the THERESA KRETZER HOME (L); she is supposed to have emulated Barbara Fritchie (*see Frederick*).

During the Battle of Antietam, SHARPSBURG, 0.2 *m.* (425 alt.,818 pop.), was the scene of so many important events that the engagement was called the Battle of Sharpsburg by Southerners. Several of the stone and log houses built when Joseph Chapline founded the town in 1763 are still standing. The town was named in honor of Governor Horatio Sharpe and soon became a trading center for farmers in the fertile valley, a position it still retains.

Left from Sharpsburg 3.2 *m.* on the Harpers Ferry Road to ANTIETAM (350 alt., 150 pop.). During the Revolution many cannon balls and cannon were cast in the Antietam Iron Works, which operated here from 1765 to 1880 but are now in ruins. In 1785 James Rumsey built some of the machinery here for what is considered by many to have been the first steam-propelled boat successfully to navigate upstream.

On State 34 at 0.9 *m.* is the marked site of LEE'S HEADQUARTERS (R) during his army's occupation of Sharpsburg. Rows of maples line the road for more than a mile, intertwining overhead to make a beautiful arch.

MT.AIRY (L), 1.5 *m.*, a plain brick mansion erected in 1800, was visited by President Lincoln two weeks after the Battle of Antietam when wounded were being cared for in it.

FERRY HILL (R), 3.3 *m.*, commanding a view of the Potomac where a ferry once crossed, is a substantial brick house built by Colonel John Blackford in 1813. General Robert E. Lee's son was brought here after being wounded at Antietam. State 34 crosses the West Virginia Line, 3.7 *m.*, at the far end of the bridge over the Potomac River to Shepherdstown,W.Va.

At 7.3 *m.* on State 65 a lane leads (R) to an observation tower and to Bloody Lane (*see above*).

An annual tilting tournament is held (*3rd Sat. in Aug.*) in TILGHMAN-TON, 11.8 *m.*, a crossroads settlement named for Colonel Frisby Tilghman, who settled here late in the eighteenth century on the 10,000-acre estate, Rockland.

ROCKLAND (R), 12.6 *m.*, is a rambling 24-room brick mansion erected in 1808 by Colonel Frisby Tilghman. In the rear wing several rooms are said to have been used since the Civil War. The violent deaths of several slaves quartered in them gave rise to a legend that this part of the house is haunted.

At LAPPANS (Jones' Crossroads), 13.2 *m.*, is the junction with State 68 (*see Tour 2c.*)

At 14.2 *m.* is a junction with a dirt road.

Right on this to ROXBURY, 1 *m.* (495 alt.,20 pop.), where the MARYLAND STATE PENAL FARM has introduced the honor system in penology. Prisoners till the soil, attend the dairy stock, and do household duties under the guidance of unarmed guards.

Most of the building construction was done by prisoners in 1929. The prisoners are not committed directly but are selected for good behavior from the penitentiary in Baltimore and the House of Correction at Jessups.

At 15.9 *m.* is the junction with macadamized St. James Road.

Left on this to the six buildings housing St. James School, 1.7 *m.*, a Protestant Episcopal preparatory school opened in 1842. It was first housed in Fountain Rock, the home built here in 1792 by General Samuel Ringgold on his 17,000-acre estate. Henry Clay and Presidents Madison and Monroe were among the noted guests at Fountain Rock.

HAGERSTOWN, 20.1 *m.* (552 alt.,30,861 pop.) (*see Hagerstown*), is on US 40 (*see Tour 2*).

Tour 2E

Cumberland—Oldtown—(Paw Paw,W.Va.); State 51.

Cumberland to West Virginia Line, 26 *m.*
Concrete-paved roadbed, two lanes wide.
Western Maryland R.R. roughly parallels route.

For most of its length State 51 parallels the meandering Potomac River through a narrow valley with steep, wooded sides. The country is sparsely settled and lightly cultivated, but rich in anecdotes of frontier days and the Civil War.

State 51 branches southeast from its junction with US 40 (*see Tour 2*) in CUMBERLAND, 0 *m.* (626 alt.,37,747 pop.) (*see Cumberland*).

Near the highway at 3 *m.* is the marked site (L) at which in October 1755 Mrs. Jane Frazier was captured by Indians.

A detailed narrative preserved by her descendants, and said to have been written by Jane Frazier herself, tells that while on a buying trip to Will's Creek—later Cumberland—with Bradley, the hired man, she was seized by savages. Being pregnant, she was permitted to ride her own horse all the way to their village on the Miami where she was adopted into the tribe and treated as an Indian squaw; and when her son was born, the tribe raided a settlement to obtain a proper layette for the white child. The child died, however, and was buried in these clothes in a bark coffin. Nearly a year later, while the warriors were off raiding, she escaped with two white men who had managed to obtain some provisions and a rifle. They managed well until 'the men shot a turkey and being so very hungry they foundered themselves and next morning neither one of them was able to travel.' Mrs. Frazier went on alone, living on bark and herbs.

After traveling more than 300 miles she finally reached friends in Old-town (*see below*) who told her that her husband, believing her dead, had remarried. Nevertheless, 'the next morning they had about fifty men, women and children and a couple of flags . . . and having dressed me in good style, placed me on the horse and away we went as a surprise party, blowing horns, men and women singing and dogs barking . . . Nearing the house my husband came out very frightened at the parade . . . then coming near he saw me and grabbed me off the horse shouting with all his power, "The lost is found, the dead alive," and so would not let me go for some time fearing it was all an apparition. We went into the house and I met his second wife. She seemed a very nice woman but he told her he could not give me up again, that as I was living their marriage had been illegal, but he would still support her as he had promised . . . and she being a woman of good sense took it all in good part, wishing me luck and said she would come some time and hear me tell all about my captivity.'

The FORT CUMBERLAND GOLF CLUB (L), 5 *m.*, has an 18-hole course (50¢ *one round or* 75¢ *entire day*).

State 51 passes under the tracks of the Western Maryland R.R. at 5.8 *m.* and skirts the jutting ends of Nicholas and Collier Mountains. Below (R) is the weed-choked bed of the Chesapeake and Ohio Canal. The gates of an old canal lock, 6.8 *m.*, hidden in bushes and undergrowth, are rotting but the heavy masonry walls are solid.

The road passes again under the railroad and crosses Walnut Ridge, a succession of low, wooded hills. A few log houses and barns, whitewashed and isolated, stand near the road in the shallow valleys.

OLDTOWN (R), 15.5 *m.* (564 alt.,200 pop.), stretches along a single street squeezed between the railroad and the canal.

Before white men settled America members of widely separated Indian tribes transacted business here at a camping ground where a branch of the Warriors' Path forded the Potomac. This path, Athiamiowee (Path of the Armed Ones), started in the Iroquois country in what is now New York State, and was a main artery between North and South.

In 1692 when a band of Shawnees led by Martin Chartier crossed Maryland on their way from the Illinois to the Susquehanna, some must have remained at this camp ground, for a Shawnee village of some size existed here in the last decade of the seventeenth century. About 1711 Opessa, a Shawnee chief, returned here from the Susquehanna and this village became known as King Opessa's Town. The Shawnees abandoned their settlement shortly thereafter and in 1741 the first white settler, Colonel Thomas Cresap (*see below*), arrived. He laid out the town that has alternately flourished and declined as a transportation point. When the westbound pioneers were traveling this way in numbers Oldtown pros-pered, but when the Cumberland Road was opened ten miles to the north it declined. It revived when the canal was dug and the stream of traffic paused for the Oldtown lock, but languished when paralleling railroads hurt the business of the water route and the canal was abandoned. In the earliest days of the Civil War the headquarters of the Second Regiment, Potomac Home Guard, was established here. Three men of Company B, wounded in a skirmish with the Confederates on a march to Springfield, Virginia, are believed to have been the first Marylanders to shed blood for the Union.

In the center of the town stands the MICHAEL CRESAP HOUSE (R), a worn stone building with stucco sloughing from its face. Its gable wall rises from the falling diagonal of the ground to a squat brick chimney, an unbroken cliff of masonry. A spindly porch is perched over the high basement and the front windows are of modern glass; but the original woodwork remains in the low ceiled rooms. The house was built by Michael Cresap about 1765; a brick addition dates from about 1780.

Except for a few years when he went to Baltimore for an education, Michael Cresap (1742-75), youngest of Thomas Cresap's sons, spent his entire life trading, clearing the wilderness, and fighting Indians. Though Thomas Jefferson's charge that Cresap was infamous for his many Indian murders drew fire from Luther Martin, Cresap's son-in-law, and has since been proved unjust, Michael Cresap was so prominent in the Indian fighting in Ohio in 1774 that the campaigns were spoken of as 'Cresap's War.'

At the beginning of the Revolution, when he was appointed captain of a Maryland company of rifles, men from all along the frontier came to serve under him; he and his band, some of them painted Indian style, attracted considerable attention on their way to Boston. But failing health forced Captain Cresap to resign his command and start for home. He died in New York City and is buried in Trinity Churchyard.

1. Left from the Cresap House in Oldtown on a dirt road crossing the canal to the site of CRESAP'S FORT (L), 0.5 m., in a field overlooking the river. Only the ruins of a stone chimney remain of the fortified dwelling and trading post built in the 1740's by Thomas Cresap. In March 1748 George Washington, sixteen-year-old surveyor in the employ of Lord Fairfax, forded the river. He intended to spend only one night at Cresap's but, according to his journal, floods delayed him and he had to spend four more. Thus began for America's most famous overnight guest a lifetime of visiting in Maryland.

Thomas Cresap (c.1702-c.1800) arrived in Maryland from Yorkshire around 1717. In 1729 when he took up land under Maryland patent, in what is now York County, Pennsylvania, a border dispute that had existed for 50 years became a bloody conflict. With arrogance and an aggressive faith in Lord Baltimore's claims, Cresap defied the Pennsylvanians. In 1736 they captured him by burning him out of his house, but even then their troubles were not over. They had on their hands a youth so muscular that even when shackled he tossed his captors around with ease. Philadelphia turned out to see the prisoner. When a jeerer, safe in the crowd, asked Cresap how he liked the town he replied that he found it the finest city in Maryland. The Pennsylvanians soon wished they had not captured the 'Maryland Monster' and he got his revenge by refusing freedom for nearly a year. He was finally released.

After he settled his family at King Opessa's abandoned town, Cresap became one of the most prominent figures on the western frontier. He cleared land, ran a trading post, and made friends with the right Indians. With the aid of his sons he removed the troublesome ones and in general ran the Maryland wilderness to his own and the province's profit. Every traveler to the West stopped here, since his dwelling was almost the only one in a wide area. He ladled out food with such a generous hand that the Indians named him 'Big Spoon.' He was a stockholder in the Ohio Company in 1749. A year later, with the help of Nemacolin, an Indian who was his friend, he cleared a trail through the wilderness from Will's Creek to what is now Brownsville, Pennsylvania, on the Monongahela. The French, watching the advance of the English with concern, ordered Cresap to abandon his outpost, which they considered to be on their territory. Instead of obeying, he involved himself in events that led up to the French and Indian War. During Braddock's campaign he acted as a commissary and in May 1755 the troops camped at this place. General Braddock probably lodged at Cresap's house and one of his officers wrote of the place, 'there lives Colonel Cressop, a Rattlesnake Colonel, and a d———d Rascal; calls himself a Frontiersman . . .'

With Braddock's defeat Cresap's Fort became a refuge for the scattered settlers, but eventually the Indians and the French forced him out and with his family he retreated to a place near the site of Williamsport. Here he stood out against the Indians when the rest of the whites had fled. In 1767 he returned to Oldtown and with his son Michael divided the site into building lots, which they advertised in the *Maryland Gazette*. Legends have it that he took a trip to England when he was seventy, remarried when eighty, visited Nova Scotia when a hundred and died at the age of one hundred and six.

Major Andrew Ellicott—who had achieved fame as a Revolutionary soldier before he became a surveyor (*see Tour 2b*)—after spending an evening with the 'Celebrated Col. Cressap,' wrote: 'Now more than 100 Years Old he lost his Eye sight about 18 months ago; but his other faculties are yet unimpaired his sense Strong and Manly and his Ideas flow with ease. . . .'

2. Right from Oldtown 1 *m*. on a dirt road to the OLD POTOMAC FORD, now crossed on a concrete toll bridge (*25¢ one way, 35¢ round trip*). In August 1864 McCausland's and Johnson's cavalry brigades returning to Virginia after the raid on Chambersburg were closely followed by Federal cavalry under General Averill. The advance under Major Harry Gilmor and his Maryland battalion had run into an ambuscade in a heavy fog at dawn and had been forced to retire. General Johnson's troopers came up and attempted a dash across the canal bridge in the lifting mists, but were repulsed by heavy fire from the wooded ridge between Oldtown and the river. Three of McCausland's regiments, having crossed the canal farther up, now appeared and drove the Federals across the Potomac. Here they crowded into the cars of an armored train on the Baltimore and Ohio tracks directly in line with the ford. Gilmor charged across the stream and drew up his squadron, knee deep in water, under the west Virginia bank, which they were unable to mount. A battery was brought across the canal to shell the train. Even though the gunner, George McElwee, was under heavy fire, he sighted coolly and struck the locomotive with his first shot. The boiler exploded and the Federals stampeded. After the third or fourth shot entered the porthole of the armored car and dismounted its gun, the Confederates crossed the river and demanded and received the surrender of the Federals in a blockhouse beyond the disabled train. This opened the path back to Virginia.

State 51 skirts the southern end of GREEN RIDGE STATE FOREST (*see Tour 2d*) between 21.1 *m*. and 25 *m*. Several dirt roads (L) branch off into the reservation.

At 24.5 *m*. is the junction with a dirt road.

Left on this road 1 *m*. to the Chesapeake and Ohio CANAL TUNNEL, which pierces the slopes of Anthony Ridge and cuts six river miles from the old waterway.

State 51 crosses the WEST VIRGINIA LINE, 26 *m*., on the Potomac River Bridge into Paw Paw, W. Va.

Tour 3

Elkton — Chestertown — Wye Mills — Easton — Salisbury — Ocean City;
152.8 *m.*, US 213.

Concrete or asphalt-paved roadbed.
Branches of the Pennsylvania R.R. serve the region.
All types of accommodations in larger towns; limited elsewhere.

Along this route, which traverses all but the southern tip of Maryland's Eastern Shore, agriculture and the sea-food industry are the chief source of income, though lumbering is important, especially toward the south. A series of short navigable rivers and bays indent the whole Eastern Shore, so that no farm or hamlet is more than a few miles from a landing. The waterways were the main arteries of travel and transportation from the earliest days of settlement down to the advent of railroads in the middle nineteenth century; highways have now largely superseded both. Negroes, forming about one-third of the population, do most of the manual labor ashore and on the fishing boats.

Mild climate, easily-worked soil, and abundance and variety of fish have created a pattern of living that has persisted with little change for three centuries despite nearness of the industrial North and the entrance of modern devices of many kinds. Tradition governs almost everything: methods of farming and fishing, styles of architecture, cooking, and relations between whites and Negroes. Allegiance to the Democratic Party is hereditary and the political warfare is carried on between the local factions. Life on the Eastern Shore is peaceful, self-assured, unselfconscious, concerned over local interests alone; and Eastern Shoremen, loving it, see no reason for a change.

Section a. ELKTON to WYE MILLS; 60.7 m.

Between Elkton and Wye Mills is a generally flat country, relieved in the northern part by the low Cecil County hills. Most of the land is under cultivation and towns are small, functioning chiefly as county seats and centers of rural trade.

US 213 branches south from Main St. on Bridge St. in ELKTON, 0 *m.* (29 alt., 3,331 pop.), which is at the junction with US 40 (*see Tour 2a*).

HOLLY HALL (L), 0.3 *m.*, a two-and-a-half-story brick mansion with hip roof, was built before 1820 by Major James Sewall, later a general, who commanded a battalion at Fort Defiance, a mile below Elkton, when the British Admiral Cockburn attacked Elk River points in 1813. The house, so-called because of a large grove of holly trees that once surrounded it, is now owned by the Society of the Divine Saviour of the Roman Catholic Church. Across the highway is the Sewall family vault.

At 1.1 *m.* is the junction with a dirt road.

Right on this road 1.8 *m.* to the old FRENCHTOWN TAVERN, a two-and-a-half-story brick dwelling by Elk River. This is the only remnant of Frenchtown, which before 1837 was a busy port and point of relay on the main line of travel between Philadelphia and Baltimore. Because a land trip of 16.5 miles between Frenchtown and New Castle, Delaware considerably shortened the water journey between the North and South, a freight line established in 1806–07 used this port as did the Union Line of passenger and freight stagecoaches, organized in 1818.

When the town was bombarded by the British on April 29, 1813, the wharf, fishery, and warehouses—valued at $30,000—were plundered and burned, together with five vessels in the harbor. Frenchtown defenders were driven from the redoubt at the landing place after twice repulsing the enemy. But Frenchtown rallied quickly; the *Chesapeake*, first steamboat on Chesapeake Bay, docked here on her maiden voyage from Baltimore, June 21, 1813.

In 1827 the New Castle and Frenchtown Turnpike and Railroad Company was chartered in Maryland (before any other passenger railroad had started operating in the United States) and a similar charter was granted by Delaware in 1829. The line was constructed with stone sleepers and iron-faced wooden rails in 1831, but the first locomotive did not operate satisfactorily, and on July 4, 1831, horses pulled the cars at the official opening. It was not until September 10, 1832, that a locomotive, the *Delaware*, with two cars attached, made the initial service trip.

Travel grew heavy, and the passengers landing here on their journeys included Andrew Jackson, Daniel Webster, Henry Clay, Davy Crockett, and Stonewall Jackson. But after the railroad route by way of Elkton was completed around the head of the bay in 1837, this tiny land link in water transportation could not long survive; the line was dismantled in 1858.

At 3 *m.* on US 213 is the junction with a dirt road.

Left on this road to BRANTWOOD (R), 0.2 *m.* The main section of this brick dwelling was built in 1839, the remainder much earlier. An ingenious arrangement conducted the smoke of the fireplaces to a third floor room, which was used as a smokehouse. At the entrance to Brantwood two spiked cannon are partly buried, one with muzzle down, the other with breech down. They are believed to have come from the Frenchtown redoubt demolished by the British in 1813.

CHESAPEAKE CITY, 5.9 *m.* (17 alt.,1,016 pop.), on Back Creek, is the Maryland terminus of the Chesapeake and Delaware Canal, first opened for navigation in 1829. The canal, whose existence was predicted as early as 1661 by Augustine Herman (*see below*), was a lock canal for nearly a century; now as a sea-level route, toll free, 27 feet deep and 14 miles long, it shortens the route between Baltimore and Philadelphia by 286 miles. All but the largest liners and battleships can be accommodated, so the canal is an important link in the seacoast defense.

The original cost of the canal was $2,200,000; it was purchased by the Federal Government in 1919 for $2,500,000 and lowered to sea level in 1927 at a cost of more than $10,000,000; many more millions have been expended in improvements until it has become a 'twenty-five million dollar ditch' between the two great bays. Chesapeake City came into existence with the canal and its fortunes have fluctuated with it. When the lock system was changed to the sea-level course, necessitating removal of the bridge from the main street to the western edge of the town, a new main street was established. The C.& D. Canal is an important link in the nation's inland waterway from Maine to Florida, hundreds of pleasure craft using it for the cruise both north and south. The town's chief business besides that connected with the canal is the servicing and provisioning of the many small craft that cruise on Chesapeake Bay.

On the Government reservation (L) in the stone PUMPHOUSE (1837) is a waterwheel 40 feet in diameter that formerly ran day and night lifting water into the canal to replace water lost every time a vessel passed through the lock.

At 6.3 *m.* is the junction with an asphalt-paved road.

Left on this road to ST.AUGUSTINE, 3 *m.* (70 pop.), and the small frame ST.AUGUSTINE PROTESTANT EPISCOPAL CHURCH of Bohemia Manor, erected about 1838 on the site of the 'Mannour Chapple' of 1692. In the cemetery is the grave of Colonel Edward Oldham, who served in the Continental Army under General Greene. A walled grave contains the remains of a dissolute young man who, when dying in 1861, requested that his coffin lid be left unscrewed, no dirt be thrown over the coffin, and a brick wall be set up about the grave with one brick left out, in order that he might escape if the Devil came after him. Bricks still disappear, though mortared into the space from time to time by sextons of the church.

A bulb-shaped dome and cross surmount the GREEK CATHOLIC CHURCH (R), 6.9 *m.*, serving a small colony of Ukrainians who settled here about 1900 and converted a wilderness of swamp and scrub into rich farm land. The original group of 40 immigrants has increased to 300 persons, with close-knit family life and Old World customs. Their Julian-calendar Christmas, January 7, is celebrated with a three-day festival including European dances.

At 7.2 *m.* is the junction with a dirt road.

Right on this road to COURT HOUSE POINT, 3 *m.*, site of the second courthouse of Cecil County. As a matter of convenience the first courthouse, at Jamestown on the Sassafras, was superseded in 1717 by a building here, in which court was held until 1781. Ephraim Augustine Herman, the builder, received 38,000 pounds of tobacco for his services. Tradition has it that bricks from this structure were used in building its successor at Elkton. The ferry from Elk Ferry on Oldfield Point to Court House Point became one of the most important in the county. General Howe's invading army landed at Elk Ferry on August 25, 1777, and on August 28 Howe marched with part of his army to Head of Elk. Generals Knyphausen and Agnew crossed to Court House Point on August 30; their men removed some court records but left the building intact. There is a local story that 19 deserting Hessians were captured and shot at Welsh Point, across the mouth of Back Creek from Court House Point, and buried in a common grave; a depression at the spot, said to be the grave, is called 'The Hessians' Hole.'

The hamlet of CAYOTS, 9.6 *m.*, marks the northern edge of the La-badie Tract. This fertile farmland formerly belonged to a colony founded by the followers of Jean de Labadie, religious mystic of the seventeenth century who advocated community of property. In 1679 after several forced migrations in Europe, the Labadists sent Jaspar Dankers and Peter Sluyter, two of their leaders, to New Netherlands in search of land. They met and converted Ephraim Herman, son of Augustine Herman; then visited Bohemia Manor, and were granted a tract of more than 3,000 acres. The final deed to Dankers, Sluyter, and Peter Bayard was dated August 11, 1684. Colonists came from Holland and a few from New Amsterdam (New

York), but the community never exceeded 100. Men and women dined at separate tables. Suggestion was made as early as 1688 for division of the property; many colonists left and Sluyter became sole proprietor by 1698. When he died in 1722, a wealthy man, the colony was almost forgotten.

Right from Cayots on an asphalt-paved road to BENTON, 1.5 *m.*, an estate of R.R.M.Carpenter, Dupont executive and breeder of Chesapeake Bay retrievers. The Chesapeake Field Trials (*3 days, end of March*) held here bring in the best water dogs in North America.

At 2.7 *m.* is the junction with a dirt road; R. on this road 0.6 *m.* to the fishing village of PORT HERMAN (*public beach*) (135 pop.), with adjoining HOLLYWOOD BEACH, a popular summer resort. The tract on which the village stands was once leased (1713) in return for the payment of one ear of Indian corn, if demanded in November, provided the lessee had 'two hunting hounds that were to be a part of the cry of hounds that the lord of the manor then kept.'

On the asphalt-paved road at 4 *m.* is TOWN POINT where Augustine Herman planned in 1661 to erect a town to be called Ceciltown in honor of Cecil Calvert. The town was never built here.

On BOHEMIA MANOR (R), 11 *m.*, along Bohemia River, is a large brick house of the modern Georgian Colonial type erected by Thomas F. Bayard, U.S. Senator from Delaware (1922–29), on part of the far greater Bohemia Manor of his ancestor Augustine Herman. Both the manor and river are named for Herman's birthplace. Close by is the site of his house. His grave is also here, marked with the original stone which is broken and has been set in marble to preserve it.

Augustine Herman first came to Maryland in 1659 when, with Resolved Waldron, he served as envoy from the Dutch at New Amsterdam (New York) to St.Marys. Herman was so charmed by this region that he applied to the Calverts for a large tract, offering in return an 'exact mapp' of the entire province. The Calverts accepted and Herman spent ten years surveying and defining shore lines and other boundaries for his excellent map of Maryland and Virginia. Many place names he added have survived to this day.

On June 19, 1662, Herman was granted 4,000 acres here; his chosen site was regranted as a tract of 6,000 acres, Bohemia Manor, on May 11, 1676. St.Augustine's Manor, contiguous to Bohemia Manor, was a tract of uncertain acreage in Delaware that was made a manor in 1684, when granted to Herman's son and heir Ephraim. Augustine Herman died in 1686, entailing Bohemia Manor and other lands forever (after the decease of his elder son) on the eldest male of his second son's descendants. In order to hold land, Herman was decreed a denizen of Maryland in 1660; his naturalization took place in 1666.

Herman's vast holdings—his property exceeded 15,000 acres—coupled with his shrewdness and keen grasp of the conflicting claims of Baltimore and Penn (*see History*) made him the most important man of his day on the Eastern Shore. In true manorial style, he kept open house—roaring hearthfires and an abundance of meat and drink greeted the visitor. Herman maintained a deer park, kept a coach-and-four, and owned many slaves.

In 1661 Herman proposed construction of a canal connecting the

Chesapeake and Delaware bays and agreed to clear half of a cartroad joining Bohemia Manor with New Castle, Delaware.

A great-grandson of Augustine Herman, who in time owned Bohemia Manor, was Richard Bassett (1745–1815); he was a Delaware signer of the Constitution and served as a governor of Delaware, as well as U.S. Circuit Court Justice. His daughter Ann married James A. Bayard (1767–1815), Delaware statesman and signer of the Treaty of Ghent at the end of the War of 1812. Both Bassett and Bayard were buried here but later were re-interred in Wilmington, Delaware. When the manor vault was opened no traces were found of the coffins or bones of Herman or his wife.

The highway crosses Bohemia River, 11.6 m., a broad and lovely estuary.

At 12.1 m. is a junction with a dirt road.

Right on this road to HACK'S POINT BEACH, 0.2 m., where a group of summer cottages extends along the south shore of the Bohemia River. This resort's name comes from the Hack family, which settled in this section in the seventeenth century. Sepherin (sometimes Stephen) Hack received his first patent in 1658; the property next passed to Dr. George Hack, who was naturalized the same year as Augustine Herman.

On the dirt road is CHERRY GROVE, 4.7 m., the ancestral home of the Norman family of Veasey. The house was built in 1670 in two parts, one with clapboarded frame and one of logs. Thomas Ward Veasey, Governor of Maryland (1836–38), is buried in the adjoining Veasey burial plot.

LITTLE BOHEMIA, formerly Milligan Hall (L), 13 m., built 1743–45, is almost concealed by its grove of trees. The tract, first granted to Hugh McGregory (1689), was bought by John Baldwin (1751) and deeded by him to his daughter Catherine and her husband George Milligan. The detail of the rectangular, five-bay painted brick house conforms to the early Georgian tradition. On the front is a small hip-roofed portico extending across a slightly projecting central pavilion. Above the portico a group of three windows, faintly suggesting a Palladian motif in their arrangement, breaks through the lower part of the triangular eave pediment. In the center of the pediment is a bull's-eye window, with four key blocks. The façade has a wide stringcourse and corner pilasters of brick. Double key blocks cap the windows of the first story and of the central pavilion. Within is a beautiful stairway of unusual lattice design; some rooms are decorated with plaster ornaments in French motifs.

BENTON FARM (L), 13.6 m., belonging to R. R. M. Carpenter (*see above*), has gently-rolling fields that from November to early April are swarming with wild Canada geese in one of the greatest concentrations of the Atlantic flyway. Brown carpets of the large birds feed on young wheat and eat wagonloads of cob corn spread for them. Often flocks circle in to feed or leave at night to sleep on the bay; their honking is audible for miles. A few geese are shot by the owner and his guests. Until recently a wire-enclosed trap for catching and banding geese was operated here by the U.S. Biological Survey, which was making a migration study.

ANCHORAGE MANOR HOUSE (R), 14.8 m., a brick and frame farmhouse, was built about 1835 by Commodore Jacob Jones (1768–1850), hero of the naval battle between the *Wasp* and the *Frolic*. Born in Smyrna, Delaware,

Jones entered the Navy in 1799 and at the opening of the War of 1812 was in command of the sloop-of-war *Wasp*. On October 13, 1812, he attacked the British brig *Frolic* and captured her as a prize. Although both vessels were taken the same day by the British 74-gun *Poictiers*, Jones's exploit aroused great enthusiasm among Americans. Subsequently he was made a commodore. He became a resident of Maryland when he married Ruth Lusby of Cecil County. At his death his body was buried in St.Stephen's Cemetery near Cecilton, but in 1850 it was removed to Wilmington.

In CECILTON, 16.2 *m.* (458 pop.), a village with several houses of the Revolutionary period, is an asphalt-paved crossroad.

1. Left on this road to WARWICK, 5.3 *m.* (200 pop.), on Middle Neck, a point of land between two forks of the Bohemia River. Here is the BIRTHPLACE OF JAMES RUMSEY, inventor of an early steam marine engine. On the Potomac in 1787, two decades before Robert Fulton operated his *Clermont* on the Hudson, Rumsey ran a boat propelled by a stream of water forced from its stern by a steam pump (*see Tour 2B*).

Left from Warwick 2.1 *m.* on an asphalt-paved road to ST.FRANCIS XAVIER (OLD BOHEMIA) CHURCH, a brick Roman Catholic shrine built in 1912. The congregation was organized in 1704 when the Jesuit, Thomas Mansell, established a Roman Catholic mission on the Eastern Shore. Bohemia Academy (1745) on this site was the alma mater of John Carroll, first American Catholic archbishop, and of Charles Carroll of Carrollton, signer of the Declaration of Independence. A military field mass is held at this church (*Sundays in June*).

2. Right from Cecilton on the paved crossroad to ST.STEPHEN'S PROTESTANT EPIS-COPAL CHURCH, 5.6 *m.*, whose parish, one of the 30 established in Maryland in 1692, was first called North Sassafras. St.Stephen's has been rebuilt several times; the present edifice was completed in 1873.

The State road ends at WHITE CRYSTAL BEACH, 7 *m.*, a popular bathing resort by Elk River.

Greenfields or GREENFIELD CASTLE (L), 17.1 *m.*, is a brick house with a large central square chimney, a hip roof and Georgian façades. It is on a tract patented by Colonel John Ward about 1664. The Ward burying ground near by contains graves of the Lusbys and Pascaults, later owners.

FREDERICKTOWN, 19 *m.* (95 pop.), on the north bank of the Sassafras (*pronounced Sasfres*) River, which divides Cecil and Kent Counties, builds boats and does boat repairing; many yachts are seen at moorings here. Georgetown and Fredericktown, directly opposite on the south bank, were named for the British prince, who became George III, and for his brother.

At the northern end of the bridge over the Sassafras is a stone monument, commemorating the exploration of this region (1607–09) by Captain John Smith.

GEORGETOWN, 19.5 *m.* (50 pop.), once a busy port of entry, was a base for supplies during the Revolution and a popular stop on the colonial post route between Annapolis (via Rock Hall) and Philadelphia. During the War of 1812 both villages were almost totally destroyed by a landing party from Admiral Cockburn's fleet; all but two houses in Georgetown were burned to the ground. The KITTY KNIGHT HOUSE, a brick dwelling (R) at the bridge end, is said to have been saved by young Kitty Knight, who repeatedly beat out the fires with a broom as soon as the soldiers set them; finally an admiring officer ordered the house spared. The old house has floors at different levels, stairways in odd places, and numerous fire-places and cupboards. The other house that survived is now part of the Kitty Knight house.

In GALENA, 21 m. (265 pop.), formerly Down's Crossroads, is the SITE OF WILLIAM DOWN'S TAVERN, famed in the heyday of colonial post travel. The tavern burned in 1893 after 130 years of business.

Here is the junction with State 313 (see Tour 4).

SHREWSBURY CHURCH (R), 26.1 m., is one of the oldest centers of worship in Kent County; the present brick building of 1832 occupies the site of the edifice erected in the last years of the seventeenth century. In the churchyard is the GRAVE OF GENERAL JOHN CADWALADER, a staunch friend of George Washington. When the 'Conway Cabal' was brewing against Washington, Cadwalader challenged the leader, General Thomas Conway, to a duel and wounded him in the mouth. It is said that when Cadwalader saw Conway lying on the ground with the blood gushing from his mouth, he exclaimed: 'I have stopped the damned rascal's lying tongue at any rate.' Conway survived and penned an abject apology to Washington. The eulogy on Cadwalader's tombstone was written by Thomas Paine, long a bitter political opponent.

Bordering the highway are the lawns of BLAY'S RANGE (L), 26.2 m., which has a large brick house with the date 1727 in glazed header bricks in the south gable end. The hand-carved woodwork in this mansion is notable. The land was granted to Colonel Edward Blay in 1676.

In KENNEDYVILLE, 28.5 m. (160 pop.), is the junction with a macadam and gravel road.

Right on this road 2.1 m. to SUFFOLK, a two-and-a-half-story brick house with a front wall laid in Flemish bond. It is built on part of a tract of the same name, granted to James Staveley in 1681, and has long been the home of the descendants of Matthew Howard, who came from Virginia in 1660. One of them, B.Howard Haman, was the author of the law under which the oyster beds of Chesapeake Bay and streams running into it were surveyed and plotted for the first time. At 3.2 m. (L) is another of the brick houses built by the Howard family.

JANVIER HOUSE (R), 3.8 m., is by Turner's Creek; the story-and-a-half section built of logs in the late 1600's, with central chimney and fireplaces back-to-back, was enlarged by the larger brick section about 1800. The stairway is noteworthy.

KNOCK'S FOLLY (R), 4 m., a story-and-a-half brick dwelling with hipped dormers and fine paneling, was erected about 1738.

BENNET'S DELIGHT (L), 4 m., once the home of General Cadwalader (see above), is similar in design to Knock's Folly but has an unusual recessed chimney.

At 29.9 m. is the junction (R) with a concrete road (see Tour 3A).

The long, narrow, whitewashed THOMAS PERKINS HOUSE (R), 30.6 m., was built in 1720 by Thomas Perkins, whose son Colonel Isaac Perkins was known as 'The Flaming Patriot.' Colonel Perkins with Robert Morris supplied Washington's starving soldiers at Valley Forge with flour ground at the mill on this farm. In the burial ground is the grave of Thomas Perkins's daughter Mary, whose ghost is said to walk on the anniversary of her death, January 8; many believe that wishes made in good faith at her grave will come true. Perhaps she was the young woman of the legend who, after leaping safely from a window of the house to elope, ran down the lane, fell, and struck her head on a rock, dying instantly. From that time until the stone was removed by a road crew 'bloodstains' showed on the rock in spite of repeated efforts to remove them. Why any one wanted to remove them is not explained by those who tell the tale.

A soil conservation program has been conducted on this farm by the Civilian Conservation Corps, which has terraced hillsides and planted trees.

A mill and the miller's house are all that mark URIEVILLE (L), 30.9 *m.*, where 40 buildings formerly housed the workmen in the grain mills. Its heyday was in the 1870's when a branch railroad was being constructed. On holidays groups of Irish laborers and Negroes boxed and wrestled here; the sport often ended with showers of brickbats from the Irish. When the proprietor of the large general store received a barrel of whisky, he diluted part of it with water and sold full-strength, half-strength, and quarter-strength whisky, at prices that varied accordingly. After the railroad by-passed the village, it soon declined.

At 32.6 *m.* is the junction with a concrete road.

> Right on this road 1 *m.* to the brick BETSY TURNER HOUSE (L) on a tract known as Duncan's Folly. Each gable end has a chimney, and in the kitchen wing is a fireplace of the pyramid type; even the cellar has a fireplace. The old strap hinges extend almost the width of the doors.

ROSE HALL (R), 34.2 *m.*, one of several houses built on the Eastern Shore by the Ringgold family, later belonged to the Biddles. It has a double stringcourse at the second floor level. Its once-noted gardens and lake have disappeared.

CHESTERTOWN, 36.5 *m.* (22 alt.,2,809 pop.), a gracious old place facing the broad and tranquil Chester River, is the seat of Kent County and the very essence of the Eastern Shore with its mellow combination of sights, feelings, tastes, and smells that recall centuries of pleasant living. Old brick houses with second-story porches overlooking the river, a row of one-story offices bearing the faded shingles of generations of lawyers having the same names, and the business and professional men's after-lunch naps are typical of the region.

Chestertown is personified by its well-groomed women of middle age, walking with heads well up, doing the marketing, playing bridge, or discussing their favorite subjects: people and food. Social life and sport are all-important. Lawyers, doctors, and merchants drop work for a week at a time to live in a shack on Eastern Neck Island, shooting ducks and geese by day, playing poker by night. Everyone has a boat of some kind—a little sloop, a speedboat, or a cabin cruiser for fishing or moonlight excursions. Town and county spend three days (*late April or early May*) showing visitors houses and gardens during the tour of the Federated Maryland Garden Clubs. On 'A Day in Old Chestertown' (*2nd Sat. afternoon in May, adm.* $1), 30 or more town and country houses are open to the public. Late in July the Chester River Yacht and Country Club is host to scores of sailing and power boats here for the Chester River Regatta, one of the series held on the bay.

Before 1920 few Kent Countians had much money. There has since been an influx of wealthy Northerners who have bought and restored old plantations. In addition to its legal offices, Chestertown has fertilizer and clothing factories and canneries; a hospital, an armory, and a library are among its institutions.

When in 1696 it was decided to remove the Kent Courthouse from New Yarmouth (see Tour 3A), a site was selected several miles down river from here, but soon abandoned in favor of this site, then called New Town. A courthouse was built in 1698 and streets were laid out in 1706. New Town in 1708 was made a port of entry for Cecil, Kent, and Queen Annes Counties. When the charter was revised in 1780 the present name was adopted. Planters began to come here for horse racing and to attend the drama brought by traveling theatrical groups. In the Reverend Francis Asbury's journal is the notation made in 1786, 'Sunday 9. I preached at Kent Old Chapel . . . in the afternoon and at night in Chestertown. I always have an enlargement in preaching in this very wicked place . . . '

A tea party similar to the Boston variety was staged here on May 13, 1774, when the tea brought into port by the brigantine *Geddes* was thrown overboard after an indignation meeting. A little later Chestertown sent vessels loaded with provisions to the Boston population suffering from the Boston Port Bill.

On September 25, 1910, fire swept the business district, destroying twenty stores and six houses, causing a loss of $90,000.

WASHINGTON COLLEGE, N. end of Washington Ave., on an eminence overlooking the river and town, has a 20-acre campus and 10 major brick structures—William Smith, East, Middle, West, Reid, and Hodson Halls; College Dining Hall, the James W. Cain Gymnasium, the Bunting-Foxwell Library, and the Dunning Science Hall. Washington College is coeducational and nonsectarian, conferring degrees of A.B. and B.S. The number of students is approximately 300.

The college was founded in 1782 by the Reverend William Smith, an Anglican clergyman, and named for the then commander in chief of the Continental forces, who visited the institution two years later and contributed fifty guineas to its endowment. The predecessor of the college—which was intended to be a part of the University of Maryland—was Kent County Free School, established in 1723 although its roots extended beyond 1707. Dr. Smith had taken over direction of Kent County School while serving as a rector in Chestertown. He was one of the very few clergymen of the Established Church to cast his lot with the province when the Revolution—and disestablishment—came. Late in 1780 he had sent out a call to the faithful to meet in Chestertown in an attempt to revive the church; only two other clergymen and 24 laymen responded, but his efforts had more success in the following years.

The first Washington College commencement was held in May 1783 when six graduates delivered their orations in Latin and French. The college gave Washington in absence the honorary degree of doctor of laws in 1789. In October 1933 at the inauguration of Gilbert W. Mead as president of the college, President Franklin D. Roosevelt delivered an address and was awarded a similar degree.

The first building was burned in 1827, and college exercises were conducted in town quarters until the construction of Middle Hall in 1844. Until 1849 the institution suffered like other small colleges from lack of funds. East and West Halls were erected in 1854.

The CIVIL WAR MONUMENT in front of the Kent County Court House was erected in 1917 by Judge James Alfred Pearce to honor the soldiers of Kent who fought for the Blue or the Gray. The inscription for the Federals faces north and for the Confederates south.

EMMANUEL PROTESTANT EPISCOPAL CHURCH, High and Cross Sts., a brick building with Victorian embellishments, was erected in 1768, the people of Chestertown contributing £500. A tablet commemorates the fact that the denominational title—The Protestant Episcopal Church of America, as distinguished from the Church of England—was adopted in this church on November 9, 1780, at a meeting of clergy and laity.

The very old PALMER HOUSE, 532 W.High St., was built of stone brought into port as ship's ballast by the Captain Palmer who erected it, using parts of his own retired sailing vessels for timber. The one-and-a-half-story building has walls two feet thick, hand-carved mantels, random-width flooring, and paneled window frames. A picture of the house is on the silver service presented to the Battleship *Maryland*.

The former WHITE SWAN TAVERN (c.1750), 231–35 E.High St., a two-and-a-half-story brick structure with dormers and wide end chimneys, is now called the Eliason Building.

The WILLIAM BARROLL HOUSE, 108–110 E.High St., now a duplex dwelling, was erected in 1735 by William Barroll V. It is three stories high, of brick laid in Flemish bond, and has wide chimneys at the gable ends. Notable paneling has been retained in remodeling the old structure.

The WICKES HOUSE, 100 E.High St., a three-story brick mansion built before the Revolution, was once a tavern conducted by Samuel Beck. Noteworthy are the cornice in the library, the mantels in the drawing room, and the window and door moldings, all hand-carved.

WIDEHALL, High and Front Sts., a well-preserved three-story brick house now ivy-covered, was built sometime between 1732 and 1762. The doorway is hand-carved and the short pavement from the street was laid more than 150 years ago. Victorian modifications were removed by a recent owner, who added an Ionic portico on the side where the lawns sweep down to the river.

Inside the house has beautifully carved mahogany woodwork and a hanging staircase on one side of the wide side hall, which is really a room in itself. Keystoned arches, doors with dropped silver handles, and old mahogany furniture add to its charm. The detail of the woodwork is noteworthy.

The PERKINS HOUSE, 115 N.Front (Water) St., with a lawn sloping to the Chester River, is built of brick in all-header bond, and occupied by a descendant of David and Daniel Perkins, who were seated in Kent County in the early eighteenth century. There are fireplaces in nearly all its rooms, and the mantel in the living room is hand-carved.

The METEER HOUSE, 110 N.Front (Water) St., built in 1780, as the town home of the Frisby family, is a large brick dwelling with wide chimneys, and large porches of recent origin. It contains a hand-carved mantel and some of the original hardware.

The CHESTERTOWN CUSTOMHOUSE, 101 S.Front (Water) St., a long, three-story brick building painted yellow, was a warehouse erected in 1694 by the Ringgolds, early merchants who built three vaults under the terrace for the storage of valuable goods; one was perhaps used on occasion as a dungeon for slaves. The Ringgolds rented a room here to the port authorities for a custom house. The building is now divided into apartments.

The ABBEY, also called the Ringgold-Pearce House, 100 S.Front (Water) St., recently restored, massive and ivy-covered in the corner of a high-walled garden, has brick walls two feet thick in all-header bond. It was erected in 1735, either by Nathaniel Hynson or by Thomas Ringgold. When the exquisite paneling of the drawing room was taken to the Baltimore Museum, a faithfully executed reproduction was substituted. The house has many details characteristic of the larger Maryland colonial dwellings, and a double stairway in the wide hall with a fireplace before which the king's officers warmed themselves when this was a bachelor's hall for gay bloods on colonial duty.

West from Chestertown on Queen St. and the Quaker Neck Rd. to White House Farm or RADCLIFFE MANOR (R), 0.2 *m.*, a two-and-a-half-story brick house painted red. The burial plot near by contains graves of the Wilmers, who long owned this property. A picture by Charles Willson Peale shows the Reverend Simon Wilmer on horseback, and his wife, 'the beautiful Miss Ann Ringgold,' seated on the porch. The Radcliffe Racetrack, now a short distance north, was once on this tract, which includes part of the site of Chestertown, granted to Dr. Richard Tilghman, early settler.

At 2.1 *m.* is the junction with a graveled road; L. here 0.5 *m.* to PINEY GROVE (L), one of the early houses on Godlington Manor (*see below*). It has an old-fashioned garden and much boxwood.

On the graveled road at 0.7 *m.* is a country lane; L. on this 1 *m.* to GODLINGTON MANOR, a gambrel-roofed clapboarded mansion surrounded by boxwood. It was built for Thomas Godlington on the 1,000-acre tract granted to him in 1659. This building, believed to be the original manor house, has visible post construction; within is a log-linteled fireplace. Close by is the mansion erected by the present owner.

POMONA, 4.3 *m.* (50 pop.), is at the junction with a dirt road (*bad in wet weather*); R. on this 1 *m.* to the two-wing brick THOMAS HILL HOUSE (L), sometimes called Hill-top, built in 1711 by William Thomas, whose father, also named William, received his grant of 1,000 acres before 1686. The house has hand-carved mantels, a huge kitchen fireplace, and wide floor boards; in the cellar is a 10-foot chimney and an old wine closet.

On the dirt road at 2 *m.* is a fork; R. (straight ahead) 0.5 *m.* to AIRY HILL (R), a brick house built about 1701–05, and also owned by the Thomas family. It has outside mahogany window sills, a 10-foot fireplace, and great hand-hewn, smoke-blackened beams supporting the kitchen ceiling.

On the Quaker Neck Road is brick BOND CHAPEL (L), 4.7 *m.* In the woods opposite, a pair of monkeys, fugitives from a gas station, took up residence late in 1938. They were fed from time to time by housewives and throughout the winter warmed themselves during chapel services by sitting on car radiators. A baby monkey, born in the woods, survived the cold weather.

On the Quaker Neck Road at 5.2 *m.* is a side road; R. here 1.5 *m.* to WALNUT POINT, a steep-roofed, two-story whitewashed brick house on the east branch of Langford Bay. It was built by the Trew family late in the eighteenth century. The estate has a shore line of several miles.

At 6 *m.* is the SITE OF QUAKER NECK MEETING HOUSE (L), erected by Friends living in the area between the Cecil Meeting at Lynch (*see Tour 3A*) and the Third Haven Meeting at Easton (*see Tour 3b*).

RELIEF (R), 6.3 *m.*, a two-wing brick house with partition walls of solid brick, was built about 1724 by Thomas Wilkins, a merchant. There is a chimney in each gable end and one in the center, providing fireplaces for every room. REWARD (R), 6.6 *m.*, built in 1698 for Cornelius Comegys, is well preserved.

PROVIDENCE (R), 7 *m.*, a two-and-a-half-story brick house with walls laid in Flemish bond with glazed headers, bears the date 1781. Though its first occupant was Bartus Trew, a Quaker, it contains paneling with fluted pilasters and dog-ears, and a dog-eared fireplace. The property is still owned by a member of the Trew family, which settled in Quaker Neck in 1668.

Well preserved RIPLEY (R), 42 *m.*, a two-and-a-half-story brick dwelling built about 1800, is the second on a 950-acre manor granted to Stephen Tulley by Cecil Calvert in 1673. It has large, high-ceilinged rooms and box window seats.

CHURCH HILL, 43.6 *m.* (232 pop.), a center for rural trade, is named for the venerable ST.LUKE'S PROTESTANT EPISCOPAL CHURCH around which it grew. This brick church was erected in 1731 at a cost of 140,000 pounds of tobacco. The most interesting features of the exterior are the heavy gambrel roof, the glazed headers in the Flemish bond walls, and the arched windows between narrow buttresses along the sides. At the rear is a circular apse also with gambrel roof and arched windows. The entrance is through the base of the front tower in the manner of the English parish church. On both sides of the chancel hang tablets, one of the Lord's Prayer and the other of the Ten Commandments, said to have been the gift of Queen Anne of England. A solid silver chalice and flagon, presented by Major John Hawkins, bear the name of the donor and the respective dates 1716 and 1717. Long dilapidated, St.Luke's was repaired in 1842 and restored completely in 1881 by George Hawkins Williams.

At 44.9 *m.* is the junction with a dirt road.

Right on this road to KENNERSLEY (L), 1.8 *m.*, built in 1704. This three-story brick house has wings on both sides (connected with the main dwelling by bridgeways), 14-foot ceilings, broad mantels, and hand-carved woodwork.

At 45.6 *m.* on US 213 is the junction with a dirt road.

Right on this road, turning sharp left at 3.2 *m.* to READBOURNE (R), 4.4 *m.*, on a knoll overlooking the Chester River, a massive two-and-a-half-story brick dwelling with wings in the rear. It was built in 1734 by Colonel James Hollyday on part of a 2,000-acre tract patented in 1659 by George Read. Sarah Covington Lloyd Hollyday, widow of Edward Lloyd of Wye House, is said to have supervised the building of Readbourne from plans Lord Baltimore had helped her to prepare. The main part of the building is little changed though the paneling has been removed. A beautiful stairway leads from the high ceiled hall to the upper floor, and a great fireplace dominates the living room.

At 5.3 *m.* the dirt road turns L.; R. (straight ahead) to another dirt road at 6.4 *m.*; R. on this 0.2 *m.* to the lane (L) of POPLAR GROVE, home of the Emory family for the past five generations. The low rambling two-and-a-half-story brick house painted yellow is on land granted to Arthur Emory, and was built by his son John in the early 1800's. The big cross-shaped, terraced garden contains enormous old boxwood. The Emory burial ground close by is overgrown with myrtle and trailing vines.

The southern end of BLOOMFIELD (L), 50.9 *m.*, a large dwelling with a red roof and buff stucco walls, was built about 1760 by William Y. Burke. It has high ceilings, a broad hall, and many fireplaces.

CENTERVILLE, 52.9 *m.* (61 alt.,1,291 pop.), county seat of Queen Annes, is well paved and well kept, though the population decreased by almost 500 between 1920 and 1930. In this typical Eastern Shore town, life moves along quietly even during the quarterly court sessions. Many of the stores as well as dwellings have upstairs porches in the front.

Though business consists chiefly of supplying the needs of public officials and farmers, there are tomato and pea canneries, a flour mill, and one weekly newspaper.

The first act to remove the county seat from Queenstown (*see Tour 5*) to this place was passed in 1782, but owing to defects in the law, the courthouse was not completed until 1792; the town was laid out that year. Two fires burned many old buildings, but a few remain.

On Courthouse Square is the brick QUEEN ANNES COUNTY COURTHOUSE, painted cream. Victorian alterations include a handsome iron balcony. The grassy lawn has boxwood bushes and flowers.

ST.PAUL'S PROTESTANT EPISCOPAL CHURCH, South Liberty St., a stuccoed brick structure erected in 1885, is the fourth church of the parish. Bricks and timbers from the third church, which was near Centerville, were used in this building. The chalice and flagon of the church were presented by Queen Anne.

The MOTHER OF SORROWS ROMAN CATHOLIC CHURCH, W. side of Chesterfield Ave. near the town limits, is a stone structure of the Gothic type erected in 1933. The church and the adjacent rectory were the gift of John J. Raskob who has a country estate near by.

The YELLOW BRICK HOUSE, NE. cor. Water St. and Banjo Lane, a small brick residence, was built in the colonial period by Judge Richard Nette Carmichael. Another old brick structure is the PALMER HOUSE, W. side of Commerce St., S. of Water St., now the Blue Lantern Tea House.

The BROWN GARDENS on Wharf Lane are arranged according to the color of the flowers.

Right from US 213 in Centerville on Broadway to the asphalt-paved Corsica Neck Road, 0.6 *m.*; L. here, passing Centerville Landing—from which freight is carried on a branch of the Pennsylvania Railroad—to the junction with a dirt road, 2.5 *m.*; R. 0.8 *m.* on this to OLD FORT POINT, a remnant of the fortifications thrown up by the citizens of Centerville during the War of 1812.

On Corsica Neck Road at 3.1 *m.* overlooking Corsica River is MELFIELD (R), a two-story brick house with a two-story Doric portico that was added many years after the dwelling was erected. The structure was built before the Revolutionary War by James Tilghman, and is clearly but one part of the proposed mansion. On the lawn is a huge white-oak tree with branches spreading 150 feet.

PIONEER POINT, (R) 3.4 *m.*, formerly called Winton, has a three-story brick mansion and belongs to John J. Raskob, financier and Dupont associate, who houses blooded Guernsey cattle here in elaborately equipped barns. The former mansion was burned about 1910.

At 53 *m.* on US 213 is the junction with the Ruthsburg Road.

Left on this road to the PRATT MANSION, 6.5 *m.*, an early show place that since 1832 has been the county almshouse. In the hall is a sounding post, which carried voices from the lower hall to the master's bedchamber above. Its last private owner put it out of commission when, upon departing, he fired a bullet through it.

At 53.7 *m.* on US 213 is the junction with State 18.

Right on State 18 to a dirt road, 2.7 *m.*; R. on the dirt road 1.8 *m.* to WALNUT GROVE (L), a little whitewashed brick house with steep-pitched roof on the banks of Reed's Creek, possibly the oldest dwelling in Queen Annes County. Solomon Wright, ancestor of the present owner, built it between 1681 and 1685 of logs and brick, with hand-riven poplar shingles that still cover the logs of the front and rear walls. The headers in the west wall have a glaze an inch deep, the unusual depth the result of the kind of clay used in making the bricks; when the afternoon sun strikes them, they glitter brilliantly. The living room paneling and other woodwork were sold some years ago for $16,000—it was handcarved and put together with wooden pins; the little office adjoining has been left intact, with paneled chimney breast and tiny cupboards opening above the mantel. The oldest part of the house has two rooms downstairs and two up; an incongruous addition with gambrel roof, of much later construction, contains kitchen, pantries, and a bedroom.

REED'S CREEK HOUSE, 2.8 *m.* on State 18, is a two-and-a-half-story brick dwelling with a lower two-story wing. It was built in 1776 by Colonel Thomas Wright, a member of Solomon Wright's family (*see above*). Colonel Wright was a Revolutionary leader who commanded a Queen Annes County regiment. In his house, which was a rendezvous for the fox hunters and duck shooters of the section, canvasback ducks and diamondback terrapin were served at huge tables. Near Reed's Creek it was not uncommon to shoot 100 ducks in a few hours, and other foodstuff was equally plentiful. The house, still in the hands of the Wrights, has wide floor boards, hand-hewn floors, paneled walls and enormous fireplace. The entrance is particularly notable.

On State 18 at 3.2 *m.* is the junction with a dirt road leading into Tilghman Neck; R. 1.1 *m.* on this road to a fork.

1. Right from the fork 2.7 *m.* to a lane (L) of THE HERMITAGE, ancestral home of the Tilghman family. The three-story mansion of brick covered with cement is on land granted in 1659 to Dr.Richard Tilghman, first of the family in America. His grandson Matthew Tilghman was prominent in Revolutionary days, and a delegate to the Continental Congress from Maryland. Lieutenant Colonel Tench Tilghman (*see Tour 3D*) was a member of this family. The Hermitage burned in 1832, was rebuilt in 1859, and has since been altered. The Tilghman burying ground here contains the grave of Dr.Richard Tilghman, who died in 1675.

2. Left from the fork 1.3 *m.* to BLAKEFORD (L), a two-and-a-half-story, L-shaped dwelling partly weatherboarded and surrounded by beautiful park land. Parts of the house are more than 200 years old but it has been entirely remodeled. When Lord Baltimore gave to Henry DeCourcey (Coursey), secretary of the province, as much land as his thumb would cover on a certain map, the extreme tip of his thumb extended across Queenstown Creek and included this tract, which was later sold to a man named Blake. The place was first called Blake-fort for a fort erected as defense against Indians, and then Blake-ford because of a ford to My Lord's Gift (*see Tour 5*).

State 18 continues to QUEENSTOWN, 6 *m.* (288 pop.) (*see Tour 5*).

PEACE AND PLENTY (L), 55.6 *m.*, a two-and-a-half-story brick mansion, built in the colonial period by the Wrights (*see above*), is similar to Reed's Creek House. It is still owned by the family. The large drawing room has six ample windows with eared frames and carved cornices; the wainscoting is carved with recessed squares. It is said that the name was selected by the wife of the Wright who built it—her own home had been called Hungry Hill.

WYE MILLS, 60.7 *m.* (125 pop.), at the junction with State 404 (*see Tour 5*), grew up about a gristmill; it is on the boundary between Queen Annes and Talbot counties. The WYE OAK (R) is the largest white oak in

Maryland and one of the largest in the United States. Believed to be over 400 years old, it is 95 feet high with a horizontal spread of 165 feet. The trunk is more than 21 feet in circumference. WYE CHAPEL (R) was consecrated on St.Luke's Day, October 18, 1721, according to a letter still extant from a Reverend Wilkinson to the Reverend James Williamson, inviting him to assist at the consecration and to lodge with the writer 'ye night before.' The little brick structure is well preserved and cared for.

Section b. WYE MILLS to SALISBURY; 60.3 m.

South of WYE MILLS 0 m., US 213 crosses slightly rolling land of a grain-growing section. Southeast of the Choptank River the route passes through the low-lying truck-farming areas.

At 2 m. is the junction with a dirt road.

Right on this road to KING HAYS FARM (L), 2.2 m., with an odd brick house whose construction began in 1730. The smallest section is a story-and-a-half high, the middle section is two stories, and the end with a gable facing Wye River is two-and-a-half-stories. In this gable end are ten windows, allowing a river view from each room.

An old dock and warehouse mark WYE LANDING, 2.7 m., once a busy shipping point for this farming section.

In LONGWOODS, 7.1 m. (45 pop.), on US 213, is the junction with a graveled road.

Right on this to WYE HEIGHTS (Cleghorne-On-Wye), 2 m., with a three-story structure built in 1823 and recently enlarged. The extensive lawns along the Wye River contain many kinds of trees; and the walks and drives are bordered with English box. This estate, one of the finest dairy farms on the Eastern Shore, is part of the first (1660) land grant to Edward Lloyd.

At 7.4 m. on US 213 is the junction with the Tunis Mills Road (see Tour 3B).

At 10.4 m. on US 213 is the junction with a dirt road.

Right on this to a dirt road, 1.1 m.; R. here to another dirt road, 1.6 m.; L. on this to MYRTLE GROVE (L), 2 m., ancestral home of the Goldsboroughs. The frame wing, built in 1734, was the wedding gift of Robert Goldsborough to his son Robert; it has wide clapboarding over logs. The main brick section, two-and-a-half stories high, was built in 1789 by the third Robert Goldsborough, a judge. A portrait of Judge Goldsborough and his family, painted here by Charles Willson Peale, hangs in the central hall. Near the old cedars in front of the house is a one-story building in which Richard Bassett (see above) studied law.

On this estate, one mile west of the entrance lane, is ASHBY, a frame house erected in 1854 for a member of the Goldsborough family. North of Ashby is the family burial ground.

Easton, 12.6 m. (35 alt.,4,092 pop.), county seat of Talbot, near the Tred Avon River, is a trading center for local farmers as well as for the numerous wealthy people from New York, Pittsburgh, and other cities who have bought water-front plantations near by since the World War. These newcomers and their guests are manna to Easton's genealogists, tearooms, and antique shops. At mail time, shiny station wagons cluster about the post office as their owners, in riding breeches, greet each other and exchange jokes. Like others of the Eastern Shore, this town has canneries, a lumber mill, and a garment factory.

Many of the houses are large and spacious on regularly laid-out streets and most of them are surrounded by shady lawns, As in other Eastern Shore towns, most Easton residents, including the thousand Negroes, are native-born.

The electric, gas, water, and sewage systems are owned and operated by the municipality.

After Third Haven Meeting House was erected here in 1682–83, a little Quaker community arose close by but grew slowly until 1710 when it became Talbot Court House. In 1789 the present name was adopted, presumably in memory of Easton on the lower Avon River in England. Families of wealth and prestige built substantial houses and lawyers settled near the courthouse.

TALBOT COUNTY COURTHOUSE, Washington and Dover Streets, a red brick structure built in 1794, was later Victorianized. The courthouse of 1710 stood near by on two acres of land purchased from Philemon Armstrong for 5,000 pounds of tobacco. The TALBOT COUNTY FREE LIBRARY (*open weekdays*), Washington Street near Dover, is one of the oldest and most complete public libraries on the Eastern Shore.

THIRD HAVEN MEETING HOUSE (*key kept by caretaker on grounds*), south end of Washington Street, a clapboarded structure erected in 1682–83, is one of the oldest frame houses of worship in the United States. William Penn once held meeting under one of the massive oaks of the adjoining yard. The simple old building has broad-plank floors and straight-backed benches. The stove was a source of contention in 1781 when some members thought that religious zeal should give sufficient warmth without a stove. The old structure is no longer used but meetings are held in the brick meeting house adjacent. The records, which go back to the first meeting held in October 1683, have been carefully preserved.

FOXLEY HALL, Aurora and Goldsborough Streets, a three-story brick dwelling, was built about 1794. Tradition has it that Charles Dickinson, killed by Andrew Jackson in a duel, was born in Foxley Hall. It was the residence of Colonel Oswald Tilghman, a gallant officer of the Confederate Army, and is now occupied by a Tilghman.

The three-story brick BULLITT OR CHAMBERLAIN HOUSE, Dover and Harrison Streets, now painted brown, was erected about 1780 by Thomas James Bullitt, ancestor of William C. Bullitt, ambassador to the Union of Soviet Socialist Republics (1933) and to France (1936).

On the corner of Washington and Gay Streets is THE REST, home of Franklin Buchanan (1800–74), an admiral of the Confederate Navy (*see Tour 3B*).

Easton is at the junction with State 17 (*see Tour 3C*) and with the Cambridge Road (*see Tour 3E*).

TRED AVON AIRPORT (L), 16 *m.*, has planes available for sight-seeing or trips to distant points.

The yellow stucco building (R), 16.5 *m.*, is a substation of the Maryland State Police (*information and first aid*).

A farm lane (L) passes through extensive apple orchards to TROTH'S FORTUNE, now Orchard Knob, on the Choptank River, whose story-and-a half hip-roof brick dwelling was built soon after 1676 by William Troth, a prominent Quaker. In 1682 he was attacked in this house by an Indian named Poh Poh Caquis. The Indian was arrested and his trial was set down at length in the minutes of Lord Baltimore's Council. The 'greate men amongst the Indians' were convened by the commissioners, Colonel Henry Coursey and Colonel Philemon Lloyd; according to Troth and his witnesses, Poh Poh Caquis, let into the house to warm himself at the fire, threatened that 200 Senecas were near by, to which Troth replied: 'Pish! Doest thou believe him when he talks of Sinniquois; for he Lyes.' Insulted, the Indian fired at Troth, whose back was turned, but missed him. Then he made for the white man with his tomahawk, but was frightened away when Troth called for his 'gunn.'

In his defense, Poh Poh Caquis said he was drunk or otherwise he would not have 'shott' at Troth. The 'greate men' and their king, Ababco, could not justify the prisoner's actions. The court explained that the death penalty would have been dealt out by a Christian court, but that 'the rigour of the Lawe' would be relaxed and a sentence of 20 lashes substituted. This was executed by one of the Indians upon Poh Poh Caquis, but as his good behavior was not guaranteed he was ordered banished. Later on King Ababco and his men gave pledge that the prisoner would thereafter behave himself, and Poh Poh Caquis' sentence was remitted.

Whitewashed brick walls and the steep sweep of dormered roof mark the house of DOVER FERRY FARM (L), 17.7 *m.* This early colonial house, which stands close to the Choptank has an unusual 'porch chamber' above its sagging front porch. The paneling of the main room has been sold to a collector.

The road crosses the Choptank River, 17.9 *m.*, on the Dover Bridge. On the west bank, two miles downstream (R) is DOVER, once a port but now only a name. Seagoing vessels tied up at its wharves to let the fresh water kill the barnacles on their bottoms. In 1778 the Maryland legislature authorized the building of the Talbot County Courthouse at Dover, but the act seems to have been disregarded and the county seat was placed at Talbot, now Easton. With changing shipping routes and the shoaling of the harbor, Dover joined the list of vanished ports on Chesapeake Bay.

The Choptank, longest navigable river on the Eastern Shore, widens toward its mouth into a bay. Waving cattails of the marshy shore reach up to a fringe of trees.

At 19 *m.* is the junction with a dirt road.

Right on this to FRAZIER'S FLATS HOUSE, 3.2 *m.*, a high two-and-a-half-story brick dwelling by a broad bend of the Choptank. The steps that led to the entrance, which has elaborately fluted pilasters and modillioned pediment, have dropped away, but this is still one of the finest formal Georgian houses on the Eastern Shore. Captain William Frazier, who built it, was born about 1756 and served in the Revolution, but is better remembered as a leader of Methodism in this section. Francis Asbury, circuit-riding preacher and bishop, mentions many visits to Frazier's house in the journal kept on his trips between Massachusetts and Georgia. Religious meetings were often held here and the second-story front room is still called the 'church room.' The family burial plot is on the right of the entrance lane.

For the few weeks of every Christmas season the rural quiet of BETH-LEHEM, 20.8 m. (80 pop.), is interrupted. The cedar (L) growing at the crossroads near the general store and the church are decorated with colored lights, visible for miles across the fields. The little post office, usually as peaceful as the maple-shaded road that is the town's main street, is choked at Christmas time with envelopes from all over the country, sent here to be postmarked.

PRESTON, 24.3 m. (316 pop.), looks newer than most Eastern Shore towns. In its central section one or two old houses remain from the days when it was a tiny settlement called Snow Hill. Paved streets radiate toward the surrounding fields, and concrete sidewalks link houses built in the latest styles.

The BETHESDA METHODIST CHURCH (L), a white clapboarded structure with square belfry, at the junction of State 16 with Main Street, is on the site of one of the first Methodist churches in America, the Bethesda Chapel, more commonly known as Frazier Chapel in remembrance of Captain William Frazier who helped establish it. Its records have been kept since 1810.

In 1892 the town that grew around the chapel was granted a charter under the name of Preston; one clause stipulated that every able-bodied man should give one day of each year to working the city streets or pay the bailiff $1. Growth and prosperity came with modern transportation. Preston is now the marketing center of a large truck-raising district with several canning factories and canned-goods brokerage houses.

LINCHESTER, 25.4 m. (19 alt.,50 pop.), one of the oldest settlements in Caroline County, was formerly called Murray's Mill because of the gristmill (R) established here in 1681, but by legislative act was renamed Linchester, a combination of parts of the names of Caroline and Dorchester Counties. Murray's Mill supplied flour to Maryland troops during the Revolution; tradition has it that the existing frame structure is the original mill; it stood farther upstream but during a flood was swept from its foundations to its present site.

HURLOCK, 32 m. (45 alt.,765 pop.), a busy and thoroughly modern town in the midst of a prosperous farming country, developed around a railroad station built here in 1867. It was named for John M. Hurlock, who erected the first store in 1869 and the first dwelling in 1872, 21 years before the town was incorporated.

Hurlock's industries are varied, but canning and the manufacture of cans are important. The American Stores Company has its only vegetable canning factory here; the pack in good years by this plant exceeds half a million cases of fruits and vegetables. Here also are flour mills, shirt and dress factories, lumber yards, and dairies.

In 1923 the State Department of Health opened a bacteriological laboratory here, serving five Eastern Shore counties.

The HURLOCK FREE LIBRARY, established in 1900, is the oldest public library on the Eastern Shore.

SHILOH CHURCH, 34.9 m., now dilapidated, stands by a camp-meeting ground still in use. At the four corners of the tabernacle are fire-stands in which pine knots are burned during camp meetings as protection against insects; before the days of electricity the torches served as lights.

VIENNA, 43.3 *m.* (311 pop.), along the Nanticoke River, has been a port since it was established in 1706. Some streets are paved with stone brought here as ballast by vessels docking for cargo, chiefly tobacco and white oak for ship construction. The CUSTOMS HOUSE, erected in 1791 when this was a port of entry, was in use until 1866. The large electric power plant (L) supplies current to a wide area, towns as well as farms. Three canneries, lumber, flour and feed mills, a pickling plant, and a shirt factory are also operated here.

In 1698 an early Nanticoke Indian Reservation of more than 5,000 acres, covering this site, was established. One hundred acres at Emperor's Landing was bought in 1706 from the Indians for 5,000 pounds of tobacco and laid out as the town of Vienna. In 1780 a British gunboat fired upon the town from the river, doing minor damage. In the War of 1812 when British vessels entered the river, a company of militia quickly threw up breastworks to repulse the expected landing, which did not occur. A ferry was operated across the river until 1828, when a wooden bridge was constructed as a link in an important transpeninsula stage route, but after several years the ferry was revived. The concrete span now carrying traffic over the line has been dedicated to the World War veterans of Dorchester and Wicomico counties.

Vienna is at the junction with State 344 (*see Tour 3E*).

Right from Vienna on a dirt road to Lewis Landing Road, 6 *m.*; L. on this to WES-TON, 7 *m.*, the home of John Henry, who was the first U.S. Senator elected in Maryland; he had been a member of the Continental Congress and later governor of Maryland. The most interesting feature of the large five-bay house is the large entrance with graceful fan and sidelights. A former brick residence here was raided and nearly wrecked by a British landing party in 1780; it later burned. The Reverend John Henry, grandfather of the statesman, was a Scottish Presbyterian minister who succeeded Francis Makemie as pastor of Rehoboth Church in Somerset County (*see Tour 6B*).

US 213 crosses the NANTICOKE RIVER at 43.7 *m.*; this second long-est river on the Eastern Shore follows a southwest course from the head of navigation at Seaford, Delaware, 20 miles upstream, to its mouth 25 miles downstream on Tangier Sound. Until the end of steamboating in the 1920's the Nanticoke was an important channel of commerce and travel. Though Seaford and Baltimore are only 70 miles apart as the crow flies, the river-and-bay voyage of 150 miles took at least 16 hours. Small Diesel-powered freighters and an occasional schooner, usually bearing fertilizer materials or oil, are among the few craft now using the river. But the Du-pont Company's construction (1939) of a nylon plant here is bringing re-newed water activity; the deep Nanticoke, of value in bringing raw material for the new synthetic-fiber product, was a determining factor in selecting the site.

In MARDELA SPRINGS, 47.8 *m.* (370 pop.), is a little octagonal Springhouse (R) built before the Civil War, when the clear waters at-tracted carriage loads of well-to-do people from distant places, and the village of Barren Springs, at the head of Barren Creek, became something of a health resort. The name Mardela was later coined to include the first letters of the words Maryland and Delaware (the southwest corner of Delaware is only two miles east). Several unsuccessful attempts have been made to sell the water on a large scale.

At 48.2 *m.* is the junction (L) with State 313 (*see Tour 4*).

SPRING HILL CHURCH, 53.2 *m.*, is a small frame structure (R) erected in 1771–73 as a chapel of ease in Stepney parish, then in Somerset County (*see Tour 3H*). An old account book states that the construction cost was £509, which was duly paid—except for £3 deducted 'for bad work.' This building became the church of the new Spring Hill parish created from Stepney in 1827. It stands on or near the site of a Spring Hill Chapel built before 1725.

Right from the church on an asphalt-paved road is HEBRON, 1.2 *m.* (805 pop.), founded in 1890 when the railroad was built between Claiborne and Salisbury. A lumber mill, shirt factories, and a cannery employ several hundred persons here. The BOUNDS GARDEN on the southwestern edge of town, hidden from the street, is noted for its long vistas of formal beds between lines of evergreens; exotic waterlilies bloom in small pools.

SALISBURY, 60.3 *m.* (23 alt.,10,997 pop.) (*see Salisbury*).

Points of Interest: Poplar Hill Mansion, State Teachers' College, and others.

Salisbury is at the junction with US 13 (*see Tour 6*), and State 349 (*see Tour 3H*).

Left from Salisbury on Lake Street, a paved road to (R) the WICOMICO STATE GAME FARM, 1.4 *m.*, where quail are propagated by the State Conservation Department. After the bumblebee-sized chicks are hatched in incubators they are put out of doors in long rows of small brooders heated by electricity. Thence they go to rearing pens. Laying hen-birds often produce 50 eggs apiece annually and there is a record of a single hen's laying 150 eggs in one year. About 6,000 mature bobwhites were raised here in 1938 and distributed throughout the State.

Section c.   SALISBURY to OCEAN CITY; 31.8 m.

Between Salisbury and the Pocomoke River are small farms producing truck crops and berries. East of the river and its swamp, the flatlands of Worcester County are more heavily pine wooded; nearly every farm has its 'br'iler plant'—a long, low building for rearing broiler chickens for sale in Northern markets. Despite new crops, this section retains an isolated backwoods flavor. Women wear old-time slat bonnets as they 'horry' the corn. Moonshine stills operate in the swamps—until discovered by officers.

US 213 branches east from Division Street, 0 *m.*, in Salisbury.

PARSONSBURG, 7.7 *m.* (211 pop.), is in a truck-raising section.

PITTSVILLE (L), 10.7 *m.* (217 pop.), has hatcheries, nurseries, a cannery, and a basket factory and is one of several towns in an area packing and shipping large quantities of holly and other Christmas evergreens. During November and December dealers wearing long white coats and gloves purchase thousands of holly wreaths ('reefs') brought in by white and Negro farmers whose families have worked late by coal-oil lamps with holly twigs, wire, and little hoops. 'Reef-wrappin'-time' is always jolly in backwoods kitchens; songs are sung and bets are made as to who can wrap the most wreaths in a given time. In recent years most of the wreaths have been dipped in a preservative paint of an unnaturally brilliant green hue that keeps the leaves from curling and is supposed to improve their color, and natural berries have been replaced by artificial ones several times as large and shiny, which are supplied by the dealers, who pay 3¢ to 6¢ apiece for the finished wreaths.

The village was named for Dr.H.R.Pitts, a president of the little Wicomico and Pocomoke Railroad completed in 1869 from Salisbury to Berlin as a continuation of the line from Claiborne.

WILLARDS, 14.3 *m.* (217 pop.), near the Pocomoke Swamp, also began as a railroad station, named for Willard Thompson of Baltimore, an officer of the line. A big business, until recently, was the cutting and shipping of mine props of loblolly pine to coal mines in Pennsylvania and elsewhere. Willards, a strawberry marketing center, has a shirt factory and basket plant.

US 213 crosses the narrow Pocomoke River (Ind., black water) at 15.9 *m.* From its source in the Great Pocomoke Swamp of Delaware and Maryland, this deep treacherous river twists and doubles for 33 miles through the pine, gum, white cedar, bald cypress, and holly of the ever-broadening Pocomoke River Swamp, to its mouth in Pocomoke Sound southwest of here.

Since early colonial days the chief activity of those living near both swamps was the making of cypress shingles, riven out by hand with heavy iron blades called frows and then drawknifed to the required thinness. Most of the old-time Pocomoke shingles were 30 inches long or longer (modern shingles are 18 inches) and were used throughout this region not only for roofs but also for sheathing walls. The shipping of redwood shingles from the West has ended the shingle industry here. Many houses of the region still have shingled walls more than a century old. The hand-shaved cypress shingle wears out in time—becoming paper-thin—but it never decays.

Bald cypress and white cedar logs were mined for many years in the Great Pocomoke Swamp, which covers about 50 square miles chiefly north of the Delaware Line. By 1860 most of the old-growth standing timber had been removed, but layers of windfalls were found in the deep peat of the swamp floor. Rotting vegetation and sphagnum moss had preserved the trunks perfectly for hundreds of years. When winter rains flooded the swamp, men and oxen scooped the muck off the logs, which then floated to the surface and were dragged to the crosscut saws. The large cylinders were split into bolts, the bolts into shingle blocks from which an expert with a drawknife could rip out 500 long shingles a day. When he had 1,000 he could trade them at the store in Whaleyville for $2.50 worth of calico, sugar, tobacco, whisky, or other commodities.

In 1930 after drainage and drought had lowered the water level, a great fire (presumedly started by an exploding moonshine still) burned for several months underground through five to ten feet of tinder-dry peat and destroyed most of the remaining buried cypress and cedar. In the vast burned area is nothing but water and blackened snags; foresters say it will take several thousand years for the swamp to regenerate itself. The fire even spread to near-by fields of growing corn.

Bear, deer, and wildcats survived in the depths of the Great Pocomoke Swamp until mid-nineteenth century, long after virtual extinction everywhere on the Peninsula. Locally-forged bear traps are still kept by the sons and grandsons of trappers.

At 17.2 m. is the junction with a paved road.

Left on this to WHALEYSVILLE, 0.5 m. (300 pop. est.), named for Captain Seth Whaley who settled here late in the eighteenth century, a descendant of Edward Whaley (or Whalley), who was possibly the English regicide (see Tour 7A). At the edge of the Great Swamp, this place was a center of the shingle industry. Now by-passed by the highway, it is little more than a ghost village of old cypress-sheathed houses and stores.

On the dirt-road extension of the main street at 0.8 m. from US 213 is (R) the old WHALEYSVILLE NEGRO SCHOOLHOUSE, an abandoned, sagging frame structure; across the road is PULLITT'S CHAPEL, a neat, white-painted Negro church, whose Methodist congregation in 1926 called on the talents of their white friend and fellow townsman, P. Dale Wimbrow, to raise funds for an addition. Wimbrow—who, under his own name and as Old Pete Daley of Whaleysville, has since become known for his phonograph records and for his radio performances with the orchestras of Paul Specht, Abe Lyman, and Gustave Haenschen—agreed to put on the show for the Negroes partly because a home-town recital at the Lodge Hall had brought out only 'eight people including the dog under the stove.' As Mr. Wimbrow recalls the affair:

'Those colored people plastered posters from Curtis's Chapel to Sugar Hill. Every telephone pole shouted in red letters that "The Real Honorable Mister Peter Dale Wimbrow Esquire" would entertain at Whaleysville Schoolhouse—looked as if I was running for sheriff in a Democratic primary. On the night appointed they came from Parsonsburg in busses, from Jenkins Neck in carryalls, from the swamp in oxcarts and one-lung jalopies. They were jammed in the schoolhouse and standing about fifty deep outside . . .

'So I uked—and New York never heard that much uking from me. I sang, danced, whistled, told stories, and did impersonations for a solid hour. When I had to sign off, limp and wet with sweat . . . up came the master of ceremonies, all worried, and whispered: "what we gonna do about all de folks dat couldn't git in?" So I told him to clear the hall and let in another helping. There was a second show from start to finish, and a third. The money they raised not only put the new wing on the church—it painted the whole works.'

BERLIN, 23.8 m. (45 alt., 1,480 pop.), is at the junction with US 113 (see Tour 7).

On US 213 is GLEN RIDDLE FARM (L), 27.7 m., the 1,500-acre estate of Samuel D. Riddle, noted breeder and racer of thoroughbred horses. This Maryland farm is his principal training-ground for young animals. War Admiral, son of Man O'War, was trained here; the latter, now at stud on Mr. Riddle's Kentucky farm, was beaten only once in the 21 major races of his second and third years (1919–20) and has earned more than $2,600,000. In 1937 War Admiral won the American Triple Crown for three-year-olds—the Kentucky Derby, the Maryland Preakness, and the Belmont Stakes. Other noted race horses trained here include Crusader, Big Blaze, American Flag, War Hero, Battleship Grey, Edith Cavell, and Maid-at-Arms. Usually about 40 yearlings are brought here from the

Kentucky breeding farm to be trained during the winter and spring. Animals of least promise are converted into hunters. There are from 60 to 75 trainers, grooms, and exercise boys.

OCEAN CITY, 31.8 m. (5 alt.,946 pop. in winter), Maryland's large seashore resort and only port directly on the ocean, a noted headquarters for marlin fishing, has a summer population that reaches 30,000 or more over 4th of July and the Labor-Day week end. Most of the summer people come from Baltimore, Washington, the Eastern Shore, and Delaware. Conventions of many organizations bring thousands of delegates and their families for short visits. It is primarily a hotel and apartment-house resort, with 40 or more beach-front hotels (American plan) operated mostly by Eastern Shore natives. There are also private cottages, generally occupied for the season by owners or tenants. A boardwalk extends two miles along the beach, the southern end lined with amusement places and refreshment stands. The surf bathing is excellent and protected by lifeguards and safety ropes. There is a semipublic golf course near by on the mainland. Small sailboats of the Chincoteague-bateau type are available for use on Sinepuxent Bay here.

Some of the streets of Ocean City were laid out in 1872 by a group of promoters, but not until 1875 was the first hotel, the Atlantic, opened. Early patrons were ferried on a scow across Sinepuxent Bay until the railroad was extended from Berlin and a bridge built across the bay. Every hotel had its hacks, driven by white or Negro men whose duty it was to corral at the depot as many guests as possible. In the 1920's the highways had undermined the railroad's passenger business so much that the destruction of the railroad bridge in the storm of 1933 was no great hardship to the resort. Though that storm damaged watercraft and wharves, it also opened the long-closed inlet here. Since then more than $900,000 in Federal and State funds have been spent on improvements to the inlet and to inner harbors at Ocean City.

Built upon a quarter-mile-wide, three-mile-long section of the sandy, treeless coastal Barrier Reef, Ocean City is separated from the Worcester County mainland by a narrow arm of Sinepuxent Bay. At the southern end of the resort the sand dunes are broken by the rock-jettied Ocean City Inlet, 12 feet deep and 200 feet wide, which gives entry to many harbors with their scores of commercial fishing trawlers, high-powered cruisers chartered for big-game fishing, and numerous private yachts of many kinds.

Though many species of fish, including croakers, bluefish, and weakfish (trout), are caught by anglers in the surf and still-fishing from boats on ocean and bay, it is the big-game fishing that has brought Ocean City its greatest fame in recent years. Channel bass (drum) and tuna of great size are taken frequently, and white marlin, averaging 70 pounds, are found (*June–Sept.*) from 20 to 30 miles out at shoals called the Jack Spot, the Tide Rips, Fenwick's Ridge, and Winter Quarter.

For white marlin fishing, cruisers are equipped with tall, flexible outrigger poles fastened upright amidships; from the angler's rod the heavy line goes to the top of an outrigger for trolling outside the wake. The marlin strikes the bait with its long, sharp bill, knocking the line from the clothespin on the outrigger. For an instant the bait lies at the surface before the fish takes it. Then follows a terrific fight as the big fish leaps from the water time after time, played by the angler who uses both arms and nearly all muscles. If the marlin stays hooked it is finally brought to the boat after from twenty minutes to two hours of battle, and is pulled on deck by its bill. A marlin caught from Ocean City in 1937 weighed 130 pounds. Several hundred are caught annually and it is a rare day when none of the boats has any luck. (*Charter cruisers should be reserved in advance; party usually limited to four persons; boats leave about 6 a.m.; usual charter fee, $35.*)

Tour 3A

Junction with US 213—Fairlee—Eastern Neck Island; 32 *m.*, State roads 292–298–20–21–445.

Asphalt and concrete-paved roadbed; graveled on Eastern Neck Island; entrance lanes often impassable in wet weather.
Tourist homes and hotels in summer.

This route, never at any great distance from the broad Chesapeake (glimpsed now and then) passes through excellent farming land devoted to general farming and dairying. In summer the area becomes a playground for Baltimoreans, who make regular excursions to Betterton and Tolchester for bathing and to Rock Hall for sport fishing. Oyster dredging and commercial fishing are the only commercial activities.

State 292 branches west from a junction with US 213 (*see Tour 3*), 0 *m.*, at a point 1.5 miles south of Kennedysville.

RUNNYMEDE (R), 0.5 *m.*, a two-and-a-half-story whitewashed brick house, is believed to have been built in 1692 by Zachariah Cooper, a vestryman of Shrewsbury Church. The old tree-bordered lane leading to the house is no longer used.

SHEPHERD'S DELIGHT (L), 1.6 *m.*, built about 1682 on a part of the Camelsworthmore tract, was the home of the Reverend Sewell S. Hepburn, onetime pastor of I.U.Church (*see below*) and grandfather of Katharine Hepburn, the actress. Its walls, with brick nogging, are clapboarded but only six inches thick. The hall is paneled with vertical random-width boards. The living room has a mantel carved by hand with 19 sizes of auger bits (these bits are still in use) and a chair rail with 5,000 handmade holes. The kitchen's hand-hewn rafters are still visible, but the old brick floor has been covered with flooring and the fireplace bricked up. Behind the house is much boxwood. Across the fields can be seen HEBRON, owned by the Hebron family (also called Heborne and Hepburn) but built by James Corse, Quaker son of Colonel Henry DeCourcy, secretary of Maryland in 1660. The land was patented in 1683 for James Heborne.

At 2.8 m. is the junction with a dirt road and with State 298 which becomes the main route.

1. Right on the dirt road to LAMB'S MEADOWS (R), 0.8 m., whose simple house was built in 1733 by the Quaker, Pearce Lamb, on land inherited from his father.

2. Right (straight ahead) on State 292 to STILL POND, 0.9 m. (79 alt.,205 pop.), where Tom Hyer in 1841 won the first American heavyweight boxing championship by defeating Yankee Sullivan for a purse of $10,000.
At 2.6 m. from the junction with State 298 on State 292 is State 443, Coleman Road; L. here 0.9 m. to COLEMAN, a crossroads hamlet.
a. Left (straight ahead) 1.9 m. from Coleman on an improved road to STANLEY'S HOPE (L), a tract assigned in 1669 to William Stanley. The walls of the house were laid in English bond and brick headers in a gable give the date 1743.
b. Right from Coleman on a dirt road to the BARTER LADY'S ORCHARD, 3 m., which contains 40,000 pear, apple, and peach trees. The estate was owned by Mrs.Evelyn Harris, who wrote *A Woman Sees It Through*. In this book she told her experiences during the years she fought for the control and success of her three farms while rearing her five small boys. In 1926 Mrs.Harris made airplane trips with produce to New York in her fight against commission merchants; this and other tactics are recorded in her book as suggestions to farmers for solving their financial problems and obtaining better results for their labor. Mrs.Harris gained her nickname—'the barter lady'—from some of the barter-deals she made in lean years.
State 292 ends at BETTERTON, 3.9 m. (60 alt.,296 pop.), a summer and fishermen's resort. First settlers here were the Crews, who were aided by Indians in erecting their home, the former Fish Hall. Betterton has an excellent beach and is popular with Baltimoreans. Many pleasure craft touch at this resort.

The main route, State 298, turns L. and at 4.2 m. is the junction with State 561 (Lynch Road).

Left on this road which passes Camelsworthmore Manor (L), CAMELSWORTHMORE, 0.3 m., built in Revolutionary times by John Angier, has been greatly altered by recent remodeling, but the formal boxwood garden, beautiful wainscoting, and hand-carved mantels and doors still attest the excellent taste of the Angiers.
DUNCAN'S FOLLY (R), 1.2 m., is a whitewashed brick house built in 1687.
State 561 continues to the junction with US 213 (*see Tour 3*), 2.5 m.

At 4.4 m. on State 298 is (R) the SITE OF THE CECIL MEETING HOUSE (1698) adjacent to a Friends burial ground (L).
At 5.4 m. is the junction with an improved dirt road.

Right on this road to DRAYTON MANOR (R), 3.3 m., whose seventeenth-century house has been remodeled beyond recognition. It is now the mansion of Wayne Johnson's large Churn Creek estate, with sunken gardens containing thousands of tulips and many rare plants. A racing stable is maintained. The first house here is believed to have been built by Charles James who received the grant in 1677.

OLD I.U.CHURCH, 5.7 m., was so named because of initials found on a large boundary stone near by. The church was built in 1868 to replace an older structure (1768). The churchyard contains some graves nearly as old as the parish, which was established in 1765.

Prize-winning Angus-Aberdeen cattle are raised for the beef market at ANDELOT STOCK FARM on Worton Point, 5.8 *m.*, owned by Lammot du Pont Copeland. Recently the president of the Dominican Republic purchased a herd of these prize cattle.

At 6.2 *m.* is the junction with a dirt road.

Right on this road through SMITHVILLE and turning L. through NEWTON to WORTON MANOR (L), 3.3 *m.*, whose two-and-a-half-story brick house is on a grant of 2,300 acres made to Colonel Edward Carter. The one-mile lane leading to this place is impassable in wet weather.

At 6.3 *m.* is the junction with State 297.

Left on this road to BIG MEADOW (R), 0.6 *m.*, sometimes called the Rufus Park Place. The two-and-a-half-story brick house has a stone foundation five feet thick that extends above the ground, and wide chimneys at each gable end. Among the details that remain unchanged since the house was built about 1784 are hand-carved mantels, strap hinges on heavy doors, woodwork fastened with wooden pins or hand-made nails, and a graceful stairway with heavy oak newel post and handrail extending to the third floor.

In WORTON, 0.7 *m.* (62 alt.,100 pop.), is the junction with a dirt road; L. on this 0.4 *m.* along railroad tracks to MUDDY BRANCH (L), whose dignified brick farmhouse has a seven-and-a-half-foot dining room fireplace topped by a nine-foot mantel, old oak woodwork, fireplaces in all the second floor rooms, strap hinges on many doors, and ten-inch hand-hewn ceiling beams that run the entire length of the house on the first and second floors. The dwelling was built for William Thomas, member of the family for whom Mount Hermon was surveyed in 1730, and owner of Thomas Hill and Airy Hill in Quaker Neck (*see Tour 3*).

At MELITOTA, 9.9 *m.*, is a junction with a graveled road.

Right on this 1.8 *m.* to the entrance (L) of GREAT OAK, a large modern estate. Old Great Oak Manor, part of which is included in the present estate, was granted to John Van Neck in 1673. The British overran the manor in 1814, shortly before the battle of Caulk's Field (*see below*), and forced a captured slave to guide them to the American camp.

CARVILL HALL, by Fairlee Creek on the modern Great Oak estate, is a two-and-a-half-story brick structure now rented. It was built before the Revolution by the Carvill family. A secret brick-walled basement room was recently discovered.

On HANDY POINT, 3.6 *m.*, an estate, is an L-shaped house built in 1740 by Marmaduke Tilden II. It contains beautifully executed paneling and woodwork. The porch with hanging balcony is a recent addition of some interest.

Witch Coach Castle or WYCH COTE HALL (L), 11 *m.*, is one of the homes built on old Fairlee Manor in the colonial period. It is a two-story brick house with flat-roofed dormer windows extending from the ridge pole, and chimneys at each gable with bases seven feet wide, affording fireplaces in several rooms. The narrow stairways leading from each of the five first-floor rooms to the room above are unusual. 'Wych Cote' was medieval English for 'elm cottage.'

At 12.7 *m.* is the junction with a dirt road.

Right on this road to BIG FAIRLEE FARM, 2.4 *m.*, a subdivision of a manor granted to James Brown in 1674. The two-and-a-half-story, two-winged house, built about 1674, retains many of its early features; the living room and parlor are paneled and have wide fireplaces and hand-carved mantels. The kitchen has a fireplace eight feet wide, old-fashioned cupboards and wainscoting, and battened doors with old strap and H-hinges.

FAIRLEE, 13 *m.* (78 alt.,150 pop.), is the trading center for a section where some farms have been under cultivation continuously for more than 250 years.

Straight ahead from Fairlee on State 20, which becomes the main route. At 14.7 *m.* is the junction with State 21, which in turn becomes the main route; and with an improved dirt road.

Left on the dirt road through SANDY BOTTOM, 0.8 *m.* (50 alt.,30 pop.), to ST.PAUL'S CHURCH (L), 1 *m.*, a structure with ivy-covered walls and well-preserved masonry. This church, completed in 1713, is believed to be the oldest church in Maryland used continuously as a place of worship. Thirty-four pews were constructed in 1714 and rented for a stipulated number of pounds of tobacco. An entire pew could be bought outright forever for 1,000 pounds of tobacco; one of these is today occupied by the tenth-in-line from the purchaser. The vestry house, built 1766, stands a few yards away. The seven oaks in the churchyard were at least a century old when the first white settlers arrived.

1. Left at St.Paul's 0.9 *m.* to a dirt lane (*impassable in wet weather*) leading to RINGGOLD'S FORTUNE (R), now called Violet Grove. The two-and-a-half-story brick building was erected in 1762 for James Ringgold. Many of the interior fittings have been sold, and the house is dilapidated. The three-roomed cellar with peephole windows is said to have been used as slave quarters.

2. Right from the fork at St.Paul's Church to BROADNOX (L), 1 *m.*, a one-and-a-half-story house of whitewashed brick, with two side wings. The land upon which it stands was surveyed for Thomas Broadnox in 1659 and later acquired by Robert Dunn, who built the house in 1708. The interior is notable for its oak paneling of various widths, hand-carved mantels, large fireplaces, and leather hinges extending the entire width of the doors on the first floor.

At 2.9 *m.* is the junction with State 20; L. on this now main side route.

In the crossroads hamlet of EDESVILLE, 4.8 *m.*, is the junction with a dirt road; L. on this, 0.8 *m.*, to MY LORD'S GIFT (R), whose one-and-a-half-story log and frame house has lost its antique appearance by the application of shingles. The paneling and old mantels indicate that the house is at least 200 years old.

The dirt road continues to BUNGAY HILL (L), 1 *m.*, a two-story brick house with a low kitchen wing. In the gable end, in large headers burned black, appears '1757 by C.P.' The fireplaces, doors, and mantels have interesting details.

The exact age of KIMBOLTON (L), 1.6 *m.*, is not known, but Colonel Hans Hanson, who became prominent in Kent County government, purchased the house in 1679. The brick center section is older than the frame wings. The original dormer windows, batten window shutters, and some of the fireplaces are still intact. The kitchen and cellar have hand-hewn beams, and under the windows on the second floor are unusual small cupboards.

State 20 continues southward to ROCK HALL, 7.1 *m.*, at the junction with State 445 (*see below*).

The main route continues from the junction on State 21 (*see above*). At 15.3 *m.* is the junction with a dirt road.

Right on this road to the CAULK'S BATTLEFIELD, 0.1 *m.*, where a granite monument marks the scene of a skirmish between English and American forces, August 31, 1814. Sir Peter Parker (a grandson of the Peter Parker who was repulsed at Charleston in 1776) landed near Tolchester with a force of 260 men to have what he termed 'a frolic with the Yankees.' The British attacked twice and were repulsed with a loss of 14 killed and 28 wounded. American losses were three wounded. After Parker died from a thigh wound, the British retired, not knowing that the Americans were out of ammunition. For many decades Kent County Negroes called the battle 'Marse Peter Parker's War.'

At 17.1 *m.* is the junction with State 445; L. on this, now the main route.

Right (straight ahead) on State 21 to the MITCHELL HOUSE (R), 0.2 *m.*, a two-section house with large chimneys, now called Lotus Inn. Here Sir Peter Parker died of wounds received at Caulk's Field. Although the interior has been modernized, the old hand-carved mantels, large fireplaces, mouldings, and locks remain.

At 0.5 *m.* is the mile-long entrance lane (L) to GRESHAM HALL, a brick and log house built early in the eighteenth century. It was once called Gresham College, perhaps for Gresham College in England. The brick section has been burned down and rebuilt; the log section, which contains the dining room and kitchen, has wide doors with strap or H-hinges, an old-fashioned mantel, and a stairway whose handrail, newel post, and spindles are of walnut. The estate is now owned by a corporation which has constructed a group of summer cottages near by, on the bay shore.

TOLCHESTER BEACH, 0.9 *m.* (*amusement park, bathing, fishing; summer ferry service to Baltimore twice daily*, $2 *for car and driver*), is a bay side resort, started in 1877 and long popular with Baltimore excursionists. This was part of the Tolchester Farm, patented to William Tolson in 1672.

A shaded entrance lane (R), 18.9 *m.* on State 445, leads to HINCHING-HAM, a two-and-a-half-story structure built in 1774. The manor of more than 2,000 acres was granted to Thomas Hynson in 1659. The interior of the house contains much mantel paneling and roundheaded cupboards (now with glass doors) and scrolled shelves.

At 19.6 *m.* is the junction with a dirt road.

1. Right on this road to HINCHINGHAM FARMHOUSE (L), 0.3 *m.*, built about 1675 by Michael Miller. It has log walls.

MILLER FARMHOUSE (L), 0.5 *m.*, a two-story brick and frame house erected in the early eighteenth century, contains several hand-carved mantels, interesting door paneling and hinges, and two stairways with handmade spindles, rails, and newel posts.

DRIFTWOOD (R), 1.4 *m.*, is a brick and weatherboard house built about 1750. Near by is an observation tower from which observers for the Aberdeen Proving Grounds watch the performance of long-range guns.

TAVERN CREEK HOUSE (L), 2.9 *m.*, a two-and-a-half-story brick and frame house, was built before the Revolutionary War. The inside chimney of the kitchen and the hinges on some of the doors are noteworthy.

The road continues to SWAN POINT, a long sand bar extending into the Bay. This is one of the leading oystering areas in Maryland.

2. Left on the dirt road to SPRINGFIELD (L), 3.1 *m.*, built before the Revolution. It has a two-story main section and a steep-roofed lower wing, used as a kitchen. The house is set off with boxwood and shade trees.

ROSEDALE (R), 21 *m.* on State 445, is one of the homesteads of the Pages, leaders in Kent County affairs in the eighteenth century. The two-story brick house contains many old locks and brass knobs, several large fireplaces, one with an intricately carved mantel. Slave quarters and the family burial lot are near by.

LIBERTY HALL or Humphrey's Point (R), 21.4 *m.*, a two-and-a-half-story brick residence, was the home of the Hodges. Colonel James Hodges, a member of George Washington's staff, was born here on the same day as his chief—February 22, 1732. The house has two wings and a large basement with heavily barred windows. Much of the interior mahogany woodwork remains and there are excellent examples of hand-carving. The family burial ground is near the house.

BOXLEY (L), 22.2 *m.*, a two-and-a-half-story whitewashed brick house, long the home of the Blakistons, is built on the tract purchased by Ebenezer Blakiston from Lawrence Symonds and William Davis in 1674.

ROCK HALL, 23 *m.* (15 alt.,714 pop.), on the shore of Chesapeake Bay, offers excellent facilities for fishing and is one of the leading points shipping fish, crabs, and oysters. The name is said by some to have been Rock Haul originally, so called from the large hauls of rockfish taken there; however, the historic marker erected by the citizens states that the town was named for Rock Hall Mansion, which stood at the landing a mile west of the town. Used as a landing as early as 1707, Rock Hall was long the Eastern Shore terminus of the post road from the North, and thus the point of departure for passengers for Annapolis and the South. George Washington crossed here many times, and Lieutenant Colonel Tench Tilghman crossed on the Rock Hall ferry in October 1781 as he was taking the news of Cornwallis' surrender at Yorktown to the Continental Congress sitting at Philadelphia. Ferry service has been discontinued.

At Rock Hall is the junction with State 20 (*see above*).

HUNTINGFIELD (R), 25 *m.*, a modern frame dwelling, stands upon a tract granted to Colonel Thomas Ringgold in 1659. Near by are the ruins of former mansions which bore the same name.

By Gray's Inn Creek, 25.1 *m.*, is the SITE OF NEW YARMOUTH (L), Kent County's first town. In 1674 Charles Calvert directed the removal of court sessions from Kent Island to Eastern Neck. About a year later a town was laid out and named, perhaps, after Great Yarmouth, England. In 1683, when the first known court sessions were held here, the town had a courthouse, a prison, and two shipyards. New Yarmouth rapidly declined after the county seat was moved to New Town (Chester Town) in 1696. The ruins of St.Peter's, the first Anglican church established in the county, lie beneath the waters of the creek.

ELLENDALE (R), 26.3 *m.*, destroyed by fire before 1850, was rebuilt with a frame second story on the old walls. The double chimneys are more characteristic of southern Maryland than of the 'Sho.' The ceilings are 12 to 14 feet high, and the kitchen is in the basement. At the rear of the house are two log buildings, formerly slave quarters.

Opposite Ellendale is the junction with a dirt road.

Left on this road to NAPLEY GREEN, 0.9 *m.*, whose colonial house has been converted into a hunting lodge by its owner, Eugene E. du Pont, of Delaware. The two-wing frame structure has been modernized but retains a huge fireplace and an inside pyramid chimney.

TRUMPINGTON (R), 27.9 *m.*, a two-and-a-half-story brick house, was built in 1723 on land granted to Thomas South in 1658. The main structure has a large T-shaped chimney at each end and two windows that nearly bisect the rafters in the gable ends.

A wooden bridge, 28.8 *m.*, crosses to EASTERN NECK ISLAND where the roadbed is graveled.

At 30.4 *m.* is the junction with a farm lane.

Right on this lane to INGLESIDE, 1 *m.*, a two-wing brick house erected in 1792 and containing old corner cupboards, wide fireplaces, hand-carved mantels, and broad window recesses. The kitchen fireplace is built inside the room.

In pre-Revolutionary times WICKLIFFE, 30.9 *m.*, now a hunting lodge, was the home of the Wickes family. Lambert Wickes was commander of the American vessel *Reprisal* that carried Benjamin Franklin to France. After capturing several British merchantmen, Wickes went down with his ship off Newfoundland in 1777.

HAIL POINT, 32 *m.*, the southern point of Eastern Neck Island, was so called because here the proprietary's officials stopped all inbound vessels for customs and health inspections. A gun club now owns the land.

Tour 3B

Junction with US 213—Tunis Mills—Junction with State 17; 13.2 *m.*
Unmarked roads and State 370.

Graveled roadbed, short macadamized sections; difficult in winter and early spring.
The houses on this route, with one exception, may not be visited without permission from the owners.

This route follows country roads that twist among the rich flat fields and silent woods of Miles River Neck, never more than a mile from tidewater; there are frequent glimpses of the inlets that cut back into the level country in an intricate pattern of rivers and coves. At times a mast or a sail is seen, apparently gliding across fields as a boat travels a hidden creek.

The unmarked graveled road branches west from US 213, 0 *m.* (*see Tour* 3), 5.8 miles north of Easton.

At 1.6 *m.*, the main route turns R. at the junction with a dirt road.

At 3 *m.* is the junction with a dirt road.

Right on this road to PRESQU'ILE, 2.5 *m.*, a frame house built by Governor Edward Lloyd for his son Murray. One pedimented façade faces the long, straight entrance avenue; the other looks across a level lawn to a wide stretch of the Wye River. Beside the house is an old boxwood garden.

On the main route at 3.5 *m.* is the entrance lane (R) to GROSS' COATE, which has belonged to the Tilghman family for six generations. The large brick house, its main section a full three stories high, stands among trees that tower above its roof. To its oldest section, built between 1755 and 1760, each succeeding generation has made additions. Behind the house is a very old brick stable with small barred windows, and a smokehouse from which is still taken the monthly 'lay-in,' a ration of smoked meat which, together with an allowance of cornmeal, is part of the wages of the families living on the place. The custom, still in practice on a few old Eastern Shore farms, has come down from the days of slavery. At the edge of the gardens an ivy-hung wall encloses the family graveyard.

Gross' Coate was granted to Roger Gross in 1658. In 1687 it was acquired by the Lloyds, from whom it was inherited by the Tilghmans. In 1790 Charles Willson Peale visited here to paint several portraits that still hang in the house. His portrait of Mary Tilghman is considered by some critics as one of his finest. During the sittings, tradition has it, artist and subject fell in love, but the opposition of Mary's brother, because Peale was a middle-aged widower with several children, broke up the romance.

The main route bears right at 3.9 m. and right again at 5.4 m.

At 6.1 m. is the junction with a dirt road.

Right (straight ahead) on the dirt road to the iron gates of WYE HOUSE (R), 0.8 m., which has belonged to the Lloyd family ever since the grant of many thousands of acres to the first Colonel Edward Lloyd in 1658. Thick shade subdues the red of the stone-capped brick piers. Beyond the entrance gates stretches a formal avenue lined with oaks and beeches whose branches permit a vista of the white portico on the lovely house, three-quarters of a mile away. The two perfectly balanced lower wings of the frame house stretch into a long façade that rises from smooth turf. The pedimented gable that crowns the façade of the main building is repeated on the pavilions, an unusual motif in the five-part house. Worn stone steps lead up to a small Palladian portico. In all the first-floor rooms paneled overmantels extend to the high ceilings, and the woodwork throughout has beautifully executed detail. The porch across the back of the house faces a bowling green beyond which is the ORANGERY. This building, of the late colonial period, has a decidedly French Renaissance character. It is designed in three sections. The two-story, hip-roofed central portion, four bays in length, has walls of rusticated stonework on the first story and very tall floor-length windows. The second story windows are small and square. The flanking hip-roofed wings, raised just one step above grade, have equally large arched windows, giving the effect of glass-enclosed arcades. Until about 70 years ago in this stuccoed brick building, orange and lemon trees were grown in square tubs identical in design with those at Versailles.

On both sides of the bowling green are secluded formal gardens as extensive as any left from colonial America. Parterres and walks are bordered with wide box hedges that have been growing at least 200 years. At one side stands a low whitewashed brick house—probably built before 1700—and believed to be the north wing of the original Wye House. In it lived the captain of the sailing vessel that served the Lloyds not only as a freighter but also as a yacht to carry them back and forth to their town house in Annapolis. Often on such occasions it was fitted with soft pillows and rugs, for the Lloyds lived in luxurious style and entertained in a manner that would have aroused envy among many of the English gentry of their day.

On March 13, 1781, a landing party of British raided Wye House and took many things, including large pieces of silver plate which years later came into the possession of the British royal family and, identified by their coats of arms, were returned to their American owners. Contrary to a recent story that survives every denial, Wye House was not burned by the raiders. The present house was built between 1770 and 1792 by Colonel Edward Lloyd (1744–96), who was a delegate to the Continental Congress and a member of the Maryland Council of Safety. The garden and orangery are older.

Through an arched gate in a high brick wall behind the orangery is a family graveyard, with a stone marked 1684. Here are buried descendants to the tenth generation of the first American Edward Lloyd (d.1696), and also two sons-in-law of Governor Edward Lloyd (1779–1834), Admiral Franklin Buchanan (see below) and Commander Charles Lowndes, and his grandson, General Charles S. Winder.

Beyond the east wing of the house surrounding a service yard are the dairy, a large smokehouse, and the loom house where cloth was woven to clothe the plantation's hundreds of slaves.

At 1.4 *m.* is the entrance to BRUFF'S ISLAND. Inside the gate where the road reaches the shore is the site of DONCASTER, 2.1 *m.*, a town laid out in 1683, used as a port for a few years, and then abandoned. The foundation of one building remains, hidden in marsh grass and undergrowth.

The main route turns left from the junction at 6.1 *m.* through COP-PERVILLE, 7.1 *m.* (10 alt.), a tiny Negro settlement.

At 7.3 *m.* is the junction with a graveled road and a macadam road that becomes the main route.

1. Straight ahead on the gravel road between the tall loblolly pines to the gate lodge of CAPE CENTAUR (L), 1.3 *m.* The large modern house of pink stucco, flat-roofed and designed in the modern Spanish-Moorish style, stands on a point overlooking Miles River.

The graveled road ends at the entrance to FAIRVIEW, 1.5 *m.* The house is said to have been built in 1729 but its present Classic Revival lines date from the early nineteenth century. The boxwood hedges of the old parterres behind the house have grown to large billowing mounds of green. Beyond the thick trunks and low branches of old trees is the wide sweep of Eastern Bay. Fairview, granted in 1683 to Andrew Skinner, belonged to an Andrew Skinner for two centuries. It is liberally endowed with ghosts.

2. Right on the macadamized road to a dirt road, 0.5 *m.*; R. on this 0.9 *m.* to HOPE HOUSE (*adm. to gardens* 25¢), one of the most unusual five-part houses in Maryland. Between the red brick façade of the main building and the flankers are pavilions with serpentine rooflines sweeping down in a cyma or ogee curve. Since the burning of Winton (*see Tour 3*) the curved roofs of these connecting passages have been unique. The main unit, said to have been constructed in 1748, is all that remains of the original building. The wings were rebuilt between 1906 and 1910. The new flankers were made higher, and though the roofs of the connecting pavilions were raised, the curved lines of the cornices were accurately restored. Dense planting encloses extensive boxwood gardens which, though planted only three decades ago, seem as old as the house.

Hope House stands on a grant made in 1666 and later sold to Colonel Philemon Lloyd (1646–85) of Wye House (*see above*) by its two bachelor owners 'for a case of spirits.' Several men met here under a beech tree to witness the contract. They finished off the spirits and one of the sellers forgot to sign his name. He died soon after and Colonel Lloyd instituted chancery proceedings in order to clear the title. The property passed by inheritance to succeeding generations of the Lloyd and Tilghman families for over 200 years.

The main route continues L. on the macadam road from the junction at 7.3 *m.*

The narrow head of LEEDS CREEK, 7.5 *m.*, is crossed on a wooden bridge; the placid surface of the water is sparsely dotted with anchored skiffs and canoes belonging to fishermen and oystermen. A cargo boat or schooner sometimes ties up at the remnants of the wharf from which a steamer ran to Baltimore in the days before branch railroads penetrated this area.

TUNIS MILLS, 7.8 *m.* (10 alt.,100 pop.), was once a shopping center and post office for farmers.

At 8.3 *m.* the main route turns R. on a macadamized road; this road at 9.5 *m.* turns L. on another.

Straight ahead at this junction 0.4 *m.*, to the entrance lane of KNIGHTLY (R), whose rectangular brick house, with a lower wing, stands by Leeds Creek. This was the birthplace of Charles S. Winder (1829–62), a West Point graduate who served on the western frontier, was made a brigadier general in the Confederate Army, and commanded the Stonewall Brigade during Jackson's Valley Campaign in 1862. He was killed at Cedar Mountain on August 9, 1862.

Brick gateposts mark the entrance to MARENGO, 1 *m.*, whose first house burned in 1847. For many generations this was the home of the Gibson family (*see Tour 3D*). Fayette Gibson, the last of his name to live here, was, according to local historians, the inventor of the first reaper. His machine was exhibited at the Easton Fair Grounds in 1833 and examined there by Obed Hussey (*see Tour 16A*), whose reaper, patented in December of that year, is generally considered the earlier. Gibson's machine and his models were destroyed when the Marengo house burned.

The main route, turning L. at the junction, 9.5 *m.*, passes neat fields and thick woods.

At 11.3 *m.* on the main route is the junction with Bracco Road.

Right 1.5 *m.* on Bracco Road, which parallels Miles River, to the whitewashed brick gateposts that mark the entrance to VILLA PHOMA (L), a modern white frame cottage hidden from the road by woodland. It is the summer home of John Charles Thomas, Metropolitan Opera and concert singer.

At 11.7 *m.* the main route turns R. on macadam State 370.

On a lawn almost level with the waters of Miles River is THE ANCHORAGE (R), 12.1 *m.* Two low frame wings extend from the main part of the house to form a symmetrical five-part dwelling. Within the central building is incorporated an old house built, probably by Richard Bruff, in the middle of the eighteenth century. In 1763 the property was bought by the Reverend John Gordon, a noted rector of St. Michael's parish. Behind his church several miles down the river, Parson Gordon maintained a racetrack at which he and his congregation bet on each other's horses after services.

Directly across the road is ST. JOHN'S PROTESTANT EPISCOPAL CHURCH (R), so close to the shore that on still days the river gives back the reflection of its low crenelated tower. Its high lancet windows are boarded up; vines climb walls that are beginning to crumble; and young trees are thick in the weed-choked grounds.

In 1839 the wealthy planters of Miles River Neck built this chapel to save themselves a long trip to their parish church. Part of the congregation arrived by coach or on horseback; others came in boats rowed by one or two slaves, thus maintaining a custom of colonial days when the wealthy Eastern Shore families went visiting in luxurious barges rowed by from four to a dozen slaves. In 1900 the dwindling congregation, unable to afford repairs to an unsafe roof, decided to abandon the church.

A concrete bridge spans the Miles River, originally called St. Michaels in honor of the saint upon whose feast day the semiannual rents for lands granted the colonists were payable to the lord proprietor. Owing largely to the influence of Quaker settlers, the word 'Saint' was dropped and the name corrupted to Miles. The first ferry at this point was a log canoe for the occasional pedestrian in days when nearly all Eastern Shore travel was by water, and roads had not yet linked the widely separated plantations.

Later a flat scow pulled by a rope carried coaches and oxcarts across; in 1858 a bridge was built.

In a grove of trees on the south shore of the river is THE REST (R), 12.5 *m.*, a frame house built to replace the Buchanan house, destroyed by fire in 1863.

Franklin Buchanan (1800–74), born in Baltimore, entered the United States Navy at fourteen. When he died it was said that he had seen more varied sea service than any other man in the navy. During the Civil War he distinguished himself greatly and was made an admiral, the ranking officer of the Confederate Navy. Commanding the *Virginia (Merrimac),* he was seriously wounded the day before the encounter with the *Monitor,* which prevented him from taking part. Buchanan was defeated by Farragut in the battle of Mobile Bay, August 5, 1864, again seriously wounded, and taken prisoner. Returning to The Rest, he died here in 1874 and was buried in the Lloyd cemetery at Wye House.

At 13.1 *m.* is the junction with Glebe Road.

Left on Glebe Road, past pinewoods and level fields separated from the highway by the somber green masses of fence-row cedars, to a dirt road, 1.7 *m.*; L. on this to another dirt road, 2.1 *m.*; L. on this road to FAULSLEY WOOD FARM (L), 2.2 *m.*, whose house, a narrow two-story structure in a ring of shade trees, has meager windows, heavy two-panel doors, simple mantels in low rooms, and a narrow enclosed stair, indicating that it was built in the late seventeenth or early eighteenth century. Tench Tilghman (*see Tour 3D*) was born here in 1744.

A modern colonial-type frame house (L), 3.7 *m.*, has attached to its service wing by a paved areaway a low building so short as to look like half a house. Within its white clapboarding are included brick fragments of an old house that—according to tradition—was ENDING OF CONTROVERSY, the home of the Quaker Wenlock Christison. After having suffered extreme persecution in the Massachusetts colony, he came to Maryland about 1670, took a prominent part in the establishment of the Society of Friends in this county, and acquired lands and honors. At the time of his death (*c.*1678), he was a member of the Maryland House of Burgesses; it is possible he was the first Quaker to hold political office in America.

At 3.8 *m.*, the road is blocked by a gate through a tall hedge of Osage orange trees, latticed into a wall by honeysuckle. Points of light reflected from Miles River glint through the tangled grove beyond and outline the square masses and bracketed Victorian cornices of THE VILLA. The turreted house, forbidding and gloomy, has a history of lost or squandered fortunes, of failures and tragedies. It was built just before the Civil War, its vanished Italian gardens laid out to celebrate the fortune acquired by Richard France, Maryland's lottery king, who subsequently died in poverty. During the winter of 1876 The Villa is said by gossips to have been the hideout of Boss Tweed of New York when he escaped jail.

At 13.2 *m.* is the junction with State 17 (*see Tour 3C*), 2.5 miles west of Easton.

Tour 3C

Easton—Claiborne; 15.3 *m.*, State 17.

Concrete-paved roadbed, two lanes wide.
Limited accommodations between terminals.

State 17, part of a much used route between Ocean City and the Annapolis ferry, passes through the flat fields and pine woods of Miles River Neck, skirting the headwaters of creeks that are favorite resorts of yachtsmen, hunters, and fishermen.

In EASTON, 0 *m.*, State 17 branches west from US 213 (*see Tour 3*) at Washington and Gay Streets.

At 1.1 *m.* is the junction with a gravel road.

Left on this road to the catalpa-bordered lane (straight ahead) of RATCLIFFE MANOR (*visited by appointment*), 0.7 *m.*, whose large ivy-covered brick house facing Tred Avon River was built in 1749 by Henry Hollyday on a tract patented by Captain Robert Morris in 1659. The five-bay structure with its jerkin-head roof and pedimented dormers is typical of Georgian Colonial design. The roof is pierced by four large end chimneys and the entrance is now protected by a small, one-story pedimented portico. The high-ceilinged rooms contain some fine paneling and excellent wood carving.

At 2.5 *m.* is the junction (R) with State 370 (*see Tour 3B*).

NORTH BEND (R), 2.6 *m.*, a frame residence, has been the Dixon home for nearly 100 years and contains many old mahogany furnishings. The 1,000-acre grant was patented (1659) to Samuel Tilghman. The Betty Cove Meeting House was built here by a congregation of the Society of Friends organized in 1673 by George Fox, the society's founder.

At 3.3 *m.* is an asphalt-paved road.

Left on this road to OLD BLOOMFIELD, 1.1 *m.*, a whitewashed brick dwelling built about 1700, with a roof extending more than four feet beyond the northwest wall.

At 4.7 *m.* is the junction with bituminous-surfaced State 329.

Left on State 329 is ROYAL OAK, 1.4 *m.* (6 alt.,150 pop.), named for a giant tree that stopped two British cannon balls during the bombardment of near-by St.Michaels in 1813.

At 2.4 *m.* is the junction with the Bellevue Road.

Left on this asphalt-paved road 2.4 *m.* to a gravel road; R. 0.6 *m.* to CLAYLANDS (*visitors*), a rambling, telescope-type house built about 1700.

CLAY'S HOPE, 2.6 *m.* on the Bellevue Road, is a whitewashed brick dwelling built in 1720. In 1936 it became the Home for Aged Women of Easton.

BELLEVUE, 2.9 *m.* (5 alt.,150 pop.), by the Tred Avon River, manufactures fertilizer and is a terminus of the Bellevue-Oxford ferry.

ST. MICHAELS, 10 *m.* (8 alt.,1,043 pop.), on a neck of land between the Miles and Broad rivers, is a summer resort. In early times it produced many of the clippers that were to establish Baltimore as a leading port; more important to the farmers of Talbot were the numerous buckeyes, commonly called 'bugeyes,' produced here. These fleet sailing vessels speedily carried the grain, farm produce, and seafood of the Eastern Shore to Baltimore at low cost. The wide, shallow hull of the bugeye enables it to pick up farm cargo in small tributaries of the bay. It is also used extensively in oyster dredging.

In 1813 the town escaped damage in a British night bombardment by putting out all light near the ground and hanging lanterns in upper stories and treetops. This ruse caused the British to take a false range and overshoot.

CANNON BALL HOUSE on Mulberry St., the oldest house in the town, was so named because a ball dropped through the roof and bounced down the stair past the owner's wife without doing great harm. The AMELIA WELBY HOUSE, on Mulberry St., was the birthplace in 1819 of Amelia Ball Coppuck, the poet praised by Poe. CHRIST PROTESTANT EPISCOPAL CHURCH, Talbot St., serves a congregation that had a rector as early as 1672, though the parish was not given formal recognition until 1692. The present building was erected in 1878.

PERRY CABIN (R), 10.6 *m.*, built before the Revolution on part of the Martingham tract, was given its present name by Samuel Hambleton, paymaster on Commodore Perry's flagship in the battle of Lake Erie. The wings were added in 1860 and 1870.

At 11 *m.* is the junction with a graveled road.

1. Right on this to the MILES RIVER YACHT CLUB, 0.5 *m.*, where the annual Miles River Regatta (sail and motor) is held in August.

2. Left on this road to ROLLE'S RANGE, 1 *m.*, a gambrel-roofed two-and-a-half-story brick house built in 1740 on a grant surveyed in 1670. Repeated attempts have been made to find the legendary Spanish loot buried here.

WEST MARTINGHAM, 12.1 *m.* (*open to visitors*), built about 1670, is a low two-part, white clapboarded house with small windows and a single dormer in each section. The West Martingham tract, with the adjoining East Martingham, was patented in 1659 to Samuel Hambleton. The present owner of the house, residing in Easton, is his descendant and namesake.

ELBERTON, 12.3 *m.*, a low rambling white clapboard structure built in Colonial times but thoroughly modernized, contains a large collection of old pewter.

At 12.7 *m.* is the junction with State 304.

Left on this road to LOSTOCK, 3.7 *m.*, built before 1700 and the home of the Caulk family for nearly 250 years. Major William Caulk, an officer in the War of 1812, is buried here. His son John Caulk, a sea captain, is credited with the introduction of Muscovy ducks into this country.

State 17 crosses BAY HUNDRED election district. This name remains from the former division of the Province of Maryland into Hundreds for administrative, elective, and military purposes. In Anglo-Saxon times the English Hundreds contained ten families, ten estates, or 100 fighting men. The Hundreds here were more important in local government than the counties until well after the American Revolution.

At 14 *m.* is the junction with asphalt-paved State 451 (Tilghman Island Road).

Left on State 451 to WEBLEY, 2.4 *m.*, an old house with modern wings. In the 1830's it was the residence of Dr.Absalom Thompson, who rode bareback and barefoot on a mule, carrying a jar of calomel, a lancet, and a syringe with a nozzle like a 12-bore shotgun. His practice became so extensive that he opened a hospital in his home, the first on the Eastern Shore.

At 6 *m.* is the junction with a shell road; R. here 0.4 *m.* to LOWE'S LANDING. POPLAR ISLAND, 2 miles offshore, was held in William Claiborne's time by Richard Thompson, who lost his family in an Indian massacre here, and later by Alexander D'Hinoyossa, Dutch director of Delaware, who came to Maryland when the English captured New Amstel (New Castle) in 1664. The 1,000-acre tract of Thompson's time has been cut into three small islets by tidal erosion. The Jefferson Rod and Reel Club and the Poplar Island Club are the present owners.

The bridge, at 9.4 *m.* on State 451, crosses Knapps Narrows to TILGHMAN ISLAND, a three-and-a-half-mile stretch of low sandy ground much frequented by hunters and fishermen. The only villages on the island are TILGHMAN, 9.5 *m.* (4 alt., 700 pop.), AVALON, 10 *m.* (4 alt.,65 pop.), and FAIRBANK, 11.5 *m.* (4 alt.,150 pop.). Packing is carried on in low board structures that are gradually surrounded by huge heaps of oyster shells. The inhabitants also engage in fishing, crabbing, and oystering. Boats and guides are obtainable throughout the fishing season in summer and the shooting season in the autumn.

At 15.1 *m.* on State 17 is the junction with a graveled road.

Right on this road a few yards to a fork; R. here to MIRACLE HOUSE, 0.2 *m.*, established in 1919 by the Maryland Tuberculosis Association Inc. as a preventorium for undernourished children; more than 2,500 have been treated here but no active cases are accepted.

RICH NECK MANOR (*open Wed.*), 0.3 *m.*, was patented in 1651 to Captain William Mitchell. The two-story house, overlooking the Miles River and Chesapeake Bay, was the home of Matthew Tilghman, delegate to the Continental Congress and president of the Maryland Constitutional Convention. In his time it was partly burned and the present main building was erected, the original house becoming a wing. Rich Neck was the birthplace of Lloyd Tilghman, a general in the Confederate Army. On the grounds are an ivy-covered brick chapel and gray-walled burying place with a headstone marked 1692.

CLAIBORNE, 15.3 *m.* (5 alt.,156 pop.), was established in 1886 by the Baltimore & Eastern Shore Railroad as a ferry point on its line. At present it is the eastern terminus of the Roanoke-Claiborne ferry, a part of the route to Annapolis by way of Matapeake.

Tour 3D

Easton—Oxford; 9.6 *m.*, State 333.

Two lane concrete-paved roadbed.
Pennsylvania R.R. parallels route throughout.

This route crosses three small peninsulas cut by the Tred Avon River and its branches. The low, flat land, thickly wooded along the stream banks, is well adapted to farming, which, with fishing, furnishes livelihoods for most of the residents. Sport-fishing and yachting attract summer visitors. A few of the seventeenth- and eighteenth-century houses are still owned by the families who built them.

State 333 branches (R) at 0 *m.* from the junction with State 331 (*see Tour 3E*) at a point 0.7 miles south of Easton. Along the banks of narrow twisting Peachblossom Creek, 2.9 *m.*, are many country houses amid dense woods.

At 3.2 *m.* is the junction with a graveled lane.

Right on this to the TALBOT COUNTRY CLUB (L), 0.1 *m.* (*golf and tennis*), on land formerly called Llandoff and owned by Richard Tilghman Goldsborough.

At 3.5 *m.* on State 333 is the junction with a macadamized road.

Right on this, one of the wide tree-bordered avenues that cut back from the highway across level fields to the white houses of country estates on the banks of the Tred Avon. The road ends at a brick and marble gatepost, the entrance to AVONDALE, 2.7 *m.* The east wall of the three-story T-shaped brick residence is the only remaining part of the house that was built about 1770. In one gable end the twin chimneys project at the base and incline so sharply inward near the roof that they become almost flush with the wall. The land, granted in 1659 to William Turner, a Quaker, was long known as Turner's Point. After Turner's death and before 1697 Thomas Skillington established a shipyard here that launched seagoing vessels, among them the ship of a Captain Martin who, returning from southern voyages, 'would bring sufficient coin to cover the large dining room table over with Spanish dollars a foot deep.'

In TRAPPE STATION, 6.1 *m.* (14 alt., 10 pop.), a railroad shipping point, is the junction with a graveled road.

Right on this to (R) the iron grilled entrance gate of DEEP WATER POINT (*private*), 1.5 *m.*, whose three-towered chateau was erected in 1928. In the log cabin south of the chateau John Gill wrote *In His Own Country* (1935) and other works of fiction.

Hidden from view by a high thorn hedge is OTWELL (R), 2.3 *m.*, for more than two centuries a Goldsborough estate. The gambrel-roofed sections of the two-story T-shaped residence were built about 1670 of vari-colored brick burnt on the farm. Three other gabled sections were added a few decades later, giving the whole a long rambling appearance. Little change has been effected in the physical aspect of the building and much of the woodwork is fastened with wooden pegs. The step ends of the black walnut stairway are carved in tulip designs. This estate was patented to William Taylor in 1659; John Goldsborough, the third owner, acquired it in 1720.

The oldest section of ANDERTON (R), 6.6 *m.*, built about 1660, is a long story-and-a-half frame wing with dormers. Its main entrance door is only four feet in height and other doors are of less than average size; one bedroom is 19 feet long but only 5 feet wide. The estate of 600 acres was a grant to John Anderton in 1659; in 1719 it belonged to Major Nicholas Lowe, who owned the first coach in Talbot County. William Thomas acquired the estate in 1740.

JENA (R), 7.9 *m.*, a small brick dwelling erected before 1700 on the Anderton tract, was so named by Jacob Gibson, its owner during the Napoleonic wars. Gibson admired Napoleon so much that he named his various estates in Talbot County after victories won by Bonaparte: among them Jena, Austerlitz, Marengo, and Friedland. When Gibson was soundly thrashed by a political opponent, the latter in derision named his own farm Waterloo.

During the War of 1812 Gibson owned Sharp's Island near the mouth of the Choptank River. When the British cruisers under Admiral Warren raided the island and carried off some of Gibson's cattle, the owner in turn boarded the admiral's flagship and succeeded in getting paid for the property taken. Gossips said Gibson had sold out to the enemy. With feeling against him at high pitch and the whole bayside country expecting an attack from the British, Gibson sailed into St.Michaels harbor with a red bandanna at the masthead and an empty rum barrel for a drum. The town thought the attack had arrived; women and children were sent into the country, and the militia was assembled before the prank was discovered. Here Mr.Gibson's career almost ended but, being a man of courage, he boldly confronted the angry townsmen and was allowed to depart unharmed.

At 8.0 *m.* is the junction with a graveled road.

Left on this to a farm lane, 0.3 *m.*, that leads to COMBSBERRY (L), erected in 1740. The front of the three-story central section is laid in all-header brick. The wide windows are sunk in panels of glazed headers, and a similar effect is introduced in an arrangement beneath the window sills. The expansive lawn, studded with trees and an abundance of shrubbery, extends to Island Creek. Though the house has been completely modernized the cellar contains an old slave dungeon.

PLIMHIMMON (R), 8.9 *m.*, is best known as the residence of the widow of Colonel Tench Tilghman. After her husband's death in Baltimore in 1786, the widow (a first cousin) was given the estate by her father, Matthew Tilghman, and she resided here until her death 57 years later. Tilghman himself never lived here. Plimhimmon is a subdivision of the Hir-Dir-Lloyd grant to Edward Lloyd in 1659. The two-and-a-half-story dwelling, of old English-mold brick, was erected about 1736; the frame wing was added later.

At 9.0 *m.* is the junction with a shell road.

Right on this road to the OXFORD CEMETERY, 0.3 *m.*, in which is the TILGHMAN MONUMENT, erected to the memory of Tench Tilghman and his wife by their descendants. Tilghman, a merchant in Philadelphia, had liquidated his business at the approach of the Revolution and was shortly made Washington's aide-de-camp. After the surrender of the British Army at Yorktown he was sent with this news to the Congress in Philadelphia. Washington said of him: 'He left as fair a reputation as ever belonged to a human character.'

BONFIELD (L), 9.2 *m.*, is the home of Hervey Allen, author of *Anthony Adverse* (1933). The former house, erected in 1772 by Samuel Chamberlaine, Jr., was burned in 1927. It stood on a hill said to have been made by slaves who brought the earth on their backs from near-by Boone Creek. Between the residence and the guest house is a formal garden and sunken pool.

OXFORD, 9.6 *m.* (1 alt., 915 pop.), is on the southern tip of a peninsula between the Choptank and Tred Avon rivers, and has a land-locked harbor that now protects a large fishing and oyster fleet. In the middle of the eighteenth century, this port rivaled Annapolis as the busiest in the province. Most of the adult males are now engaged in the sea-food industry. The town today bears little evidence of age, nearly all the buildings having been erected within the last century; but the shipyard has survived two and a half centuries. A half dozen inns and tourist homes cater to sport fishermen. The Tred Avon Yacht Club holds an annual three-day regatta here about the middle of August.

In 1668 William Stevens (*see Tour* 7) deeded 30 acres of land here to the proprietary for the erection of a town, which in the following year was proclaimed a port of entry by Charles Calvert. Its first name was Thread Haven, perhaps because it was a depot for cordage and ship supplies, including thread; later it became Third Haven and is found under that name on old maps. (Third Haven River by another sea change became Tred Avon.) In 1683 Oxford was officially laid out in 100 lots on land then owned by Colonel Nicholas Lowe whose mother, Margaret Lowe, left by will certain tracts to the new town. The act was repealed but re-enacted in 1694; a new survey was requested and the name changed to Williamstadt in honor of William of Orange. The name Oxford was resumed when Queen Anne ascended the throne.

Large London and Liverpool commercial houses established branches here for trading with the colonists, exchanging articles of necessity for cargoes of tobacco. Two record books of the port collectors, kept between 1747 and 1775, show that at one time almost 200 vessels were registered at the customs house. As other ports in the province grew, Oxford's trade declined. By 1790 one chronicler wrote: 'Oxford's streets and strands were once covered by busy crowds ushering in commerce from almost every quarter of the globe. The once well-worn streets are now grown in grass, save a few narrow tracks made by sheep and swine; and the strands have more the appearance of an uninhabited island than where human feet have ever trod.'

An early Oxford tradesman was Robert Morris, whose son and namesake became the financier of the American Revolution. The senior Morris (*see Tour* 3E) came to Oxford in 1738, leaving his young son in Liverpool. The younger Morris arrived in 1747 at the age of 13; after private tutoring he was sent to Philadelphia, where he attained fame as one of the great merchants of his day but later was sentenced to debtors' prison.

The town's memorial to the Morrises (the name of its principal street) is an extension of the State highway to the water front. The street along the water front is still called The Strand.

All that remains of the MORRIS HOUSE (1774) at Morris St. and The Strand is a frame story-and-a-half structure with dormers, now part of an old hotel, deserted except for a store and a restaurant.

The old RIDGEWATER HOUSE, north side of Morris Street two doors east of the post office, has corner fireplaces, paneling, and a handmade stairway. On the south side of Morris St., five doors from The Strand, is an inn called GRAPEVINE HOUSE, for the large grapevine that was planted on its lawn in 1775 continues to bear an abundance of grapes each season.

Tour 3E

Easton—Cambridge—Vienna; 31.6 *m.*, State 331, State 16, State 344.

Concrete- and asphalt-paved roadbed.
Usual types of accommodations.

This route runs through the grain-growing section of Talbot County and the truck-raising farmlands of Dorchester. It is a region abounding in legend, folklore, and well-preserved seventeenth- and eighteenth-century buildings.

Section a. EASTON to CAMBRIDGE; 15.3 m.

State 331 follows Washington Street south from its junction with US 213 (*see Tour 3*) in EASTON, 0 *m.* (*see Tour 3B*).

At 0.7 *m.* is a junction (R) with State 333 (*see Tour 3D*).

The hexagonal structure, 2.8 *m.*, is PEACHBLOSSOM CHURCH (L), built in 1881 and formerly used by Methodist, Reformed Lutheran, Swedenborgian, and Church of the Brethren congregations every fourth Sunday. According to tradition, the six-sided edifice was built 'so that the devil would have no corner to sit in and hatch evil.'

At 3.3 *m.* is the junction with an asphalt-paved road.

Left on this road at 2.3 *m.*, opposite a canning factory, is the graveled Lloyd Landing Road; L. on this to OLD MANOR FARM HOUSE, 4.5 *m.*, a high peaked story-and-a-half brick dwelling built about 1740 when this was a shipping point on Choptank

River. Its interior woodwork, projecting window seats, and twenty-four-pane windows are unchanged.

The crossroads hamlet of HAMBLETON, 5.8 *m.* (52 alt.,20 pop.), has been called Hole in the Wall for more than two centuries because tradition says sailors formerly sold smuggled goods through a hole in a wall here, the buyer and seller concealed from each other.

Left from Hambleton on a dirt road to the ruins of WHITE MARSH CHURCH (L), 0.3 *m.*, which may have been built as early as 1685. A mutilated parish record shows that White Marsh had an acting rector of the Church of England in 1690. The church was abandoned during the Civil War, and partly burned in 1896. Annual services are now held here. In a corner of the churchyard is the GRAVE OF ROBERT MORRIS,SR., who died July 12, 1750. He was the father of Robert Morris, the Revolutionary War financier.

Among provincial rectors of White Marsh was the Reverend Thomas Bacon, compiler of *Bacon's Laws*, a compendium of Maryland's colonial statutes which for many decades was an authoritative guide for the State's courts. Another rector was the Reverend Daniel Maynadier, Huguenot fugitive who fled to America after Louis XIV of France revoked the Edict of Nantes. It is told that the night after Maynadier's wife was buried in the churchyard, two strangers opened her grave to steal a valuable old ring from her hand. Unable to slip it off, they severed her finger. The shock revived her, she arose, gathered up her shroud, and made her way to the rectory, surviving for several years after the ordeal.

TRAPPE, 8.4 *m.* (56 alt.,300 pop.), an inland farming community with vegetable canneries and a lumber mill, is known to baseball fans as the home of J.Franklin (Home Run) Baker. Baker was born here March 13, 1886, and attained fame as third baseman with the Philadelphia Athletics '$100,000 infield.' During the World Series of 1911 with the New York Giants, Baker won two of the games by timely home runs. He now lives on a farm outside of Trappe.

In Trappe is the junction with a road that serves as the town's northernmost intersecting street.

Right 2.5 *m.* on this road to a fork.
   1. Right (straight ahead) from the fork 1 *m.* to ISLAND CREEK HOUSE (R), an early eighteenth-century dwelling recently restored. The central section has frame sides and glazed brick laid in Flemish bond, the bricks zigzagged where chimney and ridge pole meet. A 'curtain' connects the middle section with a two-story frame kitchen wing.
   At 2.9 *m.* is a lane (straight ahead) leading to CHLORA POINT HOUSE, with brick ends and clapboarded sides, said to have been erected in 1678. The site, overlooking the Choptank River, was part of a grant to Edward Lloyd in 1659. A ferry once operated to Castle Haven, on the opposite side of the Choptank.

   2. Left 0.8 *m.* at the fork to a lane (L), leading to HAMPDEN, erected in 1665 on the Hir-Dir-Lloyd grant by Thomas Martin. The roof was pitched low to conceal the house from roving Indians. Diagonally battened doors, huge elliptical fireplaces, and ogee arches are interesting features.
   THE WILDERNESS (L), 2.3 *m.*, with its attractive old boxwood gardens and trees, is the former home of Daniel Martin, twice governor of Maryland (1828–29 and 1830–31) and grandson of Captain Daniel Martin of the 38th Maryland Militia in the Revolutionary War.

At 9 *m.* on State 331 is the junction with a macadam road (L) and a graveled road (R).

1. Left on the macadam road to a dirt road, 2.2 *m.*; L. on this to SAULSBURY HOUSE (L), 4 *m.*, a two-story yellow brick structure built in 1663, its hip roof, placed cross-wise, forming a distinctive landmark. In 1871 Jesse Cryer, a hermit who lived on the shores of near-by Miles Creek, attempted unsuccessfully to fly by strapping two homemade wings to his arms and leaping from a shed.

2. Right on the graveled road 1.8 *m.* to the long lane (L) of CROSIADORE, home of the Dickinson family since 1669. The name is an Anglicization of the French Croix d'Or. It was the birthplace of John Dickinson (1732–1808), whose *Letters from a Penn-sylvania Farmer* (1767) stirred up antiparliamentary feeling before the Revolution. Dickinson advocated conciliation with the mother country; however, when the break came he espoused the Colonial cause and became a signer of the Constitution for Dela-ware. John Dickinson, appointed U.S. Assistant Attorney General in 1935, is the pres-ent owner.

A lane (R) at 2.5 *m.* on the graveled road leads to COMPTON, erected in 1760 by John Stevens, who entertained lavishly here. His grandson, Samuel Stevens, Jr., governor of Maryland (1822–25), continued the family tradition for hospitality. While governor he invited General Lafayette to visit Maryland, and through him the marquis and his male heirs forever were voted citizenship by the General Assembly.

PERRY FARM HOUSE (L), 13.4 *m.*, on the shore of Choptank River, is a frame hip-roofed residence with broad chimneys, built about 1687. It was once an inn at the terminus of a ferry between this point and Cambridge.

The GOVERNOR EMERSON C. HARRINGTON BRIDGE across the Choptank is the longest (8,737 ft.) concrete span in the State and was completed in 1935 at a cost of $1,500,000, one-third defrayed by the State and the re-mainder by the Public Works Administration.

CAMBRIDGE, 15.3 *m.* (20 alt.,8,544 pop.) (*see Cambridge*).

Points of Interest: The Point, La Grange House, Glasgow, Courthouse, Phillips Pack-ing Co., and others.

In Cambridge are junctions with State 16 (*see Tour 3G*) and State 343 (*see Tour 3F*).

Section b. *CAMBRIDGE to VIENNA;* 16.3 *m.*

In CAMBRIDGE, 0 *m.*, State 16, now the route, follows E. Washington Street eastward.

SHOAL CREEK HOUSE (L), 1.1 *m.*, was built before 1750 presumably by Joseph Ennalls from whose family it was acquired by Charles Golds-borough, governor of Maryland (1818), and it long provided the setting for lavish entertainment.

EASTERN SHORE STATE HOSPITAL (L), 1.2 *m.*, cares for the mentally ill. At 2.1 *m.* is the junction with graveled Bucktown Road.

Right on this road to another graveled road, 4.2 *m.*; L. on this 1.2 *m.* to PITT'S DE-SIRE (R), a log house built before 1700 and recently faced with weatherboarding and shingles, though the interior is little changed. The Reverend Freeborn Garretson (1752–1827), a Methodist evangelist and organizer, was conducting services here dur-ing the Revolution when he was imprisoned for teaching 'toryism.'

Left from BUCKTOWN, 7.4 *m.* (4 alt.,48 pop.), on another graveled road. A wide lane leads to Yarmouth or WHITE HOUSE FARM (L), 10.2 *m.*, by the Transquaking River. This was the homestead of the Ecclestons, whose names appear frequently in the county's early records. The two-foot brick walls appear to be as substantial as when laid more than two centuries ago; the corner fireplaces and much of the original panel-ing are intact.

On State 16 at 2.5 *m.* is a lane (L) to WARE NECK HOUSE, erected during the Revolution by Henry Ennalls (*see below*) on part of the former Choptank Indian Reservation. It contains a notable stairway and old mantels.

The lane (L) at 3.5 *m.* leads to BONNY BROOK (1762), a dilapidated frame house with brick gable ends and broad chimneys. A few traces remain of the once elaborate garden on the shore of Hurst Creek.

Ferry Lane (L), 4 *m.*, is the entrance to WHITE HALL, now a summer residence. The two-and-a-half-story brick section was built about 1750 by one of the Ennalls family. Imbedded in the cellar floor are two tombstones, bearing the date 1854; no explanation is given for their presence. In antebellum times White Hall is said to have been used by Patty Cannon as a hiding place for Negroes she had kidnaped in order to sell.

At 4.3 *m.* is the junction (straight ahead) with State 344, which becomes the main route.

Left 3.7 *m.* on State 16 to SHERMAN INSTITUTE or Sherwood (L), erected in 1825 as part of a private school by Captain Thomas Sherman for the education of his two sons. Instructors were hired and soon scions of other prominent families were admitted. When the school was discontinued the building became a private residence.

At 3.8 *m.* is a graveled road; L. on this 0.4 *m.* to a turn and a dirt road; L. (straight ahead) on the dirt road 0.5 *m.* to VUE DE LEAU, which has, as the name implies, an excellent view of the Choptank River. Once a part of the Choptank Indian Reservation, this tract was purchased in 1799 by Samuel LeCompte; later, it was the home of the Stewarts and the Dixons. The present structure is the result of 125 years of extension and renovation. The face of the 16-room structure is now shingled; the north end or main entrance is said to be built of gum logs with walnut sills. North of the house is an Indian shell mound, indicating the site of an Indian village; to the south is a spring used by the red men. Century-old boxwood and a sandy bathing beach add charm to this place, which from November to March is a sanctuary for white swan.

The graveled road continues 0.9 *m.* to GOOSE CREEK HOUSE (L), a high two-story brick building. It was built about 1750 on a tract bought from the Choptank Indians in 1693 by Frances Taylor, wife of Thomas Taylor. The indenture, which is in the Cambridge Courthouse, contains the signature marks of Chief Hachwop, his Queen, and five of his 'greate men.'

At 4 *m.* on State 16 is a junction with concrete-paved State 14, an alternate route to East New Market (*see below*). Left on State 14 1.7 *m.* to the fishing town of SECRE-TARY (361 pop.), supposedly named for Henry Sewall, secretary of the province under Charles Calvert. Near the end of a short street is MY LADY SEWALL'S MANOR HOUSE, now a children's nursery operated by the State. It was erected shortly after the grant of 2,000 acres by Lord Baltimore to Secretary Sewall in 1661. After her husband's death Lady Sewall married Lord Baltimore. The fine paneling, probably installed by Major Nicholas Sewall, is in the Brooklyn (N.Y.) Museum of Art.

WARWICK FORT MANOR, overlooking Secretary Creek opposite the village, was formed in 1720 when Colonel Henry Hooper combined My Lady Sewall's Manor with adjacent tracts. The old brick Colonial manor house burned a decade ago; some of the original English-mold bricks were used in the present Spanish-type bungalow which occupies the site.

On State 14 at 2.8 *m.* is ROSE HILL (L), one of the seven Rose Hills in Maryland. This two-and-a-half-story brick building, now somewhat marred by the passage of years, formerly was the home of the Webster family.

State 14 continues to EAST NEW MARKET, 3.3 *m.*, and thence eastward to the junction with US 213 (*see Tour 3*) at SHILOH CHURCH, 5.8 *m.*

On State 16 is EAST NEW MARKET, 5.6 *m.* (222 pop.), a center of a productive farming area. This quiet town, with easy access to water and railway transportation, was formerly the seat of the New Market Academy, founded in 1818.

FRIENDSHIP HALL (R), 0.2 *m.* from Main St. on State 14, was built about 1790 by James Sulivane, quartermaster general of Dorchester County during the Revolution.

The front of this two-and-a-half-story mansion has brick pilasters apparently supporting the stringcourse and two oval windows in the pediment of the west gable. A frame and brick dwelling with four corner chimneys, opposite Friendship Hall, occupies the site of Maurice Manor, another contemporary Sulivane house.

MANNING HOUSE (R), on Main St. south of State 14, is a three-story painted brick dwelling formerly the East New Market Hotel. It is sometimes called the Old House of the Hinges because of the great hinges on the meat house to the rear. The cornice has tapering modillions with guttae below. Said to have been built by one of the Ennalls, it came subsequently into the possession of Anthony L. Manning, an officer in the War of 1812.

State 16 continues to the junction, 9.6 m., with US 213 (*see Tour 3*) at a point about 15 miles north of Vienna.

State 344 continues from the junction with State 16 southeastward to the junction with US 213 (*see Tour 3*) in VIENNA, 31.6 m. (*see Tour 3*).

Tour 3F

Cambridge—Ragged Point Island; 14.6 *m.*, State 343 and a country road.

Concrete-paved roadbed to Hudson; graveled beyond.

State 343 runs through a level peninsula formed by the Choptank and the Little Choptank Rivers. The permanent inhabitants are engaged in the sea-food industry, agriculture, and catering to summer residents whose estates contrast with the drab homes of the tenant farmers.

State 343 follows Washington Street in CAMBRIDGE, 0 *m.*, west from its junction with State 331 (*see Tour 3E*) and State 16 (*see Tour 3G*).

At 2.2 *m.* is the junction with a macadamized road.

Right on this road to the CAMBRIDGE COUNTRY CLUB (*for members only*), 0.7 *m.*, by the Choptank River. The club has a nine-hole golf course and tennis courts.

The entrance (R), 1.6 *m.*, leads to HORN'S POINT, estate of Coleman du Pont (1863–1930), U.S. Senator, industrialist, and pioneer in modern road-building. The handsome dwelling, now owned by a son, faces both the river and the broad greensward that stretches to the highway. Near the entrance, bordered by 300-year-old trees, is a private flying field. On the gateposts are concrete figures of the prize Merino ram, Don Pedro, whose arrival in 1801 was an event.

As early as 1785 the Society for the Promotion of Agriculture of South Carolina offered a medal for the first flock of Merino sheep kept in the State. Yet no importation of these superior wool bearers is recorded in Carolina or the other States till 1793, when William Foster of Boston smuggled two Merino ewes and one ram aboard Captain John Atkin's ship the *Bald Eagle*. Shortly after their arrival Foster went to France and left the sheep with a man named Craigie—who ate them and pronounced them delicious. Years later Foster encountered Craigie at an auction where Craigie was paying $1,000 for a Merino ram.

In 1801 the importations were more successful. Mr.Seth Adams of Dorchester, Massachusetts, and Colonel Humphreys both claimed to have the first pair. The controversy was finally settled by giving Adams a $50 prize and the colonel a medal.

Don Pedro, who cost $1,000, was the only survivor of four Merino rams shipped from Spain by E.I.du Pont and M.DeLessert. After a year on the du Pont farm Don Pedro was used for four years on DeLessert's place. DeLessert sold his sheep at auction in 1805 and du Pont's agent bought Don Pedro for $60. When the ram died in 1811 Thomas Jefferson wrote a letter of condolence to du Pont; the latter had a wooden image of Don Pedro made from which the figures on the present gateposts were cast.

The house of JARVIS HILL (R), 4.5 m., is identified by the wide twin chimneys of the south wing. The central brick structure was built about 1735 and the wings shortly after. The fireplace paneling in the older section and the 18-inch window recesses and doorjambs taper towards the floor. Jarvis Hill is part of a grant made in 1659 to Anthony LeCompte, who left France at the time of the conflict between Richelieu and the Huguenots and went to England where he won military distinctions during his eleven years in the army. He came to Calvert County, Maryland before 1655. Jarvis Hill was built for his descendant, John LeCompte. The ancient LeCompte graveyard and the slave burial lot are north of the dwelling.

WINDMERE (L), 5.3 m., the summer home of George L. Radcliffe, elected to the U.S. Senate in 1934, occupies the site of the ancestral home of the Radcliffes. The main section is modern. The east wing, built in 1700 on Taylor Island and recently moved here, is still called Aunt Polly Critchett's House. During the War of 1812 Aunt Polly had one of her slaves take her across the bay to the British flagship, where she demanded and obtained the return of her husband's vessel, seized by the invaders. Her house retains the original exposed rafters, paneled fireplace, and mantel. On the lawn of Windmere is a one-room schoolhouse built at near-by Castle Haven by Senator Radcliffe's father more than a century ago.

SPOCOT (L), 5.7 m., is a T-shaped frame dwelling with five broad chimneys, and 13 dormers. The southern section was erected soon after the land was patented to Stephen Gary in 1662. The Indian Council Oak on the land is said to be more than 400 years old.

The house was once the center of a self-contained community with a shipyard, gristmill, general store, blacksmith shop, and large slave quarters. All of these have disappeared except two of the slave houses, now combined to form a tenant house. Spocot is now owned by Senator Radcliffe, a descendant of Stephen Gary.

LLOYDS, 5.9 m. (2 alt.,30 pop.), is a crossroads hamlet.

At 6.2 m. is the junction with a graveled road.

Right on this road to POKETY LODGE (R), 1.6 m., owned by Walter P. Chrysler, automobile manufacturer. Since its purchase in 1929, the estate has been converted into a showplace with old boxwood for the lawns, formal gardens, an orchard of fully grown fruit trees, a sandy bathing beach, and a swimming pool. The low rambling frame and brick lodge, recently erected, faces the Choptank River. At Todd's Point, on the estate, Mr.Chrysler maintains an extensive wild fowl preserve that attracts thousands of birds every year.

At 2.3 *m.* is the entrance to CASTLE HAVEN, a castle-like brick structure once considered by President Hoover for his summer home. Here Anthony LeCompte (*see above*) came in 1659 to take possession of his first grant of 800 acres, named Antonine, later St. Anthony's. It was said several vessels were required to transport his retainers and goods. After the brick central section was built in 1730, several wealthy families spent lavishly to improve the place. At one time it was a camp for girls, attended by daughters of socially prominent families. The land-locked harbor is often used by boatmen as a refuge.

At 6.4 *m.* on State 343 is a junction with the graveled Morris Neck Road.

Left here to TRAVERS HOUSE (R), 0.3 *m.*, built before the Revolutionary War and largely furnished with furniture of that period.

On the Morris Neck Road at 2 *m.* is the old SEWARD HOUSE (R), constructed between 1725 and 1730. The roof is still covered with hand-rived shingles.

Morris Neck Road ends at CHERRY ISLAND, 3 *m.*, former summer home of Alfred I. du Pont (1864–1935). The Nemours Foundation, established by du Pont, now maintains Cherry Island as a summer convalescent home for crippled children. The five-acre island on which it stands was formerly the southern tip of the mainland.

At 7.5 *m.* on State 343 is the junction with a graveled road.

Left on this to MAYHEW FARM (L), 1.3 *m.*, the home of William Mayhew, composer of popular songs. The oldest part of the Mayhew home was built about 100 years ago as the one-room Beckwith School.

At 9.6 *m.* is the junction with a graveled road.

Right on this road 1.1 *m.* to a private entrance into COOK POINT. Before 1661 Sir Andrew Cooke (the 'e' was later dropped by the family) came to Maryland from England to take possession of land here called Maulden. His son, Ebenezer, was Maryland's first recognized poet (*see Literature*).

Concrete-paved State 343 ends at 10 *m.*, and the main route becomes a graveled road.

The HUDSON–JAMES Community, 10.2 *m.* (1 alt.,400 pop.), actually one settlement, extends along both sides of the road for about a mile.

The road forks at 11.1 *m.*; the route follows the right hand road.

MARGARET'S DELIGHT, or Spedden's Regulation (R), 11.6 *m.*, has a frame story-and-a-half house erected about 1750. The dining and living rooms have large old fireplaces and old furnishings.

The road forks at 13 *m.*; L. here on a road that ends at 14 *m.*, where a private wooden bridge extends to RAGGED POINT ISLAND. William A. Starrett, a member of the firm that constructed New York's Chrysler Building, converted this isolated, low-lying island into a modern show place. It is still owned by his widow, who occupies it infrequently. Like many other islands of the Chesapeake, this was formerly connected with the mainland and was gradually detached by tides.

Tour 3G

Cambridge—Church Creek—Hooperville; 30.4 *m.*, State 16 and State 335.

Concrete-paved roadbed between Church Creek and Golden Hill; elsewhere graveled or asphalt-paved.
Tourist homes and boarding houses in towns.

The route runs through tidewater country, popular for duck hunting and fishing. The sea-food industry and the packing and canning of sea-food and tomatoes are the chief means of livelihood for the permanent population; truck farming and muskrat trapping provide employment in season. Droning buzzsaws and huge piles of sawdust at intervals along this route indicate how rapidly the pine and oak are being cleared.

State 16, called Church Creek Road, and following Race St. in CAMBRIDGE, 0 *m.*, branches south from State 343 (*see Tour 3F*).

At 2.9 *m.* is the junction with a dirt road.

Right on this to another dirt road 0.3 *m.*; R. here 0.3 *m.* to a dirt lane (L) leading to WOOLFORD HOUSE, sometimes known as Hull House, a late seventeenth-century dwelling of modest proportions. The dining room chimney has a space back of it where slaves in the old days would remain during intervals between waiting on table.

CHURCH CREEK, 6.3 *m.* (5 alt.,300 pop.), laid out about 1700, was once surrounded by large forests of white oak and pine and early did considerable shipbuilding. Today, its quiet, shaded main thoroughfare is lined with the homes of retired farmers, most of them descendants of early English settlers. At the entrance to the village, on the lawn of the M.E. Church, is the ancient TREATY OAK, under which a treaty was signed between the settlers and the Indians.

In Church Creek concrete-paved State 335, the Hooper Island Road, becomes the main route.

Right from Church Creek on State 16 to the WYVILL HOUSE (R), 0.3 *m.*, home of Dr.Dorsey Wyvill, one of the founders of the Medical and Chirurgical Faculty of Maryland. The frame house contains many fireplaces, gracefully carved mantels, decorative panels, and unusual plaster work.

OLD TRINITY PROTESTANT EPISCOPAL CHURCH (R), 0.9 *m.*, believed to have been built before 1680, was restored in 1850 when it was named Trinity. Its high-doored box pews, sounding board, and high pulpit disappeared in the course of alterations. The church still possesses a silver chalice, part of a communion service given by Queen Anne, and a red velvet cushion on which Queen Anne is said to have knelt at her coronation. In earlier times the cushion was so highly regarded that it was kept on the altar. A newly arrived church dignitary, questioning its place there, exclaimed: 'If Queen Anne were here would you set her on God's altar?'—and threw the cushion on the floor. These relics are now shown only on special occasions.

Agriculture

WATERMELON TIME AT THE DOCKS

FARMSTEAD

HARVESTING WHEAT

Holmes I. Mett

SILO FEEDING, BELTSVILLE

HAYING

BEAN PICKER

Rothstein: Farm Security Administration

THE COUNTY AGENT VISITS

SOW AND SHOATS

BULL EXERCISER, AGRICULTURAL RESEARCH CENTER, BELTSVILLE

CANNING FACTORY, EASTON

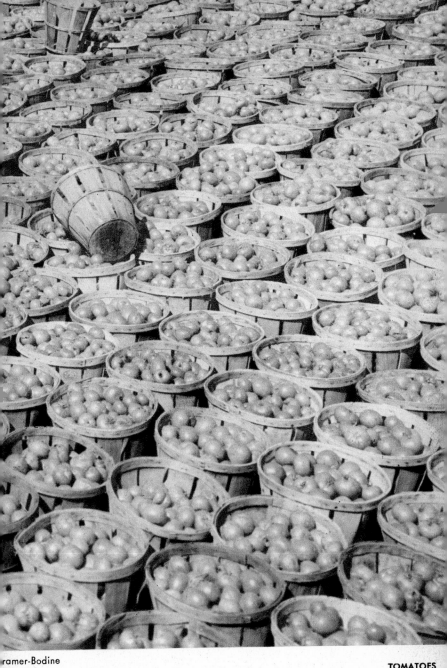

ramer-Bodine

TOMATOES

STRIPPING TOBACCO

Kramer-Bodin

In the churchyard millstones at the head and foot appropriately mark The Miller's Grave. Distinguished Marylanders, including Thomas King Carroll, governor of Maryland 1830–31, are buried here.

The BUSICK HOUSE, 1.2 *m.*, sometimes called the Roger Jones House, is a story-and-a-half farmhouse on a cove of Church Creek. The oldest part of the house was built about 1700, the remainder a few years later. The interior contains some fine woodwork, including vertical paneling of the type used in large sailing vessels of the day.

MADISON, 4.5 *m.* (3 alt.,200 pop.), formerly a shipping and boat building community, now depends entirely on the sea-food industry. The village was first called Tobacco Stick, because of the feat of an Indian who, while being pursued by white settlers, jumped across the channel at the mouth of the cove with the aid of a tobacco stick. Emerson C. Harrington, governor of Maryland 1916–20, was born here.

A farm near Madison was the home of the incorrigibly stubborn white mule of legend who successfully resisted every attempt to harness him. The tale is that a Negro once sought to do so by a ruse and fell to the ground in a coma—proof that the mule was an incarnation of Satan. The mule is said to have galloped about the neighborhood at night, until finally driven onto the marshes by a posse; here he sank from view. But his ghost later appeared before the town drunkard, who was so overcome by the experience he gave up intoxicating liquor and became a parson.

The ruined HODSON HOUSE (R), 5.2 *m.*, is believed to have been the first courthouse of Dorchester County. From 1669 to 1673 the first courts were held in private homes; this house, built by John Hodson, an early justice, was not only used for trials but as the county jail. As late as 1814 it still served the latter purpose; members of the crew of a British tender, captured in 1814 near James Point, were kept here for a time.

State 16 ends at the Slaughter Creek Bridge, 9.4 *m.* A shell road continues to the village of TAYLOR ISLAND, 9.7 *m.* (3 alt.,750 pop.). The point of land called Taylor Island, of which the village is the social center, was settled about 1659 and named for an early inhabitant. At present it is renowned for fishing and duck hunting and is popular as a summer resort.

At 10.1 *m.* the road branches. The left branch formerly led to Hooper Island but a bridge, washed out years ago, has never been repaired, so the road is impassable. The route follows the right branch.

The mile-long entrance lane (L), 11.4 *m.*, leads to MULBERRY GROVE, the Pattison estate for the past 250 years. The land, originally called Dover, received its present name when an early eighteenth-century attempt was made to establish a silk industry here by importing mulberry trees to nourish silk worms. The story-and-a-half center section erected in 1684 had brick walls 54 inches thick. These walls are now partly plastered and partly clapboards fastened with wooden pegs. The foundation is built of cedar blocks two feet square. The interior contains large fireplaces and old pine paneling. The small structure behind the house was the first schoolhouse on Taylor Island, built in the late 1700's.

Near a brick church is the junction (R) with a dirt road, 13.6 *m.*, which becomes the main side route. The OLD LECOMPTE HOUSE (L), visible from the road at 14.4 *m.*, was built in 1710. In 1781, at the invitation of the owner, Moses LeCompte IV, the meetings of the newly organized Methodist congregation were held here until a chapel could be erected on the island. In 1801 the place was acquired by the Cator family, from whom it received its alternate name. The dilapidated old mansion is used as a storage house.

HOOPER POINT GUN CLUB (L), 15.2 *m.*, maintained by a group from Boston, is one of many sportsmen's clubs in this section. The Hooper family cemetery is near by.

State 335 continues southward from Church Creek, crossing the Big Blackwater River at 11.3 *m.* The BLACKWATER MIGRATORY BIRD REFUGE, an 8,000-acre marsh along the Big and Little Blackwater Rivers, was established by the Federal Government in 1931. Black ducks, blue-winged teal, and gray mallards are bred on this important waterfowl sanctuary.

The Blackwater marshes rank high in the production of black muskrat pelts.

At 16.1 *m.* State 335 turns sharply R. at the junction with concrete-paved State 336.

> Left on State 336 to a shell road (*impassable in wet weather*) 7.9 *m.*; R. 0.9 *m.* on this to LAKE COVE, a small house built in 1739. Near the house is a dilapidated old wind-mill once used for grinding grain. The millstones and ratchet wheel survive.
> State 336 ends at WINGATE, 9.7 *m.* (2 alt.,800 pop.), a truck farming, oystering, and canning community on the Honga River.

State 335 continues westward to the junction with a dirt road at 18.1 *m.*

> Right on this road to the village of GOLDEN HILL, 0.1 *m.* (2 alt.,275 pop.), where the APPLEGARTH HOME stands. A section of this house was built in 1675 but the living room was not added until 1820. The great fireplaces and interior finish of the older section remain unchanged.
> Burials in a near-by cemetery are made in vaults above ground because of the marshy land.

On State 335 is ST.MARY'S STAR OF THE SEA CHURCH (L), 19.6 *m.*, built in 1872. Opposite the church a wooden structure, now a garage, was once St.Mary's Chapel—the first Roman Catholic chapel in Dorchester County, built in 1769.

At 20.3 *m.* is the junction with a shell road that runs north to Taylor Island (*see above*).

The route crosses Fishing Creek on a wooden drawbridge, 22.5 *m.*, to Upper Hooper Island and the village of HONGA (90 pop.), consisting of fishermen's cottages, a 'crab factory,' and a general store. Many boats tie up at the wharf including commercial craft as well as those for rent to fishing parties. Honga has one of the few legal diamondback terrapin pounds in Maryland.

The HOOPER ISLANDS are in the midst of one of the greatest concentration areas for wild ducks and geese in the United States; iron bars on larger windows are primarily to prevent wild fowl, attracted by lights at night, from breaking the window panes.

Most of the inhabitants of FISHING CREEK (893 pop.), 23.7 *m.*, the main settlement on Upper Hooper Island, are watermen. The town has five crab-packing plants, and two vegetable canneries, as well as several boat yards.

Concrete paving ends at Fishing Creek; the route now follows a winding shell road across marshland and passes numerous duck blinds in Tar Bay. A long wooden bridge leads to HOOPERSVILLE, a watermen's town on Middle Hooper Island, where the men fish, crab, and oyster. Crab packing, tomato canning, and boatbuilding also provide income.

Lower Hooper Island, isolated since the connecting bridge washed away several years ago, is frequented only by gunners, who cross to it in private boats. The Hooper Island Gun Club occupies the only undeserted building on the island. Applegarth, a small village of watermen here, was abandoned during the World War because of high wages in the industrial centers.

Tour 3H

Salisbury—Nanticoke; 20.2 *m.*, State 349.

Macadamized and concrete-paved roadbed.
Accommodations limited.

Typical of the bay side of the lower Eastern Shore, the low level pine-wooded neck penetrated by this route lies between the Wicomico River on the south and the Nanticoke River and its creeks on the north and north-west. Like other necks of this region, this one has a threefold character. Along the solid bluffs of the upper reaches of navigable (or once-navigable) streams are old plantation houses on land that has been tilled for about 275 years. On lower ground alternating with marshes, beside the broad lower reaches of the rivers, are the watermen's villages, strung out so close to the water's edge that it seems as if a sudden noise behind them might send them sliding in, like alarmed terrapin off a log. Inland along the highway, old farmhouses occupied by elderly couples are scattered among the newer and more prosperous-looking houses and barns of the truck-crop, dairy, or poultry farmers.

In SALISBURY, 0 *m.*, State 349 follows Isabella St. west from its junctions with US 213 (*see Tour 3*) and US 13 (*see Tour 6*).

At 0.1 *m.* is the junction with the slag-covered Anderson road.

Left on this to the lane (L), 2.1 *m.*, leading to small brick, gambrel-roofed PEMBERTON HALL, built in 1741 by Colonel Isaac Handy of the Maryland militia, whose family had settled in the latter part of the seventeenth century in what was formerly Somerset County. Occupied now by tenants and in a state of disrepair, this notable old house near the Wicomico has a small kitchen wing and a single tiny dormer window on each side of its steep roof. For the size and age of the house, the paneling of the living room is unusually fine, extending from floor to ceiling on opposite walls—a rough partition has been erected across one end of the room to make a hallway. Grooved pilasters decorate the corners flanking the eight-foot fireplace, which has a dog-eared molding around it. The huge cupboard formerly at the left of the fireplace was recently sold.

At the beginning of the Civil War Captain Allison Parsons, who lived here, made the house a secret rendezvous for Confederate sympathizers though Union troops were stationed in near-by Salisbury. But his attitude was soon known because he fired a small cannon at the news of each Confederate victory. After he had defied ultimatums from Union commanders, they raided Pemberton Hall only to be told the secessionists' arsenal of small arms here had been buried. The defiant captain, his brother Milton Parsons, and a loyal slave all took the secret of the burying place to their own graves. Much digging has failed to reveal it.

The slag surface on the Anderson Road ends at 3.2 *m.*, and the road turns R.

Left (straight ahead) is a rough dirt private road that twists its way 0.8 *m.* to NEW NITHSDALE by the Wicomico. This little house, with walls laid in Flemish bond under pent eaves, was erected about 1732. The shingled rear wing and dormers are recent additions.

In 1730 Captain Levin Gale, who owned this farm, was homeward bound in his vessel from Glasgow, Scotland, and put in at Bermuda for water and supplies. The Negroes of the island were in revolt and several white residents engaged Captain Gale to take them to Baltimore. That night their baggage came aboard, accompanied by a four-year-old boy and a six-year-old girl. After waiting for the other passengers, the captain, fearing seizure of his ship, finally hoisted sail and departed. The children knew their names only as John and Frances, but the name North appeared on a trunk and some books; other articles bore a family crest. The seaman brought the children to this farm. The next year he returned to Bermuda but could find no trace of the parents. In their foster father's new house, John and Frances North grew up. John was lost at sea when a young man. Frances married Captain William Murray, a Scottish sea captain, who called this place New Nithsdale after his native Nithsdale in Scotland. From them descended William Murray Stone, elected in 1830 as the third Episcopal Bishop of Maryland.

On State 349 at a spot in the woods marked by two large oaks is the site of ROCKAWALKING PRESBYTERIAN CHURCH (L) 3.4 m., erected in 1767 as the successor to the structure built about 1740 at Upper Ferry (see below). Only two headstones remain here, but the place is marked by a monument of bricks from the ruined foundation of the building.

At 4.8 m. is the junction with the dirt Upper Ferry road.

Left on this to UPPER FERRY, 1.3 m., by the Wicomico, one of two places on the river where a small scow takes passengers and vehicles from shore to shore (free to residents of Wicomico County between sunrise and sunset; fee of 50¢ charged all other vehicles; service uncertain after hours). Pull sticks are available to persons willing to help the ferryman haul the scow across by the wire cable.

On a knoll (L) above the ferry, the white-painted frame ANDERSON HOUSE is still a landmark for vessels today as the older rear section of it was late in the eighteenth century. Though the kitchen has a huge old fireplace, most of the cooking in old times was done in the separate little brick kitchen near by, where an even larger fireplace is still used during hog-killing season on windy days. Lard is rendered in great iron pots suspended from cranes.

CATCHPENNY CORNER, 6.6 m., two or three houses on State 349, was probably named for an early-patented tract of land.

Left on concrete-paved State 352 to the end of the pavement, 4.5 m., and a junction with the Whitehaven road; L. to a fork, 4.9 m., where the Whitehaven road turns R.

1. Left at the fork (straight ahead) on a dirt road 0.7 m. to GREEN HILL EPISCOPAL CHURCH (named St.Bartholomew's in 1887), on a high and commanding bluff above the Wicomico River (annual service on St.Bartholomew's Day, Aug. 24). This well-preserved church has never been altered inside or out since its construction in 1733. It has brick walls laid in Flemish bond, one story high, with four arched windows on each side. This, the second parish-church building of Stepney parish in old Somerset County, succeeded one built a few yards away before 1698, the year the first minister of the parish, the Reverend John Huett, died.

Inside are the original high box pews, high pulpit, and clerk's desk. The massive silver service used on St.Bartholomew's Day includes a flagon 20 inches high said to have been presented by a pastor about 1750. Old Green Hill, as the church is affectionately called, stands on the site of Green Hill Town which in 1706 was ordered laid out by the Maryland Assembly as a port of entry and commerce. No trace of the town exists.

2. Right 8.5 m. from the fork to WHITEHAVEN (5 alt.,115 pop.), one of the few landings on the Wicomico still regularly visited by vessels. Small Diesel freighters have succeeded sailing vessels and steamboats here as elsewhere on Eastern Shore

rivers. Though the shipbuilding that flourished here late in the nineteenth century is gone and fishing has declined, the frame houses of the village are spick-and-span—because the town is near enough to Salisbury for the residents to commute to work there daily.

At 7.2 *m.* on State 349 is the junction with State 347 (*see Tour 3b*).
At 12 *m.* is the junction with a slag road.

Right on this to the lane (L), 1.4 *m.*, leading to the small brick-ended STEWART HOUSE, built by Wetipquin Creek in the early eighteenth century. The great doors and the paneled hallway are noteworthy.

At 14.8 *m.* on State 349 is the junction with a graveled road.

Left on this to the story-and-a-half brick house (L), 1.5 *m.*, built in 1787 on a tract called McCANTIRE'S CHANCE in the seventeenth-century deed that is preserved by the present owner.

At 16.2 *m.*, at a fork, State 349 turns L.

Right from the fork on a slag road, to TYASKIN, 1 *m.* (23 alt.,153 pop.), a declining waterside village by Wetipquin Creek near the Nanticoke River. When the last Nanticoke River steamboat was running between Baltimore and Seaford, Delaware, in the 1920's, the timetable indicated a stop at Tyaskin, 'tide permitting'—so shallow was the water up to the wharf. It was a matter of professional pride with the captain, however, never to take advantage of that excuse for passing by. As his propeller churned up the mud, backing and going ahead, crowds on shore shouted taunts or encouragement. But Cap'n Billy always made it.

BIVALVE, 17.2 *m.* (15 alt.,310 pop.), and NANTICOKE, 20.2 *m.* (10 alt.,400 pop.), are characteristic Chesapeake Bay oystering, crabbing, fishing, and muskrat-trapping villages, occupying the narrow strip of fastland along the southeast shore of the mouth of the Nanticoke River where it flows into Tangier Sound. Until about 1920 most of the oysters caught in the river and sound were sent on sailing vessels up the 40 miles of river to Seaford, where they were shucked and packed for shipment north by rail. Now most of the local oysters go to Deal Island (*see Tour 6A*) for shucking and shipment in cans on refrigerated trucks and vessels. Many other oysters from this section are sold to 'run-boats' from Baltimore and Washington.

Around such places as Nanticoke obsolete expressions of speech and old local customs persist strongly. All conversation has the flavor of the salt water about it. A polin'-skiff, for instance, is a small boat in which a man stands at the bow, propelling it with the reversed handle of his crab-net; seeing a soft crab on the bottom, he can quickly twirl the handle to scoop it up. When someone feels that whisky has affected his speech, he says he has a 'slip-hitch' on his tongue. All white persons live on the same democratic level, often resenting the economic competition of the Negroes, but usually getting along well enough with them.

Tour 4

Galena—Denton—Federalsburg—Mardela Springs; 77.2 *m.*, State 313.

Narrow concrete-paved roadbed.
Pennsylvania R.R. roughly parallels route north of Greensboro.
Limited accommodations in towns.

This route along the western Delaware border crosses the slightly rolling terrain of Kent County and the table-top flatness of Caroline. In Kent and Queen Annes Counties the wealthier farmers sow their broad acres with wheat or use their fields for turkey raising; many of the smaller farms grow diversified truck crops. Cedar and pine predominate in the stretches of wooded territory, often scarred by shabby houses in ragged clearings. The route is dotted with villages that have grown very little since they were first settled, and is crisscrossed with roads that run through pine-wooded stretches to the marshy shores of creeks where waterlilies bloom in season.

State 313 branches south from US 213 in GALENA, 0 *m.* (*see Tour 3*) to a junction with State 290 at 1 *m.*

> Right on State 290 to CHESTERVILLE, 4.2 *m.*; R. 1.8 *m.* from Chesterville on a concrete-paved road to a lane leading (R) to MT.HERMON, a two-and-a-half-story red brick dwelling erected in 1727 by William Thomas, a Quaker. It has a one-and-half-story wing and end chimneys. A winding stairway extends from beside the kitchen fireplace to a second-story spinning room. The estate was part of a grant made to John Baker in 1685 and called Cheapside.
>
> On State 290 at 5.2 *m.* is a sharp and dangerous **Z** turn. Here on a high bank overlooking the Chester River is VIENNA (R), a house built in 1706 by a Dutchman named Comegys, who had settled on the Hudson about 1654, later moved to Virginia, and as a member of the Religious Society of Friends reached the Eastern Shore with other Quakers in 1661. The main section is of brick cast in English-type molds; its roof, a semigambrel, reaches to the first floor ceiling both on the 'broken' half and on the slope. The log kitchen, now stripped of weatherboarding, probably antedates the rest of the house.

In MASSEY, 4.3 *m.* (64 alt.,150 pop.), is a railroad junction.

The HENDRICKSON HOUSE (R), 7 *m.*, probably built about 1700, is believed to have been the first dwelling on the London Bridge tract. The frame house, painted white, has dormers, an outside chimney, and a red gambrel roof. The original huge locks and strap hinges that are the width of the door are still in good working order. The heavy battened doors are paneled, some vertically and others diagonally, and the fireplace in the living room has a handmade mantel.

LONDON BRIDGE (L), 7.2 *m.*, two-and-a-half stories high, is a brick structure said to have been built shortly after the tract of more than 700 acres was patented to Daniel Massey in 1754. The main wing has a double chimney at one gable end and a wide chimney at the other. This house has batten window shutters on the brick section, strap hinges extending across the width of the battened doors, and the original H and L hand-wrought hinges and large brass locks.

MILLINGTON, 8 m. (27 alt.,406 pop.), at the headwaters of the Chester River, is on part of the London Bridge tract. The brick HIGMAN GRIST MILL (1760) is (L) the sole remaining water-wheel mill of the six or more around which the town grew. The original foundation, floor, and grindstone are still in use. Milling declined when the village was rebuilt after a fire had destroyed half the village in 1872.

SUDLERSVILLE, 14.4 m. (279 pop.), is perhaps best known as the birthplace of Jimmy Foxx, major league baseball star. Two tomato canneries give the town seasonal business activity. St.Andrew's Church is on the site of St.Luke's Protestant Episcopal Church, built in 1728. The town that grew about the church was formerly called Sadler's Cross Roads, a misspelling of Sudler, the name of a family whose descendants retain large holdings here.

GOLDSBORO, 28.1 m. (63 alt.,211 pop.), a quiet town with neat homes and shaded streets, is on the direct trucking route between the middle Eastern Shore and the northern cities and is a shipping point for a prosperous agricultural district. Called Oldtown when there were but few houses, it grew rapidly after the railroad reached the section in 1870 and canneries were established. The name was changed at that time to Goldsborough (now Goldsboro) in honor of Dr.G.W.Goldsborough, who owned most of the land surrounding the community.

1. Left from Goldsboro on State 311 is MARYDEL, 6 m., on the Maryland-Delaware Line. It was the scene on January 3, 1877, of a duel between James Gordon Bennett, owner of the *New York Herald*, and Frederick May, clubman and explorer. When the two—who had quarreled in New York City over the breaking of May's engagement to Bennett's sister—met at this strategic spot between the two States, both fired wildly; neither was hit.

2. Left from Goldsboro on State 287 to a dirt road, 1 m.; R. here 0.4 m. to CASTLE HALL (L), a red brick house of four sections. It was completed in 1781 by Thomas Hardcastle, eldest son of Robert Hardcastle, who acquired the tract in 1748 and whose family was prominent in colonial Maryland's military, legal, and medical affairs. The exterior of the house has been altered at various times but the reeded mantels and four-pane cupboards still decorate the interior.

GREENSBORO, 33 m. (40 alt.,760 pop.), near the headwaters of the Choptank River, is one of the oldest inland towns on the Eastern Shore. Its chief income is from a large condensed milk plant and an ice cream factory. Greensboro's homes are comfortable and well kept, and its tree-shaded streets well paved. An act passed in 1732 called for the laying out of this town which was first known as Choptank Bridge, then Bridgetown. When resurveyed in 1791, the name was changed by legislative act to Greensborough. On Main Street near Four Corners a pair of Ailanthus trees planted over a century ago by the owner of the house and his bride form the AILANTHUS GATEWAY. With their massive trunks and foliage these 'bride and groom' trees now form a natural archway before the house.

South of Greensboro the trees change from hardwoods to evergreens; the sedge grass is dotted with pine seedlings, and a few loblolly pines are sprinkled among the short-needle pines that thrive in this sandy soil.

DENTON, 40.4 *m.* (40 alt.,1,604 pop.), seat of Caroline County, is the trading center for a fairly wide agricultural area; its industrial plants include vegetable canneries, a basket and crate factory, fertilizer, overall, and pearl button plants. In the days when commerce between the Eastern Shore and Baltimore was chiefly by water, Denton wharf on the Choptank River was a busy loading point. Today, most shipments are made by railroad and motor truck.

The town began as a tiny settlement on Pig Point, which projected into the Choptank. About 1773 the settlement was called Eden-Town in honor of Sir Robert Eden, the colonial governor who was an ancestor of Captain Anthony Eden, contemporary English statesman. Soon after the Revolution the name was contracted to Edenton, and in 1791, when the county seat was moved here from Melvill's Warehouse farther up the river, it was again shortened.

There are few landmarks of note in the town, since most of the early buildings were destroyed by fire in 1863, when Union soldiers, celebrating the Fourth of July, fired a skyrocket that landed on the roof of a combination cotton-and-flax storehouse and rum shop.

The BRICK HOTEL, Second and Main Sts., has been in continuous operation for more than 150 years, and counts Andrew Jackson among its famous guests. The building was damaged by the fire of 1863 but was rebuilt and a third story added. The present hip-roofed brick building, painted yellow, has a two-story gallery covering the sidewalk on two sides. This old house began its career as an ordinary, under the tavern rules laid down by the county court about 1775: That the tavern keeper maintain 'good rules and orders, and does not suffer loose, idle or disorderly persons to tipple, game or commit any disorders or other irregularities in his ordinary.'

In Denton is the junction with State 404 (*see Tour 5*).

On the outskirts of Denton is THE NURSERY (R), 41 *m.*, the birthplace of Sophie Kerr (1880), author of *Painted Meadows* and many other books. The white frame building, set back from the road and surrounded by hedges, shrubbery, and trees, was so-named because Miss Kerr's father was a nurseryman.

Adjacent to the Nursery is PLAINDEALING (R), 41.2 *m.*, a two-story brick structure, now with a Victorian bay window. It was built in 1789 as the Caroline County poor home and in 1823 was purchased by James Dukes. It has long been a social center for the community.

At 45.4 *m.* is a junction with an asphalt-paved road.

Right on this to the POTTER MANSION (L), 0.4 *m.* The small brick house erected about 1730 by Captain Zabdiel Potter is the kitchen of the present house, which was built in 1808. The main section of this telescope-type brick structure is two-and-a-half stories high with dormer windows and first- and second-story porches across the entire front. After Captain Potter came up the Choptank and took over Coquerious Fields, a tract surveyed in 1673, his residence became a commercial center. Ships sailed direct from here with tobacco cargoes to England and France, and brought back supplies. Nathaniel Potter, a grandson who became one of the founders of the University of Maryland School of Medicine, was born here. Colonel John Arthur Willis bought the home about 1847 and the name of the port was changed from Potter Town to Williston.

At 46.6 m. is the junction with a dirt road. In the southwest corner of the intersection is the brick foundation of the FREEDMAN'S BUREAU, a two-story frame building erected in 1865 by the Federal Government as part of a program for the care of emancipated slaves. One activity of the bureau was the assigning of 40 acres from the confiscated or abandoned lands of the Confederate States to each male freedman. When work on the program was discontinued in 1870, the local building was used as a Negro school, then as a church until it was destroyed by fire in 1938. The section about the building is still called the Bureau. It is said the Bureau was erected here because a Choptank River boat captain unloaded the lumber at a near-by wharf instead of at Denton as intended.

Right 0.5 m. on the dirt road to TWO JOHNS, a large, dilapidated Victorian frame mansion overlooking the Choptank. In the 1880's this house was extensively enlarged and equipped with a roof-top observatory by John Stewart Crossey and John Hart, noted comedians of the period. The two Johns each weighed more than 300 pounds, and one of their later shows was called *The Fat Men's Club*. This landing became a regular stop for the Baltimore-Denton steamers, and trains brought stage folk for gay holidays that included dancing in the 'round-house' on the shore. Neighboring farm families were fascinated but reserved.

FEDERALSBURG, 57.2 m. (10 alt.,436 pop.), is a busy town with some industrial activities and modern stores. As Northwest Fork Bridge, it developed around the general store opened by Clonsberry Jones in 1789. Although the water was too shallow to launch boats, a ship-building business using top-grade white oak flourished here until the Civil War. Boats were conveyed on lighters and scows to Chimney Point, about four miles down the river, for launching. Tanbark, cordwood, and mill products were other sources of income as well as a large slave-trading station in an old tavern at the east bridgehead. The name of the town was changed to Federalsburg in 1812 at a mass meeting of the Federalist Party held here.

In FINCHVILLE, 62.2 m., is the junction with State 392.

Left on this road to RELIANCE, 3.5 m. (50 pop.), a drowsy hamlet, once the head-quarters of Lucretia (Patty) Cannon, notorious female kidnapper of free Negroes. The Smith house, a two-story gray frame dwelling built about 1885, is on THE SITE OF JOE JOHNSON'S TAVERN. The house is said to contain some of the framing from the old tavern, which was operated by Patty and her son-in-law and partner in business and crime, Joe Johnson.

ELDORADO, 65.7 m., is at the junction with State 14 and a shell road.

Right on the shell road to the entrance (L) of REHOBOTH, whose square two-and-a-half-story brick dwelling houses a collection of old cannon and firearms made by Francis W. Breuil. The row of cannon on the lawn, among them an ornate Spanish piece used by Malay pirates, is the overflow of a large and varied assortment. The house, in a heavily wooded section, was built on a tract of more than 2,300 acres surveyed in 1673 for John Lee, son of Colonel Richard Lee, founder of the Lee family of Virginia.

At SHARPTOWN, 70.7 *m.* (10 alt.,727 pop.), State 313 crosses the Nanticoke River, where pinewoods reach to the marshy shores. Water hyacinths bloom here in profusion in the summer.

At 77.2 *m.*, in MARDELA SPRINGS, is the junction with US 213 (*see Tour 3b*).

Tour 5

(Bridgeville,Del.)—Denton—Matapeake; State 404. Delaware State Line to Matapeake; 42.9 *m.*

Asphalt-paved on Kent Island; elsewhere concrete-paved; two lanes wide.
Hotels and tourist homes in larger towns.

This route is a link in the most direct route between Baltimore and the Delmarva Peninsula ocean resorts. Travelers from Ocean City, Maryland, and Rehoboth and Bethany Beaches, Delaware, to Baltimore have a choice of two ferry routes connecting the Western Shore with Kent Island.

Between one of the later-settled sections of the Eastern Shore and the site of Claiborne's trading post established in 1631, on the flat and now sparsely-populated Kent Island, State 404 passes through the gently rolling and prosperous farming districts of Caroline, Talbot, and Queen Annes counties.

State 404 crosses the MASON AND DIXON LINE, 0 *m.*, 7.2 miles northwest of Bridgeville, Delaware.

At 6.3 *m.* is the southern junction with State 313 (*see Tour 4*) with which the route unites to DENTON, 8.9 *m.* (40 alt.,1,604 pop.) (*see Tour 4*).

At 13.1 *m.* is a junction with State 312.

1. Right here, this road joins State 480 at RIDGELY, 2.6 *m.* (67 alt.,703 pop.), a busy forwarding point for farm products, shipping particularly large quantities of strawberries. Ridgely has vegetable canneries and a very large strawberry-preserving plant, operated by the Armour Company. Baskets, crates, and strawberry boxes are also manufactured in large quantities.

The first attempt to lay out Ridgely as a town in 1867 in a land promotion scheme failed though there was definite planning of beautiful streets before any buildings were erected. Such foresight is evident in the town of today, with its broad Main Street with double roadway. The advent of the Queenstown and Harrington Railroad a little later revived the project and Ridgely grew rapidly along the planned lines. The town was named for the Reverend Greenbury W. Ridgely, one of the moving spirits in its inception.

Left from Ridgely 2.8 *m.* on State 312, a concrete-paved road, to OAK LAWN (L), a brick house erected in 1783 by Benjamin Sylvester. An unusual feature is the arcade of four arches connecting the main house with a two-story kitchen wing and servants' quarters. Mrs.Mary M. Bourne, who inherited the estate in 1797, built The Plains, a summer home northwest of Greensboro and now part of St.Gertrude's Academy. Oak Lawn was once the residence of the Reverend Greenbury W. Ridgely, who, before he became a clergyman, was a law partner of Henry Clay in Lexington, Kentucky.

Opposite Oak Lawn is CEDARHURST, erected in 1782, with interior woodwork showing the craftsmanship of carpenters and joiners of the period. Two-and-a-half-stories high, the stuccoed dwelling is connected by an areaway with a back wing at a right angle. A long porch extends across the front.

2. Left three miles from State 404 to THAWLEY HOUSE, built by Thomas Daffin in 1783. The house is noted as the scene of the first meeting between Charles Dickinson and Andrew Jackson who was a guest here when Thawley House was the home of Dickinson's sister. In 1806 Jackson and Dickinson quarreled over an insult to Mrs.Jackson and later met in a duel on the banks of Red River, Kentucky. Jackson allowed Dickinson to shoot first; then, ignoring his own wound, he took deliberate aim and killed Dickinson. Jackson was severely criticized for his cold-blooded strategy.

HILLSBORO, 16.2 *m.* (49 alt.,200 pop.), is on the banks of Tuckahoe River, which divides Caroline from Queen Annes and Talbot counties. Hillsborough Academy, erected here in 1797, served the community for 75 years.

QUEEN ANNE, 16.8 *m.* (21 alt.,250 pop.), in Talbot County, is across the river from Hillsboro, the two villages practically constituting one settlement. Queen Anne is at the junction of the eastern branch of the Pennsylvania R.R., and the Baltimore & Eastern R.R. from Love Point.

At 23.8 *m.* is the junction with US 213 (*see Tour 3a*).

At 25.4 *m.* is an improved dirt road.

Left on this to CLOVER FIELDS, 1 *m.*, a large brick house built about 1730 on·the bank of Wye River by William Hemsley, high sheriff of Queen Annes County. His granddaughter married into the Forman family and in the burying ground at Clover Fields are graves of many generations of both families. The house was originally in two sections consisting of the symmetrical two-story main block with its square stair tower at the rear, and the one-and-a-half-story kitchen wing. The two-story lean-to at the rear and the lower two-story unit now connecting it with the kitchen are of later date. The exterior is notable for its patterned glazed brick and the zigzag string-course. The interior has fine woodwork. Especially notable is the late Georgian decoration of the banquet hall. Here the mantel is richly carved with scrolls and figures in the sophisticated Chippendale mode. The marble fireplace and the overmantel are framed with dog-ear trim and flanked at the corners of the chimney breast by fluted Ionic pilasters.

At 27.4 *m.* on State 404 is a junction with a side road.

Left on this to the village of CARMICHAEL, 2.3 *m.* At 3.1 *m.* is a lane (R) leading to CHESTON-ON-WYE, granted to the DeCoursey family in 1658 by the second Lord Baltimore and held by them for 250 years. Its 800 acres of land are among the most productive in Queen Annes County. The original house burned to the ground in the early part of the present century and has been replaced by a modern dwelling.

At 4.3 *m.* is the entrance lane to the old WYE PLANTATION of William Paca (1740-99), signer of the Declaration of Independence and twice governor of Maryland. (Paca's town residence was the Paca House, now Carvel Hall, in Annapolis.) The house, a long structure of vaguely Dutch appearance, was built by Colonel Edward Tilghman in 1747 on an elevation overlooking Wye River. The linden-studded terraces, falling away to the water's edge, are old. The plantation today contains about 1,000 of the 1,400 acres in the original gift. In the graveyard near the house is the tomb of William Paca who died, and was first buried, at Wye Hall on Wye Island. General Lafayette, the two Charles Carrolls, and Colonel Tench Tilghman were among the noted guests at Wye Plantation, which for generations was associated with the Tilghman and Paca families. Though united solidly during the War of Independence, the family was split by the Civil War. At the close of the war the Unionist William B. Paca of Wye Hall attempted to take over the lands of Edward Paca, of Wye Plantation. In the resulting feud two members of the Edward Paca family were killed, and William Paca, though acquitted after a trial for murder, soon died. Shortly afterward two of his sons committed suicide, and a daughter died of poisoning.

WYE HALL, on Wye Island directly opposite Wye Plantation, is reached by a bridge across Wye Narrows at 5.1 *m*. The first Wye Hall, designed by James Hoban, architect of the White House, was built by William Paca the elder for his son John and was famed for its lavish entertainment. After fire destroyed it in 1789 a new structure was built, but it too was burned in the late 1920's. The present house follows roughly the outlines of the old foundation.

BLOOMINGDALE, 27.5 *m*. (R), one of the finest old red brick houses of Georgian design in Queen Annes County, is on a site long known as Seth's Mill. The central section was built in 1792; the southeast wing is much older, and the miller's house on the property, built before 1698, outdates the main dwelling. The mansion has a fine hall.

At 29.8 *m*. is a junction with a dirt road.

Right on this road to QUEENSTOWN, 0.5 *m*. (5 alt.,288 pop.), the first seat of government in Queen Annes County. Although never more than a village, its shipping facilities on the then-navigable Queenstown Creek made it an outlet for cargoes of grain, hemp, and tobacco and a receiving point for manufactured goods from Europe. As such it was considered important enough by the British in the War of 1812 to warrant a joint attack by their land and sea forces. Two miles south of the village the British encountered a band of pickets who, though greatly outnumbered, checked their advance appreciably at Slippery Hill, a large dune of loose sand. Queenstown has few landmarks. Recent excavations in the former jailyard unearthed a skeleton with handcuffs riveted about the wristbones. Gallows Field, on the outskirts of Queenstown, survives in name as a memento of the days when the gallows, stocks, and pillory were in regular operation in this former court town.

Left from Queenstown 1.1 *m*. on State 18 (*see Tour* 3) to MY LORD'S GIFT (R), the principal estate in the so-called 'thumb' grant, in which the third Lord Baltimore gave Henry DeCoursey as much land as the latter's thumb covered on a map of the Province. Part of this grant was later apportioned to Blakeford, across Queenstown Creek (*see Tour* 3). The old house on My Lord's Gift (built *c.*1658) survived until recent years.

At 1.2 *m*. on State 18 is the junction (L) with State 404.

At 30.3 *m*. is the junction (*see above*) with State 18, which unites with State 404 for 9.4 miles westward.

GRASONVILLE, 33 *m*. (10 alt.,754 pop.), trade center of a fruit-growing area, serves as shipping point for much of the crop.

A bridge crosses KENT NARROWS, 35.8 *m*., the narrowest part of the estuary separating Kent Island from the mainland. On the southern tip of Kent Island William Claiborne established a trading post in 1631, three years before Lord Baltimore's settlement at St.Marys, thus making Kent Island the first place of settlement within the present Maryland boundaries. Claiborne traded here by permission of the governor of Virginia and became Lord Baltimore's most troublesome rival, having finally to be evicted by force (*see History*). Among other things, he changed the name of the island from Winston's (as it had been on John Smith's map) to Kent.

The island was populous enough at one time to be represented by a burgess elected to the Virginia Assembly, for Claiborne insisted his outpost was part of Virginia.

STEVENSVILLE, 39.7 *m.* (400 pop.), is the principal town on Kent Island. Though the sea-food industry supplies an important share of the local income, this section is also noted for its peaches; some of the orchards are along the route. Broad Creek Church built in 1652, stood until 1880 in a grove of venerable oaks at a spot about one-and-a-half miles from the village.

Right 4 *m.* from Stevensville on State 18 to LOVE POINT, a summer resort with a hotel, several boarding houses, and bathing facilities, on the northernmost tip of Kent Island. It is the terminus of a ferry line to Baltimore (*$2 for car and driver, additional passengers 50¢ each*). The adjacent waters of the Chesapeake are popular with sportsmen because of the abundance of bluefish, rock and black bass.

At 42.5 *m.* is a junction with an asphalt-paved road.

Left (straight ahead) on this road through MATTAPEX and FREDERICK–TOWN to a private lane (R), 3.5 *m.*, leading 0.5 *m.* to CARVILLE HOUSE, a huge unoccupied mansion. The men of the Carville family who built it in 1789 disdained public office, preferring the name and role of gentleman farmer. The estate is now the property of the Claiborne-Annapolis Ferry Company, though the land is tilled by Roland Carville, a descendant of the builders.

At 4.5 *m.* on the asphalt-paved road is the junction with a dirt road.

Right on this 2.4 *m.* to BLOODY POINT, on the southwestern coast of the island, about a mile north of the southern tip. The three legends that explain the name tell of a massacre of Indians by white settlers who had lured them to a parley, a fight during the Claiborne Rebellion, and the hanging of a notorious French pirate who had been apprehended in Norfolk.

KENT FORT MANOR, 2.9 *m.*, about 150 yards from the road but plainly visible, was built sometime between 1638 and 1640, and is said to be one of the oldest structures now in Maryland. After Claiborne's settlement was burned in 1638, this building was among those erected on the site. It is a modest building of brick and clapboard, one-and-a-half-stories high, 40 feet long, and 20 feet wide. Windows are on the long sides, and two dormers on each slope of the roof. Both gable ends have chimneys, which provide fireplaces in each of the downstairs rooms. The hall has vertical paneling and the stairway in it a clearance of less than five feet. The house, now tenanted by Negroes, stands on a slope a few yards from the cove known as Kent Creek. An unmarked brick tomb was recently uncovered in the dooryard. This site was part of the 1,000 acres granted to Captain Giles Brent in 1639.

On the asphalt-paved road at 5.7 *m.* is a ferry to Claiborne (*see Tour 3C*) (*$2 for car and driver, additional passenger 65¢ each*).

In MATAPEAKE, 42.9 *m.* on the western shore of Kent Island, is a terminus of the Annapolis ferry (*$1.50 for car and driver, additional passengers 50¢ each*).

Tour 6

(Laurel,Del.)—Delmar—Salisbury—Princess Anne—Pocomoke City—(Accomac,Va.); US 13. Delaware Line to Virginia Line, 40.5 *m*.

Concrete or macadam roadbed.
Pennsylvania R.R. parallels route.
Hotels and tourist homes in larger towns; few tourist camps.

US 13 crosses the southernmost part of Maryland's Eastern Shore, connecting towns on navigable or once-navigable reaches of Chesapeake rivers that push in from broad estuaries and sounds a few miles to the westward.

In this, the only part of the Eastern Shore of Maryland that extends to the Atlantic Ocean, there early arose the terms Bay Side and Sea Side to differentiate the two areas of original settlement—terms still in common use (*see Tour 7*). On the river-separated necks just west of US 13 the seventeenth-century settlers built their first small, plain houses and with the help of a few slaves cleared small patches of pineland for crops that were shipped out on vessels. These early settlers were mainly English-Virginians: small farmers, artisans, adventurers, or religious nonconformists including Quakers and Presbyterians (the latter Scots and Scotch-Irish) to whom the Virginia government was unfriendly at the time. Pioneering in this region lagged somewhat behind the upper Eastern Shore, where the higher bluffs offered more tempting homesites and the land was generally richer and better drained. Rivers in this southern section were more often separated from the fastland by broad expanses of marsh.

East of US 13 was nearly all wilderness until the railroad came through after the Civil War and made feasible the moving of forest and farm products. There are still large areas of second-growth or cutover pinelands (mostly loblolly), but the central section, as well as the old settled necks, now contain huge acreages devoted to food crops for Northern markets: sweet and white potatoes, strawberries, asparagus, broccoli, tomatoes, melons, cabbages, and other products. Trucks and trains filled with fresh vegetables and fruits roll northward throughout the harvest season. Canneries are numerous but face competition with producers of fresh foods along the Atlantic coast to the south. Farm laborers are for the most part Negroes, who compose about one-third of the total population and whose numbers are supplemented from farther south at harvest time.

The fringes of most of the necks along the Bay are dotted with fishing and oyster villages, many declining because of the concentration of the sea-food industry at two or three larger ports (*see Tours 6A* and *6B*), or because more money can now be earned in agriculture.

US 13 crosses the Delaware Line in DELMAR, 0 *m.* (57 alt.,2,018 pop.; 1,180 in Md.), a town with two mayors, two town councils, and two school systems, though the post office address for both sections is Delmar, Delaware. State Street, the main thoroughfare, follows the State boundary.

The site was a pine forest in 1859 when the Delaware Railroad reached here and opened repair shops. In 1884 the New York, Philadelphia and Norfolk Railroad was extended to Cape Charles and a ferry line established to Norfolk, after which Delmar enjoyed a period of fast growth. Not long after the Pennsylvania Railroad took over the whole line in 1918, its business began to feel the competition from trucks on the new paved highways, and the town became increasingly dependent on the surrounding farmlands and their large cantaloupe crop.

The State boundary here was surveyed in 1750–51 by John Watson and William Parsons for Pennsylvania—Delaware then being the Three Lower Counties—and by John Emory and Thomas Jones for Maryland, who ran it from the ocean 35 miles westward to the center of the Peninsula. In 1764 Charles Mason and Jeremiah Dixon, English surveyors employed jointly by the Penns and the Calverts, started north from that point and ran the Delaware-Maryland boundary northward 100 miles to Pennsylvania. Thence westward across the mountains they ran what became the Pennsylvania-Maryland boundary which, as the Mason-Dixon Line, became the imaginary line between free and slave States.

SALISBURY, 7.1 *m.* (23 alt.,10,997 pop.) (*see Salisbury*).

Points of interest: Poplar Hill Mansion, State Teachers' College, and others.

Salisbury is at junctions with US 213 (*see Tour 3*), with State 349 (*see Tour 3H*), and State 12 (*see Tour 7*).

Right from Salisbury on Camden St., the northern part of an 11-mile alternate, partly concrete paved. TONYTANK MANOR (R), 2.4 *m.*, a large white frame mansion with an imposing Doric portico, was erected beside Tonytank Creek in the early nineteenth century.

At 3.2 *m.* on this alternate is the junction with a macadamized road; R. on this 1.3 *m.* to CHERRY HILL, overlooking the Wicomico River, a brick house built before 1757, and owned for many years by the Somers and Gunby families. Though the house has been altered to some extent, the old wide flooring and other interior woodwork have been preserved. On the grounds is a noted garden and a private golf course.

At 3.9 *m.*, the alternate turns R. on an asphalt paved road to ALLEN, 7.7 *m.* (10 alt.,150 pop.), a village of one winding street formerly on the main road between Salisbury and Princess Anne.

Right from Allen on a macadamized road 2.6 *m.* to the entrance lane (L) of the PAUL JONES HOUSE (1733) by Wicomico Creek; this story-and-a-half, five-bay, gambrel-roofed brick dwelling is notable for its old heart-pine paneling and the intricate interlaced diamonds formed by glazed header bricks in the Flemish-bond walls. The land was patented as Jones Hole by James Jones, a Welsh Quaker, who moved here from the Eastern Shore of Virginia where he had for a time defied the officers collecting church levies. In 1672 George Fox, the Quaker organizer, held at least one meeting here—'a large and glorious gathering' he called it in his journal.

At 3.6 *m.*, from Allen, the macadam ends; straight ahead 0.7 *m.* on the dirt road to the CHASE HOUSE, an elongated frame structure with dormer windows. The Rev-

erend Thomas Chase was living here in 1741 when his son Samuel, the signer of
the Declaration of Independence, was born. Upon this fact was based the assertion,
later refuted, that the signer was born here (*see below*).

On the alternate to US 13 at the southern edge of Allen, the road, here concrete-
paved, crosses Passerdyke Creek. Near the bridge a grassy bank (R) is all that remains of bridge abutments constructed in 1835 for what was to have been the Eastern
Shore Railroad between Elkton and the lower Eastern Shore. After great celebrations
it was realized that the cost of the line, $8,000,000, was too great for the State to bear,
and in 1837 the project was abandoned.

Visible from the road at 9.2 *m.* is BRENTWOOD FARM (R); the brick part of the house
was built in 1738. Near by is a brick cave 10 feet wide and 15 feet high, built apparently at the same time. According to local tradition, it was a hideaway for use during
Indian raids and was later used to secrete slaves on the Underground Railway.

A lane (R) at 10 *m.* leads to the Tull farm on which is a large brick dwelling sometimes called the ANDERSON HOUSE because it is believed to have been built about 1730
by a man of that name who owned land here on upper Wicomico Creek. Neglected but
distinguished, this two-and-a-half-story structure, partly yellow-plastered, is a monumental relic of early prosperity. The gable ends are extended to form end walls of a
long, two-story front porch. Windows and doors are arched in the very early manner;
the belt course and water table are bold.

At 11 *m.* is the southern junction with US 13, 5.1 miles south of Fruitland.

FRUITLAND, 10.5 *m.* (42 alt.,300 pop.), on US 13 is a busy canning
and shipping center that started as the hamlet of Forktown. In 1867 the
railroad brought civic pride and a new name.

At 16.6 *m.* is the southern junction with the shorter alternate route (*see
above*).

At 19.3 *m.* is the junction with a concrete-paved road.

Right on this to MONI (pronounced m'nye), 3.6 *m.*, by the shoaled-up headwaters
of Moni (or Monie) Creek. The large, square, brick house (R) marked by plastered
quoins at the corners was built soon after 1741 by Captain Henry Waggaman who
came here from Accomac County, Virginia. Though his grandfather, Hendrick Waggaman of Amsterdam, Holland, had already settled in Virginia, the captain was born
in London in 1709 while his parents were living abroad. Inside the dilapidated mansion are a handsome stairway and other woodwork, but the paneling of the drawing
room was sold by the county commissioners of Somerset, who use the place as the
county poor farm.

At mealtime, there emerges from the one-story frame barracks, at one side of the
lawn, a slow file of aged Negro women, each carrying her tin plate and cup to be
filled by the overseer's wife in the old kitchen of Moni. When the simple meal has been
dished out, back they go to their quarters to sit down and eat. Besides the Negro
women, there was only one other inmate in early 1939—an old white man who 'got
tired of living by himself in the woods' and is now quartered happily in a little outbuilding.

All that is now left of old HACKLAND (L), 3.8 *m.*, is a small brick outbuilding.
On this place in the late seventeenth and early eighteenth centuries lived Levin Denwood, whose house was designated by the court as a Quaker meeting house. To it
came many pioneer leaders of the Society of Friends, including in 1672 its founder,
George Fox. Denwood was on the committee of 1682 that selected the site of the
Third Haven Friends Meeting House in Talbot County—the little building still
standing at Easton.

At 5.4 *m.* the concrete road ends at a junction with a shell road; R. on this and L.
at 7.1 *m.* on the Reading Ferry (dirt) road to the entrance lane, 7.3 *m.*, of the probable SITE OF THE BIRTHPLACE OF SAMUEL CHASE (1741–1811), signer of the Declaration of Independence and later an Associate Justice of the U.S. Supreme Court
(1796–1811). The house, now destroyed, belonged to his maternal grandfather. The
question of where Chase was born was long in dispute, but recent research indicates
that his mother was here at her father's home at the time of her child's birth.

PRINCESS ANNE, 20 *m.* (18 alt.,975 pop.), seat of Somerset County, at the head of the Manokin River (pronounced m'*no*-kin) is in the center of a highly-cultivated truck-crop area. Except for the cotton-garment factory controlled by Northerners—nearly every Peninsula town has or is trying to get one—its canneries, flour-and-feed mills, lumberyards, and other small plants near by, all depend on products of the surrounding country. As late as 1900 three-masted schooners were able to approach the broad main street to unload fertilizer and manufactured goods and to carry away farm and forest products to Baltimore and other markets. But the river bed is now so completely filled with silt washed from denuded timberland and cultivated fields that a row boat can scarcely navigate it at low water. Nevertheless Princess Anne changes little. The magnificent sycamores of Somerset Avenue and Prince William Street are symbols of the age, dignity, and repose of a town rich in traditions of gracious living and unplagued by ambition.

Though Somerset County (then including the territory of Somerset, Worcester, and Wicomico counties) was organized in 1666, and Princess Anne was ordered laid out in 1733, it was not until 1742, when Worcester County was cut off, that the village became the seat of the shrunken parent county. The town was named in honor of Anne (1709–59), daughter of King George II.

Just north of the bridge on Somerset Ave. (US 13) is MANOKIN PRESBYTERIAN CHURCH (R). The red-painted brick walls are nearly all that remain of the structure erected in 1765; the tower was added in 1888. Presbyterian meetings have been held near this spot since 1672 when Robert Maddox was called by the Somerset grand jury to preach at Christopher Nutter's house. Organization of the Manokin congregation was effected about 1686 under the Reverend Thomas Wilson, a co-religionist of the Reverend Francis Makemie (*see Tour 6B*), and it is believed a church building was here in 1690. The graveyard's stones bear the names of many noted county families: Handy, Dennis, and others. A member of the church was Lieutenant Oliver T. Beauchamp (pronounced *beech'm*), killed in the World War and immortalized in *Heaven High, Hell Deep* by Norman Archibald, 1935. Memorial Bridge over the Manokin was built in 1921 and has a bronze tablet bearing the names of all Somerset County citizens, white and Negro, who participated in the War; an adjacent grassy plot contains a tree planted in honor of Lieutenant Beauchamp, which is ringed by five more trees for the other World War dead. Funds for the bridge were raised by a house-to-house canvas.

The two-and-a-half-story, white-painted frame WASHINGTON HOTEL (R), on US 13 between Broad and Prince William Sts., has a fairly recent signboard giving the year of erection as 1744. The pair of large outside chimneys at the north end show evidence of age, as do the dormers and other exterior details, though the interior has been altered. It was a tavern at least during late colonial days and a rendezvous for prominent men including Judge Samuel Chase.

Princess Anne's most noted house is TEACKLE MANSION, blocking off the western end of Prince William Street. This two-hundred-foot-long, austere, heavily-proportioned brick structure has a two-story central part with pedimented gable and unusually long two-story pavilions connecting it with gabled wings. Littleton Dennis Teackle built it in 1801 to face the river, but a frame addition on that side covered up the doorway in later years. Teackle Mansion (or Hall) served as the very core of the plot of *The Entailed Hat*, George Alfred Townsend's realistic novel (1884) of Peninsula life in the early nineteenth century, when Patty Cannon and her gang (*see Tour* 4) were kidnaping free Negroes and selling them at high prices into Deep-South slavery. A Delawarean attempted to buy up and destroy an edition and some old families still complain about the obvious similarities between characters in the book and prominent residents of Princess Anne and this area.

At the eastern end of Prince William St., facing Teackle Mansion, is EAST GLEN, a large yellow-painted frame house in the Adam style, built about 1795 by Colonel Mathias Jones. Here Ellen Dashiell (pronounced d'sheel) wrote *Under the Shade of the Maples* and other volumes of poetry. The BOXWOOD GARDEN, SE. cor. Somerset and Washington Aves., was laid out by General George Handy in 1844. The E.HERRMAN COHN HOUSE, SE. cor. Somerset Ave. and Antioch St., built in the refined Federal style about 1800 by William W. Johnston, a merchant, is a weatherboarded white house whose broad gable front faces Antioch Street. An addition was built about 1834. The fanlighted double front door is flanked by boxwood, apparently quite as old as the house. Inside, the stairway with curly-maple spindles and mahogany rail is a duplicate of that in the Peale Museum in Baltimore. Between the living room and dining room is a fine beaded arch. The handsomely furnished house contains twelve finely-made British locks bearing brass medallions of the time of George IV.

ST.ANDREW'S EPISCOPAL CHURCH, NE. cor. Washington and Beckford Aves., though Victorianized, retains the Flemish-bond brick walls and part of the gallery of the building erected in 1770–73 as a chapel of ease in Somerset parish. The parent parish church stood down the Manokin at Almodington (*see Tour 6A*). While rector at St.Andrew's, the Reverend Clayton Torrence compiled his scholarly and detailed *Old Somerset* (1935), the standard source book on the history of the region's early settlements.

Opposite the western end of Washington Ave., at Beckford Ave., is BECKFORD, approached by a curving private lane. This imposing Georgian mansion of brick, with a hip roof and a pair of huge central chimneys, ranks as one of three or four truly great houses on the Eastern Shore of Maryland below the Nanticoke River. A huge pecan tree stands near the southwest corner of the house. Beckford ('beck' is an old word for brook) was erected in 1776 by Henry Jackson, a merchant and planter, on land first patented by Colonel William Stevens (*see Tour 6B*) in 1679. Everything about Beckford is on a sumptuous scale, from the great brass locks on heavy paneled doors to the 12-foot ceilings bordered by well-proportioned cornices. Mantels and other woodwork are elaborate.

In the house is a small but heavy chair said to have been used in one of the seventeenth-century courthouses of the county and declared by connoisseurs to be of sixteenth-century (or earlier) manufacture, already an antique piece when brought from England. Another prized possession is a tall wooden device with adjustable headpiece called a 'slave-measurer'— used for a century or so by the sheriff when auctioning slaves in front of the courthouse in settlement of legal actions.

In Princess Anne is the junction with State 363, Deal Island road (*see Tour 6A*).

1. Left from Princess Anne on Broad St. which becomes a dirt road to PRINCESS ANNE COLLEGE (R), 0.4 *m.*, a coeducational State institution for Negroes. The 200-acre farm and buildings of the former Princess Anne Academy, founded under Methodist auspices in 1886, were bought by the State in 1935 to take advantage of land-grant appropriations under the Morrill Act. Constructed by PWA in 1939 are three large buildings of modified Georgian design. Four-year courses are offered in agriculture, mechanic arts, and home economics, and a two-year course in arts and sciences. Enrollment in 1937–38 was 90.

2. Left from Princess Anne on Antioch St. and the West P.O. Road, concrete-paved, to a dirt road 1.7 *m.*; R. here to the lane (R), 2.3 *m.*, of PEACHBLOSSOM, the Williamson place, a compact little story-and-a-half brick dwelling of the early eighteenth century.

At 20.6 *m.* on US 13, at the southern end of Princess Anne, is the junction with the asphalt-paved Old Pocomoke City road.

Left on this 1.6 *m.* to the unmarked SECOND SITE OF WASHINGTON ACADEMY, in a field (R) just south of marshy Jones Creek. The first building, about three miles south on another stream, from 1767 housed what was called simply the School on Back Creek; it burned in 1795. When the classes moved in 1800 to a large brick building here, a year after the first president's death, it was renamed Washington Academy. After the Civil War the school was abandoned. In 1891 its bricks were used in building a public school in Princess Anne, which in turn was torn down in 1939; the same bricks became backing in the walls of the new Washington High School there.

An early resident tutor of the academy was Luther Martin, who was the first attorney general of Maryland (1778–1805). A member of the Constitutional Convention of 1787, he opposed the Constitution as written and refused to sign it. His alliance with Federalists brought him into frequent clashes with Thomas Jefferson, who in 1807 referred to him as the 'Federal bulldog.' Martin's ability was best demonstrated by his part in the successful defense of U.S. Supreme Court Justice Samuel Chase during the impeachment trial before the U.S. Senate in 1804–05 and in the trial of Aaron Burr in 1807 for treason. Improvident throughout his brilliant career, Martin in later years became penniless. He served again as attorney general of Maryland from 1818 to 1822, when he resigned. In that year the Maryland Legislature passed a resolution requiring every lawyer in the State to pay an annual license of $5 to be used in pensioning Martin. He was born in New Brunswick, New Jersey, on February 9, 1748, and died at Burr's home in New York on July 10, 1826.

KING'S CREEK, 22.9 *m.*, is a hamlet at the junction of the Crisfield branch of the Pennsylvania Railroad.

The entrance lane (R) to BEVERLY OF SOMERSET, 23.1 *m.*, used to be part of the Revell's Neck road, laid out in 1708 by order of the County Court.

Visible from the highway, Beverly of Somerset (so-called to distinguish it from Beverly in Worcester County) would be a 'great house' anywhere. Here it represents the tremendous wealth in land and slaves of its builder, Nehemiah King II, and compares favorably with the important houses of its time in Annapolis. King (1755–1802) supervised the construction of the house for ten years until its completion in 1796; his own forests supplied the wood necessary, and the English-mold bricks were baked on the place.

The style of the house is Georgian, featured by a two-story octagonal entrance bay in the center of the front façade, a hipped roof, and two large inside chimneys. The broad central hallway has an arch in keeping with the Adam-style delicacy of the stairway and the rest of the woodwork, all of which was made to match as closely as possible the original, destroyed in 1937 when the house, then newly restored, was gutted by fire. A Negro formerly employed here confessed to spraying the house with coal oil and setting fire to it because another Negro had been hired in his place.

The house figured in one of the many schemes to rescue Napoleon from St.Helena Island. In 1803, while awaiting opportunity to return to the scene of Bonaparte triumphs, Jerome Bonaparte, brother of Napoleon, had married Elizabeth Patterson of Baltimore; when he was able to return to Europe two years later he had the marriage annulled to further his dynastic ambitions, though she had already borne a son to him. Despite the annulment he retained the friendship of many Americans, including the Kings of Beverly. When Napoleon was finally confined to St.Helena, various admirers, among them Mayor Girod of New Orleans, plotted to rescue him. Funds were raised to build a fast sloop, plans of the island and its fortifications were studied, and details of the attempt carefully rehearsed. The plan was to hide Napoleon in a secret room at remote Beverly until the hunt for him should subside and he could be safely taken to New Orleans. Before the sloop sailed in 1821, word came of Napoleon's death.

At 23.7 *m.* is the junction with the graded-dirt Revell's Neck road.

Right on this road, which becomes macadam-paved at 2.7 *m.* and goes down Revell's Neck, between the Manokin River and Back Creek. CLIFTON (R), 4.7 *m.*, from a knoll overlooks the river. This two-and-a-half-story brick house was in a state of near-ruin when the present owner set about restoring and enlarging it in 1939. Though it is said to have been built in 1700, the details of its construction and remaining woodwork resemble those of houses built in this region about 1800. Clifton is on the site of the Somerset Town ordered laid out by Governor Charles Calvert in 1688 as the first town and port of entry in the newly-erected county of Somerset, on the Double Purchase tract of Mrs.Anne Toft and Randall Revell (*c.*1613–86). What are said to be foundation stones of the first courthouse are still visible off the point at low tide. From Virginia in 1662 Revell transported Anthony and Mary Johnson, who were among the first free Negroes in Maryland.

Described in early Virginia records as a cooper, Revell in 1661–62 was Lord Baltimore's head officer and land agent for the Manokin settlement, which, with the mainly Quaker colony of Annemessex near by, formed the nucleus of settlement on the lower Eastern Shore of Maryland. Revell was relieved of his position after he became too friendly with Edmund Scarburgh, surveyor general and treasurer of Virginia, who was pressing Virginia's claims to land as far north as the Wicomico River. The Maryland authorities held that their charter placed the boundary at the Pocomoke River. In October 1663 Scarburgh and 40 horsemen, riding up from Virginia, placed the 'broad arrow of confiscation' on houses in the settlements. However, after conferences between higher authorities of the two Provinces, the Maryland contention was accepted and the boundary to the ocean was run in 1688.

The two brick houses directly across the Manokin here are Elmwood and Almodington (*see Tour 6A*).

At 25 *m.* is the junction with State 413 (*see Tour 6B*).

The GREEN HILL FOREST FIRE TOWER (R), 27.2 *m.*, is in a public picnic ground (*tables and benches*).

At 31 *m.* is the junction with a shell and dirt road.

Left, on this road crossing the railroad tracks, to a dirt road, 1.1 *m.*; R. here to Ivy Hill, or HAYWARD'S LOTT (R), 2.3 *m.* Most of the other early eighteenth-century brick houses of the region were small, story-and-a-half structures built on a simple rectangular plan. But when Thomas Hayward erected this house in 1720 he made it two-and-one-half stories in height—a fine large dwelling for the region and time. The pitch of the roof is very steep; a stringcourse and a fine water table of brick are notable details of the weather-worn Flemish-bond walls. The great lawn trees were all destroyed in a recent hurricane. Hayward's Lott (as it was called in the patent) has never been out of the Hayward family or name.

At 34 *m.* is the junction with Dividing Creek road (*see Tour 7*).

US 13 crosses the Pocomoke River (Ind.: black water) at 34.3 *m.* On the west side of the river (R) is a large white steamer whose bow points into the river and stern extends back into the cypress swamp. Amidships, the former paddle-wheel box is glass-enclosed and displays a large neon sign— GRILL. Aloft, the smokestack projects tall and white from the superstructure, and the gilt-decorated wheelhouse bears the name Governor Emerson C. Harrington. Now a hotel, the 216-foot sidewheeler—built in New York in 1901—for several years plied Chesapeake Bay as a ferry between Claiborne and Annapolis. Unprofitable there, she was bought in 1938 by the present owner who sold her engines and towed her up the Pocomoke to this slip which he had dredged out of the river swamp. Here she floats, made fast by ordinary mooring lines; rising and falling with the two-foot tide; she is entered over a gangplank. The proprietor ('Cap'n' to the help) sometimes has to explain matters to tourists who take rooms for the night and leave calls to be awakened 'in plenty of time before we get to Norfolk.'

POCOMOKE CITY, 34.8 *m.* (8 alt.,2,609 pop.), usually called merely Pocomoke, is the largest town in Worcester County. It was established as Meeting House Landing about 1700. Later called Warehouse Landing, and still later (1780–1878) New Town, the place has steadily developed as an agricultural shipping center. The once-heavy river traffic has waned because of the railroad and the highways, but some canned goods go out and oil and fertilizer come in by vessel. The women workers in the local clothing factory refer to the factory as the sewing room—a term they consider more dignified.

In spite of the town's age, it has almost no old structures, fires in 1888, 1892, and 1922 having destroyed them. Streets, except the business section of Market Street, are narrow but shady and trim, and the houses have the comfortable air that goes with the steady prosperity of a town that is frankly commercial and proud of it. Individual residents, however, have the qualities of Eastern Shoremen everywhere. The CITY HALL, E. side of Clarke Ave. near Market St., a handsome brick building of the modified Georgian Colonial type, was erected in 1936 as a PWA project.

Right on 4th St., a concrete road, to its end, 5 *m.*; R on a graded dirt road to Beverly of Worcester or THRUMCAPPED, 6 *m.* a large five-bay, painted brick Georgian Colonial house by the Pocomoke River, three miles above its mouth in Pocomoke Sound. The estate, which extends across the Virginia Line, was the home of the Dennis family for about 250 years following a brief settlement in Virginia. The two-story brick structure was completed soon after the death of Littleton Dennis (1728–74), planter and lawyer, the great-grandson of Donnoch Dennis, the Irish immigrant. The lower service wings are of frame. On the landward side is a white-columned portico, a Greek Revival addition; on the river side is a delicate iron grillwork arch carrying a lantern that for many years was lighted at night to guide vessels on the narrow, winding stream.

Inside, the original heart-pine paneling is as it was when completed by the local craftsmen who laboriously carved it with the aid of English patterns. The riverside drawing room is paneled to the ceiling. The house has been carefully restored by the present owners. Generations of Dennises lie in the family graveyard near the house. John Dennis, who went to Congress at 25, was one of five Federalists who switched votes to Jefferson to break the deadlock with Aaron Burr. John Upshur Dennis (1793–1851), whose ships carried Pocomoke cypress and West Indian molasses, had three wives and 21 children, winning the third wife in competition against his oldest son; a legend is that the tombstone for his second wife came to Beverly on the same vessel with a carriage bought for his third.

At 35.9 *m.* on US 13 is the junction with US 113 (*see Tour 7*).

In a small woodland clearing stands the simple white frame PITTS CREEK PRESBYTERIAN CHURCH (R), 39.8 *m.*, erected early in the nineteenth century. Two other churches have stood on the site; the first was built, it is believed, by one of the six congregations founded between 1683 and 1707 by the Reverend Francis Makemie (*see Tour 6B*).

US 13 crosses the VIRGINIA LINE, 40.5 *m.*, 21 miles north of Accomac, Va. (*see Virginia Guide*).

Tour 6A

Princess Anne—Deal Island—Wenona; 18.8 *m.*, State 363 (Deal Island Road).

Concrete-paved roadbed to Deal Island, macadam and shell on the island.
Boarding houses at Deal Island.

On the neck between the Wicomico River on the north and the Manokin River on the south, this route crosses a truck-farming section, large areas of woodland, and broad salt-marsh lowlands to fishing island settlements.

The route branches west from US 13 (*see Tour 6*) in PRINCESS ANNE, 0 *m.*, and follows Prince William St.; R. at the end of Prince William St. one block, L. on State 363.

At 4.2 *m.* is the junction with a graveled road.

Right on this 0.3 *m.* to the plain, green frame ALL SAINTS' EPISCOPAL CHURCH (R) of Somerset parish. A church built here in 1710 was wrecked by a hurricane in 1879. The first church of the parish was on the Manokin River shore.

HABNAB, 1 *m.*, a run-down hamlet, is still called by its old name though it became Venton officially in 1921 when the inhabitants sought a more dignified name. Hab Nab was the name of an early land grant.

At 5.5 *m.* on State 363 is the junction with an asphalt-bound graveled road.

Left on this 1.2 *m.* to a dirt road; L. on this 0.6 *m.* to the lane of ALMODINGTON, by the Manokin, whose large, plain brick house was erected, it is said, by Arnold Elzey (d.1733). John Elzey, father of Arnold, came here from the Eastern Shore of Virginia in 1661 and was a member of Lord Baltimore's commission to establish the Manokin settlement. In 1918 the New York Metropolitan Museum of Art purchased the woodwork of the Almodington living room for its American Wing. The woodwork dates between 1750 and 1775, the mantelpiece between 1800 and 1810.

Visible offshore at very low tide is part of the foundation of the original Somerset Parish church. The Manokin has cut away a broad strip of shore since the little building was erected about 1697. Directly across the river, where the house of Clifton now stands on the point of Revell's Neck, was the site of Sommerton or Somerset Town, ordered laid out in 1688 (*see Tour* 6).

At the end of the dirt road, 2.2 *m.*, is the lane (L) of ELMWOOD, formerly belonging to the Jones and Fitzgerald families. The large gabled front section of the brick house overlooking the Manokin from a low, tree-shaded lawn was built about 1810, supposedly by Arnold Elzey Jones, planter and member of the Maryland assembly. His son, Arnold Elzey (1816-71)—who dropped the name Jones—was born here, was graduated from West Point, served in the Seminole and Mexican wars, and became a major general in the Confederate Army.

On State 363 is DAMES QUARTER, 11.9 *m.* (2 alt.,565 district pop.), a typical Chesapeake Bay fishing-and-farming village of small frame houses on streets that are little more than the original winding roads or cow paths. This area was formerly known as Damned Quarter—perhaps because of its proximity to Devil's Island. Here the great marshes come almost up to the road as the neck narrows toward its end.

CHANCE, 14 *m.* (2 alt.,628 pop.), at the tip of the neck, has a name smacking of an early land patent. (There were many early farms with Chance, Folly, Adventure, or Hope as part of their names, indicating doubt, if not downright pessimism, on the part of patentees.) At Chance is a large oyster-shucking-and-packing plant.

The somewhat rickety wooden bridge across Deal Island Narrows, 15.1 *m.*, is paralleled (R) most of the year by the sterns of a score or more skipjacks and a few bugeyes and schooners, moored side by side; a rare and arresting sight in Chesapeake waters today, when sail is fast giving way to power. They are the largest vessels of the great Deal Island fleet of oyster and crab boats, second only to the fleet at Crisfield (*see Tour* 6B). There, however, very few sailing vessels are in use; the Deal Island fleet, though including many powerboats, has the greatest array of sail left on the bay.

These large vessels are all oyster craft, equipped with iron-pronged dredges that are let down overside to scrape along the bottom during the fall-to-spring harvesting season and during the spatting season in May when oysters are caught on the State beds for transplanting to leased grounds. All the craft are painted white with their names across the sterns. On the bows names and designs carved in relief are decorated with gold leaf and colored paint.

The skipjacks are one-mast, sloop-rigged vessels of several lengths between 60 and 30 feet; the small ones are used in winter also to scrape hard crabs out of the mud. Big and little, there are (1940) about 150 skipjacks here; there remain only six two-mast schooners with tall mast aft, and two bugeyes with masts of the same height and no topsails.

DEAL ISLAND, 15.5 m. (2 alt.,1,237 district pop.), in Tangier Sound, is about half marsh. Most of the people live on the higher strip, a mile wide and three miles long, on the western side. Directly or indirectly the entire populace makes its living by catching, packing, and shipping oysters and crabs, trapping muskrats on the great marshes, and carrying out parties of salt-water anglers in summer. Most of the houses are small frame buildings with white-painted walls and bright red roofs. Even a prosperous oyster packer lives in a small very neat, red-roofed house with a small lawn. Harbors are filled with many kinds of craft. Besides skipjacks (called sailing bateaux at Crisfield) and boats built for power engines, there are a number of the distinctive sailing canoes (called *cunners*) that were made long ago of hewed-out logs of cypress or heart-pine and are now for the most part dismasted and power driven. In spring every waterman has his boat blocked up for painting on the beach in front of his house.

Four oyster-packing plants shuck and ship about one-fifth of all the oysters caught by Deal Island boats; the rest are sold to 'run-boats' from Baltimore and elsewhere. More important, however, is the crab business. Thousands of barrels of hard crabs come in annually by boat and truck. They are steamed in huge vats and the meat is picked out by women who are paid about 6¢ a pound; if the crabs are fat, an expert can pick 100 pounds of meat in a day. On the island and at adjacent villages in 1938 nearly 2,000,000 soft-shell crabs were packed alive in wet grass and shipped to Northern cities. During the duck-hunting season in late fall, guides are available by advance arrangement; blackheads (scaup) and canvasback are the principal species shot.

The earliest land patent recorded for the island is that of Thomas Rowe's North Foreland of 1676.

Near the south front corner of the old Methodist Church, 16.1 m., is (L) the GRAVE OF JOSHUA THOMAS (1776–1853), called the Parson of the Islands. Thomas more than anyone else was responsible for establishing Methodism as the deep-rooted faith of lower Chesapeake Bay people (*see Tour 6B*). The most famous act of his career was his preaching to the British expeditionary force encamped on Tangier Island, Virginia, during the War of 1812, when he had the hardihood (divine guidance, the islanders say) to predict that they would not succeed in taking Baltimore.

It was an elder of this church who had the name of the island changed from Devil to Deal to avoid any implication 'of Satan having some right to, or property in the island.' Why it was originally called Devil's Island is not known.

A narrow road winds southward to WENONA, 18.8 m. (3 alt.,300 pop.), a fishing village at the lower end of the island.

Tour 6B

Junction with US 13—Crisfield—Smith Island; 27.8 *m.*, State 413 and boat.

Concrete and asphalt roadbed.
Pennsylvania R.R. parallels road.
Hotels and tourist homes in Crisfield; boarding houses on Smith Island.

This route at the southernmost tip of the Eastern Shore of Maryland is on the neck of land between the Annemessex and Pocomoke Rivers, which empty into Tangier Sound in Chesapeake Bay. The route passes through a strawberry and truck-crop section and terminates at the busy and salty headquarters of the Maryland and Virginia sea-food industry. Much of this level, pine-bordered farmland has been tilled since late in the seventeenth century, when Eastern Shore Virginians came in search of land, adventure, or liberty to dissent from the tenets and evade the tax-levies of the Church of England. The rivers and sounds and marshes of the bay that the Indians had found rich in fish, fowl, and fur animals have continued to supply their bounty to the people of the Eastern Shore.

State 413 branches south from US 13 (*see Tour 6*), 0 *m.*, at a point about 5 miles south of Princess Anne.

WESTOVER, 0.8 *m.* (14 alt.,150 pop.est.), is a rail and highway shipping point for farm and forest products in the heart of the truck-crop country. It has a cannery and a flour and feed mill.

In May hundreds of Negro berry pickers, men and women, work in the great flat strawberry fields, their backs bent as they move slowly in groups down the rows, talking, laughing, and singing. Some are local Negroes, but most are 'bought' at 50¢ a head from labor agents on the Norfolk docks, transported up the Eastern Shore in trucks, and housed in rough, often crowded, and primitive barracks. They do their cooking in the open. Mostly from the Virginia mainland and North Carolina, they follow the berries and other crops—peas, beans, tomatoes—up the peninsula and drift back and forth as labor is needed. Pay is by the quart of berries, and pickers can earn $3 or $4 a day if the berries are not dwarfed by drought.

At 1 *m.* is the junction with the concrete-paved Potato Neck road.

Right (straight ahead) down Potato Neck—sometimes called Fairmount Neck— where a number of old brick and frame houses stand in more or less disrepair along the shores of the Annemessex, Manokin, and Back Creek. MANOKIN, 2.7 *m.*, (9 alt.,60 pop.) is a post office hamlet.

The lane (L) at 3.7 *m.* leads to the solid, square brick house of POPLAR GROVE overlooking the Annemessex. It was built about 1780 on land patented in 1663 by Colonel William Waters of Accomac County, Virginia.

TUDOR HALL (L), 4.4 *m.*, also approached by a lane, is said to have been built by Richard, a son of Colonel Waters. Richard Waters was a leader among the Quakers from the Eastern Shore of Virginia who composed most of the very early Annemessex settlement of dissenters. This once handsome two-and-a-half-story brick house is also known as the Ballard or Loockerman place.

UPPER FAIRMOUNT, 5.7 *m.* (8 alt.,500 pop.), is a scattered community dependent on farming and the sea-food industry.

At 6.2 *m.* the concrete gives way to shell. The lane (L), 6.6 *m.*, leads to the BALLARD HOUSE, a two-and-a-half-story brick structure with the date 1802 on the chimney. FAIRMOUNT, 6.7 *m.* (5 alt.,500 pop.), is a farmers' and watermen's village on the edge of the great marsh bordering Tangier Sound.

On State 413 is the little WATERS HOUSE (R), 3.4 *m.*, built with walls laid in Flemish bond early in the eighteenth century on one of the many tracts of the Waters family.

When the once noted and now forlorn KINGSTON HALL (R), 3.6 *m.*, was built early in the eighteenth century, the upper Annemessex was easily navigable. The long, yellow, two-and-a-half-story brick mansion has a double veranda that is a later addition and is surmounted by a square frame cupola added before the Civil War as a lookout from which to watch the Negroes at work in the fields. From the west end extends a brick colonnade and a two-story servants' wing. Many of the great boxwoods have been removed from the lawn—some to the Walter P. Chrysler estate near Cambridge. Years of neglect and tenant occupancy have not entirely robbed Kingston Hall of its former elegance as the home of the Kings (*see Tour* 6) and later of the Carrolls and the Dennises. The builder of the house was probably Colonel Robert King III, who died in 1750. At his death the place went to his grandson Thomas King whose daughter married Colonel Henry James Carroll of St.Mary's County; their son was Thomas King Carroll, later governor of Maryland (1830–31), who lived here amid scores of slaves until 1840. His daughter, Anna Ella Carroll (1815–94), was called 'the great unrecognized member of Lincoln's cabinet.'

This Baltimore belle of the 1840's, who had early developed a keen interest in law and politics, decided slavery was the root of the country's trouble, and freed her own slaves at heavy personal sacrifice. When Senator Breckinridge of Kentucky made a speech designed to bring about Maryland's secession, Anna Carroll distributed 50,000 copies of her pamphlet accusing Southern leaders of having prepared for war since the time of John C. Calhoun. President Lincoln, noting the widespread effect of her tract in stimulating enlistments in the Union Army, encouraged her to continue writing and later sent her to St.Louis to write of the proposed Federal expedition down the Mississippi. When she reported that the river was too heavily fortified to serve as a means of invading the Deep South and urged that the best line of attack was by way of the unfortified Tennessee Valley, her strategy for the campaign was accepted by the President and his cabinet. Even after success had vindicated her judgment the generals, it is said, were never told they had been advised by a female civilian. When the capture of Vicksburg seemed impossible, Miss Carroll drew plans for attacking it from the land; in 1863 Vicksburg fell by land attack. Congress never rewarded her, and after Lincoln's death she was almost forgotten. For the last years of her life she was paralyzed and was supported by a sister who was a Government clerk.

At 4.4 *m.* is the junction with a concrete-paved road.

Right on this through KINGSTON, 0.9 *m.* (8 alt.,120 pop.), and along a dirt road, winding toward the Annemessex River. GREENWOOD (R), 2.7 *m.*, by Gale's Creek is a very long frame house—21 rooms and a ballroom—containing very fine stairways and paneling. It was built by the Williams family before the Revolution. Another Williams house, apparently of the early eighteenth century, stands near by on the shore of the creek.

The land was patented as Coulbourne in 1663 by Stephen Horsey (*c.*1620–71), a cooper who settled here about 1661 and was the first person of record to make a permanent home in the newly-opened region of the Eastern Shore below the Choptank River. A man of much vigor and independence, he had migrated to Northampton County, Virginia, about 1643 and later became a member of the Virginia House of Burgesses. As an agitator for the rights of the common people of Virginia he was once 'thrown out by ye Assembly for a factious and tumultuous person, a man repugnant to all Govmt.' In 1652 he was on the committee of six that entered the celebrated 'Northampton Protest'—which opposed taxation without representation nearly 125 years before the Declaration of Independence was signed. After repeated arrests for refusing to pay Church of England levies, he moved to Maryland and became a defiant leader of the Annemessex settlement in resisting Colonel Edmund Scarburgh's attempts to make the settlers swear allegiance to Virginia (*see Tour 6*). Later he served as a judge, as sheriff, and in the Maryland Provincial Assembly.

At 5.9 *m.* on State 413 is the junction with a concrete-paved road.

Left on this, which is paved after 1 *m.*, to a fork, 2.3 *m.*; R. here 0.4 *m.* to the ruins of COVENTRY PARISH CHURCH (R), in the hamlet of REHOBETH, beside the Pocomoke River. Adjoining the site of a church erected for the parish about 1697 are the vine-covered brick walls of the ruined second church, which was built here in 1784–92, though a bronze plate erroneously gives the date 1740. The building continued in use until 1900. In 1928 the ragged walls were capped with cement and an altar was built of brick within the roofless rectangle. One of the walls still exhibits the two tiers of windows that lighted this once-fine structure.

The small brick REHOBOTH PRESBYTERIAN CHURCH (L), 2.8 *m.*, is venerated as the oldest house of worship (1705–06) in the United States that has been used exclusively by the Presbyterians and as one of the early church buildings erected through the zeal of Reverend Francis Makemie (*c.*1658–1708), the founder of the sect in America. Because he had it built on his own property, it is known as Makemie's Own Church. Though the Flemish-bond walls contain Victorian windows and the original furnishings have been replaced, the little church retains much of the aspect and atmosphere of an early day.

Francis Makemie (pronounced M'Kemmy), born of Scottish parentage in Ireland, came to Maryland in 1683 when Colonel William Stevens requested a Presbyterian minister to settle in Somerset County. Aided by the Reverend William Traile, the Reverend Samuel Davis, and the Reverend Thomas Wilson, who soon followed him to America, Makemie presently had five other places of worship under his guidance in the county. The name Rehoboth (there is room) was applied by Colonel Stevens to the tract he patented in 1665 near here along the Pocomoke. Besides holding important public offices—he was a justice and a member of the provincial council—Stevens (1630–87) profited greatly by having the inside track on the patenting of land, acquiring huge acreages for little or nothing, and selling to settlers coming in from Virginia and elsewhere.

MARION STATION, 10 *m.* (7 alt.,650 pop.), has a block where in May an auctioneer cries the sale of hundreds of thousands of dollars' worth of strawberries brought in all sorts of vehicles. The region annually supplies about 50,000,000 young strawberry plants to growers for transplanting here and in the North, and also quantities of tomatoes picked green in early summer for shipment to distant markets.

CRISFIELD, 16.8 *m*. (5 alt.,3,850 pop.), actually a loosely-knit community of 7,500 if the environs are included, is a distinctive town that derives its livelihood from oysters, crabs, and fish. All the waters of lower Chesapeake Bay are its salty domain. To this self-styled Sea Food Capital of the Country come hundreds of vessels of many sizes and rigs, under power and sail, bringing thousands of tons of marine edibles from many directions. They come from the Bay islands and sounds, the rivers and coves of the Eastern Shore of Maryland and Virginia, the waters of the Western Shore in Southern Maryland, and the great rivers below—the Potomac and the Rappahannock of the Virginia mainland.

The upper part of the town resembles other Eastern Shore settlements, having narrow, tree-lined streets, a modest business section, and neat frame houses. There is a well-equipped hospital, a public library, and a new post office and customhouse. The people are mostly Methodists and Baptists, more interested in old-time sermons than in the shows at the lone moving-picture theater.

Upper Crisfield is on tracts surveyed in 1663 for John Roach and Benjamin Summer (Somers); the latter's name is preserved in Somers Cove, which was formerly the name of the wharf-hamlet here. In 1868 a rail line was brought in and the town, renamed for John W. Crisfield, a promoter of the railroad, began its steady growth. As a result of seven disastrous fires between 1883 and 1928 that swept the frame buildings and sheds of the town, especially near the water front, many of the old structures have been replaced with brick buildings.

It is the straggling, odorous lower section at the water front that gives Crisfield its character. The town here is more of the water than of the land. Even the site is made of oyster shells, the residue of 70 years of oyster shucking along the marshy shores. Almost every street leads briefly to a wharf or a marine railway or a marshy cove where boats of many kinds cluster at anchor while others move continually back and forth, propelled by oars, poles, motors, or sails. Many of the 'gas-boats' are dismasted sailing bateaux or bugeyes. Crisfield's sailing bateau is called a skipjack at Deal Island, only 14 miles away (*see Tour 6A*). Very few sails are now visible in Crisfield waters, though in 1910 the place had one of the largest registries of sailing vessels in the United States.

The railroad track runs down the middle of South Main Street to the railroad pier, where refrigerated express cars receive cases of fish and soft-shell crabs from the 'run-boats' (small freighters) moored alongside. From this pier small freight-and-passenger vessels leave for Chesapeake islands beyond the horizon. They leave on schedule—unless the preacher or some other island notable has forgotten something his wife wanted and has to go back to a store for it.

Near the water front along the Little Annemessex are the wooden or concrete-block buildings where oysters and crabs are made ready for shipment up the Peninsula by train and truck. In 1938, 1,000,000 bushels of oysters, 200,000 barrels of hard crabs, and 1,000,000 dozen soft crabs were handled here. No machines have been devised to shuck oysters or pick the meat out of hard crabs—operations done only by the knives and deft fingers of hundreds of workers, white and Negro, male and female. The extremely perishable nature of crabs and oysters require the most rigid sanitary and protective regulations, enforced by State and Federal inspectors. Speed and cleanliness are the goading anxieties of every sea-food packer.

Crab meat—graded from backfin to claw—is picked from boiled hard crabs, mostly by Negro women working over stainless-metal tables in large sheds. Shells and other residue are collected daily by fertilizer makers. Shuckers are usually Negro men and women, who rapidly stab and open the oysters at the risk of gashing fingers with sharp, heavy oyster knives. When a good voice starts the refrain of a spiritual, others take it up gradually, and soon the melody spreads through the large shed, rising and falling in smooth cadenced rhythm as knives scrape and shells rattle.

Though oysters have always been a mainstay of Crisfield, crabs are of great and increasing importance as the basis of a year-round industry. In winter the sailing or power dredges plow the mud bottoms for hibernating crabs; the rest of the year small boats lightly drag the surface of the bottoms with basketlike rakes. From May to October is the soft-crab season; growing crabs, that have shed their shells in quiet waters or in the shedder-floats of crabbers, are brought here for live shipment packed in marsh grass and crushed ice. Fishing is also important. In spring and summer hundreds of barrels and boxes of shad, herring, croakers (hardheads), and other fish are sent to market, and sportsmen-anglers are taken in party-boats to the fishing grounds of Tangier Sound.

Crisfield also manufactures oyster tongs, oyster dredges (metal-pronged devices dragged over a vessel's side), oyster knives, muskrat traps, sea-food packing cases, and clothing. A shipyard and several marine railways build boats and repair and paint them. At the TAWES COLD STORAGE PLANT, on the water front, tons of frozen fish, crab meat, soft crabs, shad roe, shrimp, and other sea foods are stacked like cordwood from floor to ceiling to await an expected rise in prices.

In the marshy section called Jersey, across a bridge (SW) from the lower part of South Main Street, is the TERRAPIN POUND of the Holland Sea Food Company. Within a partitioned enclosure of board walls extending into tidewater, the heads of hundreds of diamondback terrapin appear above the surface. They are purchased from watermen around Crisfield and along the south Atlantic coast. They are shipped out of here alive as the rarest and most expensive of all American marine delicacies. The principal consumers of diamondback today are old conservative clubs in large Eastern cities, noted old hotels, and households able and willing to pay from $20 to $50 a dozen for them. In the 1890's no formal dinner in Baltimore, Wilmington, Philadelphia, or New York was truly epicurean without terrapin, sometimes served with a sherry wine sauce.

At one end of the pound is a sand bank where the terrapin crawl up to drink fresh water and to lay eggs for hatching by the sun. Baby diamondbacks are allowed to escape under water through the wide cracks in the walls and return to the marshes. The terrapin are fed daily (*about noon, except Sun. and Mon.*) on the rich yellow-green fat removed from steamed crabs at the picking plants. The firm also packs unseasoned terrapin meat in cans. Like cattle, terrapin are heifers, cows, and bulls; the last never grow as large as the cows, which sometimes measure ten inches along the lower shell.

The native arts of Crisfield are marine. One of them is the carving and painting of amazingly lifelike decoy geese and ducks. Another is the art, now almost lost, of carving, painting, and gilding the fancy nameboards under the bowsprits of sailing vessels—against a background of red or green enamel, letters and decorative scrolls in relief are painstakingly covered with gold leaf.

East from Somerset Ave. on Main St. to a shell road, 1.1 *m.*; L. here to MAKE-PEACE (*adm.* 25¢), 1.7 *m.*, overlooking the green marshes (L) of Johnson's Creek, which empties into Pocomoke Sound. Of the late seventeenth or early eighteenth century, this story-and-a-half house with walls laid in Flemish bond stands on the 150-acre farm which John Roach in his patent of 1663 called Makepeace—in memory of a peace made, tradition says, with the Indians of the region at the time of the Anne-messex settlement.

The house is one of the finest and best preserved of its modest, early-Virginia type on the Peninsula. Two front doors side by side lead into the two large rooms of the first floor; the gable ends are noted for their glazed header bricks in a diamond-grid pattern on one end, an inverted V pattern on the other. Inside are two enormous fire-places. The fine paneling and stairway, similar to the paneling of Eastern Shore houses of the Revolutionary period, may have replaced earlier woodwork. A frame colonnade and kitchen adjoin the east end.

At the railroad pier, foot of Main St., are the berths of the boats for Smith Island and for Tangier Island, Virginia. (*Two or three boats carrying passengers, freight, and mail, but no vehicles, leave daily at* 12:30 *p.m. for Smith Island returning at* 7–8 *a.m.; round-trip fare for non-islanders,* $1. *One boat direct to Ewell, another to Tyler and Ewell, another irregularly to Rhodes Point only. At Ewell trucks for hire for* 2-*mile drive to Rhodes Point and boats for hire for inter-island trips and fishing guides for angling and duck shooting.*)

West from Crisfield across Tangier Sound 11 *m.* to SMITH ISLAND (2 alt.,777 pop.), the most remote and distinctive of all Maryland islands in the Chesapeake. Named for Captain John Smith (1580–1631), who explored the bay in 1608, Smith Island is actually a compact little archipelago about eight miles long, north and south, and four miles wide; nearly all salt marsh or meadow, it is cut and indented by dozens of thoroughfares, guts, ditches, and coves. The southern fringe of the island is in Virginia.

Several times great storm tides have flooded the whole island, damaging truck-patches, oyster boats, and crab houses, and even drowning islanders caught unaware at work on the bay or sound. After the waters recede, however, these hardy, fatalistic, and strongly religious people go on living in the isolated pattern of their ancestors.

As a boat approaches Smith Island there appear beyond the marshes the villages of EWELL, TYLERTON, and RHODES POINT, each separated from the others by a mile or more of marsh and water. A few sparse pine groves are seen, but the most prominent objects are the three Methodist churches, each rising high above the small frame dwellings of its village. Almost without exception the people are of British ancestry (there are no Negroes). Offshore along the front of each village is a row of small build-ings on piling; these are crab houses where soft crabs are packed in ice for shipment to Crisfield. Between and behind the crab houses are the fenced crab pounds, in which are scores of latticework shedding-floats containing, in summer, thousands of crabs that are carefully separated daily according to their stage in shedding the hard shells. At Tylerton the effect is that of a main street of water, one side of it the line of crab houses and pounds, the other side the houses and stores on shore, each with its little pier. The freight-and-passenger boat and the busy traffic of small boats move up, down, and across this 'street.' The nearest approach to a main street on land is the seven-foot-wide alley at Ewell, bordered by white picket fences in front of houses with grassy yards and large fig trees. There can be no wide streets in a place where every square foot of soil must have its use. Only three or four old pick-up trucks, without license tags, use the two miles of shell road between Ewell and Rhodes (originally Rogue's)Point, and they run only on special and infrequent occasions. Because these self-reliant men build their own roads, the State does not enforce the law re-quiring license plates. There is no moving-picture house. Most of the fire-wood and much food must be brought by boat from the mainland. The island has no wire to the mainland. Radios have brought welcome enter-tainment—especially when the island is locked up by the occasional freezes lasting several weeks. On the other hand the radio is causing discontent among young people and it threatens the continuance of their piquant seventeenth-century mode of living.

Either and *neither* are used everywhere in ways that leave the visitor gasping from the attempt to unscramble the double and triple negatives. 'I didn't ketch neither fish'—a comparatively simple form—means the speaker had no luck at all. 'She's the first girl I ever walked with' is said naturally in a place where taking a girl for a walk is the chief available means of courting.

From the settlement of the island in the middle seventeenth century until about 1800 the people here were more or less neglected by Govern-ment and church alike. A good deal of hearty lawlessness, violence, and drunkenness was an expression of their fierce independence as they strug-gled to make a living from the surrounding waters. (In more serene years two brother-patriarchs, Richard and Solomon Evans, were called 'King Richard' and 'King Solomon.') The change came after a young fisherman of Potato Neck settled on Tangier Island and became a leader in Method-ist revivals and camp meetings on that and other islands. As the Parson of the Islands, Joshua Thomas (1776–1853) went about Tangier Sound in his sailing log canoe *The Methodist* with a religion that exactly suited the islanders.

Today all are Methodists and attend church every Sunday. When a stranger has satisfactorily answered the question, 'What is your business here?' and appears not to be a game warden or other undesired visitor, a group of a dozen or more persons of all ages will escort him to the church, take him inside, and then wait for his favorable comments on its appearance and size. All three congregations are served by one preacher whose salary is raised by an assessment on every head; he is the most respected figure of the island, an arbiter and counselor as well as a man of God. Religious faith is powerful. When the church in Ewell burned in 1938 and the wind changed in time to save the rest of the village, the entire population, which had been kneeling in the road for hours, believed their prayers were answered. Besides the preacher, other important men of the island are the resident doctor—whose salary also comes from a voluntary head tax—and the magistrate. There is no mayor, council, or jail. Children attend public schools here through the grammar grades; for high school they are boarded by the State in Crisfield.

The spirit of independence is as strong as ever. Though the Black and Jenkins Award of 1877 forced Maryland to give Virginia 23,000 acres of fine oyster bottoms, chiefly at the behest of Tangier Island, the Smith Island men kept on dredging there for 50 years despite repeated attacks by Virginia patrol boats and inter-island battles in which oystermen on both sides were killed and wounded. The warfare ended only when the oysters in the area died. (In this the islanders saw the hand of God protesting strife.) Although killing wild ducks for market has been outlawed by Federal enactment since 1918, Smith Island remains a source of anxiety to the United States Biological Survey. Wardens risk their lives when drawn to the lonely island marshes by the deep booming of swivel guns mounted in sneak-boats—artillery that throws a pound of shot at a blast to kill and cripple ducks by the hundreds. To spot wire-enclosed duck traps, wardens in airplanes drop streamers of paper for the guidance of wardens in boats who attempt to make arrests, sometimes successfully, sometimes not. The islanders are sure that God has given them the ducks, oysters, fish, and crabs to take as they wish and they bitterly resent man-made game laws.

Tour 7

(Georgetown,Del.)—Berlin—Snow Hill—Junction with US 13; US 113
Delaware Line to Junction with US 13, 38.5 m.

Concrete- and asphalt-paved roadbed.
Pennsylvania R.R. parallels route.
Hotels and tourist homes in larger towns.

This route along the Sea Side of Maryland's Eastern Shore runs through
Worcester County between the coast and the Pocomoke River, which approaches within a few miles of the ocean, yet empties into Chesapeake
Bay. This area was settled—mostly by Eastern Shore Virginians—late in
the seventeenth century as part of Somerset County, and by 1697 a road
here extended as far north as Indian River (now in Delaware); Worcester
County was cut out of Somerset in 1742.

Between the eastern chain of small, salty bays, noted for fish, oysters,
and waterfowl, and the Pocomoke's cypress swamps, the country is low,
flat, and largely wooded. The old-growth loblolly pine that made the paneling and wide flooring of the old houses is nearly exhausted, but second-
growth pine keeps sawmills humming and crews busy cutting piling and
coal-mine props. Much piling used to support buildings at the New York
World's Fair of 1939 came from Worcester County. Holly abounds and is
a source of pre-Christmas revenue.

Because of the tempering effect of the ocean and the Chesapeake, the
growing season (210 days average) is as long as that of inland regions much
farther south. When the sandy soil is heavily fertilized it produces two
crops of Irish potatoes on the same land in one season; sweet potatoes,
strawberries, corn, wheat, and legumes are important crops. There are
large peach and apple orchards, canneries, and nurseries. The production
of broiler ('briler') chickens, spreading from Delaware, has become common in the northern part of the county.

Worcester County, despite its age in settlement, retains many qualities
of its early frontier days. Isolated by geography and until recently by
poor roads, the people live to themselves, indifferent to events in other
parts of Maryland, resenting any 'meddling' from Annapolis or Baltimore,
obeying the laws they respect, and ignoring those they disapprove. They
are friendly, hospitable, and full of polite curiosity toward strangers. The
speech of cultured as well as uncultured persons is spiced with archaic
words and phrases. The peculiar emphatic rhythm and slurring of common
speech sometimes make it unintelligible to a Baltimorean. Men call each

other 'honey' on first acquaintance as casually as a New York policeman calls a stranger 'buddy.'

Thirty-one per cent of the population is Negro, mostly tenant farmers and watermen.

US 113 crosses the DELAWARE LINE, 0 *m.*, at a point 22 miles south of Georgetown, Delaware.

This boundary was not surveyed first by Mason and Dixon, as locally supposed, but by an earlier commission (*see Tour* 6).

At 1.7 *m.* is the junction with a concrete road.

> Left on this road to BISHOPVILLE, 1.7 *m.* (23 alt.,275 pop.), a neat, white-painted trading center for near-by farms; it originated as Milltown at a dammed headwater of St.Martin's River, an estuary of Isle of Wight Bay. Bishopville Prong is now very shallow, but as late as 1900 small sailing vessels carried lumber and farm products out to sea and up to Philadelphia and other ports.
> Right from Bishopville on a slag and dirt road down St.Martin's Neck to ISLE OF WIGHT, 6.8 *m.* On this small island of woods and marsh, connected to the neck by a causeway, an 'oil well' was driven in 1915 by men who extracted a fortune from a trusting speculator before he discovered the well was salted. No oil in commercial quantities has ever been found on the Peninsula, but wells are still sunk from time to time.

SHOWELL, 3.9 *m.* (24 alt.,131 pop.), on US 113 was named for one of the largest slaveholding families of the region. The old two-story white frame house (L) is part of the much larger SHOWELL HOUSE that formerly stood farther back from the road.

ST.MARTIN'S EPISCOPAL CHURCH (*key at St.Paul's Church, Berlin*), 4.5 *m.*, is on a pine-wooded knoll (R) above the south prong of St.Martin's River. This simple structure, almost square and of brick laid in Flemish bond, was erected between 1756–59 as the mother church of Worcester parish. Beneath a pitched roof and cove cornice, the door and shuttered windows are very tall. Inside, the box pews, gallery, and chancel have been little changed since they were installed in 1763. Part of the colonial silver service is kept at St.Paul's and part at St.Mark's Church, Millsboro, Delaware. In the old vestry book of St.Martin's the construction of this building is recorded as costing 80,000 pounds of tobacco (about $4,000) raised by a levy on all taxable inhabitants of the region, of whatever sect. A chapel of ease for Snow Hill parish was here as early as 1703. Worcester parish was erected in 1744 and organized in 1753.

Within the crossroads settlement, 6.6 *m.*, called JONES on most maps but FRIENDSHIP locally, is the small story-and-a-half EVANS HOUSE (R). Built in the late eighteenth century with outside chimney, it is one of the many old houses in this region that are sheathed with hand-riven bald cypress shingles from the near-by Great Pocomoke Swamp (*see Tour* 3).

At 9.2 *m.* is the junction with US 213 (*see Tour 3c*).

BERLIN (pronounced Berl'n), 9.9 *m.* (45 alt.,1,480 pop.), is a pleasant place of shady, winding, very narrow streets that radiate from a compact little business section. Comfortable Victorian-styled houses along the older streets are interspersed with handsome residences built during the first third of the nineteenth century. Except for two of brick, these houses are weatherboarded and painted white, notable for their classic doorways and cornices but especially for pedimented gables that stretch the length of the façades.

Berlin's principal source of income is HARRISON'S NURSERIES, established in 1873. The orchards of the nurseries, chiefly apple and peach, are among the largest in the country and border all near-by roads (*peach trees bloom March or April, apple trees late April*). The village has other nurseries, a chicken-dressing plant, and a barrel factory. Unskilled farm labor seldom receives more than 10¢ an hour, and much of the work is seasonal. Small factories turn out cheap clothing, taking advantage of low wages, taxes, and power rates. Berlin has a public library and its own electric, water, and sewerage systems.

The first village in this upper Sea Side region arose at a gristmill on near-by Trappe Creek (*see Tour 7A*), but the main highway by-passed to the westward and the settlement that became Berlin grew up in the early nineteenth century around a public stable, blacksmith shop, and tavern. It was built on land patented by Colonel William Stevens (*see Tour 6B*) in 1677 as Burleigh. Even after the spelling was changed to that of the German city, the accent stayed on the first syllable. Some have supposed the name to be a contraction of 'Burleigh Inn.'

Buckingham Presbyterian Church was organized near by in 1683 or soon afterwards by the Reverend Francis Makemie (*see Tour 6B*). The first and second church buildings stood in Buckingham Cemetery at the southern edge of town—the second, of brick, was blown down in 1857; the third burned in the Berlin fire of 1904, and the present granite BUCKINGHAM CHURCH, west side of Main St., was completed in 1906.

BURLEIGH COTTAGE (L), on Main St. north of Burley, overlooking a garden of boxwood, flowers, and old trees, is of brick painted a soft yellow; it is almost square and much larger than it looks from the street. Built in 1834 by Captain John Selby Purnell, this story-and-a-half house has a small pediment on the porch and at each end a pair of large outside chimneys. Kitchen and servants' quarters were in the spacious cellar. The removal of wallpaper in the living room exposed an antique paper with applied velvet that is believed as old as the house.

It is said that old Captain Purnell was sometimes annoyed by his grandsons' returning late after drinking too freely. His test for the boys' sobriety was their answer to his command: 'Say "*National Intelligencer*, sir"!' The hardest part was putting the required 'sir' on the end of the name of a journal published in Washington.

On Main St., south of Burley, is BURLEIGH MANOR (L) on a broad and shady lawn. This handsome, dignified mansion of brick that has been plastered, was built in the early part of the nineteenth century by John P. Mitchell. The kitchen wing joins a rear corner of the house in an unusual way. Furnishings of the house are in keeping with the beauty of the woodwork and other decorations.

In a peach orchard east of Decatur St., on the eastern outskirts, is a wooden sign marking the site of the birthplace of Stephen Decatur (1799–1820), whose daring exploits in the Tripolitan War and the War of 1812 made him one of America's naval heroes. When the British occupied Philadelphia in 1778, Stephen Decatur, a prosperous shipping man of that city, had his young wife come here for safety to the farm of Isaac Murray. Young Stephen was born January 5, 1779. Four months later his mother took him home to Philadelphia. Later, as a handsome, athletic midshipman, Decatur fought his first duel at 20. Both as a lieutenant and a captain fighting Tripolitans in the Mediterranean in 1804, his fame reached a peak for victories won by his dashing leadership and his hand-to-hand combat with pirate crews. His record in the War of 1812 added to his honors. It was at a dinner in Norfolk in 1815 that he offered the toast: 'Our country! In her intercourse with foreign nations may she always be in the right; but our country, right or wrong!' When Decatur was 41 he was mortally wounded in a duel with a suspended naval officer. His body lies in St. Peter's churchyard, Philadelphia.

In Berlin is the junction with the Sinepuxent Road (*see Tour 7A*).

At 11.9 *m.* on US 113 is the junction with the slag and dirt Newport Neck Road.

Left on this road to NEWPORT CREEK, 1.4 *m.*, in colonial days a deep stream. At one time there were granaries and warehouses here on the east side of the creek, where inspectors graded tobacco for export and received it in payment of levies for government and church expenses.

At 2.2 *m.* the Newport Neck Road forks.

1. Right (straight ahead) to HENRY'S LIME KILN (L), 2.8 *m.*, a building of stone lined with brick. It was constructed before the Civil War by Zadok P. Henry II, to burn imported limestone and oyster shells to make fertilizer. A small tree grows from the top of the crumbling structure.

2. Left 0.8 *m.* from the fork to the large brick ISAAC PURNELL HOUSE (L), overlooking lower Trappe Creek. Erected about 1790 by John Ratcliffe, it is a duplicate of Sandy Point, his home two miles southeast on the bay shore of Sinepuxent Neck. Ratcliffe was said to have been on his way from Newport Neck to Sandy Point when he was murdered by his abused slaves (*see Tour 7A*).

This house with its spacious rooms, fine stairway, handsome mantels and fireplaces, delicate cornices, and dog-eared paneling was going to ruin when new owners began its restoration in 1938. Purchased with it was the adjoining farm, including the white frame GEORGE PURNELL HOUSE, which is visible a mile northeast and has similar proportions and even finer interior woodwork. The new private road built across a marsh between the two places has created a 40-acre lake where hundreds of Canada geese feed in winter and furnish sport for the owners.

The hamlet of IRONSHIRE, 13 *m.* (37 alt.,81 pop.), on US 113 was called Poplar Town before it was renamed for a family of the neighborhood.

The railroad station at NEWARK, 17.6 *m.* (35 alt.,250 pop.), is given the local Indian name Queponco to avoid confusion with other Newarks. Near by there lived a number of the intelligent and respected 'Moors' or Yellow People—of mixed blood including, it is believed, an Indian strain —who were related to the group still living along Indian River, Delaware. At both places the same legend of their origin is related: that they were descended from local Indians and from Spanish (or Moorish or Portuguese) seamen wrecked long ago on the Delaware coast. Local whites and Negroes and the Government census takers regarded them as Negroes.

The large rectangular brick building was erected in 1837 as the WORCES-

TER ALMSHOUSE (R), 22.6 *m*., but was sold by the county in 1917, and since has been used as a barn and as quarters for seasonal laborers on the large farm—formerly the Poor Farm—where it stands. In a large room on the second floor, where insane or violent inmates were kept, is a stout timber with old leg irons. Convicts hanged by sentence of the court were buried in the woods back of the building.

SNOW HILL, 25.7 *m*. (20 alt., 1,604 pop.), founded in 1686 on the southeast side of the Pocomoke River, has been the seat of Worcester County since its formation in 1742 and is both the southernmost county seat in the State and also the one least affected by modern commerce. The business section is tucked away, almost apologetically, in a small space between the neoclassic WORCESTER COURTHOUSE (L) on Market Street and the deep, narrow river, where the cypress swamp crowds up to the lumber mill and the fertilizer plant. There are several canneries, a basket factory, a shirt factory, and other minor industrial plants.

With its long, straight, shady streets laid out at right angles, Snow Hill is peaceful, gracious, and unselfconscious. If the elderly editors of the *Democratic Messenger* (founded 1879) conduct no trade-boosting campaigns, it is because the paper, like the people, has an agricultural outlook and income, and is county-minded rather than town-minded. No loud protests are made over the gradually declining population and civic pride is expressed not in showing signboards at the town limits but in white-painted houses and well-tended gardens. The town government is efficient and public utilities are well administered.

The site was part of a tract that Colonel William Stevens patented in 1676 and called Snow Hill after a London surburb of the time; two years later he sold it to Henry Bishop for 15,000 pounds of tobacco. The Maryland Assembly's Act for the Advancement of Trade in 1683 called for the founding of five towns in Somerset County, and the Snow Hill tract was selected in 1686 as the site of a trade-and-export town on the Pocomoke. Here early townsmen were Scottish merchants—Martins, Spences, and others—who dealt in tobacco and crops produced in this new seaside region by immigrants from Virginia and the Chesapeake country. The river is only seven miles from Chincoteague Bay, and a freight road built to the east formed a short overland link between the Chesapeake and north Atlantic ports.

In 1742 when Worcester County was erected, Snow Hill became the county seat. Slavery was firmly established. The pattern of life that developed did not at first include schools. Later schools for the children of planters and merchants were established. Union Academy in Snow Hill was not opened until 1834.

Bad fires swept the village in 1834 and 1893. Of the surviving old houses most are frames; many have the large outside chimneys, separate kitchens, and 'colonnades' characteristic of the early nineteenth-century plantation houses of the lower Peninsula; several have second-story galleries. Victorian houses are numerous and, like the HARGIS HOUSE on east side of Federal St., north of Morris St., often handsomely furnished. Next door south is the one remaining large old brick house of Snow Hill, now called BOXHAUL by its owner, a retired naval officer. (To boxhaul a square-rigger is to tack her smartly by putting the head yards abox, or aback.) Called Ingleside and Chanceford by former owners, this white-stuccoed house was apparently built in three different periods. The large front section, with pedimented gable end facing the street, was erected in the latter eighteenth century by James Rounds Morris, clerk of the court. Inside this fine mansion the hall is across the front and has entrances in the center and each end. Behind this hall are a living room and dining room. A square ballroom with similar hall has been added in the rear. Mantels and cornices are delicately ornate.

The WHALEY HOUSE, SW. corner Federal and Morris Sts., is a two-story white frame house with square columns and two outside chimneys at each end of the main wing and another on the kitchen wing. The upstairs gallery has a lattice railing. Also on Federal Street, at the NW. corner of Dixon's Alley, is CHERRYSTONE, formerly called the Teagle Townsend House, built about 1814. Set well back from the street in spacious grounds, this house has a great chimney at the south end and a separate kitchen connected by an enclosed passage. The garden here is notable.

On the northern side of town at the end of Park Row is the BURRIS HOUSE, with three great outside chimneys, a fanlighted doorway, and an upper porch; it was erected early in the nineteenth century and is now in poor condition. The little white THEBAUD HOUSE, Spence St. near Market, has blue shutters and trim, and a large chimney on the small wing. The large, white-walled PAYNE HOUSE, west side of Market St. between Church and Bank Sts., two-and-one-half stories, is ornamented in the Adam style; it has delicate dormers and a handsome doorway.

The exterior of ALL HALLOWS CHURCH (Episcopal), NE. corner Market and Church Sts., remains about as it was in 1756 when, after eight years of work, it was completed. Its brick construction was authorized at a cost of 80,000 pounds of tobacco. Changes have included the replacement of the old pews and woodwork in the 1870's, a new recessed chancel and slate roof in 1891, new windows in 1899. When the new roof was put on, the bell was placed on a bracket between two cedars in the churchyard. It is still there. Within the door, in a glass case, is a Bible, the gift of Queen Anne, dated 'London, 1701.'

The present brick MAKEMIE MEMORIAL PRESBYTERIAN CHURCH, east side of Market St. near Bank St., built in 1890, is a successor to the 'plain country building' erected here sometime between 1686 and 1697 during the pastorship of the Reverend Samuel Davis, who served with Francis Makemie as one of the first Presbyterian ministers in America.

Good cooking is a Snow Hill tradition, whether the food is terrapin in chafing dishes, steamed oysters opened in the back room of a soda fountain, or the noted Sunday-pone of Worcester County. The latter is a damp but digestible form of corn bread (also called sweat-pone) that is cooked slowly all night in large iron pots. Nowadays the pone pot and its mixture of meal and molasses is put in the stove oven, but in old times it was set in the fireplace, covered with embers, and left until morning. The pots were also used to heat the family's Saturday-night bath water.

Usually undemonstrative, the people of Snow Hill were deeply aroused during the two years' period between the arrest of Euel Lee, a Negro, in October 1931 for the murder of a local family of four whites, and his execution in Baltimore on October 27, 1933. Feeling against Lee ran high from the start but became violent when his defense was assumed by a Baltimore attorney of the International Labor Defense League. On November 4, 1931, a mob, failing to seize Lee, grabbed and beat the attorney and two companions in front of the courthouse here before they were rescued and escorted from town. After trial in Baltimore County in January 1932, Lee was sentenced to hang; a mistrial was declared because there were no Negroes on the jury, but he was convicted the next September after Negroes drawn had been successfully challenged by the State. The case was carried to the Court of Appeals and then to the U.S. Supreme Court, which refused to review it.

1. Left from the northern limits of Snow Hill on the concrete-paved Public Landing road to PUBLIC LANDING, 6.3 *m.* (10 alt.,12 pop.), on the shore of Chincoteague Bay, here five miles wide. Until the railroad era, the place was a busy shipping point for freight going the short distance overland between vessels here and at Snow Hill. It is now primarily a summer resort, with a hotel, private cottages, and amusements. The MANSION HOUSE (R), with an eighteenth-century section at right angles to the later main wing, all painted white, belonged until recently to the Spence family, long notable in Maryland public life. Many stories are told about Ara Spence (1793–1866), a Maryland judge who spent a long widowerhood here with his servants and numerous cats. One story concerns a little Negro of the household whose laziness and impudence survived the judge's rage; Judge Spence collared the boy and ordered his father, the butler, to 'Take him down to the shore, tie a rock to him, and dash him in the bay.' The boy thought fast, and protested, 'Bless Gawd, Mass' Ara, don' drown me—I ain't had ma breffas' yit!'

Right from Public Landing 1.2 *m.* on a graded dirt road to MOUNT EPHRAIM (L), a story-and-a-half brick house built early in the eighteenth century on a great tract patented by the Purnell family. Legend says Mount Ephraim, like other very old houses on the coastal bays, was saved from destruction by pirates (or the British in the Revolution or the War of 1812) through a ruse: occupants and slaves paraded back and forth with guns and cornstalks to simulate a large force of soldiers.

On the dirt road is (R) WATERMELON POINT or Simperton, 1.5 *m.*, built by a Purnell about 1712. The gambrel-roofed house is of brick except for the north wall, which blew out in a gale and has been replaced by a shingled wall. A great outside chimney stands at the south end of the main house. Old pine paneling is covered by wallpaper. Human bones constantly come to the surface in the yard—whether of whites, Negroes, or Indians, no one knows.

2. Right from Snow Hill on State 12, the Salisbury road, to the junction with concrete-paved State 354 (R) and an asphalt road (L), 1.2 *m.* This crossroad is on the Askiminokonson Indian Reservation established by the Maryland Assembly in 1686 at 'Indian Town' where a tribe of Nanticokes had what is said to have been the largest Indian settlement in Maryland.

a. Right on State 354 to a dirt road; L. here to the Shockley Farm Lane, 4.1 *m.*; R. on foot through the farm and woods (*guide required*) to the INDIAN HEAP beside a long disused road. Until about 1915 nearly every passerby, riding or afoot, tossed a twig or branch upon a brush heap that would often become many feet high before being destroyed by a brush fire. Not to add to the 'Old Injun Heap' was bad luck. In 1939 the heap was only a foot high. A legend explains the ancient mound as a memorial erected by an Indian to his dead sweetheart.

b. Left from State 12 on the asphalt road 6.9 *m.* to MILBOURNE LANDING (L), a recreational area (*picnicking facilities*) developed by the Resettlement Administration on a large tract along the west side of the Pocomoke River. A new pier is used by small boats, but the river here is considered too treacherous for public bathing.

The asphalt paving becomes concrete; at 8 *m.* is the entrance (L) to the CELLAR HOUSE by the Pocomoke. This early eighteenth-century frame house has brick ends and much primitive paneling. The great fireplace in its living room has no mantel, and the heavy doors are battened diagonally inside. In the peak of the south gable is a 'lay-on-your-belly' window, so-called because the lookout watching down the river had to do just that. No two windows in the house are the same size. It is not certain who built the house.

The name of the place is explained by a legend that an underground passage runs from the cellar to the river and emerges under the bluff where a grassy mound is said to mark the former entrance. The story goes that pirates or other river thieves brought loot to be stored in the house until sold. Other versions speak of kidnaped free Negroes being shipped South from the landing, or the antithesis—runaway slaves being sent North by the Underground Railroad. There is also the ghost of a woman murdered by her French husband, an owner of the place, for accepting the attentions of a visiting pirate.

The road crosses DIVIDING CREEK, 10.8 *m.*, which has separated Worcester County from Somerset County since 1742. On the west bank stood the Somerset Courthouse, built in 1694 or soon afterwards, in use until the partition of the county.

At 13.6 *m.* is the junction with US 13 (*see Tour 6*).

Back on State 12, at a point 4.1 *m.* northwest of Snow Hill, is a graded dirt road; L. here 1.1 *m.* to a second dirt road; L. here a few yards to the tall, crumbling, brick stack of NASSAWANGO FURNACE, erected in 1832 to smelt the bog ore of Nassawango Creek. More than 100 houses, a hotel, and stores were built here and served the short-lived boom town; the project lost money owing to competition with better iron ores elsewhere. The furnace was abandoned in 1847. One of its leading promoters and investors (with his wife's money) was Judge Thomas Spence of Princess Anne. Near the furnace lived a huge Negro named Samson Harmon, whose great prowess, both muscular and amatory, is still a lusty Worcester tradition though he died about 1900. Samson is said to have run down a buck deer after an all-day chase.

At 2.2 *m.* on the second dirt road is the WARREN MANSION (R), built over a period of years in this clearing in the pine wilderness by Frank A. Warren (d.1934), whose murals decorate public and semipublic buildings in various cities. The large and spreading rustic structure of concrete follows no set architectural style. Flying buttresses jut from yellow-stuccoed walls to the ground; the dining room is 100 feet long, the concrete dining table 32. A sunken fireplace accommodates 12-foot logs. Warren's numerous children, growing up here, helped build the house. They studied their lessons while riding to and from the Snow Hill school in a covered mule cart lighted with a lantern. As the older ones left school and got jobs, they sent the younger ones to school and college. Warren was killed by a train, but his wilderness home remains; his children, a successful and self-sufficient group, frequently return for visits.

State 12 continues northwest to SALISBURY, 17.5 *m.* (*see Salisbury*), and the junction with US 213 (*see Tour 3*) and with US 13 (*see Tour 6*).

3. Left from Snow Hill on State 12 (Church Street) to GIRDLETREE, 6.3 *m.* (34 alt.,375 pop.), a shipping point for farm products and sea food.

STOCKTON, 9.4 *m.* (33 alt.,400 pop.), is a railroad shipping point for large quantities of Chincoteague Bay oysters and about 100,000 soft-shell and peeler crabs annually.

Left 2.9 *m.* from Stockton on a macadamized road to the piles of oyster shells, the boats, wharves, and packing houses that form GEORGE'S ISLAND LANDING on Chincoteague Bay, two miles north of the Virginia Line. Because the waters here are too shallow for the skipjacks (one-mast sailboats) used on Chesapeake oyster grounds, the tongers use small square-end scows to 'catch' the celebrated George's Island oysters. On a wharf here is Captain Ben Disharoon's STEAMED OYSTER HOUSE, advertised only by a crudely-lettered sign but known throughout several counties. Customers remove coats and vests and call for oysters well-done, medium, or hot-raw (epicures say 'hot-raw'). Small iron baskets of 'selects' go into a steam box connected to a boiler stoked by a Negro fireman; a row of Negro shuckers behind a long, low table make knives fly as they flip oysters into saucers of vinegar or melted butter as fast as the customers can eat them.

The shore of Chincoteague Bay is believed to be that described by Giovanni da Verrazano, Florentine navigator, as one of his landing places in 1524 after first touching somewhere to the southward. Historians believe he entered Chincoteague Inlet near by, sailed up into Sinepuxent Bay, and out another inlet on his explorations up the coast.

On US 113 at 31.2 *m.* is the entrance (R) to a CCC camp in the POCO-MOKE STATE FOREST, whose 1,700 acres border the river. A road leads to a picnic ground on the shore.

At 38.5 *m.* is the junction with US 13 (*see Tour* 6), one mile east of Pocomoke City (*see Tour* 6).

Tour 7A

Berlin—Sinepuxent Neck—South Point; 10.9 *m.*, State 376 and Sinepuxent Neck Road.

Concrete, slag, and graded dirt roadbed.
No accommodations.

On the Sea Side of the Eastern Shore, this route penetrates Sinepuxent Neck, a very low, wooded, marsh-fringed section about nine miles long and less than two miles wide, separated from the mainland by Ayres and Trappe creeks and Newport Bay, and bounded on the east by Sinepuxent Bay.

What 'the auld country' is to the Irish, Sinepuxent Neck is to many old families of Worcester County whose Fassitt, Henry, Purnell, Robins, Spence, or Whaley forebears dwelt here. A chronic homesickness for The Neck leads them to visit and revisit it. Negro tenants of the old houses—who often wear the names of the former owners—are used to hearing strangers from distant States tell children solemnly, 'This is where your people came from.'

Late in the seventeenth century, settlers mostly from farther down the Peninsula were clearing the hardwood forest (pines came later) and planting corn, tobacco, and flax. Despite marauding pirates, mosquito-borne fevers, and occasional ruinous storm tides from the Atlantic, they prospered while they could replenish the fertility of the sandy, often poorly drained soil. Colonial and post-colonial descendants built the brick and frame plantation houses that still stand here and in Newport Neck (*see Tour* 7) as the most important group on the Maryland Sea Side. Several of the houses were hit by cannonballs, possibly during April 1813 when the British blockading fleet was sending small armed craft through the inlets to forage for food supplies.

As elsewhere along the Peninsula's tidal shores, the system based on slavery and water transport was undermined by exhaustion of the soil, loss of cheap labor, and the building of rail lines inland. Most of the old houses of Sinepuxent Neck show the ravages of long tenant occupancy.

Mules have never been replaced by tractors or trucks and even yokes of oxen, rare now in Maryland, are still preferred for hard going on wet lands. The making of outlaw whisky here did not begin or end with National prohibition and stills are officially sledge-hammered at intervals. The Neck is a favorite place for fox and 'coon hunting, afoot, in cars, and on horseback, by day and by night; marshes are leased in season for duck shooting. Recently mosquito-control work has been carried on by the CCC.

State 376 follows Pitts Street east from its junction with US 113 in BERLIN, 0 m. (45 alt.,1,480 pop.) (see Tour 7).

The old gristmill and hamlet of TRAPPE, 1.7 m., is at the head of Trappe Creek; this old trading place declined as Berlin developed in the early nineteenth century on the new stage route.

The magnificent tree (R), 3.9 m., resembling a white oak, is the AYRES ELM whose 18-foot girth and lofty crown of gnarled branches make it a landmark for boatmen coming up Chincoteague and Newport bays. It shades the old house of GOLDEN QUARTER, built by an Ayres beside Ayres Creek; the small kitchen wing of brick antedates the two-story frame house of the Revolutionary period in which the fine heart-pine paneling and carved mantels are well preserved. The ivy and the elm are said to have grown from seedlings brought from England by a woman of the family, and the name Golden Quarter referred to the yellow English daisies that she planted.

In the hamlet called LEWIS'S STORE, 4.5 m., concrete State 376 ends and the main route turns R. on the gravel-and-slag Sinepuxent Neck road.

1. Left from Lewis' Store on a dirt road to MAYFIELD (R), 0.1 m., a white-painted brick house erected about 1785 on bayshore land of William Fassitt (see below). His descendant, the present owner, has a collection of mounted specimens of wild life taken near by, including a swan, a bald eagle, and that rare summer visitor, a brown pelican. He also has a collection of shotguns, rifles, and pistols, all kept oiled and fully loaded.

2. Straight ahead from Lewis' Store at the end of the concrete road is the woods lane leading to the FASSITT HOUSE (or Rounds), overlooking the bay. This small story-and-a-half brick house was built by William Fassitt (d.1734) or by a son-in-law named Rounds, early in the eighteenth century, and displays what an authority has called 'probably the most interesting Colonial brickwork in Maryland.' Dark glazed-header bricks make fanciful diamond and zigzag patterns.

Fassitt was a planter, vessel owner, and an early Presbyterian follower of the Reverend Francis Makemie (see Tour 6B). A tale recalling an episode in Uncle Remus is told of him: Pirates had captured his vessel, chained his crew, and were chaining him when he cried out piteously, 'Do anything you want to, boys, only don't throw me overboard—the water's full of sharks!' The pirates heaved him overboard. In the water he was as much at home as Br'er Rabbit in the brier patch and swam safely to Fenwick's Island beach.

A legend about another Fassitt of Sinepuxent Neck is that he fired the fatal shot that struck the British General Braddock in the back during the western campaign of 1755 against the French and Indians; Braddock had cut down Fassitt's brother for advancing behind trees and not in the open, and revenge was quick.

On the Sinepuxent Neck road at 5.8 *m.* is the junction with a dirt side road.

    Left on this road 0.7 *m.* to (L) HENRY'S GROVE (or the Julie Henry House), built near the shore by a Fassitt in 1792, according to a plate in the south wall. This is an example of the best Sea Side type of brick mansion—plain, solid, rectangular, two stories high with fine woodwork and stairway.
    On the dirt road at 0.9 *m.* is the slip of the SINEPUXENT BAY FERRY (*round trip $1.50 for car & driver, 50¢ each passenger; use signal flag if ferry is at other side*). A motor-scow ferryboat crosses the bay, one-and-a-half-miles wide here, to the Coastal Barrier Island, which stretches 35 miles between Ocean City Inlet on the north and Chincoteague Inlet on the south; the southern 12 miles, in Virginia, is called Assateague Island.
    An automobile can usually be driven the entire length of the hard beach of the surf bank. (*Tires should be partly deflated, cars should carry reserves of fuel and water and an old sail or heavy cloth to provide traction. Emergency phone calls may be made from Coast Guard stations*). This long narrow island, a primitive wilderness of beach, sand dunes, and wind-twisted stunted pines on the western side, has marshes abounding with wild life. There are occasional gunners' and fishermen's shacks but the only human inhabitants are the Coast Guard crews at North Beach and the Pope's Island, Virginia stations.

On the Sinepuxent Neck Road is WILLIAMS GROVE (L), 6.4 *m.*, a long, gray house. The small north end with dormers was built about 1800 as a tavern for the shipping trade then using the deepwater landing here. Vessels sailed out with exports for Northern markets and returned with limestone to burn, manufactured goods, and silk dresses for Christmas balls and soirées. Williams Grove, neglected, wears a melancholy aspect as it overlooks the bay.

SANDY POINT (L), 7.5 *m.*, with buff-plastered brick walls and a makeshift pyramidal roof replacing the old pitched roof, was formerly one of the finest homes on the Sea Side but is now occupied by tenants and appears forlorn. The builder was John Ratcliffe, said to have been educated in London and Paris. As the roof was being put on during the Revolution, a British landing party set fire to the house. Ratcliffe's restoration included a ballroom with floor made springy for dancing, and his parties were famous among Sea Side society. No less famous was his cruelty to his slaves in a region where kind treatment was usual; one night in 1799, as he was coming home from Newport Neck, his Negro men sprang upon him and murdered him in his own lane (*see Tour 7*). In 1929 the house was again gutted by fire—this time from a secretly-operated still. The place is part of the great Genezir tract (*see below*).

In the dilapidated shell of SCARBOROUGH HOUSE (L), 8.5 *m.*, a shingle-walled, gambrel-roofed dwelling erected about 1780 for Thomas Purnell, fine mantels and paneling survive. A lady had finished dressing here, it is said, for a ball at Sandy Point when she tripped on her skirt, fell downstairs, and died of a broken neck. Her ghost is a source of concern to the Negroes who live here.

Rising sheer, gaunt, and bare, yet strangely appealing in its somber decay, is GENEZER (R), 9.4 *m.*, most noted of all the houses in Sinepuxent Neck. The combined length of the two-story main wing, the colonnade, and the kitchen wing is 80 feet, but the width of this brick structure is but 19 feet throughout—a long, slim building unlike any other in the region. Patched spots in a wall are said to be bullet marks. The house is on a tract of more than 2,000 acres patented under the name Genezir in 1684 by Edward Whaley (*see below*) and Charles Ratcliffe. It was built by Major John Purnell (pronounced Purn'l) in 1732.

The road ends at SOUTH POINT, 10.9 *m.*, a landing where oysters in season are forked from boats to trucks. A modern dwelling (R) on the site of South Point, is the home of the influential Robins family. About 1840 one of the sights of the Neck was the Robins girls being driven in a great coach on Sunday to St.Martin's Church, 15 miles north (*see Tour 7*). A clump of trees just south of the house is said to mark the GRAVE OF EDWARD WHALEY. The tradition about Whaley is the most popular in Worcester County and has inspired much research, off and on, for at least 75 years.

This Edward Whaley, some historians believe, was the Edward Whaley (or Whalley), a cousin to Oliver Cromwell, who served under Cromwell against the Royalists as a cavalry general and was later one of the judges who sentenced King Charles I to death; with another regicide he fled to America when Charles II assumed the throne, and landed at Boston in 1660. Tradition takes it up here to say that Whaley, still pursued, went to New Haven and thence to the Eastern Shore of Virginia, and moved about 1678 to Sinepuxent Neck under the name Middleton, not resuming his true name until the accession of William and Mary in 1688 made it safe to do so.

Records have been cited to show that the Whaley, who was a co-patentee of Genezir in 1684, was in Maryland when the regicide judge was believed to be in New England. The legend, however, is a strong one and goes on undiminished, even though the local Edward Whaley would have been 103 at his death in 1718.

Tour 8

Baltimore—Annapolis—Prince Frederick—Solomons Island; 83.7 *m.*, State 2.

Concrete-paved dual highway between Baltimore and Annapolis; elsewhere macadam, two lanes wide.
Baltimore and Annapolis R.R. parallels route between Baltimore and Annapolis.
First class hotels in Baltimore and Annapolis; small hotels and tourist homes elsewhere; few tourist camps.

Section a. BALTIMORE to ANNAPOLIS; 25.6 m.

State 2, the main route between Baltimore and the State capital, is paralleled for most of the distance by narrow winding old State 2. The new route, without a curve for three quarters of its length, rises and dips across low rolling Anne Arundel County. Side roads lead to the Magothy and the Severn Rivers and to water-front resorts ranging from fashionable Gibson Island to clusters of week-end shacks.

The light sandy soil, where it is not covered with second-growth pine, is divided chiefly into truck farms. In season vegetables and small fruits are offered for sale in roadside stands. In spring stooping men and women workers move slowly along the neat rows of strawberry fields and from this region come the 'Annarannle strawberries,' which have been cried in Baltimore for generations.

South of BALTIMORE, 0 m. (*see Baltimore*), State 2, the dual highway is named for Albert Cabell Ritchie (1876–1936), four times governor of Maryland. Three weeks after he was born in Richmond, Virginia, Ritchie was brought to Baltimore and he spent the rest of his life in Maryland. He was graduated from Johns Hopkins University, then studied law at the University of Maryland, where he later held a professorship until he became assistant city solicitor of Baltimore, his first public office, at 27. He became a popular hero in 1914 when, as a private citizen, he instituted an action before the public service commission to compel the Consolidated Gas and Electric Company of Baltimore to improve the quality of its gas or reduce its rates. The commission sustained him and the company accepted lower rates. In 1915 he was elected attorney general of Maryland, in 1917 was appointed chief counsel to the War Board in Washington, and three years later became governor of Maryland for the first time. His personal charm and popularity, his position as governor of Maryland, and his leadership in anti-prohibition sentiment made him a national figure for many years.

451

In GLENBURNIE, 7.8 *m.* (*see Tour 9a*), is the junction with macadam State 3 (*see Tour 9a*).

At 12 *m.* is the junction with State 177, a concrete-paved dual highway.

Left on State 177 to JACOBSVILLE, 4.3 *m.* (105 alt.,42 pop.), at the junction with a concrete-paved road; L. here to FORT SMALLWOOD PARK, 3.7 *m.*, named in honor of General William Smallwood (*see Tour 12*). In 1896 the United States Government acquired 100 acres on Rock Point and erected barracks here at the mouth of Rock Creek. The property was sold in 1926 to the City of Baltimore for a public park. From the road skirting the river are seen smokestacks of industrial Sparrows Point (*see Tour 2a*) and (L) abandoned FORT CARROLL, a man-made island built in 1848 on a shoal, called Sollers Flats, in the middle of the Patapsco River. Robert E. Lee, then a brevet colonel of engineers in the United States Army, supervised construction of this fort that was intended as a full military post but was never completed. Today the forbidding stone walls though well supplied with warning lights, bells, and horns are a menace to navigation.

State 177 continues to the gate, 11 *m.*, at the end of the causeway to GIBSON ISLAND, a quiet, fashionable resort open only to members and their guests. Smooth lawns stretch down from white painted summer cottages to an anchorage dotted with yachts and to the sandy shores of the bay. The Gibson Island Club, formed in 1921, has become the chief center of yachting in the Chesapeake (*see Sports and Recreation*). Much futile digging for Captain Kidd's treasure has been done on this island.

State 2 crosses the crest of a hill, 23.4 *m.*, from which the Severn River and Annapolis are seen. The massive gray buildings of the Naval Academy, dominated by the dome of the Chapel, stand at the water's edge, and behind them red brick chimneys and sharp steeples cluster about the white painted cupola of the State Capitol. Beyond the mouth of the river (L) is a wide view across the Chesapeake to the low wooded bank of the Eastern Shore. Hydroplanes drone overhead or taxi over the surface of the tidal inlet. On spring afternoons Navy eight-oared shells, followed by the coach's launch, slide up and down the river. In summer groups of sailboats, filled with landlubber plebes getting their first taste of salt water, move among the private pleasure craft. The white sails of warm weather give way in winter to the patched gray sails and raking masts of oyster dredges.

At 23.7 *m.* is a junction with macadamized old State 2.

Left on this to the NAVAL ENGINEERING EXPERIMENT STATION and RADIO STATION (R), 0.4 *m.* The latter is one of the most powerful on the coast and its nine towers are visible from the bay and from points on the low-lying Eastern Shore nearly 30 miles away.

At DULLS CORNER, 0.8 *m.*, is macadamized and concrete-paved St.Margaret's Road.

Right on this to ST.MARGARET'S PROTESTANT EPISCOPAL CHURCH (R), 1.7 *m.*, a white frame building with a low, shingled tower. Erected in 1895 it is the fourth to house this congregation since 1673. Because the modern parish is called Westminster and the church generally spoken of as St.Margaret's, Westminster, many believe it is named for the famous church in London.

Under the chancel of the third church was buried Sir Robert Eden, last governor of the Province of Maryland. Eden, accompanied by his brother-in-law Henry Harford, proprietary heir-at-law, returned to Maryland after the Revolution to press claims for the Calvert estates which had been confiscated by the State of Maryland. He aroused resentment by issuing patents to vacant lands and taking fees of office until the governor and council took legal steps against him. When he died at the home of Dr.Upton Scott on September 3, 1784, no mention of the fact was made in the press. Owing to public sentiment and the attitude of the vestry it was decided not to bury him at St.Anne's, Annapolis, and interment is believed to have taken place secretly at this country parish church. In 1923, the Society of Colonial Wars identified the grave on the site of the third church, which had burned in 1802, and removed the remains to St.Anne's (*see Annapolis*).

At 2.8 *m*. is a dirt road; L. 0.6 *m*. on this to ST.MARGARET'S HUNT CLUB (R), where horse shows are held in spring and on Labor Day and members ride to hounds in season. A tilting tournament, followed by the crowning of a queen of love and beauty, is held (*Labor Day*) for the benefit of St.Margaret's Church.

At 4 *m*. on St.Margaret's Road is a dirt road; R. 1 *m*. to WHITEHALL, a five-part, brick house, nearly 200 feet long built on rising ground so that its entrance façade is three stories high and its garden façade only two. The main house, only one room deep, contains a dining room, drawing room, and a central great hall that extends through two floors. Arcaded walls stand between the main house and square two-story pavilions whose pyramidal roofs rise to central chimneys. On the south front is a monumental Corinthian portico, one of the earliest constructed in this country. It faces a long lawn and the Chesapeake Bay. Whitehall was built about 1766 by Horatio Sharpe, one of the last governors of the province. According to legend the elaborate carving of the interior woodwork—modillioned cornices, fluted Corinthian pilasters, consoles, acanthus leaves, frets—was executed by a young redemptioner who had been transported to the colony for some crime. His youth and intelligence aroused the interest of the governor, who took him into his household and promised him freedom if he would carve the decorations for the new house. The promise was never carried out as the craftsman died just as he completed his task, six years later.

Sharpe planned the house as a summer seat, but lived here throughout the year from the time of his unwilling retirement as governor in 1769 until his return to England in 1773. On his death in 1790 he deeded the estate to John Ridout, his former secretary, who had come from England with him in 1759.

Sharpe held Ridout in high esteem and helped secure the latter's appointment to the house of delegates. The friendship between the two continued even after young Ridout was Sharpe's successful rival for the hand of Mary, daughter of Governor Samuel Ogle.

In SKIDMORE, 5.2 *m*. (10 alt.,100 pop.), is a macadamized road.

Left on this to LOG INN, 1.2 *m*., a bathing and fishing resort on a bluff above Chesapeake Bay.

St.Margaret's Road continues straight ahead to the entrance of HOLLY BEACH FARM, 5.8 *m*., a 2,500-acre estate acquired by the Labrot family in 1907 and maintained as a model breeding farm for cattle and race horses.

State 2 crosses the Severn River, 24 *m*., on a concrete draw bridge and passes the Naval Hospital (L) and the Naval Academy Golf Course (R).

ANNAPOLIS, 25.6 *m*. (40 alt.,12,531 pop.) (*see Annapolis*).

Points of Interest: U.S. Naval Academy, State House, St.John's College, Hammond-Harwood House, Chase Home, and others.

Annapolis is at the junction with US 50 (*see Tour* 10).

Section b. *ANNAPOLIS to SOLOMONS ISLAND;* 58.1 *m*.

This section of State 2, called the Solomons Island Road, winds through rolling country that has large stretches of woodland and many abandoned fields sparsely covered with young pines. More and more of the farmland is being planted in tobacco, as in early days. Some fields are surrounded by snake fences, overgrown with catbriars or honeysuckle, and corners are choked with dogwood, sassafras, and chinquapin. At Solomons a ferry with regular service crosses the Patuxent River to St.Marys County (*see Tour* 11).

Between ANNAPOLIS, 0 *m.*, and PAROLE, 2.3 *m.*, State 2 unites with US 50 (*see Tour* 10), then branches L.

South River, 4.8 *m.*, is almost half a mile wide here between high banks. On the south shore, close to the highway, is a summer colony. To the east, down the widening river, is a view of Chesapeake Bay.

At 6.2 *m.* is the junction with State 214, Central Avenue (*see Tour* 10*A*).

The RUINS OF ALL HALLOWS CHURCH (R), 8.1 *m.*, are in a grove of oaks on a knoll beside the road. Only the shell of the simple rectangular brick building, erected in 1727, remains, the ancient edifice having been destroyed by fire February 11, 1940.

Under the Anglican Establishment, All Hallows became one of the richer Maryland parishes, but for a time after the Revolution it had no rector. In 1784 young Mason Locke Weems (1759–1825), a relative of Dr. William Smith who was trying to reorganize the Anglican churches, was installed, but voluntary contributions for support of a rector were so small that he was forced to conduct a school and also take to book selling to support himself. By 1792 Parson Weems had shown himself too liberal to please vestrymen and when he failed of reappointment to a parish he took to the road in clerical garb, carrying a stock of books and a fiddle. For 33 years he traveled through the South, in a special wagon, preaching, fiddling, selling books, and collecting stories that he wove into highly moralizing tracts and biographies. He is remembered today chiefly for his bit of fiction concerning George Washington and the cherry tree, but his biography of Washington has gone through more than 70 editions and is still in circulation. This *History of the Life and Death Virtues and Exploits of General George Washington* helped to fix the image of an impossibly cold and inhuman figure that later biographers have had much difficulty in dispelling. His moralizing pamphlets were forerunners of modern 'sob sister' writing. Typical of these was a work entitled *The Bad Wife's Looking Glass, or God's Revenge against Cruelty To Husbands—exemplified in the awful history of the beautiful but depraved Mrs. Rebecca Cotton, who most inhumanly murdered her husband John Cotton, Esq., for which horrid act God permitted her, in the prime of life and bloom of beauty, to be cut off by her brother, Stephen Kennady, May 5, 1807, with a number of incidents and anecdotes most extraordinary and instructive.*

At All Hallows is the junction with a dirt road.

Left on this road 1.3 *m.* to the SOUTH RIVER CLUB, a simple gabled white frame building housing a gentlemen's society organized in 1722 or earlier, probably the oldest active social club in the United States. Within are a big silver punch bowl used since 1776, old chairs and china, and a set of brass quoits given by Mr. Ingersoll of Philadelphia in 1742. The framed rules of the club have hung on the wall since 1793 or possibly earlier. It has always been forbidden here to discuss either religion or politics, and Mason Weems attempted in vain to introduce debating. Records reveal that in September 1777 the club did consider 'the alarming situation of this State, occasioned by an invasion of the British Fleet.' On October 2, 1777, it resolved: 'that this club be continued as usual.' Though the Revolution was not allowed to interfere with meetings, the races at Annapolis and the Civil War did. In early days there were 37 members and meetings were held every two weeks; then monthly after 1742. At times there were only three members and from 1874 to 1895 no meetings were held.

The 25 men who belong at present are all descendants of former members; they hold four all-day dinners each year. One of these has been on the Fourth of July since 1776. The dinners are provided by members in rotation, though the rules say: 'The steward that appears not in person or by proxy at the usual place of meeting, provided with two-and-one-half gallons of spirit with ingredients of toddy, by one o'clock, and a sufficient dinner, with clean pipes and tobacco, shall serve the following club day for such default.'

At 13.8 *m.* on State 2 is the junction with macadamized State 255.

Left on this 3.1 *m.* to a QUAKER BURYING GROUND (L), surrounded by a white fence. The West River Friends Meeting was one of the largest in the province and its meeting house, which stood here, is often mentioned in the journals of the day. Here is the marked grave of Captain James Dooley who had been a Friend but carried on privateering during the War of 1812 and continued the practice after the treaty of peace—when it became piracy.

At the Quaker Burying Ground is the junction with a second macadam road.

Left on this 0.4 *m.* to (R) TULIP HILL (*open during Garden Club week*), an estate patented to Richard Talbot in 1659 as Poplar Knowl. The five-part brick house, visible from the gate only in winter, was built by Samuel Galloway, probably in 1756. The two-and-a-half-story central unit has a low gambrel roof surmounted with chimneys pierced by arches, a feature of few colonial houses. On the pediment of the entrance portico is a dancing Cupid in high relief and in the larger eave pediment is a bulls-eye window balanced by carved white panels set into the brick. From each side of the main house an arcaded gallery extends to a low two-story gabled wing. Over the door in the garden front is an arched hood with carved brackets, cresting, and a conventionalized tulip as the fineal. The terraced garden overlooks West River and Chesapeake Bay.

A fine open-string stairway with delicate scrolls rises at one side of the wide central hall.

Though the Galloways were Quakers they lived in luxury here. The first Samuel owned Selima, finest horse of his day, and, as long as the family lived here, a portrait of the Godolphin Arabian, ancestor of many western thoroughbreds, hung above the dining-room mantel.

At 0.5 *m.* on the macadamized road is a dirt road; R. 0.3 *m.* on this to CEDAR PARK (R), whose house was built before 1700 by Richard Galloway soon after his arrival in America. The oldest part of the low rambling thick-walled house is a brick story-and-a-half structure with brick pilasters on the front. Its steep gable roof, pierced by tiny dormers and flanked by wide end-chimneys, sweeps down over a pent at one end. The interior woodwork and paneling are simple. A high holly hedge encloses two sides of the garden and around the other two is a rose hedge more than a century old.

From the Quaker Burying Ground the main side road continues to GALESVILLE, 4 *m.* (10 alt.,260 pop.), on the shore of West River. In 1682 William Penn attended a Friends' meeting here at the home of Thomas Hooker.

TUDOR HALL (L), 16.0 *m.*, is a frame telescope house with a two-story gallery on the approach front; the oldest section, the low kitchen wing, was built by Edward Hall in 1722 or earlier. The central section and its porch were probably built after 1800.

ST. JAMES CHURCH (L), 18.5 *m.*, locally called Herring Creek Church, belongs to an Anglican parish laid out in 1694. The walls of the simple rectangular building are laid in all-header bond and the arched windows and doors are unusually wide. On the south front is a brick entrance porch and near by among the trees a wood frame supports the church bell. In the churchyard are the tombstones of Christopher Birckhead and his wife, dated 1666—the oldest known in Maryland.

The public notice of the church contract of 1762 read: 'Likewise Mr. John Weems has undertaking the building of a breek church in the sd

Parrish according to the draft of the plan that was this day layd before the vestry, and is to build the sd church att fourteen hundred pounds cur without any further charges to the said Parrish in any shape whatever, in case the vestry git ann act of Assembly for what tob. will be wanting of the sum that is to build the said church; for as they hant tob. enufe in hand for the finniching of the sd church.'

In 1765 the church was completed by Weems, who was probably a cousin of Mason Locke Weems. Mason Locke Weems' birthplace was east of the church near Herring Bay.

At SEAR'S CORNER, 18.7 m., is the junction with macadamized State 258.

Right on this to PORTLAND MANOR (R), 2.5 m., a former 2,000-acre estate granted to Jerome White in 1667. Later half of it was given to Colonel Henry Darnall, who held many important offices under the lord proprietary. He was secretary and council member, and sat with Lord Baltimore at the conference with William Penn over the Maryland-Pennsylvania boundary in December 1682. He served sometimes as deputy-governor, and later was judge and register of the land office. The present simple two-and-a-half-story structure was built after the first Portland manor house burned before 1800.

At WEBB, 21.2 m., is the junction with a macadamized road.

Left on this to FAIRHAVEN, 2.2 m. (10 alt.,31 pop.), a handful of houses that look out over the bay where it is more than 10 miles wide and only Poplar Island breaks the horizon. Off Fairhaven a minor naval skirmish took place on April 4, 1865, five days before the surrender at Appomattox.

FRIENDSHIP, 22.6 m. (150 alt.,185 pop.), is at the junction with a macadam road.

1. Left on this to HOLLY HILL (R), 1.5 m. The T-shaped brick story-and-a-half house, visible from the road, has a steep roof, narrow dormers, small window panes, and massive chimneys. The oldest part was built about 1704 by Richard Harrison.

2. Right from Friendship on the macadamized road, paved only a short distance, to TRENT HALL (L), 0.2 m., a tall two-and-a-half-story frame house with a two-story gambrel-roofed wing. The main house was built by Dr.Benjamin Carr about 1800.

At 0.7 m. on the dirt road is another dirt road; R. here 1.2 m. to MAIDSTONE (L), a story-and-a-half house with a steep roof and dormers. Its construction was begun by Samuel Chew and completed in 1778. The dining room is paneled and painted a dark red, now almost black. There is a legend that the ghost of Anne Chew, dressed in gray, with a long scarf blowing behind her, walks in the garden in the evening.

At 28.4 m. on State 2 is the junction with macadamized State 262.

Right on this 4.4 m. to LOWER MARLBORO, (20 alt.,150 pop.), by the Patuxent. This was an important port before the river silted up with the top soil of formerly fertile fields.

At the eastern end of the village is the GRAEME HOUSE (R), on a tract patented in 1661 to John Bogue as Patuxent Manor. About 1743 Malcolm Graeme built this small, steep-roofed, story-and-a-half house. The brick is laid partly in Flemish, partly in English bond and there are dormers in the front and a chimney at each end. Paneling from the hall and the three downstairs rooms has been sold.

Ivy covers the walls of ALL SAINTS CHURCH (L), 28.6 m., and partly hides the high surface arches of the side walls. The first services were conducted here by the Reverend Henry Hall, rector of St.James, Herring Creek, in a building erected between 1694 and 1696. The first rector, the

Reverend Thomas Cockshutt, arrived in 1697. The first church here burned in 1776 and the present one was built in 1815, to replace the second. In 1696 the church received one of the libraries Commissary Bray sent to the Maryland parishes. Near the north wall is the CLAGETT SUN DIAL. Thomas John Clagett (*see Tour 9b*), who was rector here (1767–76, 1788–92) presented it to the church when he left after being made a bishop.

South of All Saints, tobacco is the one staple cash crop. Oxen are still used and few motorists fail to meet at least one springless wagon or a two-wheeled cart drawn by slow-moving beasts.

HUNTINGTOWN, 31.9 *m.* (170 alt.,150 pop.), is near the site of old Huntingtown on Hunting Creek, a stop on the post route between St. Marys City and Annapolis. A gristmill built by General James Wilkinson added to its prosperity but tobacco was, of course, its mainstay. It had a public tobacco warehouse and carried on considerable trade with European countries, when Hunting Creek, now silted into sluggishness, was deeper. During the War of 1812 Huntingtown was burned by the British and never recovered its importance.

At 38 *m.* is the junction with macadamized State 231.

> Right on this 3.2 *m.* to the junction with a macadamized road.
> Left (on this road) to the TANEY PLACE (L), 0.7 *m.* The solid, square, two-story house stands above the Patuxent on the west side of Battle Creek. Its front and rear brick walls are clapboarded.
> The early history of the house is obscure. Michael Taney arrived in Maryland in 1660 as an indentured servant but prospered and became sheriff of the county. Here Roger Brooke Taney (*see Frederick*) was born on March 17, 1777.
> In 1819 John Magruder and the 70-year-old Michael Taney V quarreled here over a woman. According to one story, Magruder slapped Taney in the face while they were at the table during a hunt breakfast, and Taney stabbed Magruder through the heart. Taney escaped and, with the help of his people, crossed into Virginia, where he spent the remainder of his life. After his death, when his body was brought home for burial, one of the Magruders smashed the old man's face with a stone as he lay in his coffin.
> State 231 ends at HALLOWING POINT, 5.6 *m.* (20 alt.,15 pop.), the Calvert County side of the ferry crossing the Patuxent to Benedict (*see Tour 11*). It was formerly necessary to 'hallo' to the ferryman if he was on the far side of the river. (*No regular schedule.*)

PRINCE FREDERICK, 38.2 *m.* (150 alt.,300 pop.), seat of Calvert County since 1723, is a collection of white houses lining a single street that extends for half a mile along the road. On Saturday nights or on court days there is hardly room to get between the parked cars and wagons. The place was called Williams Old Fields until 1725 when it was named Prince Frederick, for one of the English princes. The town survived the Revolution unharmed, but was burnt by a British raiding party in 1814, and in 1882 was so completely destroyed by fire that no old buildings remain.

At 42 *m.* is the junction with macadamized State 264.

> Right on this 0.5 *m.* to CHRIST CHURCH (L), on a knoll. Christ Church parish was one of the three into which Calvert County was divided at the time the Anglican church was established in the province. The present building bears on its front the dates 1772, 1881, 1906. The Victorian surfacing of dark stucco and brown-painted bracketed cornices obscures the lines of the old buttressed walls.

In MUTUAL, 2.3 m. (160 alt.,50 pop.), is the junction with a macadamized road.

Left (on this road) to PARROTT'S CAGE (R), 4.2 m., whose small story-and-a-half house has dormers and brick walls laid in Flemish bond with glazed headers so dark they give a checkerboard effect. The house was built by William Parrott about 1652, when The Cage, 250 acres, was surveyed for him.

Right from Mutual on State 264 to BROOME ISLAND, 4.2 m., (20 alt.,81 pop.), a water-front community of oystermen and fishermen, some of whom act as guides for sportsmen. The 'island' is a narrow point jutting into the Patuxent and has a view that extends miles up and down the river.

At 43.1 m. is the junction with macadam State 509.

Left on this to KENWOOD BEACH, 1 m., by the bay. The tiny summer community has an excellent view of the CLIFFS OF CALVERT, which extend along the bay shore for 30 miles from Chesapeake Beach to Cove Point and range in height up to 150 feet. Embedded in them are fossil-bearing layers. Captain John Smith noticed the cliffs in his explorations up the Chesapeake in 1608.

LUSBY, 50.6 m. (100 alt.,10 pop.), is at the junction with State 266.

Right on this 2 m. to a dirt road; L. 0.7 m.; and R. 1.2 m. to PRESTON–ON–PATUX-ENT. The gable roofed, story-and-a-half brick house is thought to have been built in 1650 by Richard Preston, one of the commissioners appointed by Cromwell in 1652 to govern the colony. The seat of government was moved to his dwelling a year later. In 1654 the proprietary's forces attacked Preston, and, although they did not recover control of the province, they carried the records back to St.Marys City. In the struggle the Great Seal of the Province was lost. In 1656 at the trial here of Judith Catchpole, one of America's first juries of women was impaneled. The prisoner had been accused of infanticide and the court appointed eleven women 'to search the body of the said Judith.' Their report stated '[we] have according to our charge searched the body of Judith Catchpole, doe give in our verdict that according to our best judgment that [she] hath not had any child within the time charged.' They also found 'the party accusing not in sound mind, whereby it is conceived the said Judith Catchpole is not inditable.'

State 266 continues to SPOUT FARM, 3.2 m., on the bluff above St.Leonard Creek. The land was granted in 1652 to John Sollers, a justice of the peace from 1680 to 1685. The old two-and-a-half-story frame house now has a two-story porch and a story-and-a-half wing. The outside chimneys on the east end of the building narrow at the third floor line and are connected by a two-story windowless pent. A small square cupola with pyramidal roof breaks the ridge of the house roof.

At the foot of the bluff at SOLLERS WHARF, 3.3 m., is a spring that has been in use for almost 300 years.

MIDDLEHAM CHAPEL (L), 52 m., stands in a grove of shellbark hickory trees. In the high gable end of the simple brick building is the date 1748. Its predecessor, a chapel of ease of Christ Church, stood about nine miles to the north. In 1746 the vestry petitioned the assembly to levy the sum of 80,000 pounds of tobacco to build a new chapel of ease because the old one 'is by Length of Time become ruinous and by increase of the Inhabitants, too small for the congregation.' Their request was granted and the present cruciform building erected. Middleham has no regular services.

BERTHA, 52.9 m., is at the junction with macadamized State 497.

Left on this 1 m. to a narrow, rough dirt road; R. here 0.4 m. (bear L. at a fork) to the GREAT ELTONHEAD MANOR HOUSE, a large two-story brick structure built about 1750. Except for brick stringcourses and a molded brick base, it is severely plain. About 1880 when the house was gutted by fire, the interior was refinished. In 1649 Edward Eltonhead, barrister of London, was given a patent for 10,000 acres of land on the usual terms—that he bring 50 people into the province within two years and a half, and 50 more within a second two-and-a-half-year period. In 1651 he had a re-grant, this time with a seven-year limit. The lapse of the grant in 1658 suggests that he did not collect his hundred immigrants. The builder of the present house is not known.

A mile across fields from the house and 100 feet above Chesapeake Bay are the ruins of the house from which was taken paneling now in the Baltimore Museum of Art. It is sometimes called the first Eltonhead Manor House, but a more reasonable supposition is that it was a hunting lodge. When the present owner purchased it in 1910, only the paneling of the great room and a staircase were worth salvaging.

From the fork leading to Eltonhead, the main dirt road continues to (R) Rousby Hall, 4.7 *m.*, on the shore of the Patuxent; it is more easily reached by boat from Solomons (*see below*). The long, low story-and-a-half whitewashed home has walls covered with wide clapboard and a steep roof that sweeps down over the porches. Near by are the outbuildings of a big brick house that stood until about 1810 on the site of the present house. Left of the entrance lane is the well-preserved brick ledger tomb wherein 'lies Interr'd the Body of Mr.John Rousby (only sone of the Honble John Rousby, Esqr.) who departed this Life the 28th day of January Anno Domini 1750 in New Style, 1751 Aged 23 years and 10 months.' Near the tomb are the ruins of a barn built of brick laid in Flemish bond with glazed blue headers. On a line with the house are the old meat house and a small whitewashed building that was an office.

At 56.7 *m.* is the junction with a dirt road.

Right on this to POINT PATIENCE, 1.3 *m.*, a grant made to John Ashcomb (Ascham) in 1661 or a little earlier. John Ashcomb was the great-grandson of Roger Ascham, the Greek and Latin scholar who tutored the Princess Elizabeth and later, when she was Queen of England, wrote many of her official letters. The estate was confiscated at the time of the Revolution because the Aschams were Loyalists. The house, which stands on a long point affording a beautiful view of the river, has been so much al-tered that its age is hardly recognizable.

SOLOMONS, 58.1 *m.* (10 alt.,550 pop.) (*boats, guides, sport fishing equipment for hire*), is on an island connected by a causeway with the mainland. On the Patuxent front the harbor is two miles wide and has a depth of 150 feet. Here the drydock *Dewey* was tested in 1905 before it went to the Philippines and here for many years were stored four German vessels confiscated by the United States in 1917; they were ordered sold in December 1939. One, renamed the *George Washington*, in 1918 carried President Wilson to the peace conference at Versailles. The land-locked harbor on the other side of the island is the anchorage of a large fishing and oystering fleet.

On the eastern shore of the island is the HOUSE OF SOLOMON, once the home of the island's first settler.

The CHESAPEAKE BIOLOGICAL LABORATORY, maintained by the State Conservation Commission, is a large two-and-a-half-story brick water-front building with a 750-foot pier. For underwater observation the station has a bentharium (home in the depths), which permits two persons to work safely below the surface. The murkiness of the Chesapeake has made this less valuable than was hoped. The marine life of the bay is studied chiefly during sessions of a summer school.

The ferry to Millstone Landing ($1 *for car and driver, passengers* 25¢) leaves from the creek side of the island (*see Tour* 11A).

Tour 9

Baltimore—Glenburnie—Upper Marlboro—La Plata—Rock Point; 84.5 *m.*, State 3.

Macadam roadbed, two lanes wide; short stretches concrete-paved.
The route is paralleled between Baltimore and Bel Alton by the Pennsylvania R.R., and between Baltimore and Glenburnie by the Baltimore and Annapolis (electric) R.R.
Accommodations in towns.

State 3 is a winding road and though it is hedged for many miles with second-growth timber, it has frequent vistas of rolling farms where tobacco has been grown for more than two centuries. The new and the old are sharply contrasted on these farms. A mule with canvas and chain harness may be pulling a plow near a twentieth-century farmhouse or a tractor may be at work in a field enclosed by a vine-covered rail fence. The soil is sandy and much of it has been exhausted by the one-crop system used from almost the first years of settlement. Except on the old farms there are few large trees, and many patches of woodland are only thin saplings in a tangle of vines and underbrush. Though few of the houses along the highway are exceptional in interest, the narrow side roads pass luxurious dwellings built 200 years ago when the soil was rich enough to yield fortunes in tobacco.

Early in May just before the planting season, the tobacco seed beds, covered with cheese cloth, make white patches on the hillsides and in the woods.

Section a. BALTIMORE to UPPER MARLBORO; 36.9 m.

Between Baltimore and the junction with State 178 this route roughly follows a road laid out about 1770 and used by Washington in 1783 on his way to Annapolis to resign his commission as commander in chief of the Continental Army.

Between Baltimore and Glenburnie are commuters' homes and little hillside farms where cantaloupes, watermelons, and vegetables are grown. Between Millersville and Upper Marlboro are many tobacco farms, identified at any season by their drying barns with hinged ventilating boards in the side walls.

State 3 branches south in BALTIMORE, 0 *m.* (20 alt.,804,874 pop.) (*see Baltimore*).

ENGLISH CONSUL, 4.5 *m.* (100 alt.,400 pop.), just outside the city limits, is a modern village almost entirely inhabited by commuters.

The DAWSON HOUSE (L), foot of Oak Grove Ave., a two-and-a-half-story white house of Georgian Colonial design, was built by Will Dawson, who came to Baltimore in 1816 as the British Consul. The modern village is named for this place. Frederick Dawson, brother of William, committed a crime in England for which he was sentenced to banishment in Australia. Through family influence the sentence was changed so that he could live in Maryland, provided he received 30 lashes on each anniversary of the day the crime was committed. He lived in this house until his death and each year superintended his own beating, ordering a servant to bind him to a tree and lay on heavily.

In PUMPHREY, 6.1 m. (50 alt.,500 pop.), at the crossroads, is the HOLLY RUN METHODIST CHURCH (R), built in 1828 of bricks from a powder magazine abandoned after the War of 1812. It is a small square, red-brick building with a white doorway and a wide white, wooden cornice. The interior is frescoed and lighted with oil lamps.

GLENBURNIE, 9.7 m. (56 alt.,1,044 pop.), developed and named for John Glenn, who acquired an estate here in the 1880's, is a suburban town of medium-sized homes.

In Glenburnie is the junction with State 2 (see Tour 8a).

Near the junction of the old Annapolis-Baltimore Road and a road laid out by Charles Carroll from Doughoregan Manor to Annapolis, is the marked SITE OF THE WIDOW RAMSAY'S TAVERN (L), 16.3 m., where Washington breakfasted in 1773 and again in 1775.

At DORR'S CORNER, 16.6 m., is the junction with concrete-paved State 178.

Left on State 178 to the RISING SUN INN (R), 2 m., a two-and-a-half-story, ivy-covered, frame building with part gable and part gambrel roof. The bricks of the gable ends are laid in all-header bond. This inn, built about 1753 on the estate of Edward Baldwin, was recently restored and is maintained as an inn by the Daughters of the American Revolution.

The CROWNSVILLE STATE HOSPITAL FOR NEGROES (R), 3.9 m., caring for mentally ill men and women, was established in 1911.

At 4.6 m. is (L) the dirt entrance lane of BELVOIR, whose two-and-a-half-story brick house was built in 1730 by John Ross, great-grandfather of Francis Scott Key. The original six-bay T-shaped house, with gabled and white-painted entrance portico placed slightly off center on the front façade and flanked by ancient boxwoods, has been greatly altered. The former gambrel roof of the front section of the house has been changed to a gable—the front brick wall clearly showing the mark of this alteration. The clapboarded and gambrel-roofed wing at the right is of recent construction. The walls are fully five feet thick at the foundation. In the garden is the fenced-in grave of Ann Arnold Key, Francis Scott Key's grandmother.

At 8.2 m. on State 178 is the junction with US 50 (see Tour 10).

In MILLERSVILLE, 18.3 m. (120 alt.,101 pop.), is the junction with concrete-paved State 180.

Right on this to ODENTON, 3.5 m. (160 alt.,400 pop.), founded in 1867 and named for Governor Oden Bowie (see Tour 10).

At 4 m. is FORT GEORGE G. MEADE, a 7,500-acre army reservation established in 1917 as Camp Meade for training World War troops. A permanent garrison of about 2,000 is maintained.

At 20.8 m. on State 3 is the junction with a dirt road.

Left on this to WHITE HALL (R), 0.8 m., the birthplace of Johns Hopkins (see Baltimore). It is a two-story, white-painted, frame and brick house built about 1761. The frame wing and porches were added after 1812.

At 23.7 *m.* State 3 unites briefly with US 50 (*see Tour* 10). State 3 bears L. at 24.2 *m.* where US 50 branches R.

South of WELLS CORNER, 35.4 *m.*, State 4 unites with State 3 for 1.5 miles.

> Left on State 4 to COMPTON BASSETT (L), 0.8 *m.*, whose large square two-story stucco-covered brick house has a hip roof. It stands on a slight rise overlooking the Patuxent River—at this point hardly more than a creek. In 1699 Clement Hill, a deputy surveyor of the province, took up this tract of land but the present attractive house was built in 1789 by his great-grandson. The little brick structure near by was a private chapel during the days when public services by Roman Catholics were not permitted.

UPPER MARLBORO, 36.9 *m.* (39 alt.,450 pop.), named for the Duke of Marlborough, has been a tobacco town since it was founded in 1706. Tobacco auctions are held here two or three times a week in late spring. All the townsmen know and talk tobacco; and many business buildings display prize leaves during the sales. In the lobby of the new post office is a large mural showing tobacco leaves being loaded on wagons in the fields. As tobacco is always harvested by stalks rather than leaves the citizens are quite critical of the picture.

Tobacco, one of the most demanding of field crops, requires 15 months care; the second crop must be in the ground before the preceding one is ready for market. In March—as soon as the frost is out of the ground—the Maryland farmer plants his seedbeds either under cheesecloth on a protected slope, or in the shade of woods. Farmers who can afford to sterilize the ground with live steam use the same spot year after year, but the rest find new spots annually to avoid pests likely to be in ground previously disturbed. Land is then plowed, and the farmer watches the weather anxiously, inspecting his seedbeds and the previous crop which still hangs in the barns. Ideal weather is warm with even rainfall; too much rain is likely to spoil the crop in the barns; too little injures the young plants and also makes transplanting difficult. This transplanting takes place in June about the time when the previous crop must be marketed.

Tobacco plants require very careful hand cultivation; a machine passing between the rows would bruise the leaves. By September harvest begins; all leaf must be in before the first frost. The stalks are cut and fastened into bunches by bands near the bottom of the stalk; they are taken at once to the tobacco barns and hung upside down from poles. In a bumper year the overflow goes into attics, sheds, and other emergency shelters. Wherever the crop is stored the air must circulate freely and the farmer must watch constantly to remove spoiled stalks before they contaminate others; he must also change the position of the bundles to bring the inner ones nearer the ventilators. As drying proceeds he carefully strips the leaves from the stalks and ties them together at the base into clusters that are placed on the drying bars again. The stalks go back on the fields for fertilizer.

In the past the farmer has sorted the leaves and packed them in bundles in accordance with his idea of the three grades—bright, second, and tips. (In other States there are as many as seven or eight grades.) The buyers now favor looseleaf buying because farm grading was not very accurate and some less scrupulous producers sent bundles that were deceptive in appearance.

Until ten years ago nearly all Maryland tobacco was exported, largely to France. Now it is bought by domestic manufacturers for blending in cigarettes. It has been found better than the famed white burley because it holds fire better, has a pleasanter taste, and, according to experts in the Department of Agriculture, has the lowest nicotine content of any tobacco grown in America. No one has been able to find out why Maryland tobacco has these qualities but Maryland farmers say it is because their land has been used for no other purpose for the last 300 years. Formerly cigarette manufacturers gave best prices for the yellow-brown leaves because they most resembled the white burley, but they have found the Maryland tobacco at its best is reddish brown.

In 1938 a great change took place in Maryland tobacco marketing; formerly the growers either shipped directly to the buyers in Baltimore or, more often, sold through local factors who advanced loans for seed and fertilizer to those who needed them, and then collected the crop in trucks or at their local warehouses for marketing. Under this system the few who did not need advances were often at a disadvantage because the factors were often too busy collecting the crops on which they had liens to bother with the more independent producers. Markets in Upper Marlboro and elsewhere have put many factors out of business but, though offering a saving to the farmers, this arrangement has not entirely satisfied them. After hearing for the first time the auctioneers' mysterious jargon and watching the faint signs by which buyers and appraisers indicated the price to be paid for a lot, the growers made such complaints as, 'Why don't they talk English? What are they putting over?'

Profits on crops depend in part on how much fertilizer is used—the more prosperous growers believe that about $20 worth is needed for each acre but the poor tenant skimps by with about a quarter of that. Profits also depend on how much must be paid for credit on seed and fertilizer and, in the past, how much went to the factor. Current prices and quality are also important. The average gross return on an acre is $100 to $150—occasionally $200.

Experiment stations and growers are working with a new variety of plant—the Maryland Mammoth. It has a better leaf than the prized reddish brown, but flowers so late that its seed does not mature until the frost comes—which ruins the leaves.

The marked SITE OF JOHN CARROLL BIRTHPLACE (L) is near the courthouse. John Carroll (see Baltimore), who became the first bishop and archbishop of the Catholic Church in the United States, was born here in 1735. This house was also the birthplace of Daniel Carroll, his brother, who was a delegate from Maryland to the Constitutional Convention of 1787, and a signer of the Constitution.

The old MARLBORO HOUSE (R), Main St. across from the courthouse, is said to have been built about 1732. It is a long narrow, badly-neglected building with an antique shop in one end. It was at one time an inn and, according to tradition, when George Washington stopped here on his trip north he always occupied room number seven on the second floor. Lafayette was also a guest and it is said that Major General Robert Ross, commander of the British Army during the War of 1812, stopped here. Whether it was built as an inn is doubtful, for it is of distinguished Georgian Colonial design and seems much too elaborate for a tavern of the period.

Section b. UPPER MARLBORO to ROCK POINT; 47.6 m.

(A bridge across the Potomac west of Newburg to be completed late in 1940 will cause highways to be slightly rerouted. Inquire at Upper Marlboro.)

South of UPPER MARLBORO, 0 m., the patches of saplings and brush give way to open fields and to woodlots where trees have attained considerable height, yet the country is quite unlike the southern Maryland of which an early colonist wrote: 'Fine groves of trees appear, not choked with briers or bushes and undergrowth, but growing at intervals as if planted by the hand of man, so that you can drive a four-horse carriage, wherever you choose, through the midst of the trees.'

WESTON (R), 2 m., is a two-and-a-half-story brick house with dormers and a gable roof. The first house on this site was built about 1700 by Thomas Claggett and restored by the Claggett family in 1939 after it had been damaged by fire.

At 3.2 m. is the junction with macadamized State 382.

Left on State 382 to a dirt road, 2.3 m.; L. on this 0.2 m. to a second dirt road; L. here 1.2 m. to a third dirt road, and L. 1.2 m. to MOUNT CALVERT, a large square, two-and-a-half-story brick house, built probably late in the seventeenth century. The brick work in the oldest part is laid in an unusual bond with four headers and four stretchers. On a tract of land surveyed here for Philip Calvert in 1652 and erected into a manor in 1657, a town called Charlestown developed and became the seat of Prince Georges County in 1695. In 1732 Upper Marlboro became the county seat and this house is all that remains of Charlestown.

State 382 continues southeastward to CROOM, 3.9 m. (200 alt.,27 pop.), a straggling village on a low ridge. It was named for an estate patented to Thomas Claggett, Calvert County coroner in 1789.

Left from Croom 0.1 m. on a dirt road to ST. THOMAS CHAPEL (L), built in 1732 under direction of the Reverend John Eversfield. The small, red brick building in a grove of oaks was at first a plain rectangular structure, but additions have made it cruciform. When the church tower was added it was made a memorial to Bishop Thomas John Claggett (*see below*).

At 1 m. on this dirt road is a narrow dirt lane leading R. 0.4 m. to MATTAPONI (L), a two-story, stuccoed brick house on a high basement; it has two balanced one-story wings, added when the dwelling was rebuilt in 1820. William Bowie, son of the first owner of the land, erected the original house in 1745. A wide hall runs the length of the first floor and there is a finely-proportioned staircase in a cross hall at the front.

At ROSARYVILLE, 5.4 m. (200 alt.,62 pop.), is the junction with a dirt road.

Right on this to the DOWER HOUSE (R), 0.9 m., once known as Mount Airy. In 1931 fire destroyed all of the original structure except a one-and-a-half-story brick wing built in 1660 as a hunting lodge of the Calverts. The rest of the house has been completely restored. It is a T-shaped structure consisting of the early story-and-a-half, gambrel-roofed wing, and a two-story gabled section. The five-bay central section has slightly lower flanking wings. The roof of the lodge, pierced by small dormers and two clustered chimneys, is hipped at the ends. Its brick walls are laid partly in all-header and partly in Flemish bond. The main section of the mansion has a wide recessed, two-story gallery porch on the front with two columns raised on pedestals. The wine cellar under the main house has a high vaulted ceiling.

A long tree-bordered road leading from the gate terminates in a circular drive edged with boxwood in front of the old house. To the right lies a terraced garden planned by Major Pierre Charles L'Enfant, designer of the city of Washington. Charles, fifth Lord Baltimore, gave this estate to his natural son, Benedict (Swingate) Calvert, who built the former two-story brick house that joined the old lodge at an angle. In 1748 Benedict married Elizabeth, daughter of Governor Leonard Calvert. Washington frequently recorded in his diary that he and his family had visited Mount Airy. In 1774 his stepson, John Parke Custis, married Calvert's daughter Eleanor, a match that did not have Washington's approval because of the youth of the pair. The last of the Calverts to live here was Benedict's granddaughter Eleanor who died in 1902 at the age of 95.

At 2.7 m. on the dirt road is the junction with another dirt road; L. here to beautiful POPLAR HILL (L), 3.5 m., built before 1735 by George, fourteenth Earl of Shrewsbury, for his niece and ward, Anne Talbott, on the occasion of her marriage to Henry Darnall. The house consists of a large central building balanced by smaller story-and-a-half wings, the three parts connected by low arcades. The structure, about 150 feet long, has brick walls laid in a variety of bonds. The approach front and the garden front are nearly identical, both having Palladian windows on the second floor over white doorways reached by low flights of stone steps. The entrance portal is much more elaborate, however, with a fanlight over the recessed door and the recess itself framed by pilasters and a richly carved pediment. The right wing was for nearly two centuries a Roman Catholic family chapel, and the left wing has always contained the kitchen. The central hall is so well proportioned that its great size is not unduly striking. Along it are the carved doorways of the drawing room and dining room. The wide staircase with carved balustrades and mahogany handrail leads to unusually large rooms with ceilings and windows as high as those on the first floor. Nearly all of the richly handcarved original woodwork has been preserved.

At CHELTENHAM, 7.2 m. (237 alt., 250 pop.), is the junction with a macadamized road.

Right on this to CHELTENHAM SCHOOL FOR BOYS (L), 0.3 m., established in 1870 as a privately maintained reformatory for delinquent Negro boys. In 1937 it was taken over by the State.

At 10.6 m. on State 3 is T.B. at a junction with macadamized State 381 (see Tour 19).

Left on State 381 to CEDARVILLE, 4.8 m. (240 alt., 115 pop.); R. 0.7 m. on a macadamized road to another macadamized road; R. here 0.4 m. into CEDARVILLE STATE FOREST (picnic areas and hiking trails), a 3,000-acre tract (L) of woodland and swamp.

State 381 continues southeastward to another macadamized road, 6.1 m.; L. here 0.4 m. to BADEN (220 alt., 165 pop.), and ST.PAUL'S PROTESTANT EPISCOPAL CHURCH, a cruciform brick structure whose construction began in 1733 on the site of a frame church (1692). The transepts were added soon after the main structure was erected; the nave with walls laid in Flemish bond followed and finally the chancel with walls laid in running bond. The low gable roof is modern, but the roundheaded windows are believed to have been in the original structure. The sun dial above the entrance was added in 1753, and the marble baptismal font was installed in 1754. The one memorial window honors Thomas John Claggett, who was born at White's Landing near Lower Marlboro in 1742 and was ordained in London in 1767. He was rector of St.Paul's from 1780 until 1786 and in 1792 was consecrated Bishop of Maryland, the first Episcopal bishop consecrated in the United States. Since the county lacked an ecclesiastical outfitting shop at the time, his family made his miter from a hat; it is preserved in Baltimore. Claggett again served as rector of St.Paul's until 1808, when he became rector of Trinity Church in Upper Marlboro. He died at Croom in 1816.

State 381 continues to the junction with State 231 (*see Tour* 11) in PATUXENT, 15.8 *m.*

At 10.9 *m.* is the junction with State 5 (*see Tour* 12) which unites with State 3 southward to Waldorf.

WALDORF, 16.5 *m.* (200 alt.,700 pop.), has modern houses with wide, well-kept lawns. It developed after 1870 as a trading and shipping center of tobacco growers, but now serves chiefly as a shopping center for Washington workers who have moved into the county to escape the Capital's high rents. At Waldorf, State 5 (*see Tour* 12) branches L.

At 22.4 *m.* is the junction with a macadamized road.

Right on this to MOUNT CARMEL (L), 2 *m.*, founded in 1790 as a Carmelite convent. In 1831 the nuns took up residence in Baltimore and Mount Carmel was abandoned. Of the original seven frame buildings two, recently restored, remain.

At 2.4 *m.* is LINDEN (R), a two-and-a-half-story frame house built by John Mitchell late in the eighteenth century. The house has a pair of huge outside end chimneys of brick; one wing, the oldest part of the house, is of logs, now clapboarded. On the south are great clumps of boxwood.

LA PLATA, 24.9 *m.* (192 alt.,332 pop.), came into existence shortly after the Pope's Creek Railroad was built in 1868 and was made the seat of Charles County in 1895. The highway makes a slight jog to cross the single wide main street, where filling station and other signs almost obscure the buildings. On November 9, 1926, a tornado demolished a two-room schoolhouse here killing 15 children and injuring many more.

La Plata is at the junction with State 6 (*see Tour* 12) and the Mason Springs Road (*see Tour* 12).

BEL ALTON, 30 *m.* (160 alt.,250 pop.), grew up in the 1890's after the railroad was built. John Wilkes Booth and his accomplice, Herold, hid in the woods near here while trying to cross to Virginia after the assassination of Lincoln.

Right from Bel Alton on a macadamized road to ST.IGNATIUS ROMAN CATHOLIC CHURCH and ST.THOMAS MANOR HOUSE (L), 2.1 *m.* Members of the Society of Jesus could not hold land as individuals but Father Phillip Fisher, who managed the property of the Maryland mission, claimed the land under the name of Thomas Copley as an importer of settlers. He assigned 4,000 acres to Thomas Matthews. A chapel built in 1662 was replaced by St.Ignatius Church in 1789. In 1741 the Jesuit Father George Hunter built the present house, a solid two-story structure of brick with stone quoins. The road ends at CHAPEL POINT, 2.5 *m.*, an amusement park (*adm.* 25¢).

At 31.4 *m.* on State 3 is the junction with macadamized State 424.

Right on this to POPE'S CREEK, 3.1 *m.* (10 alt.,25 pop.), at the confluence of Pope's Creek and the Potomac River. In this village are the terminus of the Pope's Creek branch of the Pennsylvania Railroad and the power plant of the Tri-County Electrification Co-operative. The single daily passenger train takes several hours to wander down from Baltimore and the passengers are accommodated in a combined coach and freight car. Long before the white man came to Maryland, Indian tribes camped by Pope's Creek annually to eat oysters; the shell heap that had accumulated for centuries once covered 30 acres and at places was 15 feet high. In recent years most of this great accumulation has been trucked away for use in road building or for fertilizer. Archaeological excavations here have uncovered artifacts of people who lived long before the arrival of the whites.

At 34.1 *m.* on State 3 is the junction with State 234.

Left on State 234 to SARUM (R), 4.7 *m.*, a one-and-a-half-story house with brick ends and wide clapboards, built before 1724.

In WICOMICO, 6.4 *m.* (160 alt.,165 pop.), is the junction with a macadamized road; L. here to TRINITY PROTESTANT EPISCOPAL CHURCH (L), 2.8 *m.*, a small, brick building painted gray, with lancet windows. It was built in 1793.

CHAPTICO, 12.4 *m.* (20 alt.,60 pop.), on State 234, was named Calverton when it was surveyed by command of Lord Baltimore in 1651 but was later renamed for the friendly Chaptico Indians. It became a shipping point for a time, second in importance to St.Marys City.

Right from Chaptico 0.1 *m.* on macadamized State 237 to CHRIST CHURCH (R), built about 1736. During the War of 1812 British cavalrymen stabled their horses in the church and wrecked the interior. In the cemetery is the GRAVE OF CAPTAIN GILBERT IRELAND, the High Sheriff of St.Marys County in 1745, who was buried in an upright position at his own request.

State 237 continues to SOUTHAMPTON (R), 0.9 *m.*, ancestral home of the Bond family, now a two-and-one-half-story clapboarded house, with a gambrel roof and porches along the front and rear. The ivy clinging to the huge double brick chimneys —which have a pent between and pents flanking—is said to have been brought from Kenilworth Castle shortly after Southampton was built by Richard Bond in the seventeenth century. The wall-of-Troy panel above the fireplace is the only carved wall panel remaining. The old 'witch door' has H hinges, a brass lock, and a pendant handle.

DEEP FALLS (L), 1.6 *m.*, was built by Major William Thomas about 1745 and is owned by his descendants. Wide piazzas with massive pillars now run the entire length of the front and rear of the frame house. Great chimneys tower above its roof. Behind the house five long terraces, each ten feet deep, lead down to an old-fashioned garden. In the family graveyard near the house are several stones more than a century and a half old.

At 2.9 *m.* is a dirt road; R. 0.9 *m.* to HURRY, a hamlet that belies its name. At 1.6 *m.* is BACHELOR'S HOPE (R), a small unusual seventeenth-century brick house having a two-story central section topped with jerkin-head roof, and lower, flanking, hip-roofed wings. The most interesting feature of this house is a one-story recessed portico extending the full width of the central section, with four capless and baseless columns. Between the columns are segmental arches forming a crude arcade. Above the colonnade is a narrow classic entablature. The entrance portal is flanked by square-headed windows, the right partially obscured by a steep outer stairway, rising to the second floor.

On State 237 at CLEMENTS, 4.6 *m.* (20 alt.,75 pop.), is macadamized State 242; R. 4.5 *m.* on State 242 to State 239; R. 1.3 *m.* to OCEAN HALL, a small brick and stone house erected by Richard Booth about 1684 on part of the manor of St.Clements. Its interior contains much of the original woodwork. Over the drawing room mantel is a painting on wood, for which the artist was paid in tobacco.

State 242 continues southward to COLTON POINT, 8.9 *m.* (20 alt.,200 pop.), a small summer resort.

Off ST.CLEMENTS ISLAND (*no ferry*), also called Blakistone Island, a short distance from Colton Point in the Potomac River, the *Ark* and the *Dove* dropped anchors in March 1634. The colonists lived on the *Ark* while the governor went up the river to treat with the Indians. The island belongs to the Government and has a lighthouse on it that is no longer used. The large cross commemorating the mass held here by the Catholic group can be seen plainly from the mainland.

From Chaptico State 234 continues northeastward to State 5 (*see Tour 11*), 16.2 *m.*, at a point 2 miles north of Morganza.

In NEWBURG, 36.7 *m.* (120 alt.,35 pop.), are junctions with a narrow graveled road and with macadamized State 230.

1. Right on the graveled road to the chimneys and part of the end wall of the LUDLOW FERRY HOUSE (L), 2.1 *m*. The ferry was discontinued in 1847. In his diary Washington called it Laidler, Ledler, and Laidlaw ferry.

The bridge being constructed across the Potomac at this point will link southern Maryland and Virginia and provide a short cut between the North and the South.

2. Left from Newburg on State 230 to MT. VICTORIA, 3.8 *m*. (100 alt.,15 pop.); L. on a dirt road 0.5 *m*. to HARD BARGAIN (R), on a ridge above the Wicomico River. The brick house of two-and-a-half, two, and one-story units was built before the Revolution by Gwynn Harris for his brother Tom. From the river side the three parts of the building appear to be telescoped into each other. At the rear of the hall in the main section a wide staircase curves to the floor above. The doors and window frames on the first floor have a simplified robe molding; practically all the interior trim is in good condition though the house has long been occupied by tenants.

According to tradition, Gwynn Harris and his brother Tom were bitter rivals for the hand of Kitty Root. Gwynn won and during the marriage celebration he had an expansive moment in which he offered to build Tom a fine house if Tom would kiss Kitty. Tom kissed the bride and Gwynn built Hard Bargain. No one now knows whether it was Tom or Gwynn who considered the bargain hard.

Brick gate posts (R) at 5.1 *m*. on State 230, marked the entrance to WEST HATTON. The present brick house, second on the site, was built in 1790 by Major William Truman Stoddert, whose grave is in the garden (L). The central part of the house is two stories high, with end chimneys connected by a roof curtain. Two flanking wings, one lower than the other, seem to have been added at a later date.

MOUNT REPUBLICAN (R), 37.6 *m*., a large brick house, with a lower wing, was built in 1792 by Theophilus Yates. From each gable end rises a pair of inside chimneys with a roof curtain between them, and the end walls continue a little above the roof to form parapets. Both fronts of the main section of the house are exactly alike, with off-center wide white doors framed by sidelights and transoms.

In WAYSIDE, 38.6 *m*. (10 alt.,30 pop.), behind a low brick wall is WAYSIDE CHURCH (R), a plain little brick building erected before 1750 and remodeled in 1871. It is the second to stand on the site since the parish was created in 1696. Communion silver, imported from England in 1740, is still in use.

Right from Wayside on macadamized State 229 to MORGANTOWN, 3 *m*. (10 alt.,40 pop.), and the ferry to Colonial Beach, Virginia (*fare $1 for car and driver; passengers 25¢*).

Right 0.5 *m*. from the ferry landing on a dirt road to CEDAR POINT (*open June-Sept.; parking 50¢*), an amusement park. Washington's diary records that on August 25, 1768, he fished here 'all day for Sheephead but catched none.'

At 44.6 *m*. on State 3 is the junction with a graveled road.

Right on this 0.8 *m*. to WOLLESTON MANOR (L). The manor house was destroyed by fire about 1900 and the site is now occupied by a clubhouse. Captain James Neale came to the province about 1635 and a few years later was trading with the Indians, carrying a stock of cloth, knives, scissors, bells, hoes, and axes. Most of these transactions were carried on with peake—small polished cylinders made of clam or mussel shells—or with roanoke—bits of flat shell pierced for stringing. In 1642 the lord proprietary granted him 2,000 acres and the right to kill Indians who stole his cattle. Neale played an important part in colonial affairs. His four children, born in Spain and Portugal, were among the first persons naturalized in the colony.

ROCK POINT, 47.6 *m*. (10 alt.,300 pop.), is a summer resort of cottages at the confluence of the Wicomico and Potomac Rivers.

In the Counties

Work Projects Administration

GATE, OLD CHESAPEAKE AND OHIO CANAL

AUNT LUCY'S BAKE SHOP (c. 1700), ANNAPOLIS

CHAPEL (1908), U. S. NAVAL ACADEMY—JAPANESE BELL IN FOREGROUND

STATE HOUSE (1772), ANNAPOLIS

WEST PATRICK STREET, FREDERICK

CUMBERLAND

LOCUST STREET, HAGERSTOWN

HOUSES ALONG THE WESTERN MARYLAND RAILROAD, HAGERSTOWN

HILL WOMAN, GARRETT COUNTY

COUNTRY SCHOOL

SAWMILL, GARRETT COUNTY

AIRVIEW, CAMBRIDGE

H. Robins Hollyda

AIRVIEW, GREENBELT HOUSING PROJECT

Farm Security Administration

Tour 10

Annapolis—Bladensburg; 27.5 *m.* US 50.

Winding, two-land asphalt- or concrete-paved roadbed.
Accommodations limited.

East of Bladensburg this road was built in 1926 to replace an older and much longer one, and because it links the U.S. Naval Academy with the National Capital, it was called the Defense Highway. It passes through a rolling wooded country with here and there a patch of level ground on which tobacco or vegetables are grown, but for the most part pine-covered clay bluffs and some swampy ground dominate the scene east of Bowie. Sycamores, pines, dogwood, sumac, and honeysuckle flourish in this region.

West of ANNAPOLIS 0 *m.* (40 alt.,12,551 pop.) (*see Annapolis*) at a junction with State 2 (*see Tour 8a*) is PAROLE, 2.6 *m.* (70 alt.,315 pop.), a settlement of scattered houses at a second junction with State 2 (*see Tour 8b*).

In 1861 when General Burnside's brigade camped here, one of his regiments, called D'Epeneuil's Zouaves, was made up entirely of Frenchmen from New York uniformed in baggy red pantaloons, bright crimson fezzes, and short jackets over shirts with puffed sleeves. Dress parade of the Zouaves at the camp was a romantic spectacle, but action in the field quickly revealed that the gay uniforms made perfect targets, and the Frenchmen changed to more sober attire. Later in the war the Government constructed a prison camp here for Union soldiers of uncertain loyalty. It had been discovered that some of the drafted men were permitting themselves to be captured by the Confederates, and when such soldiers, paroled by the Confederates, had been picked up by Union forces they were sent to this and similar camps. Thus the place came to be called Camp Parole. The population of the camp, increased by wounded men, at one time approached 30,000.

THREE MILE OAK (L), 3.5 *m.*, at the junction with State 178 (*see Tour 9a*), is a blackened stump of a tree set in concrete. Here, while on his way to Annapolis to resign his commission, General Washington was met by General Gates and Smallwood and a delegation of Annapolitans.

At the eastern end of the North River Bridge, 7.3 *m.*, is a junction with a smooth surface road.

Right on this road to a clay road, 0.8 *m.*, L. here 0.5 *m.* to (R) MT. TABOR CHURCH (1893) of the South River Methodist Circuit.
ST. STEPHEN'S CHURCH, 3.4 *m.*, on the surfaced road is a rectangular brick building (1842) with a wooden entry porch under an open frame belfry. Connected with the

church by a brick ambulatory is the parish house (1898), a memorial to Edith Woodward, daughter of William Woodward (1835–89), benefactor of the church. Between the church and the parish house is a Celtic cross of white marble, erected in 1899 in memory of Woodward by his wife. In front of the church are one male and one female Ailanthus tree. Near them is a memorial font showing St.Francis feeding the birds.

According to local tradition, a parishioner one night saw what appeared to be a ghost bobbing up and down in the cemetery behind the church, and he aroused the neighborhood. Investigation revealed a sheep, which had fallen into a newly dug grave and was trying to leap out.

At 12.6 *m.* is a junction with State 3 (*see Tour 9a*), which unites with US 50 to a junction at 13.1 *m.*, where US 50 turns sharply R. Small culverts elevate the concrete roadbed above the flood level of this low section along the Patuxent.

At 13.8 *m.* is the junction with a dirt road.

Left on this up a steep hill to WHITEMARSH CHURCH, 0.3 *m.*, a rectangular brick building erected in 1856 on the foundations of a church erected in 1742. On the south wall is a vertical sundial. Heavy iron rods, installed in 1874, brace fire-weakened walls. To the right are a school and a farmhouse rectory. Whitemarsh was built on a 2,000-acre tract bequeathed with 100 slaves to the Society of Jesus by James Carroll in 1728. Since Maryland law forbade the willing of property to any religious group without consent of the proprietary, Carroll left the property to the Port Tobacco Jesuits as individuals.

In 1783 a delegation of the Roman Catholic clergy met at the first church here to draw up a plan for the government of the church in the newly created United States of America. Here on May 18, 1788, Father John Carroll was nominated first bishop of the Roman Catholic Church in America. The fire that destroyed the old church in 1855 also destroyed the early records of the congregation. In 1933 Whitemarsh was made a mission church in charge of the diocesan clergy at Bowie, but the Society of Jesus still owns the land and receives the rents.

At 14.1 *m.* on US 50 is the junction with an asphalt-bound graveled road.

Right here 0.8 *m.* to BOWIE RACE TRACK, financially one of the most successful of Maryland's four major one-mile tracks. The plant, established by the Southern Maryland Agricultural Association in 1914, includes the track, a concrete and steel grandstand seating 14,500, a clubhouse, and stables for several hundred horses; two meets are held here, one of 12 days during the first part of April and the other of 13 days during the last half of November. The grandstand, with pari-mutuel booths under both decks, overlooks the homestretch, which is 90 feet wide.

From the road passing the backstretch and bordered by privet hedge and a hedge fence is a view across the infield to the grandstand. During meets the road is littered with racing forms, newspapers, and tip sheets. Stablehands, youths, touts, and professional race-track followers cluster in groups near the stables discussing 'inside dope.' Peddlers shout their wares—hot dogs, oyster sandwiches, fish cakes, and crab cakes.

Right from the road around the backstretch on a clay road lined with low rambling stables and farmland to the MARYLAND NORMAL AND INDUSTRIAL SCHOOL (*see below*), 1.6 *m.*

Massive stone posts holding iron gates mark the entrance (L) to BELAIR (*private*), 15.1 *m.* The main section of the five-part brick house, approached by a long double avenue of venerable tulip poplars, is two-and-a-half stories high with a curb roof. This section was built in 1746; the two-story wings were added after 1900 to replace earlier flankers that had been destroyed. On both façades central pediments, flanked by a square dormer on each side, break the roof above a heavy modillioned cornice. Flanking the square stair hall are large and small parlors; a music room overlooks the garden terrace. The walls of the first floor are lined with pictures of celebrated horses. The gardens are simple but charming.

Belair was built for Governor Samuel Ogle (1694–1752), who was 47 when he brought 18-year-old Anne Tasker here as a bride. In his day he had English deer in a preserve on the estate, but his passion was fine horseflesh. Though he raced his own horses he was chiefly interested in improving the breed. He had brought with him from England in 1747 two famous thoroughbreds, Spark and Queen Mab, the latter a brood mare. From these two horses have descended much stock that has made Maryland famed on American tracks. The next occupant of Belair was Benjamin Tasker, Jr., Ogle's brother-in-law, who was the owner of the notable Selima. The present owner is William Woodward.

At COLLINGTON, 15.9 m. (141 alt., 130 pop.), is the junction with a clay and graveled road.

Right on this road, bordered by rolling fields of tobacco and corn, to the MARYLAND NORMAL AND INDUSTRIAL SCHOOL, 2.7 m., locally called Bowie Normal. It gives teachers' training to Negroes.

BOWIE, 3.3 m. (149 alt., 694 pop.), at the junction of the main line of the Pennsylvania R.R. and the Pope's Creek Branch, is a small village with a few frame houses, a shop or two, and an Odd Fellows' Hall.

The road continues to LAUREL, 12 m., on US 1 (see Tour 1b).

At 16.3 m. on US 50 is the junction with a clay road.

Left on this road to FAIRVIEW (R), 1.6 m., a big stucco-covered brick house in a thick grove of oaks. In a wing are kitchen and serving quarters. The house was built about 1785 by Baruch Duckett, who left it to William Bowie, his son-in-law, and to Bowie's heirs, but with unusual restrictions. The Bowies were to hold Fairview only as long as they refrained from cutting down certain trees near the house. Oden Bowie, who was governor of Maryland from 1868 to 1872, lived here, devoting much of his time to rearing and running such horses as Catesby, Compensation, Belle D'or, Oriole, and Crickmore.

At 17.5 m. on US 50 is the junction with a clay and graveled road.

Right on this to HOLY TRINITY CHURCH (1836), 0.1 m., a brick building covered with ivy and surmounted by a belfry. In the early 1700's Mareen Duvall, a Huguenot, built a small family chapel deeded by his son to the newly formed Queen Anne Parish in 1705.

At 18.9 m. on US 50 is the junction with a dirt road.

Right on this road to MARIETTA, 0.3 m., a large two-and-a-half-story T-shaped building with walls laid in Flemish bond and woodwork of some interest, but in poor condition. Boxwood borders the top of the terraces. Gabriel Duvall, who in 1811 was appointed to the U.S. Supreme Court lived here for a number of years and died here in 1844.

At 19.5 m. on US 50 is the junction with a macadamized road.

Right on this road to GLENDALE SANITARIUM, 0.4 m., which has accommodations for about 700 indigent tubercular patients from the District of Columbia.

At 25.5 m. on US 50 is Landover Road.

Left on this to BEALL'S PLEASURE (R), 1.6 m., a brick house of Georgian Colonial design built about 1795 by Benjamin Stoddert, first Secretary of the Navy.

BLADENSBURG, 27.3 m. (20 alt., 817 pop.), though the home of many Washington workers, is not merely a suburb. It was chartered in 1742 as

Garrison's Landing on the Anacostia River and was named for Sir Thomas Bladen, governor of the province. The town was a very busy port, shipping tobacco and flour until about 1800 when the Anacostia filled with silt eroded from the recently cleared lands, and large vessels could no longer come upstream. Though Bladensburg was no longer a port, it retained some prosperity by virtue of its position on the main coach road between the North and the South. Later when Congress forbade the railroads to enter Washington, Bladensburg became a terminus of the Baltimore & Ohio R.R. and freight and passengers for the Capital were discharged here. But in 1835 Congress was induced to lift the ban and local business declined.

On August 25, 1814, an engagement of the War of 1812 took place near here (see Tour 1b). On the outskirts of town is a field where prominent and fashionable gentlemen of Washington met on the field of honor when words or actions finally led to duels. One of the most notable of the many fought here was that in which the former Commodore James Barron shot and killed Commodore Stephen Decatur. Here, too, Colonel John Mc-Carty killed his cousin, Brigadier General Armistead Mason. McCarty as the challenger first suggested that he and Mason leap from the dome of the Capitol; when that was refused, he proposed that both sit on a keg of gun-powder and be blown up. The second suggestion was refused also, as was his third, that the combatants fight hand to hand with dirks. The final agreement provided for shotguns at 10 paces, but this was modified to rifles at 12 paces 'to the death.'

The MEMORIAL CROSS was erected in 1925 to the Prince Georges County men who died in the World War. It is surrounded by filling stations, billboards, and hot dog stands.

On Maryland Avenue, which runs north from Peace Cross Plaza, is (L) the GEORGE WASHINGTON TAVERN, built in 1732 and called the Indian Maid.

PARTHENON HEIGHTS on a wooded hill high above the road is a frame house built by Christopher Lowndes about 1769.

The SHIP BALLAST HOUSE, River Road, a small, low-roofed house with casement windows, is hidden from the road by trees. It was built about 1750 of stone said to have been brought in ships as ballast.

The BOSTWICK HOUSE, on a terraced hill (L) at the end of River Road, was built in 1746 by Christopher Lowndes for his bride, Elizabeth Tasker. The initials of the builder and the date are in wrought iron on the south chimney. The paneling of the drawing room is of black walnut.

On US 50 west of the junction with River Road is the MAGRUDER HOUSE (R), a two-and-a-half-story brick house built about 1743. Wood-work and metal hinges, as well as locks stamped with the lion and unicorn, are well preserved.

The ROSS HOUSE (R), a brick building 200 yards west of the Magruder House, was erected in 1749 by Dr. David Ross, an officer and supply pur-veyor in the French and Indian War. The fine Georgian Colonial structure is now as shabby as its surroundings.

US 50 turns L. at Peace Cross Plaza, uniting with US 1 (see Tour 1b).

Tour 10A

Junction with State 2—Hall—(Washington,D.C.); State 214. Junction with State 2 to District of Columbia Line, 19.8 *m.*

Concrete roadbed, three lanes wide.
Accommodations limited.

State 214, an east-west highway crossing tobacco country in Anne Arundel and Prince Georges counties, is the most direct of three routes between the National Capital and the Annapolis area.

State 214 branches west from State 2 (*see Tour 8b*), 0 *m.*, at a point about 5.5 miles southwest of Annapolis.

DAVIDSONVILLE, 3.6 *m.* (185 alt.,54 pop.), is a scattered farming community.

The DUCKETT HOUSE (R), 4.4 *m.*, among trees on a slight elevation, is a white frame house more than a century old, with two tall brick chimneys at each gable end. Until the beginning of the present century it was the home of the Igleharts, prominent in this vicinity. It is now known by the name of its present owner.

State 214 crosses the Patuxent River to a junction with a dirt road at 6.6 *m.*

Left on this road 1 *m.* to the SITE OF QUEEN ANNE, a town of the early eighteenth century caring for travelers on the road between Annapolis and the Potomac settlements of Maryland and Virginia. Only small tenant houses are now here. Local Negro tradition—in the face of Queen Anne's failure to visit America—is that the sovereign once stopped here to comb her hair, thus giving the place its name.

GOODWOOD, 1.4 *m.*, a large brick house with almost flat roof, was built early in the nineteenth century for Bernard Moore Carter. The wings were added by Carter's son Charles Henry in 1830.

At 8.6 *m.* on State 214 is the junction with State 3 (*see Tour 9a*) and at 11 *m.* a junction with a dirt road.

1. Left on this road to BOWIEVILLE (L), 1.1 *m.*, a large brick house surrounded by oaks and standing on a hill. The estate, granted about 1760 to Charles Boteler, came into Governor Robert Bowie's possession in 1800. When Mary Bowie, his daughter, married her cousin Thomas Contee Bowie in 1809, the governor deeded the land to her and ordered the house built.

SAINT BARNABAS CHURCH, 1.8 *m.*, serves a parish (Queen Anne) formed out of St.Paul's, Patuxent River, by an act of assembly in 1705. Construction of the first brick church, replacing a wooden chapel, was begun in 1708. Its decorations were the work of Gustavus Hesselius, the Swedish artist who painted in America from 1711 to 1755 (*see The Arts*). The altar piece, a *Last Supper* painted in 1721-22, is the first religious painting known to have been done to order in English America. When the old Protestant Episcopal church was rebuilt in 1774 during the rectorship of the Reverend Jonathan Boucher, the picture disappeared and was not rediscovered until

1911. Now privately owned, the painting in 1940 was on display at the American Swedish Museum, Philadelphia.

The present building, dating from Reverend Boucher's day, is of brick laid in Flemish bond. That the structure is either a faithful reproduction of the one built in 1708 or a restoration is indicated by the design, which belongs to the early Georgian Colonial period. The mass is unrelieved in its severity. Broad walls support a high shingled, gambrel roof flaring at the eaves; the cornice and the white trim of the narrow windows are extremely simple; the entrances are without ornament, though each door has five panels.

The belfry, a small separate structure of brick, was erected in 1930 in memory of Dr.John Contee Fairfax, eleventh Baron of Cameron (*see below*).

The parish has a communion set dated 1714.

2. Right from State 214 on the dirt road to MULLIKIN'S DELIGHT, 1.4 *m.*, a low rambling house built late in the seventeenth century for James Mullikin, former governor of a West Indian island. It is well cared for and has a delightful garden.

NORTHAMPTON (R), 14.3 *m.*, is an estate patented in 1673 to Thomas Sprigg, high sheriff and justice of Calvert County. A house built in 1704 was burned in 1909 and replaced by the present white clapboarded structure. Gardens laid out in 1788 with the aid of L'Enfant are still kept up. Osborne Sprigg, a descendant of Thomas, was a member of the State Constitutional Convention in 1776 and of the convention that ratified the Federal Constitution in 1788. Northampton was the refuge of President Madison during and after the Battle of Bladensburg, August 24, 1814. Samuel Sprigg, another descendant of the patentee, was governor of Maryland from 1819 to 1822. In 1869 Dr.John C. Fairfax, then owner of the house, succeeded to the title of Baron Fairfax of Cameron, in the Scots peerage, and moved to London; the estate is still owned by his family.

LARGO, 14.9 *m.* (175 alt.,135 pop.), is at the junction with State 202.

Left on State 202 to MOUNT LUBENTIA (R), 1.3 *m.*, a large hip-roofed brick house with balustrade along a platform on the ridge of the roof. The estate was patented by Ninian Beall in 1696 and named for his birthplace in Fifeshire, Scotland. Beall had been captured at the battle of Dunbar and transported to America, but as soon as his years of servitude were over he began to patent land and to take part in civil and military affairs. He several times served as commissioner to the Indian leaders, commanded frontier guards, and eventually became commander in chief of the armed forces of the province. The estate passed by marriage to the Magruders, one of whom built the present house some time before 1770.

From 1770 to 1774 it was rented to Jonathan Boucher, the clergyman who had with him three boys he was tutoring—Washington's stepson Jackie Custis, Benedict Calvert's eldest son Charles, and Master Overton Carr, of Virginia. These boys named the house Castle Magruder. While there Boucher married Nelly Addison, niece of Henry Addison. Boucher, a man of violent temper, strong prejudices, and an ardent Tory had left Virginia because of the unpopularity he had stirred up there against himself. He was no more popular in Maryland, as he himself recorded in a book he wrote on America after his return to England. When he came to St.Barnabas Church from St.Anne's, Annapolis, in 1770, his reputation had preceded him and, as he recorded, 'the very first Sunday I found the church doors shut against me; and not many Sundays thereafter a turbulent fellow had paid eight dollars for as many loads of stones to drive me and my friends from the church by force.' A neighboring blacksmith found Boucher's horse in his cornfield and lamed it with swan shot, then swaggered up to the clergyman with his gun in one hand and a large stick in the other. 'I struck him but once, when "prostrate he fell, and measured o'er a length of ground," boasted Boucher. Thus 'settled not pleasantly,' he determined to safeguard his family and bought 'The Lodge' on the Potomac. There in 1774 he engaged energetically in farming. Early in 1775 he left St.Barnabas' and became a curate to his brother-in-law, the Reverend Henry Addison at St.John's Church (*see Tour 12*). There 'for more than six months I preached, when I did preach, with a pair of loaded pistols lying on the cushion.' When a public fast was proclaimed, he felt it his duty to preach in his own church. Osborne Sprigg, with 200 armed men, crowded into the church to prevent him. 'Seeing myself thus circumstanced, it occurred to me that things seemed now indeed to be growing alarming, and that there was but one way to save my life. This was by seizing Sprigg by the collar, and with my cocked pistol in the other hand, assuring him that if any violence was offered to me I would instantly blow his brains out, as I most certainly would have done. I then told him that if he pleased he might conduct me to my horse, and I would leave them. This he did, and we marched together upwards of a hundred yards, I with one hand fastened in his collar and a pistol in the other, guarded by his whole company, whom he had the meanness to order to play on their drums the Rogues' March all the way we went, which they did.' Boucher decided to leave the province after the Revolution broke out, and sailed September 10, 1775. His memoirs are notable for their contempt of the colonials and the low opinion he held of Washington's abilities.

At 18.7 *m.* on State 214 is the junction with State 389 (Chapel Road).

Right 0.9 *m.* on State 389 to ST.MATTHEW'S CHURCH, often called Addison Chapel. It is visible (straight ahead) on a hilltop as the road crosses a creek on a narrow wooden bridge. The land was donated about 1696 for a chapel of ease by John Addison, uncle of the essayist Joseph Addison. The early frame chapel was replaced by the present brick building shortly before the War of 1812. The local version of the English-brick legend relates that the bricks, brought over as ships' ballast, came from one of the razed royal palaces. In the Protestant Episcopal cemetery is the GRAVE OF BENJAMIN STODDERT (1751–1813), first Secretary of the Navy.

CAPITOL HEIGHTS, 19.5 *m.* (125 alt.,1,611 pop.), is a suburb of Washington.

State 214 crosses the DISTRICT OF COLUMBIA LINE, 19.8 *m.*, about five miles east of the Zero Stone behind the White House.

Tour 11

(Washington,D.C.) — T.B. — Waldorf — Leonardtown — Point Lookout; 79.2 *m.* State 5.

Macadamized, concrete-paved, or graveled roadbed, two lanes wide.
Hotels and tourist homes in towns; few tourist homes and camps along highways.

This route cuts down through the peninsula between the Potomac and Patuxent rivers, the first region of settlement in Lord Baltimore's province.

Near Washington the clay and gravel soil is cultivated by truck farmers, but farther south tobacco has been the chief product for 300 years.

State 5 crosses the DISTRICT OF COLUMBIA LINE, 0 *m.*, at a point 5.4 miles southeast of the White House. Enclosed by an iron cage is (R) one of the stones set up in 1791–92, to mark the boundary between the Federal District and the State of Maryland.

CLINTON, 7.6 *m.* (240 alt.,200 pop.), is still locally known as Surrattsville; the name was changed after Mrs.Mary E. Surratt was hanged for participation in the Lincoln assassination plot. The SURRATT TAVERN was supposedly the place where the plot was hatched. Mrs.Surratt was hanged July 7, 1865, along with others convicted as accomplices in the plot. Booth, on his flight from Washington, is supposed to have stopped here for a gun and ammunition before continuing on to Dr.Samuel Mudd's (*see below*) to have his broken leg set.

Right from Clinton over rolling hills and through woods on a road much used in colonial times to PISCATAWAY (*see Tour 12*), 6 *m.*

T.B., 12.6 *m.* (225 alt.,100 pop.), was named for a boundary stone bearing the initials of Thomas Brooke, a leading landholder.

At 13.1 *m.* is the junction with State 3, which unites with State 5 to WALDORF (*see Tour 9*), 18.7 *m.*, where State 5 branches L.

In BEANTOWN, 20.3 *m.*, is the junction with State 233.

Left 3.7 *m.* on State 233 to (L) the MUDD HOUSE (*adm.* 25¢), a two-story frame building with gable roof and one low wing. In the parlor of this dwelling on the morning of April 15, 1865, Dr.Samuel Mudd set John Wilkes Booth's leg. Mudd, found guilty as an accessory to the crime and sentenced to life imprisonment at Fort Jefferson in the Dry Tortugas, was pardoned in 1869 by President Andrew Johnson, after having rendered great service during an epidemic of yellow fever at the fort.

In HUGHESVILLE, 29.5 *m.* (193 alt.,500 pop.), a tobacco auction center, is the junction with macadamized State 231.

Left on this road to PATUXENT, 2.1 *m.* (184 alt.,10 pop.), and a junction with State 381 (*see Tour 9*). At 7 *m.*, on State 231 is BENEDICT (5 alt.,111 pop.) and a ferry that crosses the Patuxent River (*see Tour 8b*). The settlement founded in 1683 as a customs center soon became an important shipping point for tobacco but had lost its prominence by December 26, 1812, when British ships anchored here while blockading the Potomac River and Chesapeake Bay. In August 1814 British troops under General Ross landed here shortly before the march on Washington. Benedict, now a small summer resort, also does some boat building.

CHARLOTTE HALL, 33.6 *m.* (167 alt.,67 pop.), established in 1698, was usually called Ye Coole Springs of St.Maries. It was the first health resort of the province, popular because of the healing properties attributed to the water of its spring.

The school of CHARLOTTE HALL (R) was opened under charter of 1774 and named for Queen Charlotte of England. It became a military academy about 1797. The main building is a light gray, two-story square structure with a tall portico.

In 1939 seven Amishmen of Pennsylvania bought farms near Charlotte Hall and about 100 will have arrived by 1940. They decided to migrate because land in Pennsylvania had become too expensive for those now establishing homes and also because of trouble they had been having with Pennsylvania laws, which keep children in school longer than the Amish believe is necessary. Maryland demands completion of the seventh grade only.

NEW MARKET, 33.7 *m.* (180 alt.,294 pop.), is at the junction with macadamized State 6.

Left on State 6 to ALL FAITH CHURCH (R), 2.5 *m.*, a rectangular brick building erected in 1765. The first church here was built when the Anglican parish was laid out in 1692. In the gable of the present building is a Palladian window and in the body of the church are single arched windows. The frame belfry is a modern addition.

Close to the church, at 2.6 *m.*, is a dirt road; L. here 5.4 *m.* to THE PLAINS, a house bearing the scars received when it was the center of a skirmish between Maryland militiamen and a British naval landing party during the War of 1812. The stuccoed brick dwelling, built in the early eighteenth century, is of two stories with ten rooms, and is on land granted as Chesley Hill but later called Orphans Gift.

MECHANICSVILLE, 36.9 *m.* (165 alt.,300 pop.), sprang up around a crossroads tavern conducted by the Adams brothers next to their blacksmith shop and forge. The tavern (R), near the center of town, has been remodeled for a store.

The Mechanicsville neighborhood has long been notable for food in the high Maryland tradition; the region even now has an inn where such food is served—an unusual rural institution whose address is revealed only to choice friends of its discoverers. Traveling salesmen, telephone linemen, and tourists all sit at one long table. That the inn has no plumbing is accepted without a murmur for the sake of breakfasts beginning with fruit and cooked cereal, and working through fried chicken, ham and eggs, and hot breads to that mysterious but delicious black meat concoction called 'pudding.' Dinners and suppers are even more astonishing; food is brought to the table without special order and new visitors, having filled themselves beyond prudence with oysters on the half shell, oyster broth, fried oysters, and perhaps some other trifle—shad, clams, and so on in season—are overcome by the discovery that these were mere appetizers to prepare them for duck, chicken, steak, or whatever the cook's inspiration has provided.

At 39.3 *m.* is the junction with Three Notch Road (*see Tour 11A*).

In HELEN, 41.9 *m.*, is a junction with State 234 (*see Tour 9*).

At 49.8 *m.* is the junction with State 243.

Right on this road to ST.FRANCIS XAVIER CHURCH (L), 4.7 *m.*, erected in 1767 on the approximate site of a church built about 1654; between the graveyard and the road a few old bricks mark the site of St.Ignatius Chapel, constructed in 1662. About 1668 the Jesuits built a large chapel here dedicated to St.Francis Xavier. The present church is a simple frame structure with sacristy, square bell tower, and cross. The bell is inscribed ' St.1691. S.T.Joannes Arden.' Except for the removal of the slave gallery and choir loft the interior resembles that of early days, although the building has had much restoration. The ceiling is triple-vaulted. An undated but well-preserved painting of St.Francis Xavier hangs above the altar. The church is on Newtown Manor, an estate acquired by the Jesuits in 1668, not actually a manor, though on former manor land. A two-and-a-half-story parish house was built in 1740. A school, founded in St.Marys City by Father Andrew White, was transferred to Calverton Manor in 1640 and to this place about 1677.

In colonial times on GIBBETT HILL (L), 49.9 *m.*, also called Golgotha Hill, criminals condemned to death were placed in an iron cage hung from a tree and left to starve. A guard prevented the delivery of food or drink to the condemned and, as a warning, the body of the victim was often left to rot in the cage until only the skeleton remained.

The twentieth century has made little impression on LEONARD–TOWN, 50 *m.* (90 alt.,697 pop.), where oxen trundle tobacco along the tree-lined lanes to the warehouses and boat landings, and the warm hospitality of the people has not yet been commercialized. In 1708 the assembly ordered Seymour Town laid out here on a ridge overlooking Breton Bay, an estuary of the Potomac. A log courthouse was built and in 1710 succeeded St.Marys as the county seat. When the assembly renewed its order in 1728 and provided means for carrying it out, Seymour Town—named for Governor Seymour of the province—was renamed in honor of Benedict Leonard Calvert, fourth Lord Baltimore. In addition to its two-century-old trade in tobacco, Leonardtown ships oak and gumwood logs for piles and railroad ties.

TUDOR HALL (L), near the courthouse, was built in 1780 by Abraham Barnes. A plain rectangular stuccoed brick structure with a low hip roof, Tudor Hall has one feature unusual in Maryland Georgian design—a deeply recessed entrance portico at ground level with four oddly capped Doric columns. Also distinctive, though perhaps a later addition, is a small square platform between four chimneys in the middle of the roof ridge. The builder directed in his will that his 300 slaves should be freed on condition that they assume his family name. The new Barneses were so fruitful that theirs is now the most common surname among the Negroes of St.Marys County.

ST.MARYS ACADEMY was opened in 1885 by the Sisters of Charity.

St.Marys Beacon, a Democratic weekly, occupies a house constructed in 1704. In this house, originally of seven rooms but enlarged to 21, the court sat until the log courthouse was built.

At 52.5 *m.* is the junction with macadamized State 244.

Right on this road to MULBERRY FIELDS (R), 2.3 *m.* Although the history of this manor was lost when the records of St.Marys were burned in 1831, it is believed that the old mansion of the type known as 'big house, little house, colonnade and kitchen' was built by William Somerville between 1760 and 1770. Its exterior, unaltered since 1832, is an interesting example of Georgian Colonial design. The red brick walls are laid in an all-header bond and the hand-carved paneling of the interior is two inches thick. The bottom lands of the estate are divided into three fields by two lines of enormous mulberry trees, stretching three quarters of a mile from the house to the river. These rows appear parallel but are actually twice as far apart at the river as at the house. The old brick building at the entrance to the garden was originally used in the small silk industry the mulberry trees supported.

At 58.6 *m.* on State 5 is the junction with macadamized State 249.

Right on State 249, 3.2 *m.* to State 250; R. here 0.4 *m.* to ST.GEORGE'S CHURCH (L), built in 1750 near the site of Poplar Hill Church, which was erected in 1642 by an Anglican congregation organized in 1639.

At 3.4 *m.* on State 249 is State 251; L. here 2.9 *m.* to PORTO BELLO (R), a large frame three-unit building of the telescope type with shingled gambrel roofs. The main section has double chimneys at both ends. William Hebb is said to have built the house in 1740; the Hebb burial ground is in the rear. Another story has Edwin Goode as the builder. The house, used at one time for a boarding school and then neglected for years, has been restored.

At 7.6 *m.* on State 249 is the junction with State 498; R. here 1 *m.* to PINEY POINT (*hotel, bathing, duck hunting, year-round fishing*), a resort that was the summer social center of Washington dignitaries between 1820 and 1853. President James Monroe stayed first in the hotel and later in a cottage that became a summer White House; it was demolished by a hurricane in 1933. John C. Calhoun, Henry Clay, Daniel Webster, President Franklin Pierce, and President Theodore Roosevelt also visited here.

State 249 continues to ST.GEORGE ISLAND (*hotel, bathing, fishing*) 10 *m.*, which is reached by a narrow wooden bridge.

At 65.2 *m.* beside the junction with a dirt road is the FATHER WHITE MEMORIAL, a stone erected to one of the Jesuits who arrived with the first Maryland settlers.

Right on the dirt road to the JESUIT MEMORIAL ALTAR (L), a concave brick wall surmounted with a white stone slab, dedicated in 1933 by the Pilgrims of Maryland Society to Fathers White, Altham, and Gervase.

At 66.9 *m.*, where State 5 bears L., is ST.MARYS CITY. Since Maryland's Tercentenary Celebration in 1934 this site has been maintained by the State in co-operation with various organizations.

In March 1634 (O.S.) Leonard, brother of Cecil Calvert, the lord proprietor, dropped anchor with his company of adventurers and indentured servants from the *Ark* and *Dove* by St.Clements Island (now Blackistone). While most of the company continued to live on the ship the governor went up the Potomac to treat with the Emperor of the Piscataway (*see The Indians*) and arrange for the company to settle peaceably on the Indian land. Later, on March 27, the little ships sailed up St. George's River (now St.Marys) for about six miles to the village of the Yoacomico Indians, members of the Piscataway Confederacy who were beginning to evacuate in fear of the Susquehannock. The colonists took over the Indian village and paid the natives with axes, hatchets, farm tools and a few bolts of cloth for their houses and fields. St.George's Fort was soon erected, 'a Pallizado 120 yards square with flour flankes,' and on Lord Baltimore's plans an orderly town was laid out. The little group of colonists increased and prospered to the point that in 1676 they erected a statehouse here for the provincial assembly. This place was the capital of Maryland until 1694 when Annapolis was laid out as a more convenient site. A few years later St.Marys lost its status as the county seat to Leonard Town and declined rapidly. Few traces of the town remained in 1934 though it had had some of the finest buildings in the colonies in its day.

In the Y of the junction is the FREEDOM OF CONSCIENCE MONUMENT, a massive limestone figure of a youth with face heavenward. It was designed by Hans Schuler, the Baltimore sculptor.

ST.MARYS SEMINARY (R), near the junction, is a preparatory and junior college for girls. The long, narrow two-story red brick structure has a gambrel roof with dormers. Within the recessed portico with its six free columns is a railed second-story porch. The present structure, a restoration made after a fire in 1924, is an exact copy of the building erected here in 1840 when the school was established. Its charter provided that the board of trustees should consist of five Catholics, five Methodists, and five

Episcopalians and these denominations should be represented on the faculty. The site of the old county jail and gallows is said to be on the seminary campus.

TRINITY PROTESTANT EPISCOPAL CHURCH, near the seminary, was erected in 1829 with bricks salvaged from the first statehouse here. It is a small structure with steeply-pitched gable roof, wooden belfry, and brick entrance porch. In the churchyard, the LEONARD CALVERT MONUMENT marks the site of a tree near which the settlers from the *Ark* and *Dove* are believed to have assembled to hear the Royal Charter read soon after their arrival. This was the official act establishing settlement.

The COPLEY VAULT, at the rear of the church, is believed to hold the dust of Sir Leonard Copley and his wife. Copley (1693) was the first royal governor of Maryland. For many years it was assumed that Governor Leonard Calvert and his wife were buried here.

The ST.MARYS STATEHOUSE, on Middle Street a few yards from the church, was built in 1934 by the State, with bricks from the ruins of several old buildings near by. It is a small cruciform, gable-roofed structure and has free-top end chimneys. Interior furnishings and decorations are careful copies of seventeenth-century pieces. The original building was erected in 1676 by Captain John Quigley 'at a cost of 300,000 lbs. of tobacco and cask.' Cannon, some of them unearthed after being buried for centuries, are at the covered entrance and on the lawn high above the water.

About 200 yards east of this building is a dirt road (R) on which, a few hundred feet off the highway, are the RUINS OF SMITH'S TOWN HOUSE, erected in 1647. Here legislative meetings of the colony were held in 1662. Only crumbled stone and bricks and slight excavations remain. Fort St.Marys with breastworks and cannon stood across the road from Smith's Town House.

On State 5 at 66.4 *m.* is a junction with a lane and with Mattapany Street (pronounced Mat-a-pan-eye), which follows Mattapany Path (*see Tour 11A*) that led from the Yoacomico village to a Mattapany village near the mouth of the Patuxent River.

1. Left on Mattapany Street 0.1 *m.* to the GOVERNOR'S SPRING (R). The brick wall erected around the spring in 1640 has crumbled.

2. Right from State 5 on the dirt lane to the SITE OF SISTERS FREEHOLD (R), 1 *m.*, the home of Margaret Brent who was born in Gloucester, England, in 1601. With her sister Mary, she accompanied their brothers Giles and Fulke to America in 1638. Within a year she had patented in St.Marys, 70 acres of land, which she named Sisters Freehold. From time to time she accumulated more land by transporting small groups of settlers. Ten years later upon furnishing proof of having brought in five menservants and four maidservants in 1638, she and her sister Mary each received 1,000 more acres. When Governor Leonard Calvert died in 1647 he made her his executrix. As his attorney she collected rents, paid soldiers, settled his estate, and attended to affairs of the province. She appeared before the assembly on January 21, 1648, requesting a voice in its councils and demanding two votes, one as landowner in her own right and one as the attorney for Lord Baltimore. The pleas were denied by the governor. This was the first time in America that a woman sought legal rights comparable to those being exercised by men.

In 1650 Mistress Brent, very much annoyed by the attitude of the proprietary (after she had quieted a rebellion by paying soldiers from Leonard Calvert's funds), moved to Virginia, where she built a new home and named it Peace. She still retained her estates in Maryland, however, and returned to them once a year to collect rents from her tenants. The exact date of her death is unknown, but her will, dated December 26, 1663, was probated May 19, 1671.

At 66.6 m. on State 5 is the junction with a narrow dirt road.

Right on this to CLOCKERS FANCY (L), 0.5 m., a small one-and-a-half-story white brick house built before 1681. The gabled roof is extended forward over a long porch. Small clapboard wings are late additions. The house stands on land patented by Daniel Clocker who on March 23, 1649, 'demandeth 100 acres of land viz: 50 for himself as servant to Captain Cornwalleies and 50 in right of his wife who was servant to Mistress Margaret Brent within this province.'

ROSE CROFT, 1.8 m., a mansion with high roof, brick gable ends, and dormers, was built about 1706. It is on a bluff at the confluence of the St.Inigoes Creek and St.Marys River, a site occupied earlier by the home of Daniel Wolstenholme, Lord Baltimore's collector of revenue at the port of St.Marys. The estate is noted for its ancient boxwood.

At 67.9 m. on State 5 is the junction with a dirt road.

Left on this 0.3 m. to ST.PETER'S KEY (L), an estate named for the key-shaped creek on whose banks it lies. The basement and free-standing double chimney with one-story pent are part of a house built about 1650. In 1640 a tract of 50 acres was patented to John Harris and Thomas Allen, assigned by Allen to Harris and sold by Harris to Roger Oliver. Oliver, killed by Indians aboard ship in 1643, left St.Peter's Key to his widow, Blanche Harrison Oliver. A few years later this lady, having committed willful perjury, was sent to the pillory and deprived of both her ears. The ignominy of the family was perpetuated by a decree that her cows, assigned to her children, should be identified by a cropped left ear and two slits in the right ear.

At ST.INIGOES, 69.5 m., is the junction with a dirt road.

Right on this 1.3 m. to a second dirt road; R. here 0.3 m. to FENWICK'S FREE (L), granted in 1651 to Cuthbert Fenwick, who had been a member of the first assembly. The name is undoubtedly a contraction of 'Freehold.' In the manor house, which has long since disappeared, Captain Prescott was tried in 1659 for hanging a witch on his ship, the *Sarah Artch*. John Washington, immigrant ancestor of George Washington, was on the ship and was called as a witness. He did not testify, however, because on the day he was called he had a previous engagement—'I intend to git my young sonne baptized, all ye company and gossips being all ready invited.'

At 0.9 m. on the second dirt road is the entrance (L) to CROSS MANOR, whose house is the oldest brick structure in Maryland. Despite many alterations and additions—including two-story porches—enough survives of the structure built in 1643 to validate its antiquity. The present roof, gabled with arched dormers, replaced a high gambrel, as the bricks in the end walls clearly show. It stands on the grant made in 1639 to Thomas Cornwallis, one of the richest men in the colony. The gardens, toward the water, are approximately as old as the house and contain great masses of boxwood, some of them 45 feet in circumference.

On the first dirt road is ST.IGNATIUS CHURCH (R), 1.7 m., the third on this site, which is part of the manor of Little Bretton granted to William Bretton in 1637. He gave this land to the Catholics among the colonists for their chapel.

PRIEST MANOR (R), 2.2 m., once a part of St.Inigoes Manor, was patented to Thomas Copley, the Jesuit who was taken to England in chains during the Ingle invasion. The Jesuits were not supposed to hold lands personally but Lord Baltimore was unwilling to allow any religious group to build up estates—least of all a Catholic body—since one of the charges he had to meet from enemies was that he was establishing a Roman Catholic State on English soil. The Jesuits had begun acquiring lands from the Indians soon after the arrival of the settlers; the governor promptly informed them that only the proprietary could make grants and that grantees, regardless of their status, must pay the usual rents to Lord Baltimore and accept the usual responsibilities of those receiving land in the province. Copley and Father Philip Fisher, the business manager of the Jesuit missionaries, fought this ruling by every possible means; it was finally somewhat circumvented by the registration of lands in the names of the priests and members of their household. This tract, like Newtown, was not really a manor, though the tracts from which these lands were donated were manors in fact. The house is said to have been built about 1750 with bricks from the Catholic chapel at St.Marys City. The dwelling, which had four great outside chimneys and a large sweep of roof, was recently destroyed by fire. Near the ruins is a very old brick stable with two tiers of loopholes piercing the walls above the big double doors in the middle of the long sides.

In RIDGE, 72.3 m., is the southern junction with Three Notch Road (*see Tour 11A*).

The oldest part of the brick house on ST.MICHAEL'S MANOR (L), 76.4 m., is thought to have been built in 1687. The larger section, built before 1800, has fine mantels with dog-eared trim and unusual diamond motifs in the carved decorations. The front door opens into the main room instead of the usual hallway.

At 76.5 m. is the junction with a macadamized road.

Left on this to SCOTLAND BEACH (*camping, crabbing, boating*), 1 m., a summer resort.

On POINT LOOKOUT, 79.2 m., is a lighthouse built in 1830 and still an important beacon for Bay and Potomac River navigators. The cemetery here is on the site of a fort where more than 3,000 Confederate prisoners died. It was one of two forts built to defend the mouth of the Potomac and Chesapeake Bay and was later made a prison camp. Sanitary precautions were not well understood, and death from fever, dysentery, and other diseases claimed a large daily toll.

Tour 11A

Harpers Corner—Jarboesville—Ridge; 31 m., State 235.

Oiled-gravel roadbed, three lanes wide, well maintained.
Roadside accommodations limited; shore resort accommodations plentiful in summer.

This alternate to State 5 between Harpers Corner and Ridge is only about two miles shorter, but it has fewer steep grades and crossroads. It parallels the lower western bank of the Patuxent River, passing through a sparsely settled and little cultivated area; many side roads lead to shore resorts, wharfs, and campsites along the water.

Between 1642 and 1650 when numerous houses were built along the south bank of the Patuxent, all communication was by water. In 1672 a trail was extended north and south from Mattapany Landing near the mouth of the Patuxent through the Patuxent settlements. In 1702 a road-marking law prescribed three equidistant notches on the face of a tree to indicate a road to a ferry; two notches with a third high above for a road to a courthouse; and two notches near the ground with a slip down the face for a road to a church. This route along the Patuxent, known as the Three Notch Road for its marking, became the chief means of communication between St.Marys and the upcountry.

State 235 branches southeast from State 5 at HARPERS CORNER, 0 *m.*, about 5 miles south of Charlotte Hall (*see Tour 11*).

At 1.3 *m.* is the junction with a macadamized dirt road.

Left on this 1.4 *m.* to DELABROOKE MANOR (R), surveyed in 1650 for Robert Brooke, then commander of Charles County and later president of the provincial council and acting governor of Maryland. Near the present house, a large brick structure with a veranda facing the river, is an excavation marking the site of the house in which the provincial council met with Governor Charles Calvert on July 19, 1662. It was destroyed by fire in 1835. An old stone springhouse still shelters the spring used continuously for centuries.

At 2.4 *m.* on State 235 is CREMONA (R), a spacious house built during the late eighteenth century and now restored. A gabled main section is flanked by large gabled wings. One of its features is the hanging staircase accessible from either end of the grand hall. A valuable collection of early American and English furnishings is housed here.

At 4.7 *m.* is the junction with a macadamized road.

Left on this to SANDGATES, 2.6 *m.* (*bathhouses, cottages, boats for fishing, crabbing, and duck hunting*).

In HOLLYWOOD, 10 *m.* (130 alt.,260 pop.), is a junction with a macadamized road.

Left on this to SOTTERLY, 2.2 *m.* The present owner has given careful study to the restoration of this early Georgian Colonial house. A later kitchen and room on the porch front were removed and a kitchen was reconstructed on the site of the original kitchen, which was one of a group of outbuildings south of the dwelling. The oldest part of the steep-roofed frame house, built in 1730 probably for George Plater, governor of Maryland (1791), is one-and-one-half stories in height. The roof is surmounted by a square wooden cupola and broken by pedimented dormers. On the face of the cupola is a plaque bearing the date 1730. The colonnaded, flagstone porch across the front facing the Patuxent River has slender paneled wooden posts supporting a long shed roof. The house contains some of the finest woodwork in tidewater Maryland. The main passage with its Chippendale stairway, the dining room, and library are all paneled in pine. The solid mahogany drawing room door is hung on large solid brass hinges. In this room is a fine fireplace with bracketed mantel and a large over-mantel panel embellished with dog-eared trim and fret motif. The deep wall recesses on either side of the chimney have carved headings in the form of large shells. In the center of the garden near the house is the Sotterly sundial, which has measured time since 1734. The owner, a New Yorker, frequently commutes to the estate by hydroplane.

At 12.1 *m.* on State 235 is the junction with a macadamized road.

Left on this to a narrow dirt road 1.6 *m.*; L. here to RESURRECTION MANOR, granted to Thomas Cornwaleys in 1650, and one of the oldest of the manorial grants. The place is neglected but the old house still stands.

CLARKS WHARF, 3.1 *m.* (*swimming, boating, fishing*), is a quiet resort with a small sandy beach on the Patuxent.

At 14.2 *m.* on State 235 is the junction with a narrow, winding graveled road.

Right on this to ST.ANDREW'S CHURCH (R), 2.3 *m.*, is one of the original Anglican parishes of Maryland. The red brick structure of unusual interest, its twin square towers now topped with steeples, was completed in 1767. On the face of each tower are two semicircular niches, one above the other. The corners of the towers are accented by brick quoins, and between the towers is an inset portico sheltering a simple arched entrance and two segmental arched windows. Two square brick columns on the front of the loggia support a slightly projecting pedimented bay at the second story. This bay finished in brick and stucco has a large Palladian window. The exterior is well preserved, but age has taken toll of some of the interior woodwork; the tower stairs crumble at the touch. The chalice and the salver purchased in 1757 are still in use. On the sides of the altar are carved wooden tablets executed by John F. Lummer, a member of the congregation when the church was built.

CALIFORNIA, 15 *m.* (115 alt.,94 pop.), is chiefly a name and a post office. Tourists like to mail letters here and in the neighboring village of Hollywood.

Left from California on a narrow dirt road 0.9 *m.* to another dirt road; R. here 0.2 *m.* to a third dirt road; L. 0.9 *m.* to KINGSTON. This old place, also called Croissant's, was part of Resurrection Manor (*see above*). The house, built in 1670 with gable roof, two end chimneys and one small chimney, is in good condition. Mysterious lights, frequently seen when the moon is high, recall the local legend of the ghost of Aunt Melie Hazel, which wanders about looking for hidden gold. Until the treasure is found, the lights will continue to shine and Aunt Melie Hazel will continue to prowl.

At 18.9 in JARBOESVILLE is the junction with macadamized State 246.

Left on this to PEARSON'S CORNER, 1.5 *m.*, and R. 1.8 *m.* on macadamized State 248 to a dirt road.

1. Left 1.1 *m.* on this road to SUSQUEHANNA, home of Christopher Rousby, king's collector killed by George Talbot in 1684 (*see Tour 2a*). The story-and-a-half frame house built in 1654 is a long, narrow structure with almost identical front and rear façades to which porches have been added. The brick ledger TOMB OF CHRISTOPHER AND JOHN ROUSBY is a few hundred yards south of the house. It is said that John died of grief over the death of his brother, to whom he was devoted.

2. Right 1.6 *m.* from State 248 on the dirt road to another dirt road; L. on this 2.9 *m.* to LONG LANE FARM overlooking Chesapeake Bay. The house, built by John Jarboe about 1648, has two pedimented dormers in the jerkin-head roof that extends over the porch. A curious chamber is concealed underneath the adjoining penthouse. According to tradition, the family planned to flee to it in event of Indian attack; access to this hiding place was by a secret stairway in the thick walls of the house. There is no evidence that the hideaway was ever needed. Near the dwelling stands the old meat house with hand-forged iron hooks. The tobacco barn, granaries, and other outbuildings are also in remarkably good condition.

Although Jarboe was a Frenchman, he rose to the rank of justice of the peace and later became high sheriff of St.Marys County. He also sat in the lower house of the Maryland assembly.

At 2 *m.* on State 246, which continues north (L) from Pearson's Corner, a view (R) of MATTAPONI (*no closer approach open to the public*). The building consists of three gabled units; the main section is a rectangular stuccoed brick building two stories high with wide, double outside chimneys at both ends. A lower, two-story frame wing connects the main house with a one-story brick kitchen at the end of which is a flush, square chimney. This brick wing, erected about 1642, was, like Long Lane, stoutly built for protection against the Indians. The rest of the house was built early in the eighteenth century.

The land on which the house stands was the site of a Mattapient Indian village presented to Father White and his associates, who established a storehouse and a mission here. The estate was reclaimed by Lord Baltimore in 1641 when he protested the Jesuits' refusal to pay quit rents to him for land they had obtained from the Indians. In 1663 Mattaponi was granted to Henry Sewall, secretary of the province, and became his widow's when Sewall died two years later. In 1666 Jane Sewall married Governor Charles Calvert, afterwards third Lord Baltimore. A fort and magazine were erected on the estate, which became the general rendezvous of the militia. When the Maryland deputies were driven from St.Marys during the Protestant Revolution they took refuge here, and here in 1689 the proprietary government surrendered to the Protestants. About 250 yards south of the present dwelling are the foundations and cellar of an old structure, probably built by Calvert, that was in a state of dilapidation by 1773. The site of the garrison is traceable about 100 yards nearer the river; and on the river bank to the rear of the present dwelling are the remains of old earthworks.

State 246 continues to MILLSTONE LANDING, 4.1 *m.*, which is connected by ferry with Solomons Island (*see Tour 8b*).

RIDGE, 31 *m.* (42 alt.,192 pop.), is at the southern junction with State 5 (*see Tour 11*), 5 miles north of Point Lookout (*see Tour 11*).

Tour 12

(Washington,D.C.)—Oxon Hill—Mason Springs—Port Tobacco—La Plata; State 224 and State 6. District of Columbia Line to La Plata, 48.6 *m.*

Asphalt-paved roadbed, two lanes wide.
Some shore accommodations in summer; limited at other times.

This route closely follows roads developed in the latter part of the seventeenth century as a means of communication between the many plantations along the Potomac River. It follows the course of the river but swings inland to avoid the wide creek mouths and occasional swamps. Today this is largely a country of wood lots and of small farms where tobacco is the chief money crop. Some of the farmers—white and Negro—are owners, others are tenants, and others farm on shares. On the whole it is not a prosperous region though its character has changed since 1933. For about a dozen miles south of the District Line Washington workers have been building tiny cottages, some close to the main route, others set well back in the thin woods. Often they erect a garage where they live until the house is built. Late in the afternoon and on Saturday and Sunday they hammer away on the parts of their houses that need less expert work, build porches, put up fences, and grade and plant lawns. These settlers are a new type of pioneer, withdrawing from Washington to escape high rents. Here, within commuting distance of the city, they are able to buy tiny plots of land, establish homes, and live without the constant fear that their children will be killed in traffic.

This countryside is only one of many in the counties between the Potomac and the bay that are undergoing rapid change. People who moved out of the city in the early years of the depression were vigorous advocates of improvement and helped to establish the Tri-County Electrification Co-operative, which went into operation with a Federal loan early in 1938. With cheap electric current for lighting, cooking, and radios the number of settlers has increased. Many fine old mansions, either deserted or falling to ruin in the hands of share croppers, have been restored by retired army and navy officers, permanent Government officials, and artists. This cheap electricity also has changed the habits of long-established families; people who never considered bathrooms and running water a necessity now buy electric iceboxes, ranges, and all the new gadgets that make city life more comfortable.

State 224, a continuation of Nichols Avenue, Anacostia, crosses the DISTRICT OF COLUMBIA LINE, 0 m., at a point 7.7 miles south of the White House.

OXON HILL, 1.5 m. (260 alt.,200 pop.), is a scattered community around two stores and a crossroads filling station.

Right here on an asphalt-paved road to OXON HILL MANOR (R), 0.7 m., overlooking the Potomac. The present beautiful house is on the site of one built in the latter part of the seventeenth century by John Addison, first in America of a family that for several generations played a leading role in southern Maryland life. John Hanson, president of the Congress of the Confederation of United States, died here on November 15, 1783. The old house burned in 1895. The gardens (*private*) here are notable.

NOTLEY HALL (R), 3.1 m., was the home of Thomas Notley, governor of Maryland from 1676 to 1679. Charles, third Lord Baltimore, later occupied the house for a brief period.

The road ends at the SITE OF FORT FOOTE, 3.8 m., one of the defenses of the Capital during the Civil War, but now only grass-covered mounds. The Potomac Parkway will pass this site.

OXON HILL SCHOOL (R), 2.5 m., serving the lower end of Prince Georges County, is an excellent example of the rural Maryland schools. The plan is modern but simple and the standard of teaching is high. A tilting tournament is held on the grounds each Fourth of July.

ST. JOHN'S CHURCH (R), 5.3 m., a rectangular, pinkish brick building with a steep roof, was built in 1723, the third church on the site. In 1820 the interior was remodeled and later colored glass replaced the earlier single panes. The parish, founded in 1692, was called Piscataway, but also was known briefly as King George's. A pew, once occupied by Washington according to tradition, is preserved.

HARMONY HALL (R), 6 m., formerly Battersea, was built by the same contractor who erected St. John's Church, and in the same year, 1723. The two-and-a-half-story red brick house has been extensively remodeled. Walter Dulaney Addison and his brother John, grandsons of John Addison of Oxon Hill, brought their brides here in 1792. The two couples happily occupied the house for a year and gave it the present name, it is said. Behind the house (R), close to the cove called Wide Water but visible from the road, is WANT WATER, a story-and-a-half clapboarded house, now in bad condition though some excellent paneling remains. A stretch of land along the river here was patented to another member of the Addison family in 1708, and it is presumed that the house was built shortly after that date. It is a low gambrel roofed structure with lines typical of the period. North of Harmony Hall on the same estate and close to the road is an old remodeled brick house moved to its present site from Piscataway.

At 6.2 m. is the junction with State 549.

Right to FORT WASHINGTON (*open; sentry at gate*), 3 m., first called Fort Warburton for the estate on which it was built. Warburton Manor, patented in 1661, was the home of the Digges family, descendants of Edward Digges, governor of Virginia (1652–89). The fort was established to protect the National Capital. In August 1814 when the British advancing up the river landed a reconnaissance party near by, the commander of the fort, an engineer, spiked his guns and withdrew to Washington without firing a shot. After the war Major Charles L'Enfant, who laid out the city of Washington in the District of Columbia, designed the present fort—one of the most interesting old military structures in the country. It is on a high promontory above the great bend in the Potomac and commands a view up and down the river for many miles. Encircled by a deep dry moat, it is entered over a drawbridge—that no longer draws up—and through a massive Roman arch trimmed with rusticated stone quoins and key block. The entrance is further guarded by a medieval portcullis and high wooden doors and is flanked by high brick guardhouses built into the thick walls. Opening onto the arched entrance passage are grim rooms with green mold on their damp stone walls. A parade ground is inside on the top of the ridge. Toward Washington are (R) the gun mounts behind parapets. At intervals the thick high walls jut starlike over the wooded river bank. Under the emplacements are powder magazines. To the left are storehouses and a few ancient barracks and dormitory quarters for married officers—tiny duplex affairs with recessed windows and doors. From the parade field steps lead to a sunken court holding more storehouses. Other steps lead to subterranean rooms and to low galleries in the base of the buttressed walls. One steep stone passageway ends at a heavy pedimented gate on the lowest level near a picturesque wooded picnic spot overlooking the river.

Outside the main entrance are modern quarters for the men and officers stationed at the post, which will be abandoned when the projected river parkway is completed; the old fort is to be preserved as a relic.

State 224 crosses Piscataway Creek, 9.4 m., now merely a trickling rill but deep enough in colonial days to float boats of considerable size to the town of Piscataway (L). Somewhere along this creek, probably (R) toward the river, the Piscataway had their village when Governor Leonard Calvert visited the 'Emperor,' chief of the confederacy (*see The Indians*) and made arrangements that later saved Maryland from the Indian terror which menaced other colonies. Excavations along the creek have uncovered hundreds of Indian skeletons and artifacts as well as evidence of early trade with Europeans. Quarts of the tiny blue trade beads with brilliant glaze—possibly the work of the Venetians brought to Jamestown—have been recovered. The oddest relics are a few small thin discs stamped with the rose and thistle—tokens used for admission to the ceremony of the 'king's touch' during the reign of Charles I; after the dethronement of the sovereign, when these bits of metal were no longer useful to people hoping for relief from 'scrofula' through the touch of the king, some canny trader doubtless decided to offer them as money to the American aborigines.

Somewhere in the neighborhood of the creek, possibly as far north as the Fort Washington reservation, a remnant of the Susquehannock built a fort of primitive European type after their defeat by the Iroquois in 1673. Raids in the area on both sides of the Potomac, possibly by the Seneca, were blamed on the refugees and Virginia sent militia under Colonel John Washington to join Maryland forces under Thomas Truman and drive the Susquehannock away. Their fort was besieged for seven weeks before five Susquehannock leaders came out to negotiate under a flag of truce. Under conditions not clear from the records the Indian leaders were murdered; their followers fled to Virginia and in revenge carried out the raids that touched off Bacon's Rebellion.

At 9.9 *m.* is the junction with the asphalt-paved Clinton Road.

Left sharply on this road to PISCATAWAY, 0.6 *m.* (25 alt.,50 pop.), one of Maryland's many little towns whose importance disappeared when silt filled the creeks that had made them ports. At the time of the Revolution it had a tavern where travelers between the Northern Neck of Virginia and Annapolis were accustomed to stop—unless they had friends living in the neighborhood. In early days few members of the southern gentry stayed at the inns, which were usually crowded and primitive. Friends and acquaintances always welcomed such guests—both for their companionship and the news they might bring—it was a reciprocal courtesy. Young Philip Fithian, the New Jersey tutor hired by Councillor Robert Carter of Virginia as an experiment when he was unable to find an English tutor for his children, noted in his delightful diary of 1774 that he spent a night here on one of his vacation trips to his home. The tavern, he said, was kept by a woman with two bouncing daughters eagerly angling for husbands among the Scottish merchants of the port. Fithian particularly noted the beauty of this deep fertile little valley.

Most of the old houses here have been torn down or removed. The single impressive building, a brick structure with white portico, was built in recent years to house a gentlemen's sport club that did not prosper.

State 224 continues over hills beautiful in the spring with dogwood and Judas tree blossoms to the junction with a dirt road at 13.6 *m.*

Right on this 0.4 *m.* to the unpaved River Road. Near the junction but reached from the River Road is CHRIST CHURCH, a little brick structure built in 1698 in St.Johns Parish and rebuilt in 1831 after long neglect following disestablishment. There is little to indicate its age. This was one of the unfortunate colonial parishes assigned a rector whose interests were worldly rather than spiritual (*see Religion*). The parishioners revolted when the Reverend Mr.Tubbman took a second wife without the formality of divorcing the one he had left in England.

Near the church is a little frame parish hall that is becoming an influential community center for Accokeek and new Accokeek Acres, scattered on both sides of State 224. In it the people hear reports on the progress and troubles of their Tri-County Electrification Co-operative, give entertainments for the benefit of the volunteer fire company, and exchange reports on difficulties with the elaborate dialing system of the telephone exchange and on the joys of the newly acquired electric irons, stoves, iceboxes, and other devices that are changing the pattern of rural life.

The graveled road continues to HARD BARGAIN, 3.5 *m.* (*visited only by written permission from Mrs.Alice Ferguson, Accokeek*). On this farm, close to the river, is MOYAONE, the Indian village marked on Captain John Smith's map with a 'king's house.' The village was burned during the reprisals following the 1622 Indian uprising in Virginia and the surviving Piscataway established their next home along Piscataway Creek, where they were living when Calvert arrived. More extensive archeological and anthropological study with the co-operation of the Smithsonian Institution has been done here than anywhere else in Maryland. More than 1,000 skeletons and large numbers of artifacts have been removed. Studies indicate that the site was occupied for many hundreds of years by people of varying cultural levels, some of them dating back possibly to the early Christian era. A small museum holds the artifacts and some of the bones and a small stone structure protects and preserves an uncovered burial pit where skeletons have been left untouched.

The graveled road continues a short distance to BRYAN'S POINT, which affords a view of Mount Vernon, slightly to the south on the opposite shore.

ACCOKEEK, 14.7 *m.*, is marked chiefly by a store holding the post office. Accokeek's volunteer fire department is very busy in the seasons when farmers start brush fires to clear their fields. The volunteers were much disappointed when, after converting an old truck into a hose cart and equipping it with a piercing siren, the first fire in the vicinity broke out on the opposite side of the Potomac. Not even rowboats could reach it because the river bank is so choked with water chestnuts and sedge grass that marine mowing machines can barely keep a channel clear.

At 17.7 *m.* is the junction with State 226.

Right to MARSHALL HALL, 4.4 *m.*, an amusement park patronized largely by boat excursionists from Washington; it is on the Marshall estate granted to William Marshall in 1690. The old brick house, now containing many relics, is of much interest. In spite of changes and additions it clearly belongs to the days of great colonial prosperity. On one side is a large brick stable with arch openings.

In scattered POMONKEY, 19.1 *m.* (160 alt.,376 pop.), is the junction with State 227 which may be developed as a route to the new Potomac bridge.

At MASON SPRINGS, 22.4 *m.* (20 alt.,50 pop.), is the junction with asphalt-paved State 225, on the northern outskirts of the village.

1. Right on this to a dirt road, 0.9 *m.*; R. on this 1.7 *m.* to CHAPMAN'S LANDING, whose one-and-a-half-story house of brick and stone, built in two sections, dates from about 1670. It stands on a high bluff overlooking the river. The ferry here was much used in colonial days. State 225 continues to INDIAN HEAD RESERVATION, 2.9 *m.* (40 alt.,1,240 pop.), established in 1892 as a proving ground for naval ordnance. A powder manufacturing plant is also here.

2. Left from Mason Springs on paved State 225 3 *m.* to a steep dirt road (R) leading up to ARABY, whose house, visible from the highway on a high hill, seems bare and unattractive. The lower view is deceptive. The carefully restored structure, consisting of a two-story unit extended by a lower wing, has great charm. The wing holds a long recessed porch at ground level, from one end of which steps rise to the main entrance of the house. The woodwork is notable, particularly in the paneled study. It is believed that the second story was added sometime after the house was built about 1720. In the informal garden is the only blue rambler rose in Maryland. The history of the estate is obscure; George Washington in his diary referred to it as the home of the Widow Elbeck whose daughter became the wife of George Mason, master of Gunston Hall across the Potomac and author of the Virginia Bill of Rights.

The paved road continues past the graveled Port Tobacco Road, 7.4 *m.* (*see below*), to LA PLATA, 9.4 *m.* (*see Tour 9b*).

State 224 continues southward to a dirt road at 27 m.

Left here 0.9 m. to the SMALLWOOD FARM. Of the tiny house only its walls of elaborately bonded and glazed brick were standing late in 1939, but the place is being restored as a memorial to General William Smallwood who commanded Maryland troops in the Battle of Long Island and covered the retreat.

At 33.1 m. is the junction with State 6.

Right on this to a junction with State 426, 4.1 m.; R. here 2 m. to one of the many pieces of real estate owned by Washington.

State 6 continues southward over a peninsula that in pre-Revolutionary times was divided into estates, among them Nanjemoy Manor, granted to William Stone, who was appointed governor of the province by Lord Baltimore in 1648. Also here was the tract called Equality, birthplace of John Hanson (see above).

State 6 ends at RIVERSIDE, 11.2 m. (10 alt.,200 pop.), one of several small river resorts of the peninsula frequented by Washingtonians in summer.

At the point where State 224 ends—its junction with State 6—another section of State 6 turns eastward; L. here on State 6, now the main route. It cuts through the Doncaster State Forest, a conservation project that is being developed for recreational uses.

IRONSIDES, 36.1 m., is chiefly a crossroads store.

Right to DURHAM CHURCH, 1.4 m., a pleasing little building erected in 1732, rebuilt in 1791, and recently restored as a memorial to General Smallwood (see above). Both Smallwood and William Stone, the governor, are buried here.

At 43.8 m. on State 6 is the junction with a graveled road.

Left on this road to RETREAT, 0.2 m., the home of Daniel of St.Thomas Jenifer, member of the Continental Congress and a signer of the Constitution. The rambling clapboarded house on a hill overlooking Port Tobacco Creek has notably tall chimneys. When Maryland's dispute with the mother country began to grow bitter Jenifer was at first inclined toward reconciliation, but when the breach came, he promptly espoused the revolutionary cause. He was president of the Maryland Council of Safety from 1775 to 1776 and first president of the Maryland Senate, 1777–81. Jenifer also rendered valuable service in raising supplies for the Continental Army. Jenifer's unusual name, believed to have been used originally to avoid confusion with another Daniel Jenifer, has been repeated through the generations.

PORT TOBACCO, 45.5 m. (25 alt.,100 pop.), was the most important of the many Maryland ports on the Potomac ruined by the silting up of the creek at its landing. Made the seat of Charles County in 1658, it continued to be the center of the county government until La Plata developed around the new railroad down the peninsula. The Indians also considered it a desirable village site, as Captain John Smith's map shows; and by 1681 it had enough settlers to be the scene of the uprising of Kendall's followers. During the Revolution Dr.James Craik established a smallpox hospital here and vigorously inoculated the inhabitants of the town to keep the disease from spreading.

Though the town, scattered along the road in a deep valley, was the county seat until 1895, nothing remains of its public buildings, though two old houses (L) of unusual interest still stand close together. One is a story-and-a-half clapboarded structure with a gambrel roof forming a slight overhang; proof of its early construction is clearly apparent. Beside the low house is a large central-halled, three-story house built in 1767 and now restored. Its history is unknown but the few mantelpieces, other woodwork, and Sheffield doorknobs not removed by vandals indicate that it must have been the home of a man of consequence. Its most astonishing feature is a brick end formed by tall brick chimneys with a brick pent broken by closet windows, rising to the level of the third floor; at the basement level this pent is further broken by a huge entrance filled by a door with long strap hinges.

At 45.7 *m.* is the junction with a graveled road.

Left on this road then sharply R. up a hill to ROSE HILL (L), 0.6 *m.*, home of Dr.Gustavus Brown, one of the physicians who attended Washington in his last illness. The large two-story house on a high foundation with clapboarded walls in front and rear and with brick ends is considered one of the finest structures along the Potomac. A slightly projecting pedimented pavilion on the garden front gives grace to the otherwise simple façade. Chimneys rise high above the ends of the main house, which is connected to one small one-story brick flanker by a brick hyphen.

The central-halled house has good woodwork and the great boxwood hedges, laid out in elaborate designs, are notable. Dr.Brown's grave is near the house.

HABRE DE VENTURE (L), 1.5 *m.*, was the home of Thomas Stone, a signer of the Declaration of Independence. The house forms a crescent with a two-story clapboarded wing projecting backward at one end. The little brick central-halled unit erected in 1742 now has a screened porch on the garden front and a Victorian canopy over the small paved terrace on the approach front. On one side is a hyphen giving entrance to the cellar and connecting the main house with a small stone flanker that may have been an office in the past. At the other end of the main house, inside steps lead down into another hyphen with a huge fireplace having a retreating breast of the Dutch type. The hyphen serves as a passageway to the two-story wing, whose nogged brick walls are clapboarded. Opening from the hall of the main house is a drawing room of much elegance; the beautiful original paneling, now in the Baltimore Museum of Art, has been carefully duplicated. In this room hangs a portrait of Stone by one of the Peales. The Signer's grave is near the house.

LA GRANGE (R), 48 *m.*, was built in 1758 by Dr.James Craik (1730–1814), who was born and educated in Scotland and served as a physician in the Continental Army. After he helped to uncover the Conway Cabal against Washington, he became his close friend and later settled in Virginia. The house, considerably remodeled during restoration, is clapboarded with brick ends to accommodate double chimneys. The stairway is of solid walnut, and each room has its own fireplace with a great mantel.

The SITE OF THE MCDONOUGH INSTITUTE (L), 48.3 *m.*, is occupied by the Sacred Heart School, a Roman Catholic high school established in 1925. Maurice McDonough, a peddler in Charles County, eventually established a store in Pomfret near La Plata. A man of some education, he served as a newscarrier for the entire section, repeating news items of the day and reading newspapers to groups that gathered at his coming. Disturbed at the widespread illiteracy, McDonough left a bequest of $2,000 for a school to educate orphans and children of indigent parents 'always and forever during the existence of this fund.' Part of the gift was used for elementary education, but the trustees decided to let the interest accumulate in order to found a school of higher learning. In 1903 when the fund had increased to about $50,000, a high school was erected here. With the development of public schools and increased costs, the school was abandoned in 1923.

At 48.6 *m.* is the junction with State 3 in LA PLATA (*see Tour 9b*).

Tour 13

(York,Pa.)—Parkton—Hereford—Cockeysville—Towson—Baltimore; US 111. Pennsylvania Line to Baltimore, 31.5 *m.*

Concrete-paved on macadamized roadbed, two lanes wide.
Northern Central R.R. (Pennsylvania System) parallels route.
Accommodations limited; tourist homes and lunchstands in towns.

This route, the York Road, runs through the Piedmont, a country of steep green hillsides in the northern part of the State, but a gently rolling terrain in the vicinity of Baltimore. Opened in 1743 as the Susquehanna Road and turnpiked about 1807, this road became an outlet to Chesapeake Bay for fertile Pennsylvania and Maryland farmlands and thus contributed considerably to the growth of Baltimore. Trucks still travel it with vegetables, poultry, and milk as well as with factory products from the industrial centers.

Numerous large estates in this section are owned by Marylanders of British descent, who carry on the traditional pastimes and customs of English county families. Tournaments, fox hunting, cross-country racing, and cock fighting are the favorite sports of the landowners and the section is one of the few in which foxhounds still are blessed before they are taken out to hunt on Thanksgiving morning. The fox hunts are strictly formal affairs, with the riders in 'pink' and the language of the English hunting field very much in evidence. The Elkridge-Harford Hunt Club, to which most of the hunters belong, pays the cost of keeping land in the Worthington-Dulaney-Green Spring Valley section under panel fence, pays farmers whose chickens are eaten by foxes, and holds annually a 'farmers' day' when the landowners of the neighborhood are the guests of the hunt club. Cross-country races held in the valley in the spring and fall attract thousands of sportsmen from all sections of the East. The races draw the best of the country's steeplechasers. Billy Barton, a starter some years ago in the famous Grand National at Aintree in England, was trained in the valley. Although the older 'Baltimore countians' fight shy of flat racing, there are a few who breed and train thoroughbreds and race on the country's major tracks.

Tournaments are modeled after the jousting contests of knights. The rider is armed with a lance and with his mount at a run must spear rings which are hung from over-arms. The most skillful rider is permitted to designate the Queen of Love and Beauty of the carnival. Riders spend much time practicing for the contests and they will pay a big price for the type of horse most likely to carry them to victory. A thick-set, short-coupled horse with a 'lot of nerve' is the choice of most riders.

Cock fighting is carried on in a more or less clandestine manner, although most bird-owners make little secret of the fact that they have a pen of 'breeding birds.' There are several pits in the county, and 'mains,' in which the Baltimore countians compete with Pennsylvanians, are held several times in a year. Horse and pony shows are held at a dozen places in the valley during the spring, summer, and fall, and children are taught to ride at an early age. Many of the 'squires' of the neighborhood have taken up cattle breeding as a hobby and some of the finest herds in the East are to be found on farms in the valley.

In recent years there has been an influx of wealthy 'outsiders' but for the most part the residents bear names well known in Maryland before the Revolution. The section through which this route passes, or which is accessible from side roads, resembles the typical English countryside and the sound of the hunting horn and the baying of hounds enhances this illusion.

US III crosses the PENNSYLVANIA LINE, 0 *m.*, 18 miles south of York, Pa.

At 0.3 *m.* is the junction with macadamized State 409, the Freeland Road.

Right on this 2.2 *m.* to an asphalt-paved road; L. here 2.9 *m.* to EKLO (790 alt., 150 pop.). In the village are the GUNPOWDER BAPTIST CHURCH (L) and OLD UNION CEMETERY, donated in 1783 by Enoch Dorsey. Interment in the cemetery is free to any one who claims a vacant lot. Slaves, veterans of the Civil War, and people of no particular category lie side by side in unmarked graves or under crude rock or slate headstones.

At 6.9 *m.* is the junction with the asphalt-paved Middletown Road.

Right on this to macadamized Molesworth Road, 1.3 *m.*; L. to concrete-paved Pretty Boy Dam Road, 2.5 *m.*; L. to PRETTY BOY DAM AND RESERVOIR, 2.7 *m.*, the main reserve of Baltimore City's water supply. This reservoir holding nearly 10,000,000 gallons of water was completed in 1935. The water falls about 130 feet.

HEREFORD, 9.7 *m.* (671 alt., 250 pop.), is at the junction with concrete-paved Monkton Road.

Left on this road to MONKTON, 3 *m.* (320 alt., 100 pop.). Between Monkton and SHEPPERD'S CORNERS, 6.2 *m.*, is the northern boundary of My Lady's Manor, a tract the third Lord Baltimore bestowed in 1713 upon his fourth wife, Margaret. The 10,000 acres are now subdivided into farms and estates.

On MY LADY'S MANOR COURSE the most important race is the My Lady's Manor Point-to-Point (*2nd Sat. in April*), a four-mile test for hunters; it has been held here since 1910. Other important races on the annual card are the Right Royal Cup, three miles over timber, and the John Rush Street Memorial, a two-mile steeplechase over brush jumps.

At 3.3 *m.* on the Monkton road is an asphalt-paved road; R. 2.9 *m.* on this to ST. JAMES CHURCH (L), a T-shaped brick structure erected about 1750. The belfry is of much later construction. This was once within St. John's Parish, the mother church of which was at Joppa Town (*see Tour 1a*). A tilting tournament in which only women may ride is held annually on the grounds of this Protestant Episcopal Church (*1st Sat. in Aug.*).

On the HEREFORD FARM (R), 11 *m.*, is the GRAND NATIONAL STEEPLE-CHASE COURSE. In the Grand National, held annually (*3rd Sat. in April*), the finest-bred jumpers compete for a duplicate of the Astor Gold Cup, which must be won three successive years for permanent possession. Eighteen fences and two water jumps make the three-mile course one of the most hazardous in the United States.

At 11.1 *m.* is the junction with a narrow asphalt-paved road.

Right on this to HEREFORD (R), 0.3 *m.*, a three-part telescope house. The central two-story section was built in 1714 by John Merryman; the stone kitchen wing was added later by Nicholas Rogers Merryman. Among the outbuildings is a group of stone huts formerly housing slaves. Near by, enclosed by a stone wall, is the family burial ground.

OLD GORSUCH TAVERN (L), 12 *m.*, is a two-and-a-half-story T-shaped brick house whose north wing was built about 1810 by Captain Joshua Gorsuch. Beneath the tavern are brick arched chambers where, it is said, Captain Gorsuch stored the silks, spices, and other goods he brought from his voyages to the East. Across the road from the tavern is the three-and-a-half-story GORSUCH STONE BARN, where Edward Gorsuch, slave-trader son of Joshua, kept his 'merchandise.' In September 1851 two of the Negroes escaped and with the aid of the Underground Railway made their way to Lancaster County, Pennsylvania. In the attempt to retake them from their protectors, Edward Gorsuch was killed and his son Dickerson and several members of their party were wounded. The incident is known as the Christiana Massacre.

The HURST HOUSE (L), 14.1 *m.*, a large two-and-a-half-story stone building with dormers, was once the Milton Academy where John Wilkes Booth and his brother Edwin received their early education. The institution, usually called Lamb's School, was founded in 1847 by John E. and Eli M. Lamb and was conducted by them until 1877. In 1885 the academy was moved to Baltimore and continued there until 1899.

The entrance lane (L), 15.7 *m.*, bordered by tall Norway spruce, leads to the gray stone JESSOP CHURCH on a high hill. The main part of this Methodist church was erected in 1811, though the present Gothic-type vestibule, the steeply pitched dormered roof, and the belfry were added in 1887.

At 16.8 *m.*, in the hamlet of MARBLE HILL (350 alt.,10 pop.) is the junction with asphalt-paved Shawan Road.

Right on this to BONNIE BLINK (R), 0.4 *m.*, a Masonic home for the aged, established in 1932. The gray stone buildings, designed in Tudor Gothic style, overlook a farm of more than 300 acres, used chiefly for dairying.

On Shawan Road at 0.9 *m.* is macadamized Western Run Road; L. on this to HAYFIELDS (L), 1.2 *m.* (*visited by appointment with N.B.Merryman,Jr., Riderwood, Md.*). On a knoll is the two-and-a-half-story house built in 1808 by Colonel Nicholas Merryman Bosley of stone quarried on the property. When Lafayette visited Maryland in 1825, he presented Bosley with a silver tankard for having the best tilled farm in the State. This was the home of Lieutenant John Merryman for whom during the Civil War the Chief Justice of the United States issued a writ of *habeas corpus* that was ignored by the military authorities.

At 16.9 *m.* on US 111 is the junction with Ashland Road.

Left on this 5.8 *m.* to Madonna Road in JACKSONVILLE (600 alt.,20 pop.); L. here 4.8 *m.* to the ELKRIDGE HARFORD HUNT CLUB (L), belonging to a group formed in 1931 by a merger of the Elkridge Hounds and the Harford Hunt Club. The stone clubhouse, kennels, and stables were formerly owned by the Harford Hunt which was organized in 1913. The Elkridge Hounds was formed in 1878 as the Elkridge Kennels with headquarters at Elkridge Landing. In the early days the huntsmen-members in their red coats, white breeches, and black boots, and the ladies riding sidesaddle were a familiar Sunday-morning sight as they rode from the Washington Monument in Baltimore toward the open country.

COCKEYSVILLE, 17.8 *m.* (264 alt.,1,515 pop.), the trade center of a large farming area, is noted chiefly for the marble obtained from quarries near by. At the south end of the Pennsylvania Railroad underpass is the SHERWOOD EPISCOPAL CHURCH (L), a stone building erected in 1830. The church was named for the English home of the Cockey family, one of whose members donated the land and money for it. In 1876 the building was enlarged and the belfry added.

Right from Cockeysville 0.6 *m.* on a macadamized road to asphalt-paved Beaver Dam Road; R. on Beaver Dam Road 0.1 *m.* to BEAVER DAM PARK (L). In the park are the BEAVER DAM QUARRIES now filled with water (*swimming, small fee*). A high grade marble quarried here for more than a century was used in the construction of the Washington Monument and the State, War and Navy Buildings in Washington, St.Patricks Cathedral in New York, the Drexel Bank in Philadelphia, and the Washington Monument in Baltimore.

On Beaver Dam Road at 1.1 *m.* is the GUNPOWDER MEETING HOUSE (R), a long, barnlike, two-and-a-half-story, stone building erected in 1773. It contains some of the original high, uncomfortable benches. Quakers hold meetings here several times a year.

TEXAS, 19.1 *m.* (300 alt.,1,009 pop.), was for many years supported by its lime kilns and quarries. These sites, now filled with water, serve as swimming pools for the people of the vicinity. One quarry was reopened in 1930. There are daily horse races at the TIMONIUM FAIR GROUNDS (R), 20.2 *m.*, during the annual fair (*beginning Labor Day*) held by the Maryland State Fair and Agricultural Society of Baltimore County.

In LUTHERVILLE, 22.4 *m.* (325 alt.,200 pop.), are several examples of the 'Carpenter's Gothic' style of architecture popular in the 1870's. The village (R) developed around the MARYLAND COLLEGE FOR WOMEN, chartered in 1853 through the efforts of two Lutheran clergymen, J.G. Norris and D.B.Kurtz. First called Lutherville Female Seminary, it was later named the Maryland College for Young Ladies; the buildings, burned in 1911, have been replaced by structures that shelter 200 students.

Right from Lutherville on Seminary Avenue 2.7 *m.* to concrete-paved Mays Chapel Road; R. on this 0.9 *m.* to FIVE FARMS GOLF COURSE, laid out by Willie Dunn for the Baltimore Country Club. The National Open and the National Amateur Championship tournaments were held here in 1928 and 1929, respectively.

TOWSON, 23.9 *m.* (465 alt.,2,074 pop.), seat of Baltimore County since 1854, was founded in 1750 by Ezekiel Towson. A local firm manufactures electrically operated portable tools for a world market.

The future site of Goucher College (*see Baltimore*), east of town on Joppa Road, is a tract of more than 300 acres purchased in 1935. On the land is the old stone EPSOM CHAPEL, erected in 1839, with material taken from an abandoned Federal arsenal near by. This chapel, now the head-quarters of a Boy Scout troop, has been used by every Protestant denomination in the town.

TRINITY PROTESTANT EPISCOPAL CHURCH, on Allegany Ave. between Washington and Baltimore Avenues, is a stone structure built in 1858 on Gothic designs. It has had only three rectors. The BALTIMORE COUNTY COURTHOUSE, Pennsylvania Avenue, completed in 1855, is of gray granite with a Doric entrance portico.

KELSO HOME, 600 West Chesapeake Avenue, a Methodist orphanage for girls, was founded in 1873 by Thomas Kelso, a Baltimore merchant who superintended its affairs until his death in 1878. Only girls between the ages of four and eleven are admitted. The children attend the public schools.

In Towson are junctions with concrete-paved Dulaney Valley Road (*see Tour 1B*) and Joppa Road (*see Tour 1A*).

The MARYLAND STATE TEACHERS' COLLEGE (R), on York Road near the southern limits of town, is a group of red brick buildings of Tudor Gothic design. Established in 1866, the school was in Baltimore until 1915.

Left about two blocks on Burke Avenue in the southern outskirts of Towson to EUDOWOOD SANATORIUM (L) for tuberculous patients, established in Baltimore City in 1896 by Mrs.Charles A. Carroll and moved to Towson in 1899. About 200 patients can be cared for in the three-story red-brick central building and the cottages. It is supported by voluntary contributions and by Baltimore City, Baltimore County, and the State.

At 24.7 *m*. is the junction with a dirt road.

Right on this to the SHEPPARD-PRATT HOSPITAL (R), 1 *m*., on a beautifully land-scaped tract. This institution for the treatment of mental and nervous disorders was opened in 1891 and named the Sheppard Asylum for its founder, Moses Sheppard. In 1898 the institution received the residuary estate of Enoch Pratt.

At 25 *m*. on US 111 is the junction with concrete-paved Stevenson Lane.
ST.VINCENT'S ORPHANAGE (R), 25.6 *m*., a large four-story red-brick building, was erected in 1909 on part of the former McCabe Farm. This institution, founded in Baltimore in 1840 by Father J.W.Gildea for boys between the ages of six and fifteen, was under the supervision of the Christian Brothers until 1899. Since then it has been managed by the Sisters of Mercy.

BALTIMORE, 31.5 *m*. (20 alt.,804,874 pop.) (*see Baltimore*).

Points of Interest: Fort McHenry, Shot Tower, Flag House, Washington Monument, Johns Hopkins University, Roman Catholic Cathedral, Druid Hill Park, and others.

Baltimore is at junctions with US 1 (*see Tour 1*), US 40 (*see Tour 2*), State 26 (*see Tour 2B*), US 140 (*see Tour 14*), State 2 (*see Tour 8*), and State 3 (*see Tour 9*).

Tour 14

Baltimore—Reisterstown—Westminster—(Gettysburg,Pa.); US 140. Baltimore to Pennsylvania Line, 41.9 *m.*

Western Maryland R.R. parallels the route.
Macadamized and concrete-paved roadbed, four lanes wide between Baltimore and Reisterstown, two lanes elsewhere.
All types of accommodations.

US 140, the most direct route between Baltimore and Gettysburg, Pennsylvania, traverses a prosperous farming section where roadside stands in season display the products of the area. Vegetables, corn, and wheat are grown south of Reisterstown, north of it is the State's butter and egg basket.

Between Baltimore and Reisterstown US 140 follows the old Patapsco Road, a pack-horse trail in use by 1741. In 1802 when the State legislature failed to provide money to pave the road, it was purchased by a turnpike company. As the Reisterstown turnpike, the road developed into an important artery between Baltimore and the back country.

In BALTIMORE, 0 *m.* (20 alt.,804,874 pop.) (*see Baltimore*), US 140 follows Reisterstown Road to Park Circle, 3.1 *m.*, and a junction with Park Heights Ave. (State 129), an alternate route to Reisterstown.

Right on Park Heights Ave., which is 4 miles longer than US 140 but avoids heavy traffic and affords views of well-kept houses, beautifully landscaped estates, horse-breeding and training stables, country clubs, and prosperous farms.

The SUBURBAN CLUB OF BALTIMORE COUNTY (L), 8.6 *m.*, has a rambling two-and-a-half-story shingled clubhouse, tennis courts, and an 18-hole golf course.

At 9.2 *m.* is the junction with Old Court Road (*see Tour 1A*) and the entrance (L) to Druid Ridge Cemetery (*see below*).

The headquarters of the Humane Society of Baltimore County, 10.1 *m.*, is in a group of stone buildings (R) resembling those of an English farmstead and including a hospital and boarding accommodations for animals.

ECCLESTON, 11 *m.* (380 alt.), has a few dilapidated Negro tenant houses.

At 11.4 *m.* is the junction with Green Spring Valley Road (State 130).

Right on this 1.3 *m.* to (L) the MARYLAND POLO CLUB (*adm. to games*, 40¢), with a modest clubhouse. The playing field ranks with the best in the country but there are no stables; spectators watch the games from parked cars.

At 13.6 *m.* is the junction with Caves Road.

Left here 0.5 *m.* to the STEMMER HOUSE (L), a two-and-a-half-story brick structure with dormers, huge chimneys, and a one-and-a-half-story wing. It was built in 1805 near Stemmers Run, 16 miles away and moved here recently.

THE CAVES (L), 13.8 *m.*, was the home of Charles Carroll (1723–83), the Barrister, framer of Maryland's Declaration of Rights and outstanding citizen during the Revolutionary period, who lived here until 1754, when Mount Clare in Baltimore was completed. This tract, Bear Run, was patented in 1710. Part of the manor house built in 1730 has been incorporated in the present stuccoed structure; one or two old outbuildings still stand.

At 16.9 *m.* the route turns L. on Worthington Avenue, which at 17.1 *m.* crosses Tufton Avenue; R. 0.8 *m.* on Tufton Avenue to concrete-paved Belmont Road, and L. 0.3 *m.* on it to BELMONT (R), whose two-and-a-half-story white brick house with dormers is one of the nine Worthington houses scattered through the valley. This house, built about 1780, has large flush end chimneys, a beautiful classic portico (probably an early addition), and a doorway with fan and side lights. One-story wings have been added and the two-story slave quarters (R) are now joined to the house. At 0.5 *m.* on Belmont Road (L) Alfred Gwynne Vanderbilt's SAGAMORE FARMS (*for adm. apply at office*), one of the best equipped horse-breeding and training stables in the country. The oval barn has about 75 box stalls and is connected with a quarter-mile indoor tanbark track for exercise and training. There is also a three-quarter-mile outdoor track.

At 1 *m.* on Tufton Avenue is (R) the western boundary of the MARYLAND HUNT CUP COURSE (*steeplechase 4th Sat. in April*). The four-mile course lies on both sides of the road. The large crowds view the race from the north slope.

On Worthington Avenue at 18.3 *m.* is the winding maple-lined lane (R) of MONT-MORENCI, whose two-and-a-half-story white stone and stucco house has dormers and paired chimneys. The interior is symmetrically arranged with a broad central hallway from which rises a winding staircase. The house was built about 1760 by Samuel Worthington. At the rear the grounds slope abruptly to an Italian garden.

West of Montmorenci Worthington Avenue becomes Butler Road. At 19.9 *m.* is the junction with macadamized Waugh Avenue; R. here 0.3 *m.* to EMORY GROVE, a Methodist camp meeting ground since the end of the eighteenth century. The hotel and cottages, equipped with bathrooms and electricity, replaced tents that from 1870 annually accommodated thousands on two-week pilgrimages.

On Butler Road is GLYNDON, 20.5 *m.* (695 alt.,490 pop.), a quiet village with plain houses on lawns dotted with old maples, oaks, and pines.

At 21.5 *m.* is the junction with State 30 in REISTERSTOWN (*see below*).

On US 140 at 9 *m.* is PIKESVILLE (516 alt.,3,570 pop.), settled before the Revolution but not named until after the War of 1812. Dr. James Smith, who owned much land in this vicinity, named the village for his friend, Brigadier General Pike of New Jersey, who had been killed during the siege and burning of York, Canada.

Near the southern end of the town among oaks are the gray stone buildings of the PIKESVILLE ARMORY (L), headquarters of the 110th Field Artillery of the Maryland National Guard. Indoor polo is played in the tanbark floored building. The excellent PISTOL RANGE (*open 8:45 to 10:30 p.m. Mon., Tues., Thurs.; 3 to 6 and 8 to 10 p.m. Fri. and Sat.; 2 to 6 p.m. Sun.; pistol rental 10¢, ammunition at cost*) is behind the armory in a soundproof building; it contains 15 shooting booths and electrically operated targets.

Near the center of town is the former MARYLAND LINE CONFEDERATE SOLDIERS' HOME (R) in a group of gray brick buildings erected by the Federal Government in 1819 as a United States Arsenal. The veterans who had occupied this site since 1888 were removed to private homes in 1932 and these buildings turned over to the county.

Pikesville is at the junction with Old Court Road (*see Tour 1A*).

In DRUID RIDGE CEMETERY (R), 9.4 *m.*, is the GRAVE OF MARY WASHINGTON, wife of Colonel L. W. Washington (1825–71), a great-grandnephew of George Washington. Colonel Washington was held as a hostage at Harpers Ferry in 1859 by John Brown. QUEEN VICTORIA MONUMENT, erected here in 1901 by the St. George's Society of Baltimore, is said to be the only monument to England's famous queen in the United States.

A private lane (R), 10.4 *m.*, leads to GREY ROCK, a large gray stone house built about 1700 and considerably remodeled in 1890. It was the birthplace of John Eager Howard (1752–1827), who served with distinction throughout the Revolution. Following Cowpens, where seven British officers surrendered their swords to him, he was awarded a Congressional medal. Colonel Howard served as governor of Maryland for three consecutive one-year terms, 1788–91 and from 1796 to 1803 was United States Senator from Maryland.

Directly opposite Grey Rock Lane is the junction with Mt. Wilson Lane.

Left on this road, which is lined with maples and honeysuckle, to MT. WILSON SANATORIUM, 1.5 *m.*, a branch of the State tuberculosis sanatorium at Sabillasville (*see Tour 15*). It was opened in 1884 as a summer resort for underprivileged children of Baltimore with part of a million-dollar trust fund left by Thomas Wilson, Quaker merchant of Baltimore.

At 10.6 *m.* is the junction with macadamized Stone Chapel Road.

Right on this 0.1 *m.* to OLD STONE CHAPEL (L), a beautifully proportioned Classic Revival structure with a Doric portico. This gray and brown stuccoed church was built in 1862 with the stones of an earlier chapel (1785). Robert Strawbridge, one of the founders of Methodism in America, preached in the first church on this site. The desk of Bishop Asbury is in custody of the vestry.

At 10.9 *m.* is the junction with macadamized McDonogh Lane and Lyons Mill Road.

1. Left on McDonogh Lane 1.5 *m.* to MCDONOGH SCHOOL FOR BOYS (1873), endowed by John McDonogh of Baltimore in 1850. This preparatory school owns more than 800 acres of orchards and arable land, where students work an hour a day. Established for 'poor, worthy boys,' McDonogh is now open to those who can pay. Student riders compete in an annual horse show held here in May.

2. Right 0.4 *m.* on Lyons Mill Road (Handboard Lane) to TRENTHAM (L), a square two-and-a-half-story stuccoed house with a hip roof, erected in 1860. Trentham stands on the site of a house built in 1746 by the Reverend Thomas Cradock (1718–70), who named his home for the Free School of Trentham in Staffordshire, England, where he had taught until 1743. In 1747 he opened a school here that was attended by boys who later achieved prominence. Between the house and the road is an octagonal bathhouse, built about 1747 and equipped with two mahogany bath tubs. Most of the Reverend Cradock's books are still in the library at Trentham.

The old TEN MILE HOUSE (L), 11.2 *m.*, a two-and-a-half-story stone tavern with a low gable roof and wide windows, was built about 1810 on land granted to the Reverend Thomas Cradock. The foundations are thick; the original staircases, fireplaces, and mantels are still in place. This was the first home of the Green Spring Valley Hunt Club and here Jake Kilrain had several workouts while training for his fight with John L. Sullivan in 1889.

At 11.5 *m.* is the junction with the macadamized Green Spring Valley Road.

Right on this to the GREEN SPRING VALLEY HUNT CLUB (L), 0.2 *m.*, organized in 1892 as the Green Spring Valley Hounds. Green Spring Valley Road continues to a junction with State 129 3 *m.* (*see above*).

The GARRISON FOREST SCHOOL (R), 12 *m.*, founded in 1910, is a private day and boarding school for girls.

At 12.5 *m.* is the junction with St. Thomas Lane.

Right on this macadamized road 0.7 *m.* to GARRISON FOREST PROTESTANT EPISCO-PAL CHURCH (L), a red-brick, cruciform building with a high-pitched roof and a cupola-belfry. The church built in 1744 forms the present nave, but has been greatly changed. After the rector of the parent church, St. Paul's in Baltimore, died in 1745 this parish took the name of St. Thomas and the Reverend Thomas Cradock became its first pastor.

At 12.6 *m.* is the junction with Painter's Mill Road.

Left on this macadamized road 0.3 *m.* to PAINTER'S MILL (L), an ivy-covered two-and-a-half-story brick building with two dormers. ULM HOUSE (R) is a two-story structure with a gable roof and a wing. It and the mill were erected by Samuel Owings in 1765. The name Ulm, derived from the Upper, Lower, and Middle Mills owned by Owings, was long the trade-mark of the flour he milled.

At 12.8 *m.* is the junction with a concrete-paved road.

Right on this road 0.2 *m.* to the long stone structure of the ROSEWOOD STATE TRAINING SCHOOL (*stop at office for permission to visit*), founded in 1888 and housing more than 1,000 feeble-minded inmates.

At 12.9 *m.* is the junction with a macadamized road.

Right on this to the GWYNNBROOK STATE GAME FARM (R), 2.1 *m.* (*stop at office for permission to visit*), owned and operated by the State for the propagation of deer, wild ducks, geese, pheasant, and quail. Quail eggs are hatched in electric incubators.

HANNAH MORE ACADEMY (R), 16.6 *m.*, is a Protestant Episcopal school for girls. The school opened here in 1832 by Mrs. Hugh Neilson was mod-eled after the schools for the poor set up throughout England by Hannah More (1745–1833). In 1873 it became a diocesan school. The oldest struc-ture on the campus, St. Michael's Chapel, was built in 1854.

In REISTERSTOWN, 18 *m.* (735 alt.,1,635 pop.), old stone houses are set close to the road, while more modern bungalows and ordinary two-story frame houses are hidden behind clumps of young maples. When John Reister, a German immigrant, acquired 20 acres of land just north of Cockey's Mill Road from the Calvert family in 1758, he named the tract Reister's Desire. The settlement that developed was largely made up of Reister's children and their families. In 1768 a near-by piece of land was purchased by Daniel Bower, also of German descent, whose children joined those of John Reister.

With the completion of the Reisterstown Road from Baltimore to Gettysburg and Hanover, this became a regular stopping-off place for passengers. Among the inns established here to care for the traffic was Forney Tavern, noted for the excellence of its liquors and food and pa-tronized by 'persons of wealth and fashion.' The Bower Inn, a commodious log house built about 1770, had rooms named for prominent towns.

BECKLEY'S BLACKSMITH SHOP and the POLLY REISTER HOUSE, SW. corner of Main St. and Cockey's Mill Road is a two-and-a-half-story brick house with a one-story wing, erected in 1779. Originally the house and the blacksmith shop were separated by a lane. The land on which the house was built was given by John Reister to his son-in-law John Beckley, the village blacksmith.

Directly across Main St. is the YELLOW TAVERN (R) built about 1804 by Jacob Medairy. It was also called the Spite House because Medairy built it to block the new road through the town. His efforts were of no avail for the roadmakers went around the house, causing the bend in the road at this point.

On Cockey's Mill Road (which follows the Indian trail from Patapsco Falls) two blocks L. off Main St. is the old LUTHERAN CEMETERY (L) surrounded by a brick wall. It developed around a log cabin used in 1765 for Lutheran services.

By the cemetery is the old FRANKLIN ACADEMY (L), now a garage. This school was established in 1820 on ground deeded by John Reister in 1773. In 1897 it became the first public high school in Baltimore County. It is said that when Edgar Allan Poe was eking out a livelihood in Baltimore, he answered Franklin Academy's advertisements in the *Baltimore Patriot* and *Federal Gazette* for a principal but was rejected.

Opposite the Post Office on Main St. is CHATSWORTH (L), a two-story stuccoed house built about 1770 by Colonel Daniel Bower, son of John Bauer (*see above*). Under each of the three front rooms is a cellar; to the rear are the smokehouse and springhouse, the latter built over a spring long used by Indians.

In Reisterstown is the junction with the Butler Road alternate (*see above*).

Right from Reisterstown on State 30 to a macadamized road, 2.2 *m.*; L. here 0.7 *m.* to a grove of oaks and pines surrounding the ANDERSON CHAPEL (R), a small, plain rectangular structure erected in 1854 for Colonel Franklin Anderson, one of the owners of Montrose (*see below*).

At 1.1 *m.* on the macadamized road is (L) the MONTROSE SCHOOL FOR GIRLS, a State training school for delinquent girls under 18. The stone buildings form a quadrangle around attractive lawns and gardens. Its own farm provides much of the produce used by the school. The institution, chartered in 1831 as the Maryland House of Refuge for boys and girls, in 1866 was incorporated as the Industrial School for Girls and was put entirely in charge of women in 1898. In 1918 the State purchased this estate for the school to which it then gave its present name.

On the eastern end of the campus is MONTROSE, now an administration building. The two-and-a-half-story stone structure with a French roof, dormers, and a belvedere is covered with ivy and flanked by enormous cedars. The estate was named for the Marquis of Montrose, enemy of religious intolerance and champion of human rights. Though the tradition that this was once the home of Betsy Patterson Bonaparte seems to have no factual support, this setting was used in 1936 for the motion picture *Hearts Divided*, a story of Betsy Patterson's romance with Jerome Bonaparte. It is known, however, that the estate was acquired by William Patterson, father of Betsy; that in 1830 he deeded it to her son, Jerome; that the latter sold it to Colonel Franklin Anderson; and that Betsy frequently visited Colonel Anderson's wife here. The property was subsequently owned by Betsy's grandson Joseph Bonaparte, who was Secretary of the Navy in the cabinet of Theodore Roosevelt.

State 30 continues through cornfields and past prosperous-looking dairy farms. Weeping willows grow in the well-kept yards around rambling, white-clapboarded farm houses. Small apple orchards are here and there on the hillsides; and between the farms, trees stand in clusters that contrast with the rows of trees along the boundary lines farther west in Carroll County.

HAMPSTEAD, 10.2 *m.* (913 alt.,905 pop.), laid out in 1786, is a station on the Western Maryland Railroad. During the day the streets seem deserted, for many of the inhabitants are skilled mechanics working in Westminster, Reisterstown, or Baltimore factories, while others cultivate surrounding lands. The townsite was part of the tract, Spring Garden, patented to Dutton Lane in 1748. The first settlers were predominantly English but were joined before the end of the eighteenth century by Germans from Pennsylvania.

Near the center of the town is the HAMPSTEAD JAIL (L), resembling a one-car garage. Except for offering occasional hospitality to unfortunate itinerants, this building has been idle for many years.

Almost opposite the jail is the OLD HAMPSTEAD STORE (R), a plain, weatherboarded, two-story building now housing a restaurant and pool parlor. It was originally a feed and grain store and is possibly more than a century-and-a-half old. Back from the road where the building forms an ell are an old pump and watering trough still in use. The pump, housed in a massive wooden jacket hollowed out of a single log, is one of many such pumps on the sites of former taverns between here and the Pennsylvania Line. Some are weather-beaten and cracked, and others neatly painted, often with red, white, and blue stripes.

Despite the improved roads MANCHESTER, 13.8 *m.* (975 alt.,643 pop.), makes no bid for revenue from tourists. Steps and porches of the houses extend to the sidewalk line, brick walks are broken by roots of old trees, and nearly every house has its log pump.

Manchester is near the site of one of the Susquehannock's five towns, Cepowig, at the headwaters of the Gunpowder River. Despite the aid of the Maryland authorities with whom the Susquehannock were on friendly terms, the tribe lost in a long and bitter war with the Seneca and in 1675 was forced to seek refuge in the South. The massacre of its chiefs by Major Truman and Colonel John Washington in that year (*see the Indians*), turned its depredations into Virginia—the principal cause of Bacon's Rebellion. The surviving Susquehannocks took refuge near the southern boundary of Virginia and later migrated northward. One band settled within a mile of Manchester, in the neighborhood of their old town of Cepowig. About 1750–51 they departed again, leaving only a chief named Macanoppy and his wife.

At 15.3 *m.* on State 30 is the junction with State 86.

Right 4 *m.* on this concrete-paved road to LINEBORO, a trading point for industrious Pennsylvania-Dutch farmers. Lazarus Church, established in 1853, is occupied alternately by Lutheran and Reformed congregations. Besides being a dairy center Lineboro has had a large canning factory since 1927.

State 86 crosses the Pennsylvania Line, 4 *m.*, at a point about seven miles southeast of Hanover, Pennsylvania.

In MELROSE, 16.5 *m.* on State 30, a collection of small drab houses with recessed porches, bootleg coal trucks are often parked beside the road. From the top of the hill a panorama permits a complete review of the last few miles of this unruffled, thrifty, satisfied section of Maryland.

State 30 crosses the Pennsylvania Line, 18.5 *m.*, at a point about six miles south of Hanover, Pennsylvania.

At 20.9 *m.* on US 140 is the junction with a narrow dirt road.

Left on this to THE ELMS (L), 0.2 *m.*, a two-and-a-half-story whitewashed brick building with dormers and a two-story wing. The land on which the house was built about 1776 is part of White Oaks or Beall's Venture, a gift from one of the Lords Baltimore.

WESTMINSTER, 30 *m.* (744 alt.,4,518 pop.), the seat of Carroll County, is a prosperous, conservative community of neat homes where neither affluence nor poverty are apparent and where the village banker may live next door to the carpenter or the local lawyer may have the barber for a neighbor. The inhabitants are chiefly of Scotch, Irish, English, and German descent, with a few Negroes. Even the students of the college here come from homes where there is little money to be expended on college-boy whoopee.

In 1764 the town was named for its founder, William Winchester, but was renamed shortly after the beginning of the Revolution. Since its incorporation in 1837 it has spread over parts of additional land patents, including Kelly's Range, Pigman's Addition, and Neighborly Kindness. When the railroad came through it in 1861, Westminster had 2,500 inhabitants, 40 stores, 3 banks, and several factories and warehouses; and it was an important Union supply depot during the Gettysburg campaign. With the converging of Confederate and Union forces preceding the battle in 1863, frequent clashes between the two forces occurred throughout this area. More than a hundred men of the 1st Delaware Cavalry were dispersed here by Confederate General J.E.B.Stuart's cavalry on June 29, 1863. Of the 67 Union men lost, several were buried here.

MAIN COURT INN, SW. corner of Main St. and Court St., built in Revolutionary times, is now occupied by shops and apartments. It is a two-story, L-shaped structure with dormers. The rear courtyard was the transfer point for stagecoach passengers, horses, and baggage. Beneath the building are cells in which slaves were confined while awaiting sale.

On Main St., near Court St., is GOD'S WELL, now covered, which earned its name in 1806 when this section of the State suffered under a severe and protracted drought. The few fortunate owners of wells that had not gone dry locked their pumps and refused water to travelers as well as to their neighbors. Only the Misses Lydia and Betsy Winchester, aged daughters of the town's founder, threw open their gate and placed a sign on their well, 'Free Admittance to All. Water Belongs to God.' Travelers pushing westward paused to drink, as did many of the town's residents. Eventually, the story is, all wells in town except 'God's Well' went dry. The old-fashioned, moss-covered bucket was never empty, the story relates, until the drought ended.

On Court St. one block (R) from Main St. is the CARROLL COUNTY COURTHOUSE (1836), a dignified Classic Revival building with a two-story portico.

Diagonally across from the courthouse is the CHURCH OF THE ASCENSION (1844), a rectangular stone building with large arched windows. Marked by an urn here is the SITE OF THE OLD UNION MEETING HOUSE, erected in 1755 to replace a log church used by several denominations. Here Lorenzo Dow (1777-1834), the eccentric Methodist evangelist, is said to have worked his miracles of conversion with the aid of lusty and well-timed trumpet blasts delivered by assistants in near-by tree tops.

On the lawn of the WESTMINSTER POST OFFICE (R), Main St. and Longwell Ave., is a marker reciting that Carroll County was the first county in the United States to have complete rural free delivery service. Inaugurated on December 20, 1899, it operated with four two-horse wagons, each carrying a driver and a mail clerk. They provided a complete post office service over four routes.

WESTERN MARYLAND COLLEGE (coeducational), N.Main St., has about 600 students under the supervision of the Methodist Church. Founded as a private academy in 1860, it was reorganized as a college in 1866. About 20 buildings stand on a hilly wooded campus in the northwestern outskirts of town. Western Maryland College was the first school in the State to employ trained athletic instructors and to build a gymnasium. In a modern three-story building on the campus is the WESTMINSTER THEOLOGICAL SEMINARY, founded in 1882. It is not a part of the college.

In Westminster are junctions with State 32 (*see Tour 15*), State 31 (*see Tour 15*), and State 27 (*see Tour 2A*).

At 37.1 *m.* is the junction with a dirt road.

> Right 0.1 *m.* on this to SHRIVER MILL, erected in 1796 to replace an earlier mill. It has been in continuous operation since it was built and is still controlled by descendants of the first owners.

UNION MILLS, 37.4 *m.* (700 alt.,225 pop.), developed at about the time of the Revolution around a flour mill built by Adam and Daniel Shriver.

US 140 crosses the PENNSYLVANIA LINE, 41.9 *m.*, beside a Mason-Dixon marker at a point 12.5 miles southeast of Gettysburg,Pa.

Tour 15

(Gettysburg,Pa.)—Frederick—(Leesburg,Va.); US 15. Pennsylvania Line to Virginia Line, 41.6 *m.*

Macadamized or concrete-paved roadbed, two lanes wide.
Baltimore & Ohio R.R. roughly parallels route.
Ample accommodations.

This route follows the eastern slope of the Blue Ridge Mountains through the fertile wheat farms and apple orchards of the Monocacy Valley. Many small streams along the route are stocked with trout and black bass.

US 15 crosses the PENNSYLVANIA LINE, 0 *m.*, about nine miles southwest of Gettysburg,Pa.

EMMITSBURG, 1.7 *m.* (400 alt.,1,235 pop.), was not settled till 1834, 25 years after the Sisters of Charity founded their order and established St.Joseph's School near here (*see below*). Some of the inhabitants are employed in St.Joseph's, others in Mount St.Mary's College, and some in a garment factory.

> Left from Emmitsburg on State 32 to a steel bridge, 5.3 *m.*, over the Monocacy. North of this spot Dr.James Mitchell of Mount St.Mary's College in 1895 discovered

several dinosaur tracks in sandstone. Some slabs are at the college and others in the Maryland Academy of Sciences at Baltimore.

TANEYTOWN, 8.7 *m.* (493 alt.,938 pop.), was founded in 1740 by Frederick Taney. Muskets were made here during the Revolutionary War and there is evidence that Eli Bentley produced some of his noted clocks here in the early nineteenth century. The principal products now are men's clothing and rubber shoes.

In the CARROLL COUNTY FAIRGROUNDS (R), 10.1 *m.*, an annual county fair is held (*Aug.*).

BIG PIPE CREEK PARK (R), 11.2 *m.*, is an amusement and picnic ground with a swimming pool.

WESTMINSTER, 20.3 *m.* (774 alt.,4,463 pop.) (*see Tour* 14), is at the junction with US 140 (*see Tour* 14).

On US 15, at 2.3 *m.*, is ST.JOSEPH'S COLLEGE (L), an accredited college for women founded in 1809 as a Roman Catholic girls' boarding school by Elizabeth Bayley Seton (1774–1821), who had opened a small school for girls on the grounds of St.Mary's Seminary in Baltimore the year before. Mrs.Seton, a widow with five children and a convert to Catholicism, also founded the Sisters of Charity at Emmitsburg and was named Mother Superior of the order by Bishop John Carroll. James Cardinal Gibbons in 1880 introduced her Cause to the Holy See, which was accepted, thereby making her Venerable. The log cabin where she lived and taught is still preserved. Mother Seton and her nephew James Roosevelt Bayley, Archbishop of Baltimore from 1872 to 1877, are buried in a chapel on the campus.

MOUNT ST.MARY'S COLLEGE (R), 4 *m.*, the second oldest Roman Catholic college in the country, was founded in 1808 by Father Dubois, later Bishop of New York. Its stone buildings of modified Gothic design at the foot of Catoctin Mountain blend with the background. The seminary, with an enrollment of 400 pupils, is an accredited college and confers degrees in several branches of the arts and sciences. The first American Cardinal, Monsignor John McClosky, studied here as a youth, as did Chief Justice Edward D. White (1845–1921).

At 4 *m.* is the junction with macadamized State 76.

Left on State 76 to MOTTERS, 2.1 *m.*; L. on a dirt road 0.4 *m.* to CLAIRVAUX, an old stone dwelling, believed to have been built by monks forced to flee from Clair Vaux, France, during the French Revolution. For many years it was the home of Paul Winchester (1851–1932), writer and journalist.

THURMONT, 9.6 *m.* (519 alt.,1,185 pop.), whose first settler was Jacob Weller in 1751, was earlier named Mechanicstown, a name not justified until 1811. West on Main Street, which follows an old Indian trail, is the Watson House, where in 1825 the first friction matches in the United States were made.

1. Right from Thurmont on State 81 through SABILLASVILLE, 6.6 *m.* (1,134 alt.,250 pop.), to a macadamized road, 7.7 *m.*; R. on this 0.5 *m.* to the STATE SANATORIUM, a group of red brick buildings on a 200-acre tract, that accommodates 500 tubercular patients.

BLUE RIDGE SUMMIT, 8 *m.* (1,407 alt.,500 pop.), a mountain summer resort lying partly in Maryland and partly in Pennsylvania, has diplomats among its summer visitors. Left from Blue Ridge Summit on macadamized State 92, now the main side route to CAMP RITCHIE, 9.2 *m.* (1,500 alt.), the Maryland National Guard's camp named for Governor Albert C. Ritchie (1876–1936).

At 10.1 *m.* is the junction with a macadamized road; R. here 0.9 *m.* to PEN MAR (1,245 alt.,125 pop.), a mountain resort and amusement park straddling the Maryland-Pennsylvania line. The Appalachian Trail crosses the highway here.

Left from the park 1.9 *m.* on a road, paved for the first mile, to HIGH ROCK PAVILION (1,822 alt.); L. here on a rough and narrow road to QUIRAUK, 3.2 *m.* (1,445 alt.). From both High Rock and Quirauk are excellent views.

State 92 crosses the Pennsylvania Line, 11.2 *m.*, at a point 1.3 miles south of Rouzerville, Pennsylvania.

2. Left from Thurmont on State 77 to APPLE'S CHURCH (R), 1 *m.*, mother church of both Lutheran and Reformed denominations in this section. The log structure, built around 1770, was replaced by the present stone building in 1826. In 1857 the Lutherans moved to a separate church in Thurmont, but the Reformed congregation continued to meet here until 1879.

GRACEHAM, 1.9 *m.* (450 alt.,150 pop.), has stores, a grain elevator, and a separator building. Its tree-lined streets, old houses with gardens in the rear, and the old Moravian church mark the tempo of its life. The Moravian Congregation of Monocacy, an offshoot of Apple's Church, purchased 30 acres here in 1782, and divided 12 of them into half-acre building lots which were leased to members of the church for an average of 88¢ a year. The first house in the village was erected in 1782, and in 1792 a man named Moeller received permission to bake gingerbread, brew small beer, and dispense the latter 'under strict regulation.' In 1822 the present brick church replaced a log structure.

DETOUR, 8.4 *m.* (350 alt.,104 pop.), was so called because the former name of Double Pipe Creek was too long for Western Maryland Railway timetables. A sawmill was recorded here in 1770 near this site, but the village developed around another sawmill and a woolen mill built in 1794 by Joshua Delaplane, a French settler. The woolen mill was in operation until 1849. Today Detour maintains two general stores, a bank, a grain elevator and coal yard, a blacksmith shop, and a dairy employing about 50 people.

Left from Detour 2.3 *m.* on a macadamized road through KEYSVILLE (420 alt., 32 pop.) and R. 0.8 *m.* to TERRA-RUBRA, birthplace on August 1, 1779, of Francis Scott Key, author of 'The Star Spangled Banner' (*see Baltimore*). The tract, patented to Francis' English grandfather, Philip Key, was named for the color of the soil. The first house, completed in 1770, was destroyed by a storm in 1850 and replaced by the present brick building. Half of the land was confiscated from the Tory uncle of Francis, who joined the British Army during the Revolution. The other half, including the mansion, was inherited by John Ross Key, father of Francis and an officer in the Continental Army.

After Francis Scott Key was graduated from St. John's College in Annapolis in 1796, he studied law there under Judge J.T. Chase. In 1801 Key and Roger B. Taney (*see Frederick*), later Chief Justice of the United States, practiced in Frederick. Taney married Key's sister, and Key later married Mary Taylor Lloyd and moved to Georgetown, where he practiced law with his uncle, Philip Barton Key. From 1833 to 1841 he was district attorney for the District of Columbia.

Although himself a slave-owner, Key in 1816 became a director of the American Colonization Society, whose purpose was to promote 'a plan for colonizing (with their consent) the Free People of Colour residing in our country, in Africa or such other place as Congress shall deem most expedient.'

The main side route continues straight through Detour on an unnumbered concrete-paved road to concrete-paved State 71, 10.4 *m.* Here the unnumbered road becomes State 85.

Right on State 71 2.5 *m.* to LADIESBURG (464 alt.,55 pop.), founded about 1820. Legend attributes its name to the disproportion of seven women to one man in its early population.

On State 85 at 11.5 *m.* is MIDDLEBURG (462 alt.,112 pop.), where detachments of the Army of the Potomac made several raids during the Gettysburg campaign in 1863.

UNION BRIDGE, 15 *m.* (402 alt.,862 pop.), on Little Pipe Creek, was settled in the 1730's by William Farquhar, who became prosperous making buckskin breeches.

The village received its present name when the settlers, many of them Quakers, built a bridge here uniting the hitherto scattered Pipe Creek settlements. From early time Union Bridge showed industrial initiative. A linseed oil mill and the first nail factory in the State were operating here about 1800 and a resident, Jacob R. Thomas, invented a mechanical reaper that was unsuccessful in its trial in 1811, but was later perfected by Thomas's cousin, Obed Hussey. A large cement plant, a shirt factory, a men's clothing factory, and the machine shop of the Western Maryland Railway continue the industrial tradition. A farmers' marketing co-operative organized in 1817 is still in existence.

Right 0.5 *m.* from Union Bridge on a dirt road to another dirt road; R. here 1 *m.* to the farmhouse that was the BIRTHPLACE OF WILLIAM HENRY RINEHART (1825–74), the sculptor. After leaving his father's quarry, Rinehart worked for a Baltimore firm of stonecutters, opened a studio, and attended art courses at the Maryland Institute. The sculptor later studied in Italy for two years, to which country after a short period in Baltimore he returned for the rest of his life. *Clytie*, usually considered his finest piece, is in the Peabody Institute in Baltimore.

From Union Bridge the side route follows State 75 east to concrete-paved State 31 at 19.9 *m.*

a. Right 0.1 *m.* on State 31 to BLUE RIDGE COLLEGE (coeducational), founded in 1846 as Calvert College and chartered about 1900 as the Maryland Collegiate Institute.

NEW WINDSOR, 0.3 *m.* (450 alt.,503 pop.), was settled in the early nineteenth century. First called Sulphur Springs, it was renamed in 1844. The town has a cannery, an apple packing and drying plant, and a clothing factory.

At 2.1 *m.* on State 31 is macadamized Marston Road.

Left 0.4 *m.* on this to a dirt lane, and R. 0.3 *m.* to the site of SAM'S CREEK MEETINGHOUSE (R), probably the first Methodist meeting house in America, built here in 1764 by a congregation organized by Robert Strawbridge, who had been converted to Methodism in his native Ireland, and who came to Maryland some time after 1759. After the little square log building was razed in 1844, the congregation started using the present Bethel Chapel, built in 1821 and remodeled in 1860. Strawbridge, who preached in various parts of the province, died in 1781 at Towson and is buried in Mt.Olivet Cemetery, Baltimore.

State 31 continues to State 26 (*see Tour 2A*), 9.8 *m.*

b. Left on State 31 from the junction with State 75 to the junction with US 140 in WESTMINSTER, 27.2 *m.* (774 alt.,4,465 pop.) (*see Tour 14*).

US 15 continues through the 12,000-acre Catoctin Recreational Area, being developed by the Federal Government with camping centers, picnic grounds, and swiming pools.

In CATOCTIN, 12.9 *m.* (389 alt.,150 pop.), several old log houses are the only remnants of a thriving community that grew around an iron furnace opened in 1774. During the Revolutionary War, the Catoctin Furnace supplied cannon balls for the siege of Yorktown. Parts of the engines for Rumsey's steamboat were also cast here, as well as plates for the iron-clad Union vessel, *Monitor*.

LEWISTOWN, 16.7 *m.* (402 alt.,300 pop.), settled about 1745, became the home of several Hessian soldiers who had been captured during the Revolutionary War. The STATE FISH HATCHERY, at the southern edge of the village, propagates brook trout and black bass and is the largest of three similiar establishments operated by Maryland.

In the PETER KEMP HOUSE (R), 19 *m.*, 14 ministers of various denominations in 1800 organized the United Brethren in Christ. In this house and its barn, known as 'meeting places' as early as 1790, Otterbein, Newcomer, Boehm, Asbury, and the eccentric Lorenzo Dow preached. The main section of the stone structure is rectangular with the long axis across the front, and two-and-a-half-stories high. It is flanked by two wings, one of which has a two-story porch. The living room occupies the entire first floor of the main structure. At each end of this room is a fireplace capable of taking a six-foot backlog.

RICHFIELDS, (L) 21.9 *m.*, was the home of Thomas Johnson, member of the Continental Congress from Maryland, who nominated George Washington for commander in chief of the colonial armies on June 15, 1775. Johnson later became Maryland's first State governor.

Winfield Scott Schley, born at Richfields in 1839, was graduated from the United States Naval Academy in 1860 and 24 years later won national acclaim when an expedition under his command rescued a party of explorers. In 1898 during the Spanish-American War, while temporarily in command of the American fleet, he bottled up the Spanish fleet under Cervera in the harbor of Santiago, then destroyed it when Cervera attempted to escape.

Schley was hailed by the press of the nation as the hero of Santiago, but he was officially reproved for having failed to obey an order of Commodore Sampson. The Sampson-Schley controversy continued for some time, but both the officers were made rear admirals in 1899. Schley died in New York in 1909.

At 23.4 *m.* is the junction with State 26 (*see Tour 2A*).

FREDERICK, 25.9 *m.* (296 alt.,14,434 pop.) (*see Frederick*).

Points of Interest: Maryland School for Deaf, Mt.Olivet Cemetery, Barbara Fritchie House, Roger Brooke Taney House, and others.

Frederick is at junctions with US 40 (*see Tour 2c*), US 340(*see Tour 2B*), and US 240 (*see Tour 16*).

In LIME KILN, 30.1 *m.* (284 alt.,185 pop.), founded in the middle of the eighteenth century, the most important landmark is the SPRING HOUSE, a structure apparently erected as a refuge against Indians. The limestone walls, two feet thick, were built around a spring. In both house and barn are loop holes.

BUCKEYSTOWN, 31.6 *m.* (300 alt.,375 pop.), was settled at the time of the Revolutionary War by German families who developed a leather-tanning industry. Today many of the townsmen work in near-by lime kilns.

At 31.6 *m.* is the junction with a macadamized road.

Left on this 3 *m.* to a dirt road, and R. to Park Mills, 5.6 *m.*, the SITE OF THE AMELUNG GLASS WORKS. Here in 1785 John Frederick Amelung and a group of workmen from Bremen, Germany, produced some of the finest early American glass (*see The Arts*).

At 33.4 *m.* is the junction with a dirt road.

Left on this to LILYPONS, 1.5 *m.* (75 pop.), a tract of more than 100 acres, largely covered with water and devoted to the production of pond lilies and ornamental fish. Millions of fish, including specimens of the prized fringetail calico are marketed every year. Among the 50 varieties of water lilies is the lotus of the Nile, which often attains a diameter of two feet. The French coloratura for whom the farms were named sends her Christmas cards from the Lilypons post office. The unusual name of the place and the fact that stamps are canceled here by hand have attracted the interest of philatelists.

At 37.3 *m.* is the junction with State 28.

Left on State 28 2.5 *m.* to a narrow dirt road, and R. here to the MONOCACY AQUEDUCT (L), 1.5 *m.* This stone-arched causeway, 438 feet long, carried the Chesapeake and Ohio Canal over the Monocacy and when constructed in 1837 was the longest of its type in the country.

At 2.8 *m.* is the junction with a dirt road. L. here 0.3 *m.* to the JOHNSON HOUSE (L), built during the War of 1812. Its thick stone walls, wide door jambs and window casings, high hand-carved mantels, and graceful front staircase are in excellent condition.

Isolated SUGAR LOAF MOUNTAIN (1,300 alt.), to the north, is largely of brown sandstone with heavily-wooded slopes. Lookouts were placed on it during the Civil War. The entire area is now a park, open to the public without charge.

Right from BEALLSVILLE, 7.1 *m.* (515 alt.,70 pop.), on State 109 2 *m.* to CHISWELL MANOR HOUSE (Gray Haven Manor), erected in 1796 by Newton Chiswell. Slight alterations have been made, but the thick walls, massive chimneys, and wide window frames are well preserved. Inside are doors with hand-wrought hinges, high mantels, and a beautiful hand-carved stairway. An attic stairway has a Chinese Chippendale balustrade.

In POOLESVILLE, 2.4 *m.* (475 alt.,197 pop.), is the junction with State 107. Right 2.5 *m.* to KILLMAIN (R), the main part of which was erected before the Revolutionary War by Daniel Carroll, signer of the Constitution. Of most unorthodox design, the main house is constructed of field stone set with little regard for symmetry.

A flatboat, guided by an overhead cable, still crosses the Potomac River at WHITE'S FERRY, 5 *m.*, established in colonial times.

At 5.9 *m.* on State 28 is DARNESTOWN (450 alt.,170 pop.). Right here on concrete-paved Seneca Road 3.5 *m.* to a dirt road, and R. 1 *m.* to MONTEVIDEO (R), a brownstone house that was the home of John Parke Custis Peters, grandson of Martha Washington. Brownstone quarried near by was used in the construction of the Smithsonian Institute, Washington,D.C.

ROCKVILLE, 24.7 *m.* (421 alt.,1,422 pop.), is at the junction with US 240 (*see Tour* 16).

From the junction with State 28, US 15 continues straight ahead to a point at 41 *m.* where the site of the Indian town of Canarest, on a Potomac island, can be seen. Now called Heater's Island, it was occupied by the Tuscarora during their flight from South Carolina to join the Five Nations in New York. The tribe stayed here for two years (1711–13).

POINT OF ROCKS, 41.5 *m.* (230 alt.,500 pop.), is well known to bass fishermen. The town was not laid out until 1835, but the name sprang into national prominence in 1830 when the Baltimore & Ohio Railway and the Chesapeake and Ohio Canal fought over the right of way on the narrow strip of land here between the base of Catoctin Mountain and the Potomac. After a long legal battle a compromise was reached that lasted until 1867, when the railroad tunneled the mountain.

Point of Rocks was a strategic site during the Civil War. Although no major engagements took place here, there was much skirmishing and raiding; and it was here that Hooker received telegraphed orders to turn over the Army of the Potomac to General Meade just before the Battle of Gettysburg.

Near Point of Rocks is a quarry of the unusual calico marble from which were taken several columns for the Capitol in Washington.

US 15 crosses the VIRGINIA LINE, 41.6 *m.*, at the southern end of the Point of Rocks Bridge spanning the Potomac River, at a point 12 miles north of Leesburg,Va.

Tour 16

Junction US 15—Rockville—(Washington,D.C.); US 240. Junction US 15 to District of Columbia Line, 36.7 *m.*

Concrete and macadam roadbed, two lanes wide.
Baltimore and Ohio Railroad, Frederick Branch, roughly parallels route in north.
All types of accommodations.

US 240 roughly follows an Indian path, later a colonial road, that was used by General Braddock on his way West in 1755. It crosses the Monocacy battlefield, a few miles south of Frederick and continues through gently rolling country chiefly used for dairy farming. Between Rockville and Washington are suburban real estate developments, largely for people of good income.

US 240 branches southwest from a junction with US 15 (*see Tour* 15), 0 *m.,* at a point 1.1 miles south of Frederick.

The northern boundary of MONOCACY NATIONAL MILITARY PARK, established in 1934, is at 1.1 *m.* On July 7, 1864 General Lew Wallace, with 2,700 men under General E.B.Tyler, took up a position at Monocacy Junction, planning to check the advance of General Jubal Early and his 15,000 Confederate troops. On July 8 Wallace was joined by 3,350 men from General Rickett's division. The bloody battle fought the next day ended in a decisive Union defeat but the delay it caused Early probably prevented the Capital from falling into the hands of the Confederates. The Federal casualties were 1,880, the Confederates lost between 600 and 700.

In BEST'S GROVE (R), 1.3 *m.,* Confederate troops under Jackson and Longstreet camped September 5 and 6, 1862, when they crossed the Potomac River into Maryland ten days before the Antietam campaign. Here on September 8 Lee drafted his proclamation assuring Marylanders that they would not be molested by his troops and urging them to support the Confederacy.

Between the point marked by the CONFEDERATE MONUMENT, 1.8 *m.,* and Frederick Junction, General Stephen Dodson Ramseur's Confederates were engaged with Union skirmishers.

By an overpass crossing the Baltimore & Ohio Railroad tracks, 2.2 *m.,* is the junction with a dirt road.

Left on this road to the BALTIMORE & OHIO IRON BRIDGE, 0.1 *m.,* built in 1831–32 at Frederick Junction. When the Union forces fled across this bridge after the Battle of the Monocacy, some fell between the ties to the Monocacy 40 feet below, but the Confederates held their artillery fire and many crossed in safety. On the banks of the river (L) at Braddock's Pass are the ruins of the OLD FORT FURNACE. Here in 1755

Major General Edward Braddock held a conference with provincial officers to plan his Fort Duquesne campaign.

Just south of the overpass is the NEW JERSEY MONUMENT (R), a granite shaft surmounted with the figure of an infantryman, commemorating the action of the 14th New Jersey Volunteer Infantry.

On the bank of the Monocacy near the steel and concrete highway bridge, 2.4 *m.*, is the WORTHINGTON HOME (L), a two-and-a-half-story brick house, used to care for wounded Confederates after the Battle of the Monocacy.

On the lane to BOSCOBEL (L), 2.5 *m.*, is a small cottage built by Colonel John McPherson in 1830 as part of the ARABY FLOUR MILL. During the battle this building was the Union post office. A number of soldiers killed in the fight were buried on the hill back of the house, which also sheltered the wounded.

At 2.6 *m.* is the junction with a dirt road.

Right on this road to the PENNSYLVANIA MONUMENT (L), a 35-foot granite shaft surmounted with a large polished granite ball. It commemorates the action here of the 67th, 87th, and 138th Regiments of the 6th Corps of the Army of the Potomac.

At the junction with the Baker Valley Road, 2.9 *m.*, is the VERMONT MONUMENT, a rectangular block of granite which marks the position of the 10th Vermont Infantry in the battle.

Right on the Baker Valley Road to the THOMAS HOUSE (R), 0.5 *m.*, a two-and-a-half-story brick dwelling built about 1780 by James Marshall. When this house was bombarded during the Battle of the Monocacy, the Thomas family and neighbors took refuge in the cellar. General U.S.Grant, General David A. Hunter, and General Philip Sheridan conferred here on August 5, 1864, and decided on the Virginia campaign against General Jubal Early.

In URBANA, 6.3 *m.* (425 alt.,250 pop.), a village settled about 1730, is LANDON, a long two-story frame house of 28 rooms erected in 1846 and used by the Reverend R.H.Phillips as a seminary for girls. Later it became a military school. The material for Landon was brought by boat from Fredericksburg, Virginia to Washington and then hauled in oxcarts. In 1862, the year Samuel Hinks, the Baltimore mayor, bought the property, Confederate General J.E.B.Stuart's officers held a dance here; at its height Federal cavalry advanced on the house but were repulsed and the Confederates continued their party.

Near HYATTSTOWN, 10.3 *m.* (450 alt.,103 pop.), founded in 1800 by Jesse Hyatt, are quarries said to have supplied slate for roofing the old Capitol in Washington. In 1862 General Stonewall Jackson had an artillery skirmish here with General N.P.Banks.

CLARKSBURG, 14.1 *m.* (700 alt.,150 pop.), said to be on the site of an Indian trading post, has two stores, two garages, and a few residences and tourist homes set back in pleasant gardens.

On the marked SITE OF DOWDEN'S ORDINARY (L), 14.6 *m.*, Michael Dowden built a tavern in 1750 that was torn down in 1920. The troops raised by Governor Sharpe to assist General Braddock camped here in the spring of 1755.

Ducks, pheasants, and quail are bred at the MONTGOMERY COUNTY GAME REFUGE (R), 19.5 *m.*, a 76-acre tract on the left bank of Seneca Creek.

GAITHERSBURG, 21.6 *m.* (512 alt.,1,068 pop.), on the Deer Park tract surveyed in 1722, is a milling and trading point in a stock-farming area. On Observatory Hill is the U.S. COAST AND GEODETIC OBSERVATORY. This small frame structure with a removable roof is one of five observatories in the world—others are in California, Japan, Turkistan, and Italy, all at 39° 8' north latitude from observation of fixed stars—for recording the wobble of the poles and resultant shift in the equator and changes in latitude. In 1899 the International Geodetic Association and the International Astronomical Union financed and founded observatories for this special study. Since then Congress has provided an annual appropriation for the work and has placed this and the station in Ukiah, California under the Coast and Geodetic Survey.

ROCKVILLE, 26.9 *m.* (421 alt.,1,422 pop.), has been the seat of Montgomery County since 1777. First called Montgomery Court House and later Williamsburg, the town took its present name in 1804. In the Civil War it was frequently raided by Confederate troops in search of horses. After General Lew Wallace's defeat on the Monocacy, General Jubal Early's forces passed through on their way to and from the attack on Washington. Today Rockville is a town of tree-shaded lawns surrounding attractive homes.

The SITE OF THE OLD HUNGERFORD TAVERN is one block south of the modern hotel bearing the same name. A great event in the life of the old inn was the meteor shower of November 1833. It had a powerful effect on the guests in the card room, according to the records. 'When they first saw the raging meteoric shower cast its globes of fire on the ground, and against the outside walls and the windows of their room, they rushed from the card table, cast their cards in the fire, and knelt in prayer before a long-neglected throne of mercy.'

Right from Rockville on State 28 (*see Tour* 15) to State 189 (Falls Road), 0.4 *m.*; L. on Falls Road to POTOMAC, 6.1 *m.* (164 alt.,150 pop.), a crossroads village little changed since its founding in the eighteenth century. The SITE OF TUSCULUM ACADEMY at the southern end of town is now occupied by the Potomac Methodist Church. The academy was conducted by the Reverend James Hunt in pre-Revolutionary days and closed in 1781.

Left from Potomac 1.5 *m.* on State 190 (River Road), which roughly follows an old Indian path, to the NATIONAL CAPITAL HORSE SHOW GROUNDS (L), the scene of an annual four-day show and of fox hunts, in season. The riding academy is open throughout the year.

At 2.1 *m.* on River Road is the junction with a macadamized road; L. here 1.2 *m.* to the NATIONAL WOMEN'S COUNTRY CLUB. The club house is a long, low, white building. Membership is restricted to women but men are allowed to play the nine-hole course.

The CONGRESSIONAL COUNTRY CLUB (R), 2.2 *m.* on River Road, was organized in 1924 with Herbert Hoover as its first president. It has an 18-hole course.

The STONEYHURST QUARRY (L), 2.9 *m.*, has supplied mica schist for a number of residences and public buildings in Washington.

The BURNING TREE GOLF CLUB (L), 3.6 *m.*, was named for the brilliant autumn color of a large oak on the grounds. In the two-story stone clubhouse are framed photographs of Ambassador Joseph E. Davies golfing in Europe with the king of Belgium and of King Albert's acceptance of an honorary membership in this club to which only men are admitted.

The LOUGHBOROUGH PLACE (R), 7.2 *m.*, a stone house built about 1808, has for its east wing a trading post built about 1700.

River Road crosses the District of Columbia Line, 7.8 *m.*

At 8.6 *m.* on Falls Road is Conduit Road, so-named because it is built over two conduits that carry Washington's water supply.

1. Right 1.4 *m.* on Conduit Road to GREAT FALLS and GREAT FALLS PARK. From here there is an excellent view of the cataracts of the Potomac, which are particularly scenic. The park contains recreational areas and the sites of several of George Washington's enterprises. A part of his iron foundry is standing, and the walls of his mill are well preserved. A section of the abandoned Chesapeake and Ohio Canal is used here for boating.

2. Left on Conduit Road to CROPLEY, 1.7 *m.* (150 alt.,100 pop.), a hamlet near which gold was discovered in 1864 by members of a regiment of California volunteers. One of these, John Clear, returned after the Civil War and organized the Maryland Mining Company which mined small quantities of gold between 1869 and 1880. Operations were resumed in 1935 after revaluation of the metal. In the river below Cropley is PLUMMER ISLAND, a biological observation station. Plant and animal types from the uplands mingle here with those of the Coastal Plain, and hitherto unknown species have been discovered among them.

At 4 *m.* are (R) the huge semicircular buildings of the TESTING LABORATORY OF THE U.S. NAVY DEPARTMENT. The CABIN JOHN BRIDGE, 5 *m.*, built between 1857 and 1863, is a single arch of masonry 220 feet in length. The construction of this bridge was started during Franklin Pierce's administration, when Jefferson Davis was Secretary of War. Davis' name was erased from the bridge when he became President of the Confederacy but restored during Theodore Roosevelt's administration.

The BANNOCKBURN GOLF CLUB (L), 5.3 *m.*, has an 18-hole course.

The CLARA BARTON HOUSE (R), 5.9 *m.*, (now an apartment house) is a white clapboard structure with only its two steeple-roofed towers visible from behind a parking lot. Clara Barton (1821–1912), who founded the American Red Cross, was Red Cross director during the 1889 Johnstown flood and in appreciation the city of Johnstown constructed this house for her in 1897, using lumber from emergency buildings put up after the flood. The house was the headquarters of the American Red Cross until 1904.

GLEN ECHO PARK (R), 6.1 *m.* (*open May to Sept.*), is an amusement park with swimming pool, dance pavilion, and other recreational facilities.

Conduit Road crosses the District of Columbia Line at 8.5 *m.*

GEORGETOWN PREPARATORY SCHOOL (R), 31.2 *m.* on US 240—the nucleus from which Georgetown University in Washington developed—was established by the Jesuits at Georgetown in 1789 and transferred to this place in 1919. The buildings are Georgian Colonial in appearance, the chapel Italian Renaissance; all are of brick with limestone trim.

At 31.2 *m.* is the junction with macadamized Forest Glen Road.

Left on this to FOREST GLEN, 3.7 *m.* (308 alt.,1,000 pop.), once a trading post on an Indian path. The land is part of a grant made in 1680 to an ancestor of Archbishop John Carroll. It was the home of Daniel Carroll, a cousin of Charles Carroll of Carrollton.

In Forest Glen is ST.JOHN THE EVANGELIST CHURCH, a brick building erected in 1894. A reconstruction of the first frame structure,built in 1774, is in the Forest Glen Cemetery as a memorial to Archbishop Carroll.

The OLD BETHESDA PRESBYTERIAN CHURCH (R), 32.6 *m.*, was built in 1848 to replace a building destroyed by fire.

In BETHESDA, 34.6 *m.* (340 alt.,200 pop.), a suburb of Washington developed around and named for the Bethesda Presbyterian Church, is a

MADONNA OF THE TRAIL MONUMENT, a red sandstone figure of a pioneer mother and child. There is also a memorial honoring General Richard Montgomery (*c.*1736) who succeeded to Schuyler's command in the Canadian invasion in 1775 and was killed leading the attack against Quebec that same year. Montgomery County was named for him.

The CHEVY CHASE COUNTRY CLUB (L), 36.1 *m.*, has a white-porticoed, stone building, an 18-hole golf course, 14 tennis courts, and an outdoor swimming pool.

US 240 crosses the DISTRICT OF COLUMBIA LINE, 36.7 *m.*, at a point about 5 miles northwest of the Zero Stone behind the White House.

Tour 17

(Chambersburg,Pa.)—Hagerstown—Williamsport—(Martinsburg, W.Va.); US 11. Pennsylvania Line—West Virginia Line, 12.7 *m.*

Concrete-, bituminous-, and asphalt-paved roadbed.
Cumberland Valley R.R. and Western Maryland R.R. parallel route.
Tourist homes, camps; hotels only in Hagerstown.
Toll bridge over Potomac River.

US 11 traverses the fertile fruit-producing Hagerstown Valley after crossing the PENNSYLVANIA LINE, 0 *m.*, at a village called State Line, which is about 16 miles south of Chambersburg,Pa.

The HAGERSTOWN MUNICIPAL AIRPORT (R), 0.7 *m.*, is a modern flying field where planes manufactured in Hagerstown at the Fairchild Aircraft Plant are tested.

REST HAVEN CEMETERY (R), 3.7 *m.*, was formerly Bellevue, one-time estate of Major Charles Carroll, cousin of Charles Carroll of Carrollton. Major Carroll was one of the developers of Rochester, New York, to which he moved about 1810. Behind the cemetery is the transmitting tower of WJEJ.

HAGERSTOWN, 5.5 *m.* (552 alt.,30,861 pop.) (*see Hagerstown*).

Points of Interest: Washington County Museum of Fine Arts, Rose Hill Cemetery, Washington County Free Library, Moller Organ Plant, Mt.Prospect, and others.

Hagerstown is at junctions with US 40 (*see Tour 2*), State 65 (*see Tour 2D*), State 64 (*see Tour 2C*), and State 60.

Left on State 60 to a macadamized road, 1.6 *m.*; R. 0.8 *m.* on this to FIDDLES-BURG (500 alt.,300 pop.), where nearly all the houses are of logs with yards enclosed by stone walls; each has its vegetable and flower garden. The settlement is said to have been named for a group of itinerant fiddlers who in early days played at all social affairs in this section.

At 2.6 *m.* on State 60 is Marsh Turnpike; L. here 2.9 *m.* to LONG MEADOWS, patented to Thomas Cresap and one of the earliest grants made by the proprietary in this section of Maryland. Cresap came here from Oldtown (*see Tour 2E*) after Braddock's defeat; he built a fortified house and opened a trading post.

The ONE HUNDREDTH MILESTONE, one of the crown stones of the Mason and Dixon Line, stands where Marsh Turnpike crosses the Pennsylvania Line, 4.5 *m.*, about five miles southwest of Waynesboro, Pennsylvania.

The DOWNING HOUSE (L), 3.6 *m.* on State 60, built in 1750, is a two-and-a-half-story stone structure with gabled roof. It is one of the oldest houses in western Maryland.

LEITERSBURG, 7.2 *m.* (596 alt.,300 pop.), in a wheat- and fruit-growing district, was named for Jacob Leiter, a German immigrant who purchased land here in 1762 and whose grandson, Andrew Leiter, laid out the townsite in 1815.

Left 0.3 *m.* from Leitersburg on Greencastle Road to the LEITER BURYING GROUND (L), at the far end of which is STRITE'S MILL (R), erected in 1792 on Leiter land. The mill, still used to grind flour and feed, is owned by descendants of Christian Strite, who purchased it in 1843.

At 1.7 *m.* on Greencastle Road is MILLER'S MENNONITE CHURCH (L), where since 1835 the congregation has held its semiannual love feasts (*May, Oct.*).

At 7.4 *m.* on State 60 is the junction with State 418; R. 3.1 *m.* to RINGGOLD (769 alt.,340 pop.), settled when John Cresap built a log cabin here in 1825. Originally called Ridgeville it was renamed in 1850 for Major Samuel Ringgold, a local resident who was mortally wounded in 1846 in the battle of Palo Alto. Here is the only church in Maryland of the Brethren in Christ, or River Brethren. Also in Ringgold is the neat brick FRANZITE CHURCH of New Mennonites. Ringgold's position along a line of the Underground Railway permitted some of its inhabitants in pre-Civil War days to do a lucrative business in slave catching.

At 9.4 *m.* is a dirt road; L. here 1.3 *m.* to JACOB'S LUTHERAN CHURCH on a tract called Martin's Good Hope, patented to Martin Jacobs in 1790. This congregation, organized in 1791, met in a log structure that was replaced by the present brick building in 1841.

State 60 crosses the Pennsylvania Line, 9.4 *m.*, at a point about 2.5 miles southwest of Waynesboro,Pa.

TAMMANY (R), 10 *m.* on US 11, named for the Indian chief, is a two-and-one-half-story structure with one wing, built by Matthew Van Lear in 1789 of square brick burned on the premises. Rude batten shutters hang from strap hinges; a T-shaped chimney rises above the wing, which also has the typical end chimney of the period.

A tree-lined lane leads to SPRINGFIELD (L), 11.2 *m.* (*visited on written application to C.W.Humrichouse Estate, Hagerstown*), on a tract patented by Thomas Cresap early in the eighteenth century as the Garden of Eden. The central part of the house, made of stone and brick now weatherboarded, was built in 1750. The brick right wing was added by General Otho Holland Williams, founder of Williamsport (*see below*), and the large square brick left wing was added about the time of the Civil War. Scratched on a window pane is 'Edward Williams and Ann Williams, 1821.' The gray limestone springhouse served as a stout refuge in early times.

WILLIAMSPORT, 11.6 *m.* (380 alt.,1,775 pop.), has a large tannery, a silk mill, a broom factory, brick kilns, limestone quarries, and an electric power plant. The commercial briskness contrasts sharply with the peaceful air of the town, whose streets are unusually wide and lined with substantial brick and stone houses. Set on high ground at the confluence of the Potomac and Conococheague Creek, this place was at a junction of important early trails; the major part of Braddock's army used one of them in 1755 on the retreat to Frederick. In 1786 the town was laid out by General Otho Holland Williams for whom it was named. Williamsport, already a busy shipping point, petitioned Congress to be selected as the 'Federal City,' and was inspected by Washington in October 1790; the fact that the Great Falls of the Potomac prevented large vessels from ascending the river was one cause given for denial of its petition.

The post office stands on the SITE OF THE BLUE CORNER TAVERN, built in 1787 of stone, stuccoed and painted a vivid blue. It was operated until 1881 when it burned.

> Right from Williamsport on Clearspring Road, crossing the old stone Conococheague Creek Bridge, 0.1 m., to the SITE OF JEREMIAH JACK'S CABIN (L), 0.6 m., on the Byron Tannery property. Jack, who had been granted a tract of 175 acres in 1739, built a substantial log cabin near the much-used Indian path. In 1750 some Delawares met and slaughtered all but one of a band of Catawbas near here. He, according to legend, sought refuge with Jack, who sheltered him and persuaded the Delawares to let him depart unmolested. At 1 m. is (L) the Washington County Polo Association field.

Rotting on the weed grown banks of the WILLIAMSPORT FORD (L), 12.2 m., and the abandoned Chesapeake and Ohio Canal (L), are canal boats that once played important parts in Williamsport life.

US 11 crosses the WEST VIRGINIA LINE, 12.7 m., on a toll bridge (*cars 15¢*) spanning the Potomac River at a point 13 miles northeast of Martinsburg, W.Va.

Tour 18

(Bedford, Pa.)—Cumberland—McCool—(Keyser, W.Va.); US 220. Pennsylvania Line to West Virginia Line; 27.2 m.

Concrete, bituminous and asphalt roadbed.
Hotels in Cumberland; few tourist camps.
Baltimore & Ohio R.R. and Western Maryland R.R. roughly parallel route south of Cumberland.

This route, attractive for its scenery, goes through mountainous country with well-kept farms and occasional wooded sections north of Cumberland and south of it, skirts the Appalachian apple belt and follows the narrow, winding Potomac River valley.

US 220 crosses the PENNSYLVANIA LINE, 0 *m.*, about 25 miles southwest of Bedford,Pa., and follows a road cut by Continentals in 1758 through virgin forest between Cumberland and Bedford, during the campaign against Fort DuQuesne in the French and Indian War. Forbes, in command of the campaign, was persuaded by Pennsylvanians to build the road. Washington's protests were ignored and the slow pace necessitated by the construction almost caused Forbes to abandon the campaign.

CUMBERLAND, 5.8 *m.* (626 alt.,37,747 pop.) (*see Cumberland*).

Points of Interest: Washington's Headquarters in Riverside Park, Site of Fort Cumberland, Rose Hill, the Dent House, and others.

Cumberland is at the junction with US 40 and State 51 (*see Tour 2E*).

South of Cumberland US 220 (the McMullan Highway) is a broad asphalt boulevard lined with bronze-topped granite markers. The precipitous walls of Dan's Mountain (R) rising in places to almost 2,000 feet above the highway are balanced on the West Virginia side of the Potomac River by the slopes of Knobly Mountain. Dan's Mountain was named for Daniel Cresap, pioneer and soldier.

A ten-day racing meet (*end of Aug.*) is held at the ALLEGANY COUNTY FAIRGROUND (L) 9.6 *m.*

In case of war the CELANESE CORPORATION OF AMERICA PLANT (*no admittance*), 11.3 *m.*, which covers approximately 100 acres and employs almost 10,000 persons, could produce ammunition.

CRESAPTOWN, 12.6 *m.* (780 alt.,500 pop.), is named for the sons of Daniel Cresap who settled here shortly after the Revolution. On the night of February 21, 1865, a small Confederate cavalry detachment surprised a Union outpost here and then rode on to Cumberland where it captured two Union generals.

At 13.7 *m.* is a junction with dirt road.

Left to PINTO, 0.5 *m.* (780 alt.,300 pop.), headquarters of the Appalachian Orchard Company, which employs 125 pickers during the apple harvest.

RAWLINGS, 17.7 *m.* (707 alt.,104 pop.), named for Colonel Moses Rawlings, soldier of the Revolutionary War, was originally called Hickory Flats. The surrounding country is famous for apples. Orchards line the hillside above the highway.

At 26.6 *m.* is the junction with State 135, the Westernport—McCool road.

Right on this road through the narrow gorge of the North Fork of the Potomac River where mine shaft entrances are visible high on the mountain slope. From these openings the coal mined here is carried by tramways down to the railroad tracks on the West Virginia side. These mines tap the Georges Creek Coal Basin that lies for the most part between Dan's Mountain and Savage Mountain.

WESTERNPORT, 4.5 *m.* (*see Tour 18A*), is at the junction with State 36.

McCOOL, 26.8 *m.* (825 alt.,300 pop.), a suburb of the larger Keyser across the river, was called Keyser before West Virginia was formed.

US 220 crosses the WEST VIRGINIA LINE, 27.2 *m.*, on a bridge across the Potomac River to Keyser,W.Va.

Tour 18A

(Bedford,Pa.)—Corriganville—Frostburg—Lonaconing—Westernport—
(Piedmont,W.Va.); State 35 and State 36.
Pennsylvania Line to West Virginia Line, 29.5 *m.*

Macadamized and concrete-paved roadbed; two lanes wide.
Cumberland & Pennsylvania R.R., and Western Maryland R.R. roughly parallel
route.
Limited accommodations in towns.

The abundance of coal in the region traversed by this route and the development of transportation led to the establishment during the early
nineteenth century of many small industrial plants, employing Irish and
Welsh immigrants. The companies built houses for them of stone and logs.
These remain in a country that still is to some extent a wilderness.

State 35 crosses the PENNSYLVANIA LINE, 0 *m.*, at a point about
33 miles southwest of Bedford, Pa.

Though three railroads pass a few hundred yards from CORRIGAN-
VILLE, 2.3 *m.* (715 alt.,500 pop.), at the confluence of Jennings Run and
Will's Creek, the nearest passenger station is almost one mile southwest at
Kreigbaum. Limestone quarries furnish much of the local employment,
and east of the town is the DEVIL'S BACKBONE, a serrated formation of
up-ended limestone.

The main route follows State 36 R. from Corriganville.

Left from Corriganville on State 35 to a junction with US 40, 2.2 *m. (see Tour 2e).*

MOUNT SAVAGE, 7.4 *m.* (1,206 alt.,3,500 pop.), on State 36 was a
roaring industrial center when the first American-made solid track rails
were produced here in 1844. Church Hill, the modern residential section,
overlooks the hollow where company-built, century-old, one-story houses
line Old Row, New Row, and Jealous Row—names given to the streets
when throngs of laborers, predominantly Irish, came here to man the iron
works and rolling mill in 1839 and 1841. The FIRE BRICK PLANT of the
Union Mining Company, established in 1841, uses the high grade plastic
and flint clay mined in the hills northwest of town. James Roosevelt,
father of Franklin D. Roosevelt, was the company head in the 1880's. The
Cumberland and Pennsylvania Railroad repair shops employ many
skilled mechanics. John Charles Thomas, operatic baritone, was once a
choir boy in the Mount Savage Methodist Church.

At 9.8 *m.* is the junction with State 638 in MORANTOWN, a gasoline-
station crossroads.

Left 3 *m.* on State 638 to the junction with US 40 in ECKHART MINES (*see
Tour 2e*).

In FROSTBURG, 12.2 *m.* (1,929 alt.,5,588 pop.) (*see Tour 2e*), is the junction with US 40 which unites briefly with State 36. At 12.7 *m.* State 36 turns L.

OCEAN, 17.8 *m.* (1,735 alt.,75 pop.), now almost a ghost town, had more than 1,200 residents during the peak of coal production in 1907. Some of the citizens of this vicinity now support themselves by mining bootleg coal.

Most of the workers in MIDLAND, 17.9 *m.* (1,715 alt.,865 pop.), are of Irish and Dutch ancestry and are employed by the five large coal companies, a large bakery, and a shirt factory.

Left from Midland 0.4 *m.* on State 55 to a dirt road; L. here 3.3 *m.* to the summit of DAN'S ROCK. (*Caution—jagged rocks project from sides where road ascends stiff grade.*) From this peak rising 1,100 feet above the valley floor are seen the valley of the Potomac, the ridges of West Virginia, and Will's Mountain far to the east; to the west, Big Savage Mountain and crests of other ridges tower in the blue haze beyond the Georges Creek Valley; and heavily wooded peaks and knobs of Dan's Mountain rise to the north and south. The mountain was named for Dan Cresap.

LONACONING (Ind., where many waters meet), 20.9 *m.* (1,560 alt., 2,426 pop.), developed around coal mines opened in 1835. An overwhelming majority of its inhabitants are of Scottish descent and many cling to the customs and habits of their ancestors, such as 'first-footing'—the compulsory treatings of the first visitor with fine liquor on New Year's Eve. Coal mining remains the major industry but silk manufacturing adds to local income.

WESTERNPORT, 29.1 *m.* (922 alt.,3,440 pop.), at the head of navigation on the Potomac River, was a point where traders and adventurers left the river during pre-Revolutionary days to strike out over Indian paths and trails toward the Ohio River. The ANDREW MULLINS HOUSE on Main Street is pointed out as a stopping place used by Washington on one of his late western expeditions. The town grew rapidly with coal mining which sent thousands of tons downstream on huge flatboats before the coming of the railroad. After local production dwindled, many of the inhabitants found employment in the near-by pulp and paper mills and in Cumberland.

Right from Westernport on an unnumbered road to BLOOMINGTON, 2 *m.* (1,040 alt.,369 pop.), at the confluence of the Savage River with the North Branch of the Potomac. The town was called Langollen when the Langollen Coal Company established a company town here, but laborers laying the Baltimore & Ohio Railroad tracks across dreary Backbone Mountain (R) called this settlement 'blooming town,' for its many early blossoms. Bloomington declined rapidly when local coal production diminished but pulp and paper mills at Luke, one mile to the east, give work to many of its inhabitants.

Left from Bloomington on the dirt River Road to the BRANT GUN FACTORY SITE (L), 0.5 *m.* A log cabin here is reputed to have been the home of John Brant who established a gun factory here in 1811 and contracted 'to manufacture 2,375 muskets with bayonets complete to be delivered at the United States armory at Harper's Ferry.' The gun stocks were made of black walnut. Some of these old Brant flintlocks, changed to fire percussion caps, are still owned by local mountaineers.

Left from Westernport 4.8 *m.* on State 135 to the junction with US 220 in McCOOL (*see Tour* 18).

State 36 crosses the WEST VIRGINIA LINE, 29.5 *m.*, at the south end of the bridge across the Potomac River to Piedmont, W.Va.

Tour 19

(Somerset,Pa.)—Keyser's Ridge—Oakland—(Elkins,W.Va.); US 219. Pennsylvania Line to West Virginia Line, 49.7 *m.*

Two-lane macadamized and concrete-paved roadbed.
All types of accommodations in summer; limited accommodations in towns in winter.

This route in the westernmost county of the State follows the crests of high wooded ridges and traverses 'glades,' broad valleys and marshy grasslands that supported buffalo and much other wild life in the early days. Cattlemen from Virginia and Pennsylvania paid local landowners for their use as summer pastures until overgrazing destroyed most of the buffalo grass and precipitated a cattlemen's war, in which thousands of cattle were killed by the settlers.

Potatoes are now the principal crop in the glades; hay, corn, and small grains, especially buckwheat, are grown on the rocky hillsides; and maple sugar is produced in fair quantities. The region is still a favorite resort of hunters. A large part of the population is of conservative Pennsylvania-German stock, who show little concern for the outside world. There are extensive recreational areas, both State-owned and private. Warm days and cool nights are the rule in summer; subzero temperatures and heavy snows are not uncommon in winter.

US 219 crosses the PENNSYLVANIA LINE, 0 *m.* about 29 miles south of Somerset,Pa.

At 2.1 *m.* is the junction with US 40 (*see Tour 2e*) which unites with US 219 between this point and KEYSER'S RIDGE, 11.2 *m.* (*see Tour 2e*).

COVE HILL, 14.1 *m.* (2,440 alt.), overlooks The Cove (R), a natural amphitheater extending several miles westward. This valley is part of the Grantsville maple sugar district (*see Tour 2e*).

At 16.3 *m.* is the junction with State 42 and an unnumbered road.

1. Left on the unnumbered road to KAESE MILL (R), 0.5 *m.*, where the original overshot wooden water wheel has been replaced by a steel wheel and wheat is ground by steel rollers. Stone burrs, however, are still preferred for buckwheat.

On the unnumbered road is the BEAR CREEK FISH HATCHERY AND REARING STATION, 1.5 *m.*, maintained by the State Conservation Department on the banks of one of the best trout streams in the State. In the six rearing ponds brook and rainbow trout are bred to stock the streams and lakes of the State.

2. Right on State 42 to FRIENDSVILLE, 7 *m.* (1,500 alt.,600 pop.), at the confluence of Bear Creek with the Youghiogheny River. It was named for its first settler, John Friend, who came from the Potomac in 1765 with his six sons and bought a Shawnee village site. An iron furnace and gristmill were here in the early days, but the town had little growth until 1890 when the extension of the railroad down the Youghiogheny River started a lumber boom. Much of the larger timber has been cut,

but there is enough second growth to keep a modern planing mill in operation. The town's second occupation is the trade in fishermen's supplies.

Right from Friendsville 3 m. on macadamized Somerfield Road to SELBYSPORT (1424 alt.,150 pop.) once at the head of navigation on the Youghiogheny River. It was named for Evan Shelby, captain of a company of rangers in the French and Indian War and father of General Isaac Shelby, first governor of Kentucky (1792). Evan Shelby had a tract surveyed here in 1772 and laid out lots in 1798. When the hunter, Meshach Browning, who had been commissioned a captain during the War of 1812, ordered his company to muster in 'Selby's Port,' a group of Democrats here refused to serve under a Federalist officer, attacked him, and precipitated a riotous conflict that began on the banks and ended in the waters of a millrace. Aided by his brothers and friends, Browning won the battle but was so badly injured that his military career was ended.

Blooming Rose Tract, extending west from Friendsville along State 42 between the Youghiogheny and Buffalo Run, was opened in 1774 and settled by migrants from tidewater Maryland who continued the social gayety of their earlier homes.

At 16.4 m. US 219 crosses Bear Creek, so-called because of the many bears that formerly inhabited the caves along its banks.

At 18.1 m. is the junction with an asphalt-paved road.

Left on this road, 0.3 m., to the DRANE HOUSE, a one-and-a-half-story weather-boarded log structure, thought to be the oldest house still standing in this part of the State. The smaller section was built before 1800 by James Drane who brought a few slaves here and raised tobacco for several years. His son Thomas Lamar Drane (1789–1874) fought in the War of 1812 and was noted in this section for his fiddling until he joined the Methodists and renounced country dances and other sins of the flesh.

In ACCIDENT, 18.4 m. (2,400 alt.,350 pop.), a village with frame houses clustered around a Lutheran Church, a few stores, and a black-smith shop, such names as Bach, Speicher, Spoerlein, and Spruce indicate the German descent of many of the inhabitants. In 1774 when William Deakins marked *by accident* the same land that Brooks Beall had marked the day before, the present name was given to this site and later to the town that was established here about 1800. In *Forty-four Years of the Life of a Hunter* Meshach Browning (*see below*) said this was 'the summer camp of Indians and abounded in deer, bears, panthers, wolves, wildcats and foxes, and in all streams trout without numbers.'

The road follows the northern shoreline of DEEP CREEK LAKE (*good fishing*), 24.3 m., an artificial lake, covering more than 4,000 acres, formed by the dam of the Youghiogheny Hydro-Electric Power Company.

At 24.9 m. is the junction with a dirt road.

Right on this 3.5 m. to a stone chimney, the only remnant of MESHACH BROWNING'S HOUSE. Meshach Browning (1781–1859) was a farmer and hunter who estimated his total kill as '1800 to 2000 deer, 300 to 400 bears, about 50 panthers and catamounts, with scores of wolves and wildcats.' He relieved the monotony of shooting by wres-tling with a full-grown buck or boxing with a bear. At his death, moreover, he was mourned by 122 descendants. Browning's favorite hunting rifle is in the Smithsonian Institution in Washington.

McHENRY, 25.3 m. (2,480 alt.,150 pop.), is a summer resort on the flat, grassy shores of Deep Creek Lake. The settlement was named for James McHenry (*see Baltimore*), who purchased land about 1805 in what was then called Buffalo Marsh and Cherry Tree Meadows.

At 27.3 *m.* is the junction with a dirt road.

Left on this, 1 *m.*, to the entrance of the THAYER GAME REFUGE (R), a tract of more than 1,000 acres used by the State for propagation of game.

At 18.8 *m.* is the junction with a macadamized road leading 1 *m.* to LAKEWOOD BEACH (*bathing and fishing*).

When white oaks were abundant here, barrel hoops were a chief product and US 219 between Deep Creek Lake and Oakland was called the Hoop Pole Road. Most of the ridges now are covered with second-growth pine, maple, and oak trees.

At 31.1 *m.* is the junction with Swallow Falls Forest Road.

Right on this dirt road 5.1 *m.* to SWALLOW FALLS STATE FOREST.

SAND FLAT, 31.9 *m.* (2,686 alt.,10 pop.), is the junction with State 38.

Left on State 38 to DEER PARK, 5 *m.* (2,450 alt.,249 pop.), a village that grew around the agricultural and lumbering enterprises of U.S. Senator Henry G. Davis and became during the late nineteenth century a noted summer resort.

DEER PARK HOTEL, built by the Baltimore & Ohio Railroad in the 1870's, was for a time one of the most fashionable resort hotels in the United States. Presidents Grant and Harrison were among its guests and President Cleveland and his bride honeymooned in one of the adjoining cottages in 1886.

Right from Deer Park 0.5 *m.* on a dirt road to a second dirt road; L. (on foot) 1 *m.* to the summit of OBSERVATORY HILL (2,767 alt.).

At a fork in the gap (2,880 alt.), 2.5 *m.* on the first dirt road is a rough dirt lane; L. (*on foot*) 1.7 *m.* to EAGLE ROCK (3,162 alt.) and views of several mountain ranges in Maryland and West Virginia.

East of Deer Park, State 38 follows the base of Backbone Mountain.

At 7.5 *m.* is concrete-paved State 537; L. 4 *m.* on this to SWANTON (2,300 alt., 126 pop.), formerly an important shipping point on the Baltimore & Ohio Railroad for white and yellow pine timber, especially in the form of ship spars 60 to 80 feet long. It was named for Swan's Mill.

State 537 becomes the dirt Bittinger road and crosses the southern boundary of the SAVAGE RIVER STATE FOREST, 10.6 *m.* (*see Tour 2e*).

East of the junction with State 537, State 38 continues to ALTAMONT, 8 *m.* (2,626 alt.,35 pop.) on the Appalachian Divide, the highest point on the Baltimore & Ohio Railroad.

Near the overpass above the railroad tracks is OUR FATHER'S HOUSE (L), built in 1934 of chestnut logs with cement seams. During a trial in Oakland in which a moonshiner's wife was accused of poisoning her husband, a witness exclaimed: 'God? Why, we folks at Altamont don't know nothin' about Him!' To introduce God to the community, this little building was erected. Though undenominational at first, it was served by the Episcopal rector from Oakland and is now a Protestant Episcopal chapel.

Near the summit of BACKBONE MOUNTAIN, 11 *m.*, on State 38 is the entrance (L) to the northern section of the POTOMAC STATE FOREST, more than 4,000 acres of rugged, mountainous country set aside for recreational purposes.

At 11.1 *m.* on State 38 is a posted foot path; R. here 3 *m.* along the mountain crest to EAGLE ROCK (*see above*).

KITZMILLER, 16.7 *m.* (1,100 alt.,827 pop.), in the bottomland along the Potomac River, is chiefly a mining settlement with narrow streets and frame houses.

The town, named for Ebenezer Kitzmiller, one of the pioneer settlers, expanded when the railroad reached this point in 1882 and brought a lumber boom. The local development of coal mining 20 years later gave further impetus to the community, and added Italians and Slavs to the population that had been chiefly of English, Irish, and German stock.

Right on Spring Street in Kitzmiller is the OLD WILSON MILL, constructed of hewn logs in 1800. The stone burrs were carried over the mountains by Indians.

State 38 bears right in Kitzmiller to cross the West Virginia State Line, 16.8 *m.*, on the Potomac River Bridge to Blaine,W.Va.

OAKLAND, 37.4 *m.* (2,461 alt.,1,583 pop.), seat of Garrett County and its largest town, is in a small valley at the southern end of Hoop Pole Ridge. The east branch of the Youghiogheny River skirts the southern limits of Oakland under the brow of a wooded hill. A business center for the surrounding farming country and for the summer resort colonies to the north and south, Oakland lies in part of what was the westernmost of Lord Baltimore's manors. The town was established in 1851 and incorporated in 1861. On Second St. at the BROWNING HOUSE (L) is a collection of ancient firearms and Indian relics.

At 39.1 *m.* on US 219 is the junction with State 41, Mountain Lake Park Road, which continues L. to the junction with State 38 in Deer Park (*see above*).

A dirt road at 42.1 *m.* follows McCulloch's Path, an Indian trail between the Youghiogheny and the Potomac. In his diary for September 1784 Washington wrote: 'McCulloch's path . . . owes its origin to buffaloes, being no other than their tracks from one lick to another.'

REDHOUSE, 46.7 *m.* (2,550 alt.,14 pop.), is a crossroads hamlet with several roadhouses. The RED HOUSE (R) was once a tavern for cattle drivers following the Northwest Pike (US 50).

Left 2.4 *m.* from Redhouse on US 50 which follows an old buffalo trace used by Indians and packhorse trains and crosses BACKBONE MOUNTAIN (3,095 alt.), at the highest point on any road in Maryland. Here a gravel path leads around the Table Rock Inn (*parking and picnic grounds*) to TABLE ROCK, from where there is a broad view of the glades to the south and west and of the mountains of West Virginia in the far south and east.

At 2.5 *m.* on US 50 is a rough stone road (*difficult for cars*) to a wooden OBSERVATION TOWER, 0.3 *m.*

The hillsides along the road are pock-marked by entrances to small independent coal mines.

US 219 crosses the WEST VIRGINIA LINE, 49.7 *m.*, at a point 47 miles northeast of Elkins, West Virginia (*see West Virginia Guide*).

PART IV
Appendices

Chronology

1608   During June, Captain John Smith reaches what is now Maryland on his first exploration of Chesapeake Bay.

1625   King James I elevates George Calvert to the Irish peerage (Baron Baltimore of Baltimore).

c.1631   In August William Claiborne (with about 100 men) establishes a plantation on Kent Island; first permanent white settlement in Maryland.

1632   April 15, first Lord Baltimore dies before Maryland charter receives Great Seal of England.

June 20, Cecil (second Lord Baltimore) becomes first Lord Proprietary.

1633   Cecil appoints his brother Leonard governor of Maryland.

October 18, *Ark* sails from Gravesend, England.

November 22, *Ark* and *Dove* sail from Isle of Wight for 'Capes of the Chesapeake Bay.'

1634   January 24, *Ark* and *Dove* leave Barbados.

In March *Ark* and *Dove* arrive at St.Clements Island (now Blakistone Island), off the north shore of Potomac River.

March 25, settlers land briefly on island, take formal possession, hold divine services, and erect large cross to commemorate event.

March 27, Governor Leonard Calvert buys Indian village site and founds St.Marys.

1635   April 23, battle on the Pocomoke between forces of Claiborne and the Province.

1638   In February, Governor Calvert and Captain Cornwallis proceed with a military force against Kent Island.

April 4, Board of Commissioners for Plantations (London) awards Kent Island to Lord Baltimore.

1642   Population, 207 tithables: St.Marys Hundred, 28; St.Georges Hundred, 30; St.Clements Hundred, 20; St.Michaels Hundred, 45; Mattapanian Hundred, 14; Kent County, 70.

1644   Captain Richard Ingle captures St.Marys. Governor Calvert flees to Virginia. Claiborne recovers Kent Island.

1646   Calvert returns from Virginia with a small army, surprises and defeats rebels at St.Marys.

1649   Puritans from Virginia settle at Providence April 21.

Assembly passes Toleration Act.

1650   Anne Arundel County erected.

1652   During March, Commissioners Bennett and Claiborne proceed to reduce 'all the plantations within the bay of Chesapiaik' to obedience to the Commonwealth. Treaty with Susquehannock Indians.

1654   February 7, Governor Stone issues proclamation concerning oath of fidelity (alleged cause of civil war that took place in province shortly afterwards).

During October, the 'act of reducement of this province by commission from the Council of State in England to Richard Bennett, esqr., Colonel William Claiborne, and Edmund Curtis, was fully acknowledged by the whole assembly.'

Calvert (then Patuxent) County erected.

1655   March 24–25, Puritans defeat Governor Stone's forces in Battle of the Severn.

1655   July 10, Lord Baltimore commissions Josias Fendall governor of Maryland.

August 13, Puritans imprison Fendall.

1658   March 22, Proprietary governor negotiates with Puritans, who surrender.

Charles County erected.

1659   Baltimore County erected.

1661   Population of province about 10,000.

Talbot County erected.

1663   August 3, Lord Proprietary concludes articles of peace with Delaware Bay Indians.

1666   Somerset County erected.

1668   Dorchester County erected.

1671   Population of province about 20,000.

October 10, an act for marking 'Highwaies and makeing the heads of Rivers Creekes and Branches & Swamps passable for horse and foote.'

1674   Cecil County erected.

1675   Population 6,610 tithables.

November 30, Cecil Calvert dies.

1683   November 6, General Assembly passes act for advancement of trade.

1689   Province comes under direct supervision of the Crown.

William Nuthead establishes printing press at St.Marys.

1691   In March, William III commissions Sir Lionel Copley royal governor of Maryland.

1692   June 9, Church of England becomes established church of province.

1694   Population 9,847 taxables.

Sir Francis Nicholson (appointed lieutenant governor in 1691) arrives from England.

February 28, assembly held in Annapolis by order of Nicholson.

October 18, an act for the encouragement of learning.

1695   Population 10,390 taxables.

First public post route established.

1697   Population 11,030 taxables.

1699   July 22, Doctor Thomas Bray establishes parochial and provincial libraries.

1701   Population about 25,000.

King William's School opened to students.

1702   March 25, English Toleration Act for Dissenters extended to Maryland.

1704   October 21, assembly passes act 'to prevent the growth of popery.'

1706   Queen Annes County erected.
1707   Prosecution of Roman Catholic priests conducting services in private houses suspended 'during the Queen's pleasure.'
1711   Crown refuses petition by Charles Calvert (third Lord Baltimore) for restoration of province.
1713   Sending of letters by private hand or special messenger abolished.
1715   Population about 30,000.
       February 20, Charles Calvert dies; Benedict Leonard succeeds him, dies on April 15.
       In May, proprietary government restored to Charles Calvert, fifth Lord Baltimore, a minor.
1716   July 17, assembly passes stringent oaths of 'allegiance to the King,' of 'abhorrency' against supremacy of Pope, and 'adjuration' of claims of Pretender. No person refusing to take these oaths to exercise any public office.
1720   In February, Charles Calvert, uncle of Lord Baltimore, commissioned governor.
1723   Courts of assize, composed of two provincial court justices for each shore, are organized; for the ensuing 20 years they exercise certain powers superior to those of county courts.
1726   Governor Charles Calvert dies. Benedict Leonard Calvert succeeds him.
1729   July 30, Baltimore Town founded.
1732   May 10, Lord Baltimore and John, Thomas, and Richard Penn, sons of William Penn, agree on settlement of boundary dispute between Pennsylvania and Maryland.
1735   Thomas Schley and 100 German families settle in Frederick region.
1740   June 3 and July 26, assembly provides for £7,562 to enlist 500 men to assist in expedition against Spanish West Indies.
1745   September 28, Baltimore and Jones Town are combined and called Baltimore Town.
1746   Province organizes 300 men to join forces against the French and Indians.
1748   Population about 130,000.
1751   April 23, Charles Calvert (fifth Lord Baltimore) dies. Frederick, only surviving son, a minor, becomes proprietary.
1756   Population 154,188.
       French from Acadia, exiled by British, seek refuge in Baltimore Town.
1763   Mason and Dixon begin survey. (Complete task in 1767.)
1765   During August, citizens of Annapolis refuse to let Zachariah Hood, stamp tax collector, land and drive away his vessel.
1769   June 5, Sir Robert Eden, brother-in-law of the sixth and last Lord Baltimore, becomes governor.
1770   Population 199,827.
1771   Frederick Calvert, sixth and last Lord Baltimore, dies in Italy; Henry Harford (natural son) succeeds him as Lord Proprietary.
1774   October 19, indignation meeting protesting against the 'most daring insult' of bringing *Peggy Stewart* in with 2,000 pounds East India tea results in burning of vessel and cargo.

1775   Population 225,000.

July 26, Association of Freemen in Convention at Annapolis takes government of province into its hands.

December 7, Maryland Convention reassembles at Annapolis and passes resolutions for raising troops.

1776   June 23, Governor Eden leaves.

July 3, assembly adopts 'A Declaration of the Delegates of Maryland.'

November 3, Declaration of Rights and State Constitution adopted. All holders of Christian faith placed on equal footing.

November 25, first election in Maryland as a State held in Leonardtown.

December 27, Congress in session at Baltimore grants George Washington extraordinary powers for prosecution of war.

1777   February 5, first General Assembly of State meets at Annapolis and on February 14 elects Thomas Johnson governor.

April 11, Washington calls on Governor Johnson for more troops; State raises five more regiments, doubling Maryland's quota.

1778   March 17, Assembly provides for gathering of supplies for use of an American army 'for the service of the United States.' Maryland troops protect Washington's retreat from the Battle of Monmouth.

1780   Quit rents, considered incompatible with absolute sovereignty of State, abolished.

1781   John Hanson of Maryland becomes 'President of the United States in Congress Assembled.'

1782   Population 254,050.

Stagecoach line established between Baltimore and Philadelphia.

1783   November 26, Annapolis becomes temporary National Capital.

December 23, George Washington resigns commission in Annapolis as commander in chief of the Continental Armies.

Importation of slaves into State forbidden.

1784   December 25, Methodist Episcopal Church organized in Baltimore; Francis Asbury appointed superintendent.

1785   January 22, act chartering St. John's College, Annapolis, is signed.

May 17, Potomac Company, with George Washington as president, begins operations designed to establish water transportation by canal boats 'to Fort Cumberland Md. or beyond.'

1787   April 10, special session of Maryland Assembly appoints delegates to represent State at Philadelphia constitutional convention.

December 3, James Rumsey makes test of his steamboat with six passengers aboard on Potomac River.

1788   April 28, State Convention at Annapolis ratifies Constitution of the United States.

1790   Population: State 319,728 (white males 107,254, females 101,395, other free persons 8,043, slaves 103,036); Baltimore 13,503.

August 15, John Carroll consecrated Bishop of Baltimore, first Roman Catholic bishop in United States.

1791   March 30, Maryland cedes District of Columbia to the United States.

1792   Thomas John Clagett consecrated Bishop of Maryland—first Protestant Episcopal bishop consecrated in United States.

1793   During July more than 50 vessels arrive at Baltimore with 1,500 refugees from uprising in San Domingo.

1793-4   Three hundred and forty-four Baltimoreans die of yellow fever.

1794   A fort built at entrance to Baltimore harbor and named for James McHenry.

1795   Library Company of Baltimore organized; acquires large and valuable collection of books.

1796   December 31, Baltimore Town incorporated as a city.

1797   Frigate *Constellation* built in Baltimore.

1800   Population: State 341,548; Baltimore 31,514.
Baltimore becomes third commercial port in United States.
Anatomical Hall, Baltimore, demolished by mob objecting to lectures on anatomy and surgery. Lectures continued at County Alms House.

1804   General court is abolished and chief justices of separate courts constitute a court of appeals.
May 2, excavation of Chesapeake and Delaware Canal begins.

1807   June 22, naval battle between U.S. frigate *Chesapeake*, and *H.M.S. Leopard* off Annapolis.

1810   Population: State, 380,546; Baltimore, 46,555.

1811   Contracts awarded and work started on Cumberland Road.

1812   June 18, war declared against Great Britain.
Numerous sailing craft for use in the war are constructed in Maryland. Baltimore vessels harass English shipping.
Charter granted to University of Maryland.

1813   April 13, City Council appropriates $20,000 for defense of Baltimore as enemy vessels are lying off the port. Havre de Grace and other near-by towns sacked and partly burned by British. The first steamboat on Chesapeake Bay launched in Baltimore; on June 21 it begins regular trips to Frenchtown.

1814   August 18, British fleet enters Chesapeake Bay.
August 24, Americans lose Battle of Bladensburg.
British burn public buildings in Washington.
August 30, Maryland troops win Battle of Caulk's Field near Tolchester.
September 12, British repulsed at Battle of North Point.
Attack on Baltimore by land fails.
September 13–14, British Fleet bombards Fort McHenry but is repulsed. Francis Scott Key writes 'Star Spangled Banner.'
The war has reduced the State's exports for this year to $248,434.

1815   July 4, cornerstone of Washington Monument at Baltimore laid.
September 12, cornerstone of North Point Battle Monument at Baltimore laid. State's exports exceed $5,000,000.

1817   February 5, the Baltimore Gas Lighting Company, organized by Rembrandt Peale and a group of citizens, receives first charter in America to provide illuminating gas.
The Protection Society, to promote 'abolition of slavery and for the relief of free Negroes and others unlawfully held in bondage,' is chartered.

1820   Population: State 407,350; Baltimore 62,738. Yellow fever epidemic in Baltimore.

1821   May 31, Archbishop Marechal consecrates Baltimore Roman Catholic Cathedral, first in America.

1824   Peter Cooper builds first locomotive in vicinity of Canton.
Chesapeake and Ohio Canal Company chartered in Virginia.

1826   Assembly passes bill granting Jews right to hold office in State.

1827   Baltimore & Ohio Railroad chartered.

1828   July 4, formal beginning of work on Baltimore & Ohio Railroad and Chesapeake and Ohio Canal.

1829   August 9, cornerstone of the Baltimore & Susquehanna R.R. laid.
October 17, Chesapeake and Delaware Canal opened.

1830   Population: State 447,040; Baltimore 80,625.
August 28, Peter Cooper's steam car *Tom Thumb* makes first trip, Baltimore to Ellicott's Mills.

1831   January, the Maryland State Colonization Society formed for freeing Maryland slaves and finding refuge for them.
July 4, Baltimore & Susquehanna R.R. opens its first division (seven miles).

1834   August 25, Baltimore & Ohio R.R. opens branch line between Relay and Bladensburg.
December 1, first (Baltimore & Ohio) regular passenger train arrives at Harpers Ferry from Baltimore.

1835   July 20, Baltimore & Ohio R.R. inaugurates train service to Washington.

1839   April 4, Baltimore-built *DeRosset*, first iron vessel constructed in the United States, is registered.

1840   Population: State 470,019; Baltimore 102,313.

1842   November 5, Baltimore & Ohio R.R. completes line to Cumberland.

1843   In November, express company organized to operate between Baltimore and New York.

1844   First telegraph line constructed—between Baltimore and Washington.
May 24, Baltimore receives first message over line.
Regular packet ship service established between Baltimore and Liverpool.

1845   October 10, United States Naval Academy opened at Annapolis.

1846   May 11, the *Baltimore Sun* transmits by telegraph the complete Mexican War message of President Polk.

1850   Population: State 583,034; Baltimore 169,054.

1851   Second State constitution adopted.

1853   January 1, Baltimore & Ohio R.R. completes track to Ohio River, becoming longest railroad in world.

1857   Strike interrupts Baltimore & Ohio R.R. service. Riots at Ellicott City quelled by militia.

1858   Baltimore's first steam fire-fighting engine placed in service.

1859   July 12, the first streetcar, drawn by four horses, operated by City Passenger Railway.

1860   Population: State 687,049; Baltimore 212,418.

1861   April 19, Baltimore's southern sympathizers attack Sixth Massachusetts regiment as it marches across Baltimore.
April 23, James Ryder Randall (1839–1908) wrote 'Maryland, My Maryland.'

A regiment is formed to fight for the Union.

1864 June 7, Abraham Lincoln nominated for a second term by Union Republican national convention at Front Street Theatre.

July 9, General John B. Gordon, C.S.A., routs General Lew Wallace at Monocacy. Baltimore erects barricades.

November 1, a State constitution abolishing slavery in Maryland is adopted.

1865 George Peabody of Baltimore donates $2,000,000 for founding and maintaining schools in South.

1867 During May, fourth State constitution adopted.

1870 Population: State 780,894; Baltimore 267,354.

1874 Legislature passes act for establishing a normal school for training Negroes.

1876 In October, Johns Hopkins University opens with 89 students.

1877 July 20, State troops called out to cope with rioters in railroad strike.

1880 Population: State 934,943; Baltimore 332,313.

1882 Enoch Pratt gives Baltimore $1,083,333.33 to found a circulating library, subject to the city's creating annuity to maintain it.

1885 August 10, electric traction used for streetcars between Baltimore and Hampden.

1888 March 12–14, blizzard cripples commerce of Baltimore.

1889 May 7, Johns Hopkins Hospital opens.

1890 Population: State 1,042,390; Baltimore 434,439.

1893 Johns Hopkins Medical School opens.

1894 June 5, two regiments of troops are sent to the Frostburg-Cumberland area to cope with rioters in soft-coal miners' strike.

1897 August 7, Columbia Iron Works constructs two submarine boats, John G. Holland's *Plunger* and Simon Lake's *Argonaut*.

1899 February 12–13, worst blizzard in history of State; temperature reaches 15° below zero.

1900 Population: State 1,188,044; Baltimore 508,957.

1901 Drydock *Dewey*, largest floating drydock ever built, is launched at Sparrows Point.

1902 First workmen's compensation law in United States passed by Maryland legislature.

1904 February 7–9, the great Baltimore fire; property loss about $125,000,000.

1910 Population: State 1,295,346; Baltimore 558,485.

November 6, aviation meet opens at Halethorpe.

1917 In April, Maryland Council of Defense organized.

1918 Maryland contributes 62,133 men and 435 nurses to World War forces.

1920 Population: State 1,449,661; Baltimore 733,826.

1925 Survey shows manufacture of men's clothing leading industry of State.

1930 Population: State 1,631,526; Baltimore 804,874.

1932 State provides aid for special education of children physically and mentally handicapped.

1933 January 4, General Assembly provides for issuance of $12,000,000 in bonds by Baltimore for relief of the city's needy for two years.

1935   October 8, Federal Government grants $9,180,000 additional for relief of destitute in State.

1936   March 17–19, Potomac River valley flooded; damage in excess of $5,000,000; 8,000 homeless.

1937   November 14, new Baltimore Municipal Airport chosen by Pan-American Airways and Imperial Airways as summer alternate and winter base for Bermuda service.

1938   Legislature passes laws covering the first State income tax and a $15,000,000 Federal Housing Project.
March 16, Baltimore-Bermuda air mail service begins.

THE LORDS PROPRIETARY

George Calvert (*c*.1580–1632); several times member of parliament; marries Anne Minne, 1604, Joane ———, after 1622; knighted, 1617; a Principal Secretary of State, 1619–1625; first Lord Baltimore, 1625. A man of affairs—shrewd, energetic, cautious, and practical, with considerable political talent.

Cecelius Calvert (1606–75); marries Lady Anne Arundel, *c*.1628; second Lord Baltimore and first lord proprietary, 1632. Less energetic and more cautious than his father but with all his shrewdness, practicality, and breadth of vision.

Charles Calvert (1630–1715); marries Jane Sewall, 1661; governor, 1661–75; succeeds his father, 1675; governs in person, 1679–84. An able administrator, but inclined to be haughty and arbitrary.

Benedict Leonard Calvert (1678–1715); nominal governor, 1684–88; marries Lady Charlotte Lee, 1699; member of parliament, 1714; succeeds his father, February 1715; dies April 15.

Charles Calvert (1699–1751); succeeds his father, April 1715; Fellow of the Royal Society, 1731; Gentleman of the Bed Chamber to Frederick, Prince of Wales, 1731; governs in person, 1732; member of parliament, 1734, 1741, 1747; Junior Lord of Admiralty, 1741. 'The best and honestest man in the world, with a good deal of jumbled knowledge, but not capable of conducting a party.'———*Walpole*.

Frederick Calvert (1731–71); last Lord Baltimore, 1751; marries Lady Diana Egerton, 1753; author of several prose and poetic works of no merit. 'He was a fast young man, and did not live to be an old one.'———*J.G.Morris*.

Henry Harford (1762–?); natural son of Frederick by Mrs.Hester Wheeland; last Lord Proprietary, 1771.

Bibliography

DESCRIPTION AND TRAVEL

Appleton's Handbook of American Travel; The Southern Tour . . . by Edward
H. Hall. New York, D.Appleton & Co.,1866. 141p. 'Maryland' p.1–20.

Browning, Meshach. *Forty-Four Years of the Life of a Hunter*. Rev. and illus. by
B.Stahler. Phila., J.B.Lippincott Co.,1883. 400p. The career of a Maryland
Nimrod in early western Maryland.

Earle, Swepson. *The Chesapeake Bay Country*. 4th ed.rev., Baltimore, Thomsen-
Ellis,1934. 522p., illus.,map.

Eddis, William. *Letters from America*, 1769–1777. London, printed for the author
1792. 455p. Maryland before the Revolution.

James, Henry. *The American Scene*. New York, Harper & Bros.,1907. 442p.
A chapter on Baltimore.

Steiner, Bernard Christian. *Descriptions of Maryland*. Baltimore, The Johns
Hopkins Press,1904. 94p. (Johns Hopkins University Studies in Historical
and Political Science . . . Series xxii, nos.11–12.)

———'A Frenchman's Impression of Maryland and Virginia in 1791.' *Sewanee
Review*, January 1904, vol.12:52–72.

Stieff, Frederick Philip. *Baltimore-Annapolis Sketch Book*. Baltimore,1935. 128p.,
photographs.

Wilstach, Paul. *Potomac Landings*. Garden City, New York, Doubleday, Page
& Co.,1921. 376p.

NATURAL SETTING

Besley, F.W. *Forest Trees of Maryland*. 2nd ed. The University of Maryland,
State Department of Forestry . . . in co-operation with the Forest Service, U.S.Dept.of Agriculture,1938. 100p.

Clark, William Bullock. *The Geography of Maryland*. Baltimore, The Johns
Hopkins Press,1918. 167p. (Maryland Geological Survey. Special Publication, vol.x,part 1.)

Clark, William Bullock, and Mathews, Edward B., with the collaboration of
others. *Report on the Physical Features of Maryland*. Baltimore, The Johns
Hopkins Press, 1906. 260p. (Maryland Geological Survey, vol.6,part 1.)

Pearson, T. Gilbert. *Some Birds of Maryland*. Baltimore Game Division, Conservation Department,1929. 70p.,col.,illus.

Shreve, F., Chrysler, M.A., Blodgett, F.H., and Besley, F.W. *The Plant Life of
Maryland*. Baltimore, The Johns Hopkins Press,1910. 533p. (Maryland
Weather Service, vol.3.)

Truitt, R.W., Bean, B.A., Fowler, H.W. *The Fishes of Maryland*. Baltimore, State of Maryland Conservation Department,1929. 120p. (Conservation Bulletin no.3.)

ABORIGINAL MARYLAND

Ferguson, Alice L.L. *Moyaone and the Piscataway Indians*. Washington,D.C., privately printed,1937. 44p.,map and illus.

Hancock, James E. 'The Indians of the Chesapeake Bay Section.' *Maryland Historical Magazine*, March 1927, vol.22:23–40.

Hanna, Charles S. *The Wilderness Trail*. New York, G.P.Putnam's Sons,1911, 2 vols.,maps and illus.

Marye, William S. ' "Patowmack above ye Inhabitants" ' *Maryland Historical Magazine*, March, June 1935, vol.30:1–11;114–37.

———'Piscataway.' *Maryland Historical Magazine*, September 1935, vol.30: 183–240.

Semmes, Raphael. 'Aboriginal Maryland.' *Maryland Historical Magazine*, June, Sept. 1929, vol.24:157–72;196–209.

Smith, John. *The True Travels, Adventures and Observations of Captain John Smith etc*. From the London ed. of 1629. Richmond, republished at the Franklin Press,1819. 2 vols., map.

HISTORY

General:

Andrews, Matthew Page. *History of Maryland: Province and State*. Garden City, New York, Doubleday, Doran & Co.,1929. 721p.,maps.

Dodd, William E. *The Old South; Struggles for Democracy*. New York, Macmillan,1937. 312p.

Lantz, Emily Emerson. *The Spirit of Maryland*. Baltimore, Maryland, Waverly Press,Inc.,1929. 361p.

McSherry, James. *History of Maryland*. Ed. and cont. by B.B.James. Baltimore, Norman, Remington Co.,1904. A detailed history of the province and State from the beginning to the end of the Revolution.

Richardson, Hester Dorsey. *Sidelights on Maryland History*. Baltimore, Williams & Wilkins Co.,1913. 2 vols.

Scharf, John Thomas. *History of Maryland*. Baltimore, J.B.Piet,1879. 3 vols., illus.,maps. A standard reference work but not always reliable.

———*History of Western Maryland*. Philadelphia, Louis H. Everts,1882. 2 vols. The settlement of western Maryland.

Early:

Andrews, Charles McLean. *Our Earliest Colonial Settlements*. New York, New York University Press,1933. 'Maryland: A Feudal Seignory in the New World.' pp.141–67.

———*The Colonial Period of American History*. New Haven, Yale University Press,1934–38. 'Proprietary Maryland,' vol.2:274–379.

Andrews, Matthew Page. *The Founding of Maryland*. Baltimore, Williams & Wilkins Co.,1933. 367p.,maps. The first 60 years of Maryland's history.

Brown, William Hand. *George Calvert and Cecilius Calvert*. New York, Dodd, Mead & Co.,1890. 181p. The first two Barons of Baltimore.

———*Maryland; the History of a Palatinate*. Rev. & enl.ed. Boston, Mifflin & Co.,1912. 318p. Maryland to the outbreak of the Revolution.

Claiborne, J.H. *William Claiborne of Virginia*. New York, G.P.Putnam's Sons, controversy from the Claiborne standpoint.

Covington, Harry Franklin. 'The Discovery of Maryland or Verrazzano's Visit to the Eastern Shore.' *Maryland Historical Magazine*, Sept. 1915, vol.10: 199–217.

Hall, Clayton Colman,ed. *Narratives of Early Maryland*, 1633–1684. New York, Charles Scribner's Sons,1910. 460p. Reprints of original documents relating to Maryland's early history.

McCormac, Eugene Irving. *White Servitude in Maryland*, 1634–1820. Baltimore, The Johns Hopkins Press,1904. 112p. (Johns Hopkins University Studies in Historical and Political Science . . . Series xxii,nos.3–4.)

Mereness, Newton Dennison. *Maryland as a Proprietary Province*. New York, Macmillan,1901. 530p.

Semmes, Raphael. *Crime and Punishment in Early Maryland*. Baltimore, The Johns Hopkins Press,1938. 334p.

Steiner, Bernard Christian. *Beginnings of Maryland*, 1631–1639. Baltimore, The Johns Hopkins Press,1903. 112p. (Johns Hopkins University Studies in Historical and Political Science . . . Series xxi,nos.8–10.)

———*Maryland during the English Civil Wars*. Baltimore, The Johns Hopkins Press,1906–07, 2 vols. in 1. (Johns Hopkins University Studies in Historical and Political Science . . . Series xxiv,nos.11–12; series xxv,nos.4–5.)

———*Maryland under the Commonwealth*. Baltimore, The Johns Hopkins Press, 1911. 178p. (Johns Hopkins University Studies in Historical and Political Science . . . Series xxix,no.1.)

Later:

Heysinger, Isaac W. *Antietam and the Maryland and Virginia Campaigns of* 1862. New York, Neale Publishing Co.,1912. 322p.

Marine, William M. *The British Invasion of Maryland*. Ed., with an appendix containing 1,100 names, by Louis Henry Dielman. Baltimore, Society of the War of 1812 in Maryland,1913. 519p.

Sullivan, Kathryn. *Maryland and France* 1774–1789. Philadelphia, University of Pennsylvania Press,1936. 195p.

GOVERNMENT

Bond, Beverly W.Jr. *State Government in Maryland*, 1777–1791. Baltimore, The Johns Hopkins Press,1905. 118p. (Johns Hopkins University Studies in Historical and Political Science . . . Series xxiii,nos.3–4.)

Niles, Alfred S. *Maryland Constitutional Law*. Baltimore, Hepbron & Haydon, 1915. 587p.

Silver, John Archer. *The Provisional Government of Maryland*. Baltimore, The Johns Hopkins Press,1895. 61p. (Johns Hopkins University Studies in Historical and Political Science . . . Series xiii,no.10.)

Steiner, Bernard C. *The Institutions and Civil Government of Maryland*. Boston, Ginn & Co.,1899. 410p.

Stieff, Frederick Philip, compiler. *The Government of a Great American City*. Baltimore, Roebuck,1935. 379p.

SOCIAL AND ECONOMIC DEVELOPMENT

Agriculture and Commerce:

Blood, Pearl. 'Factors in the Economic Development of Baltimore, Maryland.' *Economic Geography*, April 1937, vol.13:187–208. Illus.,map.

Fairbanks, W.L., and Hamill, W.S. *The Manufacturing Industry of Maryland*. Baltimore, The Maryland Development Bureau of the Baltimore Association of Commerce,1932. 210p.

Gould, Clarence P. 'The Economic Causes of the Rise of Baltimore.' (*Essays in Colonial History*. Presented to Charles McLean Andrews by his students. New Haven, Yale University Press,1931, pp.225–51.)

Hamill, W.S. *The Agricultural Industry of Maryland*. Baltimore, The Maryland Development Bureau of the Baltimore Association of Commerce,1934. 332p.

Morriss, Margaret S. *Colonial Trade of Maryland*, 1689–1715. Baltimore, The Johns Hopkins Press,1914. 147p. (Johns Hopkins Studies in Historical and Political Science . . . Series xxxii,no.3.)

Steiner, Bernard Christian. *Maryland, Its Resources, Industries and Institutions*. Baltimore, Sun Job Printing Office,1893. 504p.

Transportation:

Chapelle, Howard Irving. *The Baltimore Clipper*, Salem,Mass., The Marine Research Society,1930. 192p.,illus. The origin and development of the Baltimore Clipper ships.

Daniel, Hawthorne. *The Clipper Ship*. New York, Dodd, Mead & Co.,1928. 227p.,illus. The history and romance of the clipper ship, including a chapter on Baltimore clippers.

Hungerford, Edward. *The Story of the Baltimore & Ohio Railroad*, 1827–1927, New York, G.P.Putnam's Sons,1928. 2 vols.,illus. An absorbing account of the rise of the 'Iron Horse,' with many details of Maryland and Baltimore history.

Searight, Thomas B. *The Old Pike*. Uniontown,Pa., the author,1894. 384p. A history of the old National Road.

Sioussat, St.George Leakin. 'Highway Legislation in Maryland and Its Influence on the Economic Development of the State.'(In Maryland Geological Survey, Baltimore, The Johns Hopkins Press,1899, vol.iii,part 3.)

Ward, George Washington. *The Early Development of the Chesapeake and Ohio Canal Project*. Baltimore, The Johns Hopkins Press,1899. 113p. (Johns Hopkins University Studies in Historical and Political Science . . . Series xvii,nos.9–10–11.)

Labor:

Andrews, John R. *Labor Problems and Labor Legislation*. 4th ed.rev., New York, American Association for Labor Legislation,1932. 135p.

Commons, John Roger,ed. *Trade Unionism and Labor Problems*. 2nd Series. Boston, Ginn & Co.,1921. 838p.

Janes, George Milton. *The Control of Strikes in American Trade Unions*. Baltimore, The Johns Hopkins Press,1916. 131p. (Johns Hopkins University Studies in Historical and Political Science . . . Series xxxiv,no.3.)

Lauchheimer, Malcolm H. *The Labor Law of Maryland*. Baltimore, The Johns Hopkins Press,1919. 166p. (Johns Hopkins University Studies in Historical and Political Science . . . Series xxxvii,no.2.) A study of Maryland's labor legislation.

Singleton, Evelyn Ellen. *Workmen's Compensation in Maryland*. Baltimore, The Johns Hopkins Press,1935. 130p. (Johns Hopkins University Studies in Historical and Political Science . . . Series liii,no.2.)

Press:

Johnson, Gerald W., Kent, Frank R., Mencken, H.L., and Owens, Hamilton. *The Sunpapers of Baltimore*. New York, Alfred A. Knopf,1927. 430p.

Wheeler, Joseph Towne. *The Maryland Press, 1777-1790*. With an introduction by Lawrence C. Wroth. Baltimore, The Maryland Historical Society,1938. 226p.

Winchester, Paul, and Webb, Frank D., editors. *Newspapers and Newspaper Men of Maryland Past and Present*. Baltimore, F.L.Sibley & Co.,1906. 178p.

Wroth, Lawrence C. *A History of Printing in Colonial Maryland, 1686-1776*. Baltimore, Typothetae of Baltimore,1922. 275p.

Education:

Adams, Herbert B. *Public Educational Work in Baltimore*. Baltimore, The Johns Hopkins Press,1899. 47p. (Johns Hopkins University Studies in Historical and Political Science . . . Series xvii,no.12.)

Gilman, Daniel Coit. *The Launching of a University*. New York, Dodd, Mead & Co.,1906. 386p.

Potts, P.C. *Secondary Education in Maryland before 1800*. Baltimore,1930. 160p. A typewritten thesis submitted to the Johns Hopkins University for the Ph.D. degree.

St.Johns College (Annapolis,Md.). *Catalogue for 1937-1938*. Contains an explanation of the new 'too best books' educational policy.

Steiner, Bernard C. *History of Education in Maryland*. Washington, Govt.Print. Off.,1894. 331p.

Religion:

Altfeld, E.Milton. *The Jew's Struggle for Religious and Civil Liberty in Maryland*. Baltimore, M.Curlander,1924. 211p.

Bibbins, Mrs.Arthur B. *The Beginnings of American Methodism*. Baltimore, The Book Depository of the Methodist Episcopal Church, c.1916. 48p.

Dennis, Alfred Pearce. 'Lord Baltimore's Struggle with the Jesuits, 1634-1649.' In American Historical Association, *Annual Reports*, 1900. Washington, Govt.Print.Off.,vol.1:105-125.

Skirven, Percy G. *The First Parishes of the Province of Maryland*. Baltimore, The Norman, Remington Co.,1924. 181p.

Steiner, Bernard C. 'Maryland's Religious History.' *Maryland Historical Magazine*, March 1926, vol.21:1-20.

Wroth, Lawrence C. 'The First Sixty Years of the Church of England in Maryland.' *Maryland Historical Magazine*, March 1916, vol.11:1-41.

Social Studies:

Bell, Howard M. *Youth Tell Their Story.* Washington,D.C., American Council on Education, 1938. 273p. A study of the conditions and attitudes of Maryland youth between the ages of 16 and 24, conducted for the American Youth Commission.

Peters, Iva L. 'A Social Interpretation: Maryland.' (113 entries) *Social Forces,* March 1926, vol.4:510–519.

RACIAL GROUPS

General:

Duncan, H.G. *Immigration and Assimilation.* Boston, Heath & Co.,1933. 890p., maps.

Fairchild, Henry Pratt. *Immigration, A World Movement and Its American Significance.* New York, Macmillan,1925. 520p.

Young, Donald. *American Minority Peoples.* New York, Harpers,1932. 621p.

English:

Latani, John Holloday. *The History of the American People.* Boston, Allyn & Bacon,1938. 'English Colonization, 1584–1660.'

Muzzey, David Saville, and Krout, John A. *American History for Colleges.* Boston, Ginn & Co.,1933. 'The English Migration.' pp.3–18.

German:

Hennighausen, L.P. 'Early German Settlements in Western Maryland.' In Society for the History of the Germans in Maryland, *Annual Reports,* 1887–92, vol.6:11–25.

Morris, J.G. 'The Germans in Baltimore.' In Society for the History of the Germans in Maryland, *Annual Reports,* 1894–96,vol.8:9–19.

Jewish:

Jewish Encyclopaedia: 'Maryland.'

Wiernik, Peter. *History of the Jews in America.* 2nd ed.,rev. and enl. New York, Jewish History Publishing Co.,1931. 465p.

Negro:

Brackett, Jeffrey R. *The Negro in Maryland; a Study of the Institution of Slavery.* Baltimore, The Johns Hopkins Press,1889. 268p.

Douglass, Frederick. *Life and Times of Frederick Douglass.* Boston, De Wolfe and Co.,1892. 752p.

Green, Lorenzo J., and Woodson, Carter G. *The Negro Wage Earner.* Washington,D.C., The Association for the Study of Negro Life and History,Inc., 1930. 388p.

Reid, Ira DeA. *The Negro Community of Baltimore.* Baltimore, The Baltimore Urban League,1934. 229p.

Wright, James M. *The Free Negro in Maryland* 1634–1860. New York, Longmans, Green and Co.,1921. 347p.

Others:

Evening Sun, (newspaper), Baltimore. 'Around the World in Baltimore,' by Lee McCardell, March 10–23, 1938. A series of articles on the racial groups in Baltimore.

FOLKLORE AND CUSTOMS

Bullock, Mrs.Waller R. 'The Collection of Maryland Folk-Lore.' *Journal of American Folk-Lore*, Jan.–Mar. 1898, vol.11:7–16.

Dahlgren, Madeleine V. *South-Mountain Magic*. Boston, J.R. Osgood & Co., 1882. 218p. A narrative of South Mountain traditions, superstitions, magic, etc.

Ingraham, Prentiss. *Land of Legendary Lore*. Easton,Md. Gazette Publishing House,1898. 308p.illus.,map. Sketches of romance and reality on the eastern shore of the Chesapeake.

Seip, Elizabeth Cloud. 'Witch-Finding in Western Maryland.' *Journal of American Folk-Lore*, Jan.–Mar. 1901, vol.14:39–44.

Whitney, Annie W., and Bullock, Caroline C. *Folk-Lore from Maryland*. New York, American Folk-Lore Society,1925. 239p. An omnium-gatherum of Maryland folklore.

Wrenshall, Letitia Humphreys. 'Incantations and Popular Healing in Maryland and Pennsylvania.' *Journal of American Folk-Lore*, Oct.–Dec. 1902, vol.15: 268–274.

TOWNS AND CITIES

Annapolis:

Norris, W.B. *Annapolis, Its Colonial and Naval Story*. New York, Thomas J. Crowell Co., 1925. 323p.,illus.

Smith, Delos Hamilton. 'Annapolis on the Severn.' *The Monograph Series*. 1929, vol.15,no.7:143–63.

Stevens, William Oliver. *Annapolis, Anne Arundel's Town*. New York, Dodd, Mead & Co.,1937. 339p.,illus.

Baltimore:

Hall, Clayton Colman, editor. *Baltimore; its history and its people*. New York, Lewis Historical Publishing Co.,1912. 3 vols.,maps.

Janvier, Meredith. *Baltimore in the Eighties and Nineties*. Baltimore, H.G.Roebuck & Co.,1933. 312p.

————*Baltimore Yesterdays.*

Scharf, John Thomas. *The Chronicles of Baltimore*. Baltimore, Turnbull Bros., 1874. 756p. A history of 'Baltimore town' and Baltimore city from the beginning to the 1870's.

Sioussat, Annie Leakin. *Old Baltimore*. New York, Macmillan,1931, 249p.,maps. Baltimore's first 100 years.

Stockett, Maria Letitia. *Baltimore: A Not Too Serious History*. Baltimore, The Norman, Remington Co.,1928. 336p.

Cumberland:

Loudermilk, William H. *History of Cumberland*. Washington,D.C., James Anglim,1878. 496p.

Hagerstown:

Wilson, Leonore Hamilton. *Hagerstown, Maryland*, 1735–1935. Hagerstown, Maryland, Stouffer Printing Co.,c.1935. 21p.

Salisbury:

Truitt, Charles J. *Historic Salisbury Maryland*. Garden City, New York, Country Life Press,1932. 227p.,illus.

ARCHITECTURE

Berkley, Henry J. 'Colonial Ruins, Colonial Architecture and Brickwork, of the Chesapeake Bay Section.' *Maryland Historical Magazine*, March 1924, vol. 19:1–10.

Forman, Henry Chandlee. *Early Manor and Plantation Houses of Maryland.* Easton,Md., the author,1934. 271p. The period from 1634–1800,illus.

Rusk, William S. 'Some Buildings of Old Baltimore.' *Americana*, July 1933, vol.27:300–305.

Scarborough, Katherine. *Homes of the Cavaliers.* New York, Macmillan,1930. 392p.,illus.

Scarff, John H. 'Some Houses of Colonial Maryland.' *The Monograph Series*, 1929–30, vol.16:255–74.,illus.

Swann, Don. *Colonial and Historic Homes of Maryland.* Baltimore, Etchcrafters Art Guild,1939. 2 vols. One hundred original etchings with descriptive text.

ART AND LETTERS

Literature:

Churchill, Winston. *Richard Carvel.* New York, Macmillan,1899. 538p.

French, John C. 'Poe's Literary Baltimore.' *Maryland Historical Magazine*, June 1937, vol.32:101–112.

Harbaugh, T.C. *Middletown Valley in Song and Story.* n.p., n.pub.,*c.*1910. 173p.

Kennedy, John Pendleton. *Rob of the Bowl.* Rev.ed. New York, G.P.Putnam and Co.,1856. 43p.

Miles, Louis Wardlaw. *The Tender Realist, and Other Essays.* New York, Henry Holt & Co.,1930. 184p.

Nyburg, Sydney Lauer. *The Buried Rose: Legends of Old Baltimore.* New York, Alfred Knopf,1932. 302p.

Parrington, Vernon Louis. *The Romantic Revolution in America.* New York, Harcourt, Brace,1927. 493p. Sections on William Wirt, John Pendleton Kennedy, Edgar Allan Poe.

Perine, George C. *Poets and Verse Writers of Maryland* (1898).

Randall, James Ryder. *Poems.* Edited with introduction and notes by Matthew Page Andrews. New York, Tandy-Thomas,1910. 221p.,illus.

Reese, Lizette Woodworth. *The Old York Road.* New York, Farrar & Rinehart, 1931. 292p.

———*A Victorian Village.* New York, Farrar & Rinehart,1929. 285p.

Smith, F.Hopkinson. *Kennedy Square.* New York, Charles Scribner's Sons,1911. 504p.

Steiner, Bernard C. *Early Maryland Poetry.* Baltimore, John Murphy and Co. 1900. 102p.

Swanson, Neil H. *The First Rebel.* New York, Farrar & Rinehart,1937. 404p.

Townsend, George Alfred. *The Entailed Hat; or Patty Cannon's Times.* New York, Harper & Brothers,1884. 565p.

Turpin, Waters Edward. *These Low Grounds.* New York, Harper & Bros.1937. 344p.

Uhler, John Earle. 'The Delphian Club.' *Maryland Historical Magazine.* December 1925, vol.20:305–46.

White, Andrew. *A Relation of Maryland.* In Hall, C.C.,ed. Narratives of Early Maryland, 1633–34. New York, Charles Scribner's Sons,1910. pp.63–112. First ed. London,1635.

Index